International Relations Scholarship Around the World

It has become widely accepted that the discipline of International Relations (IR) is ironically not "international" at all. IR scholars are part of a global discipline with a single, shared object of study – the world – and yet theorizing gravitates around a number of concepts that have been conceived solely in the United States.

The purpose of this book is to rebalance this "Western bias" by examining the ways in which IR has evolved and is practiced around the world. The sixteen case studies offer fresh insights into the political and socioeconomic environments that characterize diverse geocultural sites and the ways in which these traits inform and condition scholarly activity in International Relations. By bringing together scholars living and working across the globe, Tickner and Wæver provide the most comprehensive analysis of IR ever published.

It is essential reading for anyone who is concerned about the history, development and future of International Relations.

Arlene B. Tickner is Professor of International Relations in the Political Science Department of the Universidad de los Andes, Bogotá, Colombia.

Ole Wæver is Professor of International Relations in the Political Science Department at the University of Copenhagen, Denmark, and Director of the recently created Centre for Advanced Security Theory.

Contributors:
Ersel Aydinli, Navnita Chadha Behera, Thomas J. Biersteker, Wayne S. Cox, Petr Drulák, Jörg Friedrichs, Takashi Inoguchi, Arie M. Kacowicz, Jan Karlas, Lucie Königová, Bahgat Korany, Karim Makdisi, Julie Mathews, Kim Richard Nossal, Cirino Hiteng Ofuho, Mahmood Sariolghalam, Maxi Schoeman, Alexander Sergounin, See Seng Tan, Arlene B. Tickner, Ole Wæver, and Yiwei Wang.

Worlding Beyond the West

Series Editors: Arlene B. Tickner and Ole Wæver

Universidad de los Andes, Bogotá, Colombia, and University of Copenhagen, Denmark

The *Worlding Beyond the West* series editorial board are:

Naeem Inayatullah (*Ithaca College, USA*), Himadeep Muppidi (*Vassar College, USA*), Pinar Bilgin (*Bilkent University, Turkey*), Mustapha Kamal Pasha (*University of Aberdeen, UK*), Sanjay Seth (*Goldsmiths, University of London, UK*), Qin Yaqing (*China Foreign Affairs University, China*), Navnita Chadra Behera (*Jamia Milia Islamia University, India*) and David Blaney (*Macalester College, USA*).

Historically, the field of International Relations has established its boundaries, issues, and theories based upon Western experience. This series aims to explore the role of geocultural factors in setting the concepts and epistemologies through which IR knowledge is produced. In particular, it seeks to identify alternatives for thinking about the "international" that are more in tune with local concerns and traditions outside the West.

1. International Relations Scholarship Around the World
    Edited by Arlene B. Tickner and Ole Wæver

International Relations Scholarship Around the World

Edited by
Arlene B. Tickner
and Ole Wæver

Routledge
Taylor & Francis Group

LONDON AND NEW YORK

First published 2009
by Routledge
2 Park Square, Milton Park, Abingdon, Oxon OX14 4RN

Simultaneously published in the USA and Canada
by Routledge
270 Madison Avenue, New York, NY 10016

Routledge is an imprint of the Taylor & Francis Group, an informa business

Typeset in Times New Roman by
Keystroke, 28 High Street, Tettenhall, Wolverhampton
Printed and bound in Great Britain by
CPI Antony Rowe, Chippenham, Wiltshire

British Library Cataloguing in Publication Data
A catalogue record for this book is available from the British Library

Library of Congress Cataloging in Publication Data
International relations scholarship around the world/edited by Arlene B. Tickner and Ole Wæver.
     p. cm. – (Worlding beyond the West)
   Includes index.
   1. International relations and culture.   2. Postcolonialism.   I. Tickner, Arlene B., 1964–
II. Wæver, Ole, 1960–
JZ1251.G565 2008
327.09172′4–dc22   2008025219

ISBN 10: 0–415–77235–4 (hbk)
ISBN 10: 0–415–77236–2 (pbk)
ISBN 10: 0–203–88545–7 (ebk)

ISBN 13: 978–0–415–77235–8 (hbk)
ISBN 13: 978–0–415–77236–5 (pbk)
ISBN 13: 978–0–203–88545–1 (ebk)

We dedicate this book to Hayward Alker, who sadly does not live to read it and tell us how our project might benefit from theories and authors that we are unfamiliar with. Hayward pioneered concern within the IR discipline about the provincialism of dominant perspectives. We are sure that he would have received the book with his characteristic enthusiasm and support, while also reminding us of the many exciting projects that lay ahead that can make our research agenda progress further.

Contents

Tables and figures

Tables

Figures

Contributors

Ersel Aydinli is Associate Professor and Chair of the Department of International Relations at Bilkent University, Ankara, Turkey.

Navnita Chadha Behera is Professor in the Nelson Mandela Center for Peace and Conflict Resolution at the Jamia Millia Islamia University, New Delhi, India.

Thomas J. Biersteker is Curt Gasteyger Professor at the Graduate Institute of International Studies, in Geneva, Switzerland.

Wayne S. Cox is an Assistant Professor in the Department of Political Studies at Queen's University, Kingston, Ontario, Canada.

Petr Drulák is Director of the Institute of International Relations, Prague, Czech Republic.

Jörg Friedrichs is a Lecturer in the Department of International Development at Oxford University, England.

Takashi Inoguchi is Professor in the Graduate School of Public Policy at Chuo University, Tokyo, Japan, and will be President of the University of Niigata Prefecture from 2009.

Arie M. Kacowicz is Associate Professor and former Chair in the Department of International Relations at the Hebrew University of Jerusalem, Israel.

Jan Karlas is Head of the Research Department in the Institute of International Relations, Prague, Czech Republic.

Lucie Königová is an interpreter and yoga instructor, and a former researcher with the Institute of International Relations and Charles University in Prague, Czech Republic.

Bahgat Korany is Professor of International Relations and Political Economy at the American University in Cairo, Egypt, Director of the AUC Forum, and Research Professor at the University of Montreal, Canada.

Karim Makdisi is Assistant Professor of International Relations in the Department of Political Studies and Public Administration at the American University of Beirut, Lebanon.

Julie Mathews is Assistant Professor and Director of the graduate program in the Teaching English as a Second Language Program at Bilkent University, Ankara, Turkey.

Kim Richard Nossal is Sir Edward Peacock Professor of International Relations in the Department of Political Studies at Queen's University, Kingston, Ontario, Canada.

Cirino Hiteng Ofuho was formerly Associate Professor of International Relations and Politics at the United States International University, Nairobi, Kenya, and is currently Undersecretary (Deputy Minister) of the Ministry of Regional and International Cooperation of the Government of Southern Sudan (GoSS) in Juba, and Visiting Professor at the National Defence College, Nairobi, Kenya.

Mahmood Sariolghalam is Professor of International Relations in the School of Economics and Political Science at the Shahid Beheshti (National) University of Iran, Teheran.

Maxi Schoeman is Head of the Department of Political Science at the University of Pretoria, South Africa.

Alexander Sergounin is Professor of Political Science in the Department of International Relations, Theory and History, St. Petersburg State University, Russia.

See Seng Tan is Associate Professor of International Relations in the S. Rajaratnam School of International Studies at Nanyang Technological University, Singapore.

Arlene B. Tickner is Professor of International Relations in the Political Science Department of the Universidad de los Andes, Bogotá, Colombia.

Ole Wæver is Professor of International Relations in the Political Science Department and Director of the Centre for Advanced Security Theory at the University of Copenhagen, Denmark.

Yiwei Wang is an Associate Professor in the Center for American Studies and Assistant Dean of the Institute of International Studies at Fudan University, Shanghai, China.

Acknowledgements

This project was begun in 2003. At the invitation–challenge of then International Studies Association president and critical theorist Steve Smith, we organized seven linked panels and roundtables, and a one-day workshop for the 2004 ISA convention in Montreal. This effort brought together a group of approximately 35 scholars from and/or working in non-core settings, along with several senior level non-mainstream scholars from the core to discuss the publication of an edited three-volume series on "geocultural epistemologies in IR." Distinct chapter drafts for these books have been presented and debated at the annual ISA meetings ever since: four panels in 2005 in Hawaii, four in 2006 in San Diego, three panels and a one-day workshop at the Chicago 2007 conference, and a roundtable in San Francisco in 2008, where we discussed the findings of this volume in particular.

We appreciate the enthusiasm, generosity and warmth with which all of the participants in the geocultural epistemologies and IR "group" – as we have fondly come to identify ourselves – have embraced this project, both those who appear in this book (and the other two volumes) and the many others who have lent their ideas, critiques, and support during crucial moments in its development. Extra thanks are due to several of the group's "core," including David Blaney, Naeem Inayatullah, and Peter Mandaville, who stepped in at various stages, suggesting and sometimes contacting potential contributors, reviewing chapters, and in other ways sharing in our editorial work.

The International Studies Association has been truer to its name than the field of International Relations normally is, by consistently backing this project. On two separate occasions we were granted ISA funding for crucial workshops, travel grants were repeatedly provided for financially strapped scholars residing in the non-core, and numerous and often prominent slots were granted to us in the convention programs. Particularly during Steve Smith's 2003 to 2004 and feminist scholar Ann Tickner's 2006 to 2007 ISA presidencies, we recognized that there is a distinctive and refreshing willingness to engage with these issues and, in so doing, to cultivate pluralism, genuine dialogue, and tolerance within the discipline.

At Routledge, Craig Fowlie not only decided to sponsor the project but did so with a zeal and insistence on its importance that contributed appreciably to keep us going through some of its more troubled phases.

During the final, hectic production phase, research assistant Anne Kathrine Mikkelsen Nyborg was an invaluable and indefatigable force. We thank her, and the Center for Advanced Security Theory and Department of Political Science at the University of Copenhagen, for funding her work.

Finally, we thank Bahgat Korany and Indiana University Press for granting us permission to reprint his article, which was originally published in 1999 as "IR Theory. Contributions from Research in the Middle East," in Mark Tessler, Jodi Nachtwey, and Ann Banda (eds), *Area Studies and Social Science: Strategies for Understanding Middle East Politics* (Bloomington: Indiana University Press), pp. 148–158. And thanks to the editor of *Review of International Studies*, Nick Rengger, and Cambridge University Press for allowing us to print a revised version of Aydinli and Mathews' "Spinning IR Theory out of Anatolia," published in the *Review of International Studies*, 34(4), 2008.

1 Introduction

Geocultural epistemologies

Ole Wæver and Arlene B. Tickner

How is the world understood around the world? How is it understood by those who are professionally dedicated to analyzing world politics, that is, by scholars of international relations? Presumably, we are all part of a global discipline studying a shared object of interest, and yet theorizing gravitates around a number of theories "made in the U.S." In addition, access to this allegedly international field is highly asymmetrical and conditioned by factors ranging from seemingly mundane issues such as library holdings, physical safety in the street, and weekly working hours, to hurdles related to language, epistemology, and perspective.

Despite its self-understanding as a global discipline studying a global reality (or the discipline of "International Relations" studying "international relations"), the scholarly community has very little knowledge about how it is itself shaped by global and international relationships of power, knowledge, and resources. Admittedly, something fairly general about this state of affairs may be found in the existing literature in the way of critique or lament. However, ironically, when this is done without a concrete study of non-dominant and non-privileged parts of the world, it becomes yet another way of speaking from the center about the whole, and of depicting the center as normal and the periphery as a projected "other" through which the disciplinary core is reinforced. In order to transcend this state of affairs, it is necessary to actually *know* about the ways in which IR is practiced around the world, and to identify the concrete mechanisms shaping the field in distinct geocultural sites, a knowledge effort which must use theories drawn from sociology (and history) of science, post-colonialism, and several other fields.

A limited number of studies have emerged on the contrast between the field of International Relations in the United States and Western Europe, but within a global perspective this is a ridiculously narrow view. In tandem with the need to enhance understanding of what IR looks like in distinct places around the globe, our basic argument is that two other types of literature must also be addressed and both of them strengthened by becoming mutually engaged. On the one hand, the discipline has been exposed to various forms of interrogation, including post-positivist critique, sociology of science-based explanations, and historiographic questioning of its self-narration. On the other hand, the study of various "third world" contexts has led to claims that key IR concepts, including the state, self-help, power, and security, do not "fit" third world realities and may not be as relevant as others for thinking about the specific problems of such parts of the world. Connecting the two should bring to light how IR knowledge is shaped by the privileging of the core over the periphery and the formation of key concepts based solely on core perspectives.

The insights and lessons from this endeavor would be helpful for thinking about both "periphery" and "center" IR. The periphery would naturally be better understood, mainly because so little has been written about IR there – and the analysis that does exist is mostly negatively defined, i.e., about the deviations from IR normality, the reality that does not fit "our" theories, and the contributions to the field that never materialize. Looking at IR in different settings, both as scholarship in its own right and within the framework of a critical understanding of the discipline as a whole, would deepen our comprehension of and receptivity to knowledge produced around the world. IR at the center would be better understood too, given that core–periphery relations are an integral part of the social structures that produce knowledge there. Therefore, studying academic practice in the less influential parts of the world does not just explain deviation from a proto-global, Western normality. It also provides key insights into how "really existing IR" as canonized at the center (on behalf of an abstract, universal disciplinary ideal) is not produced by a global discipline that is only temporarily represented by a geographically defined forerunner, but is actually the local product of a particular geoepistemological perspective. Clearly, what IR is and could be at the core is challenged by this global tour.

International Relations is interrogated in this book as both a social and an intellectual phenomenon. That is, we are interested in the discipline of IR as a *social* world, including the political and social environment that informs scholarship, the rules, rivalries, and regulations operative among people working as IR scholars, and their working conditions and criteria for individual success and professional survival. At the same time, this focus also sheds light on the *intellectual* products of these people, namely theories and analyses of IR. The social organization influences intellectual patterns: how scholars work, what they are recognized and rewarded for, and what kinds of practices rule the field, are important factors determining what kinds of scholarship are eventually produced and which, among these, comes to count as superior scholarship. Conversely, intellectual structures impact upon social relations: the form of knowledge and especially the dominant conceptions of (social) science and of theory are important elements in the social regulation of scholars. The social and intellectual structures are closely connected, but nevertheless distinct interests. Whether one is interested in understanding the world of IR scholars or the world of IR theories, the analyses in this book should help to obtain a more global answer – the social dimension can be a tool to understanding the intellectual dimension, while conversely, an understanding of the intellectual patterns helps to clarify the social structure of the IR discipline.

Achieving this kind of insight into the geocultural dimension of the IR discipline is a larger task that will be continued in two other edited volumes, as well as a book series titled "Worlding beyond the West." This first book has the very explicit purpose of satisfying many scholars' curiosity by explaining "what goes on" in IR in other parts of the world that is difficult to follow due to linguistic and publishing barriers, among other factors. When teaching IR theory, most of us probably field questions from students about how this is seen from other parts of the world: "Is there a Chinese approach?", "Are conflicts between the West and parts of the Islamic world rooted in different views of international relations?", "Do African scholars think about the world based upon the specific problems of the continent?", and so forth. As a student or scholar of international relations, one ought to have some sense of how the discipline looks on a global scale, but so far there has been no such overview available.

Two maturing literatures that need to meet

Since Stanley Hoffmann's 1977 seminal depiction of International Relations as an American social science, it has become commonplace to affirm that IR is not "international" at all, but rather characterized by the pervasiveness of Anglo-American modes of thought and their respective conceptual and spatial boundaries (cf. also Alker and Biersteker 1984; Holsti 1985). Recent research on the state of the field suggests that the overall nature of IR has changed very little (Wæver 1998; Aydinli and Mathews 2000; Smith 2000; Crawford and Jarvis 2001; Friedrichs 2004). IR's primary conceptual tools, although sorely inadequate for understanding key global problems and dynamics, do not get updated through innovative input from new circles; few contributions from the non-core are recognized as legitimate ways of thinking about international politics; and scant dialogue exists among competing perspectives.

Notwithstanding attempts within International Relations to reflect critically on itself and to use these reflections constructively for the sake of developing the field, the center–periphery axis has been particularly underexplored. During the past ten years, systematic efforts have been made to analyze the discipline. Debate concerning the irrelevance of standard IR terminology, perspectives, and theories for many "peripheral" situations has also grown considerably, but on a separate, parallel track. The former has taken four basic forms: post-positivist critiques of IR (Lapid 1989; Walker 1993; Smith 1995); historiographic questioning of its disciplinary self-narration (Schmidt 1998, 2002; Wilson 1998; Holden 2001, 2002, 2006; Ashworth 2002); explanation of the existing state of the discipline drawing on sociology of science (Guzzini 1998; Wæver 1998); and exploration of national variations, many of which confirm the continued status of IR as an "American social science" (Wæver 1998; Smith 2000; Crawford and Jarvis 2001; and a number of articles on single cases, many by the contributors to this volume).

Although most of the relativization of the U.S.-centric view has been rooted in comparisons between the United States and Europe, such studies often mention the need to expand this work into non-Western and "third world" contexts. The work actually done about IR theory and the third world has included: analyses of the misfit between numerous core concepts (among them power, security, sovereignty, and the state) and narratives with peripheral realities and problems (Ayoob 1995; Blaney 1996; Inayatullah 1996; Neuman 1998; Chan *et al.* 2001; Tickner 2003b; Agathangelou and Ling 2004; Inayatullah and Blaney 2004); the examination of national and regional IR perspectives different from those of the United States and Europe (Chan 1996; Cox 1997; Alagappa 1998; Chan 1999; Rajaee 1999; Dunn and Shaw 2001; Inoguchi and Bacon 2001; Euben 2002; Geeraerts and Jeng 2001; Tickner 2003a); and the identification and analysis of representational practices in IR discourses and their role in perpetuating subordinate relations between core and periphery (Escobar 1995; Doty 1996).

As mentioned previously, little has been done in the way of combining these two increasingly dynamic areas of research – critical, disciplinary self-reflection at the core and the periphery's revolt against IRs concepts – and exploring how the IR discipline and the knowledge it prefers are shaped by core license over the periphery and how the rethinking of concepts in non-core contexts interacts with and influences disciplinary developments at large. We are not saying that this has never occurred. From the pioneering cultural analyses of Ali Mazrui (1990, 1996) to works emerging from post-colonialism and feminism on the role of geocultural factors in molding epistemological perspectives (Harding 1998), important observations have been made. However, this nexus remains systematically understudied. The discipline seems to be heading – slowly and reluctantly – towards increased sociological reflexivity, but one major aspect is still missing: the core–periphery structure so deeply entrenched within it. In turn, analyses of IR from the periphery could also benefit from being connected more systematically to historiographic, sociological and epistemological debates that have focused mainly on the discipline at the core.

Around the world

Our basic premise is that the first step towards addressing this lacuna is simply to ask what the state of IR is in different corners of the world. Similar questions have been posed before, normally in relation to only one country or region, and a few relatively brief summaries of larger parts of the globe. However, no study has covered all parts of the world, and none has tried to draw systematically upon sociology of science, post-colonialism, and other helpful disciplines in mapping the field's global contours. This effort becomes more complicated as soon as one starts to think about the circularity of the question: How does one ask about IR in different places without assuming either some a-spatial and a-temporal conception of the field or privileging core IR as normality? In what sense do the different efforts unearthed constitute "IR" and what would it take for the discipline to recognize them as such?

The choice of a geographical strategy in this volume is meant to be an interpretative grid rather than a claim about "the Indian approach" or "the Chinese school." Although we aim to bring to light the varied approaches that exist and compete in distinct locales, this is best achieved by moving around the world and shifting the geographical reference point chapter by chapter. On a more concrete level, the selection of countries and regions for the book's distinct chapters involves a choice among a spectrum of possible scales and their ensuing delineations. This ultimately comes down to pragmatic judgments about which areas can be covered within one chapter and which demand more extensive treatment – for example, one chapter for China, one that covers Japan, Korea, and Taiwan together, two chapters for Africa, and only one for Latin America. The drawing of lines is not meant to be a deep ontological statement *à la* Huntington about natural regions or civilizations, and along the arch from Turkey to India especially we could have made other choices – for example, we might have created a "Muslim countries" category and pulled Pakistan and Iran in with the Arab states (creating problems in Southeast Asia), or defined Israel into a larger Middle East. However, the ultimate criterion had to be (our pre-book knowledge of) the nature and conditions of IR scholarship in these sites, where it seems reasonable to consider both Turkey and Israel distinct from the Arab world, to look separately at Iran, and to treat South Asia as an integrated region. Similarly controversial is the decision to group the United Kingdom, Canada, Australia, New Zealand, and Ireland together as "the Anglo core," emphasizing its global position as "almost center" or "post-imperial non-core" more than contiguity or other forms of internal coherence in the group. The cuts between both Canada and the United States, and the British Isles and the rest of Europe are in some respects unnatural, but in others the chapter captures extremely well the shared condition of being in the English-speaking developed world, and thus as privileged as can be without being in the United States as such. Although there is no one correct way to do to this, we believe that we have created a 16 case study structure that is both exhaustive and non-overlapping, in which each chapter is meaningful within its own borders, be they national or regional.

A likely question is whether a project of this nature shows the discipline of IR as particularly self-examining. Other fields, such as anthropology, have been even more soul-searching, partly due to self-doubt about their scientific status and methodology (i.e., similar to IR but only more so), but also because their subject matter has raised obvious moral dilemmas about "us" studying "them" (in the interests of whom? colonial administrators? our own self-construction through contrast to "them"?). This example suggests that the "self-examining" involved in our project is derived naturally from *our* subject matter: the international. In IR, it is more problematic than in other fields that the discipline *is not international* in its own practices. While many other disciplines (including the natural sciences) are probably just as unequal, this state of affairs carries a particular irony for so-called "International Relationists."[1] Namely, the study of international relations is conducted primarily from a specific geopolitical site (the United States) that happens to be the most powerful country in both international affairs and the discipline itself. To a significant degree, this influences the way our discipline sees the world and also how it contributes to policy making and thereby to the world's very shape.

A single snapshot of the state of the IR discipline suggests that indeed there is "a problem," that the field is skewed, and that it makes a huge difference to a scholar's global visibility and prestige whether she or he works at Berkeley or Benin. Figure 1.1 (an update of Wæver 1998: Table 2) simply illustrates the distribution of authors of articles in three leading journals in terms of their current university. Neither their origin in biological or educational terms is counted both for reasons of simplification and because place of academic employment is actually the strongest measure of what gives access or not to the leading scholarly organs. Although Figure 1.1 does not reveal the "life prospects" of an IR scholar born in a specific part of the world, it does exemplify the global visibility and circulability of work conducted as a member of different geographical IR communities. The numbers speak clearly about the invisibility of the "rest of the world." Obviously, this is only a quantitative measure – it only shows that the journals surveyed cultivate a skewed representation of IR scholarship and not whether the resulting knowledge is also (mis)shaped as a result. In order to answer the latter question we would need a similar analysis of how academic interests or approaches vary geographically. Since this is a more complicated exercise, we prefer that it transpires through the chapters that follow, and be picked up in the conclusion. However, a partial response – in similar snapshot format – may be found in the chapter on the United States, where Tom Biersteker shows that in the syllabi of basic IR courses taught at the top U.S. universities there is not only an absence of non-Western authors (Table 17.4, p. 320), but also a very high profile for "methodologically sophisticated" studies, i.e., rational choice and quantitative works (Table 17.3, p. 318). These are almost totally absent in the rest of the world, so if the discipline defines itself through U.S.-style IR, this does mean a specific form of IR, not just the American part of a discipline that does the same elsewhere.

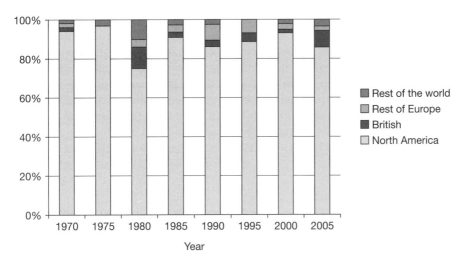

Figure 1.1 Articles in three leading U.S. journals, 1970 to 2005, authors from U.S./Canada, U.K., rest of Europe, rest of world. Journals: *International Organization, International Studies Quarterly* and (since 1980) *International Security*.

Geocultural epistemologies: theoretical underpinnings

Before we discuss the structure and rationale of the book, we briefly present two bodies of theory particularly relevant to the geocultural dimension of IR that this project aims to explore – post-colonial theory and sociology of (social) science. In doing so, our aim is not to set up an active analytical terminology which the authors of the distinct chapters then apply. Rather, we are interested in exploring the diverse modes of thinking, reflections, and problematizations that have been part of the numerous discussions sustained by the geocultural epistemologies and IR "group," and that inform the kinds of questions asked in each chapter in more or less explicit ways. Presenting, however crudely, these large and complex fields is furthermore intended to help students who may want to engage with this book and related analyses of the discipline and search for theoretical frameworks through which to deepen or counter the types of interpretation put forward by the different contributors.

Post-colonial theory

Increasingly, reflections in the discipline – both at the core and in the periphery – have gained a vocabulary for reflecting on the conditions and options for IR in "most of the world" (Chatterjee 2004). Helpful inspiration comes from post-colonial theory and subaltern studies. Post-colonialism emerged primarily out of literary studies as reflections on literature produced in former colonies, spreading rapidly to writings authored by immigrants in the West, to fields of study other than literature – from art to the social sciences – and not least into an accelerating philosophical sophistication and reflexivity. [2]

Edward Said's book *Orientalism* (1979) was a catalyst for wider dissemination of basic arguments – so powerful that they often became trivialized – about the way Western gazes on a non-Western "other" had constituted both the categories for that other to reflect itself through, and the understandings of the Western self. An increasingly critical literature scrutinized the paradoxes and problems of such self–other dynamics, and the performative peculiarities of expressing oneself from sites constituted through this kind of global cartography. Among them, the cultural search for authenticity and a politics of nationalism often ended up recycling not only Western but colonial perspectives. Namely, the categories through which to articulate oneself in a different way continued to be the established ones, and – most clearly in the case of nationalism (Chatterjee 1986, 1993, 2004; Fujiwara forthcoming) – the "trap" had been sprung from the start, so to say, given that nationalism works by way of a serial rhetoric of difference that appears as similarity and replication when seen from outside – not only in the post-colonial world, but since the birth of nationalism itself (Anderson 1983). In the post-colonial context, further ironies are added due to the powerful asymmetries and complexities of intertwined histories.

Highly relevant to IR theory is the way Western thinking has shielded itself from the influence of the non-West by the basic distribution in *space* of subject and object, and in *time* of developed and developing:

> [T]he colonised appeared as passive, for the West was the subject of history, and the colonies were the inert object it acted upon. But just as the colonies were subjected to governance, exploitation, and other processes of transformation, the colonisers too were transformed by the colonial encounter. Not only did the elites of the metropolitan countries grow fat on colonial profits, not only did these profits facilitate the industrial and other transformations which shaped the West anew; the administration and exploita-

tion of the colonies shaped the West's sense of self, and created new forms and regimes of knowledge. A huge array of data was collected, to enable rule and exploitation; the non-western world was represented in a burgeoning literature and art; and whole new disciplines were born, such as anthropology. In short, the new ways of perceiving, organising, representing and acting upon the world which we designate as "modern" owed as much to the colonial encounter as they did to the industrial revolution, the Renaissance and the Enlightenment.

(Seth *et al.* 1998: 7)

Within International Relations, there has been a consistent inclination to see East–West issues, most prominently the Cold War, as much more foundational than North–South questions, not to speak of South–South ones. For instance, in the subdiscipline of security studies, Tarak Barkawi and Mark Laffey (2006) have shown how the conceptualization of warfare has been defined by "Northern" wars instead of war in the South or "expeditionary warfare" – from colonial war proper to the war in Iraq – conducted by the North. The invisibility of a large portion of global warfare makes it easy to delegitimize Southern resistance by labeling it as "terrorism," and to place it on a lower moral scale than Western war and policing. A proper understanding of current world politics demands a perspective that acknowledges "the mutual constitution of European and non-European worlds and their joint role in making history" (Barkawi and Laffey 2006: 329; see also Barkawi and Laffey 2002).

Whereas earlier post-colonial theory might be viewed as part of the identity politics that dominated leftist humanities departments in the United States in the 1980s and 1990s, and thereby came dangerously close to reifying cultural categories and in-group authenticity – as occurred with both gender and race in cultural studies – subsequent rounds have incorporated a much stronger awareness of the fluidity of categories and the paradoxes of articulating identity. In particular, post-colonialism was instrumental in developing and deepening understandings of hybridity. By definition, post-colonial writings are both writing "away from" and "back to" the center in terms that cannot originate independently of the relationship to the latter. Nor can they be the same. Whereas early reflections exposed but also made extensive use of dichotomous categories, later theory has increasingly undermined and challenged them. In doing so, post-colonialism often draws upon post-structuralist philosophy but also manages to transcend it. The gain on "ordinary post-structuralism" often comes from a social grounding of positions of enunciation which imports a concrete heterogeneity that much post-structuralism declared in principle but has found it hard to live up to in practice, due to its (ironic) penchant for abstraction and grand theory. When theory is taken down to earth and linked to concrete lived conditions in specific locales, it naturally becomes different, but in a way that hardly allows for grand summaries of a systematic and consistent "difference," however much this is longed for by radical theorists who have vested their hopes for a new transcendent subject in post-Western social forces.

This is not to suggest that post-colonial studies are uninterested in critical, political engagement, only that such reflections are not conducted via classical categories. Subaltern studies in particular have focused on writing history from below, discovering new forms of political action and opposition that do not appear on the screen (at least not as "political") when viewed through the lens of categories derived from Western political philosophy. Terms such as social class, democracy, civil society, and representation take on new meaning in life situations where power and resistance are pervasive, but the main institutions and actors of politics did not emerge through the route that gave these concepts their particular meaning in the modern West.

In a famous 1988 article, Gayatri Chakravorty Spivak asked "Can the subaltern speak?" An important component of her argument was that attempts to establish a collective category of "the subaltern" were ultimately self-defeating because they forced homogeneity on to the subaltern through a collective, cultural category defined in relation to the core, reinforcing dependence upon Western intellectuals to speak for it. Within this framework, the post-colonial critic acquires the role of "local informant," and the entire relational structure ends up replicating colonial patterns.

In a dangerous move, many attempts to privilege subaltern perspectives play off "experi-ence" against "theory" (such excesses are performed less by the founding theorists and more as popularity generates mass production of "post-colonialism"). If the subaltern's claim to authority is "concrete experience," this risks excluding the possibility that the subaltern can have culture and theory, and not only inarticulate, concrete experience. When this line of argument is deepened by attempts to claim supreme access to lived realities by the oppressed that are impossible for others to grasp, the end result is a form of romantic nationalism and closed culture in which the subalterns are, paradoxically, further silenced, because their "culture" is not one of words but experience.

Feminist standpoint theory, which shares many of post-colonialism's concerns and inspirations, offers a potential exit to this cul-de-sac by focusing on the role of social location in knowledge formation. According to Sandra Harding (1986: 189), individuals involved in different kinds of social activity have distinct cognitive styles and worldviews. Instead of posing experience against theory, this approach argues that recognizing the social situated-ness of beliefs and knowledge in everyday life leads to more systematic, wider descriptions and knowledge of the world. The fact that subordinate or subaltern subjects are "outsiders" to the established order of knowledge production, and that they bring with them distinct accounts of reality emerging from their everyday experience, maximizes the "objectivity" of scientific inquiry precisely by recognizing the subjective character of all knowledge-building enterprises (Harding 1991: 124).

Spivak also illustrated the centrality and complexity of any concept of *subject*, while showing that Western post-structuralism had not pushed its deconstruction and decentering far enough. "Who is really giving voice to whom?" turns out to be an inherently fraught question. John Beverley (1999: 40), for instance, suggests that subaltern studies largely carried out by middle- or upper-middle-class academics at major research universities in the United States naturally do not claim to "represent" or "speak for" the subaltern:

> Subaltern studies registers rather how the knowledge we construct and impart as aca-demics is structured by the absence, difficulty, or impossibility of representation of the subaltern. This is to recognize, however, the fundamental inadequacy of that knowledge and of the institutions that contain it, and therefore the need for a radical change in the direction of a more democratic and non-hierarchical social order.

As a scholarly movement, "post-colonialism" became a privileged, hyper-academic, institu-tionalized practice, and ultimately a "first world anchored" one. Hence, there is a high risk of repressive tolerance producing a nicely carved out niche for it (Spivak 1985; Seth *et al.* 1998: 9; Dirlik 1999; Chun 2000; Wai 2004). Geocultural conditions find expression here as a problem of epistemology, in the sense that the whole university system in which post-colonialism, as a theory and a form of scholarship, has to be valued comes not from nowhere, but from Europe. As a result, the form of knowledge that is relevant for the post-colonial challenges easily comes into tension with the demands on form raised by the academic institutions.

To quote again from the editors of the first issue of the journal *Postcolonial Studies*:

> How, then, might postcolonialism circumvent the authorising signature of its European inheritance, or even articulate its heady desire for self-invention without always already speaking back to the West? For all its apparently oppositional energies, can the post-colonial project ever liberate the cultures/histories it represents from the shadow of "alterity", from the consolations of "difference", from the language of "otherness"? Indeed, how far is the postcolonial intellectual implicated in the relentless "othering" of her own cause? And, additionally, is it possible to dissolve the disabling oppositions of centre/margin, metropolis/province, West/rest without submitting to the feeble consolations of "hybridity" and "syncretism"? Can we imagine, instead, a situated dialogue between competing knowledges; a coming face-to-face of old antagonists in the aftermath of colonial violence?
>
> (Seth *et al.* 1998: 9)

In line with the argument that colonialism and post-colonial relations were not a one-way street but influenced both sides, attempts have been made to transgress dichotomies by emphasizing how cultures interact, transgress, and transform each other. Homi Bhabha, in particular, pushed the concept of "hybridity" by arguing that those factors that cannot be represented in the dominant dichotomies of the colonizer produce an ambivalence and anxiety at the center that challenge the authority of power (Bhabha 1994; although also sharply criticized, see, e.g., Dirlik (1999) and a more balanced assessment in Beverley (1999); for different developments of the concept by other authors, see, e.g., Néstor García Canclini (1995) and Walter Mignolo (2000)). While seemingly productive in terms of showing how specific practices can break dominant binaries, celebrating hybridity without sufficiently interrogating the power relations involved in its construction and operation runs the risk of complacency.

Finally, when we talk about "worlding"[3] in our book series, this is to emphasize that these intersecting practices of colonizing, resisting, and reshaping mean that we are all engaged in imagining and creating *worlds*. While one form of global order might be hegemonic in particular registers – as the neoliberal economic model, U.S. geomilitary power, and standard IR theory – the world *is not* this one version, or at least it can be challenged by other "worldings against empire" (Wilson 2007). Worlding is at stake in all the myriad processes by which we determine who we are in relation to "others." Disciplines that study these others always institutionalize specific global imaginaries. IR as we know it is an effect of a specific mode of worlding.

Here, worlding is meant to invoke a situation in which we live as neither homogenized and global, nor separate and local, but place-based yet transnational (for important related ideas see Childs 2003; Gillman *et al.* 2004; Wilson 2007; Wilson and Connery 2007).

The notion of worlding has been usefully employed in gender studies, where "Worlding Women" (Pettman 1994) and "Worlding Men" (Jones 2006) have pointed, foremost, to the need to move from a first phase of de facto studying gender issues for white, Western, privileged subjects towards attention to gender issues for "Southern" women and men. Simultaneously, in the core, worlding is often a way of reminding ourselves about the relevance of post-colonial insights. In American studies, for instance, a move from a nation-state-based frame to an understanding of the United States as shaped by interactions in the world, including imperialism, has been presented as a worlding of the field (Adams 2001).

While used in this context as another way to restate "standard" post-colonial arguments, the term has also been given a critical accent vis-à-vis post-colonial studies. For example, without critical attention to the way in which a world is pulled together from a particular angle, post-colonial literary studies risked performing an imperial operation parallel to those taking place in the economic and political spheres and simply importing "the third world" into distinct academic disciplines (Spivak 1985; Wilson 2007). In contrast, an emphasis on worlding brings to light the question of the situatedness of knowledge and experience in relation to the dominant reading of world globalization, and simultaneously constitutes a call for reconnecting to particular anchorings of practices in social situations, for "worldliness" (Said 1983).

The so-called era of globalization is not about a single global reality (or world) being experienced and responded to in different ways. Global interconnectedness is created and sustained by actions originating from myriad sites, driven by different visions of the world, projects, and conceptions (Karagiannis and Wagner 2006). In this sense, we take up the challenge that IR is not "global" in the sense commonly assumed by the universalizing mainstream discipline, nor is it simply local and about inward-looking variation. Rather, the field is constituted by numerous intersecting academic practices that are all about the world and all making their own worlds (cf. Appadurai 1996; Muppidi 2004). Indeed, within the particular world of IR scholarship, it could be that *the world is becoming world* through the processes that we are exploring here!

Sociology of social science

What do we mean by "sociology of (social) science"? Surely, it is not a very common term to come across in a text on international relations. There is an unfortunate tendency in the discipline to assume than anyone who wants to talk about any kind of theoretical reflection on "science" refers to one particular mode of addressing this – and one then walks to the shelf containing first-semester books about positivism, critical rationalism, hermeneutics, and critical theory; and this is not what we are getting at. Although terminology varies across disciplines, schools, and languages, it is important to distinguish between "epistemology," "philosophy of science," "history of science," and "sociology of science." Epistemology – in Germanic and Scandinavian languages often called *theory of science* – usually refers to different understandings about how scientific knowledge is achieved and what status is guaranteed by which methods – examples include schools such as logical positivism, critical rationalism, hermeneutics, critical theory, and pragmatism (for useful overviews, see Diesing 1991: part I; Blaikie 1993). Thus, it deals largely with questions of epistemology (in its Anglo-Saxon sense, not the French tradition of the same name). Quite often this is called philosophy of science. However, in order to illustrate the wider field of perspectives that exist, the term *philosophy of science* is reserved in this text for the genre of writings that are associated today with a debate between Popper, Kuhn, and Lakatos (and should perhaps be labeled something like "processual philosophy of science").[4] In this case, the perspective on science is not the single act of knowledge gathering – be it observation, deduction, testing, or interpretation – as in epistemology/theory of science, but rather the processual question of what attitude should be adopted towards data anomalies and what relationship among scholars in terms of deep questioning versus joint framework for a discipline to flourish. Do disciplines develop by rigorous falsificationism, or by socialization into paradigms left unchallenged for a period and thereby allowing cumulation, only to be replaced by a revolutionary change to another paradigm – and what are the implications for the rules of the game that should be adopted more at the collective, disciplinary level for how to assess theories and shape research programs? (For IR application, see Elman and Elman 2003.[5]) Philosophy of science evolved largely out of *history of science*, primarily because it was by studying the actual trajectories of theories that rationalized principles were devised for understanding how science progresses most productively.

Finally, *sociology of science* (including "Science Studies," "Sociology of Scientific Knowledge," and "Sociology of Science and Technology") examines the social mechanisms at play in the social universe of researchers – *internally* in each community as coordination, control, and contestation, *between* fields in processes of delineating disciplines and superseding them interdisciplinarily, and vis-à-vis the *external* worlds of economic and political interests. Here the world of scientists is not studied through the lens of devising principles and rules of the game ensuring progress. Instead, the social object is to be understood in its own right, in order to grasp its peculiar features and dynamics. This analysis provides for understanding about how different kinds of knowledge are produced at various times and places, why disciplines are more or less integrated (both conceptually and socially), and why activities in distinct disciplines are organized around various types of institution (journals, foundations, top professors, or associations).

There is strikingly little disciplinary sociology done in and on International Relations. *Theory of science/epistemology* is often covered in introductory courses, *philosophy of science* has gradually found a place within the mainstream (cf. declarations by Keohane (1986) about the importance of Lakatos, and by Waltz (2007) about the importance to his work of "philosophy of science," and systematically investigated in Elman and Elman (2003)), but *sociology of science* has only been employed explicitly in very few cases (Diesing 1991: part II, entitled "Social Science Studies Itself"; Wæver 1998, 2003; Büger and Gadinger 2007). Conversely, *histories* of the IR discipline, of key episodes or specific authors, are numerous, and increasingly these develop from being ad hoc and "innocent" to the inclusion of explicit reflections on method and historiography, thus touching on some of the same issues as the sociology of the discipline, including questions about internal versus external causes (cf. Guzzini 1998; Schmidt 1998, 2002; and not least a quite sophisticated debate on the historical construction of a so-called "first debate" in the discipline (allegedly between "realism" and "idealism" in the 1930s): Wilson 1998; Ashworth 2002, 2006; Vigneswaran and Quirk 2005).

Today, this has created the somewhat curious situation that reflections on the social mechanisms at play in IR are mainly studied as part of the *history* of the discipline, as if it were only its past that lent itself to such insights. In addition, this unusual arrangement means that sociological factors are mainly assessed in relation to their potential for explaining the development of theories, while it is largely overlooked that we can understand and explain many other aspects of the discipline than why certain theories came to prosper, including why some institutional loci (including journals, universities, and individual theorists) are more powerful than others that carry greater weight in other disciplines (such as professional organizations and exemplary empiricists).

So what *are* the theories of the sociology of science? A simplified overview goes like this:

Merton

Modern sociology of science developed in the 1950s and 1960s under the strong influence of work conducted in preceding decades by Robert K. Merton (1942, 1957, 1973, 1977). The theory is functionalist in that it sets out the criteria necessary for a research community to operate as the subsystem of society doing its particular thing: search for truth and cumulatively develop a better understanding of various subject matters. Particularly important to achieving this goal is a sufficient degree of external autonomy and, internally, adherence to a specific ethos, the (in)famous CUDOS values (Communism, Universality, Disinterestedness, and Organized Skepticism). Science is made historical and social – to a degree. It emerged as an institution at a given time and place due to specific social and political conditions (in seventeenth-century England), and it feeds back into society both its products and a certain support for Western democracy due to an affinity between scientific and democratic norms.

However, its main external link is a delinking: the autonomy of science is a precondition for the particular social institution to operate and produce its results. Therefore, external factors have no impact upon the internal shape of science, meaning that there are not different kinds of science due to different social conditions. The content is shaped by "reality" – social, external conditions are necessary only for this particular truth-seeking institution to come into place. Similarly, internal social factors are necessary for science to work, but there is no theory for explaining different outcomes within the sphere of science itself, only more or less success at being scientific.

Among the *weaknesses* of this theory was a limited empirical accuracy of both the internal and the external stipulations – the actually operating norms and the nature of autonomy. More importantly, the basic structure of the theory black-boxes the content of science and only produces a theory about the conditions for science to emerge. Among the theory's *strengths*, and the reason for presenting it here, is that it opened the door to studies of the specific institutions of science, including refereed journals, scientific societies, research training, and hiring patterns.[6] For our purposes, this strand of the sociology of science remains important because it enables us to see the peculiar dynamics of a social system regulated not mainly by direct political orders, or by economic competition for profit, but through the institution of peer recognition for the production of scientific originality.

In the chapters that follow, a key question that emerges is whether or to what extent local IR disciplines achieve "professionalization," whereby the field comes to be guided by the peculiar scientific institutions and criteria that Merton depicted almost as an ideal type. This is not to imply that the Mertonian format for science is innocent or necessarily ideal, but it is a particular kind of regulation with distinct effects and should therefore be explored, basically in order to have a clearer benchmark against which to judge when other forms of regulation and relationships shape the field more strongly, most importantly economic or political actors external to the university world.

Kuhnian interlude

Thomas S. Kuhn (1970), with his theory of paradigms that described interchanging periods of normal science and revolutions, is probably the best-known theorist on science to scholars of IR. His position in the sociology of science landscape is peculiar, because he does not develop a very precise or detailed sociological model of the mechanisms he describes – he writes more as a mixture of a natural scientist and a historian, with the social theory implied – and he is claimed by both sides across the great divide within sociology of science. For the Mertonians, Kuhn is seen to support their perspective (to the point that Merton claimed to have coined the concept of "paradigm" and lauded Kuhn's book as "merely brilliant"), due to his emphasis on the role of communities of scholars agreeing on rules of the game, jointly producing cumulative science, and thus a kind of functionalism even if no longer guaranteeing progress across paradigms. At the same time, Kuhn was also a key figure in paving the way for the anti-Mertonians, and especially for their wider reception (because the founders of the new approaches did not get their impulse from Kuhn), where Kuhn displayed much more complex and less ideal processes at play in communities of researchers. This pointed towards the possibility of studying actual academic practices in a less circular manner. However, IR is distanced from full engagement with its own sociology given its current (excessive) focus on Kuhn and follow-on authors such as Lakatos and Laudan. Thus, we just use him here as a stepping stone to the next sociology of science wave, a more thorough social science on social science.

Social constructivism

A number of approaches that differ in many other respects may be seen as jointly practicing social explanations of scientific variations, that is, of specific results and products, not only – as Merton – of a social institution that in turn produces an abstract and uniform search for truth. A heavier dose of social explanation may be derived through either external or internal channels. External explanations point to various social interests and worldviews that shape scientific content in direct and specific ways. Internal factors are explored through a number of different approaches, including ethnomethodologists, strong program, weak program, Edinburgh school, laboratory studies, and several others with or without labels. However, they all show how scientific results are reached through much more contingent and often coincidental processes of negotiating interpretations of experiments and convincing through complex social processes (Latour and Woolgar 1979; Knorr-Cetina and Mulkay 1983; for a useful summary and discussion, see Diesing 1991: 149–206).

Much of this research was focused on the natural sciences, perhaps for the rhetorical reason that this seemed to be the hard case, where it was more challenging and more demanding to prove social influences compared to the social sciences and humanities. The result has been that not much systematic work has been done on the social sciences from these approaches, a trend that was reinforced when several of its streams shifted into science and technology studies (STS).[7] Hence, although much valuable work is constructed by this community, much of it is less relevant to our discussion. For the purposes of this book, the value of these works lies foremost in the fact that they opened up the study of "science" to open-ended empirical investigation, thus interrupting the circularity of Mertonian functionalism.[8] In addition, their work pointed to a number of possible research techniques, from participant observation over questionnaires to studies of communication within a discipline, some of which are used in several of this book's chapters. None of the specific theories from this group is employed in a strict and pure form, but we draw inspiration from them.

The limit to this work is that it risks flattening our understanding of science by basing its explanation upon purely extra-scientific factors, crowding out room for science to be shaped either by the objects of study (residual realism) or by the peculiar institutions of science. The social factors invoked by social constructivists can be either macro or micro; that is, explaining science from general political, ideological, or economic forces in society, or from social explanations in "the laboratory," both of which are external to intellectual practices as such. The result is that these approaches tend to miss out on science as an institution. And the primary social context for most scholars is precisely the world of scholars.

More thoroughly sociological approaches

Again, we are dealing with a loose collection of authors who do not see themselves as forming a "school" per se, but who share a series of important traits. These more thoroughly sociological researchers use sociological theory to understand internal dynamics among researchers: basic micro-sociology, conflict theory, and organization theory, along with specific insights about science derived from the previous generations of sociology of science. In consequence, they avoid turning social constructivism into a new reductionism. Three approaches deserve special mention in order to illustrate this "third wave," those of Whitley, Collins, and Wagner/Wittrock.

Richard Whitley produced a model – drawn from theories of organizational structure – that explains variation among disciplines, specifically how particular versions of social and intellectual structures come together to regulate specific fields (Whitley 1984, 2000; Fuchs 1992; cf. IR applications in Wæver 1998, 2003, 2007). Different scientific fields are characterized by varying degrees of "task uncertainty" and "mutual dependence," and they exhibit distinct patterns both socially and intellectually. That is, they are organized differently in terms of both relationships of power, coordination, and key institutions (e.g., how powerful are local professors, leaders of the discipline, and external actors?) and how integrated knowledge in the field is (one paradigm, competing schools, canon varies from university to university, or almost total *laissez-faire*). Importantly, this theory manages to avoid reductionism between social and cognitive dimensions of science: the intellectual production of scholars in the field is neither shielded from social factors nor explained as reflections of these. Scholars in a given field struggle to produce new knowledge – and sometimes new theories – that relate to existing knowledge in the ever-difficult relationship of being both new enough to be publishable and familiar enough to make sense and seem relevant. In different fields the conditions for doing this vary, and scholars end up behaving distinctly: this is not due to their academic production being "overruled" by other rationalities, but to this peculiar form of academic motivation being channeled through the specific institutional structure of a given discipline. And it is primarily through the scientific decisions about one's own and others' work made in the networks among scholars that the future conditions are set. In other words, disciplines become variously organized systems for the production and validation of different sorts of knowledge.

Randall Collins has developed a theory geared more towards the micro-dynamics, the strategic moves made by single contributors, and the constellations that leading theorists form, their debates, and rivalries (Collins 1998; cf. Wæver 2003, 2004a). The methodological advice of Randall Collins (1998: 622) is to

> consider first . . . the clustering of ideas and the social networks among those who produced them; second, the changing material bases of intellectual production which undergirded [a specific theoretical development]; and third, the surrounding political–economic context which generated these organizational changes.

The point here is to move "inside-out."

> One layer does not reduce to another; least of all do the concerns of the philosophers reduce to the outermost material and political conditions. Intellectuals manoeuvre within their own attention space, reshaping the tools at hand from past and current controversies internal to their own sphere, while energized by the structural opportunities opening up in the material and political world surrounding them.
>
> (Ibid.)

This obviously quite demanding approach secures meaningful micro-theoretical foundations for the analysis, avoiding explanations operating "above the heads" of the actual individuals involved. Explanations have to capture how key actors in the intellectual scene make their strategic moves, career choices, write what they do, and adopt certain theories and orientations. Changes at this level will often be conditioned by changing working conditions (Collins' second circle), including funding, institutional closure or creation, and changing degrees of openness or closedness towards foreign scholars. Purely externalist explanations (circle three) that dominate the existing literature become more convincing if they can be shown to operate through concrete mechanisms in circles two and one, instead of pertaining to mysterious ways that connect broad social factors directly to intellectual products.

A third strand achieves a non-reductionist combination of social and cognitive explanations in a slightly different way. Peter Wagner and Björn Wittrock (and collaborators) have studied the relationship between the social sciences and state development. In addition to the fact that they actually focus on the *social sciences*, they have taken great care in developing an approach that avoids the "assumption that social developments by way of functional necessity somehow translate in social science inquiry" (Wittrock 1989: 501). Since the growth of the modern social sciences in the 1880s, throughout the twentieth century, different intellectual traditions have interacted in each national context with different state-building projects. During distinct phases, discourse coalitions have formed between researchers and external actors where scholarly programs and policy programs become mutually reinforcing (Wagner 1989, 1990; Wagner and Wittrock 1991; Wæver 1998). In the resulting "political sociology of the social sciences" (Wagner 1990: 24), one has to study both sociopolitical developments and debates among scholars and their theoretical production.

New production of knowledge

A final literature to introduce is the so-called "new production of knowledge" (Gibbons *et al.* 1994; Nowotny *et al.* 2001, 2003). Since the 1970s – and accelerating since the end of the Cold War – state policies for science and technology, especially in the OECD world, have shifted in the direction of more directive and systematic prioritizing aimed at improving economic welfare through innovation. Research-intensive industries demand government funding of the particular basic research relevant to their long-term prospects, whereas general support for basic research motivated previously by military demands and less differentiated economies has waned. This has led to a shift away from what the authors call "mode 1 research" towards "mode 2."[9] "Mode 1" is characterized by internal control of criteria held by academic communities, while the role of political and economic actors is kept relatively separate. With the increasing reliance on more precise justifications for public funding of research – less "general public good" – research becomes more consistently negotiated between actors inside the university and political and economic actors outside. When research becomes both too important ("knowledge economy" arguments) and too dangerous ("risk society"), it can no longer be left to the researchers (Weingart 2001; Fuller 2002; Elzinga 2003). The dominant format moves from university-based disciplines to applications-focused projects, often organized in an interdisciplinary format. Power moves from disciplinary elites to a new kind of scientific entrepreneur skilled at operating at the intersection of academe and policy, colleagues, and grant givers. It becomes gradually harder to conceive of the influence of external actors as a separate issue, only intervening, so to say, before and after the actual research – increasingly, the knowledge produced in society is negotiated between many stakeholders.

"Mode 1" versus "mode 2" is obviously too quick a dichotomy, especially given the variation among disciplines unveiled by Whitley. A much better understanding of these changes would be gained if they were treated as "circle two and three" changes in the Collins model and traced through the ensuing "circle one" processes. However, they do point to important trends.[10] Given the way that our narrative of "sociology of social science" has been organized around the role of intra-academic institutions and hierarchies within a wider social setting, it is important if general trends work to weaken these institutions and the grip of disciplinary elites (cf. Wæver (2007) on this issue for IR). Although the trends are far from complete enough to overturn all previous analyses (nor are they necessarily global), they do form part of the general picture.

We have introduced sociology of social science in more detail than post-colonialism. Among the reasons for this are that the different generations of theory are much more disparate and therefore need to be understood in individual terms and not only as variations within a common movement. In contrast, post-colonialism has been picked up in IR to a much larger extent than sociology of science, and it is thus comparatively easier for the reader to deepen our presentation above with the help of these writings, whereas the situation for sociology of science and IR remains largely one of a non-meeting.

Structure and rationale

The post-colonial and sociology of science mindset that informs our project poses three general challenges to be aware of in undertaking a comprehensive analysis of International Relations scholarship around the world. In turn, they also make this book unique in comparison to other related efforts.

IR as IR or under some other name

A common way of exploring IR in peripheral settings is to ask "Why is there no Chinese/ Turkish/Iranian/ . . . theory of international relations?" (paraphrasing, obviously: Wight 1960; cf. Acharya and Buzan 2007). Although this question should be *part* of the self-exploration of each national or regional IR community, it cannot be an exhaustive mode of asking. We should also be sensitive to theorizing that occurs in other fields – for example, literary and cultural studies, international law, economics, and sociology – which might be saying things that classify as International Relations in other places, including in parts of the (opposition within the) core. An obvious example is post-colonial theory, to which scholars in India, Africa, Latin America, and the Middle East in particular contribute significantly. However, as several of the case studies in this volume illustrate, these contributions are not widely recognized within the field of IR itself. When International Relationists *in the West* turn to post-colonial theory and it starts to be published in IR journals, it is obviously an absurdity not to register the productivity of non-Western academe just because delineations of fields work differently in distinct places.

On the other hand, it is not possible to simply forget about IR as a discipline, identify a set of issues and substantive questions, and ask who studies them in region "x," because no such laundry list making up "international relations" as a subject matter exists on a global level. Disciplines draw and redraw boundaries and constitute fields of knowledge. Therefore, statements about "IR taking place under other headings" can only be made carefully and by comparisons and connections to how fields operate elsewhere.

Thus, the study of any given locale should attempt to ask *both* about the way the "formal" field of International Relations has been constituted (or not), its origins, boundaries, relation to neighboring fields, its relation to policy making (e.g., as a chain of connected circles from think-tanks to universities, or not), and how it relates to IR at the core (import, dependence, hybridization, resistance). However, we should *also* ask what other fields have developed in ways that interrogate important elements of International Relations. A part of the solution is to explicitly ask the question: *What is locally international?* In other words, we should all ask "What is international where I live?", given that those issues, agendas, and concepts representing global issues vary from place to place.[11]

The aporia of disciplinarity

There is always disciplinarity. The question is not discipline or not, but how the discipline defines problems, and how this is articulated differently in distinct latitudes. In other words, how does disciplinarity manifest itself along a spatial dimension and how do local versions of IR articulate the universal, de facto U.S.–European center with specifically local needs and problems?

We aim to decenter the discipline by asking questions such as "What is international?" or "What is theory?", and in doing so, to expand the borders of IR and aim for a more open discussion of definitions. Everything gets inflected locally. Theory changes as it travels to different places, given that it is always a response to specific social and historical situations. Today, with more complex and accelerated travel patterns, theories change and feed back in even more challenging ways. There is not a stable constellation of theories that "are" simply themselves (in abstraction, i.e., in the center) and are "reacted to" (e.g., in the periphery), nor is this captured by a picture of local, independent realities. The particular inflections of theories have to be understood in-between the international and the local.

This is a challenge that will be confronted more directly in subsequent books in our series, but it has to be taken into account here, given that each chapter, especially in those instances of IR done somewhere "in the periphery," has to reflect upon the complex ways in which writings relate to the core in a "peripheral mode" and simultaneously modify and adjust theories and approaches from the center. Similarly, when particular local approaches are developed, it is interesting to observe to what extent and by what strategies they are defined "as IR" when presented to IR communities in the core. What is the power locally of IR status? Does it matter for the authority of a scholar in a local community whether her or his writings count as IR (or are seen as "cultural studies"), and does the road to such recognition pass through the center?

Sociology of knowledge and/or epistemology

This book is indicative of a general "sociology of science turn" or "sociological reflexivity" in IR. The discipline has undergone epistemological and ontological reflexivity, and is now increasing its sociological reflexivity (and attention to the geography of the discipline). This should only add on to reflexivity, rather than becoming the only mode for discussing issues. A plurality of analyses and debates should be nurtured, incorporating sociology of knowledge and spatiality, epistemology, and ontology.

While it is important to incorporate sociology of knowledge-based explanations, these should not be seen as replacing epistemology. Epistemology, which cannot be reduced to sociology of knowledge, points to a distinct question concerning the intellectual and epistemic constitution of fields, the premises that make it possible to speak about issues that matter. If one of our objectives is to reconstitute fields, it is necessary to work at this level as well. Without epistemology, we simply reproduce dominant strains of IR, only in a reflexive format.

Sociology of knowledge is not fit to answer epistemological queries. For instance, a number of new topics are pressing to enter the global agenda as security issues, among them poverty, drinking water, and human security. The key question is the epistemic one of how they are coded so that they can be discussed, what boundaries exist that require issues to be coded in particular ways in order to enter the debate, and how the debate is determined as a result. This is not a sociological matter.

One important example of the articulation between sociology of knowledge and episte-mology is how buzz-words become established, e.g., "governance" and "human security" in many parts of the third world today. It would be interesting to track the genealogy of how they have become so popular during the past several years that all institutes want them on their research agendas. Who are the speakers that articulate such concepts, and what are the institutional mechanisms for naturalizing them? What are the *local* mechanisms that deter-mine issues and non-issues, e.g., whether poverty is a central IR issue? How does this work in the United States versus Africa, for example?

Part of the solution to this problem is to avoid mechanistic, externalist explanations of developments within the discipline. We want to pursue explanations that respect the intellectual efforts of local scholars. Whether explaining IR in the core or the periphery – or any other discipline for that matter – it is always necessary to understand how the immediate explanation has to focus on moves made by actual scholars (cf. Skinner 2002), acting in their social context and primarily in the immediate, i.e., academic one (cf. Collins 1998; Wæver 2004a). They are influenced by economic and political factors only indirectly, both as explanations that shape their material and institutional working conditions, and as demands for specific content or use of research. By not over-sociologizing academics, we should be able to write a book about the actual doers of IR around the world.

The case studies

Each national or regional case study is written by a scholar (or scholars) who lives and works in the site studied. In identifying authors for the book we purposely sought out the greatest geocultural diversity possible in order to establish a productive dialogue among individuals who normally are not in academic contact with each other. Gathering scholars from all parts of the world contributes to our dual aims of increasing the inclusiveness and the geographical balance of the discipline, and understanding the ways in which our field is currently shaped by the privileging of core-based perspectives, assumptions, and problems. This has been a difficult task. Productive center–periphery dialogue in IR is hindered not only by seemingly irreconcilable points of view concerning global affairs. Tremendous asymmetries in working conditions, resources, and language constitute additional material barriers to initiatives such as this one, and different academic cultures and criteria make such joint production an interesting challenge.[12] Therefore, it comes as little surprise that a project like this one has not previously been carried out.

The case studies included in this book address three sets of questions: What is the situation? Why? And what does the future promise and demand?

What is the state of IR here?

The main point of departure for all of the contributions to this volume is the question "What is the general state of the discipline in each country or region under examination? What fields, works, original themes, and particular angles define the discipline *here*?" Each chapter contains some form of mapping section. However, the way in which this is done is the product of each author's creativity, ensuring the book's pluralism as a whole and an experimentation that we hope, in the long run, will generate more ideas about how to create such portraits. Chapter 14 on Central and Eastern Europe, for example, contains quite detailed statistics on different kinds of data and suggests novel ways of posing interesting questions about it in search of national patterns. The South Asia, Latin America, South Africa, Western Europe and Anglo-core and post-Imperial non-core, and U.S. chapters all point to strategies for collecting relevant data – in this case using course syllabi, journals, textbooks, and professional training of scholars as sources for sociological analysis. The mapping of the field also covers, in greater or lesser detail, the main waves of "what is studied" and their orientations and schools, as most clearly exemplified by the chapters on Russia, Japan, Korea, and Taiwan, Africa, China, and Southeast Asia.

A particularly important question posed to each author is how *theorizing* takes place locally: (1) *pure importation*: scholars are socialized abroad and teach "at home" whatever was fashionable when they studied in the United States or elsewhere; (2) *tool-box*: they pick a combination of whatever seems to work; (3) *uniqueness*: they do local analysis, given the unique quality of their particular settings; and possibly in consequence (4) they derive *theories* from their own worlds. The question of how different parts of the world relate to the theories of the core includes the kinds and degrees of intellectual "traffic," e.g., do people go to the United States to get a Ph.D. (Korea, many parts of Latin America, Israel) or not (China, Japan, the Anglo world), do they participate in international academic events such as the ISA annual conventions or not, and so forth. Are the main textbooks direct translations of Western ones (or are the English-language ones used in English), local paraphrasing or truly local? This relates, among other things, to the question of whether a tradition of IR exists (China, Japan, Latin America, Southeast Asia) or not (East Central Europe, Iran, South Asia), in which case the starting point is to import external knowledge.

Many studies point to problematic relationships between politics and the university world – either too close or too distant. Can this be seen as a kind of chain with distinct roles for think-tanks close to policy, diplomatic schools, more independent research institutes in-between think-tanks and universities, and finally universities? Does this structure work as a coherent chain or does it break down at some point – conveyor belt or division of labor? Are academics commonly appointed to positions in politics, diplomacy, or public administration? Who finances what – do think-tanks and university researchers compete for the same funding and thus try to live up to the same standards of both relevance and academic quality, or are these systems completely separate? Do the same individuals typically hold positions in both systems? How is this landscape formed in specific cases, why, and with what effects? Does it explain developments at the level of theory? (cf. Kahler 1993; Hill and Beshoff 1994; Wallace 1996; Wæver 2004b; Büger and Gadinger 2007; Eriksson and Norman 2008; Buzan and Hansen forthcoming).

Why is this the case?

The second level the case studies address is "Why?" Important factors that might be shaping the discipline in distinct geocultural settings include: (1) policy needs/foreign policy;

(2) institutional structure, financial constraints; (3) social sciences: what other disciplines are strong; maybe linked (i.e., coloring IR) or maybe covering the ground in its own terms (sociology? law? administration? humanities?); (4) the nature of the state; and (5) strong cosmologies, distinct religious–philosophical traditions.

This is a familiar list of explanatory factors that have been used in previous studies of national developments of IR (e.g., Wæver 1998; Drulák and Druláková 2000; Inoguchi and Bacon 2001; Tickner 2003a; Breitenbauch and Wivel 2004; Breitenbauch 2008). We did not want to create a strict and tight format that produced completely parallel chapters, only a "check list" which each author judged the relevance of. Most commonly included is probably the question of politically defined agendas at the national level, mainly through foreign policy orientation and general ideologies. The form of state and the kind of knowledge "it prefers" is another topic to be addressed: law? sociology? economics? Different kinds of governance/rule will naturally find better usage of different forms of knowledge. National identity also shapes the concept of science. A strong point has been made previously about how United States history and national identity favors scientism over historicism (Ross 1992); can similar connections be made in other national cases? Works by Wagner, Wittrock, and others, presented above, point to the intertwining of state history and science history, especially for the social sciences (cf. Wæver 1998). Germany and Italy went through state building (as well as unification) just before and during the period when modern social science was born. The result was a systematic merger of a professionalized law discipline and the ideal civil servant, whereas in France political science became more powerfully linked to the production of high-ranking civil servants, while the more academic IR kept interacting with sociology as the big discipline with an independent university presence. In the British Empire, the particular social function of a liberal education as "gentlemen's knowledge" left marks that show today in the system where civil servants can be trained in more or less any academic field from the humanities, social sciences or natural science, and International Relations is much more closely linked to political philosophy, history, and humanities than in most other places. Thus, the constellation of disciplines (particularly among the social sciences) within the universities interacted with the form of state apparatus, especially the preferred training for top civil servants (Wæver 1998). The majority of the case studies, in particular in the non-core, highlight the fact that the social sciences were created in order to serve the practical needs of states, meaning that knowledge is practical and policy oriented, and that theory is not as highly valued as in other sites. Conversely, it may be argued that the U.S. position in the world increases a demand for knowledge shaped as cause–effect generalizations because this enables this country to act on and try to shape the world, whereas, for instance, European allies need a more reflexive form of knowledge enabling questioning of the U.S. knowledge claims both as knowledge and as political moves (Wæver 2004b).

The relationship between or "rank" among different disciplines is also an important issue to consider. German state building led to a central position for law, in France, sociology is more important than elsewhere, and in Britain (at least until recently), history and the humanities were stronger and more closely connected to political studies than most other places. While originating in causes related to state type, this relationship becomes institutionalized *within* academia as a hierarchy among disciplines with its own reproductive mechanisms and ensuing struggles (Bourdieu 1988). Chapter 4 on Africa, for example, points out variations existing between different parts of the continent influenced by French, British, and Portuguese traditions. Very strong ruptures in cases such as Russia, Central and Eastern Europe, Iran, and South Africa raise the question of whether the academic system is reorganized in ways that link back to old patterns or in a truly new and maybe mostly imported format. These patterns matter because the kind of IR and political science one observes in a particular place tends to be strongly influenced by the disciplines it tries to measure up to.

Has the discipline obtained an internal structure, e.g., a hierarchy between theory and empirical work, the centrality of one or a few journals as criteria of status, or does it run on personalized networks? Although such patterns can be explained to a certain extent by the previous factors, they are likely to form an "intellectual and social organization" (Whitley 1984) that becomes an explanation in itself (cf. Wæver 2003). This is closely related to the study of "micro-mechanisms" such as the role of foundations, English language and disciplinary literacy, think-tanks, and regional research institutes. In terms of institutions, the most important is probably the university. The hiring practices and patterns of promotion define who the discipline's legitimate speakers are, and these practices, together with the selection of curricula, define the discipline. What is studied is influenced by who is allowed to teach IR. This in turn affects policy makers. Journals and academic associations are also fundamental.

The boundaries of what methods are accepted, what counts as knowledge, and what is credible as IR have been explored – and experienced – most clearly perhaps by feminists (Weber 1994; Tickner 1997), and their analyses point out a useful path into this part of our exploration. Some historians of political science have emphasized how, especially in the United States, disciplinary leaders police the boundaries regarding methodology and style due to worries about the standing and respectability of IR (for example, what will the economists think if we publish postmodern material that sounds like cultural studies?). In the core, epistemological and methodological correctness are more hegemonic than "content," i.e., not so much what we study as how we do it. The chapters will investigate whether this is equally true elsewhere (although it is mostly not).

In contrast to these feminist and other reflectivist writings, it is claimed by some sociology of science authors (e.g., Fuller 2002; cf. "fourth generation" presented above) that the trend goes in the opposite direction. With a decline in authority for university/science, the role of epistemology as a key disciplinary principle of legitimacy ("this is true and scientific because I followed the correct procedure") is giving way to non-epistemological legitimacy. Justification – and not least, funding – derives increasingly from policy relevance and a more general, complex field of justification where science is only one among many forms of knowledge (together with political, economic, and sometimes religious authorities).

Related to organizational and institutional questions are also the ways in which practical tasks to be performed by scholars and their everyday conditions influence the work done. This is probably a factor generally underestimated in writings on sociology of science, mostly authored from within the core and oblivious to the very down-to-earth challenges faced by most scholars in the periphery (including the most privileged) (Tickner 2004).

In countries or regions where there is a strong sense of a local cultural, religious, and/or philosophical tradition distinct from the modern West (e.g., India, China, Islamic world), how does this work its way into IR? Is it possible to have this general self-conception and at the same time import IR theories relatively unchanged from the core? Not that every scholar should invent a distinct local theory, but if the basic cosmology differs in its conception of basic categories such as subject–object, knowledge, individualism/community, and secularism, why does this *not* generate unique ways of criticizing theories – or make theory mutate in new ways, as many of the case studies suggest?

Prospects

Although we did not want to regulate how authors situated their concluding discussions, they were all asked to project their analysis forward by asking what future prospects look like, and/or to formulate suggestions for what to do. Several issues might be taken into consideration in this respect. What is the relationship between theory and empirical work? If theory often constrains research on locally pressing issues (e.g., in Africa), is the way forward to give greater priority to "facts on the ground," or will this induce problematic ontologies of "civil war," "poverty," "development," and "democracy," as long as local theoretical work is missing? The easy answer, of course, is that both theoretical and empirical work is needed, but the challenge then is how to connect the two in practice. If theory takes place in isolation from local practical challenges, it reproduces Western categories. If local empirical work is conducted without theory, it also reproduces these categories because they have not been challenged and reconfigured. "Progress" is most likely to occur when scholars discuss theory locally in a setting where they feel responsible and committed in relation to empirical and policy concerns. This brings us back to the institutional and organizational side of what kinds of institutions expose scholars to this dual demand structure as everyday practice. Neither blue-sky ivory-tower universities nor thoroughly policy-directed research centers are likely to deliver these conditions, but rather a messy combination of both with sufficient confusion to create both autonomy and overlap.

Jörg Friedrichs, in one of the few existing monographs on non-American IR (Friedrichs 2004), organizes much of his analysis around a set of different strategies that peripheries can adopt "to cope with the fundamental fact of life of American intellectual hegemony." He discusses "academic self-reliance" using France as an example, Italy as a case of "resigned marginality" and "multi-level research cooperation" in relation to Scandinavia and possibly the emerging European scene at large (Chapter 15, in this volume). These are options available in a relatively privileged semi-periphery (or semi-core) like Western Europe, but what "strategies," if any, are adopted in other places? How is the fact of U.S. dominance viewed, if in fact it is an issue or a worry at all? Does variation on this question follow the "size" (or pride) of the country, so that great powers want their own theories? Or does it simply reflect ideological distance vis-à-vis the United States, so that U.S. theory is most controversial in places where that country's influence in the world is generally resented?

Use of this book

This book is likely to be used by both students and researchers. We imagine that in undergraduate courses as part of general IR introduction it might be relevant to assign a smaller part of it, say the introduction, conclusion, and the locally relevant chapter(s). At the postgraduate level, we imagine both specialized courses oriented towards the study of the discipline as such and usage as part of courses on "the third world"/North–South and in general upper-level general IR theory courses. Currently, its subject area is not widely taught, primarily because there have been no texts to teach it from!

Courses may be constructed along different axes. One option would be to combine this book with the single articles and sub-global books that come closest to this, for a quite compact course on IR around the world. That would include Hoffmann 1977; Holsti 1985; Krippendorff 1989; Chan 1996; Cox 1997; Alagappa 1998; Chan 1999; Rajaee 1999; Smith 2000; Crawford and Jarvis 2001; Dunn and Shaw 2001; Geeraerts and Jeng 2001; Inoguchi and Bacon 2001; Euben 2002; Tickner 2003a; Friedrichs 2004; Jørgensen and Knudsen 2006; Acharya and Buzan 2007. This format could be combined with more sociology of science-like data and/or theory on the U.S.-centered discipline, including Maliniak *et al.* 2007 (the TRIP survey); Schmidt 2002; Hellmann 2003; Holden 2002[13] and possibly also a bit of history, illustrating the historiographic issue of understanding the discipline through the case of understanding the "first great debate" as myth and/or history (Wilson 1998; Ashworth 2002, 2006; Vigneswaran and Quirk 2005). In this context, particular notice should be taken of two volumes that add more detail to the picture derived from this book regarding two parts of the world, Europe and Asia: Knud Erik Jørgensen and Tonny Brems Knudsen (eds), *International Relations in Europe: Traditions, Perspectives and Destinations* (Routledge, 2006); and Amitav Acharya and Barry Buzan (eds), "Why Is There No Non-Western International Relations Theory: Reflections on and from Asia," published as a special issue of *International Relations of the Asia-Pacific* in September 2007.[14]

Another option would be to combine the book with more critical, philosophical, and normative discussions. This could mean more general literature on post-positivism and maybe post-colonialism in relation to IR, specifically Inayatullah and Blaney (2004); Chan *et al.* (2001); and a 2003 special issue of *Global Society* entitled "Locating the 'I' in 'IR' – Dislocating Euro-American Theories." The latter option could be combined with the literature mentioned in the first pages of this introduction that addresses why IR theory does not "fit" the third world (Neuman 1998; Tickner 2003b).

An important question is whether all of this is only a "social" problem (inequalities among IR scholars) or if it shapes the content of IR, because our unbalanced discipline produces a particular form of IR. One can engage with this issue vis-à-vis those that continue the discussion of IR as "an American social science," most notably Crawford and Jarvis, *International Relations – Still an American Social Science? Toward Diversity in International Thought* (SUNY Press, 2001). Despite its title, and the central message of the editors' contributions, namely that IR is *not* an American social science (but a global, pluralistic enterprise), the book is (with a few notable exceptions) about Canadian, Australian, British, and mostly U.S. scholarship! Thus, it goes nicely with the present volume, that speaks about the field by looking at what is actually done around the world and why, instead of reflecting on what the leading Western scholars have to say about it.

Notes

1 The importance of asymmetries is bigger, if the effects are not only social, distributive (scholars at the core have better opportunities than those in the periphery), but also cognitive, that is, if the asymmetries make a difference to the resulting knowledge. Most would probably deny the relevance of discussing a particular Korean quantum mechanics or a Nigerian way of nano-science. Generally, it is more immediately plausible that the place of production shapes knowledge in the social sciences and humanities. (A case can certainly be made for some social effects even in the natural sciences; cf. Bernal 1939; Sohn-Rethel 1977; Harding 1998. But in relation to the natural sciences this is a much more controversial and uphill claim to make.)

2 Explicit attempts to link post-colonial theory into IR include Darby and Paolini 1994; Ahluwalia and Sullivan 2001; Krishna 2001; Barkawi and Laffey 2002, 2006; Chowdhry and Nair 2002; Ling 2002; Agathangelou and Ling 2004; Inayatullah and Blaney 2004; Muppidi 2004; Grovogui 2006, 2007; Chowdhry 2007; Jabri 2007; Bilgin 2008 – and in an interesting indirect way through the writings on early twentieth-century (and late nineteenth-century) IR theory, where IR historians (especially in British universities) emphasize the underestimated power of colonialism: Long and Schmidt 2005; Bell 2007; Sylvest 2008.

3 The term "worlding" was originally adopted from Martin Heidegger. See Spivak (1985), Wilson (2007), and Wilson and Connery (2007).

4 These literatures are not at all separate, nor should they be. The overlap shows, for instance, when "critical rationalism" is mentioned as one of the positions in theory of science, and its inventor

Sir Karl Popper as a key figure within philosophy of science. They are distinct because each has a different problematique, but typically a specific position in one debate correlates more or less tightly with a specific position in the other genre. Critical realists, for instance, have a clear position within the debate on theory of science, a related (less distinct) position on philosophy of science, and even some elements of a sociology of scence.

5 Philosophy of science has some links to sociology of science, because an argument like Kuhn's about paradigms includes a rudimentary sociological idea of socialization and coordination, but the main format for writings like those of Kuhn and Lakatos is a combination of history of science and rationalization of a model for the evolution of scientific knowledge, the central format becoming therefore "rational reconstruction." In the words of Robert Merton: "the intricate interaction between the sociology of science and the philosophy of science has left its indelible mark on both disciplines" (Merton 1977: 23). Interaction does not mean identity. Certainly, the overlap is not big enough to make it reasonable to treat these as one debate, and especially not to let discussions around Kuhn and Lakatos crowd out all empirically based and sociologically informed knowledge about the actual mechanisms in scientific communities.

6 Quantitative studies of a bibliometric nature have become a field in its own right, and it often maps as a project in itself, or is directed towards policy needs in research policy, but much of it was originally generated by and could be made sense of in relation to Mertonian sociology of science; cf. Leydesdorff 2001.

7 STS studies how science and technology are socially embedded – shaped by social, political, economic, and cultural factors. To a significant degree, this dynamic field emerged by extending the methods and insights from science studies to technology (which is partly a materialization and outgrowth of science), merging with critical history of science. Since, however, STS studies are often driven by a concern about the development of technology and its impact on society, increasingly social science comes into the picture as part of society's ways of viewing, evaluating, and deciding on technology, but this usually only includes social science (and humanities) in relation to natural and medical science (e.g., ethics of biotechnology, risk analysis, and other technology assessments), not as studies of social science in general. See Hackett *et al.* 2008.

8 "[T]he uncoupling of historical and sociological inquiry from issues of truth, or realism, or objectivity opened the way to a remarkably productive period in the understanding of science as a human enterprise" (Golinski 1998: x).

9 A closely related literature talks about the "triple helix" of university–industry–government relations. While important methodological and theoretical differences exist between this and the "mode 2" literature, the argument is sufficiently similar for the present purpose to ignore these specificities.

10 A somewhat parallel literature on the industrialization and marketization of academe is drawn on by some critical scholars in IR. While making some of the same points as the "new production of knowledge" literature, and pointing to many relevant and often troubling changes in the world of academia, this literature unintendedly often depicts a rather naive picture of a lost world without involvement from business and state, thereby both – ironically – ignoring the internal forms of discipline in the academic world, and denying the legitimacy of society to ask for accountability from public universities. Often, this literature becomes one more version of searching for pure voices to represent an alternative to the powers of capital, this time placing hope in a purified university.

11 This question is built into the structure of our second edited volume, *Thinking IR Differently*, where thematic sections on specific concepts (e.g., "security," "authority") are supplemented by an "open" section that inquires into what the "international" is, thus highlighting different key concepts.

12 A curious illustration of the difficulty as well as the ultimate possibility is the state of the art in our neighboring discipline sociology. On the one hand, they have actually managed to produce global surveys of sociology around the world: Mohan and Wilke 1994 and Morán 1998 (and Nedelmann and Sztomka 1993 on Europe). On the other hand, even sociologists with the sociology of science close at hand have not gone much beyond mapping "who does what where", not really delving into explanations or larger patterns – neither the global structure of the discipline, nor comparative studies of local structure. Thanks to Heine Andersen for leading us to these works. An even more thought-provoking case is of course the writings within sociology of science about the state of sociology of science. Here authors are usually quite explicit about the self-exemplifying character of this case, and in a classical review of the state of "The Sociology of Science in Europe" (Merton and Gaston 1977), the contributors present the national state of affairs with varying degrees of

theoretical benefit from sociology of science, but the global structure of the discipline and its geo-cultural dynamics are left almost untouched, even in this case.

13 Especially in the journal *PS* (published by the American Political Science Association), one finds a lot of short articles on ranking of journals, publishers, and departments, and the merits of competing forms of measurement. In addition, issues like placement of Ph.D. candidates and hiring decisions are covered. This is mostly limited to the U.S. and most often written more as part of the institutional mechanisms than reflectively about them, but these articles nevertheless contain a lot of empirical data and analytical observations on the micro-mechanisms of the discipline, at least in the U.S.

14 The two works differ from ours in three important respects. First, each is only about one region, although the Acharya/Buzan volume is aimed at understanding the general non-Western issue. Second, they focus mostly on the development of IR theory in the relatively narrow, institutional sense, whereas we want to cover the dual agenda of self-declared IR theory and "IR under any other name," i.e. development of knowledge about similar issues that emerge under other disciplinary headings and in other formats as part of the variation in social formations across the globe. Third, they do not draw on theory outside IR (i.e., sociology of science or post-colonial theory) to enlighten the issues, but work in the classical mold of enlightened IR scholars reflecting in an IR manner on IR. However, given both the larger space for detail and the many good authors involved, much may be gained from these books about IR in two important parts of the world, so the three volumes will go well together in a course.

References

Acharya, Amitav and Barry Buzan (eds) (2007) "Why Is There no Non-Western International Relations Theory: Reflections on and from Asia," published as a special issue of *International Relations of the Asia-Pacific*, 7 (3; September).

Adams, Rachel (2001) "Worlding of American Studies," *American Quarterly*, 53 (4): 720–732.

Agathangelou, A. M. and L. H. M. Ling (2004) "The House of IR: From Family Power Politics to the Poisies of Worldism," *International Studies Review*, 6 (4) : 21–49.

Ahluwalia, Pal and Michael Sullivan (2001) "Beyond International Relations: Edward Said and the World," pp. 349–367 in Robert Crawford and Darryl Jarvis (eds), *International Relations Still an American Social Science? Towards Diversity in International Thought*, Albany, NY: State University of New York Press.

Alagappa, Muthiah (ed.) (1998) *Asian Security Practice: Material and Ideational Influences*, Stanford, CA: Stanford University Press.

Alker, Hayward R. and Thomas J. Biersteker (1984) "The Dialectics of World Order: Notes for a Future Archeologist of International Savoir Faire," *International Studies Quarterly*, 28 (2; June): 121–142.

Anderson, Benedict (1983) *Imagined Communities: Reflections on the Origin and Spread of Nationalism*, London: Verso (revised edition 1991).

Appadurai, Arjun (1996) *Modernity at Large: Cultural Dimensions of Globalization*, Minneapolis, MI: University of Minnesota Press.

Ashworth, Lucian M. (2002) "Did the Realist–Idealist Great Debate Really Happen? A Revisionist History of International Relations," *International Relations*, 16 (1): 33–51.

Ashworth, Lucian M. (2006) "Where Are the Idealists in Interwar International Relations?", *Review of International Studies*, 32 (2): 291–308.

Aydinli, Ersel and Julie Mathews (2000) "Are the Core and the Periphery Irreconcilable? The Curious World of Publishing in Contemporary International Relations," *International Studies Perspectives*, 16 (1): 33–51.

Ayoob, Mohammed (1995) *The Third World Security Predicament. State Making, Regional Conflict and the International System*, Boulder, CO: Lynne Rienner.

Barkawi, Tarak and Mark Laffey (2002) "Retrieving the Imperial: Empire and International Relations," *Millennium: Journal of International Studies*, 31 (1): 109–127.

Barkawi, Tarak and Mark Laffey (2006) "The Postcolonial Moment in Security Studies," *Review of International Studies*, 32 (2): 329–352.

Bell, Duncan (ed.) (2007) *Victorian Visions of Global Order: Empire and International Relations in Nineteenth-century Political Thought*, Cambridge: Cambridge University Press.

Bernal, J. D. (1939) *The Social Function of Science*, London: Routledge.

Beverley, John (1999) *Subalternity and Representation: Arguments in Cultural Theory*, Durham, NC: Duke University Press.

Bhabha, Homi K. (1994) *The Location of Culture*, New York: Routledge.

Bilgin, Pinar (2008) "Thinking Past 'Western' IR," *Third World Quarterly*, 29 (1): 5–23.

Blaikie, Norman W. H. (1993) *Approaches to Social Enquiry*, Cambridge: Polity Press.

Blaney, David L. (1996) "Reconceptualizing Autonomy: The Difference Dependency Makes," *Review of International Political Economy*, 3 (3): 459–497.

Bourdieu, Pierre (1988) *Homo Academicus*, Cambridge: Polity Press (French original 1984).

Breitenbauch, Henrik Ø. (2008) *Cartesian Limbo: A Formal Approach to the Study of Social Sciences: International Relations in France*, Ph.D. dissertation, University of Copenhagen.

Breitenbauch, Henrik Ø. and Anders Wivel (2004) "Understanding National IR Disciplines Outside the United States: Political Culture and the Construction of International Relations in Denmark," *Journal of International Relations and Development*, 7 (4): 414–443.

Büger, Christian and Frank Gadinger (2007) "Reassembling and Dissecting: International Relations Practice from a Science Studies Perspective," *International Studies Perspectives*, 8 (1): 90–110.

Buzan, Barry and Lene Hansen (forthcoming) *The Evolution of International Security Studies*, Cambridge: Cambridge University Press.

Canclini, Néstor García (1995) *Hybrid Cultures: Strategies for Entering and Leaving Modernity*, Mississippi, MI: University of Minnesota Press.

Chan, Gerald (1999) *Chinese Perspectives on International Relations: A Framework for Analysis*, New York: Palgrave–Macmillan.

Chan, Stephen (1996) *Towards a Multicultural Roshamon Paradigm in International Relations: Collected Essays*, Tampere Research Report, No. 74.

Chan, Stephen, Peter Mandaville and Roland Bleiker (eds) (2001) *The Zen of International Relations: IR Theory from East to West*, Basingstoke: Palgrave.

Chatterjee, Partha (1986) *Nationalist Thought and the Colonial World: A Derivative Discourse?*, United Nations University (reprinted in *The Partha Chatterjee Omnibus*, New Delhi: Oxford University Press, 1999).

Chatterjee, Partha (1993) *The Nation and Its Fragments: Colonial and Postcolonial Histories*, Princeton, NJ: Princeton University Press (reprinted in *The Partha Chatterjee Omnibus*, New Delhi: Oxford University Press, 1999).

Chatterjee, Partha (2004) *The Politics of the Governed: Reflections on Popular Politics in Most of the World*, New Delhi: Permanent Black.

Childs, John Brown (2003) *Transcommunality: From the Politics of Conversion to the Ethics of Respect*, Philadelphia, PA: Temple University Press.

Chowdhry, Geeta (2007) "Edward Said and Contrapuntal Reading: Implications for Critical Interventions in International Relations," *Millennium: Journal of International Studies*, 36 (1): 101–116.

Chowdhry, Geeta and Sheila Nair (2002) "Introduction: Power in a Postcolonial World: Race, Gender and Class in International Relations," pp. 1–32 in Geeta Chowdhry and Sheila Nair (eds), *Power, Postcolonialism and International Relations: Reading Race, Gender and Class*, London: Routledge.

Chun, Allen (2000) "The Institutional Unconscious; or, The Prison House of Academia," *boundary 2*, 27 (1): 51–74.

Collins, Randall (1998) *The Sociology of Philosophies: A Global Theory of Intellectual Change*, Cambridge, MA: Belknap Press.

Cox, Robert W. (ed.) (1997) *The New Realism. Perspectives on Multilateralism and World Order*, New York: United Nations University Press.

Crawford, Robert M.A. and Darryl S. Jarvis (eds) (2001) *International Relations – Still an American Social Science? Toward Diversity in International Thought*, Albany: State University of New York Press.

Darby, Phillip and Albert J. Paolini (1994) "Bridging International Relations and Postcolonialism," *Alternatives*, 19 (3): 371–397.

Diesing, Paul (1991) *How Does Social Science Work? Reflections on Practice*, Pittsburgh: University of Pittsburgh Press.

Dirlik, Arif (1999) "How the Grinch Hijacked Radicalism: Further Thoughts on the Postcolonial," *Postcolonial Studies*, 2 (2): 149–163.

Doty, Roxanne Lynn (1996) *Imperial Encounters*, Minneapolis, MI: University of Minnesota Press.

Drulák, Petr and Radka Druláková (2000) "International Relations in the Czech Republic: A Review of the Discipline," *Journal of International Relations and Development*, 3 (3): 256–282.

Dunn, Kevin C. and Timothy A. Shaw (eds) (2001) *Africa's Challenge to International Relations Theory*, New York: Palgrave–Macmillan.

Dyer, Hugh C. and Leon Mangasarian (eds) (1989) *The Study of International Relations: The State of the Art*, London: Macmillan; and previously as a special section in *Millennium*, 16 (2).

Elman, Colin and Miriam Fendus Elman (eds) (2003) *Progress in International Relations Theory: Appraising the Field*, Chicago, IL: MIT Press.

Eriksson, Johan and Ludvig Norman (2008) "Political Utilization of Scholarly Ideas: The 'Clash of Civilizations' vs. 'Soft Power' in U.S. Foreign Policy," paper presented at the ISA Convention in San Francisco, March 26–29.

Escobar, Arturo (1995) *Encountering Development. The Making and Unmaking of the Third World*, Princeton, NJ: Princeton University Press.

Euben, Roxanne L. (2002) "Contingent Borders, Syncretic Perspectives: Globalization, Political Theory, and Islamizing Knowledge," *International Studies Review*, 4 (1): 23–48.

Friedrichs, Jörg (2004) *European Approaches to International Relations Theory: A House with Many Mansions*, London: Routledge.

Fuchs, Stephan (1992) *The Professional Quest for Truth: A Social Theory of Science and Knowledge*, Albany: State University of New York Press.

Fujiwara, Kirchi (forthcoming) *The Nationalists: Advocates of Civic Nationals in Asia*, Tokyo: Kodansha.

Fuller, Steve (2002) *The Governance of Science: Ideology and the Future of the Open Society*, Buckingham: Open University Press.

Geeraerts, Gustaef and Min Jeng (2001) "International Relations Theory in China," *Global Society*, 15 (3): 251–276.

Gibbons, Michael, Camille Limoges, Helga Nowotny, Simon Schwartzman, Peter Scott, and Martin Trow (1994) *The New Production of Knowledge: The Dynamics of Science and Research in Contemporary Societies*, London: Sage.

Gillman, Susan, Kirsten Silva Greusz, and Rob Wilson (2004) "Worlding American Studies," *Comparative American Studies*, 2 (3): 259–270.

Golinski, Jan (1998) *Making Natural Knowledge: Constructivism and the History of Science*, Cambridge: Cambridge University Press.

Grovogui, Siba N. (2006) *Beyond Eurocentrism and Anarchy: Memories of International Order and Institutions*, Basingstoke: Palgrave.

Grovogui, Siba N. (2007) "Postcolonialism," pp. 229–246 in Tim Dunne *et al.*, *International Relations Theories: Discipline and Diversity*, Oxford: Oxford University Press.

Guzzini, Stefano (1998) *Realism in International Relations and International Political Economy. The Continuing Story of a Death Foretold*, New York: Routledge.

Hackett, Edward J., Olga Amsterdamska, Michael Lynch, and Judy Wajcman (eds) (2008) *The Handbook of Science and Technology Studies* (3rd edn), Cambridge, MA: MIT Press.

Harding, Sandra (1986) *The Science Question in Feminism*, Stony Stratford: Open University Press.

Harding, Sandra (1991) *Whose Science? Whose Knowledge?*, Buckingham: Open University Press.

Harding, Sandra (1998) *Is Science Multicultural? Postcolonialisms, Feminisms, and Epistemologies*, Bloomington: Indiana University Press.

Hellmann, Gunther (ed.) (2003) "Symposium: Dialogue and Synthesis in Individual Scholarship and Collective Inquiry," *International Studies Review*, 5 (1): 123–150.

Hill, Christopher and Pamela Beshoff (eds) (1994) *Two Worlds of International Relations: Academics, Practitioners and the Trade in Ideas*, London: LSE/Routledge.

Hoffmann, Stanley (1977) "An American Social Science: International Relations," *Dædalus*, 106 (3): 41–60.

Holden, Gerard (2001) "The Politer Kingdoms of the Globe: Context and Comparison in the Intellectual History of IR," *Global Society*, 15 (1): 27–51.

Holden, Gerard (2002) "Who Contextualizes the Contextualizers? Disciplinary History and the Discourse about IR Discourse," *Review of International Studies*, 28 (2): 253–270.

Holden, Gerard (2006) "Approaches to IR: The Relationship Between Anglo-Saxon Historiography and Cross-community Comparison," pp. 225–252 in Knud Erik Jørgensen and Tonny Brems Knudsen (eds), *International Relations in Europe: Traditions, Perspectives and Destinations,* London: Routledge.

Holsti, K.J. (1985) *The Dividing Discipline: Hegemony and Diversity in International Theory*, Boston, MA: Allen & Unwin.

Inayatullah, Naeem (1996) "Beyond Sovereignty: Quasi-states as Social Construct," pp. 50–80 in Thomas J. Biersteker and Cynthia Weber (eds), *State Sovereignty as Social Construct*, Cambridge: Cambridge University Press.

Inayatullah, Naeem and David Blaney (2004) *International Relations and the Problem of Difference*, London: Routledge.

Inoguchi, Takashi and Paul Bacon (2001) "The Study of International Relations in Japan: Towards a More International Discipline," *International Relations of the Asia-Pacific*, 1 (1): 1–20.

Jabri, Vivienne (2007) "Solidarity and Spheres of Culture: The Cosmopolitan and the Postcolonial," *Review of International Studies*, 33: 715–728.

Jones, Adam (2006) "Worlding Men," Introduction in Adam Jones (ed.), *Men of the Global South: A Reader*, London: Zed Books, pp, xii–xxii.

Jørgensen, Knud Erik and Tonny Brems Knudsen (2006) *International Relations in Europe: Traditions, Perspectives and Destinations,* London: Routledge.

Kahler, Miles (1993) "International Relations: An American Social Science or an International One?," pp. 395–414 in Linda B. Miller and Michael Smith (eds), *Ideas and Ideals: Essays on Politics in Honor of Stanley Hoffmann*, Boulder, CO: Westview Press.

Karagiannis, Nathalie and Peter Wagner (eds) (2006) *Varieties of World Making: Beyond Globalization*, Liverpool: Liverpool University Press.

Keohane, Robert O. (1986) "Theory of World Politics: Structural Realism and Beyond," pp. 158–203 in *Neorealism and Its Critics*, New York: Columbia University Press.

Knorr-Cetina, Karin and Michael Mulkay (1983) *Science Observed: Perspectives on the Social Study of Science*, London: Sage.

Krippendorff, Ekkehart (1989) "The Dominance of American Approaches in International Relations," pp. 28–39 in Hugh C. Dyer and Leon Mangasarian (eds), *The Study of International Relations*, New York: St. Martin's Press.

Krishna, Sankaran (2001) "Race, Amnesia, and the Education of International Relations," *Alternatives: Global, Local, Political*, 26 (4): 401–423.

Kuhn, Thomas S. (1970) *The Structure of Scientific Revolutions*, Chicago, IL: University of Chicago Press.

Lapid, Yosef (1989) "The Third Debate: On the Prospects of International Theory in a Post-positivist Era," *International Studies Quarterly*, 33 (3): 235–254.

Latour, Bruno and Steve Woolgar (1979) *Laboratory Life: The Social Construction of Scientific Facts*, Beverly Hills, CA: Sage.

Leydesdorff, Loet (2001) *The Challenge of Scientometrics: The Development, Measurement, and Self-organization of Scientific Communications* (2nd edn), New York: Universal Publishers.

Ling, L. H. M. (2002) *Postcolonial International Relations: Conquest and Desire Between Asia and the West*, New York: Palgrave.

Long, David and Brian C. Schmidt (eds) (2005) *Imperialism and Internationalism in the Discipline of International Relations*, New York: SUNY Press.

Maliniak, Daniel, Amy Oakes, Susan Peterson, and Michael J. Tierney (2007) "The View from the Ivory Tower: TRIP Survey of IR Faculty in the U.S. and Canada," Reves Center and Arts and Sciences, College of William and Mary, Williamsburg, VA, February.

Mazrui, Ali (1990) *Cultural Forces in World Politics*, London and Portsmouth: James Currey and Heinemann.

Mazrui, Ali (1996) "The Imperial Culture of North–South Relations: The Case of Islam and the West," pp. 218–240 in Karen Dawisha and Bruce Parrott (eds), *The End of Empire? The Transformation of the U.S.S.R. in a Comparative Perspective*, New York: Armonk.

Merton, Robert K. (1942) "Science and Technology in a Democratic Order," *Journal of Legal and Political Sociology*, 1: 115–126 (reprinted as "The Normative Structure of Science" in Merton 1973, pp. 267–278).

Merton, Robert K. (1957) "Priorities in Scientific Discovery," Presidential Address at the annual meeting of the American Sociological Society, *American Sociological Review*, 22 (6): 635–659 (reprinted in Merton 1973, pp. 286–324).

Merton, Robert K. (1973) *The Sociology of Science: Theoretical and Empirical Investigations*, Chicago, IL: University of Chicago Press.

Merton, Robert K. (1977) "The Sociology of Science: An Episodic Memoir," pp. 3–141 in Robert K. Merton and Jerry Gaston (eds), *The Sociology of Science in Europe*, Chicago, IL: Southern Illinois University Press.

Merton, Robert K. and Jerry Gaston (eds) (1977) *The Sociology of Science in Europe*, Chicago, IL: Southern Illinois University Press.

Mignolo, Walter (2000) *Local Histories/Global Designs. Coloniality, Subaltern Knowledges and Border Thinking*, Princeton, NJ: Princeton University Press.

Mohan, Raj P. and Arthur S. Wilke (eds) (1994) *International Handbook of Contemporary Developments in Sociology*, London: Mansell Publishing.

Morán, María Luz (series ed.) (1998) *Social Knowledge: Heritage, Challenges, Perspectives*, 11 Pre-Congress Volumes, written in preparation for the 14th World Congress of Sociology, International Sociological Association.

Muppidi, Himadeep (2004) *The Politics of the Global*, Minneapolis and London: University of Minnesota Press.

Nedelmann, Birgitta and Piotr Sztomka (eds) (1993) *Sociology in Europe. In Search of Identity*, Berlin: Walter de Gruyter.

Neuman, Stephanie G. (ed.) (1998) *International Relations Theory and the Third World*, New York: St. Martin's Press, pp. 1–29.

Nowotny, Helga, Peter Scott and Michael Gibbons (2001) *Rethinking Science: Knowledge in an Age of Uncertainty*, Cambridge: Polity Press.

Nowotny, Helga, Peter Scott, and Michael Gibbons (2003) "'Mode 2' Revisited: The New Production of Knowledge," *Minerva*, 41 (3): 179–194.

Pettman, Jan Jindy (1994) *Worlding Women: A Feminist International Politics*, New York: Allen & Unwin.

Rajaee, Farhang (1999) "Paradigm Shifts in Muslim International Relations Discourse," *Studies in Contemporary Islam*, 1(1): 1–13.

Ross, Dorothy (1992) *The Origins of American Social Science*, Cambridge: Cambridge University Press.

Said, Edward W. (1979) *Orientalism*, New York: Vintage Books.

Said, Edward W. (1983) "The World, the Text, and the Critic," pp. 31–53 in *The World, the Text, and the Critic*, Cambridge, MA: Harvard University Press.

Schmidt, Brian C. (1998) *The Political Discourse of Anarchy: A Disciplinary History of International Relations*, Albany: State University of New York Press.

Schmidt, Brian C. (2002) "On the History and Historiography of International Relations," pp. 3–22 in Carlsnaes *et al.*, *Handbook of International Relations*, London: Sage.

Seth, Sanjay, Leela Gandhi, and Michael Dutton (1998) "Postcolonial Studies: A Beginning . . . ," *Postcolonial Studies,* 1 (1): 7–14.

Shapiro, Michael J. (2004) *Methods and Nations: Cultural Governance and the Indigenous Subject*, London: Routledge.

Skinner, Quentin (2002) *Visions of Politics*, Vol. 1: *Regarding Method*, Cambridge: Cambridge University Press.

Smith, Steve (1995) "The Self Images of a Discipline: A Genealogy of International Relations Theory," pp. 1–37 in Ken Booth and Steve Smith (eds), *International Relations Theory Today*, University Park: Pennsylvania State University Press.

Smith, Steve (2000) "The Discipline of International Relations: Still an American Social Science?," *British Journal of Politics and International Relations*, 3 (3): 216–255.

Sohn-Rethel, Alfred (1977) *Intellectual and Manual Labour: A Critique of Epistemology*, Atlantic Highlands, NJ: Humanities Press.

Spivak, Gayatri Chakravorty (1985) "Three Women's Texts and a Critique of Imperialism," in Henry Louis Gates Jr. (ed.), *'Race,' Writing and Difference,* special issue of *Critical Inquiry*, 12 (1): 243–261 (reissued in book form 1986 by the University of Chicago Press).

Spivak, Gayatri Chakravorty (1988) "Can the Subaltern Speak?," pp. 271–313 in Cary Nelson and Lawrence Grossberg (eds), *Marxism and the Interpretation of Culture*, Champaign, IL: University of Illinois Press (a reworked version is [re]printed in Spivak, *A Critique of Postcolonial Reason: Toward a History of the Vanishing Present*, Cambridge, MA, and London: Harvard University Press; Calcutta: Seagull Press, 1999, pp. 198–311).

Sylvest, Casper (2008) "Our Passion for Legality: International Law and Imperialism in Late Nineteenth-century Britain," *Review of International Studies*, 34 (3): 403–423.

Tickner, J. Ann (1997) "You Just Don't Understand: Troubled Engagements Between Feminists and IR Theorists," *International Studies Quarterly*, 41 (4): 611–632.

Tickner, Arlene B. (2003a) "Hearing Latin American Voices in IR," *International Studies Perspectives*, 4 (4): 325–350.

Tickner, Arlene B. (2003b) "Seeing IR Differently: Notes from the Third World," *Millennium: Journal of International Studies*, 32 (2): 295–324.

Tickner, Arlene B. (2004) "Everyday Practice and International Relations," paper presented at the 2004 ISA Annual Meeting, Montreal, 17–20 March.

Vigneswaran, Darshan and Joel Quirk (2005) "The Construction of an Edifice: The Story of a First Great Debate," *Review of International Studies*, 31 (1): 59–74.

Wæver, Ole (1998) "The Sociology of a Not So International Discipline: American and European Developments in International Relations," *International Organization*, 52 (4): 687–727.

Wæver, Ole (2003) "The Structure of the IR Discipline: A Proto-comparative Analysis," paper presented at the ISA Convention, Portland, February 26 to March 3.

Wæver, Ole (2004a) "'Isms, Paradigms, Traditions and Theories' – But Why Also *'Schools'* in IR?," a paper that gradually mutates into "Prolegomena to a Posthumous Textbook: How Should We Teach (IR?) Theory in a Post-international Age?," prepared for ECPR Standing Group on International Relations, 5th Pan-European International Relations Conference, The Hague, September 9–11.

Wæver, Ole (2004b) "Aberystwyth, Paris, Copenhagen: New 'Schools' in Security Theory and Their Origins Between Core and Periphery," paper prepared for the 45th Annual Convention of the International Studies Association. Montreal, 17–20 March; revised version to appear in A.B. Tickner and O. Wæver (eds), *Thinking the International Differently: Worlding Beyond the West*, Vol. 2, London: Routledge.

Wæver, Ole (2007) "Still a Discipline After All These Debates?," pp. 288–308 in Tim Dunne, Milja Kurki, and Steve Smith (eds), *International Relations Theories: Discipline and Diversity*, Oxford: Oxford University Press.

Wagner, Peter (1989) "Social Science and the State in Continental Western Europe: The Political Structuration of Disciplinary Discourse," *International Social Science Journal*, 41 (4): 509–528.

Wagner, Peter (1990) *Sozialwissenschaften und Staat: Frankreich, Italien, Deutschland 1870–1980*, Frankfurt and New York: Campus Verlag.

Wagner, Peter and Björn Wittrock (1991) "Analyzing Social Science: On the Possibility of a Sociology of the Social Sciences and States, Institutions, and Discourses: A Comparative Perspective on the Structuration of the Social Sciences," pp. 3–22, 331–358 in Peter Wagner, Björn Wittrock, and Richard Whitley (eds), *Sociology of the Sciences – A Yearbook*, Vol. 15, *Discourses on Society: The Shaping of the Social Sciences*, Dordrecht: Kluwer.

Wai, Chu Yiu (2004) "Postcolonial Discourse in the Age of Globalization," pp. 37–48 in Allen Chun (ed.), *Globalization: Critical Issues*, Oxford: Berghahn Books.

Walker, R.B.J. (1993) *Inside/Outside: International Relations as Political Theory*, Cambridge: Cambridge University Press.

Wallace, William (1996) "Truth and Power, Monks and Technocrats: Theory and Practice in International Relations," *Review of International Politics*, 22 (3): 301–321.

Waltz, Kenneth N. (2007) "Kenneth N. Waltz," in Rasmus Kleis Nielsen, Ole Dahl Rasmussen, and Ole Wæver (eds), *10x10*, Cambridge: Cambridge Scholars Publishing.

Weber, Cynthia (1994) "Good Girls, Little Girls and Bad Girls: Male Paranoia in Robert Keohane's Critique of Feminist International Relations," *Millennium: Journal of International Studies*, 23 (2): 337–349.

Weingart, Peter (2001) *Die Stunde der Wahrheit? Zum Verhältnis der Wissenschaft zu Politik, Wirtschaft und Medien in der Wissensgesellschaft*, Weilerswist: Velbrück Wissenschaften.

Whitley, Richard (1984) *The Intellectual and Social Organization of the Sciences*, Oxford: Clarendon Press.

Whitley, Richard (2000) "Introduction [to the second edition]. Science Transformed? The Changing Nature of Knowledge Production at the End of the Twentieth Century," pp. ix–xliv in *The Intellectual and Social Organization of the Sciences* (2nd edn), Oxford: Oxford University Press.

Wight, Martin (1960) "Why Is There No International Theory?," *International Relations*, 2 (1): 35–48.

Wilson, Peter (1998) "The Myth of the 'First Great Debate'," *Review of International Studies*, 24 (Special Issue): 1–15.

Wilson, Rob (2007) "Afterword: Worldings as Future Tactic," pp. 209–223 in Rob Wilson and Christopher Leigh Connery (eds), *The Worlding Project: Doing Cultural Studies in the Era of Globalization*, Santa Cruz, CA: New Pacific Press; and Berkeley, CA: North Atlantic Books.

Wilson, Rob and Christopher Leigh Connery (eds) (2007) *The Worlding Project: Doing Cultural Studies in the Era of Globalization*, Santa Cruz, CA: New Pacific Press; and Berkeley, CA: North Atlantic Books.

Wittrock, Björn (1989) "Social Science and State Development: Transformations of the Discourse of Modernity," *International Social Science Journal*, 122: 497–508.

2 Latin America
Still policy dependent after all these years?

Arlene B. Tickner

Unlike the case of the United States and many countries of Western Europe, information on the field of IR in Latin America and the Caribbean is severely limited. Providing a comprehensive picture of disciplinary developments is a considerable challenge, due largely to the mix of secrecy, poor record keeping, and unwillingness to be scrutinized that characterize many academic sites. This task is complicated further by the fact that the region is comprised of 34 independent nations that are extraordinarily diverse in terms of size, history, language, culture, ethnicity, and race.

In this chapter I provide as complete a picture as possible of international relations studies throughout Latin America and the Caribbean. To this end I trace the field in historical perspective, identifying those factors that have influenced its evolution. I then map the current state of international relations studies by examining teaching and research patterns in distinct countries and institutions. Following this exercise I attempt to describe the structure of national and regional IR communities. In the final section I provide a series of explanations for the field's actual state. My primary concern is with analyzing the ways in which factors such as state needs, the nature of IR and the social sciences, and private research funding have influenced IR's development in distinct settings. I conclude by identifying several regional developments that may contribute to future transformations in the field.

Latin American IR in historical perspective

Between the mid-1800s and the end of World War II, Latin American foreign policy was focused on resolving intra-regional conflicts, dissuading foreign intervention, and participating in the nascent international system. The study of international relations reflected such concerns (Lagos 1980; Muñoz 1987; Russell 1992). With the onset of the Cold War the region's external affairs became mediated almost exclusively by its relationship with the United States, whose paramountcy grew to be a key point of reference if not the major topic of study. On the socio-economic front, the Economic Commission on Latin America (ECLA) began to analyze the correlation between Latin America's position in the international system and regional underdevelopment. ECLA-school thinking attempted to show that the role of the Latin American economies in the international division of labor as producers of primary goods was the main cause of unequal terms of trade that created asymmetrical relations with the core countries (United Nations, ECLA 1950). As a result, the implementation of inward-looking development strategies and the strengthening of regional integration mechanisms were thought to be the best remedies against existing sources of disadvantage in the global economy.

The tendency to identify the capitalist order as the primary source of Latin America's development problems and to look inward in search of solutions was strengthened even further by dependency thinking in the 1960s and early 1970s. The great majority of dependency authors highlighted the domestic manifestations of dependence and underdevelopment, including class conflict and elite class alliances, inequality and exclusion, and the deformation of the national state (Cardoso and Faletto 1969; Cardoso 1974; Santos 1968, 1973; Sunkel 1980). Nevertheless, by placing regional ills firmly within the context of international economic insertion and the existence of unequal relations of production, both dependency and its ECLA predecessor provided significant cues for thinking about Latin American international relations, given their insights on issues such as global capitalism, the state, national development, integration, and sovereignty (Tickner 2003).

On a more practical level, the two schools failed to produce viable solutions to problems of dependence, short of a flawed model of import substituion industrialization, revolution, and the adoption of socialist forms of production, or the acceptance of skewed, dependent development. Moreover, attempts to diversify Latin America's external relations and to increase its leverage vis-à-vis the United States led to new analytical needs for which existing local theories were poorly suited. The emergence of IR as a discrete field of inquiry between the 1960s and 1970s corresponded largely to these factors. During this foundational period IR's main research agenda included topics such as North–South relations and the role of the third world, economic integration and regional cooperation, comparative foreign policy, negotiation, and transnationalism and interdependence (Maira 1991: 8–10).

A key concern expressed within the nascent field of Latin American IR was related to the problem of autonomy, which was viewed as a precondition for both internal development and a successful foreign policy strategy. Autonomy became viewed from the outside in as a mechanism for guarding against the noxious effects of dependency on a local level, and from the inside out as an instrument for asserting regional interests in the international system. In both instances the primary reference point was the United States.

It was widely perceived among IR scholars that both dependency and the imported IR theories that were available, classical realism and interdependence, were of limited use individually for thinking about the problem at hand. In order to address this lacuna, a considerable amount of literature on autonomy was produced in Latin America, primarily during the 1980s.[1] Two authors, Helio Jaguaribe (1979) and Juan Carlos Puig (1980), were particularly influential in the analysis, dissemination, and practice of the autonomy concept in the region. Latin American IR scholars credit both authors with pioneering the "creative incorporation" of traditional IR principles into regional analyses of international affairs (Colacrai de Trevisén 1992: 36; Russell 1992: 10; Soares de Lima 1992: 59). This fusion of concepts from dependency, realism, and interdependence led to the creation of a Latin American "hybrid" model that was widely used to analyze global issues and that reflected the tendency, still prevalent today, to pick and choose useful categories from different theories (Tickner 2002, 2003).

The influence of dependency approaches was manifest primarily in scholarly descriptions of the international system, which was characterized in terms of hierarchical relations of domination and the role of global forces in constraining both the foreign and domestic policies of the countries of the region. The fact that the state has historically been seen as the central domain of political, social, and economic regulation, the primary expression of the "nation" and a key symbol of national sovereignty and independence also facilitated the use of dependency's reading of this actor.

One factor that distinguished autonomy writings from dependency was their faith in the role of progressive elites in mobilizing state resources in favor of a national project (Jaguaribe 1979; Puig 1980). This view meshed better with Morgenthauian realist principles concerning the statesman's role as the ultimate arbiter of the national interest (Morgenthau 1968). A second aspect borrowed from classical realism was its concern with power, although it was rephrased in terms of autonomy. Given that many of the field's main protagonists hailed from authoritarian Argentina, Brazil and Chile, and PRI-dominated Mexico, the state and power-based language that characterized realist thought allowed for scholarly engagement with the geopolitical discourse of distinct military governments and their staunchly nationalist orientation, as well as with that of the Mexican state (Tickner 2002).

Interdependence, in particular Keohane and Nye's work, was readily incorporated into Latin American discussions of IR in the late 1970s, given its openness towards economic and social issues, its optimism concerning the role of strategic resources and effective negotiating skills in boosting the international influence of weaker countries, and its acknowledgement of transnational actors as key global players.

Latin American IR received a crucial push from the Joint Studies Program in International Relations in Latin America (RIAL), a regional network of academic centers created in 1977 to promote research and teaching in the field.[2] RIAL was created by a small group of individuals – many of whom were proponents of the autonomy approach – whose professional interests and activities included a combination of academic and public service.[3] The program's twin goals were to foster interest in international studies on a regional level and, in doing so, to enhance Latin America's international negotiating capacity (RIAL 1985: 4; RIAL 1988: 2). RIAL was indispensable to the consolidation and institutionalization of the field region-wide. Before its creation, International Relations programs were concentrated in relatively few institutions in a small number of countries, namely Mexico, Chile, Brazil, and Argentina. By the height of RIAL's activities in the late 1980s, IR programs had been established in most of the Andean region and Central America, with which the regional academic network also grew.

In addition to strengthening IR studies in Latin America, the considerable activity resulting from the program and the growing interaction that it nurtured between diverse institutions and scholars lent themselves to the appropriation of new theoretical and methodological approaches to the study of global issues. One of the most interesting results of this process was the gradual "Latin Americanization" of imported IR theories, primarily through wide circulation of the Latin American hybrid model (Tickner 2002). By raising theoretical awareness, nurturing an autochthonous approach to international issues, and fostering a "critical mass" of IR specialists, RIAL also influenced foreign policy thinking in the region, mainly because a significant number of individuals active in the program went on to occupy high-level positions in their respective ministries of foreign relations.

The chronological correlation between RIAL's activities and philanthropic interest – in particular in the case of the Ford Foundation – in supporting academic initiatives in International Relations points to another key factor that explains the historical evolution of Latin American IR. Ford's concern with the underdevelopment of regional IR studies coincided with the rise of authoritarian regimes in Brazil and the Southern Cone. Between the early 1980s and the mid-1990s it actively promoted indigenous research on international issues, the training of Latin American IR specialists, the improvement of institutional infrastructures, and the dissemination of knowledge to policy-making elites and the public in general.[4]

It was strongly believed that a regional network of scholars would reinforce grant-making activities in distinct countries, with which the Foundation also began to support RIAL, whose leadership shared a similar interpretation of the problems facing Latin America globally and identified similar strategies for overcoming them. Throughout its 15-year existence RIAL's primary sources of funding were the UNDP and ECLA, which provided operational support, and the Ford Foundation, which provided grants totaling over US$800,000 between 1984 and 1992 to finance the program's annual meetings, reports, and working groups (Tickner 2002).

To a large degree, the transition to democracy in Brazil and the Southern Cone signaled a turning point in Latin American IR. Many of RIAL's major figures entered the foreign policy establishment, and since the program revolved around a small group of high-level scholar–practitioners and little attention was paid to preparing younger generations in the field, an undeniable void was created. In the mid-1990s, largely in response to the end of the Cold War and the wave of democratization in Latin America, the Ford Foundation also reoriented its priorities towards civil society development, peace, social justice, and human rights, among others. In consequence, funding provided to regional institutions specializing in IR was either cut dramatically or curtailed, leading many to reduce the scope of their activities or to simply shut down, as was the case with RIAL. Globally, these shifts coincided with renewed U.S. supremacy and the rise of neoliberal globalization, which reduced Latin America's international political leverage considerably. Both the foreign policy establishment and IR scholars abandoned the autonomy discourse that had been prevalent earlier and turned largely towards liberal-based interpretations of global affairs (Tickner 2003: 345–346).

The shape of IR in distinct national settings

Against the shared historical, intellectual, and political backdrop described above, the varied shapes acquired by IR studies in distinct national settings may also be traced to a number of structural factors. Levels of institutionalization and professionalization of academic practice; the relative weight of diverse fields within the social sciences; comparative stages of development and regional/international influence; political regime type; and the nature and strength of the foreign policy establishment and its degree of interaction with the academic sector deserve special attention.

The quality of higher education in Latin America and the Caribbean is extremely varied. A significant number, if not the majority, of institutions lack full-time staff that engage in academic activities different from teaching and the lack of "ivory-tower" autonomy characteristic of academic practice in many core countries also makes it a fairly unstable profession. Political, social, and family links continue to influence access to positions, funding, publications, and prestige in many national contexts, making the transition to less personalized, more professional forms of status and recognition difficult.

During the 1990s post-secondary education underwent significant degrees of internationalization region-wide in reaction to the challenges of globalization and to rising regional integration (Rama 2006). One result was stronger state concern with education as a cornerstone of global competitiveness, which in turn led to efforts to train professors, create research networks, and exchange human resources, in particular with Europe and the United States. However, neoliberal faith that the free market would guarantee high educational standards also led to the unregulated explosion of poor-quality private institutions (Rama 2006). Therefore, higher education in the region has become markedly imbalanced: while the most influential "core" universities, both public and private, have experienced significant degrees of professionalization and institutionalization, as measured by the number of full-time staff, graduate programs, Ph.Ds, research initiatives, publications, the gradual adoption of peer review mechanisms, and the introduction of tenure-like systems, a plethora of "garage" universities have popped up that offer substandard education and whose non-permanent staffs do not engage in academic activity writ large.

In addition to the varying qualities of International Relations programs offered in different countries throughout Latin America and the Caribbean, their respective foci exhibit high degrees of diversity, although nearly all are multidisciplinary. Contrary to the case of IR in the U.S., which was essentially born out of political science, the latter field has been comparatively weak in Latin America and developed later than International Relations in most cases.[5] Hence, international studies in the region are the offspring of a variety of other areas of the social sciences, including history, law, sociology, economics and finance, development studies, and administration. More often than not, high levels of eclecticism accompany the particular disciplinary mix characterizing distinct programs, making the field's identity throughout the region considerably fragile.

International relations studies evolved first in those countries that developed the earliest and that became regional powers, namely Chile, Mexico, Brazil, and Argentina. Between the 1960s and the early 1990s Chile was a key protagonist, to a large extent because international institutions such as ECLA and UNPD, responsible for initiating the first systematic reflections about Latin America's external relations, were located in the capital, Santiago, and because much of RIAL's leadership was Chilean in origin. During the 1970s all four countries became interested in their status as "middle powers", with which academic activity emerging from IR largely revolved around the problem of increasing national autonomy in relation to the United States. Following the signing of NAFTA in 1994, international relations studies in Mexico took a somewhat different path from that of its counterparts, given its strong focus on relations within North America. In contrast, much intellectual production in Argentina, Brazil, and Chile became more interested in exploring interactions among these countries, and with other countries in Asia and Europe.

Political regime type also played a crucial role in the development of IR in those countries subjected to authoritarian rule between the 1960s and the 1980s. Although the levels of repression directed against scholars in Argentina and Chile were much higher than in Brazil, in all three cases many individuals who would have normally aspired to participate in politics were excluded from this realm and redirected their professional interests towards the academic sector, frequently in exile within other countries such as Mexico. This process had contradictory effects. International studies received a significant intellectual push from the incorporation of important political figures that built up an incipient "academic community" region-wide, but when the dictatorships ended, many of its members deserted academia for the public sector, especially in the case of Chile. A similar situation was observable in Mexico, given the particular nature of the PRI's more than half-century rule, and the extremely high levels of interaction and movement that existed between academia and foreign policy-making circles.

Just as authoritarianism conditioned academic practice in the field, so too did the transition to democracy. Challenges related to military influence in the defense and security realms, and its continued threat to democratic stability, loomed large in most of the social sciences, including international relations studies. Hence, the relation between security, democracy, and the rule of law, as well as the role of processes such as regional integration in enriching and sustaining democracy, continue to be key research concerns in countries such as Argentina, Chile, and Brazil.

Since its inception as a field, IR in Latin America and the Caribbean has been conceived largely in terms of providing practical foreign policy advice to policy makers. In fact, throughout the region many academic programs were created with the goal of training future political elites as well as serving the interests of their respective countries more generally. However, differing levels of interaction between ministries of foreign relations and the academic sector, as well as the relative political influence of the former, determine the extent to which IR studies have been captive to foreign policy or not. For example, the Institute of International Relations of the University of the West Indies, Trinidad and Tobago, was created in order to provide academic training to diplomats of the English-speaking Caribbean shortly after independence. However, after almost three decades of nearly exclusive service to the governments of the Caribbean, the program was reformulated in order to train "generalists" in the field. In Colombia, the Universidad Externado, harboring the largest school of International Relations (government and finances) in the country, actively supervises training received at the diplomatic academy, in cooperation with the French government.[6] Similarly, the Escuela de Relaciones Internacionales was born within the Universidad Nacional in Costa Rica in response to the perception that the country lacked sufficient preparation in the area of foreign relations. For years, the Costa Rican foreign policy establishment tried, unsuccessfully, to convert this institution into a training center for career diplomats.

Although the strong levels of synergy existing between the public sector and academia in countries such as Argentina, Chile, and Mexico have provided an environment conducive to the strengthening of the field, distinct patterns of exchange between the two sectors have had differing effects. In Chile, most academics ended up in politics following the transition to democracy, while the opposite was the case in Argentina. In contrast, transit between politics and academia in Mexico exhibits a revolving-door pattern. This latter trend is extensive to a large portion of the region, in which the conviction that practical experience in the public sector is a precondition for understanding the "real world" of international relations is prevalent. A major difference that exists between Brazil and other countries is that until the 1980s the Brazilian ministry of foreign relations, Itamaraty, placed significant brakes upon the consolidation of academic programs in IR as it was fearful of losing its monopoly over the country's foreign relations (Soares de Lima 1992). Another factor that explains the relative dissociation between academia and the foreign policy establishment is the sheer size of the country and the fact that IR studies have been concentrated largely in southeastern Brazil (the most developed region) whereas the capital, Brasilia, is located in the central-west.

IR teaching and research

During the past decade IR in Latin America and the Caribbean has undergone fantastic growth, as measured by the number of academic programs, both undergraduate and graduate, students, research institutions, conferences, and publications. Much of this upswing is attributable to the marketability of nearly anything that carries the "international" label in a region deeply affected by processes and discourses related to internationalization and globalization. Table 2.1 provides a general idea of the number of institutions of higher education in each country in the region, as well as those in which there are International Relations degree programs at the undergraduate and/or graduate levels.

Quantity, however, should not be confused with quality. Relatively few institutions exist in which academics hold full-time positions and conduct research, in addition to their teaching responsibilities. In addition, only in very few countries, primarily Argentina, Brazil, and Mexico, has the burgeoning of international relations studies actually led to the consolidation of the field in terms of its disciplinary identity and the strength of its academic community. Therefore, my inventory of IR programs in the region is focused upon a group of countries and institutions in which international studies are comparatively well developed.

The countries selected also provide a representative geographical sampling of the different sub-regions of Latin America and the Caribbean, including two countries from the English-speaking Caribbean (Jamaica and Trinidad and Tobago); two from Central America (Costa Rica and Guatemala); two from the Andean region (Colombia and Venezuela); two from the

Table 2.1 Institutions granting university degrees and IR programs per country

Country	Number of institutions granting university degrees*	Number of IR programs
Argentina	99	20
Bolivia	51	1
Brazil	206	53
Chile	63	3
Colombia	263	11
Costa Rica	54	3
Cuba	64	1
Dominican Republic	35	0
Ecuador	65	3
El Salvador	26	1
Guatemala	10	2
Honduras	14	0
Jamaica	9	1
Mexico	240	18
Nicaragua	44	3
Panama	32	0
Paraguay	22	3
Peru	82	1
Trinidad & Tobago	4	1
Uruguay	13	1
Venezuela	49	4

Note
*Includes public and private universities, and other institutions granting university degrees. Variation in country figures is due largely to the fact that distinct national legislations classify institutions of higher education differently.

Sources: National Reports on Higher Education, Instituto Internacional de la UNESCO para la Educación Superior en América Latina y el Caribe (IESALC), http://www.iesalc.unesco.org.ve/. The number of institutions with IR programs was derived from personal inquiries conducted in each country.

Southern Cone (Argentina and Chile); and Mexico and Brazil. Academic institutions were identified in each of these countries based upon the longevity of their teaching programs (ten years or more); the existence and size of their IR faculties; and their national, regional, and international exposure, as measured by the formal academic training of staffs, number and types of publications and research initiatives, and participation in academic events.[7]

In addition to universities, international relations teaching, research, and dissemination takes place in several other institutional settings. The Facultad Latinoamericana de Ciencias Sociales (FLACSO), an autonomous international organization of regional scope, was founded in 1957 at the behest of UNESCO and several Latin American governments with the goal of promoting the social sciences in the region. FLACSO has academic programs in Argentina, Brazil, Chile, Costa Rica (where the General Secretariat is also located), Cuba, Ecuador, El Salvador, Guatemala, Mexico, and the Dominican Republic, among which varying degrees of interaction exist. Each local office operates with variable proportions of national governmental support, private funding and internal revenues, and different thematic emphases and graduate programs (including Masters and Ph.Ds), although they all enjoy significant degrees of recognition and influence among both the academic and policy-making communities. FLACSO Argentina, Ecuador, Dominican Republic, and Chile are the most dynamic in international studies: the first three offer graduate programs in this area and conduct considerable amounts of research on topics such as regional integration, multi-lateralism, security, development, migration, and trade, while the Chilean branch does not offer a graduate program in IR but is highly active research-wise.

The Consejo Latinoamericano de Ciencias Sociales (CLACSO) is another kind of non-governmental international institution created in 1967, also with the support of UNESCO. Contrary to the FLACSO system, CLACSO has only one branch, located in Buenos Aires, and a network of over 170 member institutions throughout the region (universities and research centers), many of which participate in working groups on a diverse array of subjects. Its influence in the field of International Relations has ranged from extremely high during the foundational stages of IR to relatively low in recent years. At present CLACSO has several working groups that address issues related to the global political economy and U.S. hegemony, mainly from Marxist perspectives. None of the IR professoriate included in my survey, with the exception of several professors from UNAM, Mexico, participate in these groups, hinting at the strong ideological divide that currently exists between Marxist-based and other forms of scholarship.

Very few independent think-tanks exist in the region, although economic specialists in countries such as Chile, Mexico, Colombia, Brazil, and Argentina have thrived in such venues, as have some defense and security experts, albeit to a lesser degree.[8] Councils of foreign relations comprised of influential associations of ex-ministers and former diplomats, with differing degrees of support from the business community and academia, exist in Argentina, Brazil, Chile, Mexico, Paraguay, and Uruguay. Their role is basically limited to agenda building, unlike their U.S. counterpart, the Council on Foreign Relations, which actively participates in knowledge-building enterprises. The direct political influence of these councils is relatively limited, given that access to policy making is usually restricted to smaller, personal networks of advisors.

Academic faculties

The levels of academic training and the geographical concentration of graduate studies – which is indicative of the sources of intellectual influence upon the professoriate – are highly variable between IR university faculties (See Table 2.2). Some of the largest full-time faculties are located at the Universidad Externado de Colombia (48), Universidad Nacional Autónoma de México (UNAM) (32), Colegio de México (24), Universidad Nacional, Costa Rica (24 including part-time staff), and Universidad de Brasília (16), all of which offer large undergraduate programs. Of the 278 professors included in my survey, only 164 (less than 60 percent) hold doctoral degrees, while nearly all have completed a Masters. The percentage of Ph.Ds on distinct university staffs ranges from 100 percent or close to it at institutions such as Brasília, Universidad Católica and PUC, Rio de Janeiro to 25 percent or under at the Universidad de Chile, Externado, and Nacional Costa Rica.

The provenance of graduate degrees held by IR professors fails to indicate a strong geographical concentration in any one country: 29 percent of the Ph.Ds were obtained in U.S. institutions; 44.5 percent in Europe, in order of importance, Spain, France, and Great Britain; and 23 percent in-house or in-country. However, individual institutions seem to favor degree holders with similar academic backgrounds, which may be related to their respective missions and global ties. Nearly all of the professors holding Ph.Ds at the Universidad Di Tella, Católica and Andes studied in the United States, while none or very few of those affiliated with Brasília, UNAM, West Indies (both Trinidad and Tobago and Jamaica), and Externado were educated in this country. Likewise, a significant number of scholars at

Table 2.2 Number and provenance of Ph.D. degrees

	Di Tella	Flacso-San Andrés	Brasilia	PUC-Rio	Chile	Católica	Externado
Full-time staff	9	17 (not all FT)	16	11	12	12 (5 do IR)	48 (not all FT)
Total Ph.Ds	7	11	15	11	3	11	12
U.S./Canada	5	3	1	4	1	9	1
Europe	2	7	7	5	2	2	9
Latin America	0	0	0	0	0	0	1
Country or in-house	0	1	7	2	0	0	1
Asia	0	0	0	0	0	0	0

Brasília, UNAM, and West Indies (Jamaica) were educated in-country or in-house, suggesting that a process of self-reproduction may have been initiated in these countries.[9]

IR theory teaching

The contents of international relations curricula provide another indication of the state of Latin American IR because they allow for observations concerning the types of texts considered authoritative in the teaching of the field. Although a more comprehensive treatment would demand looking at many more aspects of teaching programs in each country, for the purposes of this chapter the primary source of information used were the reading lists of IR theory course syllabi.[10] Given that the number of required theory courses varies dramatically among academic institutions, I included only one course per program (general or introductory IR theory). The course syllabi sampling includes IR theory courses at both the undergraduate (7) and graduate (9) levels, and is based purely upon those programs that I was able to obtain, given that virtually none are available online. Regrettably, I was unsuccessful in acquiring syllabi from either of the University of the West Indies campuses in Jamaica, and Trinidad and Tobago, or the Universidad Central de Venezuela.[11]

Table 2.3 IR theory teaching in 12 Latin American institutions

Theoretical traditions	Di Tella under-grad	Di Tella M.A.	Flacso-San Andrés M.A.	Brasilia under-grad	Brasilia M.A.	PUC-Rio under-grad	PUC-Rio M.A.	Chile M.A.
General classical	0	1	0	0	2	0	4	9
Realism	8	8	5	1	8	4	10	6
Liberalism	5	17	5	1	7	4	14	17
Marxism/neo-Marxism	3	2	2	1	0	2	3	7
Constructivism	3	4	1	3	4	3	7	0
Post-positivism	0	0	2	0	3	7	2	7
Foreign policy analysis	0	0	5	1	0	0	1	5
Other	4	6	5	5	5	0	6	33
Total	23	38	25	12	29	20	41	84

Andes	Nacional	Rafael Landívar	Colegio México	ITAM	UNAM	UWI-Jamaica	UWI-T&T
14 (3 do IR)	24 (not all FT)	18 (none FT)	24	10	32	22 (6 do IR)	9
8	4	9	18	8	26	15	6
6	2	1	6	4	0	3	1
1	1	6	8	4	13	4	2
1	0	2	0	0	0	0	0
0	1	0	4	0	12	7	3
0	0	0	0	0	1	1	0

Each of the 568 required readings appearing in the 16-course syllabi was coded into one of nine categories and assigned an equal weight. The following categories were selected on the basis of those theoretical frameworks that seem to have been the most decisive in Latin American IR studies during the past decade: (1) general classical tradition (primarily textbooks that address the so-called "major debates" and that work between the realist and liberal variants of the classical tradition without expressing preference for either); (2) realism (including classical realism and neorealism); (3) liberalism (including interdependence and neoliberal institutionalism, among others); (4) Marxism/neo-Marxism; (5) constructivism; (6) post-positivism (including feminism, postmodernism, poststructuralism, and post-colonialism); (7) foreign policy analysis; and (8) other.[12] Although many items could arguably be classified into several categories, the single classification assignment was based upon the central research questions and assumptions of each text, the focus of the specific pages assigned, and the placement of the text within the course syllabus. Following the coding of all of the items contained in a given reading list, the information was tabulated on an individual course basis. Upon completion, the results of each individual reading list were consolidated into a regional aggregate (see Table 2.3).

Católica Ph.D. en Poli Sci	Externado M.A.	Andes Grad	Nacional M.A.	Rafael Landívar under-grad	ITAM under-grad	UNAM under-grad	Colegio de Mexico under-grad	Total
9	2	3	8	7	3	13	1	62
14	3	2	5	2	13	6	6	101
22	4	1	3	4	20	2	14	140
10	1	2	0	1	7	5	0	46
0	1	0	0	0	5	0	1	28
2	3	2	1	0	5	0	0	32
14	4	0	0	1	3	5	1	40
16	2	2	9	10	11	0	5	119
87	20	12	26	25	67	31	28	568

The IR theory course syllabi contain several features that are worth noting. The great majority of texts were written by U.S. and British authors and are used in their English-language versions, even when translations in Spanish or Portuguese exist. In those courses in which Spanish-language textbooks are used they are normally authored by Spanish scholars and are revisions of classical IR theory. Conversely, texts authored by Latin Americans rarely appear in IR theory course syllabi, with the exception of the Brazilian institutions surveyed, in which several IR textbooks written by Brazilian professors are used.[13] In addition, many texts and topics not normally considered "IR theory" are also included in several of the course syllabi, most notably those offered by the Universidad de Chile, Católica, Rafael Landívar, and Nacional. Although many of the items classified as "other" – which account for approximately 20 percent of the total texts included in my analysis – belong to the English school or are IR textbooks not easily categorized as belonging to any one theoretical tradition, a plethora of other texts, ranging from Plato's *Republic* to empirical treatments of the environment and the role of the Church are also required reading in several of the courses examined.

The content analysis shows that IR theory courses in the region overwhelmingly favor realist and liberal approaches to the field. Of the 568 texts assigned on the 16-course reading lists, 62 (10.9 percent) of the items corresponded to the general classical tradition, 101 (17.8 percent) to realism, and 140 (24.6 percent) to liberalism, totaling 303 (53.3 percent). Notwithstanding the majority weight of U.S. approaches, recent debates between neorealism and neoliberalism, and rationalism and reflexivism, are given only passing attention in the syllabi examined. Moreover, texts that make use of the preferred U.S. methods, rational choice and quantitative analysis, are ignored completely.

Marxist and neo-Marxist frameworks are the third most frequently used to teach IR theory but they account for a small percentage of the texts consulted: only 8.1 percent. Tellingly, dependency occupies a comparatively insignificant place among the texts pertaining to this group notwithstanding its central influence within the social sciences in Latin America and in the field of International Relations itself. What this suggests is that dependency is simply not identified as a theory of international relations by most Latin American IR professors, probably due to its emphasis upon the domestic manifestations of dependence. Constructivist and post-positivist accounts of international affairs, including feminism, postcolonialism, and poststructuralism, are absent from over one-third of the IR theory courses analyzed and are given only passing attention in most of the other syllabi, adding up to less than 5 percent of the total readings.

Based upon the IR theory courses surveyed, it is fair to say that predominant Latin American conceptions of what constitutes "IR theory" are firmly rooted in U.S. interpretations of the discipline while failing to replicate them completely. The menu of IR theories relied upon in teaching is based upon realist and liberal readings of international affairs but strays from current developments in the United States where rationalist or behavioral scientific approaches are predominant.[14] To the extent that a large percentage of the region's IR professoriate continues to be educated outside U.S. universities, this tendency will most likely deepen. The fact that over 40 percent of professors have not received doctoral training – in which theoretical knowledge is conveyed most intensively – may explain why the most recent debates emerging within IR both in the United States and globally have not "traveled" as effectively to many countries as earlier theoretical discussions within the field. However, IR teaching has also been fairly immune to conceptual discussions taking place within other areas of the social sciences in the region itself, suggesting that its intellectual cues are not derived from indigenous sources either.[15]

Thematic trends in journals and research

Scholarly journals provide yet another picture of the state of disciplines in terms of their theoretical tendencies, major concerns, and primary debates. However, cases such as Latin America and the Caribbean suggest that rather than offering the definitive snapshot of a field (Wæver 1998: 697), journals provide just another piece of the disciplinary puzzle. This is mainly because such publications have not enjoyed the same status as vehicles of academic production and recognition, and they do not circulate easily among members of national and regional IR communities. Universities and individual scholars that are highly integrated with global academic networks tend to value publishing in a U.S. or European journal more than doing so locally or regionally, although this is certainly not the case for the bulk of the Latin American IR professoriate.[16] In addition, surprisingly few specialized journals exist in comparison to the number of teaching programs that operate in the region: with the exception of Brazil and Mexico, both of which harbor a number of long-standing IR journals, the remaining countries have either one or two, or no such publication.

In order to identify the general themes that have informed recent journal analyses of international relations, I examined the tables of contents and article summaries of six of the most prominent journals between January 1999 and June 2007. The criteria used to choose among the 20 or so journals that are currently in existence were uninterrupted publication for ten years or more; regional and international circulation; and linkage with a teaching program.[17] The journals selected include: *Contexto Internacional* (IRI-PUC Rio), *Estudios Internacionales* (IEI, Universidad de Chile), *Colombia Internacional* (Universidad de los Andes, Colombia), *Relaciones Internacionales* (UNAM, Mexico), *Foro Internacional* (CEI, Colegio de México), and *Foreign Affairs en Español* (ITAM, Mexico; now titled *Foreign Affairs Latinoamérica*) (see Table 2.4).

The entire set of articles published in the six journals between 1999 and 2007, which totaled 1,012, was classified according to its treatment of distinct topics. Following completion of this classification process, the results were aggregated for each journal and for the six publications jointly in order to identify the types of issues that receive the most attention in academic journal treatments of international relations in the region.

On average, foreign policy analyses account for nearly 25 percent of the articles published, although in the journals *Relaciones Internacionales*, *Foro Internacional*, and *Contexto Internacional* the weight of this topic is somewhat lower. Academic discussions of foreign policy seem to mirror the main concerns of each journal's local foreign policy establishment, in the sense that relations with the most important international counterparts of each are prioritized. Therefore, the Chilean journal *Estudios Internacionales* gives equal treatment to Mercosur, the European Union, and the Asian Pacific and less attention to the United States; *Colombia Internacional* looks primarily at Colombian relations with the U.S. and neighboring countries; and *Foreign Affairs en Español* is strongly dedicated to exploring Mexican and Latin American relations with Washington, as well as U.S. foreign policy in general.[18]

The second most frequently addressed subject in the journals surveyed is domestic politics and public policy, which account for 16 percent of the total articles written. This figure ascends to 43 percent in the case of *Foro Internacional*, which deals largely with public policy, and averages between 10 and 13 percent in *Estudios Internacionales*, *Foreign Affairs en Español*, and *Relaciones Internacionales*. Although this research topic is not a "natural" target of analysis for IR, it seems to take its primary cue from the distinct governance challenges faced by regional states in recent years. All the countries of Latin America and the Caribbean confront differing degrees of ungovernability, institutional weakness, political and economic instability, social unrest, and violence and citizen security that they have been

Table 2.4 Thematic trends in Latin American journals, 1999–2007

Themes	Estudios Internacionales	Foro Internacional	Relaciones Internacionales	Contexto Internacional	Colombia Internacional	Foreign Affairs en Español	Total
Foreign policy	53	37	17	17	28	94	246
International theory	4	4	10	25	18	0	61
Comparative domestic politics	7	17	1	6	21	37	89
Public policy/domestic politics	22	75	10	2	1	51	161
International law	10	0	5	2	0	0	17
Security/defense	6	0	3	2	1	22	34
Peace/conflict	9	2	4	3	6	13	37
Global trade/domestic economy	20	17	15	4	4	54	114
International institutions	5	7	2	4	0	13	31
Transnational crime	0	0	1	2	0	11	14
Globalization	3	1	2	0	1	10	17
Terrorism	4	1	1	0	0	13	19
Migration	0	3	0	0	5	15	23
Energy/resources/environment	6	0	4	2	0	14	26
Integration	9	1	3	5	1	8	27
Development	5	0	0	0	0	5	10
Global politics	10	1	3	0	0	0	14
Public health/natural disasters	0	0	0	0	0	10	10
Human rights	3	0	0	0	0	2	5
International history	2	8	1	5	1	0	17
Education	0	0	13	0	6	6	25
Other	8	0	1	0	1	5	15
Total	186	174	96	79	94	383	1012

hard-pressed to tackle effectively. Given that many of these problems are intuitively associated with neoliberal reform and globalization, it is not surprising that they have increasingly come under the purview of international relations studies.

Tellingly, only a handful of articles included in the sample, equivalent to 6 percent of the total, deal explicitly with IR theory or conceptual issues related to global politics in general. Such theoretical reflections are limited to three journals, *Contexto Internacional*, *Colombia Internacional*, and, to a much lesser extent, *Relaciones Internacionales*, all of whose sponsoring institutions and/or professoriate have demonstrated explicit concern with the conceptual debates surrounding the field in both their publications and other academic activities. This result seems particularly well suited to describe the current state of IR thinking in Latin America and the Caribbean. The overwhelming majority of the field's members favor practical, applied knowledge that would enable distinct countries to become more competitive and to insert themselves more effectively into the international system, which most likely accounts for the plethora of articles on foreign policy strategies, and on issues of democratic governance and institutions. Moreover, theory and practice are widely seen as two separate spheres of intellectual activity.

Articles on security and defense amount to even less than those dealing with theory. This is very surprising given the boom in security studies during the past decade in most of Latin America and the Caribbean. One explanation for this absence may be that the region's security and defense specialists occupy a separate professional niche which includes policy-based publications that are geared towards a distinct audience, namely the defense and practitioner communities. A considerable number of these specialists might not describe themselves as international relations experts, nor do many of them teach in IR faculties. In addition to security, other salient issues from a regional vantage point, among them transnational crime, migration and globalization, integration, and development, are barely considered either.

Nonetheless, all of the academic institutions surveyed profess research in these areas. Development issues continue to be a key concern in the Trinidad and Tobago, Jamaican, and Central American programs in International Relations, as are sub-regional integration processes. The foreign relations of small states are also a salient research topic in the former two countries. Argentine, Brazilian, and Chilean IR scholars are highly interested in diverse political and economic facets of Mercosur, including its role in nurturing a regional security community, while the North American Free Trade Agreement, and its security arrangements and migration patterns, are widely studied in Mexico. Although Andean and Caribbean integration is widely analyzed in Colombia and Venezuela, other problems such as the regionalization of the Colombian conflict, the role of the United States in the region, security and defense matters, and oil diplomacy (in the case of Venezuela) are equally important. Chile, Colombia, and Venezuela also boast a long-standing tradition of analysis in international law.

National and regional IR community structures

The aforementioned map of international relations studies in Latin America and the Caribbean says fairly little about the actual operation of the IR community in distinct sites within the region. The field may be described as a multi-tier structure in which distinct national and regional nodes coexist and sometimes overlap. To begin with, there is a small group of scholars seated primarily in Argentina, Brazil, Mexico, and Colombia at the top notch universities that is highly integrated with the discipline's core, albeit in a subordinate role, via academic training and participation in conference and publication circuits. The lion's share of what little interest the IR professoriate has in theorizing is largely concentrated among this "globalized" elite, although many of its theoretical reflections are directed towards other global interlocutors instead of local counterparts and audiences.

A second group of scholars – who represent the dominant faction of the field power-wise – is linked together through regional and hemispheric networks that are issue specific. Such is the case of a series of hemispheric groups on security and defense, whose membership is largely overlapping. The main security and defense networks are the Security and Defense Network in Latin America (RESDAL), Creating Community in the Americas and the Program on Regional Security Cooperation, the latter two of which are coordinated by extra-regional institutions, the Woodrow Wilson International Center for Scholars (with Ford Foundation funding), and the German Friedrich Ebert Stiftung, respectively. The three networks share concern with promoting the institutionalization of state security and defense policies within the framework of democratic civilian control, and with nurturing mutual confidence and cooperation between the region's countries. To this end, each group organizes workshops and seminars, publishes working papers and reports, maintains extensive databases with bibliography on diverse aspects of the security and defense problematic, and seeks to deepen interaction between experts and policy makers.

The Latin American Trade Network (LATN), funded by the Canadian IDRC, provides another example of an issue area in which substantial regional scholarly interaction takes place. LATN has approximately 35 institutional members and works with negotiators and policy makers with the aim of cultivating their trade negotiating capacity. In addition to organizing public and closed events, as do the other security and defense groups, it publishes a weekly newsletter that summarizes local, regional, and global trade news. CLACSO also sponsors a series of regional working groups, two of whose objectives include the analysis of the interface between global and local economies, the role of transnational corporations, and different sources of hegemony and emancipation in the capitalist global order. Contrary to the other groups mentioned, both of these working groups are highly anti-establishment and opposed to interaction with the policy world. Many of the academics who participate in these regional groups also attend the Latin American Studies Association (LASA) meetings, at which considerable hemispheric networking takes place.

A third tier, which accounts for the bulk of the Latin American and Caribbean IR professoriate, comprises groups of scholars that interact mainly at the local or national level. Ironically, in a considerable number of countries less intellectual exchange and communication take place at these levels than that which exists between the "globalized elite" and its international counterparts or between the members of issue-specific regional and hemispheric networks. Multiple kinds of divides constitute a major obstacle to building more encompassing IR communities at the national level: between public and private universities; between U.S. or European trained and locally or regionally trained scholars; between those who are English-language savvy and those who are not; between institutions located in capital cities and those situated in the provinces; between practical, applied scholars and those who favor theoretical knowledge; and between Marxists and non-Marxists.[19] High levels of competition and rivalry often exist between different institutions, while the lack of a deeply instilled peer review culture compounds the challenges to fruitful collaboration. Moreover, with the exception of Brazil and Mexico, no other country has an international studies association or other, similar organization capable of building more extensive communicative links between national scholars. Indeed, in many institutional sites throughout Latin America and the Caribbean, IR seems to operate within relatively self-contained micro-level communities that have little or no direct interaction with the wider national, regional, or global academic community.

Explaining IR studies in Latin America and the Caribbean

My concern in this chapter has been to paint a portrait of international relations studies in Latin America and the Caribbean and to hint at some ways in which intellectual, political, economic, social, and cultural factors have influenced the field's evolution. In this final section I would like to zoom in on a triad of interrelated factors that seem to offer the fullest explanation for the state of IR studies in the region. These include the practical policy orientation of the dominant sector of the International Relations community and of the social sciences more generally; state needs, in particular in relation to foreign policy and matters of security; and the role of philanthropic foundations in priming research agendas.

Following World War II, accelerated urbanization and industrialization led to significant economic, political, social, and cultural transformations that Latin American states were ill-equipped to manage (Wilhelmy 1980: 177). In addition, the expansion of the global capitalist system and the birth of the Cold War placed new and complex external demands upon the region. The emergence of these pressing domestic and international problems invigorated the social sciences. Their institutionalization between the 1950s and the 1960s and their role since then in the provision of knowledge susceptible to being translated into public policy formulae by Latin American and Caribbean states are not accidental (Sonntag 1998). This self-perception was nurtured largely by the state and led to a complex relationship between academia and society, characterized by ambivalence and dependence vis-à-vis the policy world (Palacios 1999: 68).

The ECLA school was one of the first to step up to the task at hand by questioning modernization-based assumptions that linked Latin American underdevelopment to the absence of modern values and institutions; by arguing that the region's position in the international division of labor constituted the central obstacle to development; and by proposing concrete steps for overcoming this problem (United Nations, ECLA 1950). Dependency thinking strengthened the social sciences' usefulness by seeking to explain Latin America's key problems in a holistic fashion, among them underdevelopment, inequality, political instability, and authoritarianism (Valenzuela 1988: 71). However, the anti-elitist, anti-establishment stance of its more radical Marxist variants was untranslatable into state policy. The founding fathers of the IR community also found it paralyzing, mainly because the majority were elite practitioners-cum-scholars whose primary interest was to produce practical knowledge of international affairs. In keeping with this objective, the RIAL regional network sought to create a theoretical and research framework that would best serve shared concerns about democracy and authoritarianism, regional integration, negotiation capacity, relations with the United States, and autonomy.

The IR discourse emerging from RIAL was especially well suited to Latin American foreign policy between the 1970s and the 1980s, given the region's transition from isolation to assertiveness in the international system. Both the perception of declining U.S. hegemony and the oil crises of 1973 and 1979 contributed to a generalized feeling of optimism concerning Latin America's relative weight as a global actor. It comes as little surprise that the Ford Foundation – the largest private donor in issues of global politics – targeted this program as part of its bid to strengthen international relations studies in the region. Given Ford's interest in supporting knowledge-building endeavors that were communicable to policy makers and/or capable of influencing the policy-making process, RIAL and many of its institutional affiliates provided a good fit. The fact that the field of International Relations in much of the region was born out of RIAL and funding incentives for policy relevant work helps explain the field's favoritism, even today, towards practical knowledge designed to serve state needs and goals, and the comparative unimportance of epistemological, theoretical, and methodological debates.[20]

With the onset of neoliberalism in the mid- to late 1980s, the flaws of global capitalism highlighted by ECLA, dependency, and the autonomy school were replaced by accusations that the state was the major impediment to well-being and development. Accordingly, neoliberal prescriptions for reform called for reduced state intervention and the reign of the free market via trade liberalization and the privatization of public goods such as education, health and public services. One result of this transition was the ascendence of "practical" knowledge purportedly designed to increase efficiency, enhance competitiveness, and synchronize Latin American and Caribbean economies and political systems with the demands of the global market. Higher education played a central role in this process, given the central importance attributed to human resources with market-based capacities and competences functional to the existing model (Mohanty 2003: 174).

The field that best illustrates this view of the academic sector is economics, in which a generation of technocrats trained abroad positioned themselves as authoritative knowers by invoking the superiority of their scientific and technical capacities. This self-perception as a prophetic policy elite allowed the technocracy to prioritize economic recovery and growth, and the reestablishment of order while extricating itself from social responsibility of any kind (Palacios 1999: 3–4). Other areas of the social sciences too experienced a shift from autochthonous, structural analyses of the "big picture" in Latin American societies towards more focused, empirical exercises of use to the neoliberal state (Sorj 1990: 109). For many, the lack of political commitment characteristic of this stage of the social sciences and their role in legitimating and sustaining the existing social order signaled a crisis from which they have yet to emerge.

In the specific case of IR, shifts in state tasks at the global level led to direct and indirect incentives to study new social, economic, and political problems. Both the end of the Cold War and the exigencies of neoliberal globalization were perceived to reduce the region's political leverage and autonomy dramatically. This, and RIAL's shutdown in 1991, largely explains the disappearance of the autonomy lexicon from both academia and foreign policy circles. Instead, problems of global insertion, competitiveness, and democratic governance came to the forefront. Economic and political integration, which had been viewed previously as a political tool for enhancing regional autonomy, was pursued by Latin American and Caribbean states, and studied by the IR professoriate in terms of its capacity to maximize globalization's full potential. Given concern in Brazil and the Southern Cone, and post-conflict Central America, in particular, with lingering military influence, security and defense studies articulated with democratic governance issues and the rule of law were also encouraged, as were those that focused on the non-traditional security agenda.

Following a cooling-off period in which the Ford Foundation reoriented grant making in Latin America and the Caribbean away from international affairs, the security problematic came to its attention, leading to concern with alternative security issues and new challenges associated with the post-Cold War context. In the case of Latin America and the Caribbean, topics such as domestic social conflict, public safety, human rights, and democracy emerged as the key human security problems funded by all of Ford's regional offices (Tschirgi 2006: 28). Similar to earlier support of RIAL, one underlying goal of its fund-making activities in the security realm has been to create a regional knowledge community on this and other global issues.

A series of recent developments may be influencing international relations thinking in ways different from the post-Cold War period. Growing U.S. unilateralism following 9/11 and attempts to impose economic and security policies that are at odds with the interests of many regional states have exacerbated anti-American sentiments throughout much of Latin America and the Caribbean. Two outcomes may be the revival of autonomy-based discourses fashionable in the 1970s and the 1980s, and increased emphasis upon counterparts distinct from the United States in foreign policy analyses. Ideological rifts within the hemisphere itself, between pro-American governments in Mexico, Colombia, Central America, and much of the Caribbean, the leftist, anti-globalization, anti-American governments of Venezuela, Cuba, Bolivia, and Ecuador, and a leftist-center bloc led by Brazil, Chile, and Argentina, constitute another potential source of change in the field of IR, especially in the latter countries. Finally, the region-wide crisis of neoliberalism, as evidenced in alarming levels of poverty and inequality, varied degrees of institutional weakness and ingovernance, and rising public insecurity is placing new demands upon the International Relations professoriate in terms of what it defines as "IR studies", and may reinforce the tendency to consider the "domestic" and the "international" as two overlapping and inseparable spheres.

Notes

1 See Tokatlian (1996) for a comprehensive review of this literature.
2 Chilean scholar Luciano Tomassini spearheaded this initiative. During the same period, the Latin American Foreign Policy Program (PROSPEL), comprising the same community of Latin American scholars, and coordinated by Chilean Heraldo Muñoz, began to publish an annual volume dealing with the evolution of regional foreign policies.
3 Many of RIAL's members hailed from Chile, Argentina, and Brazil, in which the rise of authoritarian regimes made public service careers unviable.
4 Several decades earlier the Foundation had played a similar role in the consolidation of the social sciences in Latin America, primarily through the provision of financial assistance for the development of academic programs and the training of a new generation of social scientists in the United States.
5 In those countries in which political science has a stronger footing, such as Argentina, Colombia, and Mexico, IR and political science are actually separate departments, with little or no interaction between their faculties.
6 Official French presence in the diplomatic academy and the Universidad Externado contrasts with the negligible influence that French approaches to IR have had in Colombia. This may be related to the fact that the Colombian Ministry of Foreign Relations has little political clout and its diplomatic corps is relatively unprofessional.
7 The institutions chosen include: Universidad Torcuato Di Tella (Department of Political Science and International Relations), Argentina; Facultad Latinoamericana de Ciencias Sociales (FLACSO) and Universidad de San Andrés (Humanities Department), which jointly administer their M.A. program, Argentina; Universidade de Brasília (Department of International Relations), Brazil; Pontifícia Universidade Católica, PUC, Rio de Janeiro (Institute of International Relations, IRI), Brazil; Universidad de Chile (Institute of International Studies, IEI), Chile; Universidad Católica de Chile (Institute of Political Science, ICP), Chile; Universidad de los Andes (Political Science Department), Colombia; Universidad Externado de Colombia (School of Finance, Government and International Relations), Colombia; Universidad Nacional (School of International Relations, ERI), Costa Rica; Universidad Rafael Landívar (Political Science Department), Guatemala; University of the West Indies (Department of Government), Jamaica; Colegio de México (Center for International Studies, CEI), Mexico; Instituto Tecnológico Autónomo de México, ITAM (Department of International Studies), Mexico; Universidad Nacional Autónoma de México, UNAM (Center for International Relations, School of Political and Social Sciences), Mexico; University of the West Indies (Institute of International Relations), Trinidad and Tobago; and Universidad Central de Venezuela (School of International Studies), Venezuela.

8   The burgeoning of economic think-tanks is largely due to the increased role of technocrats in public decision-making processes beginning in the 1980s. See Centeno and Silva (1998). In the case of the defense and security community, strong links to the military establishment explain its success relative to the IR academic community.

9   Although institutional information about the IR studies program offered by the Universidad Central de Venezuela was unavailable on the internet and impossible to obtain via its staff, informal conversations that I have held with Venezuelan colleagues suggest that nearly all of the professors who teach IR at the UCV and have a Ph.D. have obtained their degree from the political studies program offered in-house.

10 See Alker and Biersteker's 1984 seminal article for the first analysis of this kind, as well as Tom Biersteker (Chapter 17, this volume). IR studies programs in Latin America and the Caribbean are discussed more thoroughly in Tickner (2002).

11 In the case of the University of the West Indies in Trinidad and Tobago, a similar analysis that I performed in 1999 on a course syllabus offered there suggested that Marxist and neo-Marxist, and post-positivist approaches, especially postcolonialism, were more prevalent than classical frameworks such as realism and liberalism (see Tickner 2003: 336–338). Written and personal interviews conducted with several Venezuelan IR scholars suggest that the approach to theory offered by its School of International Studies is also quite traditional in that it highlights realist, liberal, and systemic theories of IR, while also including structuralist appproaches such as the ECLA school and dependency.

12 I conducted a similar analysis of IR theory course syllabi in 1999 (see Tickner 2002, 2003). My classification scheme distinguishes intentionally between constructivism and post-positivism in order to reflect the association that nearly all Latin American scholars make between constructivism and the work of authors such as Alexander Wendt.

13 To my knowledge, during the past decade only a small handful of general textbooks on IR have been published by Latin American scholars, basically of Mexican and Brazilian descent. Due to issues of language and size, Brazil has taken the lead in this process: between 2002 and 2007, there have been at least six different Portuguese-language textbooks, two of which specifically address the principal theoretical debates of the field. See Gutiérrez Pantoja (1997), Arroyo Pichardo (1999), Ramalho da Rocha (2002), Pontes Nogueira and Messari (2005).

14 See Tom Biersteker (Chapter 17, this volume).

15 Such is the case of a series of reflections on the geopolitics of knowledge and the coloniality of power developed by the "modernity-coloniality" network, which brings together scholars from different areas of the social sciences throughout the hemisphere and has been influenced by postcolonialism, liberation philosophy and world-system theory. Although this kind of reflection is of tremendous relevance for thinking about the "international," it is largely invisible to regional IR scholarship. See Castro-Gómez and Grosfoguel (2007: 9–23) for a brief history of the group's evolution.

16 This situation is slowly changing, as full text journal services (such as the Scientific Electronic Library Online, Scielo) have begun to alleviate the distribution bottlenecks that plague all Latin American academic journals. Growing pressure is also being exerted upon many of the "top-notch" university staff to publish in journals that are recognized by distinct international indexation services, including those published regionally.

17 Another key factor determining this selection, related to my particular working conditions, was the availability of regional IR journals in local Colombian libraries and/or online. Although *Foreign Affairs en Español* has only been in existence since 2001, the fact that it is the most widely circulated journal and that its authorship is regional in nature warranted its inclusion.

18 Some but not all of the articles that address U.S. foreign policy in *Foreign Affairs en Español* are Spanish language translations of texts originally published in the English-language version. Selection of these texts is conducted in-house by the FAE editorial staff.

19 With the exception of the UNAM (Mexico), the University of the West Indies (Jamaica) and perhaps the Universidad Central de Venezuela, there are no Marxist scholars in any of the other IR programs included in my survey. Given that international relations studies in the region are so closely wed to practical foreign policy and security concerns and to the political establishment, it comes as no surprise that this professoriate feels more at home with like-minded scholars in fields such as sociology.

20 With the exception of a handful of countries, most notably Brazil, public funding for academic research is scarce and hard to come by. Therefore, resesarch monies provided by Ford – the only

core philantroper with a region-wide presence – have significant potential to influence intellectual activity.

References

Alker, Hayward and Thomas Biersteker (1984) "The Dialectics of World Order: Notes for a Future Archeologist of International Savoir Faire," *International Studies Quarterly*, 28 (2): 121–142.

Arroyo Pichardo, Graciela (1999) *Metodología de las relaciones internacionales*, Mexico: Oxford University Press.

Cardoso, Fernando Henrique (1974) "As Tradições de Desenvolvimiento-Associado," *Estudos Cebrap*, 8: 41–75.

Cardoso, Fernando Henrique and Enzo Faletto (1969) *Dependencia y desarrollo en América Latina. Ensayo de interpretación sociológica*, Mexico: Siglo XXI Editores.

Castro-Gómez, Santiago and Oscar Guardiola (2000) "Introducción," in Santiago Castro-Gómez and Oscar Guardiola (eds), *La reestructuración de las ciencias sociales en América Latina*, Bogotá: Pensar-Centro Editorial Javierano, pp. xxi–xlv.

Castro-Gómez, Santiago and Ramón Grosfoguel (2007) "Prólogo. Giro decolonial, teoría crítica y pensamiento heterárquico," in Santiago Castro-Gómez and Ramón Grosfoguel (eds), *El giro decolonial. Reflexiones para una diversidad epistémica más allá del capitalismo global*, Bogotá: Instituto Pensar-Universidad Central-Siglo del Hombre Editores, pp. 9–24.

Centeno, Miguel A. and Patricio Silva (eds) (1998) *The Politics of Expertise in Latin America*, New York: St. Martin's Press.

Colacrai de Trevisán, Miriam (1992) "Perspectivas teóricas en la bibliografía de política exterior argentina," in Roberto Russell (ed.), *Enfoques teóricos para el estudio de la política exterior*, Buenos Aires: RIAL-GEL, pp. 19–51.

Gutiérrez Pantoja, Gabriel (1997) *Teoría de las relaciones internacionales*, Mexico: Oxford University Press.

Jaguaribe, Helio (1979) "Autonomía periférica y hegemonía céntrica," *Estudios Internacionales*, 46 (April–June): 91–130.

Lagos, Gustavo (1980) "Tendencias y perspectivas del estudio de las relaciones internacionales: Tareas para América Latina," *Estudios Internacionales*, 50 (April–June): 236–251.

Maira, Luis (1991) "Los estudios internacionales en América Latina: Las grandes tendencias y el marco teórico," in Marta Ardila *et al.*, "Los estudios sobre relaciones internacionales en Colombia y América Latina," *Documentos de Trabajo*, Instituto de Estudios Políticos y Relaciones Internacionales, Universidad Nacional de Colombia, 2 (February): 7–16.

Mohanty, Chandra Tarpade (2003), *Feminism Without Borders*, Durham, NC: Duke University Press.

Morgenthau, Hans J. (1968) *Politics Among Nations: The Struggle for Power and Peace*, New York: Alfred A. Knopf.

Muñoz, Heraldo (1980) "Los estudios internacionales en América Latina: Problemas fundamentales," *Estudios Internacionales*, 51 (July–September): 328–344.

Muñoz, Heraldo (1987) "El estudio de las políticas exteriores latinoamericanas: Temas y enfoques dominantes," in Manfred Wilhelmy (ed.), *El sistema internacional y América Latina. La formación de la política exterior*, Buenos Aires: RIAL-GEL, pp. 287–315.

Palacios, Marco (1999) *Parábola del liberalismo*, Bogotá: Editorial Norma.

Perina, Rubén M. (1985) "El estudio de las relaciones internacionales en universidades de América Latina y el Caribe," in Rubén M. Perina, comp., *El estudio de las relaciones internacionales en América Latina y el Caribe*, Buenos Aires: GEL, pp. 7–23.

Pontes Nogueira, João and Nizar Messari (2005) *Teoría das Relações Internacionais*, Rio de Janeiro: Elsevier Editora.

Puig, Juan Carlos (1980) *Doctrinas internacionales y autonomía latinoamericana*, Caracas: Instituto de Altos Estudios de América Latina, Universidad Simón Bolívar.

Rama, Claudio (2006) "La tercera reforma de la educación superior en América Latina y el Caribe: Masificación, regulaciones e internacionalización," in Instituto Internacional de la UNESCO para la Educación Superior en América Latina y el Caribe (ESALC), *Informe sobre la educación superior en América Latina y el Caribe 2000–2005*, Caracas: UNESCO, May, pp. 11–18.

Ramalho da Rocha, Antonio Jorge (2002) *Relações Internacionais: Teorias e Agendas*, Brasilia: IBRI-Funag.

RIAL (1985) "Folleto informativo," Santiago de Chile: RIAL.

RIAL (1988) "Diez años de labor," Santiago de Chile: RIAL.

Russell, Roberto (1992) "Introducción," in Roberto Russell (ed.), *Enfoques teóricos para el estudio de la política exterior*, Buenos Aires: RIAL-GEL, pp. 7–18.

Santos, Theotonio dos (1968) "El nuevo carácter de la dependencia," *Cuadernos del Centro de Estudios Sociológicos*, 10: 1–25.

Santos, Theotonio dos (1973) *Imperialismo y empresas multinacionales*, Buenos Aires: Editorial Galerna.

Soares de Lima, Maria Regina (1992) "Enfoques analíticos de política exterior: el caso brasileño," in Roberto Russell (ed.), *Enfoques teóricos para el estudio de la política exterior*, Buenos Aires: RIAL-GEL, pp. 53–83.

Sonntag, Heinz R. (1988) *Duda/certeza/crisis. La evolución de las ciencias sociaels en América Latina*, Caracas: UNESCO–Editorial Nueva Sociedad.

Sorj, Bernando (1990) "Modernity and Social Desintegration: Crisis of Society and Crisis of the Social Sciences in Brazil and Latin America," *European Journal of Development Research*, 2 (1): 108–120.

Sunkel, Oswaldo (1980) "El desarrollo de la teoría de la dependencia," in Oswaldo Sunkel *et al.*, *Transnacionalización y dependencia*, Madrid: Ediciones Cultura Hispánica del Instituto de Cooperación Iberoamericana, pp. 13–25.

Tickner, Arlene B. (2002) *Los estudios internacionales en América Latina. ¿Hegemonía intelectual o pensamiento emancipatorio?* Bogotá: Alfaomega-Ediciones Uniandes–CEI-CESO.

Tickner, Arlene B. (2003) "Hearing Latin American Voices in International Relations Studies," *International Studies Perspectives*, 4 (4): 325–350.

Tokatlian, Juan Gabriel (1996) "Pos-guerra fría y política exterior. De la autonomía relativa a la autonomía ambigua," *Análisis Político*, 28 (May–August): 22–40.

Tomassini, Luciano (1990) "El desarrollo de los estudios internacionales en América Latina: Algunas implicaciones con respecto a la docencia," in PNUD/CEPAL, *Consideraciones sobre la enseñanza de las relaciones internacionales a nivel de postgrado*, Santiago de Chile: Proyecto de Cooperación con los Servicios Exteriores de América Latina, August, pp. 51–74.

Tschirgi, Necla (2006) "Analyzing the Ford Foundation's Peace, Conflict and Security Work, 2001–2006," Final Report Submitted to the Ford Foundation for the Peace and Social Justice Program.

United Nations, Economic Commission for Latin America (1950) *The Economic Development of Latin America and its Principal Problems*, New York: United Nations.

Wæver, Ole (1998) "The Sociology of a Not So International Discipline: American and European Developments in IR," *International Organization*, 52 (4): 687–727.

Wilhelmy, Manfred (1980) "Desarrollo y crisis de los estudios internacionales en Chile," in Francisco Orrego Vicuña (ed.), *Los estudios internacionales en América Latina*, Santiago de Chile: Instituto de Estudios Internacionales, Editorial Universitaria, pp. 173–191.

3 South Africa

Between history and a hard place

Maxi Schoeman

Introduction

"Doing" IR in South and Southern Africa (teaching, research, publications) has always been preoccupied with and rooted in a triple history – colonialism, apartheid and the relationship of the region (as a region and as individual countries in the region) and the rest of the African continent, with its former colonial masters and of these countries to each other. To this triple history one can add three other determinants – let us refer to these as the contemporary drivers – closely related to the triple history, which interact with these historical factors to shape the IR environment in South Africa and the region: the end of the Cold War and of apartheid, the globalisation of the ideology of neo-liberalism and the politics of transformation in Africa, the latter being characterised by a struggle to formulate and implement an "African agenda"[1] aimed at dealing with the continent's triple history and the impact of the contemporary drivers on the field of IR. These two sets of factors (the triple history and the contemporary drivers) serve to provide the external context in which the "intellectual, institutional and political constellations" (Wæver 1998) of the discipline have developed.

This chapter deals with the development of and developments in IR in South Africa since the end of the Cold War and the demise of apartheid, taking 2 February 1990 as its starting point: the day on which (then) President F. W. de Klerk announced the unbanning of the ANC and other political organisations and the release of Nelson Mandela and scores of political prisoners from jail. In the first section I will deal briefly with developments in the pre-1990 era,[2] setting the scene for a more detailed discussion in section two of the contemporary study of IR and the context in which "doing IR" is taking place.[3]

Developments pre-1990

By the late 1980s "official" or establishment South Africa was largely isolated from the rest of the world, a result of a very successful sanctions campaign conducted by the international community with the encouragement and assistance of the external wing of the ANC, the United Democratic Front (UDF), an organisation that served as an umbrella organisation for anti-apartheid activists and internal supporters of the banned ANC, and the Frontline States (FLS) (Angola, Botswana, Lesotho, Mozambique, Tanzania, Zambia and Zimbabwe), who spearheaded the continental struggle against apartheid.

The ruling National Party's foreign policy objectives during this era were succinctly captured in the subtitle of an excellent descriptive study: *The Search for Status and Security* (Barber and Barratt 1990). The overriding aim of the government was the "preservation of a white controlled state" and it fought "to ensure the security, status and legitimacy of the state within the international community" (Barber and Barratt 1990: 1). IR scholarship was largely determined by this aim, whether in support of the government's foreign policy, or in critiquing it, though the scholarly participants were almost exclusively members of the white universities.[4] In his discussion on the role of universities and research institutes in the formation of foreign policy, Geldenhuys (1984: 168–171) points out a number of relevant aspects: political science (including IR) was in its infancy during the early apartheid years and up to the late 1960s and the two research institutes of the time, the Africa Institute and the South African Institute of International Affairs (SAIIA), carried very little weight in foreign policy making. Africa and the U.S. were the two areas in which South African academics lacked knowledge.[5] As so often happens, the development of expertise in these fields was reactive – as the U.S. began to play a significant role in the region, most notably in the case of the status of Namibia (then South West Africa) and the Angolan war, local academics began to study the U.S. and the Southern African region.

Most of the research institutes of the apartheid era were fairly close to the government, and a number of academics moved to various positions in the state bureaucracy, yet some of these institutes remained deliberately distant – SAIIA being a very good example, especially under the leadership of the late John Barratt. The apartheid era was characterised by a rather deep division between white Afrikaans speakers and their English counterparts (who were usually anti-apartheid), also in academia, but it is safe to say that during the 1980s these two groups moved closer, especially as Afrikaans academics became increasingly alarmed at the direction of the apartheid regime under P.W. Botha's presidency and as a younger generation of Afrikaans political scientists, many of them foreign-educated, started making their voices heard. Nevertheless, it was still a race-based, male-dominated intellectual elite, with white (male) academics supporting or criticising the government and its foreign policy, and no (local) black political scientists making much of an input.

IR in South Africa since the end of apartheid

The end of the Cold War and of apartheid had a profound impact on the IR community in South Africa. As will be discussed in this section, *everything* changed, yet, curiously, much also remained the same: the region's triple history would not be transcended by the new drivers; rather, these two sets of factors would serve, in a curious way, to shape South Africa, the region and the discipline of IR.

The early 1990s provided a window of opportunity, but also an imperative for change: the advent of majority rule in South Africa created expectations of a "peace dividend" in the region and, at home, demands for sweeping changes. The white face of the country – in politics, in business, in administration and in education – had to become reflective of the demographics of the country. South Africa had to be reintegrated into the international community, but more importantly into Africa – affirming its "Africanness". The end of the Cold War unleashed the exponential globalisation of neo-liberal economics, conditioning the policies of the "new" South Africa and informing Africa's response to its multiple socio-economic and political/governance crises. The struggle between the power of neo-liberal economics and an indigenous "African Agenda" had begun: the African Renaissance was declared, but it was designed, paradoxically, on the very economic system that had, during the colonial era, and later in terms of the relationship between African states and the former colonial powers, largely contributed to the continent's marginalisation, underdevelopment, poverty and insecurity.

In South Africa, the need for change and the African Agenda, embedded within a neo-liberal economic framework, yet confronted with huge development demands, impacted heavily upon the country's tertiary education sector. Universities, and particularly the former white universities, were subjected to the massification of tertiary education, resulting in huge increases in student numbers, yet without meaningful capital investments to maintain and supplement infrastructure or additional funding to cope with the expansion of the student body, increasingly including students from the rest of the continent, particularly Zimbabwe, the Democratic Republic of Congo (DRC), Mozambique, Rwanda, Burundi and Nigeria. Few, if any, departments have teaching assistants (senior graduate students) and all faculty teach at the undergraduate level, with many of them teaching both political science and IR. Specialisation in teaching is a luxury, and South African political sciences lecturers often tend to be generalists rather than specialists. As one respondent put it:

> We have not yet developed a good understanding of the pedagogy of IR. This is also because of the context in which we find ourselves – educational backwardness, heavy teaching loads, large student groups, few opportunities to use good sources.

As has happened in many other parts of the world, managerialism has become the order of the day and the teaching staff are inundated with administrative work in the wake of the bureaucratisation of academia. This bureaucratisation is inherently anti-intellectual, being driven by *form* rather than content or substance, undermining the traditional ethos of the university as a place for the development of ideas, of critical thinking and of discourse, and demanding "practical outcomes" – in the case of students training rather than education; in the case of research "practical" policy recommendations rather than publications that explore ideas and theoretical issues.

However, the above is also a rather oversimplified version of the status quo and a number of caveats are necessary before one can turn to the specific case of IR. Transformation in South Africa is aimed at dealing with the country's past (building a non-racial community), but doing so within a very specific present in which the free market ideology has permeated every corner of society, having become not only the "language of state" (see Wæver 1998) but also the language of society, in a crude and reductionist sense that is reflected in rampant consumerism. As is the case with the vast majority of sub-Sahara African states, South Africa's problems are huge and immediate: poverty, disease and unemployment are rampant, yet have to be dealt with if the country is to consolidate and maintain its fledgling democracy. At the same time, and very importantly, South Africa is attempting to Africanise – to transcend its previous image of a "white" country, out of step with and in many ways oblivious to the existence of anything north of the Limpopo River (the boundary between the country and the "rest" of Africa), except as being a threat to the survival of "white" South Africa. This vision of itself as "truly African" increasingly finds expression in the idea of the "developmental state" (see some of the comments by academics in the following section).

There is, however, an inherent tension here: the "language of state" during the first decade of the post-apartheid era was very much that of economic liberalism with its spill-over effects into academe – students became "clients", universities were selling or delivering "products", libraries became "information centres" delivering "services", and everything had to be quantified, measured, benchmarked and bureaucratised. The objectives of Africanisation and transformation (together with poverty reduction and economic development of the country and the continent the core aims of South Africa's "African agenda"), on the other hand, tend to "oppose" economic liberalism and opposition within the ruling party, coming from its tripartite allies, the trade unions (COSATU) and the South African Communist Party, forces the state into a new direction, that of the developmental state – an ideology with a different vocabulary and growth path than the one opted for when the ostensibly "ideology-free" liberal market model was adopted. Developmentalism and economic liberalism are uneasy bedfellows and while the struggle between these two ideologies continues, academics, and more specifically IR scholars, seem to be wary of both. Little wonder that their energy and effort are largely concentrated elsewhere, in a domain with which most are familiar, namely security studies (as will be discussed in a later section).

These two objectives – domestic transformation and Africanisation – have become the main demands on academia, and, more specifically, on political sciences (as political science and IR are often referred to), operating within the context of the massification and bureaucrat-isation of the tertiary sector. Yet, the two demands are also often in competition. First, labour legislation to ensure the transformation of the labour profile of the country precludes, for all intents and purposes, the appointment of qualified and experienced non-South African Africans to academic positions, while the exponential growth of think-tanks and research institutes and the private and public sectors at large constantly deplete universities of young black South Africans to be moulded into a next generation of intellectuals. Nowhere is this competition more devastating than in the political sciences: the brightest young black South Africans are enticed by high salaries into employment outside of academia and the discipline/s remain largely white and increasingly elderly.[6] One consequence of this trend (to be returned to in the following subsection) is an apparent shift of research from political science departments to research institutes and think-tanks, with academics increasingly having to concentrate on teaching rather than publishing (this is of course also related to shrinking staff numbers and increasing student numbers, referred to earlier).

Second, the legacy of apartheid South Africa's inferior system of "Bantu education" has not yet been erased. Large numbers of black[7] students from previously disadvantaged backgrounds flock to universities, educationally unprepared for the demands of university studies. Attempts to redress the inequalities inherent in the school system have so far failed and increasingly students of all racial backgrounds struggle to complete their tertiary studies.[8]

There is also a third aspect that needs attention: the Africanisation of the country's intelligentsia. The debate about the "colour" of intellectuality in the country finds its clearest expression in the "Native Club", a controversial initiative founded in 2006, based at the Africa Institute in Pretoria and chaired by former presidential advisor Titus Mofolo. The Native Club is aimed at "mobilising and consolidating South African intelligentsia as a social force", with "South African" here having a "black" connotation. The debate around the founding of this initiative is indicative of the extent to which the issue of race is still of paramount importance in South Africa, infusing all aspects of life and particularly so the realm of ideas. This initiative is perhaps the clearest indication of the intellectual drive to move away from neo-liberalism towards developmentalism; and away from overtly Western ideas and local domination by "the settler intellectual and his (*sic*) black/captive intellectual"[9] to encourage greater participation by black Africans, in particular in the socio-economic, political and cultural spheres. The Native Club engendered vigorous debate, not least within the black community, but whichever way one is inclined, its importance lies in the fact that it is an attempt to deal with the triple history and the contemporary drivers identified in the introduction to this chapter. The concern with the "Africanisation" of academe is under-standable – whites account for 9.3 percent of the population, yet 67 percent of university staff are white (down from 87 percent in 1993) (South African Institute of Race Relations 2005: 1,307).

Post-1994 South Africa is not only about non-racialism and Africanisation, though. The country's 1996 Constitution also commits the country to non-sexism and part of the history of the post-1994 era is that of the advancement of women, classified as a "designated group", whether white or black, to be targeted for employment equity. Women have therefore made significant advances in their professional lives, though the number of women in IR remains relatively small and mainly white. Although no official figures are available on the gender ratio of university staff, the number of female IR academics seems to be less than 10, but within research institutes and think-tanks this number is higher. The main reasons for this low representation of women in IR are that relatively few academic positions become vacant, universities do not create new positions, university salaries are relatively low (when compared with those in the private and public sectors) and there is therefore rather little incentive for women to plan for an academic career.

Before mapping IR in South Africa, a number of concrete aspects regarding academia and the social sciences and IR in particular will be discussed briefly. It is not possible, though, to completely divorce these "practical" or concrete issues from the intellectual activities of IR in South Africa and certain aspects of the latter will be touched upon in some of the following subsections.

The rise of the think-tank industry

The end of apartheid saw a veritable explosion in the number of think-tanks and other research institutes (many of them actually NGOs dealing with specific issues or interests, but relying on research in order to strengthen advocacy and to access funding) in South Africa. Interestingly, this industry is often region-wide or continental but based in South Africa, due largely to the relatively high level of development of the country. In other words, many of these organisations are *based* in South Africa, but draw their staff from across the continent. A good example is the Electoral Institute of Southern Africa (EISA) (dealing also with other countries in Africa), headed by a Congolese national and having a Lesotho national as its research director. Some of these organisations are international (in the sense of extra-Africa) institutes, whose work covers the whole of the region or the continent (such as the Institute for Democracy and Electoral Assistance (IDEA)), but with its regional offices in South Africa. Again, they employ researchers from across the continent.

South Africa's (and the continent's) African agenda has also resulted in a number of think-tanks originally created to deal with South Africa's international relations to broaden their remit to also study broader African issues, particularly Africa's place in the global economy and its attempts through the New Partnership for Africa's Development (NEPAD) to improve its position in the international division of labour, and African security issues. The South African Institute of International Affairs (SAIIA), the Institute for Global Dialogue (IGD), the Centre for Conflict Resolution (CCR), the Centre for Policy Studies (CPS) and to a lesser extent the Institute for Strategic Studies (ISSUP) and the Human Sciences Research Council (HSRC) are examples of these "broadened horizons" determined by the country's emphasis on its African Agenda and the importance of Africa to its foreign policy.

The real impact of the think-tank industry on IR, however, has to do with the intellectual content of the industry's activities, often shaped by and shaping the agendas of donor organisations and government. It is an issue to which we will return in the section dealing with intellectual activities in IR.

Funding opportunities

The large number of think-tanks compete for funding, and funding comes mostly from international donors. There is little competition, though, between academics and think-tanks for funding, though those think-tanks/research institutes attached to universities do compete with the non-university or so-called independent institutes for funding.[10] The main reason is that academic departments are too small and overburdened to undertake the kind of research, very often policy-driven, that donors want to see. Research funding for academics (specifically social scientists) comes from other sources: often from donors, but from different categories of funding specifically aimed at academia, from the National Research Foundation (NRF) and from the research divisions within universities. Two comments are necessary in this regard.

First, the global trend towards the "internationalisation" of universities has opened up a range of new opportunities for South African universities and specifically so for IR scholars who are now increasingly in demand to "partner" foreign universities in research projects related to Africa. Many political science departments are inundated with requests from universities (most of them rather famous) in the UK and the U.S. for cooperation agreements, usually with a view to conducting research on aspects and topics that are increasingly finding their way on to the global agenda: HIV/AIDS, poverty reduction, post-conflict reconstruction and development (PCRD), UN reform, terrorism, radical Islam, China in Africa, the U.S. in Africa and so on. Africa has become popular as a focus of international studies and South Africa as the "bridge" into the continent. But there are two problems here: the first being the lack of capacity of IR scholars to take up these opportunities, and the fact that it is not local scholars who determine the issues on the agenda, though one should hasten to admit that the issues themselves are considered important, if not crucial. Rather, the problem is that the "locals" remain largely subservient to the dictates of their "international" partners, participating in projects in which the playing fields are not level.

Contact and relations with institutions on the African continent have also increased significantly since 1994. Many academics publish with the Council for the Development of Social Science Research in Africa (CODESRIA) and the Organisation for Social Science Research in East and Southern Africa (OSSREA), and several are involved with the regular conferences and workshops presented by various organs of the African Union (AU), particularly so in the field of security and post-conflict reconstruction and development. Several African scholars, mainly from Nigeria, Kenya and Zimbabwe, hold positions in South African political science departments and research institutions, though such arrangements are not reciprocated by South African scholars.

The second aspect regarding funding opportunities for IR scholars has to do with the demands placed on academics by universities in a context in which there is a heavy emphasis both on massification of universities and on the need for local universities to become "internationally competitive", i.e. to publish in internationally accredited peer-reviewed journals. These two demands are almost contradictory in an environment of large-scale expansion in student numbers and the simultaneous stagnation, if not shrinkage, of staff numbers and the availability of qualified IR scholars. Universities are increasingly making funding available to academics in order to promote the status of their institutions as "research universities", yet seldom understand the international context in which particular disciplines operate.

The relationship between IR scholars and government

The relationship between IR scholars (here referring specifically to academics) and government plays out on two levels – informal/unofficial and official/institutionalised. Many of the country's new cadre of foreign affairs officials were trained by the current generation of IR scholars, making for a close link and fairly regular contact between them. In an effort to ensure greater interaction between academe and these officials, the Department of Foreign Affairs' (DFA) Policy Research and Analysis Unit (PRAU) established an institutionalised link between the Department and academics and think-tanks in 2005, with the various actors taking turns to present fairly regular roundtable discussions. These discussions take place on average three times per year.

At the unofficial level vibrant relations exist, with some of these officials regularly presenting seminars or guest lectures in various political science departments, and academics and officials meeting informally to discuss "matters of the day". Yet there is also at times an underlying tension in these relations, with DFA, as many other government departments, exhibiting a sensitivity to criticism of the country's foreign policy, often believing that such criticism is based on a lack of understanding of the international environment. More damning, though, from an academic perspective, is the fact that officials at times are of the opinion that "not enough" is coming from academics to assist them (DFA) in understanding and navigating the international environment. The author, for one, has often been told that "we (DFA) look to the academics for ideas", with the implication that these ideas are not forthcoming. Again, the explanation lies in the heavy teaching and administrative burden carried by academics – little time is left for genuine discussion, let alone reflection on the "state of the world and our place in it".

At a different level, two "eras" of engagement between IR scholars – be they academics or attached to think-tanks and research institutes – and government may be distinguished.[11] During the Mandela era (1994–1999), government relied heavily on the participation of civil society, and specifically think-tanks and academics, in the development of foreign policy. The reasons for this participatory role granted to academics and researchers are twofold. First, during the transition period (the Mandela presidency), the idea of participatory democracy was very strong – a kind of euphoria had taken hold of the country and the lofty ideal of "government for the people by the people" was very much in evidence. Second, and at the more prosaic and practical level, government did not have much of a choice: it lacked research capacity within its own ranks and was therefore very much dependent on the scholarly community for input into policy development. During this phase, then, in the realm of foreign policy development, the nature of the relationship between the state and civil society was collaborative, being a spill-over effect of the anti-apartheid struggle during which many civil society organisations had worked closely with the exiled liberation movements (particularly the ANC), "developing and promoting an alternate vision of the future" (Le Pere and Vickers 2004: 67).

With the advent of the Mbeki presidency in mid-1999, the era of policy development came to an end. Mbeki made it very clear that the time had come for implementation and this in itself indicated that the role of the research community would change dramatically. Added to this was the fact that by 1999 government had managed to develop its own policy research and development capacity (largely in the form of academics and researchers having taken up employment within the state sector). Opportunities for civil society engagement diminished rapidly and foreign policy issues became politicised and polarised, as is so well illustrated in the case of Zimbabwe, an issue where racial politics often raises its head: criticism is often viewed as an indication of a white, liberal, pro-Western (and by implication "anti-African") stance. Such labelling is not helpful in the development of effective foreign policy and, more broadly speaking, the watchdog role of civil society (of which academics and think-tank researchers form an integral part) and its ability to influence the broad outline and direction of foreign policy have been diluted. At the same time, though, there is no doubt that some academics and think-tanks are still taken seriously and that they have opportunities for making an input, even though such input is often indirect.

The state of IR in South Africa

In mapping the state of IR in the country, attention is paid to the way in which the study of IR is organised by providing a brief overview of its location within universities, followed by a discussion of the way in which it is studied and of the outputs of IR scholars by way of a brief analysis of two local journals which are ostensibly open to publications from IR scholars, as well as other publication outlets (e.g. books).

The location of IR within universities

In South Africa, as in many other countries, IR is largely considered to be part of political science or political studies, at the very least in terms of organisational aspects. IR is considered to be closely related to, yet also clearly distinct from, political science, with the latter constituting the intellectual basis of and for IR. Only one university in the country – the University of the Witwatersrand (Wits) – has a separate and distinct IR department. At the University of Pretoria the Department of Political Sciences hosts both political science and IR as two separate subjects. The majority of the other universities offer politics or political science degrees made up of a combination of political science and IR courses.

Despite the fact that IR is only recognised as a separate discipline at two universities, most universities in South Africa have experienced a rapid increase in students interested in IR; the reasons for this increasing interest in IR will be discussed in the following section. English is the main medium of instruction (though at the undergraduate level some of the former Afrikaans universities still teach at least some of their courses also in Afrikaans), meaning that prescribed texts are in English and there is no need for translations. Locally produced textbooks (such as the one by McGowan, Cornelissen and Nel discussed below) are few, as the market is relatively small.

The study of IR

When it comes to the *what* is studied (syllabus content), a distinction may be drawn between undergraduate and graduate approaches, as the undergraduate level reflects a largely generic offering of what is traditionally studied in introductory courses to IR, while the graduate level tends to be more reflective of specific interests and specialisations of scholars and expertise within specific departments.[12] It is at this level and in terms of publications that the extent of local IR expertise and, importantly, the scope of it become evident. Undergraduate syllabi are largely influenced by and in most cases based on Western (especially American and British) perspectives, though there are efforts to make the content relevant to domestic and African experiences and conditions. One of the respondents explained her department's approach as follows:

> In the first year course we familiarise students with Northern theories (realism, idealism, Marxism and constructivism) as a starting point, but these theories are not the canon. This introduction is a platform from which to explain Northern behaviour and criticise these mainstream theories. . . . One can argue that the difference between how we teach IR theory (proper) and how it gets taught in, say, the UK, would not differ that much except for the contextualisation.

The textbooks being used differ rather widely and three types of prescribed work may be distinguished. First, when it comes to introductory courses, most departments use "Northern" textbooks – Holsti's *International Politics: A Framework for Analysis* (1995), though long out of print, remains a favourite, as do Baylis and Smith's *The Globalization of World Politics* (2005), *Perspectives on World Politics* by Little and Smith (2001) and Kegley and Wittkopf's *World Politics: Trend and Transformation* (2004). Thus there is a mix of Northern textbooks spanning Britain and North America. For theory courses, the work of Viotti and Kauppi, *International Relations Theory* (1998), *Theories of International Relations* (Burchill *et al.* 2001) and Jackson and Sorenson's *Introduction to International Relations* (2003) are most often prescribed. Increasingly, syllabi contain sections on "non-state challenges" (concentrating on political Islam, terrorism and the rise of global civil society with, in the latter instance, the work of David Held being very popular). In the case of IPE the work of Cox, Gilpin and Strange form the core texts, with Balaam and Veseth's *Introduction to International Political Economy* (2005) often used in IPE introductory courses.

A second type of prescribed text is the production of a South African IR textbook, now in its third edition, and used by many departments at the undergraduate level: *Power, Wealth and Global Equity: An International Relations Textbook for Africa*, edited by Patrick McGowan, Scarlett Cornelissen and Philip Nel (2006).[13] This book was conceived by the Institute for Global Dialogue (IGD), a South African foreign policy think-tank under the leadership of Dr Garth le Pere, who heeded the call from local academics in the mid-1990s for an "African" IR textbook and who has been contributing financially to its publication ever since the first edition was published in 1999. The contributors to the book are a mix of local academics, scholars from elsewhere on the continent and a few "international" scholars (meaning Northern scholars who have been working regularly in Africa over several decades). A third type of prescribed text is the use of readers and study/course packs – compilations of extracts from a range of scholarly publications and textbooks, a method that allows for two things: the production of prescribed material at reasonable prices[14] and the freedom to pick and choose exactly what might be needed for a specific module.

At the graduate level, specialisation and interest become much more pronounced. Students interested in foreign policy studies tend to gravitate towards the University of Johannesburg, while the University of Pretoria runs a popular course-work Masters programme in security studies. Expertise in security studies, though, resides in most departments (see the following section). Largely descriptive and empirical studies, often in strong combination with international law, are produced at Wits, a department that also has expertise in Asian studies. Although not much IPE doctoral work has been produced in South Africa, such specialisation is to be found at Pretoria, Johannesburg, Rhodes and Stellenbosch, with the latter also producing work on more recent trends in IR, such as global cities and new spatialities of authority. There are no specialists dedicated to EU, China or U.S. studies, though the University of Johannesburg has a Centre for European Studies and the University of Stellenbosch has a Centre for Chinese Studies. Since 2005 the University of Pretoria has been presenting an annual "mini" American Studies Programme for junior faculty and senior graduate students from across the Southern African region.

Most departments have expertise in African politics, though the notion of "African politics" is rather opaque – it may denote anything from security studies, to foreign policy, to regional studies, to IPE, as long as the main focus is on Africa or an African country or region. Dissertations and theses on pure theory are few and far between, and only a very small number of scholars supervise this kind of work – mostly the emphasis is on the application of theory to the South African, Southern African or African contexts, a product of the demand for "policy-relevant" work. The intellectual climate in the country and the way in which funding (including scholarships) is structured require Masters dissertations and doctoral theses to have (policy) "relevance", meaning that topics and themes are almost exclusively based on issues directly related to South African or African politics.

The scholars who responded to questions on their views of IR in South Africa all agreed that South African IR tended to use Northern theories, but not only or largely realism, as claimed by Taylor (2000) in his overview of the discipline locally. Van der Westhuizen (2005) mentions postmodernism, critical theory, constructivism and German hermeneutics as the reflectivist impulses among at least some local IR scholars. But all the respondents lamented the fact that there was just not enough time to do "serious theoretical work", given conditions in universities and the state's transformation agenda that places so much emphasis on "policy work" (as discussed earlier) – the "tyranny of the ideology of developmentalism" as one respondent put it, while others referred to the "hegemony of neo-liberalism".

A respondent from a so-called previously disadvantaged university responded as follows to the question about the use of theory in the study of IR locally:

> In IPE, in my opinion, we part ways with dominant Northern discourses. Dependency theory forms an important part of the curriculum to explore the politics of unequal development. . . . I would argue that the way we teach (and were taught) IPE is with an intense sense of colonial and neo-colonial injustice.

The majority of the respondents, though, are rather despondent about the development of IR theory in and by South African scholars:

> We are very superficial when it comes to theory. . . . We are always busy with new security issues, but mostly doing case studies and applications, not serious theory.

These comments confirm to an extent what Peter Vale (1989: 201), a senior local IR scholar, wrote almost two decades ago:

> South Africa's contribution to the development of International Relations has been poor. This does not mean that individuals have made unimportant contributions to the discourse of facets of the discipline's "stuff"; rather, taken as a whole, the country report is unimpressive. It is interesting to note, in contrast, that some South Africans who live – by fiat or choice – outside its borders have strongly contributed to the development of International Relations.[15]

Scholarly output

Turning to publications by IR scholars, two South African journals were selected for analysis, starting with the period 1990 when the window of opportunity for change and transformation opened in South Africa. The purpose was to explore the subject matter of these publications in relation to the use of theory. The two journals are *Politikon* (the journal of the South African Association of Political Science (SAAPS)) and the *South African Journal of International Affairs* (SAJIA), published by the South African Institute of International Affairs (SAIIA). These are the two main outlets for political scientists in the country; most other journals are very specifically aimed at the Southern African region and/or Africa, such as *Strategic Review for Southern Africa*, *Africa Insight*, *Global Insight* and *African Security Review*.[16] The results of the investigation are summarised in Tables 3.1 and 3.2 below.

Table 3.1 Politikon

	Total no. of articles	IR articles*	"Pure" theory*	Applied theory*	Policy related/ descriptive*
1990–1993	62	22	2	6	14
1994–1998	45	15	0	9	6
1999–2007	118	36	4	13	19
Total	225	73	6	28	39
(%)	100	32	8	38	53

Note
* As a percentage of IR articles.

Although *Politikon* was established in the late 1970s to serve both political science and IR, the journal has, over time, become mainly political science-oriented. Of the 225 articles published between 1990 and the first half of 2007, only 73 (32 per cent) dealt with IR, and of these, only six (8 per cent) could be considered "pure theory", with half of these penned by "foreign" scholars. The bulk of IR articles in this journal deal with policy-related issues, mostly regarding descriptive-analytical accounts of South African foreign policy and security matters. It is difficult to establish the reasons for the lack of IR articles in *Politikon*, but at least four tentative reasons could be put forward. The first is that a general perception exists that the journal focuses on and is meant for political scientists, thereby creating a self-fulfilling prophecy. The second reason may be the perception that IR scholars do have "their own" journal – SAJIA – and that not much effort is therefore made to solicit IR articles. Third, the editorship of *Politikon* rotates among the various political science/s departments in the country and, since the mid-1990s, the editors have all been political scientists and not IR scholars. Finally, since 1990, political science, at least in terms of publications, has become very much equated with South African politics, and given the particular historical conjuncture in which South Africa is finding itself, especially in terms of the demand that the African Agenda should be pursued across all sectors of society, a heavy emphasis on local (and regional) issues is understandable. Yet, given the fate of SAJIA, it is understandable that there is growing concern among IR scholars about the lack of local publishing opportunities for "serious" (i.e. theoretically oriented) scholarship, especially given the increasing leadership role that the country is attempting to play in international politics.

SAJIA (formerly the *South African International Affairs Bulletin*, or *Bulletin* for short) exhibits an even more worrying trend: of the 342 IR-related articles published since 1990,

Table 3.2 South African Journal of International Affairs (SAJIA)

	Total no. of articles	IR articles*	"Pure" theory*	Applied theory*	Policy related/ descriptive*
1990–1993	38	38	5	6	27
1994–1998	102	89	0	17	72
1999–2007	202	197	0	22	175
Total	342	324	5	45	274
(%)	100	95	2	14	85

Note
* As a percentage of IR articles.

only five (2 per cent) have dealt with "pure" theory. A further 45 (14 per cent) deal with applied theory and the vast majority of articles (85 per cent) are descriptive-analytical in nature – referred to as "briefings" – short articles, often penned by in-house researchers and dealing with "topical" issues regarding South Africa's foreign relations. Contributors are a mix of local and international academics and researchers, with international authors usually having some link to SAIIA as visiting scholars/researchers or participants in SAIIA conferences and workshops presented in association with (international) donors.

The decision to structure SAJIA in such a way that it moved away from an academic focus towards "policy-relevant" matters was a conscious move on the part of the SAIIA management during the early 1990s. Whereas up until then the journal was aimed at the IR community in the country with SAIIA housing it, it was decided that, especially with a view to donors and funders (mainly international donor agencies and local "big business"), the journal had to be reoriented to reflect more "topical" discussions, thereby also providing an opportunity to influence government thinking.

Given the general publishing trends in the above two journals, respondents were asked to express their views on the question whether there was sufficient local opportunity for IR scholars to publish. On the whole, they did not think so. As one of them put it:

> We do not have much publishing opportunity – *Politikon* is for political scientists, *Politeia* for public administration and the SAJIA journal is no longer academic.

Although journals are considered to be the most direct measure of the discipline itself (Wæver 1998: 697), one could also briefly overview other publications. No effort was made to make a comprehensive study of the number of books and monographs published locally or by local IR scholars and researchers internationally.[17] Rather, books representing certain "types" of scholarship were selected.

Three strands may be distinguished. The first is "pure theory" and of this Mervyn Frost's *Towards a Normative Theory of International Relations* (1986)[18] is a good (if not only) example. This book was concerned with the question of ethics in international relations and, more specifically, the reasons why IR scholars eschewed normative theory. Frost posited a secular Hegelian ethical theory which he called "constitutive theory".

A second strand is that of applying theory to the South/Southern African context, also with a view to enhance and contribute to the development of theory. Here an excellent (though by no means only)[19] example is Peter Vale's *Security and Politics in South Africa: The Regional Context* (2003)[20] in which Vale set himself three goals: first, to "help" critical theory to take a "more empirical and policy-oriented turn"; second, to "engage with the process of ongoing anti-colonial and anti-racist struggle in southern Africa", and third, "helping to recast the idea of security as an emancipatory project rooted in a conception of regional community that makes those humans who most need security its primary referents" (Vale 2003: 3).

A third strand is to be found in the work of another senior IR scholar, Deon Geldenhuys, who has developed a number of analytical frameworks in order to describe and interpret a range of international political trends, such as the foreign relations of isolated states and the phenomenon and implications of isolation (based on South Africa's international isolation during the 1980s), and the behaviour of deviant states (Geldenhuys 1984, 1990, 2004).

In a way these three strands reflect the triple history of South African IR mentioned in the introduction to this chapter: Frost's concern with ethics and normative issues reflects the preoccupation of many "liberal"[21] academics with the wrongs of the apartheid era and the terrible damage done to people under the aegis of "separate development". Vale, as stated above, shows his deep concern with the racial and oppressive colonial and postcolonial order in apartheid Southern Africa and Geldenhuys' work, especially that published during the 1980s and early 1990s, shows his preoccupation with the negative impact that South Africa's apartheid policy had on the country's foreign relations, and its status and image.

But South African IR has been captured, in the opinion of several local scholars, by security studies and by an implied imperative to study Africa. As one respondent put it:

> If you want to build a career locally in IR you have to focus on foreign policy, conflict, security and regionalism and leave other topics for scholars in the North.

The response of another academic is interesting and quoted here extensively:

> I would identify a post-apartheid problem in the [IR] field as an over-concentration on Africa/South Africa. On post-grad level we do not encourage students to study questions that do not directly relate to Africa. I can't remember when last I heard of someone working on a theme that hasn't got "Africa" in the title. For me there is the problem that IR in South Africa may become too inward-looking or boxing itself in. We risk being one-trick ponies if everything we research is Africa-specific.

Several points regarding the study of IR in South Africa – the "*what* that is privileged" – come to the fore in the above two responses and need some unpacking. The reader is reminded of South and Southern Africa's triple history and contemporary drivers as these best explain the current state of IR in South Africa.

In 1989 the World Bank's influential and comprehensive report on sub-Sahara Africa was published – *Sub-Saharan Africa: From Crisis to Sustainable Growth*. The report chronicled and analysed the severe socio-economic and political crises that the subcontinent was experiencing at the time, not least of these the havoc and devastation visited upon South Africa's neighbours in the wake of the country's policy of regional destabilisation. The report did not pay much attention (if any), though, to the legacy of colonialism as a contributing factor to the crises on the continent. Barely a year later the end of a whole era came to pass with the end of the Cold War and of apartheid. Everywhere, but most particularly in Africa, the dawn of a new era – a new international order – was hailed. For Africa, and specifically for Southern Africa, expectations were raised as to a "peace dividend". Military security was seen to be outdated and national security was, in the view of policy makers and academics alike, in dire need of being reconceptualised to reflect a new era and new concerns, most important of which was the security of people – what would become "human security" a few years later. The work of Buzan was instrumental in the intellectual debate about security in South Africa, and practitioners (especially in the South African National Defence Force) and scholars alike explored the meaning of security in and for South Africa and the region. Increasingly, scholarly publications started to focus on "new security" issues and various think-tanks were established, dealing almost exclusively with issues and aspects of security.

However, the focus on security was not new – it had been the main objective and obsession of the white regime during apartheid. What had changed was the (political) environment in the country and internationally, and change also meant that South Africans were relinked, as it were, with the rest of the continent. National security issues were still seen to be tied to the region and the rest of the continent, as it had been under apartheid, but in a completely different way. One result was that the role of South Africa within the region and the continent would also become a major focus of local scholars – no longer would this role be one of dominance through the barrel of a gun or the manipulation of trade and transport dependencies;

South Africa would be able to use its wealth and strength to contribute to the security and development of the continent. So, the main focus of IR research has not changed much – it shifted focus, both in South Africa and the region, due to South Africa's post-apartheid status and policies and its apartheid history of regional destabilisation, but domestic and international events and processes did not ring in changes.

Little wonder then that many IR scholars in the country and across the region believe that issues of security, conflict and development (inextricably linked) dominate scholarship. How to create peace and security? How to ensure that economic growth turns into economic development? What role should South Africa play – partner or leader/hegemon? How should South Africa and Africa deal with China? How to respond to the U.S.'s announcement of the establishment of its Africa Command (AFRICOM)? What are the implications of these two superpowers' increasing involvement on the continent? How to build an effective African Union? How to rebuild the Somali state? What would be best in Sudan – a unified country or should partition between the north and south be encouraged? Can the AU solve the Darfur crisis? Can the crisis in Zimbabwe be solved? Fierce debates have taken place, with continuous meetings – conferences and workshops – between practitioners and scholars. Practitioners want solutions (i.e. "policies that will work"). Grant-making agencies, such as the National Research Foundation, and also foreign donors want to know what contribution proposed research projects would make to the resolution of South African and African problems: academics are torn between the high demands of their teaching environment and the high demands of the policy community, with little time for theoretical work and little time for participating in academic conferences.

The IR environment in South Africa and, one suspects, in many other countries in Africa is very much caught up in these real and urgent crises and calamities. From a South African perspective, the securitisation of "everything" is perhaps understandable, if not familiar, given the region's history. But there is little debate about whether securitisation is the best approach to dealing with African crises. Rather, scholarly publications tend to focus almost exclusively on analyses (and policy prescriptions) based on security perspectives. Foreign policy issues (which of course are closely related to and in many cases synonymous with these crises) are largely discussed and debated within a state-centric conception of roles and orientations *à la* Holsti.

Prospects for IR in South Africa

A number of challenges are facing the IR community in South Africa and neighbouring countries, and these challenges are inexorably tied up with the region's triple history and the contemporary drivers identified in the introduction. Poverty and underdevelopment continue as scourges, impacting not only upon the quality of life of the region's citizens, but also on the quality of students and their ability to continue with graduate studies. Increasingly, universities are turning out students with first degrees, but graduate student numbers seem to be declining.

As is the case in many other chapters in this book, much IR output is topical and largely devoid of theory. In instances where theoretical work is published, the reliance is largely on imported theories, though there are numerous attempts at "customising" or adjusting these theories to local circumstances and conditions. Yet African scholars are currently faced with what might turn out to be a tectonic shift in power relations: the rise of new power centres in the global South, challenging Africans and other Southern intellectuals to revisit Northern theories.

The old triple history paradigm through which everything is filtered through the lenses of apartheid, colonialism and postcolonialism within a post-Cold War context of the supremacy of economic liberalism is increasingly challenged by new realities, of which the rise of China, and to some extent Brazil and India, is opening up new and unchartered waters. Increasingly, African scholars have an opportunity to move out of the shadow of Northern theories and to contribute to theorising about a (coming) new world order.

Much depends on the extent to which local scholars will be able to use their international contacts and collaborators to break into international publishing and be taken note of, while at the same time not neglecting local opportunities that do exist. The increasing internationalisation of South African IR, propelled by the number of UK, European and U.S. universities interested and involved in agreements of cooperation with counterparts in South Africa, is one way of building the local IR community and allowing international scholars to share in their experience and knowledge. Imagine, for a moment, the enrichment of, for instance, constructivist theory, should some of the serious constructivists start working with African scholars in exploring the ways in which the continent and, importantly, its ideas as represented in the thinking of its intellectuals could be mainstreamed in the way in which Peter Vale used critical theory to explore the regional dimension in South African politics, enriching understandings of new forms of community developing "beyond" the state.

But as much also depends not only on whether African IR scholars are taken seriously, but on whether Africa is taken seriously as an area of the world deserving of inclusion into theorising about international relations. We might actually currently be witnessing the start of such a new trend that is being driven by some "real world events" (the font of all theoretical investigation): global climate change, the search for energy sources, forced migration, the need for the growth of consumer markets to reproduce capitalism, the scourge of HIV/ AIDS, the illegal international trade in arms, drugs, ivory and abalone, the struggle between unilateralism and multilateralism and the rise of China as a superpower might be some of the indications that "big" or "important" IR (theories and their proponents) will increasingly have to take note of Africa. But it is not only a question of addressing Africa's "long absence" in theorising about world politics as Kevin Dunn (2001: 2) has it, but about breaking the American hegemony that largely excludes others (any others, not only African scholars) from the discipline of IR: the question is whether these proponents will pay attention to the wealth of knowledge and expertise already available on the continent.

Notes

1 South Africa's African agenda forms the core of the country's governance agenda. In his State of the Nation Address to Parliament on 3 February 2007, President Mbeki summarised the aims of the agenda as follows: (1) the promotion of peace and security and the resolution of continental conflicts; (2) strengthening the African Union (AU) and New Partnership for Africa's Development (NEPAD); (3) contributing to regional and continental stability and prosperity; and (4) promoting multilateralism and South–South cooperation.

2 As far as the pre-1990 study of IR in South Africa is concerned, see Vale (1989) and Du Pisani and Van Wyk (1991). Since the early 1990s a number of further reflections on IR and political science have seen the light, including Booysen and Van Nieuwkerk (1998), Taylor (2000) and Van der Westhuizen (2005).

3 Due to time constraints the author has not been able to conduct an in-depth study of the topic, nor to conduct systematic in-depth interviews with colleagues in the field of IR, yet several colleagues (who will remain anonymous) from a range of universities kindly contributed their views and opinions and I am very grateful to them, though they cannot be held responsible for the way in which I have used their insights and comments. They were representative of the three "types" of university in South Africa: the former Afrikaans, English (both white) and black universities.

4 Afrikaans universities were "white"; the English universities were segregated in the late 1950s when new universities for the "black" community were established. See n. 5.

5 The author's chapter "The role of the public" is also of relevance in understanding the state–society relationship of the apartheid era.

6 Employment equity (EE) targets based on labour legislation make it difficult, if not impossible, to appoint young white academics. White women are still considered to be a "designated" group, yet in many instances their inclusion in junior ranks in academia (and other employment sectors) is now making it difficult to appoint them, as their numbers are outstripping those of other racial categories.

7 As was the case during apartheid, racial categories persist, due partly to the government's attempts to track black empowerment. These categories are the following: black (within which a distinction is drawn between "black African," Asian and so-called "Coloured") and white.

8 According to the South African Institute of Race Relations' South Africa Survey 2004/2005 (2006: 327–328), 50 per cent of students enrolling at tertiary institutions do not complete their studies. Some estimates put the figure at closer to 66 per cent.

9 As expressed by a participant in the debate. See www.nativeclub.org/shared/news, 14 June 2006 (accessed 13 August 2007).

10 Examples of university-based research institutes are the Centre for Conflict Resolution (CCR) at the University of Cape Town, the South African Institute of International Relations (SAIIA) at the University of the Witwatersrand, and the African Centre for the Constructive Resolution of Disputes (ACCORD) at the University of Kwa-Zulu Natal.

11 This section draws heavily on Garth le Pere and Brendan Vickers (2004: 63–80). The authors conducted a range of interviews with academics and researchers in South Africa on the role of civil society in the formulation of foreign policy.

12 This is a rather superficial claim and at most reflects a tendency, as most departments are so small that academics tend to be "generalists" rather than specialists. It is possible though to distinguish a number of specialisations – departments that have built up a reputation for expertise in specific subdisciplines.

13 An interesting mix of editors: McGowan is Professor Emeritus of Political Science at Arizona State University and Extraordinary Professor of Political Science at Stellenbosch University. Scarlett Cornelissen is an associate professor, also at Stellenbosch, and one of the new generation of young black intellectuals in the country. Philip Nel used to be chair of the Department of Political Science at Stellenbosch before moving to the University of Ontago in New Zealand in the late 1990s.

14 Due to the exchange rate of the South African currency, imported textbooks are expensive and students, the majority of whom hail from poor backgrounds, find it impossible to pay these prices.

15 The South Africans "living and working abroad" to whom Vale refers are Mervyn Frost and the late C.A.W. Manning and Sam Nolutshungu.

16 This is not to say that these journals do not publish work relevant to IR. They are however largely confined to either African issues or to security studies. Many articles published in these three journals do have some form of theoretical thrust (mainly using a theoretical framework for analysis), but the scope of this chapter and time constraints preclude a thorough content examination.

17 This would require a separate study, especially had one to also consider the rather prolific publication output rate of the large number of local research institutes who are often much dependent on such output to impress, satisfy and attract international donor funding. I here concern myself only with books published by academics, using three examples of "types" of publication – these are by no means the only books published internationally by South African IR scholars.

18 Frost emigrated to the UK in the mid-1990s. This publication was followed, in 1996, by his *Ethics in International Relations: A Constitutive Theory*, also published by CUP, while Frost was Professor of Politics at the University of Kent.

19 Another example would be Nel and Van der Westhuizen (2004).

20 Frost and Vale, together with David Weiner, made efforts in the late 1980s to "ignite a local debate on these issues [theoretical concerns]." See Vale (1989: 207).

21 "Liberal" was a label attached to any academic (or any other person) who showed opposition to apartheid. It was ascribed to all and sundry – whether communist or liberal – and was a favourite way of the ruling elite to insult anyone in disagreement with the National Party government; in a way it of course became a kind of "badge of honour" over time.

References

Balaam, David and Michael Veseth (2005) *Introduction to International Political Economy*, Upper Saddle River, NJ: Prentice Hall.

Barber, James and John Barratt (1990) *South Africa's Foreign Policy: The Search for Status and Security 1945–1989*, Cambridge: Cambridge University Press.

Baylis, John and Steve Smith (eds) (2005) *The Globalization of World Politics: An Introduction to International Relations*, Oxford: Oxford University Press.

Booysen, Susan and Anthoni Van Nieuwkerk (1998) "Political Studies in South Africa: An Assessment of the Discipline and the Profession," *Politikon*, 27(2): 207–220.

Burchill, Scott, Andrew Linklater, Richard Devekak, Jack Donnelly, Matthew Paterson, Christian Reus-Smit, and Jacqui True (2001) *Theories of International Relations*, Basingstoke: Palgrave.

Dunn, Kevin (2001) "Introduction: Africa and International Relations Theory," in Kevin Dunn and Timothy Shaw (eds), *Africa's Challenges to International Relations Theory*, Basingstoke: Palgrave, pp. 1–17.

Du Pisani, André and Koos Van Wyk, in collaboration with John Barratt (1991) "Restricted Palette: Reflections on the State of International Relations in South Africa," *International Affairs Bulletin*, 15 (1): 2–19.

Frost, Mervyn (1986) *Towards a Normative Theory of International Relations*, Cambridge: Cambridge University Press.

—— (1996) *Ethics in International Relations: A Constitutive Theory*, Cambridge: Cambridge University Press.

Geldenhuys, Deon (1984) *The Diplomacy of Isolation: South Africa's Foreign Policy Making*, New York: St. Martin's Press.

—— (1990) *Isolated States*, Cambridge: Cambridge University Press.

—— (2004) *Deviant Conduct in World Politics*, London: Palgrave Macmillan.

Holsti, Kal J. (1995) *International Politics: A Framework for Analysis*, Upper Saddle River, NJ: Prentice Hall.

Jackson, Robert and George Sorenson (2003) *Introduction to International Relations: Theories and Approaches*, Oxford: Oxford University Press.

Kegley, Charles and Eugene Wittkopf (2004) *World Politics: Trend and Transformation*, Boston, MA: Bedford St Martin's.

Le Pere, Garth and Brendan Vickers (2004) "Civil Society and Foreign Policy," in Philip Nel and Janis Van der Westhuizen (eds), *Democratizing Foreign Policy: Lessons from South Africa*, Lanham, MD: Lexington Books, pp. 63–80.

Little, Richard and Michael Smith (eds) (2001) *Perspectives on World Politics*, New York: Macmillan.

McGowan, Patrick, Scarlett Cornelissen, and Philip Nel (eds) (2006) *Power, Wealth and Global Equity: An International Relations Textbook for Africa*, Cape Town: University of Cape Town Press.

Nel, Philip and Janis Van der Westhuizen (eds) (2004) *Democratizing Foreign Policy: Lessons from South Africa*, Lanham, MD: Lexington Books.

South African Institute of Race Relations (SAIRR) (2005) *South Africa Survey 2004/2005*, Johannesburg: SAIRR.

Taylor, Ian (2000) "Rethinking the Study of International Relations in South Africa," *Politikon*, 27(2): 207–220.

Vale, Peter (1989) "Whose World Is it Anyway?," in Hugh Dyer and Leon Mangasarian (eds), *The Study of International Relations: The State of the Art*, Basingstoke: Macmillan in association with *Millennium: Journal of International Studies*, pp. 189–210.

—— (2003) *Security and Politics in South Africa: The Regional Context*, Boulder, CO: Lynne Rienner.

Van der Westhuizen, Janis (2005) "From a Culture of Insularity to a Culture of 'Competitiveness': Contextualizing the Development of IR Theory in South Africa," paper presented at the British International Studies Association (BISA) annual meeting, Fife, Scotland, 19–21 December.

Viotti, Paul R. and Mark V. Kauppi (1998) *International Relations Theory: Realism, Pluralism, Globalism and Beyond*, New York: Prentice Hall.

Wæver, Ole (1998) "The Sociology of a Not So International Discipline: American and European Developments in International Relations," *International Organization*, 52(4): 687–727.

World Bank (1989) *Sub-Saharan Africa: From Crisis to Sustainable Growth*, Washington, DC: World Bank.

4 Africa

Teaching IR where it's not supposed to be[1]

Cirino Hiteng Ofuho

Introduction

Attempts to explore and understand the study and teaching of international relations beyond the West have grown since the beginning of this century. In the African context there is a strong feeling shared by academics and practitioners alike that a detailed analysis of post-colonial societies and alternative perspectives on global issues is of fundamental importance, not only to stretch disciplinary frontiers but also to improve our analyses of the everyday problems that affect the human condition. My own lived experience, first as an African student pursuing a doctoral degree in Britain, afterwards as a professor of IR in Nairobi, and more recently as a policy-maker, seems to confirm this belief, as have my sojourns throughout most of Africa. By constantly illustrating that what I learned in a Western academic setting is not at all reflective of the world I live in, each of these provides strong evidence of the need to gain further insights into the ways in which the "international" is lived and practiced, taught and reflected upon in distinct parts of the globe.

In Africa the gap between the theory and practice of international relations seems practically irreconcilable and constitutes a source of tension between academics and practitioners. This chapter contends that this gap can only be bridged by way of a permanent dialogue between the world of theory and that of practice. In other words, the study and teaching of IR in Africa and, in fact, elsewhere must reflect and be coterminous with the "facts on the ground" as they are experienced in a particular space and time.

In order to better comprehend the complexities of the African continent and to transcend its role as a mere object to be written about by Western scholarship, I examine how African scholars have attempted to study and define IR and how the field has been taught around the continent.[2] In doing so, I argue that most of the theories that are fashionable in the global discipline are inappropriate for teaching international relations in Africa and in other non-Western societies.

Following a discussion of the development of African IR, I outline some of the early post-independence approaches to the field's study and teaching. Afterwards, the chapter describes the field's status in the continent today and poses some possible courses for future action. In addition to clarifying the nature of IR studies in Africa, my goal is to show that the kind of one-eyed glimpse of the world currently offered by Western IR, that privileges the West and its culture in terms of the worldviews, theories, and methodologies it embraces, is not only erroneous but myopic. No matter how much the West and others attempt to be culturally isolationist, addressing issues that affect the human condition in a genuine fashion necessarily compels us to look outward, beyond the vantage point of our own worldview. Indeed, this is the first step towards making IR scholarship more inclusive and truly "international."

The development of African international relations

International Relations, at least as we know it in its Anglo-American roots, became an academic discipline in 1919, in the aftermath of the First World War. Since achieving disciplinary status in the West, by definition IR has referred to myriad kinds of ties across national boundaries, including political-diplomatic, security-military, economic-developmental, and socio-cultural relations. Mirroring this view, "African IR" is not grounded in political aspects alone, but rather embraces the multiple ways in which states and societies interact.

International relations studies were first developed following African independence, when the newly emerging states faced the need to interact with the rest of the world. At this time the "international" was more of a practical notion than a theoretical one, given its rootedness in immediate problems such as the post-colonial reordering of African political life and the establishment of diplomatic relations with other countries. Given that post-independence states and ruling elites lacked expertise in international affairs, most African countries appointed academic specialists to external or foreign affairs posts. Living examples include Professor A.B. Akinyemi and his predecessor Dr. Ibrahim Gambari (Nigeria), Dr. Salim Ahmed Salim (Tanzania), and Dr. Boutros Boutros-Ghali (Egypt), to mention but a few. The fact that governments depended upon such specialists to guide their foreign relations facilitated International Relations' development as an academic subject of study.

The individuals mentioned offered the public sector expertise in diverse areas of the social sciences, including International Relations, law, economics, and political science. The fact that many of them were trained abroad was also viewed in a positive light. For example, Ibrahim Agboola Gambari graduated from the London School of Economics (LSE) and Columbia University, where he obtained his undergraduate, MA, and Ph.D. degrees in political science and International Relations during the 1960s and 1970s. Salim Ahmed Salim, who has enjoyed successful diplomatic careers both within his native country of Tanzania and continentally as Foreign Minister, Defense Minister, Prime Minister and Secretary General of the now defunct Organization of African Unity (OAU), studied international affairs at the University of Delhi and Columbia University. Similarly, Boutros Boutros-Ghali, a distinguished scholar, diplomat, statesman, and an international civil servant, specialized in international law, political science and economics at the University of Cairo and the University of Paris.

Despite widespread government acknowledgement of the importance of strengthening International Relations in order to boost state capacities abroad, it was not until 1977 that the Nigerian University of Ife established the first IR Chair in Africa, following an official order to create an institution for training national diplomats. It is not accidental that international relations studies were created first in Nigeria. Even before the country's 1960 independence, the government presented a series of policy measures in 1956 to the pre-independence Parliament that included, among others, the training of future Nigerian diplomats (Aluko 1987: 313–317). Although, initially, training was to be achieved by sending potential diplomatic representatives to foreign institutions such as Oxford, LSE, Geneva, the School of Diplomacy at The Hague, and various U.S. universities, the medium-term goal was to create a local training center.

Advancement in the teaching and research of international relations in Nigeria during the 1970s was enhanced by two major factors. First, the interventionism of numerous foreign powers in the Nigerian civil war brought home to Nigerian leaders and students of international affairs that external forces could seriously endanger the country's security and territorial integrity (Aluko 1987: 315). Second, the Nigerian economy was very strong in the 1970s, due to the oil booms of 1973 to 1974 and 1979 to 1980. The Nigerian government made use of oil revenues to provide funding to universities to intensify IR studies, among other areas (Jinadu 1987). As a result of this comparative advantage, most of the few textbooks on African IR have been written and published by scholars from West African countries, particularly Nigeria, and to a lesser degree Ghana.

Although IR continues to be a field in its infancy in the African continent, there is a functioning academic community in Nigeria that is identified primarily with the realist school of thinking. A large International Relations contingent of scholars also exists in the Department of Political Science at the University of Cairo, where U.S. influence is predominant too. In Kenya, the Institute of Diplomacy and International Studies (IDIS) at Nairobi University has been the base for EU-sponsored graduate programs in diplomatic practice for many years, and an International Relations degree is also available within the Department of Government. In South Africa, IR teaching has been concentrated within departments of government, political science, or liberal studies (see Chapter 3, in this volume). In other parts of East Africa, International Relations is only offered as a minor area of study within major academic departments, including political science, government, diplomacy, and law.

Conversely, international relations studies in Francophone Africa have mirrored the French tradition of political economy, which integrates faculties of law, political science, and economics, and is well-known for its empirical emphasis (Groom 2005). In Yaoundé, Cameroon, a program similar to that offered by Nairobi University for training diplomats is also available for Francophone countries. Although a detailed analysis of such programs in terms of how academia has been influenced by state needs and practices would require another study, both aspire to equip future diplomatic practitioners with the practical tools and training needed to represent their respective countries effectively. A distinct trend is observable in international relations thinking in countries that were once Portuguese colonies, where the main focus has been upon anti-colonialism. Such is the case of Mozambique's Samora Marcel, Angola's Holden Roberto, and Cape Verde's Amilcar Cabral.

The fact that many institutions of higher learning in Africa, such as Ife and Ibadan in Nigeria, Cairo in Egypt, Haile Selassie (now Addis Ababa) in Ethiopia, Nairobi in Kenya, Dar Es Salaam in Tanzania, or Makerere in Uganda, were created in order to reach the "international gold standard" established by universities such as Cambridge, Cornell, Harvard, Princeton, or Oxford has left a significant imprint on academic programs of study in areas such as International Relations (Ashbey 1964, 1966; Saint 1993; Jega 1995: 251–256). Namely, these institutions have been trapped in a perennial struggle to catch up with the rest of the world in terms of modernization and development. Unfortunately, due to the unstable political, economic, and social situation that characterizes most of the continent, the majority of them have experienced partial or total collapse, and none is in a capacity to compete with the Western institutions mentioned in terms of curricula, resources, and academic productivity.

In general terms African universities are grossly underfunded, understaffed, ill-equipped with the facilities required for top-notch teaching and research, and subject to extensive political interference on the part of the state. Even worse, they were all built as copycats of institutions in their colonial metropolis, dooming them to failure. Moreover, the predominant tendency among the earlier scholars was to replicate what they had learned from the Western world. Instead of being critical and innovative by looking inward, states, university administrators, and academics alike looked outward for guidance from their imperial examples.

Early approaches to IR

During the first stages of African IR, the field was captive to the continent's external relations and its general rush to catch up with the rest of the world in terms of modernization. Thus, early approaches to the study of international relations were all rooted in post-colonial African politics that were in turn heavily influenced by the Cold War context. Its outbreak and intensification between 1947 and 1989 transformed the newly independent African countries into proxy battlefields between the superpowers. Even with the end of the bipolar conflict, little consensus emerged among analysts as to how to probe the complex inter-connections that exist between politics and society in Africa.[3]

Notwithstanding this observation, since independence the social sciences have in fact searched for conceptual frameworks that might afford fuller insights into the dynamics of the continent. These, in turn, have influenced academic thinking about international relations. Three classical approaches borrowed from Western, southern, and continental sources deserve mention here. The first approach revolved around the concept of modernization and emerged in the aftermath of independence in the 1960s. Modernization theories provided a hopeful general framework of progressive development toward "modern" statehood, conceived largely in a Western mold.[4] The basic proposition underlying this approach was that African societies were in the process of becoming modern rational entities in which efficiency and scientific logic would replace traditional values and belief systems. Therefore, modernization was viewed as providing the basis for African countries to achieve some measure of stability and autonomy, in ways similar to the trajectories followed by the Western industrialized world. After a decade it was apparent that notions of modernization were, at best, only a partial guide to understanding the political and economic conditions of the continent.

In the 1970s, social scientists borrowed from the Latin American *dependentista* school to develop their own approach to local problems. African-based dependency scholars such as Samir Amin and Walter Rodney (who taught at Dar Es Salaam University) preoccupied themselves with the analysis of the causes of Africa's underdevelopment (Rodney 1974; Amin 1974, 1977, 1990). In keeping with Latin American dependency and the world-systems approach developed by Immanuel Wallerstein (1974), most African representatives of this school highlighted the external constraints imposed on African societies and focused their attention on emerging class conflicts. Although providing new insights into the role of capitalism in constraining African development, this approach was not in vogue for long. Dependency theory imposed uniformity in the study of contemporary Africa, thus treating the continent as if it were a homogenous entity. In concentrating upon external sources of dependency, it also failed to consider the intricacies of the domestic political upheavals that engaged the continent during the 1970s and the 1980s.

Due to the failure of dependency analysis, a third approach emerged in the late 1970s and early 1980s whose main objective was to reassess the role of the state. The statist school viewed the state as the primary motor force of social and economic life throughout the continent (Cooper 1981: 1–86; Young 1982; Bayart 1987). Thus, state leaders were held accountable for the political and economic deterioration that Africa experienced in the early 1980s. Primarily, they were accused of having created structures of domination that enabled them to misuse their offices for personal gain at the expense of the pressing needs of the bulk of the population. Thus, African leaders were held responsible for catastrophes such as the food crisis of the early 1980s, the debt crisis, and the generalized crisis of governability.

Between the late 1980s and the early 1990s a new analytic framework emerged, that of pluralism, which argued that the state–society relationship was central to understanding the political dynamics of Africa. Therefore, the interactions of social forces, economic activities, formal institutions, and prevalent values, among others, were identified as key factors for understanding the evolution of the diverse political, economic, and social patterns throughout the continent since independence.

In addition to these different approaches, concerning which there is little consensus in the African social sciences, another divide characterizing scholarship in the region is that which exists between those academics insisting upon so-called universalistic referents of analyses, whose studies have been highly informed by Western precepts and experiences, and those who have staked the need for a more African contextual and problem-solving perspective. A common argument offered by the latter is that individuals and governments alike are constrained by a variety of demographic, technological, ideological, global, historical, and social factors. Therefore, their aim is to identify the multiple factors at work on the African political scene and to trace their diverse dynamics over time.[5]

The study of international relations in Africa has been influenced by these conceptual developments in the social sciences, but also by Western IR debates. Major contributions to the field (Ojoegbu 1980; Ojo *et al.* 1985) are based upon the traditional, realist approach. However, a considerable number of scholars, among the most well known Samir Amin (1974, 1977, 1990) and Segun Osoba (Osoba and Akinjogbin 1980), have argued in favor of a neo-Marxist political economy approach. This latter group condemns the overwhelming majority of other scholars for being super-structural and state-centric, and mistaking the state in the developing world for an autonomous actor rather than an instrument of foreign states and global capitalism.

Nevertheless, the state-centric approach has been favored in many developing countries in Africa and Asia, due mainly to the power of the question of national unity. Admittedly, nationalism was used to create cohesion in society and as rallying ideology for successful liberation across the continent. However, the vast ethnic, regional, and religious differences that exist throughout Africa have historically weakened an already minimal commitment to national cohesion. In consequence, following the state-centric model, the study of IR has proven important for legitimating the state's role as the embodiment of the "nation." Not only has it served the purpose of uniting national populations and the continent around similar discourses, but it has also allowed the African countries to play a more realistic role in the world.

In addition to the centrality of state-centric models such as realism, the study of international relations in Africa in the 1970s and the 1980s was grounded in three main levels of analysis, partly corresponding to conceptual developments in the West (Khapoya 1975: 2). At the first, continental level, Africa was depicted as a single unit of analysis and its influence and role examined vis-à-vis the rest of the world. The creation of the OAU in the 1960s made this level particularly relevant (El-Ayouti 1975). The second, regional level entailed Africa being divided into a series of sub-regions based upon certain given criteria and analyzed accordingly. The national level, where each African state is employed as a unit of analysis, is constituted by case studies of individual countries and states. The teaching and practice of international relations was based upon these units of analysis throughout much of the Cold War.

Although most Western IR theories were not particularly well suited to explain Africa's predicament in the 1970s and the 1980s (Ojo *et al.* 1985: 13–15), power theory, which rested on certain universal assumptions about the nature of man, was the easiest to apply. In particular, the realist emphasis on the importance of the struggle for survival, achieved through the acquisition of power (Morgenthau 1948), found sympathetic listeners in Africa. When one critically examines post-independence African politics in the 1960s, the dominance of power politics is clear. Regional states were concerned with preserving their sovereignty and independence, and their international politics were characterized mainly by a struggle for power, seen as both an end in itself and as a means to an end. For example, economic power was pursued both as a goal worthwhile in itself and as a means of producing greater military power and increased state prestige and influence. At the continental level too, African interaction largely reflected concern with power and its distribution.

Power theory was valuable for descriptive analyses of power politics within the African continent. However, dependency theory was also widely used to draw attention to outside variables that created economic and political dependence. In addition to the authors already mentioned, Ali Mazrui (1977) approached continental affairs in the 1970s from the perspectives of political philosophy and political sociology, regarding African international relations as a struggle against dependency, a situation imposed upon the continent by its historical experience.

The status of IR in Africa today

Some of the most critical issues facing Africa today – whether in cities like Abidjan and Accra, N'djamena and Addis Ababa, Cairo and Cape Town, or in rural areas from Wajir in northeastern Kenya to Ogoniland in Nigeria, or remote areas of Luxor in Egypt to those of Kwazulu Natal in South Africa – include conflict and ethnicity, refugee crises, insecurity, corruption, and bad governance, lack of democracy, militarism and *coups d'état*, poverty and underdevelopment, famine and food insecurity, HIV/AIDS, international aid and debt crises, gender and environmental issues, terrorism, the collapsed infrastructure, and gross human rights abuses. However, the conceptual tools currently available to students of IR in the continent and elsewhere are ill-equipped for understanding them.

If the study of IR is to become more useful to students in African universities and institutions of higher learning, it must be seen to equip them with the means necessary to address such critical issues. Given that International Relations in Africa still mirror developments in the North quite heavily, their utility remains a major concern. The theories that are fashionable at the global level fail to provide African scholars and students with the appropriate tools for analyzing the problems that affect their communities. In other words, how the study of realism, liberalism, postmodernism, and even Marxism and imperialism, help resolve lived problems is an unresolved question in the African context. Moreover, reservations are commonly expressed that the use of theory consists of an abstract exercise in abstruse politics and mere semantics. In order for the field of International Relations to have greater usefulness within Africa it must move from the esoteric and the abstract to the real and the concrete.

The aspiration here is to make the teaching of IR in Africa more reflective of the local conditions. These local conditions do actually indirectly affect the rest of the globe, be it in terms of disaster humanitarian relief operations such as happened in Rwanda, Somalia, and now Darfur, or the form of asylum seeking in European countries and so on. Thus, scholars and students of IR in Africa must cease viewing it just as a continuous study of a discipline whose origins are Westphalia, the First and the Second World Wars; all events that took place thousands of miles away.

What we should be striving for is a breakaway from the old approaches dominated mainly by the colonial and post-colonial literature of, say, Zartman, Mazrui, Amin, Ojo *et al.*; which are all akin very much to Western trends of analysis (see such old works: Zartman 1966; Rodney 1974; El-Ayouti 1975; Mazrui 1977; Amin 1977, 1990; Ojo *et al.* 1985; Aluko 1987: 313–317; Onwuka and Shaw 1989). Even the literature that was produced in the 1990s on Africa does not attempt to make contemporary IR theories become reflective of predominant conditions beyond the Western orbit (books such as Jackson 1990, Chazan *et al.* 1992,

Kokole (1993), and Clapham (1996) all do still reflect the old fashion of analysis of African politics).[6]

This literature suffers from the constraints of an epistemology that is tied to an exclusive tradition of thought still imprisoned in the past. None of the literature has attempted to bestow importance on the current events as major variables for making the study of IR become more indigenous. Moreover, today, events similar to those that necessitated the emergence of the IR discipline early in the twentieth century have also taken place in Africa such as the relevant incidents in the continent as in DRC, Sudan, Somalia, Ethiopia, Eritrea, among others. IR disciplinary history tells that it emerged mainly as an attempt to try to prevent the repeat of another catastrophe, particularly after the experiences of the two most devastating World Wars that have occurred in the West between 1914 and 1918 and between 1939 and 1945. Now such wars have also occurred in non-Western communities with similar devastating consequences. Had the mid-1990s war in the Great Lakes Region that drew alliances between DR Congo renegades, backed by Uganda and Rwanda on the one hand and the government forces backed by Zimbabwe, Angola, and Namibia on the other, been fought in Europe, it would have been legitimately termed a "third world war." These recent examples afford ample material to help influence contemporary research and teaching of IR in Africa. Moreover, the persistent question of "how 'international' is International Relations" has bothered a certain group of scholars in the discipline for years.

For example, in the September ECPR/ISA 1998 Conference in Vienna, Professor James Rosenau expressed disappointment at the continual use of the term "international" in conference papers and panels with much fewer international examples. Thus, on a panel of some of the big IR gurus, namely Richard Little, Barry Buzan, and K.J. Holsti on "New Frontiers of International Theory: Political Space," Rosenau argued that given the way most IR scholarship has become increasingly exclusive, there will be more justification if a shift to "inter-unit" relations, rather than the continual unjustified use of the prefix "international," is advocated. Rosenau's critics will be numerous but he has a point. Rosenau will strongly prove his argument inevitably if, for example, he points out that most instances cited to back the use of the prefix "international" are predominantly Western. There are various examples that could be used to substantiate his arguments, including such tragic incidents in Africa as Rwanda, Somalia, DRC, and Darfur. In fact, very little is often cited about the plight of the people of Darfur despite recent campaigns by some of the world's renowned celebrities; the longest civil war in Angola, the ongoing border problem between Eritrea and Ethiopia, and the perennial oppression of the Nigerian peoples by military regimes. As far as human rights issues are concerned, there is a lot to cite besides those politically linked abuses. For example, nobody cares about the business of enslaved house girls in Africa and their exportation across the Red Sea into Yemen, Jordan, or other Gulf States as cheap labor or for entertainment. Similarly, nobody pays attention to the continual slavery of the Nilotic children from South Sudan by Arab merchants, with political links to the Islamic regime in Khartoum.[7] The number of street children in African cities is growing beyond those in Latin America. Thus, not only may the inclusion of such examples increase a problem of methodology but it will also lead to the teaching of IR becoming internationally more self-reflective than ever before.

In our case in Africa, the teaching of IR must become much more reflective of what students have often pointed out to be some of the major critical issues confronting the continent. Plausibly, IR scholars and students study war, revolution, liberation movements, trade policies, diplomatic practice, regionalism and regional integration, terrorism, constitutional reforms, to mention but a few. Therefore, what we see and analyze in these actions is all about people doing things. However, it must also be noted that in IR there are difficulties involved in studying and theorizing actions. In other words, the world that IR theorists study is a social world of *meanings*.[8] This is yet a demonstration that there are difficulties encountered in our study of these actions. For example, IR scholars today engage themselves in looking at the link between theory and action in warfare (see Jabri 1996), the agency/structure debate (see Hollis and Smith 1991: 393–410, and the exchange between Jabri and Chan (1996) on the one hand and Hollis and Smith (1996) on the other), and foreign policy analysis. Analysis of such themes in the study of IR in Africa must bring to our attention current developments in the Great Lakes region, in the Horn of Africa, and the continent as a whole. These are all actions involving power and influence, be it by governmental or non-governmental actors. In Anglo-American scholarship, for example, academic disciplines advanced concurrently with the development of that part of the world. This has not been the case with Africa and other "third world" countries. Contemporary IR students in Africa, drawn mainly from East Africa, the Horn and Great Lakes region, would like to turn the study of IR to address such disparity(ies).

This should not be misconstrued as a challenge to the underpinnings of the IR discipline as a discipline, but rather should be taken as an attempt to contribute to the building of an interdisciplinary cross-fertilization of IR. One way of doing this would be through sharing ideas and examples that would lead to the enrichment of the discipline. Cross-fertilization is possible via shared publications in mainstream journals and exchange programs. I am aware that universities in the U.S., for example, have exerted efforts to offer one-year or more programs of teaching for a few African university lecturers and professors, and much of what is done is extensively on other social sciences and the natural sciences, and very minimal on IR. This is testimony to the fact that to date IR has not produced cosmopolitan legends of the Aristotelian type even within what are categorized as mainstream scholars of the discipline.

Since Aristotle, the aim of cosmopolitans has been to develop a science of politics based on concepts, theories, and empirical generalizations that travel beyond the national boundaries of any particular political system (see, e.g., Norris 1997: 17–34). This may sound ambitious but it is generally accepted that IR as a discipline refers to all kinds of cross-border transactions – political, economic, and social. These are all actions that we as individuals do incur practically and perceive cognitively. Thus, the attempt here is not just for change of content but for the improvement of the methodology and philosophy of teaching and interpretation for IR theories to become more locally reflective. However, several obstacles to this approach of cross-fertilization may be encountered. These are not severe. One of the obstacles is the professionalization of IR, a process by which a coherent body of knowledge is identified and defined as a discipline, but exclusively restricted to examples of one culture (if not a few). This state of affairs within the discipline will take time to change but "geo-cultural epistemologies" is one such critical attempt to effect such change.

Suggested typologies for the way forward

At this juncture, we should be reminded of one important point: that it has often been a turbulent experience in every field of study whenever attempts are made to breach theory and practice. For those of us who have trodden the path of IR history, it will be remembered that this view by African students is not peculiar to them alone. It may be recalled that a similar worldview became dominant in the U.S. at the end of the Second World War (see Halle 1964: 11–25): a revulsion against the utopianism that had allegedly characterized the teaching of IR, particularly in the period between the two World Wars. In that period, professors of IR had commonly been preachers and prophets. They preached international law, and prophesied the collapse of civilization in case international law and international organization were not made to prevail (Halle 1964: 1). Thus, IR scholars – the later criticism claimed – often drew more attention to the world as it should be, and in so doing often drew attention away from the world as it was. Comparatively, students in Africa have the advantage of combining theory (in fact the now more advanced theories) with practice. The teaching and study of IR in Africa has the advantage (*sic*!) of a number of examples of civil wars, starvation, dictatorship, bad governance, and so on – examples from which to learn lessons in order to alter conditions for human existence for the better. What these examples further suggest is that such work should be relevant not only to those interested in – or living in – Africa, but to all. Just as the early twentieth-century wars gave rise to a general discipline of some value to others beyond Europe, dramatic events in Africa should make us understand new features and dynamics of politics in the twenty-first century. As suggested by L. Adele Jinadu,

> globalised mainstream political science should begin to explore how data collected in and about Africa can illuminate aspects of politics in the West. In other words, the West should itself become a "laboratory" for testing data and hypotheses derived from Africa. Here again, much can be learnt about the dialectics of race and ethnic relations in the West from the work of those political and social anthropologists who studied ethnic and race relations in Africa. In the same vein, data gathered from work on patronalism, prebendalism and "bellypolitics" in Africa might provide interesting insights into the nature of similar problems in the West. This is what reciprocity demands; and this is what globalised mainstream political science should begin to address. It needs to begin to pursue the question, "what can we learn from and about African politics to help our understanding of our own politics and in developing a general theory of politics?"
>
> (Jinadu 2000: 11–12)

Thus, this chapter insists that the trend here is not to advance a parochial new methodology totally detached from the rest of the world, but rather to make IR become more meaningful and autochthonous to students in other non-Western communities by relating examples that are not just studied in classrooms, but are also practically seen, heard on radio and television, and read in the press. The aim of the project is to advance directives that can make IR become more self-reflective rather than some discipline still historically based on the Melian dialogue, Judeo-Greco-Christian Western orientation, Westphalia, or on the two World Wars. Thus the new practice may be found in many different locales, such as when we in a small private university in the Horn of Africa struggle to make the contemporary teaching of IR overcome the excesses of old theories of dependency, neo-colonialism, or neo-Marxism. The old trends and approaches should no longer be central to the teaching and study of IR but must serve as basic references for the articulation of current problems confronting the continent. Blaming backwardness and underdevelopment on colonial history is no longer fashionable. Instead, most of the critical issues identified as major impediments against progress in Africa are solely homemade. The critical issues identified should become a priority especially for those of us wishing truly to understand the intricacies of sovereignty and its limits.

That is not to say that students should not be taught how African states have managed to survive for a period of over 40 years after formal independence, within a global order dominated by states that were evidently vastly more powerful than they are (see Ojoegbu

(1980), written on the Western mould; Ojo *et al.* (1985), Mazrui (1977), and Clapham (1996), not saved from old trends of analysis).

It cannot also be denied that the international order permitted their very survival. African rulers also acted in such a way that helped their survival. Thus, the evident weakness of African states did not reduce them to a state of inertia, in which their fate was determined by external powers. On the contrary, African states were impelled to pursue measures designed to ensure their survival or at least to improve their chances of survival. This question of survival is fundamental and provides the primary focus for the study of IR in African universities. There is an adjunct point to the issue of survival, the aspect of the rulers' welfare, which brought about greed and thus self-enrichment. This is particularly important because it has affected the external relations of African countries. Their varied engagement in activities beyond their frontiers may be said to constitute a "foreign policy."

The other point to note is that the specific mechanism in which African states were created, and the peculiar emphasis which these placed on their relations with the external world, in both political and economic terms, will continue its formative influence in the study of IR. In this case, African external relations cannot be totally divorced from those of colonial influence – just as post-independence politics struggled to reflect those of pre-colonial inheritance. This is very important because it stems from the long-time state(s) and regime(s) imposition of control over the people by governments, and this has in turn created the crisis of legitimacy (see Ofuho 1998). The original modern idea of legitimacy in Western political thought is that governments should have the right to act for the good of their citizens because they operate with the consent of the people. Those in power derive their authority from the consent of the people. This has not been the case in most of Africa where, since independence (see Jackson and Rosberg 1982), it was not until the end of the Cold War that people began exerting influence upon their own governments. This lack of people's empowerment led to the proliferation of post-colonial liberation movements. This forms another important point regarding the influence of non-state actors on foreign policy (see Chan 1992; Chan and Jabri 1993; Chan and Venancio 1995). Studies on liberation movements show two different types of liberation: (1) liberation movements against colonialism (see Lan 1985; Ranger 1985; Hargreaves 1988), and (2) liberation against non-white-minority-non-colonial oppressive regimes (Mwagiru 1994; Young 1994; Ofuho 1997). The latter are of greater salience because they drew a lot of external involvement, the current example being the recently – or not yet – concluded wars in the Sudan, DRC, Angola, and South Africa. This new type of liberation movement breaks out of the standard, almost circular, categories of a dominant post-colonial discourse that has served to keep many political issues off the agenda. This more thoroughly politicized form of struggle also undermines the previous generation's constraints on forms of international involvement and therefore holds severe risks, especially internationally, at the same time as it brings important new developments domestically.

The foreign policies of African states are also another important area of research in our study of IR on the continent. It has often been difficult to establish whether most African countries deserve a "foreign policy" or diplomatic representation in many parts of the world. Foreign policy was a function of the specific nature of the state, which in turn was largely determined by the international system, and the ex-colonial powers required continued access to African states. The form which that access took in turn depended, in part, on the structure of domestic statehood imposed by relatively unchanging features of the linkages of African states with the international economy. Thus, many African states became relatively comfortable with their own identities, which were not to any great extent threatened both internally and externally. So the study of IR in African universities must also rethink the importance (or less importance) of foreign policy and diplomatic representation even in areas with less significance.

Similarly, IR students in Africa see the growing importance of security issues. Security here is not defined wholly along the realist frame. Major security concerns in Africa range from military, terrorist, and environmental to food security. There is a wide realization that the security which African states had envisaged at independence and during the Cold War was highly misleading because it rested in part on international conventions of statehood. Security concerns in Africa are derived mainly from a global power structure and, thus, insulating domestic politics from the international system. The security rationale allotted governments a highly privileged position as intermediaries between their own societies and external sources of power. This dominated the diplomacy of the people who initiated the struggle for independence. These misconceptions about actual security problems, and the modalities for achieving security, were also exacerbated by the "heroes" syndrome of the 1960s, which elevated the Nkrumahs, Nyereres, Kenyattas, Senghors, to mention but a few, to the status of international leadership. This trend of thought is radically under scrutiny and IR scholarship in Africa must seek to transform it.

Last but not least, the other topic which is already in mainstream IR scholarship is that of "International Organizations." Regional integration, in particular the formation of the OAU in 1963, marked the beginning of international African diplomacy. An examination of the OAU exposes certain positive principles that were at least formally expected to govern the relation between African states and an indication to extend relations beyond continental politics. Several reasons have been advanced explaining the weaknesses and major factors that led to the failures of the OAU (see Umozurike 1979; Mwagiru 1995, 1996), leading to its recent transformation into the African Union (AU). There is also the project of reinvigorating regional institutions like the East African Community (EAC), SADC, COMESA, among others.

Conclusion

By way of conclusion, it is clear that as a discipline IR has tended, understandably enough, to look at the world from the viewpoint of its most powerful states. It has been developed as a subject of study in the major capitalist states, and has been directed largely toward helping them to manage the demands of an increasingly complex international system. Its dominant focus during the Cold War, for example, was on the relationship between the superpowers, with a secondary but still important emphasis on relations between other industrial states such as those of Western Europe. Even the study of North–South relations characteristically had a heavy emphasis on "North–South" often within the context of superpower competition. During this period there were efforts to bridge theory and practice, or academia and professionalism (Webb 1992). The proliferation of theoretical literature seems to have overcome this consciousness about the theory–practice challenge. Theory has overtaken practice in the West, such that sophisticated theorizing has become a fashionably lucrative exercise without much regard for whether current literature will have an impact on the human condition or not, without due concern for the world beyond it.

In Africa, it must be noted that IR still means the same thing: as studied and as experienced, say, in foreign affairs or in government in general. The fundamental difference of an academic discipline distinct from this practice system that is taken as the point of departure for the construction of a whole philosophy and methodology remains absent. What is instead clearer is the fact that there is no upper case and there is no lower case of IR/ir as analyzed by, among others, Chris Brown (Brown 1996: 1). In an empirical society like ours, as in other, less modernized societies, the difference arguably ought not to exist in the first place. What this means to the African student is that IR is still empirically well understood. It is the one practice by Foreign Affairs officials; it is summitry, remains the real thing and, thus, the real thing has to be taught. This is what has motivated students in Africa to enroll for an IR degree. For example, the few we guide at the United States International University in Kenya still believe the IR degree must serve them as a master key for employment by the foreign ministry, relevant government departments, the UN and other NGOs. For them, IR must open up a privileged opportunity to access jobs, say, in the Ministry of Defense or Office of the President. This is no longer the case, for example, in Britain or in the United States where competition for jobs in the Foreign and Commonwealth Office is not a monopoly of IR or political science graduates alone – nor is this career option as clearly defining for the students. This established career pattern in the West is reinforced by recent trends in the remit of foreign policy. In Britain, foreign policy must explain mad cow disease; in the United States terrorism; in Canada it must address lesbian homosexuality, among other issues affecting society. This role is a major challenge which the study and teaching of IR in Africa must attempt to reconcile.

A great irony of the situation is thus that much of the critical literature takes Africa as the key illustration of the need to move away from a state-centric understanding. It is argued that the real issues here do not follow state-defined categories. At the same time, the institutional anchoring of the discipline in the state is in some respects stronger in Africa than elsewhere. With a look from the sociology of knowledge (or sociology of science), the actual functions and the political economy of the discipline point to the need to take the state and state practices very seriously. In this perspective it becomes visible how the tension is deepened locally between core concepts of IR and real life complexities, deepened through practical, socio-economic conditions infusing the life strategies of the actual people populating the discipline of IR.

Finally, for IR to become truly transnational, reciprocity and collaboration in terms of research projects and joint publications, particularly in Europe, must be encouraged. Comparatively, the U.S. fares better and there are now more renowned Diaspora scholars in the U.S. than in Europe. The scarcity of cross-national research data and incommensurability in development and technology are no excuse for lack of cross-cultural collaboration, particularly in this era of globalization. There should be no "scapegoating" or deliberate retreat to some kind of cultural isolationism. Transformation and interpretation of the mainstream literature including recent works that have dominated reading in IR the world over is critical. These include readings that are a continuation or a desperate attempt to improve upon the older works of IR legends such as Morgenthau, Burton, Bull, Wight, Beitz, Mitrany, and others. This type of literature leaves out the world in which we actually live and also raises the issue of relevance. Thus, the innovation that IR students in East Africa and on the continent at large are yearning for is some kind of relevant interpretative anthropology for IR and a redefinition of theories and concepts that can fit or become reflective of local conditions universally, irrespective of time and space.

Notes

1   The title of this chapter borrows from Christine Sylvester's 2001 treatment of the teaching and study of international relations in the Horn of Africa and the Great Lakes Region. Many thanks to the following who persistently encouraged me to convert my ISA Montreal paper into this chapter: Arlene Tickner, Ole Wæver, Peter Mandaville, and my mentors A.J.R. Groom, Stephen Chan, and

Andrew Williams for their altruistic interest and to ensure that I maintain contacts within the academic circles; however, all contentious issues raised in this chapter remain my own.

2　A first attempt to do just this appears in Ofuho (2003).

3　Several books on contemporary African politics have tried to break through this impasse. See Chazan *et al.* (1992) and Chabal (1994).

4　For an overview of the literature on modernization, see Huntington (1971: 55–79), O'Donnell (1973), and Higgot (1983). For a critical discussion, see Gendzier (1985).

5　In contrast, it should be noted that studies on African politics and on international relations have been spared guerrilla warfare between the traditional and the scientific writers, such as those that took place in the West during the so-called "second great debate" between, say, Hedley Bull and Morton Kaplan in the 1960s; cf. Bull 1966; Kaplan 1966; Knorr and Rosenau 1969; and for African reflections see Aluko 1987 and Chan 1989.

6　Recent developments in post-colonial theory do point in new directions – both within general postcolonialism (Mbembe 2001) and in relation to IR (Grovogui 2006, 2007) as well as in the more "applied" style of Mazrui (2002) – but so far it is highly unclear what kind of IR practice this could lead to if adopted more generally and concretely.

7　Basic information about slavery in the Sudan may be accessed from Christian Solidarity International (CSI), headed by Baroness Lady Chalker.

8　Andrew J. Williams of the Politics and IR Department at the University of Kent, Canterbury, UK organized a fascinating panel of IR scholars to discuss the difficulties of understanding what "meaning" is. Among other papers was Stephen Chan's.

References

Aluko, Olajide (1987) "The Study of International Relations in Nigeria," *Millennium*, 16 (2): 313–317.

Amin, Samir (1974) *Accumulation on a World Scale: A Critique of the Theory of Underdevelopment*, New York: Monthly Review Press.

Amin, Samir (1977) *Imperialism and Unequal Development*, Hassocks: Harvester.

Amin, Samir (1990) *Maldevelopment: Anatomy of a Global Failure*, London: Zed Books.

Ashbey, Eric (1964) *African Universities and Western Tradition*, Cambridge, MA: Harvard University Press.

Ashbey, Eric (1966) *Universities: British, Indian, African*, London: Weidenfeld & Nicolson.

Bayart, Jean-Francoise (1987) *The State in Africa: The Politics of the Belly*, London: Longman.

Brown, Chris (1996) *Understanding International Relations*, London: Macmillan.

Bull, Hedley (1966) "International Relations Theory: The Case for the Classical Approach," *World Politics*, 18 (3): 363–377.

Chabal, Patrick (1994) *Power in Africa: An Essay in Political Interpretation*, London: Macmillan.

Chan, Stephen (1989) "International Studies in Africa: The European Connection," lecture given at the European Consortium for Political Research Joint Sessions of Workshops, Paris, April.

Chan, Stephen (1992) *Kaunda and Southern Africa: Image and Reality in Foreign Policy*, London: British Academic Press.

Chan, Stephen and Vivienne Jabri (eds) (1993) *Mediation in Southern Africa*, London: Macmillan.

Chan, Stephen and Moises Venancio (1995) *Portuguese Foreign Policy in Southern Africa*, Johannesburg: South African Institute of International Affairs.

Chazan, Naomi, Peter Lewis, Robert Mortimer, Donald Rothchild, and Stephen John Stedman (1992) *Politics and Society in Contemporary Africa*, Boulder, CO: Lynne Rienner.

Clapham, Christopher (1996) *Africa and the International System: The Politics of State Survival*, Cambridge: Cambridge University Press.

Cooper, Frederick (1981) "Africa and the World Economy," *African Studies Review*, 2/3: 1–86.

El-Ayouti, Yassin (1975) *The Organization of African Unity After Ten Years*, New York: Frederick Praeger.

El-Ayouti, Yassin (ed.) (1984) *The OAU after Twenty Years*, London: Praeger.

Gendzier, Irene L. (1985) *Managing Political Change: Social Scientists and the Third World*, Boulder, CO: Westview Press.

Gottman, Jean (ed.) (1980) *Centre and Periphery: Spatial Variation in Politics*, Beverly Hills, CA: Sage.

Groom, A.J.R. (1994) "The World Beyond: The European Dimension," in Margot Light and A.J.R. Groom (eds), *Contemporary International Relations: A Guide to Theory*, London: Pinter, pp. 219–236.

Groom, A.J.R. (1995) "International Relations: Anglo-American Aspects: A Study in Parochialism," in Kanti P. Bajpai and Harish C. Shukul (eds), *Interpreting World Politics*, New Delhi: Sage, pp. 45–87.

Groom, A.J.R. (1998) "Approaches to Conflict and Cooperation in International Relations: Lessons from Theory for Practice," University of Canterbury, unpublished mimeo.

Groom, A.J.R. (2005) "The Study of International Relations in France," *European Political Science*, 4: 164–174.

Grovogui, Siba N. (2006) *Beyond Eurocentrism and Anarchy: Memories of International Order and Institutions*, Basingstoke: Palgrave.

Grovogui, Siba N. (2007) "Postcolonialism," in Tim Dunne *et al.*, *International Relations Theories: Discipline and Diversity*, Oxford: Oxford University Press, pp. 229–246.

Halle, Louis J. (1964) "On Teaching International Relations," *Virginia Quarterly Review*, 40 (1): 11–25.

Hargreaves, J. D. (1988) *Decolonisation in Africa*, London and New York: Longman.

Higgot, Richard (1983) *Political Development Theory: The Contemporary Debate*, London: Croom Helm.

Hollis, Martin and Steve Smith (1991) "Beware of Gurus: Structure and Agency in International Relations," *Review of International Studies*, 17 (4): 393–410.

Hollis, Martin and Steve Smith (1996) "A Response: Why Epistemology Matters in International Theory," *Review of International Studies*, 22 (1): 111–116.

Huntington, Samuel P. (1971) "The Change to Change: Modernization, Development and Politics," *Comparative Politics*, 4 (3): 55–79.

Jabri, Vivienne (1996) *Discourses on Violence*, Manchester: Manchester University Press.

Jabri, Vivienne and Stephen Chan (1996) "The Ontologist Always Rings Twice: Two More Stories About Structure and Agency," *Review of International Studies*, 22 (1): 107–110.

Jackson, Robert H. (1990) *Quasi-States: Sovereignty, International Relations and the Third World*, Cambridge: Cambridge University Press.

Jackson, Robert H. and Carl G. Rosberg (1982) *Personal Rule in Black Africa: Prince, Autocrat, Prophet, Tyrant*, Berkeley: University of California Press.

Jega, Attahiru (1995) "Nigerian Universities and the Academic Staff under Military Rule," *Review of African Political Economy*, 22 (64): 251–256.

Jinadu, L. Adele (1987) "The Institutional Development of Political Science in Nigeria: Trends, Problems and Prospects," *International Political Science Review*, 8 (19): 59–72.

Jinadu, L. Adele (2000) "The Globalisation of Political Science: An African Perspective," Presidential Address, June 22, 1999, in *African Journal of Political Science*, 5 (1): 1–13.

Kaplan, Morton (1966) "The New Great Debate: Traditionalism vs. Science in International Relations," *World Politics*, 19 (1): 1–20.

Khapoya, Vincent B. (1975) *The Politics of Decision: A Comparative Study of African Policy Toward the Liberation Movement*, Denver: University of Denver Press.

Knorr, Klaus and James Rosenau (eds) (1969) *Contending Approaches to International Relations*, Princeton, NJ: Princeton University Press.

Kokole, Omari H. (1993) *Dimensions of Africa's International Relations,* Delmar, NY: Caravan Books.

Lan, David (1985) *Guns and Rain: Guerrillas and Spirit Medium in Zimbabwe*, London: James Currey.

Mazrui, Ali A. (1977) *Africa's International Relations: The Diplomacy of Dependency and Change*, London: Heinemann.

Mazrui, Ali A. (2002) "Afro-Arab Crossfire: Between the Flames of Terrorism and the Force of Pax-Americana," *Occasional Paper No. 6*, Development Policy Management Forum, Addis Ababa.

Mbembe, Achille (2001) *On the Postcolony*, Berkeley: University of California Press.

Morgenthau, Hans J. (1948) *Politics Among Nations: The Struggle for Power and Peace*, New York: Alfred A. Knopf.

Mwagiru, Makumi (1994) "The International Management of Internal Conflict in Africa: The Uganda Mediation," 1985, Ph.D. dissertation, University of Kent at Canterbury, UK.

Mwagiru, Makumi (1995) "Who Will Bell the Cat? Article 3(2) of the OAU Charter and the Crisis of OAU Conflict Management," *Kent Papers in Politics and International Relations*, 4/7.

Mwagiru, Makumi (1996) "The Organisation of African Unity (OAU) and the Management of Internal Conflict in Africa," *International Studies*, 33 (1): 3–20.

Norris, Pippa (1997) "Towards a More Cosmopolitan Political Science," *European Journal of Political Research*, 31 (1): 17–34.

O'Donnell, Guillermo (1973) *Modernization and Bureaucratic Authoritarianism*, Berkeley: University of California Press.

Ofuho, Cirino Hiteng (1997) "Discourses on Liberation and Democracy in Sub-Saharan Africa: The Cases of Eritrea and Ethiopia," Ph.D. dissertation, University of Kent at Canterbury, UK.

Ofuho, Cirino Hiteng (1998) "The Legitimacy and Sovereignty Dilemma of African States and Governments: The Problems of the Colonial Legacy," paper presented at the Third Pan-European International Relations Conference, Vienna, Austria, September 16–19.

Ofuho, Cirino Hiteng (2003) "The Changing Images of a Continent: An Eclectic Survey of Writings on Africa in the International System," *Global Society*, 17 (2): 151–164.

Ojo, Olatunde J.C.B., D.K. Orwa and L.B.M. Utete (1985) *African International Relations*, London, New York and Lagos: Longman.

Ojoegbu, Ray (1980) *A Foundation Course in International Relations for African Universities*, New York: Kensington Publications.

Onwuka, Ralph I. and Timothy M. Shaw (eds) (1989) *Africa in World Politics: Into the 1990s*, Basingstoke: Macmillan.

Osaba, Segun and I.A. Akinjogbin (eds) (1980) *Topics on Nigerian and Economic and Social History*, Ife-Ife, Nigeria: University of Ife Press.

Ranger, Terrence (1985) *Peasant Consciousness and Guerrilla War in Zimbabwe*, London: James Currey.

Rodney, Walter (1974) *How Europe Underdeveloped Africa*, Washington, DC: Howard University Press.

Saint, W.S. (1993) *Universities in Africa: Strategies for Stabilization and Revitilization*, Washington, DC: World Bank.

Sylvester, Christine (2001) "International Relations where it's Not Supposed to be," paper presented at the Fourth Pan-European International Conference, Canterbury, UK, September 6–10.

Umozurike, U.O. (1979) "The Domestic Jurisdiction Clause in the OAU Charter," *African Affairs*, 78 (311): 197–209.

Wallerstein, Immanuel (1974) "Dependence in an Interdependent World," *African Studies Review*, 17 (1): 1–26.

Wallerstein, Immanuel (1976) *The Modern World System*, 2 vols., Beverly Hills, CA: Sage.

Wallerstein, Immanuel (1979) *The Capitalist World Economy*, Cambridge: Cambridge University Press.

Wallerstein, Immanuel (1982) *World Systems Analysis*, Beverly Hills, CA: Sage.

Webb, Keith (1992) "Academics and Professionals in International Relations," *Kent Papers in Politics and International Relations*, 1/12.

Wendt, Alexander (1991) "Bridging the Theory/Meta-Theory Gap in International Relations," *Review of International Studies*, 17 (4): 383–392.

World Bank (1993) "African Universities in Crisis," *World Bank News*, xii (2) (January 14): 1.

Young, Crawford (1982) *Ideology and Development in Africa*, New Haven, CT: Yale University Press.

Young, John (1994) "Peasants and Revolution in Ethiopia: The Tigray Peoples Liberation Front, 1975–1991," Ph.D. dissertation, Simon Fraser University, Canada.

Zartman, William (1966) *International Relations in the New Africa*, Englewood Cliffs, NJ: Prentice-Hall.

5 Japan, Korea, and Taiwan
Are one hundred flowers about to blossom?

Takashi Inoguchi

Introduction

International relations studies in East Asia were long regarded as something only slightly more than the disparate combination of national security analysis, area studies, and diplomatic history. The state, and its think-tanks and agencies that produced official documents, controlled developments in all three, while academia's role ranged from extremely marginal (in the case of national security), to supplying detailed country-specific information to policy makers (in area studies), to compiling and consuming historical documents (in the case of diplomatic history).

Although this is an over-simplified picture of the state of international studies in countries such as Japan, Korea, and Taiwan between the 1960s and the early 1990s, it captures quite appropriately the marginal role played by academia until fairly recently. Three factors changed this picture quite dramatically around 1989: economic development, democratization, and the end of the Cold War. East Asian economic development pushed up interest in the world economy, particularly given its export-oriented economic structure (World Bank 1994). Democratization enhanced civil society and one of its key components, the academic community (Inoguchi 2002a; Schwartz and Pharr 2003). In addition, the end of the Cold War enlarged the horizon of diplomacy and international relations available to the region (Inoguchi 2001a).

Admittedly, many differences exist between the countries of East Asia, and these forces have had varying degrees of influence upon academic fields such as International Relations. Economic development took place first in Japan, later in Korea and Taiwan, and most recently in China. Their degree of democratization varies tremendously from a long-established democracy in Japan over third-wave democracies in Korea and Taiwan (Inoguchi and Carlson 2006) to the East Asian case with its own chapter in this book: fledgling in mainland China. Although the Cold War ended in Europe, in Asia two strong, confrontational postures have remained more or less intact. Yet, this threefold development has been driving the growth of international relations studies quite steadily in each of the East Asian sites mentioned over the course of nearly 20 years.

The purpose of this chapter is to describe and examine the recent development of international relations studies in East Asia, in the light of its increased significance, in a comparative framework. Rather than developing an extended argument about the field's qualitative leap forward, my main interest is to analyze the role of the factors and historical contexts mentioned. Given my personal expertise and professional location, I look primarily at the development of Japanese studies of international relations since 1945, and only secondarily at the cases of Korea and Taiwan. However, the major *raison d'être* of the chapter lies in tracing the region-wide movement of international relations research in East Asia since the early 1990s.

The chapter proceeds as follows: in the first section, I develop a comparative framework for examining international relations studies in East Asia by posing three questions about academic autonomy, research agendas, and salient approaches to the field, and attempting to answer them one by one. I then examine the field's historical development in Japan with reference to four distinctive academic traditions: *Staatslehre*, Marxist, historicist, and American empiricist. In the chapter's third section, I explore the key framing questions underwriting Japan's international practice since 1945, and discuss some academic works that were influenced by such questions. Subsequently, the qualitative leap in international relations studies is examined in the cases of Japan, Korea, and Taiwan in terms of contexts, set menus, and new orientations. I conclude the chapter with some remarks about the future prospects for the field in East Asia.

Comparative framework

In comparing international relations studies in distinct sites within East Asia, three questions seem particularly relevant: (1) How autonomous or appendaged, isolated or fused is the professional academic community in relation to the policy community?; (2) What are the key framing questions that shape academic research agendas?; and (3) What are the salient approaches to international relations?

The first question addresses the issue of how distinctive the International Relations academic community is in relation to the policy community that deals with what is called high politics, including security, diplomacy, defense, and intelligence matters, and this is bound to be dominated by the government. Its main purpose is to gauge how much space the International Relations academic community occupies within society, and how separate and mature the civil society is vis-à-vis the state. How does the space occupied by the academic community provide a general indication of the separateness existing between civil society and the state? Without doubt, academic communities thrive where freedom of expression and of speech is abundant in civil society. Civil society prospers where the state does not suppress freedom. Given mostly recent developments in civil society in the countries discussed in this chapter, the question will therefore shed light upon the emergence of relatively vibrant academic communities in East Asia.

The second question addresses the primary concerns and interests of international relations scholars, mainly the types of subjects they are interested in tackling. It will enable us to see how similar or dissimilar the academic interests of the East Asian community are in comparison to North American, West European, or Latin American international studies, about which systematic comparative pictures have already been drawn (Wæver 1998; Tickner 2003). Similarly, the third question is important in identifying the methodological inclinations of International Relations scholarship in the region in comparison to these same counterparts.

These questions will be used to create profiles for each International Relations community in Japan, Korea, and Taiwan, following which I will evaluate the prospects for the field region wide in East Asia. However, before comparing the three cases, it would be helpful to provide, in the way of a historical background, a summary of the field's development in Japan, given that it emerged earlier here than in the other two countries.

International Relations in Japan in historical perspective

As in other societies, the field of International Relations in Japan has been strongly influenced by the major currents of the social sciences that have been prevalent in the country (Inoguchi 1989, 2001a; Nakano 2007). The first is the *Staatslehre* (teachings about the state) tradition, which greatly influenced military and colonial studies in the prewar period and remained strong in a metamorphosed form even after 1945. The main feature of this tradition is its emphasis upon rich, descriptive details that elucidate complexities of all sorts. Top priority was given to supplying ample historical-institutional backgrounds and to describing events and personalities in diverse contexts, as well as their consequences, all in minute detail. This approach was valued for analyzing trends and changes within the international system that could have affected Japan's foreign relations. Even after 1945, however, the bulk of area studies have continued in the *Staatslehre* tradition, especially when conducted by government-related think-tanks. In such cases of officially sponsored research, its main purpose is naturally to aid the government to design and implement good public policy.

In sharp contrast to the salience of this tradition in government-related research, most area studies as practiced in academia are markedly humanistic, rather than relevant to the social sciences or useful to government policy. What do I mean by humanistic versus relevant or useful? In part, this reflects the reaction of scholars to the domination of the *Staatslehre* tradition in the prewar period. Why would academic area studies develop as a reaction to this tradition? Traditionally, area studies were subordinated to the state whether the mission was to modernize Japan or to colonize adjacent space. A corollary of the centrality of the *Staatslehre* tradition within the country is its emphasis on law and economics as opposed to political science and sociology. Whereas schools of law and economy are common in Japan, there are no autonomous departments of political science or sociology. For over a century, those disciplines were most likely to be found as appendages to the faculties of law or of letters. Even at the dawn of the twenty-first century, Japan is one of the few countries in Asia which does not have an autonomous department of political science in terms of professorial appointments or budgetary allocations. Thus, when oppositional currents react against the *Staatslehre* type of area studies, the available form is not another kind of social science but the humanities.

The second current of thought that influenced the early stages of social science thinking in Japan is Marxism, which was very prominent between the 1920s and the 1960s. This tradition is associated with the conception of social science as *Oppositionswissenschaft*, or opposition science. As if to counter the *Staatslehre* tradition, a vigorous Marxist school was clearly discernible throughout this approximately 40-year period. In what ways did Marxism counter the *Staatslehre* tradition? It did so by arguing that academic research should not necessarily interiorize and revolve around the distinct missions of the state, but rather that its potential role was to unveil the subordinate nature of the *Staatslehre* and thus liberate academics from this tradition's stronghold. Marxist categories of political analysis imparted a critical coloring to the observation of political events and the recognition of the ideological biases of the observer. In the 1920s, when the term *shakai kagaku* (social science) first came to be used in Japan, it often denoted Marxism, rendering the social sciences virtually synonymous with this school. Japanese social sciences had been literally *marxisé* by the 1930s. After 1945, in the absence of prewar internal security laws, Marxist influence became even more widespread, and from the immediate postwar period through the 1960s, the social sciences, including economics, political science, and sociology, were often led by Marxists or Marxist-leaning scholars.

International Relations were no exception. Marxism was so influential and pervasive that many other social science theories, especially non-Marxist ones, were literally crowded out. Instead, within the Marxist framework, theories of international relations, such as "the second image unreversed" and "hegemonic destabilization," were put forward. Given the prevalence of the *Staatslehre* tradition and the nearly continuous one-party dominance that existed for nearly half a century beginning in the mid-1950s, it was considered natural or desirable for academics and journalists alike to form a sort of countervailing force that was critical of government conduct. After the end of the Cold War, while most Marxists have become post-Marxist, many have retained their critical view of government policy. Some have trans-formed themselves into postmodernists, radical feminists, and non-communist radicals in the post-Cold War and post-September 11 periods. In other words, when Marxism was dis-credited by the turn of historical and intellectual events it was widely believed that although it would be best to liberate scholarship from Marxist dogma, maintaining its critical stance towards social and political malaise was crucial.

The third tradition, one that has been extremely influential, is the historicist tradition. As a result, the bulk of scholarship in International Relations consists of historical research, and is therefore more akin to the humanities than to the social sciences. International relations research is historical in the sense that it is interested primarily in digging up primary historical sources but not in conceptualization. In contrast to the *Staatslehre* tradition, historicists are much less concerned with the policy relevance of their work and are normally interested in topics that involve events and personalities prior to 1945. The spirit that tends to guide much international relations research is often similar to the Rankean concept of history, *Wie es eigentlich gewesen ist*, or broadly "Let the facts speak for themselves."

Finally, post-war international relations studies have been informed by the recent introduction of perspectives and methodologies derived from American political science. In the prewar period the absorption of European social scientific thought – in the form of the works of Max Weber, Emile Durkheim, Leon Walras, and Alfred Marshall – constituted the antidote to strong Marxist influence in the social sciences. After 1945, the American social sciences played a similar role. Two components of American-style social sciences were particularly influential within the Japanese context: proclivity for the formulation of theories and for vigorous empirical testing. This intellectual tradition became stronger beginning in the 1970s and its impact has extended through the 2000s.

It is important to note that, even today, these four diverse currents are all observable in Japan's international relations studies and that they coexist fairly amicably without many efforts made towards integration. Indeed, diversity without disciplinary integration – if not without organizational integration – is one of the main features of the academic community in Japan, due in part to the strong legacy of four very different social science traditions originating from the one-and-a-half-century experience of nation building, economic development, war, and then peace.

The persistence of the four traditions, all of which are strongly embedded in the Japanese International Relations community, makes it difficult at times for the more home-grown and trained Japanese scholars to discuss matters of mutual interest with more heavily U.S.-influenced (or arguably neo-colonial) East Asian neighbors such as Korea, Taiwan and even China. However, various efforts have been underway to free Japanese academics from their slightly insulated academic community, based on a long-term accumulation of academic achievements. The most vigorous of these efforts is the launching of a new English-language journal, *International Relations of the Asia-Pacific* (published three times a year by Oxford University Press). Referees are globally distributed, depending upon the expertise of a subject matter dealt with in a manuscript. Approximately 50 percent of the journal's referees are from North America and about 30 percent from Asia, including Japan and Australia. Article submissions exhibit a roughly similar pattern of geographical distribution.

Unsurprisingly, the journal has been slowly but crucially transforming the Japanese International Relations community into an entity that is far more intensely interested in the generation and transmission of ideas and insights on a global scale than before. Publications of their works in the English language by Japanese academics have been on the steady increase. About one hundred scholars out of the community's approximate size of 2,000 have published their books in English and more than three hundred have published articles in English. Given that the number of American Ph.Ds in Japan is very small – some 6 percent of all the members of the Japanese Association of International Relations, compared to around 60 percent of the total membership of the Korean Association of International Studies – these efforts to make inroads into the global academic community are quite remarkable. Moreover, the perception of the Japanese International Relations community held by global scholars seems to be changing too.

Key framing questions in Japanese IR since 1945

In order to observe the substance of international relations research in Japan more closely, I now turn to the past half century in the development of International Relations in Japan in terms of the key framing questions that have driven intellectual agendas in the field. It is important to note at the outset that in this country the four "great debates" as conducted and narrated in the United States – realism versus idealism, behavioralism versus traditionalism, neoliberalism versus neorealism, and rationalism versus reflectivism – were not rehearsed in Japan, simply because proponents and opponents of such theoretical approaches were not very prominent among Japanese scholars in International Relations. Contrary to their East Asian neighbors, Japanese international relations studies have been much more deeply rooted in the country's own historical soils. Therefore, U.S.-derived theories needed to be historicized and contextualized first in order to generate insights and propositions that are more sensitive to Japan's historical and cultural complexities.

Although other social science disciplines such as economics and sociology were pursued in Japan since well before World War II, International Relations, as in many other places in the world, was only introduced afterwards. The historical moment, along with state needs after 1945, were determining factors that affected the development of international relations studies and its three key questions. These were: (1) What went wrong with Japan's international relations?; (2) What kinds of international arrangements best secure peace?; and (3) Why is it that so much remains to be desired in our diplomacy?

While all three questions are interrelated, it is important to note that as time passed, concern with the first question started shifting towards the other two. Concerns about Japan's international relations go back to the days when the country's external policy led to war, and then to defeat and foreign occupation, and they continue to be one of the key framing questions in the study of international relations today. This question has drawn International Relations students to study history (both diplomatic history and other aspects of modern Japanese history) in the related areas of economics, sociology, and political science.

The landmark *Road to the Pacific War* volumes are an interesting example of the above. In this work, most of the analyses developed seem to originate directly from this key question. For example, the economics perspective focuses on the productive capacity and production relationships of the Japanese economy, whose alleged distortions drove the country into a mistaken and lengthy war. The sociology perspective is grounded in the study of feudalistic social relations and state-led social mobilization that were eventually manipulated and mobilized by the state to support and sustain that war. Political science devoted its energies to the study of the pitifully insufficient democratic arrangements and institutions, among them the Imperial Diet, political parties, the bureaucracy, elections and the armed forces, and their role in the war. It is safe to say that most of the premier postwar scholarship revolved around this first key question too. In addition to the work cited, Masao Maruyama (1963) is the foremost scholar addressing the question in his *Thought and Behavior in Modern Japanese Politics*. If one had to choose only one key framing question in the Japanese social sciences during the latter half of the twentieth century, "What went wrong?" would be everyone's choice. In this sense, Japan's social science community has been living under the long shadow of World War II (belying the basis for the oft-heard chorus of "Do not forget the past"). Takeyoshi Kawashima (1978) in Japanese civil law, Hisao Otsuka (1965) in the economic history of feudalism, and Tadashi Fukutake (1954) in agricultural village sociology are just a few examples.

In the study of international relations, the key framing question that attracted students was Japan's diplomatic interactions with foreign powers. The then newly founded Japanese Association of International Relations compiled and edited the multi-volume work on Japan's "Road to the Pacific War" (*Taiheiyo senso e no michi*), mobilizing virtually all available scholars and diplomatic historians, of which some were Marxists, active in the field in the 1950s and the 1960s. The approach it employed was predominantly descriptive rather than analytical or theoretical, in sharp contrast to the other disciplines that adopted interesting mixtures of Marxism and culturalism in attempting to address similar issues.

This landmark Pacific War study asks the big what-went-wrong question and devotes chapter after chapter to tracing and examining absorbing details of the diplomatic and political dynamics of Japan's external relations. As the work is based primarily on studies of the recently released public documents of the Ministry of Foreign Affairs, the volumes are full of newly revealed details that led to the disaster. Most actors are portrayed as having done the right thing in executing their duties in those places to which they were assigned. The problem was that collectively their dutifulness and diligence did nothing to avert war with the rest of the world. Rather, the sum of each individual's actions led to collective disaster of gigantic proportions. The past presidents of the Japanese Association of International Relations (JAIR) include many who were involved in this massive study and remained leaders in the field long after the work was completed and published. In that sense as well, the key framing question had a very strong impact on the entire discipline. Diplomatic history has had a strong presence in JAIR throughout the last half century. An illustration of this is found in Table 5.1, where – in 1998 – the self-identification of Japanese International Relationists pointed to the history of Japanese diplomacy as number one. And generally, history takes several spots near the top.

In tandem with the JAIR Pacific War project, newspapers and magazines played an important role in framing the academic agenda of international relations studies. For the press, the key framing question was the second: What are the best arrangements to secure peace? Therefore, debate unfolded on the subject of peace with the allied powers. Should the San Francisco Peace Treaty have been signed? In the context of the Cold War, what was the right choice, a partial peace with the Western powers or a total peace including all the Allied powers? Nambara Shigeru, a political philosopher and President of the University of Tokyo, took the latter position in the collectively signed appeal to total peace (Tsuchiyama 2005). The former position was called realism because it placed greater emphasis on the feasibility

Table 5.1 Areas of specialization among Japanese IR scholars

Specialized areas of IR as self-identified by Association members (1998)*		
History	Japanese diplomacy	211
Theory	Theory and philosophy	200
Theory	Security studies	180
History	Diplomatic history/int'l political history	174
Theory	Int'l political economy	147
History	History, Europe	118
Area studies	Western Europe	109
History	East Asia	108
History	The Americas	107
Theory	Ethnicity	85
Area studies	North America	85
Theory	Foreign policy making	83
Theory	Peace research	79
Area studies	Southeast Asia	78
Area studies	East Asia	77
Area studies	China	69
Theory	North–South issues	68
Area studies	Japan	66
Area studies	Russia	66
History	Southeast Asia	59
Theory	International integration	53
Theory	International exchanges	47
Theory	Global environment	41
Theory	Human rights	39
Theory	World system	38
Area studies	Middle East	37
Theory	Cultural conflicts	35
Area studies	Area studies	34
Area studies	Eastern Europe	33
History	China	33
Area studies	Latin America	32
History	Russia	31
History	Middle East	30
Area studies	Africa	28
Theory	NGOs	26
Area studies	Oceania	21
Theory	International mobility	19
Theory	Regionalism	18
Area studies	Central Europe	18
History	Oceania	18
Theory	Interdependence	17
History	Africa	12
Theory	Quantitative analysis	10
Area studies	South Asia	8

Note
* Out of 2,163 members as of December 1998, 1,172 responded to the Association-led survey of members. They were asked to choose up to three specialized areas of research. On average they marked 2.5 per person. See Inoguchi and Harada (2002).

of the choice accepted by the international environment, the latter idealism because it gave priority to pursuing a higher ideal. The debate on realism versus idealism unfolded in Japan during the 1960s and the 1970s. At first glance it resembles the first great debate between idealism and realism in the United States. However, in Japan, unlike in the U.S., realism's victory over idealism was somewhat incomplete; and marked a bigger difference: the parties to the debate were not really the same, and the debate was therefore not "the first great debate."[1]

The salience of the debate on peace in the most widely read newspapers and popular magazines was such that the main arena of intellectual and political debate was journalism instead of academia. Therefore, those individuals who were involved in journalistic debates became the best-known names in the field of International Relations – also inside the IR community. Many of them received no formal training in IR or the social sciences, while some were journalists or former public officials acting as journalists. There is nothing wrong with the debate itself. Intellectuals who speak out in the media have played immensely important roles throughout the past sixty years in the Japanese context. The problem was that professionals in the academic community of International Relations ended up becoming less rigorous in their scholarship than their colleagues in other fields of the social sciences. The second framing question was basically a policy question, but given the way in which Japanese society is organized, there was little likelihood that members of academia could develop careers as experts on policy or become well versed in policy affairs and well connected to policy-making circuits. Inter-sectoral labor mobility is so limited that even scholars active in the journalistic debates over policy could not realistically aspire to active involvement in policy making as part of their careers. What seemed like policy debates, therefore, were in fact largely illusory. Ultimately, "journalist scholars" simply came to constitute a unique species within academia. This situation contrasts strongly with the case of the United States, where professionalization has made great advances over the past half century and academics have established themselves by an autonomous/autocentric dynamism.

The third framing question about the desirability of Japanese diplomacy is more recent. Although in a sense it is similar to the second question, it has led to empirical rather than theoretical investigations of what should be done. In this sense, it encouraged scholars to carry out empirical studies of an extremely detailed nature. This trend became dominant in the 1980s and the 1990s. For instance, Kusano Atsushi published meticulously researched books on Japan–United States policy discussions on the market and trade liberalization of agriculture and large retailing shops (Kusano 1983). Kusano has been quite active in commenting on policy and politics in TV programs since then. In addition, Tadokoro Masayuki published a well-conceptualized work on the international political economy of U.S. dollars and Japanese yen (Tadokoro 2001). Tadokoro too has been active as the co-editor of a monthly magazine in which he regularly contributes a policy column. Unlike empirical studies conducted in the United States, those done in Japan do not necessarily feel driven to place their research in grandiose and occasionally almost Procrustean theoretical schemes.[2]

A natural question to ask here is how the four traditions of thought highlighted previously correlate with the three key questions underlying international relations research. Over the long years since 1945, the first two traditions, *Staatslehre* and Marxist, seem to be waning in their influence. This waning correlates with the shift from the dominance of the first question and later away from the second one. Instead, the latter two, historically oriented studies and American social science-influenced studies, have been in the ascendent. This ascendent correlates with the salience of the third type of framing question. However, the basic resilience of all four of these traditions over many years has much to do with the lack of political science and International Relations departments on university campuses, and their failure to become autonomous in terms of operating as academic disciplines. Where then do political science and International Relations take place? The absence of institutionalized political science departments has much to do with the nineteenth-century tradition of priming future bureaucratic elite candidates in legal training and with the fear of producing a bundle of unemployed young elites trained in "political science" which might be subversive to the "system." Therefore, political science is normally appendaged at the undergraduate level to programs in law, whereas International Relations is taught under various umbrellas such as departments of international cooperation and of international languages and cultures.

Paradigmatic events in East Asia in 1989

In the rest of East Asia, international relations studies developed much later than in Japan. The year 1989 constitutes a turning point for the region, given that a number of events took place that helped the field make a qualitative leap in countries such as Korea and Taiwan. This genesis resulted from the combination of three factors: East Asian developmental momentum reaching a plateau; a middle-class-led civil society born in fledgling form; and the end of the Cold War in Europe bringing about a thaw of one sort or another to other forms of confrontation in the rest of the world. It would be fair to say that their convergence constituted a watershed in the development of international studies in East Asia.

The bubble economy was created in Japan around this time, due in part to the country's commitment to make massive capital flows available to New York following the Plaza agreement of 1985, whereby Japan's trade surplus was to be reduced by massively purchasing United States Treasury bonds. In 1989 a large scandal erupted within the Japanese governing Liberal Democratic Party, while in that same year President Chiang Ching Kuo of the Republic of China (Taiwan) announced that the Kuomintang's authoritarian politics would be replaced by gradual democratization. Similarly, President Roh Tae Woo of the Republic of Korea announced that military dictatorship would be replaced by democracy. By 1993, East Asian politics and economics had experienced substantial change. In Japan, the governing Liberal Democratic Party lost power for the first time since 1955 when the party was founded. In Korea the people democratically elected Roh Tae Woo as President. In Taiwan they democratically elected Lee Denghui as President. In other words, it would not be an exaggeration to say that the stage seemed to be set for the forthcoming blossoming of international relations studies in the 1990s and beyond.

Before 1993, international relations studies in East Asia had set menus. Furthermore they were narrowly focused on the highest priority subjects. In other words, similar to the case of Japan, there were key framing questions that set the scope and tone of international relations studies in each place. While in Japan, predominant international concerns at the time revolved around the country's alliance with the United States, in Korea North–South relations and reunification issues were fundamental. In Taiwan mainland or cross-strait issues captured the attention of international relations scholars. In each national context the framework imposed by the Cold War, in combination with domestic settings under military or party authoritarianism and state developmentalism, acted to confine the menu of international relations studies into a narrowly focused and fixed set of menus that were all policy relevant. Although there was hardly any space for academics to say much about the issues, to choose their topics of research or to influence the policy process, such space was the largest in Japan, followed by Korea and Taiwan, and smallest in China. In each case, however, the field began nearly anew around 1993.

Japan

Although the focus was placed on the alliance with the United States, the combination of the end of high levels of economic growth, one-party dominance, and the Cold War helped Japan's international relations studies enlarge their scope and subjects of interest quite significantly (Inoguchi and Bacon 2001). The country's foreign policy line between 1975 and 1990 centered upon playing the role of supporter of the United States-led international economic system. Conversely, between 1990 and 2005, Japan's foreign policy line shifted towards the role of a global civilian power. This transformation reflected the emergence of an enlarged space for those non-militarist powers like Germany and Japan (Katada *et al.* 2004). Along with it came the increase in interest in such topics as human security, multilateralism, regional organizations, human rights, democratization, official development assistance, free trade regimes, and historical memory. Also noteworthy was the fact that the predominant focus on Japan was replaced by increasing interest in global politics. Undoubtedly, the country's strength in area studies facilitated this transition. Although, in the past, area studies kept their distance from international relations studies, in recent years they have been more or less fused in the sense that they are now defined as part of local developments of global politics, in tandem with the tide of globalization. In turn, this transition has facilitated the integration of area studies and International Relations in departments such as international and area studies, international cultures and languages, and international cooperation.

Korea

Inter- or intra-Korean relations or reunification issues constituted the set menu for Korea.[3] Although the predominance of these topics did not change much, the scope of international relations studies in Korea was enlarged substantially following the end of military dictatorship and the bipolar conflict, as well as the resurrection of talks with North Korea. Korea's foreign policy line between 1990 and 2005 was characterized by its adroit regionalism and globalism, such as those found in the country's stance towards World Trade Organization globalism, mini-regionalism with China and Japan, Asian regionalism with the ASEAN plus Three and the APEC, free trade agreements, and regional monetary funds. A large number of American Ph.Ds teaching in Korea has enhanced this trend.

Taiwan

Cross-strait relations dominated Taiwan's international relations studies. Competition with Beijing in terms of diplomatic recognition has encouraged Taiwan to grow as an active global power with its deft use of official developmental assistance. It is a little like Israel's foreign policy vis-à-vis Africa, Latin America, and the South Pacific in that obtaining recognition is a very high priority. (Statistically, this shows (Table 5.2) in a predominance of "foreign policy" over IPE or IR theory, although it should be noticed that the score for theory is relatively high compared to most other countries outside the Western core.) Taiwan's foreign policy between 1990 and 2005 has been confronted by two dilemmas. First, that of forming a coalition of powers vis-à-vis China or joining the bandwagon on China. Second, the dilemma of enhancing economic integration through direct investment or restraining too heavy involvements in China. Facing all these dilemmas, Taiwan's international relations studies have significantly deviated from the aforementioned set menu. The large number of American Ph.Ds teaching in Taiwan has helped this change to accelerate.

Table 5.2 Fields of research in Taiwan

Subfield	State of IR research in Taiwan (1988–1993)				
	Faculty speciality self-ID	Articles	Thesis dissertations	Research projects	Courses
IR methodology	5.12	0.00	0.00	0.00	1.07
IR theory	23.33	6.01	7.58	21.88	23.53
International political economy	27.11	20.04	12.63	9.38	10.07
International organization/law	13.11	10.62	11.01	9.37	19.78
Foreign policy/relations	31.33	63.33	68.69	59.37	44.92
N	46	499	198	32	187

Source: Bau *et al.* (1994). Each column reports percentage distribution between the five subfields.

The set menus were associated with a certain set of orientations in international relations studies. Most noteworthy was a predominantly descriptive orientation. This descriptive orientation was strong in all places in all subfields of international relations studies, whether in area studies, diplomatic history, or narrowly defined International Relations. Two plausible reasons might be noted. First, the descriptive orientation went in harmony with the policy orientation of a bulk of international relations studies. Policy-oriented work needs clarity in assessing the congruence with the policy line of the government more than the descriptive work. Second, academics in these four places are less positivistically analytical in their orientation in international relations studies. They more strongly bring contextual elements into their work than American more theoretically oriented scholars in International Relations. As the menus enlarge, other methodological orientations have been increasingly adopted.

It would have been unthinkable until around 1993 to see the following kinds of theoretically informed debates conducted in East Asia. In Japan, how strongly Westphalian (stressing state sovereignty, use of force, patriotism), Philadelphian (underlining popular sovereignty, freedom, human rights, and democracy), and anti-utopian (emphasizing loss of sovereignty, failed or bankrupt, or rogue states) national actors are, is a case in point. Some argue that their distinction is more or less geographically delineated like Robert Cooper's premodern, modern, and postmodern distinctions (Cooper 2003; Tanaka 2003). Others argue that these paradigms are globally constituted and thus the geographical matching between the paradigms and a certain group of states misses the whole point (Inoguchi 1999).

In Korea, whether the seemingly vehement anti-Americanism of Koreans, as was revealed in December 2003 during the Presidential election campaign, was attributed to generational factors as younger generations did not know the tragedy of the Korean War (Kim 2005) or as a still insufficient development of a mature civil society in Korea (Moon 2003) has been debated in various forms. In Taiwan, how China's neighbors behave in response to the rise of China has been debated between those who argue that there are bound to be counterbalancing coalition formations (Taiwanese friends of John Mearsheimer and Avery Goldstein) and those who argue that most would bandwagon China (Taiwanese friends of Robert Ross and Ian Johnston).

Penetration of American international relations studies

The size of American Ph.Ds in the three sites examined can be very broadly compared. Korea and Taiwan have a very large number of American Ph.Ds among professors and some politicians. A good contrast is between Korea and Japan. Korea has 600 American Ph.Ds whereas Japan has about 60. Taiwan is comparable to Korea in this regard. In proportion to the size of American Ph.Ds in political science, translated American IR books are salient in Korea and Taiwan. In Japan translation is no less vigorous. But Japanese professors prefer to selectively digest and partially incorporate them into their own textbooks rather than translated textbooks.

This pattern points to the importance of the interaction between global and domestic structure. The Japanese structure of the discipline is generally very different from the American hierarchical one organized around top theorists and top journals structuring a large domestic market with high mobility (Wæver 1998). In Japan, the IR academy has been more "uncompetitive and decentralized, with a hierarchical reward structure based on longevity of service and fidelity to one's academic peers and mentor" (Inoguchi and Bacon 2001: 16; also Inoguchi 2002b). This again was reinforced by the institutional weakness of political science and IR, leaving scholars affiliated to a diverse mix of schools and departments, which in turn tends to weaken the institutional structures of IR, although the organization JAIR has been of growing importance. In Taiwan and Korea, in contrast, the discipline is more a product of a 1960s state-initiated effort self-consciously modeled on the U.S. and therefore leading to both a structuring of the disciplinary landscape more similar to the U.S., and internal dynamics that operate with a more permanent side view to the U.S. (Ho and Kao 2002; Moon and Kim 2002; Huang 2007).

A brief look at the outlets for products of international relations studies reveals the degree of American penetration. (1) A few get their pieces in those first-rate American journals like *World Politics*, *International Organization*, *Journal of Conflict Resolution*, and *International Security*; (2) Many get their pieces printed in their most respected local language journals; (3) Even more print their work in those journals published by departments or universities; and (4) More still get their pieces in magazines addressed to a wider audience.

The Korean and Taiwanese governments encourage academics to publish works in those journals which are taken into account in the *Social Science Citation Index*. The Taiwanese government also saw to it that what is called the *Taiwanese Social Science Citation Index* be created. The Japanese government has not taken any formal action in this regard. (On the different status of international publication scores in the three countries, see further Huang (2007).)

The publication of English-language journals of international relations studies has been motivated by the desire to get East Asian scholarship known to others abroad, the desire to create an academic forum in which debates can be conducted productively, and the desire to elevate the level of academic competitiveness through the publication of a journal. Let us take a glance at some of them, especially those published in the English language.

Japan

International Relations of the Asia-Pacific (http://irap.oxfordjournals.org) is a publication of the Japan Association of International Relations. It is published three times a year from Oxford University Press. Its founding editor is the author of this chapter. It is meant to provide an academic forum for those interested in International Relations in the Asia-Pacific. In other words, it is not primarily meant to provide a vehicle for Association members to have their research products published. The distribution of authors in terms of their residence indicates that 35 percent are from North America, 35 percent from Asia including Japan and Oceania, 25 percent from Western Europe including the UK, and 10 percent from the rest. Japanese authors amount to 10 percent for the period from 2001 to 2006. The subjects taken up by articles range widely: regionalism, alliance, energy and security, gender and military bases, state sovereignty, human rights, bilateralism, environmental agreements, and more country-specific foreign policy issues. The latest special issue is about international relations studies in Asia edited by Barry Buzan and Amitav Acharya. Available on line, it is globally sub-scribed. It has been favorably assessed in the *Times Higher Educational Supplement* (Deans 2003).

International Journal of Asian Studies (http://www.journals.cambridge.org/jid_ASI) is a humanistically oriented journal published twice a year from the Institute of Oriental Culture, University of Tokyo. It deals with historical materials such as nineteenth-century inter-national trading networks in East and Southeast Asia and twentieth-century crop production and rainfalls in India, and its editor is Takeshi Hamashita. Furthermore, it has been taken into account in the Social Science Citation Index since 2008.

Japan Review of International Affairs (http://www2.jiia.or.jp/shuppan/jr/index.html) is a journal published by a think-tank of Japan's Ministry of Foreign Affairs. It covers key issues of international security such as the Six Party Talks on North Korea, Japan's official develop-ment policy, China's rise as a global power, and the United States Middle East policy.

Asia-Pacific Review (http://www.tandf.co.uk/journals/titles/13439006.asp) is a journal published by the International Policy Research Institute, a private think-tank in Tokyo. It covers key regional issues such as the East Asian Summit, the World Trade Organization and bilateral free trade agreements, and the Japan–United States alliance.

Japanese Journal of Political Science (http://journals.cambridge.org/jid_JJP) is a very academic journal published three times a year from Cambridge University Press. Its focus is on comparative politics, especially Japan, East Asia, and beyond. It sometimes covers inter-national relations as well. Its editor is the author of this chapter. The latest special issue is the comparative political culture of East Asian societies examining quality of life, social capi-tal, governance, and democracy. It has been acclaimed in a piece appearing in the *Times Higher Education Supplement* (Connors 2003). It has also been taken into account in the Social Science Citation Index since 2008.

Korea

Journal of East Asian Studies (http://www.rienner.com/viewbook.cfm?BOOKID=1354) is a publication of the East Asia Institute, Seoul. It is published three times a year by Lynne Rienner. Its founding editor is Kim Byung-kook. Its current editor is Stephen Hagaard. It is a highly acclaimed academic journal. It is a combination of comparative politics and International Relations. It deals with democratization, environmental protection in Northeast Asia, inter-Korean issues, and international relations studies in East Asia.

Journal of International and Area Studies (http://iia.snu.ac.kr/iia_publication/iia_publication_jias.htm) is a publication of the Seoul National University's Institution of International Affairs, published by Seoul National University Press. Its editor is Chong-sup Kim. It is a very academic journal with many articles authored by professors of Seoul National University. It covers key issues of international relations theories and practices in general and those surrounding the Korean Peninsulas in particular.

Korean Journal of Defense Analysis (http://www.kida.re.kr/english2005/publications/kjda.htm) is published by the Korea Institute of Defense Analysis. It focuses on Korea. It publishes key security issues as perceived by Korean policy makers and think-tank academics and, more broadly, security experts around the world. It enjoys a high reputation.

Global Asia (http://globalasia.org/main.php) is a brand new journal featuring key regional players and policy issues, and is published by the East Asia Foundation. Its editor is Chung-In Moon, ambassador-cum-academic from Yonsei University. It is highly acclaimed.

Taiwan

Issues and Studies (http://iir.nccu.edu.tw/english/IandS.htm) is a journal published by the Institute of International Relations, National Chengchi University. It is a policy-oriented journal published four times a year. It focuses on cross-strait relations but of late it has been developing its global reach and its theoretical wings as well.

Others

International Studies (http://www.ciis.org.cn/en/publications1.asp) is a journal published by the China Institute of International Studies, a think-tank of the Chinese Ministry of Foreign Affairs. It presents the range of thinking flowing around China's foreign policy community.

The *Chinese Journal of International Politics* (http://cjip.oxfordjournals.org/) is a journal from Tsinghua University with Yan Xuetong as editor and is published by Oxford University Press. It is a very academic and yet at the same time policy oriented journal. It is very interesting because it publishes those articles originally published in Chinese for a Chinese audience. It receives high acclaim in terms of academic quality and level of translation.

World Economics and Politics (http://iwep.org.cn) is a journal published by the Institute of World Economy and Politics, Chinese Academy of Social Sciences. It is a high-quality academic journal. It covers the whole range of international relations, universal security, and international political economy. It is also noteworthy that the journal publishes articles by foreign authors even on such potentially sensitive topics as Chinese nationalism.

Contemporary International Relations (http://www.cicir.ac.cn/en/publication/cir.php) is a journal published by the Contemporary China Institute of International Relations, the Chinese Communist Party's think-tank. It covers the whole range of key international issues as perceived by China's governing elites. It is highly acclaimed as an authoritative journal on China and enables readers to take a close look at Chinese foreign policy thinking.

China: An International Journal (http://www.nus.edu.sg/sup/cij/) is a journal of the East Asia Institute, National University of Singapore. It is an academic journal published four times a year from Times Atlas. Its editor is Wang Gungwu. It is a high-quality journal on a par with *The China Quarterly*, *The China Journal* and *Modern China*. It covers international relations as well.

Asian Journal of Political Science (http://www.fas.nus.edu.sg/pol/kcommu/ajps.htm) is published by the Department of Political Science, National University of Singapore. It is an academic journal published twice a year from Routledge. Its editor is Terry Nardin. It covers Southeast Asian politics and international relations.

Contemporary Southeast Asia (http://www.iseas.edu.sg/csea.html) is published by the Institute of Southeast Asian Studies, Singapore. It focuses on each country of Southeast Asia but it often covers international relations beyond Southeast Asia. It is a highly acclaimed academic journal from many disciplines.

International Studies (http://isq.sagepub.com/) is a journal published by Jawaharlal Nehru University from Sage Publications. Its focus is on South Asia. However, more recently it has often gone beyond South Asia, reflecting the global outlook of Indian elites.

This rather detailed survey of journals in the region shows in static terms a diverse picture of journals of all kinds – from general to specialized, internationally oriented to local, anchored in the region or outside it, basic theory to policy orientated – and it shows quite a number of well-established, recognized, and well-edited journals. However, to the extent that trends and attempts can be read from especially the more recent initiatives and changes, a major change of the total picture is an increased balance of more strictly academic journals now coexisting with the already numerous, more policy-oriented journals. In addition, a trend may be discerned towards moving out of national frames and into mostly subregional or regional ones.

Conclusion

Are one hundred flowers about to blossom in the East Asian International Relations academic community? Yes, to a certain extent, given the still robust developmental momentum, the steady empowerment of civil society, and gradual and steady thaws in regionalized cold wars. To this list of structural factors I might as well add the American factor. I have briefly touched on the American penetration of International Relations concepts and methods in East Asia through translated books and articles, and via American Ph.Ds. This is one form of American democracy promotion and diffusion. Korea is definitely the most penetrated by American IR if looked at on the surface. Taiwan is the second. Japan is curiously the third. Certainly, Japan has translated more American IR books than any of the two others here, but the extent to which academics refer to American IR concepts and methods, let alone follow them, is much lower in Japan. Japan's endogenous system of training students, recruiting professors, and evaluating academic products is the most dissonant of the three with the American system. It is not quite that the Japanese skepticism of American IR knows no bounds, but has a lot to do with the proficiency of the English language among elite academics in each of the three places. Japan has been slow in making English an important language to master. Setting aside these structural factors, which this chapter has not dealt with very much, most noteworthy is the fact that American IR itself is drawn into the process of diffusion, confusion, and fusion in East Asia, and more contextualized, more culturally sensitive, and more historically grounded IRs seem to be in the offing. The idea of reappropriation in a different regional setting is one of the things that should be paid more attention to in East Asia.

Notes

1   The second great debate between traditionalism and the scientific school did not take place in Japan either, meaning that the behavioral revolution never took hold in international relations studies. Neither the third nor the fourth debates, between neorealism and neoliberalism, and rationalism and reflectivism, respectively, took place either. However, many Japanese scholars feel that they have been practicing reflectivism long before it was preached by Americans, although they were less articulate and sophisticated about methodology.

2   However, competition among international relations scholars has increased somewhat in tandem with growth in the membership of JAIR – as of January 2008, the number is slightly more than 2,200 – with which Japanese scholars may feel tempted to employ U.S.-style academic strategies.

3   For statistics on the themes of articles in the main journals and of Ph.D. dissertations, see Park and Ha (1995). However, the categories used here are not very helpful for measuring the dominance of the set menu, because such studies can fall into a number of categories (area studies, inter-Korean relations, military and security studies [East Asia], South Korean foreign policy, North Korea, etc).

References

Bacon, Paul and Edward Newman (2002) "IR Studies East and West: Some Sociological Observations," *Journal of East Asian Studies*, 2(1): 21–44.

Bau, Tzeng-ho *et al.* (1994) *Survey of Manpower Distribution in the Discipline of Political Science*, Project Serial Number NSC 83-0131-H-002-014, Taipei, Taiwan: National Science Council.

Connors, Lesley (2003) "Eastern Horizons of the Art and Science of Governing," *Times Higher Educational Supplement*, October 24, p. 32.

Cooper, Robert (2003) *The Breaking of Nations: Order and Chaos in the Twenty-first Century*, London: Atlantic Books.

Deans, Phil (2003) "Youngster in Search of an Audience," *Times Higher Educational Supplement*, April 25, p. 35.

Fukutake, Tadashi (1954) *Nihon noson shakai no kozo bunseki* (Sociological Characteristics of Japanese Peasants), Tokyo: Yuhikaku.

Ho, Szu-yin and Lang Kao (2002) "The Study of International Relations in Taiwan," *Journal of East Asian Studies*, 2(1): 89–110.

Huang, Xiaomin (2007) "The Invisible Hand: Modern Studies of International Relations in Japan, China, and Korea," *Journal of International Relations and Development*, 10: 168–203.

Inoguchi, Takashi (1989) "The Study of International Relations in Japan," in Hugh Dyer and Leon Mangasarian (eds), *The Study of International Relations: The State of the Art*, London: Macmillan, pp. 257–264.

Inoguchi, Takashi (1999) "Peering into the Future by Looking Back: The Westphalian, Philadelphian, and Anti-utopian Paradigms," *International Studies Review*, 1(2) (Summer): 173–191.

Inoguchi, Takashi (2001a) *Global Change*, London: Palgrave.

Inoguchi, Takashi (2001b) "Area Studies in Relation to International Relations," in Neil Smelser and Paul Baltes (eds), *International Encyclopedia of Behavioral and Social Sciences*, Vol. 2, New York: Elsevier, pp.707–711.

Inoguchi, Takashi (2002a) "Broadening the Basis of Social Capital in Japan," in Robert Putnam (ed.), *Democracies in Flux*, New York: Oxford University Press, pp.358–392.

Inoguchi, Takashi (2002b) "The Sociology of a Not-So-Integrated Discipline: The Development of International Relations in Japan," *Journal of East Asian Studies*, 2(1): 111–126.

Inoguchi, Takashi (2007) "Are There any Theories of International Relations in Japan?," *International Relations of the Asia-Pacific*, 7(3): 369–390.

Inoguchi, Takashi and Paul Bacon (2001) "The Study of International Relations in Japan: Towards a More International Discipline," *International Relations of the Asia-Pacific*, 1(1): 1–20.

Inoguchi, Takashi and Paul Bacon (2006) "Japan's Emerging Role as a 'Global' Ordinary Power," *International Relations of the Asia-Pacific*, 6 (1): 1–21.

Inoguchi, Takashi and Matthew Carlson (eds) (2006) *Governance and Democracy in Asia*, Melbourne: Trans Pacific Press.

Inoguchi, Takashi and Shiro Harada (2002) " Kokusai seiji kenkyuusha no sentou senryaku" (Strategies of Specialization by IR Scholars), in Yanai Haruo (ed.) *Tahenryo Kaiseki Jisurei Handbook* (Handbook of Multivariate Analyses), Tokyo: Asakura shoten; http://www.t-inoguchi.com/comp/ publish_j/bin/bin15091614339210.pdf.

Katada, Saori, Hanns Maull and Takashi Inoguchi (eds) (2004) *Global Governance: Germany and Japan in the International System*, London: Ashgate.

Kawashima, Takeyoshi (1978) *Nihon-jin no Ho-ishiki* (Legal Consciousness of Japanese), Tokyo: Iwanami Shoten.

Kim, Byung-Kook (2005) "To Have a Cake and Eat It Too: The Crisis of the Pax Americana in Korea," in Jorge Dominguez and Byung-Kook Kim (eds), *Conflict and Compliance: East Asia, Latin America and the New Pax Americana*, Boulder, CO: Lynne Rienner, pp.219–250.

Kusano, Atsushi (1983) *Nichibei Orange Kosho* (Japan–U.S. Negotiations over Orange), Tokyo: Nihon Keizai Shinbunsha.

Maruyama, Masao (1956–1957) *Gendai Seiji no Shiso to Kodo* (Thought and Behavior of Contemporary Japanese Policies), Tokyo: Miraisha.

Maruyama, Masao (1963) *Thought and Behavior in Modern Japanese Politics*, London: Oxford University Press.

Moon, Chang-in and Taehwan Kim (2002) "International Relations Studies in South Korea," *Journal of East Asian Studies*, 2(1): 45–68.

Moon, Katherine (2003) Presentation at the Conference on Korea, East Asia, and the United States, Georgetown University, Washington, DC, November.

Nakano, Ryoko (2007) "'Pre-history' of International Relations in Japan: Yanaihara Tadao's Dual Perspective of Empire," *Millennium – Journal of International Studies*, 35(2): 301–319.

Otsuka, Hisao (1965) *Kokumin Keizai – Sono Rekishiteki Kosatsu* (The National Economy: Historical Investigation), Tokyo: Kobundo.

Park, Sang-sup and Ha, Young-Sum (1995) "Trends in International Relations in the United States and Present Status of International Studies in South Korea," *Korean Journal of International Studies*, 35(1): 313.

Schwartz, Adam and Susan Pharr (eds) (2003) *Civil Society in Japan*, New York: Cambridge University Press.

Tadokoro, Masahiko (2001) *America o koeta dollar* (The Dollar Beyond the United States), Tokyo: Nihon Keizai Shimbunsha.

Tanaka, Akihiko (2003) *New Middle Ages: The World System in the 21st Century,* Tokyo: LTCB Library.

Tickner, Arlene (2003) "Hearing Latin American Voices in International Relations Studies," *International Studies Perspectives*, 4(4): 325–350.

Tsuchiyama, Jitsuo (2005) "Japanese Relations Theories: Kosaka Masataka, Nagai Yonosuke and Wakaizumi Kei," paper presented at the annual meeting of the International Studies Association (ISA), San Diego, California, March.

Wæver, Ole (1998) "The Sociology of a Not So International Discipline: American and European Developments in International Relations," *International Organization*, 52(4): 687–727.

World Bank (1994) *The East Asian Miracle*, Washington, DC: World Bank.

6 China

Between copying and constructing[1]

Yiwei Wang

Academic reflections on IR theory have entered a geo-cultural stage: perspectives sustaining the idea of "one world, many theories" (Walt 1998: 30) are gradually being replaced by those which argue that many worlds exist in which one hundred flowers are about to blossom. Globalization in its economic aspect has not overshadowed the geo-cultural diversity of the world; it brings various regionalisms along with forms of globalization. Thus, reflective IR studies that broaden our perspectives to include non-Western studies are increasingly important. China should be a major focus of this broadening process for two reasons. First, Chinese civilization is one of the most ancient and continuous in the world. Second, China's rise has been one of the most remarkable phenomena of the twenty-first century and raises growing concerns about a China threat. We might ask: Will China's geo-strategic rise also bring with it the rise of Chinese IR theory?

Unfortunately, most of the initial accounts of Chinese IR studies present only a very general overview of IR in China (Geeraerts and Men 2001) or try to assess the impact of previous field development efforts, such as the Ford Foundation report assessing its impact on the creation of Chinese IR (Johnston 2002; Wang Jisi 2002). The general overviews have usually been conducted by overseas Chinese or western China watchers and take Western IR theory as a reference point. These studies tend to ask the potentially condescending question, "Why is there no Chinese IR theory?" This concern has been echoed by Chinese scholars themselves (Wang Yiwei 2004; Su 2005). It is asked why China has no IR theory of her own but not whether China needs IR theory (Wang Yiwei 2007d). In other words, the West is assumed as the model to follow but, sooner or later, we will find that the West is not universal but local; a diversified new world is in the making.

In the information age, Chinese scholars are much better placed to express themselves on a global stage than at any time in recent memory. It is time, then, to move beyond general overviews of Chinese authors or their publications since one can easily find a large selection of papers and biographies on a website, "IR in China," established by Nankai University based in Tianjin (www.irchina.org). This site provides basic background on scholars, institutes, and the achievements of IR studies in China.[2] These achievements are the product of a long process of building IR studies in China.

With China's defeat in the Opium War, China was unable to sustain her traditional identity as the central dynasty or middle kingdom. The first challenge for Chinese thinkers of the nineteenth and early twentieth century was to open their eyes to see the world. Later, after successive revolutions, China's elites sought to establish a new Chinese identity in the world, finally succeeding with the founding of the Republic of China (in 1912) and the People's Republic of China (in 1949). After asserting its status as an independent country, Mao Zedong declared that China should make her own contributions to the world. At this point, relations between China and the world entered the stage of "constructing the world."

The great Qin Dynasty scholar, Liang Qichao (1901), classified Chinese history into three phases – "China's China," "Asia's China," and "the World's China" – corresponding to three Chinese identities. Chinese IR studies focus especially on seeking China's identity in the world and constructing a Chinese vision of the world's identity. Relations between China and the world have reached the stage of "World's China" vs. "China's World," i.e., between "China in the world" and "the Chinese version of the world." To understand the evolution of China's IR studies, it is essential to understand the relations between China and the world since the beginning of *Gaige Kaifang* (the "reform and opening-up" period).

Thus, this chapter will begin with China after 1949 but will analyze in depth the Chinese post-reform endeavor to build a Chinese IR theory as it moves through three steps: seeking the world, seeking its own identity, and constructing the world. I try to explain how China's geo-cultural background, including its recent rise, shapes Chinese IR studies. I will draw on Zhang Baijia's (2002) characterization of the Chinese logic of "Changing Itself and Influencing the World" in which China imagines the mutual impact of China and the world as the world impacts upon China through China's self-changing. The chapter is divided into four sections, reflecting phases in China's self-changing via interaction with the world. First, I examine Chinese IR in terms of its search for the world by reforming and opening up to the world. Second, Chinese IR participates in the Chinese search for itself, seeking its own identity while engaging the world. Third, Chinese IR constructs the world by seeing itself achieve its own development and peaceful rise as part of a vision of a harmonious world/region. Fourth, I draw out the implications of a geo-cultural perspective in IR studies from the Chinese experience.

Dimension 1: China in search of the world

After the foundation of the People's Republic of China, it was crucial to seek recognition of the new China in the world. Institutes of international studies and education were established to study the outside world and to prepare Chinese diplomats for the task of representing China to the world. For example, the Foreign Affairs College (today's China University of Foreign Affairs) was founded in 1955. In the beginning, Chinese IR studies focused, first, on promoting the superiority of socialism and criticizing the darkness of capitalism, especially its imperialist tendencies, and, second, on introducing the experiences of the Soviet Union and studying the history and present of the international communist movement and the situation of revolutions around the world. This second focus involved analyzing communist parties in other countries, especially their attitudes toward China, and learning how to carry out the work of external propaganda and liaison positively and respectfully (Li *et al.* 1999).

Later, the priority of Chinese diplomacy shifted to safeguarding her national security, especially when China felt threats both from the Northern Bear (Soviet Union) and the Eastern Eagle (the U.S.). When China began to reform and open up to the world in the late 1970s and 1980s, the primary task was to reform its economic and legal systems. In the 1990s, China worked to integrate with the international community, the highlight being China's entry into the WTO in 2001. Based on this evolution of events, hereafter I will divide the evolution of Chinese IR studies into four stages.

Starting-Marxism period (1960s–1980s)

Since the 1960s, great changes have taken place in the themes, methods, and analytical concepts central to the study of international politics in such fields as theory of international relations, international strategies, international organizations, and inter-state relations. These changes reveal a shift of researchers' positions from political to academic and from dogmatism to pragmatism.

In December 1963, the Chinese government issued the document "On Strengthening the Research on Foreign Affairs in China," and Peking University, Remin University, and Fudan University subsequently established their respective departments of international politics. Although some pre-existed the government initiative, new research centers for international and area studies under the Chinese Academy of Social Sciences (CASS) and other departments of ministries were established, also heralding the beginning of Chinese international politics research. A clear division of labor existed: the university system focused on education and research on the basis of translated documents; IR research institutes were placed under ministries focused on policy planning; CASS was placed somewhere in between. In addition, regions were assigned to each university. According to the arrangement, which still holds to some extent, Peking University focused on third world, especially Asian, African, and Latin American, studies, Remin University focused on the Soviet Union and Eastern European studies, and Fudan University, since it is located in Shanghai, focused on West European and North American studies.[3]

During this period, Chinese IR studies were greatly influenced by the Soviet model. Even after Chinese–Soviet relations deteriorated, China still held Marxism–Leninism as the guideline for IR studies. Class analysis and Mao's Theory of Contradiction were used widely. The studies of the West mainly involved efforts to understand Western political systems. If there was any IR theory, Chinese scholars drew on the work of Soviet scholars or cited from the classic works of Marxism–Leninism. In the eyes of Chinese IR scholars, the world was largely divided between us and others.

In 1971, China resumed her legal position at the UN and began to serve as the big brother for the third world. Following Mao's division of the world into the first, second, and third worlds, studies of developing countries, especially national liberation and independence movements, were emphasized. However, after Nixon opened the Chinese door in 1972, more and more Western countries built diplomatic relations with China. Chinese academics shifted focus to the study of the world economy, still emphasizing the total crisis of capitalism. Chinese IR scholarship tended to use the language of "revolutionary" and "counter-revolutionary" in their studies during this period.

Learning–copying period (1980s)

After the end of the Cultural Revolution, Deng Xiaoping initiated the period of openness and reform. Having been isolated from the West for such a long time, Chinese scholars were eager to learn. The introduction of Western/American IR theories began at this point, a trend that has shaped the character of Chinese IR studies up until the present. New institutes under the Ministry of Foreign Affairs, State Security, the Military, various universities, the Academy of Social Sciences, and even Xinhua News Agency were established. IR journals, such as *China International Studies*, *Europe* (now "*European Studies*"), *American Studies Quarterly*, *Contemporary International Relations* (all in Chinese), sprang up and increased in importance. Opening up to and integrating with the outside world has taken the place of revolution and overthrowing the old international order as the main topics of discussion. During this early phase of opening up, a romantic view of the West dominated, and scholars copied Western scholarship without much regard for Chinese perspectives and ideas (Wang Yizhou 2006a, 2006b).

During this period, Chinese scholars treated Western IR theory as knowledge, and were hungry to learn and introduce American IR theories to China. Scholars competent in English often studied in the U.S. or were invited as visiting scholars. These IR scholars took a leading role, publishing translations of American materials or books and articles based on English-language materials. Chinese scholars resisted the ideological influences of earlier periods, using IR concepts and theories which they borrowed from the West. As Professor Wang Jisi (2002) summarized:

> During the 20 years and more from the reform and opening-up until now, the focus of IR studies has begun to change. Internationalism with class struggle as the guiding principle before reform and opening-up has been replaced since the 1980s by rationalism with national interests at the center.

Stimulus–response period (1990s)

During this period, IR theory became a highly contested field among Chinese scholars. In addition to American IR theory, English School, Copenhagen School, *dependencia* theories and even Australian IR studies have been introduced to China, producing strong echoes and influencing scholarly debates. In the wake of the Tiananmen Square incident and the collapse of the Soviet bloc, Western theories faced a short period of intense questioning, but Chinese scholars soon enlarged their interests, moving from international relations to globalization and gradually shifting from learning from the West to thinking for themselves. Wang Yizhou's book *Dangdai Guoji Zhengzhi Xilun* (Analysis of Contemporary International Politics (1995)) is exemplary of this trend. His book was soon followed by a series on contemporary international politics begun by Shanghai People's Publishing House, which took a leading role in introducing and analyzing international relations theories in China. Some of these texts were direct responses to Western theories, such as Samuel Huntington's provocative "clash of civilizations" (Wang Jisi 1995). Some of them provided comprehensive introductions to international politics, but most focused on one school of thought or one aspect of international affairs. This series of books are still the most influential and authoritative texts and reference books for Chinese students.

Chinese academics always claim they combine theory and practice. For instance, analysis of the Democratic Peace thesis and debate produced a similarly heated debate in Chinese academic circles. NATO's bombing of the Chinese Embassy in Belgrade in 1999 during the Kosovo War led Chinese scholars to negative evaluations of new theories and practices of humanitarian intervention. These practices were seen to violate the Five Principles of Peaceful Coexistence,[4] especially the principle of non-interference in the internal affairs of other countries. The principle of non-interference is seen as more central by Chinese scholars than by most in the West, a view that China advocates in international relations. Pressed by NATO's Eastern expansion gradually closer to Chinese territory, Chinese scholars started to worry that NATO or America would apply the Kosovo model to China at some later date, so criticizing arguments that limit the weight of sovereignty has been a consistent theme. It is frequently observed by Chinese IR specialists that China has been among the strongest supporters of the Westphalian system of sovereign nation-states. Soon after the events in Kosovo, Chinese academics went on a campaign to criticize the argument that "human rights trumps sovereignty."

At the same time, China was speedily integrating with the world economically, including applying for GATT membership. Deng Xiaoping embarked on his tour to the south of China in January 1992, delivering a series of speeches aimed at clarifying the muddled idea of whether the establishment of special economic zones was capitalist or socialist in nature. Thereafter, China began to embrace a market economy totally and changed its attitude about joining multilateral international organizations. This shift revealed that China had gained the confidence that it could continue an independent foreign policy and political system while embracing globalization. Thus, after many years of deep suspicion of the international order, China's attitude toward multilateralism and especially multilateral security frameworks began to change, particularly in the 1990s, when Chinese national interests became more and more linked with international regimes.

Being both depressed by the international security environment and encouraged by Chinese economic integration with the international community, Chinese IR scholars continued to introduce IR theory from the West but now with a more critical mindset. Critical reflections on theories emerged as the key format for work in Chinese IR studies, with less emphasis given to applying theory or developing theory. In other words, Chinese publications began to review the logic and ideology of Western IR theories. The journal *Europe* emerged as a leader during this period, though *World Economy and Politics* continued to be an important site of IR scholarship.

Reflecting–constructing period (2000s)

During this period, the question of whether IR theory is a value-free instrument or an ideological tool became central to Chinese IR. Nearly all Chinese scholars agree that Western IR theory cannot solve all Chinese problems and puzzles – that the Chinese should have their own theories to explain the world, especially to theorize Chinese diplomatic practice (or foreign policy). Two measures have been taken. First, Chinese scholars resisted the growing Western discussions of a so-called "China threat," promoting instead the vision of a possible "peaceful rise" of China. Second, the move to establish a more ambitious and independent view of and from China began with the rise of the vision of a "Harmonious world." All three slogans, "China threat," "Peaceful rise," and "Harmonious world," came originally from policy circles – in the U.S. and in China – but became the object of academic analysis in both countries.

China's entry into the WTO marks a full embrace of globalization, providing great opportunities and challenges for IR scholars. IR has been a *Xianxue* (hot discipline) in China: "in the recent ten years, sixty departments of International Relations have been established" (Su 2005). Indeed, demand drives supply. Chinese interests in IR are driven by the questions that a globalized China faces. As Table 6.1 suggests, Chinese scholars apply and assess numerous theoretical traditions, including structural realism, liberal institutionalism, constructivism, feminism, and postmodernism. They address the broad range of topics associated with security studies, international political economy, diplomatic (foreign policy) decision-making, culture and identity, environmental issues, international law/organization/governance, nationalism and religion in IR.

This classification of articles in major journals suggests that Chinese IR scholars work in sync with international academics. IR scholarship has risen in political importance in China as well. In 2004, Professor Qin Yaqing from the Chinese University of Foreign Affairs and Professor Zhang Yuyan from the Chinese Academy of Social Sciences were invited to give a joint lecture to the Political Bureau members of the Chinese Communist Party. This is the first time that top Chinese leaders have displayed a willingness to learn from IR scholars. This gesture encourages Chinese IR scholars to assume the role of a guide to Chinese diplomatic

Table 6.1 Types (schools of IR theory) of articles in *World Economy and Politics* from 1998 to 2006

Year	1998	1999	2000	2001	2002	2003	2004	2005	2006	Total
Strategic/security theory	6	12	7	9	11	11	21	10	9	96
Structural realism	2	4	6	3	6	4	11	3	3	42
Liberal institutionalism	1	4	9	9	10	3	4	2	6	48
IPE	2	4	8	8	9	8	7	8	3	57
Constructivism	1	1	1	1	3	7	8	5	3	30
Regionalism		4	1	4	5	6	6	26		
Feminism		1	1	2	1	3	2	1	3	14
Diplomatic (foreign policy) decision-making		1	2	2	3	7	3	3	4	25
Culture/identity/ethnic		3	2	5	4	4	8	8	8	42
Global governance			1	2	8	3	3	3	2	23
International law and IR		1	3	2		1	2	2	1	12
Nation (ethic)/religion	1	4	2		3	1		4	6	21
Multilateralism/IO	1	2	1	10	2	1	1	9	2	29
Environmental international politics	4		5	3	5	2	2	1	2	23
Postmodern international politics theory	0	1	1	4	2	7	1	3	2	21

thinking. We now come to the second dimension of Chinese IR studies: Chinese IR in search of itself.

Dimension 2: China in search of itself

Chinese IR studies are no longer just a passive reflection of relations between China and the world, but increasingly exhibit initiative in seeking its own identity. In other words, Chinese IR studies increasingly express China not in terms defined by others, but in its own terms. This may move us beyond a situation in which outsiders to China use familiar clichés (such as nationalism) to characterize the feelings of the Chinese people (Wang Yiwei 2006).

Two basic objectives define this dimension of Chinese IR: one is to analyze the world; the other is to discover Chinese identity in relation to the process of globalization, since China feels that globalization provides both challenges to and opportunities for her sovereignty and interests. Three sentiments shape the social sciences in China and influence the way Chinese IR scholars approach these two objectives (Wang Yiwei 2002). The first sentiment is associated with scholars who may be described as "looking up to the West." With the opening up of China, it was those with the best English, often English majors, who were sent or invited to the U.S. to study IR. For instance, Professor Ni Shixiong of Fudan University took a leading role in introducing American IR theories to Chinese academics. Even today, most Chinese IR scholars' only second language is English. Deng Xiaoping's focus on the U.S. as the country from which China was to learn meant that Chinese IR studies have been greatly influenced by American IR theory. Most of the leading Chinese IR scholars spent time in the U.S., and the status of the U.S. in China improved the stature of those who could say they studied in the U.S. In addition, having established their domestic reputation based on mastery of U.S. IR theory, they gradually turned their domestic academic reputation into policy influence, especially since Chinese leaders considered relations with the U.S. to be the highest priority.

The second sentiment may be described as "looking straightforwardly at the West." In other words, these scholars look steadily toward but also critically at the West. This group includes both realists and reflectivists, but most of them are pragmatists – not in the sense of a distinct pragmatist philosophy but in the more common-sense form of moving between theories in a "non-religious" manner. These pragmatists tend to be younger and were educated in China. They came of age during the reform period and usually took their first degrees in political science. They appreciate but don't fetishize American IR theories and, since they increasingly visit both the U.S. and Europe, take a broader and comparative look at available theories, drawing heavily on English school and other non-American IR theories.[5] They are more open-minded and energetic by comparison with the first generation of Chinese IR scholars.

The third sentiment may be described as "looking down at the West." Some in this group of scholars have been labeled "nationalists" or "new leftists," including such figures as Zhao Tingyang, whose book *Tianxia System* (All-under-Heaven) (2005) has been very influential. Along with the rise of China in the world, these scholars have turned more fully to China's own historical experiences[6] and Chinese culture/philosophy as an inspiration. This so-called "New Confucianism" has rapidly grown in influence in IR studies. Support of China's claim that it is promoting a vision of a "harmonious world" is one of this group's major intellectual contributions.

The consciousness that Chinese scholars are building a Chinese IR theory is growing among all three groups. The idea that Chinese realities demand a distinctive IR theorizing has been present from the earliest phase of building IR, broached first perhaps in the book *Preliminary Inquiry into International Relations Theory* (Shanghai Association of International Relations 1991) and continues into the present (Liang Shoude 2005; Ye 2005; Yu 2005; Zhao and Ni 2006). Three impulses shape the effort to create a Chinese IR theory (Lu 2006).

Building IR theory with Chinese characteristics

This first impulse leads scholars to take American/Western IR theory as the reference point or model, but with the goal of adding Chinese characteristics into the landscape of the theoretical world. By doing so, these scholars identify Chinese theory as one of the Western family members but with differences. Thus, after being dazzled by all kinds of Western IR theory, differentiating Chinese from Western theories emerged as the first challenge and urgent task for Chinese IR scholars. Moved by Deng Xiaoping's notion of "socialism with Chinese characteristics," the impulse is to build IR theory with Chinese characteristics (Liang Shoude 1994; Callahan 2001; Song 2001).

But what is meant by "Chinese characteristics"? Some thinkers focus on Marxist IR theory (Li Bin 2005), emphasizing the Marxist–Leninist viewpoint and method, while others focus on Chinese culture and traditional diplomatic theory and practice. Because of such confusion about the exact meaning of "Chinese characteristics," other scholars have emphasized that IR is a universal science without regard to national characteristics.[7] More space for "Chinese characteristics" is opened if, as one scholar argues, IR stands "between science and art" (Wang Yiwei 2007a). In addition, because IR had already come to China as part of a process of "Americanization" – as an American mode of thinking, political culture, national mission, and national character that strongly shapes the ontological, epistemological, methodological, and axiological dimensions of IR – the U.S. is not only a country researched by IR, it is the dominant factor in creating IR studies (Wang Yiwei 2003b, 2007c; Li Yihu 2005).

A Chinese school in IR theory

Trying to go beyond the debate on whether there should be Chinese characteristics or not, a second impulse is to systematize a *Chinese* IR theory. On the one hand, scholars would continue to recognize the legitimacy of Western IR theory. On the other hand, they hesitate to simply join the Western theory family. Moved by the presence of an English School and a Copenhagen School, the idea of a Chinese School has been the focus of more and more Chinese scholars. A leading professor, Qin Yaqing (2005), reflected on the conditions of possibility of a Chinese IR theory:

> First, a Chinese School of International Relations Theory (IRT) is possible, for social theory differs from natural theory in that the former has a distinct geo-cultural birthmark. Second, three sources can provide a basis for a potential Chinese School, namely, the all-under-heaven worldview and the practice of the tributary system, the revolutionary thoughts and practices in China's search for modernity, and the ideas and practice of reform and opening-up. Third, for the past 150 years, China's greatest problem has been the identity dilemma vis-à-vis the international system. The rapid development, the great social transformation, and the fundamental ideational changes have enabled China to begin solving this dilemma fairly successfully. China's interaction with the international system and the resultant debates will inevitably lead to the emergence of a Chinese School of IRT.

But showing the possibility or necessity of a Chinese school is not the same thing as creating the conditions for the actual existence of such a school.

Chinese IR theory?

After considering further the example of the so-called "English School," a third impulse is to pull back from talk about a "Chinese School" and return to a more pragmatic way of thinking about how to theorize Chinese IR studies. Thinkers of this kind understand that it is a very long path to a Chinese School.

They begin by puzzling over the question, "Why is there no Chinese IR theory?" Chinese realists put forward the typical argument that there are no Chinese international relations theories because China is not powerful enough. Since they believe IR theory reflects the will of the leading state, only when China's national will can be expressed in her own way will a Chinese School come into being (Wang Yiwei 2003a).

Liberal theorists, by contrast, tend to focus on the logic of the discipline when they argue that an original Chinese IR theory would have three basic characteristics: first, it should be based on Chinese culture, historical traditions, and practical experience; second, it should be universally valid, transcending local traditions and experience; third, its core assumptions must be distinct from those of other theories. By these three criteria, there is still no theory that can be called a "Chinese School." But why? One of the vital reasons, argues Qin Yaqing (2005), is the lack of a core theoretical problematic. Qin Yaqin's views have been strongly influenced by Lakatos' "hard core–protective belt" argument in his theory about "Research Programs" (Lakatos 1978). Realists resist this argument, noting that liberals seek a Chinese road within a Western logic and thereby help to promote the hegemony of Western discourse.

However, Gustaaf Geeraerts and Men Jing (2001) present the state of affairs of international relations theory in China in a way which suggests that Chinese IR is already distinctive:

The basic concept of theory in China differs markedly from the one found in mainstream Western epistemology. The theory in the Chinese conception has to serve the purpose of socialist revolution and construction. Viewed from that perspective, Western international relation theory is politically and culturally bounded and only gives a partial outlook on international politics. The tradition of regarding theory as a practical guide dates to the revolutionary period in China at the beginning of the 1900s. The spread of Marxism and Leninism, and the subsequent success of the revolution with the help of those theories, convinced Chinese leaders that the importance of theoretical constructs stems from their practical applicability. Most of the younger scholars and a small number of senior scholars think that international relations theory should be a scientific framework for analyzing international politics and international relations, and so have clearly moved closer to mainstream Western conceptions of science.[8]

Keeping these differences in mind, Chinese IR scholars might try to sustain a balance between the West and China, between science and art, between modernity and traditions.

Dimension 3: China constructing the world

Traditionally, Chinese thinkers had no idea of international relations but viewed the world from the perspective of "All-under-Heaven."[9] Chinese philosopher Zhao Tingyang (2005, 2006) has pointed out that the concept "All-under-Heaven" has a triple meaning – as the land of the world; as all peoples in the world; and as a world institution – combined in the single term, indicating a theoretical project of the necessary and inseparable connections among these three elements. The "All-under-Heaven" concept emphasizes a unity of the physical world (land), the psychological world (the general heart of peoples), and the political world (a world institution). It must be admitted that the world is still a non-world in this sense, since it has not yet enjoyed a world institution representing the general heart of all peoples. Linguistically, "worldview" is a Western and mainly German term (*Weltanschauung*) after all, so the Chinese worldview must be termed the view of "All-under-Heaven" which especially emphasizes the political characteristic of a worldview (Zhao Tingyang 2006).

Different from the horizontal Westphalian system organized on the basis of sovereign equality, the concept of "All-under-Heaven" favors hierarchy – a pattern of order based on a world measure. That is to say, the issues and affairs of the world should be analyzed and measured by a world standard rather than by a nation standard and in the world context rather than from a local perspective.[10] It is an epistemological principle defined by Lao-zi (Lao Tze) as "from the standard of all-under-heaven to understand the affairs of all-under-heaven" (Tao-de-jing), or in modernized words: "the world should be seen from a view of world-size." It shows the way in which the world is considered a political entity more than a scientific object in Chinese thinking. In international relations, the Chinese perspective tends toward monism, preferring a harmonious world over a dualism or dichotomy rooted in Christianity, a culture prone to dividing the world between good and evil. For instance, Chinese scholars have persistently criticized Richard Cooper's division of pre-modern, modern, and postmodern worlds, just as they condemned Samuel Huntington's clash of civilizations which divided world civilizations in terms of a conflict between the West and non-West.

Traced back to its essence, the thinking frame of the West constitutes people as subjects able to "view/see" the world. In this theory of knowledge, every object that cannot be "converted" is assigned to the absolute: God or absolute otherness. God is identified as the source of creation; others, especially heathens, are affirmed as irreconcilable enemies. By contrast, Chinese thought supposes that there is always a method by which otherness can be changed into harmonious co-existence. In other words, all non-harmonious things can be changed from Other to Us. Hence, "the basic assumption in western philosophy is the principle of Objectivity but the assumption in Chinese philosophy is the principle of Subjectivity/Other." Western political discourse first thinks about "Who are you?" i.e., the identity problem, distinguishing friend and enemy, exploring "us" and "others"; it is a kind of splitting world outlook. The premise of Chinese political thinking is "Who are we?," creating the concept of "the whole world is one family." As a result, the Western concern is how to legally govern the possibility of fighting, while the Chinese concern is how to make harmonious co-existence possible (Zhao Tingyang 2005: 13).

Chinese epistemology was always a political epistemology because Chinese minds were inclined to investigate society while placing nature beyond analysis. The Chinese preference for political knowledge has been so dominant that Chinese minds had very little interest in the truths of nature and consequently rarely made contributions to theoretical natural sciences. It has been believed that political/ethical investigations are more important than natural science. The Chinese argument for this emphasis might go like this: the world consists of natural things and facts, but only facts determine our lives because facts are about what people have done.[11] Things are merely what we have to accept as they are and thus do not define problems for study. Nature is what should be let be, while society is what we make it to be. The world of facts concerns the relations of human beings and the problems of the world worth studying are thus found to be essentially political/ethical.

The philosophical principles of "All-under-Heaven," both when openly proclaimed and when – more often – simply implied, may be summarized as follows:

1   The world must be a political entity or the political system is incomplete.
2   The world should be the highest (in the sense of political authority/sovereignty) political entity if a political system is composed of different levels of governance.
3   The general governance of the world should be by a world institution. The most effective form would be a universal empire.
4   Political institutions at each level must be of the same essence. In other words, the political principle must be able to be universalized and transitively run throughout all political levels.
5   The legitimacy of the political institution must be rooted in the ethical.
6   The ethical justification of political governance is the representation of the general heart of peoples (Zhao Tingyang n.d.).[12]

In the eyes of China's neo-Confucians, the Chinese theory of "All-under-Heaven" is the best philosophy for world governance. "All-under-Heaven" is a deep world concept: it introduces a political principle, "worldness," that arguably transcends the principle of "internationality" and that more appropriately is seen as a "world theory" than an "international theory" (Zhao Tingyang 2006). Following this, neo-Confucians consider today's world a non-world because different peoples belong to different worlds (developing, developed; West, non-West) even if they live on the same earth. Some Chinese IR scholars are still inclined, however, to use the terminology of international politics or world politics instead of international relations to mark the difference between politics and philosophy because, in ancient China, politics is subordinated to philosophy (Wang Jisi 2006). If the New Confucianism views the world as a whole, while international relations theory thinks about different nation-states separated by their sovereignties, then Martin Wight's question "Why is there no international theory?" should be replaced by "Why is there no world theory?"

Where "world theory" is the aspiration, IR studies and diplomacy may take on quite a different character from that in the West. The theoretical problematic of American IR theory is hegemonic maintenance and the problematic of British IR theory is the formation and development of international society. By comparing British IR theory with that of the United States, Qin Yaqing (2005) draws the conclusion that a problematic of international politics dominates a specific research agenda. Taking the "harmonious world" argument as an example, the practice of Chinese diplomacy and scholarly knowledge production would aim toward the Confucian purpose of building a "Harmonious world"; that is, seeking long-lasting peace and common prosperity for the world.

When tracing the evolution of Chinese diplomatic strategies, we can see that China's foreign policy has been driven by liberalism more than anything else, as the "peaceful rise" idea indicates. Constructivism has also helped to shape the new concept of world order as a harmonious world. Of course, realists still have their influence in shaping Chinese public opinion, but this would require that China gives up a traditional concept like "All-under-Heaven" or "empire" and just integrates with the international society. Drawing on these resources, Chinese IR scholars try to construct the world.

Chinese achievements in IR studies cannot just rely on ancient thought, however. As the descendants of Confucius and Lao-zi (Lao Tze), Chinese scholars and leaders continue to put forward many new ideas for solving today's problems, thereby supporting the claim that the Chinese are constructing international relations theory in their own way. In the 1950s, for example, the Chinese Premier and Minister of Foreign Affairs Zhou Enlai, along with the Cambodian and Indian Premiers, put forward the Five Principles of Peaceful Co-existence. Deng Xiaoping's innovation of putting aside sovereignty disputes and developing territory and resources together by creating "one country, two systems" helped to solve the Hong Kong/ Macao problem. In the mid-1990s, China put forward the "New Security Concept" which takes mutual trust, mutual benefit, equality, and coordination as the core, and practiced it in the Shanghai Five and later the Shanghai Cooperation Organization (SCO).[13] In early 2004, the Chinese government put forward its peaceful rise strategy, trying to seek a new approach to avoid conflicts and other pitfalls during the power transition. Recently, China has shifted its focus from its relations with the world to imagining the shape of the world itself, which can be embodied in new thinking about Asia as a harmonious region. Being encouraged by the domestic will to build up a harmonious society, Chinese President Hu Jintao put forward a Chinese vision for world order in an important speech, "Making Great Efforts to Build a Harmonious World with Long-lasting Peace and Common Prosperity," on the anniversary of the establishment of the United Nations, September 15, 2005. He suggested that: first, we should set up a new security concept based on mutual trust, mutual benefit, equality, and collaboration and establish a fair and effective collective security mechanism; second, the UN should take tangible measures to implement the Millennium Development Goals, especially accelerating the development of developing nations and make the twenty-first century "the century of development for everyone" in a real sense; third, we should respect the right of each country to independently choose its social system and development road and support the efforts of countries to realize rejuvenation and growth according to their own national conditions; fourth, we should safeguard the authority of the UN through reasonable and necessary reform, raise the efficiency of the organization and strengthen its capacity to cope with new threats and challenges.[14] These ideas must still be fully theorized, but Chinese scholars are confident that they can be developed into a theory about the rise of Chinese soft power.

To bridge these gaps between philosophy and theory and past and present, Chinese scholars recently began to expand their efforts to theorize international relations from China's viewpoint (Qin 2006; Wang Yiwei 2006). For instance, in the Westphalia system there is a sovereignty–equality–anarchy logic, but in China the logic of world order will be a social order–subordinate–hierarchy, like that found in the traditional tributary system in which the middle kingdom enjoyed the highest position based on its culture and morality while Korea, Vietnam, and so on were subordinates. In this regard, Adam Watson's general theory of international systems seems to me very compatible with the Chinese approach. At least his approach is inclusive enough to accommodate both hierarchical and horizontal systems.[15]

Unfortunately, since these Chinese formulations rely on strong Chinese cultural traditions or characteristics, non-Chinese often find it hard to understand them and much less to accept them as ideas with universal application. When China tries to use the Western language about the rise of China to identify its strategy as Peaceful rise, others just focus on their familiar concept "rise," not what the Chinese intend as their focus: "Peaceful." Partly feeling put off by this rejection and partly facing pressure from many scholars and retired ambassadors who dislike the concept of "Peaceful rise," the Chinese authorities decided finally to use another expression, "Peaceful development," since mid-2004. This reflects China's dilemma very well. The main challenge for the Chinese endeavor to construct the world is to bridge the gap between Chinese and international languages while keeping Chinese characteristics in shaping its own theory.

Conclusions: will China's rise bring the rise of Chinese IR theory?

Chinese *Guoji Guanxi Xue* (IR discipline) is still in a process of transition (Wang Yizhou 2006a). In addition, to talk about Chinese IR theory one cannot neglect the larger situation of the social sciences in China. Only when Chinese social science has developed enough will China have her own IR theory. But the problem is: Will the geo-strategic rise of China necessarily bring with it the rise of a distinctly Chinese social science? So far, the Chinese social sciences have developed mostly by copying, learning, and catching up to the international level and they show little of what might be called Chinese characteristics.

Usually, theories of social science consist of the subject of thought (a person who observes and thinks), an object of thought (something that is observed and thought about), and the environment of thought (worldviews and conditions that shape subjects of thought). For international relations theories, the subject of thought is the theorist. His/her knowledge influences the theory that is produced, but his/her personality, including way of thinking, is even more influential. Moreover, theories reflect the ideas of the authors. Thus, many international relations theories are better identified as "hypotheses" or "arguments" or "perspectives" or "approaches" rather than as theories. International relations theories are also greatly influenced by the general atmosphere of the social sciences, including predominant philosophies of science, sociological theories, and various behavioral studies; thus, they lack an independent epistemology and methodology for themselves. IR theory's vigorous growth in the twentieth century was closely related to the full development of the social sciences more broadly. Many scholars believe that IR theory does not have its own methodology and independent disciplinary philosophy. For instance, constructivism grew up in the U.S. following the development of postmodernism and deconstruction in literature and sociology. Certain historical background factors also shape the views of social scientists, so IR theories from different cultural historical backgrounds are different.

The object of thought of international relations theories is all-inclusive, including each nation and every facet of international affairs. To some extent, the United States has been at the center of international contradictions, so the subject of thought of IR theory has mainly been the United States, which brings the American national identity into the very center of IR theory. In other words, IR theory with American characteristics thinks about what America thinks and worries about what America worries over. This is not only because America is powerful enough to produce theories, but also because of American leadership. American thinking will to some extent reflect the will of the times and current world contradictions such as globalization, emerging global issues, and so on.

The environment of thought is particularly embodied in features of the time. Since globalization is not Westernization or Americanization any more but diversification of the world, non-western schools, including a Chinese School, will come into being along with the rise of countries like the BRICs (Brazil, Russia, India and China: Wang Yiwei 2007b). During the stage of Westernization, the logic of globalization is linear, but during the non-Westernization, even de-Westernization, stage, the logic of globalization will show its diversity. This creates the legal, political, and epistemic space for the rise of Chinese IR theory.

Chinese IR theory is shaped by the personal identity of scholars, the emerging national identity of China, and broader features of the time. I have attempted to capture these factors shaping the evolution of IR in Table 6.2, which also serves to summarize my claims in this chapter. With China's opening, China was no longer veiled from the world and the process of integrating with the world began. As I have described, Chinese IR scholars borrowed IR theories principally from the United States, so a pro-Americanism was the dominant mentality among Chinese IR scholars. Many American theories and methodologies were widely introduced into China. Chinese scholars gradually distanced themselves from American IR and began a more scientific phase of thinking. As China rises we see evidence of Chinese IR taking on the task of constructing the world (Wang Yiwei 2003b). However, the rise of Chinese IR theory is based not only on China's rise (the idea of a Chinese century) but also on Asia's rise (an Asia century). In this context, China can build its IR theory on its changing role from stakeholder to shareholder in the international system. With the rise of China's comprehensive power, Chinese IR theory will serve as one symbol of the growth of Chinese soft power. The possibility of shaping Chinese IR theory also depends on the reunification of Taiwan and the Mainland: "it is hard to construct the Chinese School in IR

Table 6.2 Summary of factors shaping Chinese IR theory

National identity	Feature of the time (relations between China and the world)	Personal identity
To be others	Open to the world (1980s–1990s)	• Representative figure: Ni Shixiong • Paradigm: translation • Characteristics: pro-Americanism
Between others and us	Integrate the world (1990s–2000s)	• Representative figure: Wang Yizhou • Paradigm: theory review • Characteristics: scientism
To be oneself	Construct the world (2001–)	• Representative figure: Qin Yaqing • Paradigm: reflective • Characteristics: humanism

theory without the full reunification of China" (Wang Jisi 2006). The rise of Chinese IR theory also strongly depends on Chinese scholars' consciousness and creativeness and, thus, the total rise of the social sciences in China.

More self-reflective studies are just beginning. An example of this greater self-reflection and confidence came during the period from June 2005 to April 2006 when the editor of China's leading IR journal, *World Economy and Politics*, interviewed ten leading Chinese IR scholars in order to trace their personal identities and explore how their identities shape their IR studies. This was the first time in Chinese IR studies that the focus was the personal identity of a Chinese scholar, not a theorist from the West. Although this group is of roughly similar age, they enjoy very different personal identities and ways of studying IR. Here, personal identity refers not only to the mentalities of individual Chinese IR scholars but also to their connections with politics, including the realities of international relations and the process of Chinese diplomatic decision-making. The diversity among Chinese IR scholars is no less than among American IR scholars.

Chinese scholars look forward to a time that will bring the rise of a Chinese IR theory. Chinese IR scholars feel both puzzled and frustrated by the need to describe Chinese diplomacy in terms set by Western IR theories. Soon, they will be able to express their own feelings in the terms set by their own theories, and especially in expressions that are from China but belong to the world; that is, when Chinese expressions represent the will of our times and human beings, Chinese IR theory will have come into being.

Of course, China's geo-strategic rise will not bring the rise of Chinese IR theory automatically or naturally, but it is very clear that Chinese IR studies have left the stage of copying the West and begun to enter the stage of constructing the world. With the diversification of the world, we will witness stronger and stronger geo-cultural perspectives in IR studies drawing from Chinese experience, including its long civilization. The rise of Chinese IR theory, on the one hand, will seek common ground with Western theories since they all reflect partial truths about the world but, on the other hand, will restore Western IR to the status of local theories.

Notes

1   I am grateful to Professors Arlene Tickner, Ole Wæver, and David Blaney for their editorial assistance.
2   Institutionally, six systems jointly constitute the mainstay of IR studies in China: (1) the State Council system, represented by the China Institute of International Studies (http://www.ciis.org.cn/en/index.asp) and the China Institute of Contemporary International Relations (http://www.cicir.ac.cn/en/); (2) the system of the Chinese Academy of Social Sciences (http://www.cass.net.cn/index.html) and the Shanghai Academy of Social Sciences (http://english.sass.org.cn/); (3) the system of the national defense establishment, notably the research institutes at the National Defense University and the Academy of Military Science; (4) the university system that includes, for example, Peking University's School of International Studies (http://www/sis.pku.edu.cn/english/); Remin University's School of International Studies (http://sis.ruc.edu.cn/index/index_english.asp); Fudan University's School of International and Public Affairs (http://www.sirpa.fudan.edu.cn/en/), or Institute of International Studies (http://iis.fudan.edu.cn/); China Foreign Affairs University (http://www.cfau.edu.cn/cfauEN/index.html), and Tsinghua University's Institute of International Studies (http://rwxy.tsinghua.edu.cn/xi-suo/institute/index1.htm); (5) the Communist Party School system, represented by the Institute of International Strategic Studies at the Central Party School; and (6) the news media system, with the Center for World Politics affiliated with Xinhua News Agency being the strongest. See Wang Jisi (2002: 107) and Shambaugh (2002). See also the website organized by Nankai University, Tianjin: http://www.irchina.org/en/xueke/inchina/jigou.asp. In an attempt to connect Chinese scholars as they construct the world, the China National Association for International Studies (CNAIS) was revived in 2004 (after a 24-year hiatus). Chinese

State Councilor Tang Jiaxuan, the top leader in charge of foreign affairs in China, was elected as the president of the association. The president and vice-president of Chinese Foreign Affairs University Wu Jianmin and Qin Yaqing were elected as executive president and secretary general respectively. The association holds annual conferences usually at the end of each year in which they build a platform for scholars and officers to communicate with each other. But more important is the practice of the State Council in organizing periodic meetings on strategic issues about which Chinese leaders feel puzzled. The scholars debate both among themselves and with the officials.

3 Since China began the market economy reforms in 1992, competition has been the main theme in IR studies. Until now, IR studies have not been as tightly organized institutionally as is usual. There is no internal coherence, hierarchy, division of labor in Chinese institutes but it is shaped by the geo-cultural factor, for instance, Yunan University and Academy of Social Sciences are good at ASEAN studies while Sichuan University and Academy of Social Sciences are good at South Asian studies. Scholars shape the identity of the institutions, not just the institutions shape the scholar since more and more institutes have been established in recent years. Scholars change positions more frequently than before. This is different for scholars in political sciences (including IR) who are divided politically as left–right, new left–right.

4 The Five Principles are: mutual respect for sovereignty and territorial integrity, mutual non-aggression, non-interference in each other's internal affairs, equality and mutual benefit, and peaceful co-existence, which have been adopted in many other international documents and have become widely accepted as norms for relations between countries, which are also partly enshrined in UN Charter and documents.

5 Experience studies and issue-oriented approaches often take the English School as the model. For instance, Professor Shi Yinghong, Renmin University, focuses on grand strategy, drawing on the experience of Great Britain to serve today's Chinese grand strategy. Professor Song Xinning, Renmin University, and myself are members of the British International Studies Association (BISA). Professor Barry Buzan also included me in his English School group. China can probably learn more from the English School than from American IR theory since China enjoys more historical and cultural similarities with the UK than the U.S. In addition, the English School is more open to the idea of variations between different international systems that can accommodate non-Westphalian politics. See Zhang Yongjin (2003) on the influence of the English School in China.

6 Particularly those interested in diplomacy take Chinese history and traditions as the model. For example, Professor Ye Zicheng focuses on the traditional Chinese international system, especially the spring and autumn period (770–476 BC), while Professor Niu Jun conducts research on the diplomacy of the Chinese Communist Party since Yan'an.

7 The scientific studies approach takes American IR theory as the model. Professor Yan Xuetong from Tshingua University is taking the leading role in this field. He is the chief editor of a new journal, *Guoji Zhengzhi Kexue* (Chinese Journal of International Politics).

8 As we can see from the above, this contrast probably has much deeper historical roots than Geerarts and Jing suggest, but theirs is an accurate picture of the current situation.

9 The Chinese character 天 means sky. 下 means under, down. 天下 together, literally means under the sky. The word 天下, besides the literal meaning, is also taken by Chinese as the only way to refer to the whole world. In this context then, it may perhaps be best understood and translated as "Everything Under the Heavens." Only in modern times has the term 世界 (*shì jiè*) come into use to directly refer to the world. In classical Chinese political thought, the Emperor of China would nominally be the ruler All-under-Heaven; that is, the entire world. Although in practice there would be areas of the known world which were not under the control of the Emperor, in Chinese political theory the political rulers of those areas derived their power from the Emperor.

10 《道德经/54章》: "以身观身, 以家观家, 以乡观乡, 以邦观邦, 以天下观天下".
[Therefore just as through oneself one may contemplate Oneself, So through the household one may contemplate the Household, And through the village, one may contemplate the Village, And through the kingdom, one may contemplate the Kingdom, And through the empire, one may contemplate the Empire.] (Lao Zi).

11 The Chinese concept \" 事 \" is defined as \"what has been done\," very close to the Western word *factum*. See Huainanzi: What has to be followed is the Way, and what has been done is the facts. 《淮南子/氾论》: "所由曰道, 所为曰事".

12 The general heart of people means public opinion.

13   China's Position Paper on the New Security Concept.
     See http://www.china-un.org/eng/xw/t27742.htm.
14   Hu Jintao delivered an important speech at the UN Summit 2005/09/16.
     See http://www.fmprc.gov.cn/eng/wjdt/zyjh/t212614.htm.
15   I appreciate Professor Ole Wæver's reminder in this regard.

References

Callahan, William A. (2001) "China and the Globalization of IR Theory: Discussion of 'Building International Relations Theory with Chinese Characteristics'," *Journal of Contemporary China,* 10 (26): 75–88.

Geeraerts, Gustaaf and Men Jing (2001) "International Relations Theory in China," *Global Society: Journal of Interdisciplinary International Relations*, 15 (3): 251–276.

Johnston, Alastair Iain (2002) "The State of International Relations Research in China: Considerations for the Ford Foundation," in Ford Foundation, *International Relations in China: A Review of Ford Foundation Past Grant-Making and Future Choices.*

Lakatos, Imre (1978) *The Methodology of Scientific Research Programmes: Philosophical Papers*, Volume I, Cambridge: Cambridge University Press.

Lao-zi, see Tsu Lao.

Li Bin (2005) "What is Marxist IR Theory?", *World Economics and Politics*, 5: 37–44.

Li Yihu (2005) "On the Ontology of IR Theory: From Western Theory to Chinese Theory," *Studies of International Politics*, 1: 30–35.

Li Zong, Liu Guoping, and Tan Xiuying (1999) "Fifty Years of Chinese IR Studies," *World Economy and Politics*, 2: 5–15.

Liang Qichao (1901) "Zhongguo-shi Xulun" (An Introduction to Chinese History), *Yingbing Wenji*, 6: 1–116.

Liang Shoude (1994) "International Politics with Chinese Characteristics," *Studies of International Politics*, 1: 15–21.

Liang Shoude (2005) "Reflects on Disciplinary Construction of the International Politics in China," *Henan Social Sciences*, 1: 1–6.

Lu Peng (2006) "Analysis and Assessment on Four Approaches in Building up Chinese IR Theory," *World Economics and Politics*, 6: 52–59.

Mei Ran (2000) "Should it Be Chinese School in International Politics Theory?," *Studies of International Politics*, 1: 63–67.

Qin Yaqing (2005) "Theoretical Problematic of International Relationship Theory and the Construction of a Chinese School," *Social Sciences in China*, 3: 165–176.

Qin Yaqing (2006) "A Chinese School of International Relations Theory: Possibility and Inevitability," *World Economics and Politics*, 3: 7–13.

Shambaugh, David (2002) "China's International Relations Think Tanks: Evolving Structure and Process," *The China Quarterly*, 171: 575–596.

Shanghai Association of International Relations (eds) (1991) *Guoji Guanxi Lilun Chutan* (*Preliminary Inquiry into International Relations Theory*), Shanghai: Shanghai Foreign Language Education Press.

Song Xingning (2001) "Building International Relations Theory with Chinese Characteristics," *Journal of Contemporary China Studies*, 10 (26): 61–74.

Su Changhe (2005) "Why There is no Chinese IR Theory?," *International Survey*, 2: 26–30.

Tsu Lao (1989 [3rd–4th century BC]) *Tao Te Ching*, trans. Gia-Fu Feng and Jane English, New York: Vintage Books.

Walt, Stephen M. (1998) "International Relations: One World, Many Theories," *Foreign Policy*, 110 (spring): 29–46.

Wang Jisi (ed.) (1995) *Civilization and International Politics: Chinese Scholars' Debates on Clashes of Civilizations*, Shanghai: Shanghai People's Press.

Wang Jisi (2002) "International Relations Studies in China Today: Achievements, Trends, and Conditions: A Report to the Ford Foundation," in Ford Foundation, *International Relations in China: A Review of Ford Foundation Past Grant-making and Future Choices.*

Wang Jisi (2006) "A Humanitarian Scholar Who Makes a Point of Applying Theory to Reality," *World Economics and Politics*, 1: 55–60.

Wang Yiwei (2002) "Comparative Studies of International Relations and the Possible Chinese School in International Relations Theories," *Open Times*, 5: 17–23.

Wang Yiwei (2003a) "The End of International Relations Theories and the Rise of Chinese School", Paper presented at the annual meeting of the International Studies Association (ISA), Portland, OR, February 25 to March 1.

Wang Yiwei (2003b) "On National Identity of International Relations Theory," *American Studies Quarterly*, 4: 22–41.

Wang Yiwei (2004) "Why There is no Chinese International Relations Theory," *World Economics and Politics*, 1: 21–22.

Wang Yiwei (2006) "Seeking Chinese New Identity: the Myth of Chinese Nationalism," paper presented at the annual meeting of the International Studies Association (ISA), San Diego, CA, March 22–25 (see also *World Economics and Politics*, 2006 (2): 1–13).

Wang Yiwei (2007a) "Between Science and Art: Questionable International Relations Theories," *Japanese Journal of Political Science*, 8: 191–208.

Wang Yiwei (2007b) "The International Political Meaning of Co-rising of China and India: From Geopolitics Paradigm to Universal Harmony Paradigm," *International Survey*, 4: 10–18.

Wang Yiwei (2007c) "On National Identity of International Relations Theory: A Chinese Perspective," *ICFAI Journal of International Relations*, 1 (1): 7–24.

Wang Yiwei (2007d) "On Theorization of International Relations," *World Economics and Politics*, 4: 19–25.

Wang Yizhou (1995) *Dangdai Guoji Zhengzhi Xilun* (Analysis of Contemporary International Politics), Shanghai: Shanghai People's Publishing House.

Wang Yizhou (2006a) "Chinese IR Studies in Transition," *World Economy and Politics*, 4: 7–12.

Wang Yizhou (ed.) (2006b) *Zhongguo Guoji Guanxi Xue: 1995–2005* (*IR in China: 1995–2005*), Peking: Peking University Press.

Ye Zicheng (2005) "On China's Perspective in IR Studies," *Foreign Affairs Review*, 3: 64–71.

Yu Zhengliang (2005) "Constructing Chinese IR Theory, Building up Chinese School," *Journal of Shanghai Jiaotong University*, 4: 5–8.

Zhang Baijia (2002) "Gaibian Ziji Yingxiang Shijie" (Changing Thyself, Influencing Thy World), *Social Sciences in China*, 1: 4–19.

Zhang Yongjin (2003) "The 'English School' in China: A Travelogue of Ideas and their Diffusion," *European Journal of International Relations*, 9 (1): 87–114.

Zhao Kejin and Ni Shixiong (2006) *Zhongguo Guoji Guanxi Lilun Yanjiu* (*Studies on Chinese IR Theories*), Shanghai: Fudan University Press.

Zhao Tingyang (2005) *Tianxia System (All-Under-Heaven): Introduction to the Philosophy of World Institutions*, Nanjing: Jiangshu Higher Education Publishing House.

Zhao Tingyang (2006) "Rethinking Empire from a Chinese Concept 'All-Under-Heaven' (*Tian-xia*)," *Social Identities*, 12 (1): 29–41.

Zhao Tingyang (n.d.) "A Philosophical Analysis of World/Empire in Terms of All-under-Heaven," *Transcultural Series of Le Robert*, Vol.1: *Empire and Peace*, Part 2, available at http://www.frchina.net/data/personArticle.php?id=83.

Zi Zhongyun (ed.) (1998) *Guoji Zhengzhi Lilun Tansuo Zai Zhonguo* (*International Politics Theory Exploration in China*), Shanghai: Shanghai People's Publishing House.

7 Southeast Asia
Theory and praxis in International Relations

See Seng Tan

If modernity consists partly in mimetic reliance (or mimicry) on Western ideas and modalities, then the widespread emulation of Anglo-American methodologies in academic scholarship on the International Relations of Southeast Asia could probably be appreciated as an indication of the attempts by the region's articulators at "modernization." Such mimetic performance during the Cold War years generally assumed the form of an epistemic realism that had neither need nor tolerance for International Relations (IR) theory, although exceptions to the rule of course existed. However, the field has been gravitating, shortly before and through the post-Cold War period, toward more systematic engagements with formal theory. This shift has arisen as a result of growing interest in Southeast Asian regionalism, along with a commensurate interest among regional analysts in IR theory and its perceived relevance to the formal study of Southeast Asian international relations. As some would have it, the emerging consensus regarding the contemporary state of the theoretical enterprise of Southeast Asian International Relations is that it pivots on a realist–constructivist axis (Peou 2002; Eaton and Stubbs 2006). Again, as in Cold War Southeast Asian IR, the post-Cold War oeuvre also has its fair share of exceptions.

The aim of this chapter is to explore the social, institutional, and intellectual contexts that have facilitated the evolution of Southeast Asian International Relations (SEAIR) as a field of study. The premise here is that mimetic reliance amounts to a kind of "auto-orientalism" that permeates much of the field. Crucially, the SEAIR discipline, both in its Cold War and post-Cold War incarnations, could be apprehended as a kind of corporate institution established for managing, and thereby constructing, the Southeast Asian region by issuing statements about it, sanctioning views of it, describing and teaching it, settling or domesticating it, and of course "policing" it (Said 1979; Pettman 1998). However, the SEAIR enterprise is not a passive acquiescence to Western ideological caricatures of Southeast Asian international politics. For instance, the irreverence which many SEAIR analysts maintained toward theories of international security and political economy during the Cold War years revolved around the consensus that formal theory held little relevance for understanding, much less explaining Southeast Asian affairs (Emmerson 1987). More recently, taking on a series of influential and predominantly pessimistic Western accounts of post-Cold War Asia as an unstable and dangerous region (Betts 1993/1994; Buzan and Segal 1994; Friedberg 1993/1994; Dibb *et al.* 1999), recent studies argue instead that those Western academics had gotten their facts on Asia, including Southeast Asia, wrong (Acharya 2003/2004; Alagappa 2003; Kang 2003).

As such, the orientalism that inheres in SEAIR includes both resistive and accommodative aspects with respect to Anglo-American IR theory. Tensions exist in the efforts of regional scholars to exercise a measure of agency in their engagement with theory. The first part of the chapter examines the evolving social and institutional features of the SEAIR enterprise. The second part focuses on three particular tensions that animate contemporary SEAIR discourse.

Pedagogy, personages, and parameters

For the most part, academic practices in most postcolonial societies of the developing world have traditionally reflected ambivalence toward formal theory and the pervasive influence of a robust epistemic realism (Rosenau 1993). Such predispositions have equally affected the views of many first-generation SEAIR analysts, not least the staff of leading university departments, think-tanks, and research institutes throughout the Southeast Asian region. Not surprisingly, academic centers in the "older" ASEAN (Association of Southeast Asian Nations) members boast of more established traditions of research and scholarship compared to their "CLMV" (Cambodia, Laos, Myanmar, Vietnam) counterparts in the Association, whose long experiences with communism, totalitarianism, and/or isolationism left their societies with severely depleted academic and intellectual resources, not least institutions and analysts of international affairs.

Among the older ASEAN member countries, the political science, International Relations, and/or diplomatic history departments of the University of Indonesia, the University of Malaya (and, more recently, the University Kebangsaan Malaysia), the National University of Singapore (formerly the University of Singapore), the University of the Philippines and De La Salle University in the Philippines, and the Thai universities of Chulalongkorn and Thammasat, among others, have served as the region's intellectual crucibles for home-grown talent in security research. Arguably, these institutions pale in comparison with the Institute of Southeast Asian Studies (ISEAS), whose reputation as the region's premier producer and purveyor of SEAIR knowledge is well earned (Langford and Brownsey 1991; Yamamoto 1995). Based in Singapore, the ISEAS has since the 1970s up until the present attracted scores of prominent and upcoming analysts from Asia and beyond, whose scholarship has helped make the ISEAS imprint a notable force in the world of academic publishing. More recently, the Rajaratnam School of International Studies, a Singapore-based graduate school dedicated primarily to the study of international affairs and a first of its kind in Southeast Asia, has emerged as an alternative hub of SEAIR research. Indeed, so apparent has been the influence of these institutions in shaping the regional discourse of SEAIR that both the ISEAS and the RSIS have on occasion been criticized, fairly or otherwise, for having contributed to the perceived parochialism and provincialism of the SEAIR discipline (Jayasuriya 1994; Jones and Smith 2001a).

Many if not most of *l'éminences grises* of SEAIR studies from Southeast Asia – Muthiah Alagappa, Dewi Fortuna Anwar, Carolina Hernandez, Kusuma Snitwongse, Chan Heng Chee, Chin Kin Wah, the current ASEAN secretary-general Surin Pitsuwan, and many others – received their graduate training principally in Australian, British, and U.S. tertiary institutions. The same is generally true of the subsequent generation of analysts and scholars from the region.[1] The field of SEAIR includes those from outside the region who have made the international relations of Southeast Asia the focus of their study.[2] Chief among these would be the crucial group of prominent scholars who helped define the parameters and terms of SEAIR. For example, the late Michael Leifer had an inordinate amount of influence on successive generations of not only analysts but also practitioners of Southeast Asian countries. Other eminent long-time scholars of Southeast Asia – notably North American scholars such as Bernard Gordon, George Kahin, Donald Weatherbee, Donald Emmerson, and Clark Neher, among others – have equally exerted an impact on scholars of SEAIR from within or without the region.

Finally, it should be noted that the SEAIR enterprise is fed not only by purely academic sources, but by non-official "policy" sources as well (Evans 1994; Hernandez 1994; Simon 1996; Ball 2000; Katsumata 2003b). In this respect, another crucible of professional training is the collection of policy institutes, such as Indonesia's Centre for Strategic and International Studies (CSIS) and Malaysia's Institute of Strategic and International Studies (ISIS), that comprise the so-called "second-track" (or Track 2) regional epistemic community, which emerged in the late 1980s and grew significantly in the 1990s. In response to the perceived challenges of the security and economic environment of post-Cold War Southeast Asia, these institutes came together to form regional Track 2 networks such as the ASEAN–ISIS (Institute of Strategic and International Studies), the CSCAP (Council for Security Cooperation in Asia-Pacific), and the PECC (Pacific Economic Cooperation Council). Importantly, the emergence of concepts such as "cooperative security" and "open regionalism" may be partly attributed to the work of these policy networks (Dewitt 1994; Hassan and Ramnath 1996; Dickens 1997; Morrison 2004). By the same token, it is also their predominantly empirical contributions that form a link, if only tenuous, with the a-theoretical SEAIR enterprise of the Cold War years (Alagappa 2003). Be that as it may, it is through their participation in the regional Track 2 community that state-sponsored think-tanks from the newer ASEAN countries, such as the Cambodian Institute for Cooperation and Peace and Vietnam's Institute for International Relations, are fast emerging as places for nurturing analytical talent in mainland Southeast Asia.

SEAIR's theoretical turn?

SEAIR discourse after the Cold War reflects a greater openness to formal theory. Various factors conceivably account for this "theoretical turn," as it were, not least the diminished salience of Cold War thinking, the rise of ASEAN as a force in Asian regionalism, the apparent emergence of the Asia-Pacific as the future epicenter of global economic and political power, and the continued premium placed by many Southeast Asians (particularly budding social scientists!) on an Anglo-American tertiary education. As noted earlier, contemporary SEAIR analysts, not unlike their predecessors, are mostly Western-trained. The professional expectation heaped on academics to regularly publish their research in ranking peer-reviewed English-language publications and university presses has led many to take formal theory and methodology seriously, particularly if they hope to publish in academic journals such as *International Security*, *International Organization*, and *Review of International Studies*. Hence, despite the oft-heard insistence that Southeast Asian international relations or ASEAN regionalism is distinct from that of the West, the increasing reliance on Anglo-American epistemology and method in the study of SEAIR amounts essentially to an inordinate dependence on shared terms of reference, conceptual categories, and theoretical language. Southeast Asian affairs may indeed be distinct, but the growing congruence if not convergence wrought by the theoretical turn could mean analysts are by default "obliged to read the same story everywhere" (Barthes 1974: 15–16).

The notion of mimetic reliance implies that there is little about extant and emerging theorizing in SEAIR that is remotely indigenous or "whose provenance lies outside Europe or North America" (Mandaville 2003: 211; Crawford and Jarvis 2000; Smith 2000). If anything, the formal study of SEAIR demonstrates a persistent indebtedness to Western categories, norms, and terms of reference. For instance, two prominent scholars have lamented the dearth of an indigenous Asian IR theory (Acharya and Buzan 2007). To be sure, SEAIR has not been fully domesticated by a hegemonic discourse. Nor has its formal study been essentially simplistic and one-dimensional. Quite the contrary, the field is animated by particular tensions that parallel intellectual developments in the wider IR discipline. At the same time, those tensions arguably betray an inherent proclivity within the field for Western-influenced redactions of local knowledge that would accommodate the latter's growing appropriation of IR theory and its categories.

Historically and contemporarily, those tensions have been manifest in at least three broad areas. The first has to do with the debate over the enterprise's purported engagements with Anglo-American IR theory. The second has to do with the apparent emulation or reproduction within SEAIR of Western epistemological-cum-methodological approaches and parameters that help define the field. Third, there is the issue of whether SEAIR scholars behave more like Gramsci's traditional intellectuals who promote and preserve the interests of their political masters – in this instance, the ruling regimes of Southeast Asian countries – than organic intellectuals who serve as agents of emancipation and as the social-cum-political consciences in and of their societies. Here attention will focus on the complex relationship between Southeast Asian states and their respective intellectual communities.

Theory and SEAIR

Historically, SEAIR had little to do with IR theory given the poor fit between "Asian data" and Western theory and expectations. However, the traditional predisposition against theory has, since the end of the Cold War, been gradually supplemented (though not supplanted) by a greater appreciation for and deeper engagement with theory due to several reasons. The first has to do with the removal of the Cold War political imaginary that captivated intellectual thought and affected academic funding in SEAIR study. A second reason is the rising interest in Southeast Asian regionalism, particularly ASEAN and other Asia-wide processes. Third, the growing Americanization of IR study worldwide has affected patterns of scholarship and postgraduate education on Southeast Asian international relations and international political economy.

As noted, many SEAIR analysts writing in and about the Cold War era, whether native to Southeast Asia or based in the West, more or less share in a postcolonial ambivalence toward formal theory. Given the way in which Western and particularly American IR theories root themselves in Western philosophical traditions and debates, the relevance of Western theoretical constructs to understanding Asian calculations and behavior is not immediately apparent (Ikenberry and Mastanduno 2003: 2). In this vein the late K.S. Sandhu, an eminent observer of regional affairs, noted that he and his fellow students of SEAIR have historically understood their work as primarily involving the recognition of prevailing reality as it actually is, and assiduously avoided turning their field of study into "philosophical, methodological, disciplinary, or missionary constructs" (Sandhu 1992: 229).

To be sure, the writings of Kahin (1956) make reference to concepts such as "regionalism," while those of Leifer (1989) or Simon (1982) discuss ASEAN in terms of the "balance of power" and "regional order." On a more ambitious note, Jørgensen-Dahl's 1982 study of ASEAN explicitly employs the categories of "regional organization" and regional order. But more often than not, these scholars had little if any interest in systematic theory testing and empirical theorizing, treating such issues as modes of Western political and cultural imperialism (Rosenau 1993). The fact that IR scholars of Cold War Southeast Asia have traditionally treated their research in largely empiricist terms underscores the primacy of a "policy-relevant" focus in SEAIR – and, by implication, the perception that formal theorizing is essentially an ivory-tower endeavor with little to no bearing on real-world concerns (Jentleson 2002). In a sense, this empiricist disposition has its contemporary incarnation in the policy research of the Track 2 communities. In both instances (academic and policy communities), scholarship is informed by an epistemic realism, which views the social world as consisting in subjects and objects the existence of which is independent of ideas or beliefs about them (Campbell 1998).

Another factor that could conceivably explain the intellectual incommensurability of Cold War SEAIR with IR theory has to do with the then nascent statehood of Southeast Asian countries and their principal preoccupation with internal security considerations, which formal theories, replete with assumptions and propositions that better fit mature states in the Western mold, arguably do not accommodate (Ayoob 1988). If at all, early analysts of SEAIR demonstrated greater affinity for nationalism, nation-building and developmentalism than specific IR theories in framing their discussions of Cold War Southeast Asian affairs (Gordon 1966; Leifer 1972). In this sense, the continued salience of sovereignty and non-intervention/non-interference principles in SEAIR discourse is a measure of their perceived relevance to a region still grappling with territorial disputes and bilateral tensions, despite regional aspirations toward the building of the "ASEAN Community." For instance, recent scholarship has focused on how Southeast Asia's postcolonial societies have had to learn to behave as normal states through localizing sovereignty and non-interference norms (Acharya 2004). In this respect, post-Cold War studies on third world IR have begun preliminary theorizing that better fits the developing regions of the world, including Southeast Asia (Jackson 1990; Neuman 1998).

To the extent that Cold War SEAIR reflected any rudimentary sensitivity toward IR theory, it would likely be found (as noted earlier) in ambivalent references to power balancing, regional order, and the like. In this regard, for a region purportedly unworthy of theoretical reflection, students of Cold War SEAIR arguably adopted *realist* presuppositions, if only implicitly. For example, the writings of Brecher (1963), Colbert (1977), Gordon (1966), Gurtov (1977), and Leifer (1989) could easily be accommodated within a realist framework. Indeed, work which was institutionalist in orientation, such as those of Jørgensen-Dahl (1982) and Rajendran (1985), could arguably be seen as befitting the realist tradition, if only because of their concessions to the incessant sway of power politics and interstate rivalries among Southeast Asian nations (Collins 2000). Importantly, the realism here is more in line with the traditionalism of Hans Morgenthau or the English School of Hedley Bull and Martin Wight, the latter which had considerable influence on, say, Leifer's views on Southeast Asian regionalism (Emmers 2003a; Khong 2005; Narine 2006). Thus understood, despite the apparent disinterest in formal theory and theorizing in Cold War SEAIR, the existence therein of a sort of "pre-theoretical" appropriation of IR concepts (coupled with the salience of epistemic realism referred to earlier) could arguably be seen as *theoretical* insofar as its tacit predispositions and implicit assumptions about regional life in the Southeast Asian context are already significantly informed by a realist-oriented ontology (Chong 2007).

If Cold War SEAIR was largely characterized by a lack of engagement with formal theory, then post-Cold War SEAIR reflects a growing appreciation for the latter. While the trend's antecedents do not neatly coincide with the ending of the Cold War, the intellectual opening afforded by that crucial political development as well as a growing interest in Southeast Asian regionalism encouraged a redefinition of the concept of security and a concomitant expansion of a post-Cold War security agenda (Dewitt 1994; Woods 1997; Cheng 2006). Incipient regionalisms such as the ASEAN Regional Forum, the Asia-Pacific Economic Cooperation (APEC), and the ASEAN Plus Three facilitated efforts by SEAIR scholars to apply formal theory to their study of regional security and regional political economy. Bereft of Cold War politics, the growing significance of East and Southeast Asia as the most economically vibrant regions in the world – temporarily slowed by the regional financial crisis in 1997 – encouraged IR analysts to theorize about regional economic and security cooperation (Emmers 2003a, 2003b; Nesadurai 2003; Caballero-Anthony 2005; Acharya and Tan 2006; Goh 2007), regional identity (Acharya 2000), international regime-building (Mack and Ravenhill 1995; Dent 2003), and regional community formation (Simon 1995; Acharya 2001; Acharya and Stubbs 2006).

Moreover, growing awareness of the robust link between development, economic prosperity, and political–military security in Southeast Asia impacted upon by global forces has helped to stimulate the theoretical enterprise (Simon and Emmerson 1996; Collins 2000; Beeson 2003; Dosch 2007). By the same token, these efforts to conceptualize a wider regionalism beyond Southeast Asia – attested to by the regional discourse on Asia-Pacific security and East Asia Community, among other regional idioms (Tan 2007a) – cast a pall over SEAIR through their inadvertent subversions of Southeast Asia's "regionness," as it were (Huxley 1996).

Amid all the contemporary fascination with Anglo-American theory, a particularly interesting development has been the emerging theoretical "debate" between realist renditions of SEAIR, on the one hand, and constructivist interpretations on the other. In the immediate aftermath of the post-Cold War period, a series of influential neorealist statements on post-Cold War Asia portrayed the region as unstable and dangerous, not unlike Europe in the nineteenth century (Betts 1993/1994; Buzan and Segal 1994; Friedberg 1993/1994; Dibb *et al.* 1999). In riposte to these and extant traditionalist readings of Southeast Asian international politics, a growing coterie of constructivist scholars have raised objections against the predominantly materialist-cum-power-oriented interpretations of their realist counterparts. Following the intellectual lead provided by Amitav Acharya, scholars such as Ba (2006), Haacke (2003), Narine (2002), and Katsumata (2003a, 2004) argue the relative salience of ideational, normative, and cultural factors in Southeast Asian regionalism, particularly the regional institution of ASEAN. Their rising influence in SEAIR has been such that some have taken to describing the field as dominated by "constructivist orthodoxy" (Khoo 2004: 45). This has led to allusions of an emerging realist–constructivist axis in SEAIR (Peou 2002; Eaton and Stubbs 2006) – an idea that follows closely mainstream consensus in the contemporary IR debate (Katzenstein *et al.* 1998). The notion of a two-dimensional axis is further complicated by a growing number of critical theoretical contributions to SEAIR (Bellamy 2004; Caballero-Anthony 2005; Tan 2006).

Interestingly, these theoretical efforts are usually content to distinguish the efforts of their predecessors as not only lacking in theory but largely realist in orientation, if only to differentiate them from their own contributions. For that matter, critical contributions fare no better either insofar as their reliance on Southeast Asian realism as a point of departure is concerned. But non-realists are not the only ones who do so, since realists are equally if not more liable to do the same, as a way of laying claim to the ostensible existence of a long tradition of realist scholarship. More recently, Michael Leifer's writings, lauded by many as the quintessence of realist SEAIR research, have been subjected to close scrutiny for possible theoretical understandings that could have motivated Leifer's work (Liow and Emmers 2006). Further, several newly released efforts also highlight contemporary SEAIR as a domain more or less amenable to theoretical reflection and innovation (Acharya and Stubbs

2006). That said, these works reinforce a long-held Western bias regarding theory, no matter whether their preferred theoretical lens is realist, constructivist, or critical.

Method and SEAIR

A second broad consideration has to do with the evolving methodology in the formal study of SEAIR. As noted earlier, the epistemological-cum-methodological character of Cold War SEAIR has primarily been shaped by the intellectual, political, and strategic preponderance of the Cold War political imaginary, the traditional disciplinary emphasis on diplomatic/international history and area studies over that of IR in many of the region's institutions of higher learning, and the tacit predisposition to look to the West for guidance. In this regard, SEAIR is not entirely unlike other academic IR enterprises during the Cold War, particularly those sponsored by Western foundations and trusts (such as the Ford Foundation and the Asia Foundation) and Western governments, where historiography, ethnography, and comparative political science approaches had a fair bit of influence over country and region studies (Walt 1991). This is not to imply that the graduate education received by students of Cold War SEAIR lacked theoretical content, but that the perceived irrelevance of these predominantly IR concepts and categories to SEAIR had a likely impact on the preference for research methods with a longer heritage and greater local standing.

The post-Cold War turn to formal IR theory in SEAIR is in a sense indicative of the Southeast Asian region coming into its own as a place with a pattern of regional dynamics worthy of analytical reflection. As noted, this in no way constitutes a supplanting of historiography and ethnography, but a supplementing of these methods. For example, recent studies emphasize the efficacy of analytically diverse and interdisciplinary approaches to the study of Asian IR (Alagappa 2003; Tan and Acharya 2008).

Further, the analytical diversity that characterizes the SEAIR enterprise has raised questions over whether the field reflects rationalist or reflectivist suppositions (Keohane 1988; Walker 1989). As noted above, along with the proclivity to read Cold War SEAIR as essentially tacit exercises in realism, is an evident readiness to associate it with the tradition-alism of the English School. As such, neorealist renditions of post-Cold War SEAIR have been readily viewed by some as methodologically rationalist, which hints at emulation and hence the uncritical transplantation of some of the theoretical problems associated with the positivism of mainstream IR theory into SEAIR (Tan 2006, 2007a). The realist–constructivist axis that supposedly demarcates SEAIR calls to mind the rationalism–constructivism axis in IR (Katzenstein *et al.* 1998). As a consequence of this similarity, the squaring off between realism and constructivism, described in one instance as "the key intellectual competitors" in SEAIR (Peou 2002), has created the largely erroneous impression that most constructivist contributions could therefore be considered reflectivist in orientation, not least because they take rationalism to task for its problematic treatment of interests and identities as essentially given. For example, Acharya (2001: 22) has held that constructivism, in contrast to "rationalist" and "utility-maximizing" theories, offers a "more qualitatively deeper view of how institutions may affect and transform state interests and behavior." Thus understood, one is left to conclude that constructivism is therefore, as it were, the opposite of rationalism.

Nevertheless, this view is problematic, not least because of the equally fallacious con-clusion allowed by it, namely that realist SEAIR is thereby all rationalist. For his part, Peou (2002) seems to suggest this, since the object of his attention as the archetype of realist SEAIR scholarship is none other than the oeuvre of Michael Leifer (with that of Acharya as his preferred paragon of constructivist scholarship). Yet seldom if ever have Leifer's writings come close to aping the pseudo-scientism of neorealist interventions; their roots, as noted earlier, are better found in the English School tradition (Haacke 2005; Khong 2005; Tan 2005). And if rendering rationalism and realism as synonymous with one another smacks of crass reductionism, the same may also be said of constructivist contributions to SEAIR since most tend to reveal rather robust rationalist biases even as they claim to challenge key rationalist assumptions (Tan 2005). Indeed, that many SEAIR constructivists ultimately hew to rationalist grounds despite their best efforts underscores the view that constructivism "has shown convincingly that one does not have to swallow the contaminated epistemological water of postmodernism in order to enjoy the heady ontological wine of constructivism" (Keohane 2000: 129).

To be sure, the caricature by particular redactors of the field as primarily divided between realism/rationalism and constructivism does not take away from the fact that reflectivist SEAIR exists, particularly in the form of critical, feminist, and/or post-positivist works (Burke and McDonald 2007; Tan 2007a). Prompted by a shared dissatisfaction over the inveterate (and, in their view, injurious) dominance of the field by realist contributions, and the less-than-gratifying rejoinders from constructivist interventions, these critical efforts seek alternative lines of inquiry that have either been discounted or dismissed by the former. Nevertheless, their unapologetic appropriations of principally Western-originated ideas and modalities are as equally mimetic as their rationalist colleagues' emulation of Western epistemological-cum-methodological traditions. There are of course important exceptions; take, for example, Pettman's 2005 explorations on the implications of Taoist ideas on security, or others' efforts to transgress if not transcend Western IR. But whether a vibrant form of "indigeny" will truly take root in SEAIR remains to be seen.

Conscience and SEAIR

A final tension within SEAIR has to do with the apparent forfeiture by its participants of their privilege of critique and ostensible role as the region's intellectual and political conscience (Jones and Smith 2002). A key part of SEAIR during the 1980s and the 1990s is the lionizing of ASEAN by scholars as a paragon of third world regionalism, one decidedly distinct from Western patterns of economic and security development (Acharya 2000, 2001). Owing to reasons ranging from the purportedly dubious quality of the ASEAN brand of institutionalism to its alleged support for authoritarianism in the region, scholarly contributions which affirmed Southeast Asian regionalism – and, more recently, ASEAN counter-terrorism co-operation – became suspect in the view of some critics of that regional institution (Hamilton-Hart 2005; Jones and Smith 2007). In this respect, SEAIR is viewed by its detractors as a seriously flawed discourse, whose participants are disparagingly described as "scholar-bureaucrats" who flatteringly but fallaciously portray ASEAN as "the basis of a new regional identity and dispensation" (Jones and Smith 2001a: 844). According to these critics, ASEAN is full of talk but empty of substance and, importantly, intellectually supported and politically endorsed by the scholars who study it (Jones and Smith 2001b).

According to this reasoning, as an enterprise that provides the requisite ideological-cum-cultural ballast for political authoritarianism, SEAIR has served "to codify existing practices rather than to initiate new forms of order" and to legitimate existing and quite reprehensible political practices (Krasner 1993: 238). Do students of SEAIR speak truth to power? Do they maintain the delicate balance between intellectual orthodoxy and openness to critique and new ideas? The answer is that they clearly do not, not because they cannot but that they would not (Tan 2007b). To be sure, protests against such charges of political subservience exist, although few would argue that particular individual scholars could conceivably have, and if only inadvertently, spoken power to truth rather than the other way round (Jayasuriya 1994; Wong 1995). In doing so SEAIR participants are not unlike Gramsci's traditional intellectuals who promote elite discourse and interests. On the other hand, other observers have pointed to prospects for an emerging participatory regionalism that could potentially liberalize regional security discourse (Acharya 2003; Caballero-Anthony 2004).

The pervasiveness of auto-orientalism

That SEAIR remains indebted to Western traditions, even if it did not have a share in the historical experience which produced those traditions, is evident in the manner in which prominent intellectuals from the region, if only unintentionally, treat intellectual development in Southeast Asia as always and already defined by the West. For example, a leading IR thinker from the region argues the ability of Asians to think, insofar as they "succeed and do as well in a comprehensive sense as contemporary advanced societies in North America and Western Europe" (Mahbubani 2000: 7). To be sure, nowhere did he allow that North Americans and Western Europeans are thinkers for the same reason that theirs are advanced societies. But his text's effect, if only unintended, was such that Asians could be inferred as lagging behind in cognitive abilities relative to their Western counterparts – a point that would not have been possible unless the "West" served, for all intents and purposes, as the "other" against which "Asia" was to be measured and to which the latter was perennially beholden (Wilson and Dirlik 1995; Der Derian 1996). Accordingly, whether Asians can think is clearly not of concern as much as *how* they go about it.

In a similar vein, the issue of whether Southeast Asian analysts can theorize is equally about how they go about doing it: in an ambivalent way wherein the tensions which characterize Anglo-American IR theory are faithfully represented or emulated in SEAIR. Students of SEAIR increasingly theorize, but they continue to do so based upon the norms and parameters of Western discourse, constantly engaged in self-orientalism. Local efforts at appropriating Anglo-American IR theory to SEAIR might also be understood as "native informant" discourses that nevertheless betray traces of ambivalence. On the one hand, they attempt to resist what they regard as the ethnocentrism and imperialism of Anglo-American social science. On the other hand, in appropriating localized/indigenized categories and concepts (Katsumata 2003a; Acharya 2004), they are equally "accomplices" or "collaborators" in that project in that they are subject to the same rules, and thereby constraints of Western IR, thereby rendering them, as it were, "orientalized Orientals" (Soguk 1993). The tensions described thereby betray both a parochialism and provincialism, for no matter their ideological and intellectual preferences, they remain for the most part wedded to Western methodological categories and terms of reference.

It is possible, insofar as SEAIR begins to explore the prospects for non-Western theoretical traditions, and as attempts to instill greater, sustained, critical self-reflection into the field grow, that the chances of alternative visions of SEAIR will flourish. But it would need to begin with the recognition that while the Western IR tradition still has much to offer, it should neither be viewed as the only other to which SEAIR must answer nor to which it must live up – if only for the reason of eschewing the errors of the former while reaping its benefits.

Notes

1   For example, Rizal Sukma, Mely Caballero-Anthony, Renato Cruz De Castro, Thitinan Pongsudhirak, Panitan Wattanayagorn, Leonard Sebastian, Alan Chong, Narayanan Ganesan, Evelyn Goh, Sorpong Peou, Andrew Tan, and so on.
2   Increasingly important is the contemporary generation of analysts not native to Southeast Asia, such as Alice Ba, Jörn Dosch, Ralf Emmers, Jürgen Haacke, Hiro Katsumata, Shaun Narine, and of course Amitav Acharya, who more than most has popularized constructivism as a perspective useful to SEAIR.

References

Acharya, Amitav (2000) *The Quest for Identity: International Relations of Southeast Asia*, Singapore: Oxford University Press.

Acharya, Amitav (2001) *Constructing a Security Community in Southeast Asia: ASEAN and the Problem of Regional Order*, London and New York: Routledge.

Acharya, Amitav (2003) "Democratization and the Prospects for Participatory Regionalism in Southeast Asia," *Third World Quarterly*, 24 (2): 375–390.

Acharya, Amitav (2003/2004) "Will Asia's Past Be its Future?," *International Security*, 28 (3): 149–164.

Acharya, Amitav (2004) "How Ideas Spread: Whose Norms Matter? Norm Localization and Institutional Change in Asian Regionalism," *International Organization*, 58 (2): 239–275.

Acharya, Amitav and Barry Buzan (2007) "Why Is There No Non-Western International Relations Theory? An Introduction," *International Relations of the Asia Pacific*, 7 (3): 287–312.

Acharya, Amitav and Richard Stubbs (eds) (2006) Special Issue – "Theorizing Southeast Asian Relations: Emerging Debates," *The Pacific Review*, 19 (2).

Acharya, Amitav and See Seng Tan (2006) "Betwixt Balance and Community: America, ASEAN, and the Security of Southeast Asia," *International Relations of the Asia-Pacific*, 6 (1): 37–59.

Alagappa, Muthiah (ed.) (2003) *Asian Security Order: Instrumental and Normative Features*, Stanford, MA: Stanford University Press.

Ayoob, Mohammed (1988) "The Security Problematic of the Third World," *World Politics*, 43 (2): 257–283.

Ba, Alice D. (2006) "Who's Socializing Whom? Complex Engagement in Sino-ASEAN Relations," *The Pacific Review*, 19 (2): 157–179.

Ball, Desmond (2000) *The Council for Security Cooperation in the Asia-Pacific (CSCAP): Its Record and Its Prospect*, Canberra Papers on Strategy and Defense 139, Canberra: Australian National University.

Barthes, Roland (1974) *S/Z: An Essay*, New York: Hill & Wang.

Beeson, Mark (2003) "Sovereignty under Siege: Globalization and the State in Southeast Asia," *Third World Quarterly*, 24 (2): 357–374.

Bellamy, Alex J. (2004) "The Pursuit of Security in Southeast Asia: Beyond Realism," in Mark Beeson (ed.), *Contemporary Southeast Asia: Regional Dynamics, National Differences*, Basingstoke: Palgrave Macmillan, pp. 170–172.

Betts, Richard K. (1993/1994) "Wealth, Power, and Instability: East Asia and the United States after the Cold War," *International Security*, 18 (3): 34–77.

Brecher, Michael (1963) "International Relations and Asian Studies: The Subordinate State System of Southeast Asia," *World Politics*, 15 (2): 213–255.

Burke, Anthony and Matt McDonald (eds) (2007) *Critical Security in the Asia-Pacific*, Manchester: Manchester University Press.

Buzan, Barry and Gerald Segal (1994) "Rethinking East Asian Security," *Survival*, 36 (2): 3–21.

Caballero-Anthony, Mely (2004) "Non-state Regional Governance Mechanism for Economic Security: The Case of the ASEAN Peoples' Assembly," *The Pacific Review*, 17 (4): 567–585.

Caballero-Anthony, Mely (2005) *Regional Security in Southeast Asia: Beyond the ASEAN Way*, Singapore: ISEAS.

Campbell, David (1998) *Writing Security: United States Foreign Policy and the Politics of Identity*, Minneapolis: University of Minnesota Press.

Cheng, Joseph Y.S. (2006) "Broadening the Concept of Security in East and Southeast Asia: The Impact of the Asian Financial Crisis and the September 11 Incident," *Journal of Contemporary China*, 15 (46): 89–111.

Chong, Alan (2007) "Southeast Asia: Theory between Modernization and Tradition," *International Relations of the Asia-Pacific*, 7 (3): 391–425.

Colbert, Evelyn (1977) *Southeast Asia in International Politics 1941–1956*, Ithaca, NY: Cornell University Press.

Collins, Alan (2000) *The Security Dilemmas of Southeast Asia*, New York: St. Martin's Press.

Crawford, Robert M.A. and Darryl S.L. Jarvis (eds) (2000) *International Relations – Still an American Social Science? Toward Diversity in International Thought*, Albany, NY: State University of New York Press.

Dent, Christopher M. (ed.) (2003) *Asia-Pacific Economic and Security Cooperation: New Regional Agendas*, Basingstoke: Palgrave Macmillan.

Der Derian, James (1996) "Hedley Bull and the Idea of Diplomatic Culture," in Rick Fawn and Jeremy Larkin (eds), *International Society After the Cold War*, London: Macmillan, pp. 84–100.

Dewitt, David B. (1994) "Common, Comprehensive, and Cooperative Security," *The Pacific Review*, 7 (1): 1–15.

Dibb, Paul, David D. Hale and Peter Prince (1999) "Asia's Insecurity," *Survival*, 41 (3): 5–20.

Dickens, David (ed.) (1997) *No Better Alternative: Towards Comprehensive and Cooperative Security in the Asia-Pacific*, Wellington: Centre for Strategic Studies New Zealand.

Dosch, Jörn (2007) *The Changing Dynamics of Southeast Asian Politics*, Boulder, CO, and London: Lynne Rienner.

Eaton, Sarah and Richard Stubbs (2006) "Is ASEAN Powerful? Neo-realist versus Constructivist Approaches to Power in Southeast Asia," *The Pacific Review*, 19 (2): 135–155.

Emmers, Ralf (2003a) *Cooperative Security and the Balance of Power in ASEAN and the ARF*, London: Routledge.

Emmers, Ralf (2003b) "ASEAN and the Securitization of Transnational Crime in Southeast Asia," *The Pacific Review*, 16 (3): 419–438.

Emmerson, Donald K. (1987) "ASEAN as an International Regime," *Journal of International Affairs*, 41 (1): 1–16.

Evans, Paul M. (1994) "Building Security: The Council for Security Cooperation in the Asia Pacific (CSCAP)," *The Pacific Review*, 7 (2): 125–139.

Friedberg, Aaron L. (1993/1994) "Ripe for Rivalry: Prospects for Peace in a Multipolar Asia," *International Security*, 18 (3): 5–33.

Goh, Evelyn (2007) *Developing the Mekong: Regionalism and Regional Security in China–Southeast Asia Relations*, Adelphi Paper 387, London: IISS.

Gordon, Bernard K. (1966) *The Dimensions of Conflict in Southeast Asia*, Englewood Cliffs, NJ: Prentice-Hall.

Gurtov, Melvin (1977) "Southeast Asia in Transition," in Jae Kyu Park and Melvin Gurtov (eds), *Southeast Asia in Transition: Regional and International Politics*, Seoul: Institute for Far Eastern Studies, Kyung Nam University Press, pp. 233–238.

Haacke, Jürgen (2003) "ASEAN's Diplomatic and Security Culture: A Constructivist Assessment," *International Relations of the Asia-Pacific*, 3 (1): 57–87.

Haacke, Jürgen (2005) "Michael Leifer and the Balance of Power," *The Pacific Review*, 18 (1): 43–69.

Hamilton-Hart, Natasha (2005) "Terrorism in Southeast Asia: Expert Analysis, Myopia and Fantasy," *The Pacific Review*, 18 (3): 303–325.

Hassan, Mohammed Jawhar and Thangum Ramnath (eds) (1996) *Conceptualizing Asia-Pacific Security*, Kuala Lumpur: Institute of Strategic and International Studies.

Hernandez, Carolina G. (1994) *Track Two Diplomacy, Philippine Foreign Policy, and Regional Politics*, Manila: Center for Integrative and Development Studies, University of the Philippines Press.

Huxley, Tim (1996) "Southeast Asia in the Study of International Relations: The Rise and Decline of a Region," *The Pacific Review*, 9 (2): 199–228.

Ikenberry, G. John and Michael Mastanduno (2003) "Introduction," in G. John Ikenberry and Michael Mastanduno (eds), *International Relations Theory and the Asia-Pacific*, New York: Columbia University Press.

Jackson, Robert H. (1990) *Quasi-states: Sovereignty, International Relations and the Third World*, Cambridge: Cambridge University Press.

Jayasuriya, Kanishka (1994) "Singapore: The Politics of Regional Definition," *The Pacific Review*, 7 (4): 411–420.

Jentleson, Bruce W. (2002) "The Need for Praxis: Bringing Policy Relevance Back In," *International Security*, 26 (4): 169–183.

Jones, David Martin and Michael L.R. Smith (2001a) "Is There a Sovietology of South-East Asian Studies?," *International Affairs*, 77 (4): 843–865.

Jones, David Martin and Michael L.R. Smith (2001b) "The Changing Security Agenda in Southeast Asia: Globalization, New Terror, and the Delusions of Regionalism," *Studies in Conflict and Terrorism*, 24 (4): 271–288.

Jones, David Martin and Michael L.R. Smith (2002) "ASEAN's Imitation Community," *Orbis*, 46 (1): 93–109.

Jones, David Martin and Michael L.R. Smith (2007) "Making Process, not Progress: ASEAN and the Evolving East Asian Regional Order," *International Security*, 32 (1): 148–184.

Jørgensen-Dahl, Arnfinn (1982) *Regional Organization and Order in Southeast Asia*, London: Macmillan.

Kahin, George McTurna (1956) *The Asian–African Conference, Bandung, Indonesia, 1955*, New York: Cornell University Press.

Kang, David C. (2003) "Getting Asia Wrong: The Need for New Analytical Frameworks," *International Security*, 27 (4): 57–85.

Katsumata, Hiro (2003a) "Reconstruction of Diplomatic Norms in Southeast Asia: The Case for Strict Adherence to the 'ASEAN Way,'" *Contemporary Southeast Asia*, 25 (1): 104–121.

Katsumata, Hiro (2003b) "The Role of ASEAN Institutes of Strategic and International Studies in Developing Security Cooperation in the Asia-Pacific Region," *Asian Journal of Political Science*, 11 (1): 93–111.

Katsumata, Hiro (2004) "Why is ASEAN Diplomacy Changing?," *Asian Survey*, 44 (2): 237–254.

Katzenstein, Peter J., Robert O. Keohane and Stephen D. Krasner (1998) "International Organization and the Study of World Politics," *International Organization*, 52 (4): 645–685.

Keohane, Robert O. (1988) "International Institutions: Two Approaches," *International Studies Quarterly*, 32 (4): 379–396.

Keohane, Robert O. (2000) "Ideas Part-way Down," *Review of International Studies*, 26 (1): 125–130.

Khong, Yuen Foong (2005) "The Elusiveness of Regional Order: Leifer, the English School and Southeast Asia," *The Pacific Review*, 18 (1): 23–41.

Khoo, Nicholas (2004) "Deconstructing the ASEAN Security Community: A Review Essay," *International Relations of the Asia-Pacific*, 4 (1): 35–46.

Krasner, Stephen D. (1993) "Westphalia and All That," in Judith Goldstein and Robert O. Keohane (eds), *Ideas and Foreign Policy: Beliefs, Institutions, and Political Change*, Ithaca, NY: Cornell University Press, pp. 235–264.

Langford, John W. and K. Lorne Brownsey (1991) *Think Tanks and Governance in the Asia-Pacific Region*, Halifax: The Institute for Research on Public Policy.

Leifer, Michael (1972) *Dilemmas of Statehood in Southeast Asia*, Vancouver: University of British Columbia Press.

Leifer, Michael (1989) *ASEAN and the Security of South-East Asia*, London: Routledge.

Liow, Joseph Chinyong and Ralf Emmers (eds) (2006) *Order and Security in Southeast Asia: Essays in Memory of Michael Leifer*, London: Routledge.

Mack, Andrew and John Ravenhill (eds) (1995) *Pacific Cooperation: Building Economic and Security Regimes in the Asia-Pacific Region*, Boulder, CO: Westview Press.

Mahbubani, Kishore (2000) *Can Asians Think?*, Singapore: Times International.

Mandaville, Peter (2003) "Toward a Different Cosmopolitanism – Or, the 'I' Dislocated," *Global Society*, 17 (2): 209–221.

Morrison, Charles E. (2004) "Track 1/Track 2 Symbiosis in Asia-Pacific Regionalism," *The Pacific Review*, 17 (4): 547–565.

Narine, Shaun (2002) *Explaining ASEAN: Regionalism in Southeast Asia*, Boulder, CO: Lynne Rienner.

Narine, Shaun (2006) "The English School and ASEAN," *The Pacific Review*, 19 (2): 199–218.

Nesadurai, Helen E.S. (2003) *Globalization, Domestic Politics and Regionalism: The ASEAN Free Trade Area*, London: Routledge.

Neuman, Stephanie G. (1998) "International Relations Theory and the Third World: An Oxymoron?," in Stephanie G. Neumann (ed.), *International Relations and the Third World*, New York: St. Martin's Press, pp. 1–29.

Peou, Sorpong (2002) "Realism and Constructivism in Southeast Asian Security Studies Today: A Review Essay," *The Pacific Review*, 15 (1): 119–138.

Pettman, Ralph (1998) "Policing the Discourse on Asia-Pacific Affairs," Review Article. Available: <http://www.vuw.ac.nz/atp/policingthediscourse.html>.

Pettman, Ralph (2005) "Taoism and the Concept of Global Security," *International Relations of the Asia-Pacific*, 5 (1): 59–83.

Rajendran, Muthu (1985) *ASEAN's Foreign Relations: The Shift to Collective Action*, Kuala Lumpur: Arenabaku.

Rosenau, James N. (1993) "Thinking Theory Thoroughly," in Paul R. Viotti and Mark V. Kauppi (eds), *Realism, Pluralism, Globalism*, Boston, MA: Allyn & Bacon, pp. 20–31.

Said, Edward W. (1979) *Orientalism*, New York: Vintage Books.

Sandhu, Kernial S. (1992) "Strategic Studies in the Region," in Desmond Ball and David Horner (eds), *Strategic Studies in a Changing World: Global, Regional and Australian Perspectives*, Canberra: Strategic and Defense Studies Centre, Australian National University, pp. 224–256.

Simon, Sheldon W. (1982) *The ASEAN States and Regional Security*, Stanford, CA: Hoover Institution.

Simon, Sheldon W. (1995) "Realism and Neoliberalism: International Relations Theory and Southeast Asian Security," *The Pacific Review*, 8 (1): 5–24.

Simon, Sheldon W. (1996) "The Parallel Tracks of Asian Multilateralism," in Sheldon W. Simon and Richard J. Ellings (eds), *Southeast Asian Security in the New Millennium*, Armonk: M.E. Sharpe, pp. 13–33.

Simon, Sheldon W. and Donald K. Emmerson (1996) *Security, Democracy, and Economic Liberalization: Competing Priorities in U.S. Asia Policy*, NBR Analysis, 7.

Smith, Steve (2000) "The Discipline of International Relations: Still an American Social Science?," *British Journal of Politics and International Relations*, 2 (3): 374–402.

Soguk, Nevzat (1993) "Reflections on the 'Orientalized Orientals,'" *Alternatives*, 18 (3): 361–384.

Tan, See Seng (2005) "Untying Leifer's Discourse on Order and Power," *The Pacific Review*, 18 (1): 71–93.

Tan, See Seng (2006) "Rescuing Constructivism from the Constructivists: A Critical Reading of Constructivist Interventions in Southeast Asian Security," *The Pacific Review*, 19 (2): 239–260.

Tan, See Seng (2007a) *The Role of Knowledge Communities in Constructing Asia-Pacific Security: How Talk and Thought Make War and Peace*, Lewiston: Edwin Mellen.

Tan, See Seng (2007b) "Deconstructing the Discourse on Epistemic Agency: A Singaporean Tale of Two 'Essentialisms,'" in Anthony Burke and Matt McDonald (eds), *Critical Security in the Asia-Pacific*, Manchester: Manchester University Press, pp. 72–85.

Tan, See Seng and Acharya, Amitav (eds) (2008) *Bandung Revisited: The Legacy of the 1955 Asian-African Conference for International Order*, Singapore: National University of Singapore Press.

Walker, Robert B.J. (1989) "History and Structure in the Theory of International Relations," *Millennium: Journal of International Studies*, 18 (2): 163–183.

Walt, Stephen M. (1991) "The Renaissance of Security Studies," *International Studies Quarterly*, 35 (2): 211–239.

Wilson, Rob and Dirlik, Arif (1995) "Introduction," in Rob Wilson and Arif Dirlik (eds), *Asia/Pacific as Space of Cultural Production*, Durham, NC: Duke University Press, pp. 1–16.

Wong, Diana (1995) "Regionalism in the Asia-Pacific – A Response to Kanishka Jayasuriya," *The Pacific Review*, 8 (4): 683–688.

Woods, Lawrence T. (1997) "Rediscovering Security," *Asian Perspective*, 21(1): 79–102.

Yamamoto, Tadashi (ed.) (1995) *Emerging Civil Society in the Asia Pacific Community: Nongovernmental Underpinnings of the Asia Pacific Regional Community*, Singapore: Institute of Southeast Asian Studies and the Japan Center for International Exchange.

8 South Asia
A "realist" past and alternative futures

Navnita Chadha Behera

The realist tradition dominates the International Relations discipline in South Asia. Its foundational knowledge claims and value system tend to determine the epistemological boundaries of the South Asian discipline. In South Asia, realism's assumptions shape the answer to the question of "what counts as 'real' IR?" As such, literature produced by IR's South Asian communities remains predominantly state-centric. Even the organization and content of various IR teaching programs in universities and the research agendas of think-tanks, especially those receiving the state's support, reflect a realist bias. Even so, or perhaps owing to its derivative nature, South Asian IR remains on the margins of the larger IR discipline. Despite this marginality, some South Asian voices have made a mark in the larger discipline but these emanate from non-traditional sites of knowledge creation in IR. It is also this body of work that has the potential to chart an alternative future for regional IR disciplines. While such voices have offered critical insights both to IR's larger frame and its regional context, nevertheless, within the region, their critical creativity has yet to be recognized.

This chapter presents a comparative analysis of the state of the art of the IR discipline in several South Asian countries, analyzes reasons for its impoverishment, and identifies alternative sites for knowledge production. It concludes by assessing the prospects and challenges of producing a robust IR in South Asia.

Mapping the state of IR discipline

In assessing the IR discipline in South Asia, I ask four questions: How do IR scholars frame their questions? What contributions do South Asian scholars make to the IR literature? Which intellectual traditions shape their research agendas? And in which institutions does knowledge creation in IR occur?

Key framing questions

South Asian scholars' IR research agendas have primarily been driven by their respective states' foreign policy concerns and the role those states seek to play in the larger – regional and global – context. Since this implies pursuit of different issues and strategies for these countries, a "national" approach may yield better answers to these questions.

India

Indian IR's research agenda has revolved around three themes: India's self-conception as a "soft" and/or a "hard" power; India's assertion and preservation of its preeminence in South

Asia and the development of its power-potential in the larger Asian and global arena; and Indian attempts to restructure the international order so that it is rooted in normative values and exhibits a multipolar character. These themes have evolved with a considerable overlap and should not be viewed as excluding each other.

In the first phase, from the 1950s to the 1970s, India's first Prime Minister, Jawaharlal Nehru, envisioned India as a "soft power" that sought to forge "a confederation of independent states with common defense and economic policies" in the subcontinent (Muni 1980: 48). Nehru's normative worldview led India to denounce military blocs and Cold War politics, mobilize support for decolonization and anti-apartheid initiatives, strengthen the United Nations, seek disarmament with a universal and non-discriminatory non-proliferation regime, and, later, demand a New International Economic Order (NIEO). Non-alignment was the predominant anchor for these debates among the foreign policy officialdom as well as IR scholars.

However, India's frustrating experience with the UN over the Kashmir conflict in the early 1950s; wars with China in 1962 and Pakistan in 1965; and a collective failure of the third world countries on the NIEO front, provided reasons for change. Research agendas in the next two decades were driven by the realization that India could not be an effective power player in Asia without first mastering coercive elements of power and securing its backyard – South Asia. Such "hard" elements were articulated in the "Indira doctrine" – a doctrine based on "denying external powers a regional foothold, with military force if necessary" (Hagerty 1991: 351–352). IR scholars focused mainly on India's national security agenda with its all-out drive to develop a military muscle including nuclear, space, and missile programs. The "soft" policies of promoting regional cooperation through SAARC (South Asian Association of Regional Countries) got off to a very slow start.

In the third phase, beginning this decade, India's self-conception of being a "soft" power is again in ascendance. This time, however, it is backed by hard sources of power such as a nuclear weapons power status acquired in 1998 and an economy growing at 8 percent. With a peace process with Pakistan underway and SAARC making good progress, India's rising power in the Asian and the global context is, once again, at the center of IR debates.

Pakistan

Pakistani IR scholars frame their questions within a search for political, military, and economic parity with India and a leadership role in the Muslim world. Pakistan's Indo-centric concerns are evident in how India figures in most critical junctures of Pakistan's international relations: it has fought three-and-half wars with India in order to change the status quo in Kashmir; its military and strategic alliances with the U.S. and China have been driven by the need to counterbalance India; a key objective of its involvement in Afghanistan was to gain "strategic depth" vis-à-vis India; its decision to go nuclear following India's nuclear assertions, and finally its willingness to jettison its prodigy – the Taliban in Kabul – and join the U.S.-led war against terror were prompted by the fear that India might become America's front-line ally and damage Pakistan's strategic assets.

Political developments in the Middle East, Afghanistan, and Central Asia have been another core theme in Pakistani IR debates. Much has been written about how Pakistan's Islamic bomb vindicates Muslim pride and projects Pakistan as a moderate leader of the Islamic world. Another concern is Pakistan's strategic proximity to the Gulf and its central location for exploring new trade routes to Central Asia.

Sri Lanka, Nepal and Bangladesh

In Sri Lanka, the framing question for IR scholars, and indeed for political scientists, sociologists and economists, is the internal Tamil ethnic conflict and near-civil war conditions in the country. Nepal's foreign policy concerns emanate from its geo-political position of being a buffer (landlocked) state between the two giants – India and China. The decade-long Maoist insurgency and its internal as well as external repercussions has become another central issue of debate among its scholarly community. India also looms large over Bangladeshi IR. This is due partly to the long-standing bilateral Farakka water dispute and partly to the complications arising from the presence of Chakma refugees (from Bangladesh) on Indian soil. A common important issue of IR debates among Bangladeshi and Sri Lankan scholars concerns the security problems of small states in the international system.

Characteristic features of IR institutions and literature in South Asia

South Asian scholars' contributions to the IR literature have, with few exceptions, remained on the margins. The findings presented in this section are drawn from an analytic survey of the institutional and pedagogic structure of the field, and a critical overview of the IR literature produced in books, and a detailed content analysis of four leading research journals published by universities and think-tanks. This has been undertaken for almost the entire period of their publication except those issues that were not available for consultation.[1] *Strategic Studies* (1979–2006) published by the Institute for Strategic Studies (Pakistan) and *BIISS Journal* (1980–2003) published by the Bangladesh Institute of International and Strategic Studies (Bangladesh) were selected because no Pakistani university publishes a research journal on IR and the University of Dhaka's publication, the *Journal of International Relations*, was not available in any library at New Delhi. Nepal does not publish any research journal on IR and the *Ethnic Studies Report* published by the International Center for Ethnic Studies (Sri Lanka), which comes closest to addressing the IR problematics, was also not available locally. *International Studies* (1959–2006) – the flagship journal of the Jawaharlal Nehru University (India) – was selected from India because the *Jadavpur Journal of International Relations* – a publication of the Jadavpur University (Kolkatta) – had a much smaller sample size from 1995 to 2006. Significantly, some of the most exciting debates on IR here have taken place in non-IR-specific sites such as *Economic and Political Weekly* (EPW) and *Alternatives*. While EPW plays a critical role in the development of social sciences in India, *Alternatives* is perhaps the single most important non-Western and internationally acclaimed intellectual site for debating alternative perspectives on international relations. This is why it has been included in the following analysis. In addition, the flagship journal of the International Studies Association (ISA) (*International Studies Quarterly*) was reviewed to examine if South Asians (nationals as well as the diaspora) were represented in the larger discipline of IR. From these findings, three characteristic features of the field of IR in South Asia may be surmised.

Disciplinary IR versus area studies

The following conceptual conflation is deeply ingrained in the institutional and pedagogic structures of South Asia: discipline-oriented IR studies are thought to be the same as idiographic foreign area studies. The latter are based on the somewhat simplistic assumption that the areas being studied are "foreign." The Indian conception of IR, known as international studies, is one such peculiar product where disciplinary IR was often subsumed under the latter's rubric leading to a critical neglect of the former's development (Rana 1988a, 1988b). In JNU – the single largest School of International Studies in the region – five of its centers are devoted to area studies while only two are thematically organized. In Pakistan, most university departments also adopt an area studies approach to organize their teaching programs while paying little attention to the main fields of the discipline (Rais 2005: 47). Furthermore, the study of disciplinary IR is overshadowed by the area studies components of their syllabi. In India, Pakistan, and Nepal, IR courses mostly consist of an amalgam of diplomatic history of the two World Wars followed by a focus on the Cold War between the superpowers. The home country's foreign relations are taught in detail albeit in a chronological and narrative mode. There is little effort devoted to teaching the fundamental debates, theories, and concepts in IR. The subfields of IR including security studies, peace and conflict studies, international law, and international political economy mostly remain confined to optional courses at the Masters level, and others such as environmental studies, international ethics, globalization, and gender studies are rarely taught.

Since area studies specialists had poor grounding in disciplinary IR, this led successive generations to produce historical chronicles of the home country's relations with other states in a narrative and descriptive style all without any rigorous training in historical research methods. This is clearly reflected in the genre of literature produced by leading journals of IR in South Asia, as shown in Table 8.1.

International Studies, *Strategic Studies*, and *BIISS Journal* all reflect a decisive bent in favor of the area studies approach. Interestingly, *BIISS Journal* and *Strategic Studies* seem to do better than *International Studies* in this respect. This is perhaps due to the high priority attached to issues of environmental degradation threatening Bangladesh's security and the working of international and regional organizations such as the UN and SAARC in South Asia, which becomes clear from Table 8.2.

Nationalism and conflicts, especially ethnic conflicts, form another area of core interest in *International Studies*. Its engagement with theoretical research in IR, however, remains extremely low. This is only slightly better in the case of *Strategic Studies* whose main preoccupation remains with strategic and military issues, though it tends to peak whenever Pakistan is under military rule while during the democratic regimes led by Benazir Bhutto and Nawaz Sharif (1988–1999), its focus on strategic issue dwindles, only to rise again during General Pervez Musharraf's regime beginning in 1999. The last period also shows a much higher level of engagement with the host of disciplinary issues relating to nationalism and conflicts, international organization and law, human rights, international economy, as well as theories of IR. *International Studies* offers a sharply different picture with a consistently low level of interest in military and strategic issues of strategy, as is clear from Table 8.2. This may well be because many Indian journals such as *Strategic Analysis*, *USI Journal*, *Indian Defence Review*, and *Agni* are devoted to addressing a gamut of military and strategic issues. The first decade of this journal shows a decisive edge in debating issues of international law, which persists albeit at a lower level. This was perhaps because the founder of the JNU's School of International Studies (SIS), A. Appadorai, belonged to the British tradition of law, diplomatic history, and philosophy and hence, the foci of the School's early investigations in IR were also rooted in that tradition. In the 1970s, foreign policy issues, especially non-alignment, hogged the limelight. The overall orientation of *International Studies* has been significantly influenced by the area studies focus of the SIS, though it shows a slow albeit steady shift towards disciplinary writings in the past decade, as shown in Table 8.3. During this period, it also records a much higher level of engagement with the theoretical debates in IR. A breakdown of the area studies-oriented research in the

Table 8.1 Disciplinary IR vs. area studies focus

Year of publication	International Studies		Alternatives		Strategic Studies		BIISS Journal		Total
	Area studies	Disciplinary IR	Area studies	Disciplinary IR	Area studies	Disciplinary IR	Area studies	Disciplinary IR	
1959 – 1963	68	21							89
1964 – 1968	51	19							70
1969 – 1973	12	22							34
1974 – 1978	88	18		52				10	168
1979 – 1983	66	17	1	79	40	38	24	42	307
1984 – 1988	32	21	5	90	64	20	71	30	333
1989 – 1993	50	40	4	109	54	17	71	39	384
1994 – 1998	49	49	1	95	46	10	53	46	349
1999 – 2003	31	29	6	35	64	23	37	17	242
2004 – 2006	27	35			69	17			148
Total	474	271	17	460	337	125	256	184	

Table 8.2 Comparative analysis of disciplinary focus (issue-wise)

Year of publication	International Studies							Strategic Studies							BIISS Journal							Total
	Strategic issues	International economy	International org./Law	International theories	Nationalism/conflict	Human rights/environmental issues	Others	Strategic issues	International economy	International org./Law	International theories	Nationalism/conflict	Human rights/environmental issues	Others	Strategic issues	International economy	International org./Law	International theories	Nationalism/conflict	Human rights/environmental issues	Others	
1959–1963	0	4	11	1	0	0	8															24
1964–1968	2	1	10	4	0	1	0															18
1969–1973	0	0	1	0	0	0	0															1
1974–1978	1	5	4	6	1	0	3															20
1979–1983	1	4	2	7	2	1	16	14	0	2	5	3	0	6	5	4	4	0	6	0	2	82
1984–1988	2	1	3	5	0	1	2	12	0	0	4	1	0	0	5	2	13	2	2	1	1	59
1989–1993	1	7	5	0	8	2	9	0	3	0	5	1	0	0	3	2	8	3	6	3	5	63
1994–1998	4	8	8	6	2	5	10	2	1	2	0	1	0	3	2	5	2	0	3	2	3	75
1999–2003	4	8	5	13	1	0	3	8	3	9	5	8	2	2	6	3	2	1	2	3	4	93
2004–2006	4	2	1	5	0	0	0															13
Total	19	40	50	47	14	10	51	36	7	13	19	14	2	11	21	16	29	6	19	9	15	

Table 8.3 Comparative analysis of area studies focus (region-wise)

	International Studies					Strategic Studies						BIISS Journal					Total
	National	Regional	Third World	West	Domestic	National	Regional (South Asia)	Regional (Middle East)	Third World	West	Domestic	National	Regional	Third World	West	Domestic	
1959–1963	30	5	26	12	0												73
1964–1968	17	5	14	11	3												50
1969–1973	0*	2	7	3	0												12
1974–1978	45	13	19	11	3												91
1979–1983	10	5	42	10	1	14	16	5	6	6	1	3	4	4	6	16	149
1984–1988	7	5	18	5	1	17	15	11	15	9	0	6	28	17	11	9	174
1989–1993	15	3	21	6	0	8	21	27	4	5	1	15	30	6	11	8	181
1994–1998	9	10	25	3	1	19	24	3	8	4	0	18	32	14	8	5	183
1999–2003	11	7	12	9	0	15	17	17	6	9	2	23	22	7	3	10	170
2004–2006	9	2	16	6	0	12	25	17	6	11	1						105
Total	153	57	200	76	9	85	118	80	45	44	5	65	116	48	39	48	

*Note: No separate issues of *International Studies* were published from 1969 to 1972, as explained in note 1.

same journal shows an unwavering commitment to understand the developments in the third world followed by articles that recount India's foreign relations with other states and regions in the world.

Interestingly, the number of contributions on South Asia shows a much lower academic interest in the region especially as compared to Bangladesh as well as that of Pakistan. In Pakistan and Bangladesh's case, a separate category of research contributions pertaining to the Middle East and Gulf region was introduced, as Pakistan's scholarly interest in the Muslim world, as argued above, remains particularly high.

In a striking contrast to all the three journals mentioned above, *Alternatives* presents a site where disciplinary debates in IR have not only flourished throughout this period (see Table 8.1), but significantly, one has to amend one's disciplinary categories of analysis for this journal because the sheer diversity of issues cannot be represented by the classifications used for other journals. It proves to be difficult to "fit" many of its research papers into the conventional categories of mainstream IR such as area studies on the one hand and international law, international organization, international economy, and human rights issues on the other, which account for only 5 percent and 4 percent respectively of total articles published in *Alternatives* from 1980 to 2004. Many scholars wrote about North–South issues (9 percent), nationalism and conflicts (11 percent), social movements and grass-roots activism (4 percent), global cultures (6 percent) and world order (7 percent), global governance, democratization, ecology and development-related issues (9 percent), modern science and theology, race and culture in IR, Indian history, philosophy, literature and culture, and so on. On issues such as military and strategic affairs that accounted for 9 percent of its contributions during this period, the perspective was very different as they grappled with issues of armament, disarmament, and militarism. *Alternatives* also addressed a much wider spectrum of theoretical debates in IR illustrated by the 19 percent of its total research articles that included realism, orientalism, post-colonialism, Marxism, feminism, postmodernism, and a whole range of non-Western philosophies (4 percent), which are rarely mentioned in the mainstream IR journals. This shows that IR in South Asia is also taking place under other rubrics and disciplines that may lie outside the domain of mainstream IR.

Weak epistemic foundations: theoretical research vs. empirical narratives

Theoretical work of any kind remains a much "dreaded and despised" enterprise across the region. A comparative analysis of theoretical versus empirical research shows extremely low levels of engagement with theoretical research in all three journals – *International Studies*, *Strategic Studies*, and *BIISS Journal* (Table 8.4).[2] The picture becomes more clear from a review of their contributions to "theoretical" research in IR as a proportion of their overall research published during the respective periods of their publication, mentioned above, which stands at 0.80 percent for *Strategic Studies*, 1.72 percent for *BIISS Journal* and 7.41 percent for *International Studies*. The record for undertaking "theoretically informed" research is a little better and almost on a par among all these three journals – 17.34 percent for *International Studies*; 18 percent for *Strategic Studies*; and 19 percent for *BIISS Journal*. "Empirical" research makes up the largest share of their scholarly writings in IR. These figures are 75.24 percent for *International Studies*; 84 percent for *Strategic Studies*; and 79.26 percent for *BIISS Journal*. *Alternatives*, once again, presents a total contrast where 36.69 percent of its contributions are classified as theoretical and 57.14 percent as theoretically informed research. Only 6.16 percent of its research articles are classified as empirical research.

Table 8.4 Theoretical vs. empirical research in IR

Year of publication	International Studies			Alternatives		
	Empirical	Theoretical	Theoretically informed	Empirical	Theoretical	Theoretically informed
1959–1963	47	35	6			
1964–1968	64	1	5			
1969–1973	13	0	0			
1974–1978	93	7	10			
1979–1983	68	9	14	9	29	30
1984–1988	35	1	16	6	34	44
1989–1993	59	2	14	4	4	41
1994–1998	62	14	19	1	9	19
1999–2003	34	12	27	2	42	57
2004–2006	29	6	13	0	13	13
Total	504	87	124	22	131	204

There is, however, another side to this story, which underscores that there is no singular notion about what constitutes/qualifies as IR theory. What counts as IR depends upon the epistemological bases and ontological grounding as well as "political practices." One school of thought argues that all intellectual endeavors situated *within* Western systems of thought that seek to apply them "creatively" in their specific local contexts qualify as an exercise in IR theorizing. Arjun Appadurai refers to this process as "vernacularization," by which dominant modes of cultural production are reinscribed in peripheral contexts where they acquire a new meaning (Appadurai 1996: 110–112). In so doing, it is argued, new knowledge enriches and at times qualitatively transforms the specificities of local ground realities and value systems. South Asian scholars in IR have produced a lot of such work which Acharya and Buzan (2007) define as "exceptionalist" or "subsystemic" theorizing. This includes the literature on issues such as nuclear deterrence (Karnad 2002; Basrur 2005) or dissenting voices on the nuclear issue (Kothari and Mian 2001); regionalism in South Asia (Wignaraja and Hussain 1989) and conflicts and peace processes (Ali 1993; Samaddar and Reifeld 2001; Srestha and Uprety 2003), among others. Another genre of writings pertains to a country perspective on global issues such as international order (Bajpai 2003); globalization (Harshe 2004) and international law (Chimni 1993). These examples are clearly illustrative, *not* exhaustive; they highlight that South Asian attempts at theorizing IR are mostly at the subsystemic level.

Critics, however, point to their limitations, as most such scholars do not decide independently what to ask and how to answer; the fundamental problems of IR and theoretical frameworks for analyzing them are already "given" by Western theories. The task of local scholars is, therefore, mostly confined to collecting relevant empirical data in their respective domestic contexts and, if need be, modifying the parameters of their inquiry.

Recognition of what counts as IR theory raises other serious questions such as *who* decides what qualifies as "subsystemic" or "systemic" theorizing. Muni agrees with Cox that "theory follows reality," and Western theories of IR are dominant because they ride on the back of Western (read U.S.) power. Underlining the role of "disciplinary gate-keeping practices," Tickner notes that

Strategic Studies			BIISS Journal			
Empirical	*Theoretical*	*Theoretically informed*	*Empirical*	*Theoretical*	*Theoretically informed*	*Total*
						88
						70
						13
						110
59	0	19	38	0	15	290
70	2	12	90	2	16	328
61	2	10	83	4	16	300
49	0	7	75	1	19	275
76	0	11	65	1	19	346
75	0	11	16	0	3	179
390	4	70	367	8	88	

> IR reinforces analytical categories and research programs that are systematically defined by academic communities within the core, and that determine what can be said, how it can be said, and whether or not what is said constitutes a pertinent or important contribution to knowledge.
>
> (Tickner 2003: 297, 300)

Such claims may best be illustrated with reference to the philosophy and theoretical formulations of non-alignment. Jawaharlal Nehru is widely regarded as the founding father of non-alignment. He conceived it both as a *principle* – of exercising autonomy in foreign affairs – and as a *mechanism* or an "order-building" instrument by trying to create a "third" area of peace outside the two power blocs so as to secure a more just and equitable world order. The non-aligned movement created a coalition of more than 100 states from Asia, Africa, Europe, the Arab world, Latin America, and the Caribbean that supported the decolonization process, literally changing the world's geo-political landscape. However, this movement was never accorded status or recognition as a "systemic" IR theory. Theoretical writings on non-alignment rarely figured in the core IR journals published in North America and Europe throughout the 1950s to the 1970s. If they mentioned it all, they dismissed arguments about non-alignment as "variants of neutrality" (Armstrong 1956–1957) and made disparaging references to these countries as "uncommitted" or "neutral." They questioned non-alignment's political legitimacy (Debrah 1961; Dinh 1975). Indian scholars had little choice but to write books on non-alignment distributed by Indian publishers (Khan 1981; Jaipal 1983) or to contribute to journals such as *Indian and Foreign Affairs, International Studies, Socialist India, Seminar* and *Economic, and Political Weekly*. These publications and their arguments probably never found their way into mainstream IR journals or presses.

Likewise, Nehru's idea of non-exclusionary regionalism – the concept of *Panchsheel* and the *Mandala* theory of regionalism – received no recognition in IR's core literature. Exceptions figure only in the case of South Asian scholars based at U.S. or European universities or whose texts have been published and distributed by Western publishing houses. Mohammad Ayoob's work on the state-making processes in the third world and their security predicament is a case in point (1995) though this, too, received recognition largely in the context of the third world.

National vs. international canvass for IR research

Most South Asians write for their respective national IR journals, as is clear from Table 8.5. Furthermore, journals produced by think-tanks such as *Strategic Studies* and *BIISS Journal* primarily offer an avenue for publishing in-house research. Indian scholars also comprise the largest share of contributors to *International Studies*, though the number of international contributors to these journals has grown consistently since the early 1990s. *Strategic Studies* intermittently records a high number of international contributors but that is mostly when the journal has reproduced papers presented at international conferences organized by its parent institute, particularly in the years of 1985 to 1988 and 1991 to 1994. Only *Alternatives* can be truly characterized as an international journal with 90 percent of its contributors comprising international scholars.

South Asian presence in the mainstream IR journals is negligible at best. A detailed analysis of *International Studies Quarterly* shows that in 37 years (1967 to 2004), only one scholar from South Asia, K. Subrahmanyam's (an Indian national) work on Indian defense efforts, was published in the June 1969 issue, although it is interesting to note that Indra D. Sharma, a scholar from Punjab University (Chandigarh, India), was on the editorial board of *International Studies Quarterly* from 1967 to 1973. The South Asian diaspora has not fared much better, as only eight papers from scholars based in the U.S. universities have been published in the journal during this period.

Intellectual traditions in South Asia

From a disciplinary standpoint, the realist tradition in IR has had the most pervasive and lasting impact on research agendas in South Asia. Realist notions of state-centric power politics have been thoroughly internalized by the South Asian scholarly community. Characterizing it as the "theoretical bedrock" of much of Indian IR, Rana and Misra point out that this internalization has never been

> an explicitly self-conscious activity [but] more the result of scholars being overly impressed and influenced by state practice . . . [Even] the idea of change echoes state practice. The state is concerned about . . . realist expedients to effect change, not for change which attempts to transcend realist premises.
>
> (Rana and Misra 2004: 79)

Since several generations of IR scholars have been trained primarily in the realist tradition, a critical mass of intellects that might systematically question this paradigm has not crystallized. While the earlier generations imbibed Morgenthau's writings which were a "must-read" for all IR students,[3] those at the Delhi University were, until as late as 2004, not taught the entire genre of theoretical debates in the post-positivist phase of IR's disciplinary direction. Thus, today, theory remains essentially a positivist enterprise. This is largely true for other South Asian countries as well. Moreover, the state has proved to be complicit in privileging the realist discourses and worldview as the norms of the Westphalian state system – sovereignty, territorial integrity and non-interference in internal affairs – "fitted in admirably with powerful indigenous impulses for the maintenance of national security,

Table 8.5 National vs. international authorship of IR research

	International Studies		Alternatives		Strategic Studies		BIISS Journal		Total
	National authorship	International authorship	National authorship	International authorship	National authorship	International authorship	National authorship	International authorship	
1959–1963	80	9							89
1964–1968	61	10							71
1969–1973	11	2							13
1974–1978	96	14							110
1979–1983	81	12	8	25	51	25	47	6	255
1984–1988	46	6	13	71	53	47	103	5	344
1989–1993	54	21	14	86	51	22	91	12	351
1994–1998	68	27	7	95	43	13	80	15	348
1999–2003	53	22	4	97	84	3	61	24	348
2004–2006	30	18	0	26	83	3	10	9	179
Total	580	141	46	400	365	113	392	71	

independence and frontiers" (Rana and Misra 2004: 78). Significantly, while Nehru deeply influenced the development of the IR discipline in India, his normative worldview aroused little interest in scholarly debates. Normative traditions of IR were never seriously researched by the early generation of IR scholars and totally debunked as "wooly-eyed idealism" by the later generations that had, by then, fully absorbed the tenets of the realist approach.

In the contemporary context, several scholars using different vantage points of post-colonialism, hermeneutics, development theory, critical theory, neo-Marxism, and feminism have debated issues that lie at the heart of IR. Some scholars have, for instance, drawn upon the insights of post-colonial thought. These include Abraham's research on the making of the Indian atomic bomb (1998), Eqbal Ahmad's thoughts on the post-colonial state, and Appadurai's work on globalization (1996), who along with Bhabha highlighted the hybrid "in-betweenness" that characterizes the post-colonial subject, "allowing for the emergence and negotiation of marginal, subaltern, minority subjectivities" (Bhabha 1994: 25). Feminist analyses have been far better integrated in anthropology, sociology, and history than IR in the South Asian academe. Nonetheless, their theoretical constructions are beginning to make their presence felt in IR (Chenoy 2002; Rajagopalan and Faizal 2005), while women's involvement in conflict and peace processes (Manchanda 2001; Behera 2006) and the gendered nature of nationalism and state (Hussain *et al.* 1997) have been much analyzed.

Likewise, while the Marxist tradition of thought has flourished in South Asia, it is on a much more solid footing in the fields of economics, political science, and sociology than IR. A few neo-Marxist scholars in India and Pakistan have produced significant research that includes, for example, Dutt's formulation of "proto second tier imperialism" (1984), Alavi's conception of the Muslim salariat and Muslim ethnicity (Alavi and Halliday 1988), Harshe's work on imperialism (1997), Vanaik's work on Indian foreign policy (1995), Bastian's work on ethnicity (1994), the concepts of internal colonialism (Riaz 1994), and the colonial factor in the mode of production (Gardezi 1991).

Scholars have also highlighted the importance of culture and identity for understanding global processes because of their different knowledge traditions. Subaltern knowledge attempts to change power relations between these traditions as it seeks to acquire not only political and economic autonomy but also the power to define themselves and their aspirations. Such local voices challenge the very basis of the positivist assumption that there can be a single universalizing epistemology that holds the answers and gives *all peoples* a better life, or that "experts" and specialists, essentially from the West, have a monopoly on knowledge production (Sheth 1983; Nandy 1987). Among the earliest interdisciplinary Indian critiques of Enlightenment modernity was the work pioneered at the Center for Studies of Developing Societies (CSDS) by Rajni Kothari, Ashis Nandy, Dhirubhai Seth, and Shiv Visvanathan among others.[4] Rajni Kothari, as part of the World Order Models Project in the late 1960s, advocated structural transformation by taking into account the larger mutations of religious, ecological, and aesthetic consciousness at the popular cultural level in large parts of the world (Kothari 1979–1980: 23).

Ashis Nandy's critique of modernity, the Enlightenment project, the underlying psychological repercussions of colonialism, and especially the nature of the modern state system, all go to the heart of issues that concern this new IR (Lal 2000). He pleads for "scepticism to be directed at the modern nation-state" while stressing the need to take stock of the costs of the nation state system and the nationalism that sustains it. Nandy's seminal contribution has inspired leading scholars worldwide to conceptualize the "international" in a different light. It "challenges our habituated ways of thinking about the international as outside or between," even though he is "not usually thought of as a theorist of the international – partly, no doubt, because Nandy himself would reject any such compartmentalization of knowledge" (Darby 2003: 160). Writings of this genre are, however, an eclectic mix of these diverse intellectual traditions, admittedly few and rarely recognized as part of mainstream IR in South Asia. Nandy and Kothari's work, for instance, is much acclaimed internationally but few in India recognize it as falling within the purview of the IR discipline.

Institutional sites of knowledge creation in IR

There is a very small institutional base for "doing IR" in South Asia. Few universities teach this discipline. Only the Jadavpur University (Kolkatta) in India offers an undergraduate and a postgraduate program in IR. The Jawaharlal Nehru University, Mahatma Gandhi University (Kottayam), and Pondichery University along with the Stella Maris College at Chennai (since 2005) teach a Masters program in IR. Pakistan has three universities – Quaid-i-Azam University (Islamabad), Karachi University and Peshawar University – offering an IR degree program. Dhaka University in Bangladesh has the oldest department of IR in South Asia, which first offered the Masters program in 1947 to 1948 and five decades later, Jahangirnagar University established an IR department in 1998. In Sri Lanka, only Colombo University offers a Masters program in history and IR while in Nepal, as indeed in all other universities in these countries, IR is only taught as a subject under the rubric of political science, and sometimes economics and history. In other words, IR has not acquired the status of a separate discipline in the region.

The poor state of the IR discipline is also attributed to several pedagogical reasons, including the lack of proper teaching materials and textbooks, the insufficiency of funds, misguided educational policies, and so on. At the national and regional levels, there has been a lack of institutional strategies for sharing intellectual and literary resources for training teachers, making available locally produced good-quality textbooks in English as well as translations into Hindi, Urdu, Bengali, Tamil, Sinhala, and other regional languages; developing focused and up-to-date syllabi that take into account the geo-cultural sensitivities of the country/region in question; and establishing good libraries and archival centers in different countries in the region, and even different parts of larger countries like India and Pakistan. While the discipline merited greater attention from institutions – governmental and non-governmental – because of its importance to the contemporary global realities, the underselling of International Relations in South Asia was both a cause and a consequence of neglecting the critical task of institution building.

A healthy IR discipline would entail "a well-knit national community engaged in effective internal communion" (Rana and Misra 2004: 111). While IR scholars interact with each other, there is little evidence to show that "they have so far tried cumulatively to build a coherent edifice of work in well defined areas, related to key IR disciplinary concerns and problems in some kind of a dialectical correlation" (Rana and Misra 2004: 111). Barring Bangladesh, none has an effective, functioning professional body of IR scholars. Most conferences and seminars are organized on themes solely at the discretion of the host individual, department, or organization, which in turn are often stand-alone, disparate undertakings rarely going beyond the production of an edited volume.

With very few university departments of International Relations, those trained in this discipline have extremely limited career opportunities. The teaching responsibilities both at the college and university levels are very heavy, and teachers find little time to pursue their research. The severe shortage of a core faculty of IR also mars prospects for the discipline in most Pakistani universities. This is mainly due to "poor salary, unfriendly academic environment and lack of opportunities for higher education in social sciences" (Rais 2005: 19). An overwhelming majority of IR teachers – about 62 in six universities – are without doctoral degrees.

Most universities depend solely on state funding and those teaching social sciences are invariably facing a fund crunch. This has severely impeded the growth of IR in the region. State funding for higher education in India is highly centralized in the University Grants Commission (UGC) that is selective in what it supports while being driven by political imperatives of distributive equity and, often, the priorities of the ruling regime. Some universities are, however, beginning to seek private funds to enhance their research profile, though earlier they rarely competed with think-tanks for such private grants.

There are more think-tanks and research institutes doing IR. Their research agendas are largely determined by varying rationales, intellectual resources, and funding. One may broadly distinguish between the old and the new genre of research institutes. The old genre of think-tanks such as the Indian Center for World Affairs and the Institute for Defence Studies and Analyses; Pakistan Institute for International Affairs and Institute for Strategic Studies; Bangladesh Institute of Strategic Studies (BIISS); and the Bandarnaike Center for International Affairs in Sri Lanka were mostly set up with state patronage. Their intellectual resources are largely devoted to justifying government policies rather than recommending well-researched alternative options. Hence, their influence in shaping the governments' foreign policy agendas remains limited at best.

The growth of the new genre of think-tanks was facilitated by the availability of private funding in the 1990s. India's first Prime Minister Jawaharlal Nehru did not encourage foreign funding for IR during its formative years, but it has become much more "politically acceptable" in recent times. For example, two regional think-tanks – the Regional Center for Strategic Studies and the South Asia Center for Policy Studies – were set up in 1992 and 1999 respectively with Ford Foundation funding. Other national-level research institutes include the Institute for Peace and Conflict Analysis, Observer Research Foundation and Institute for Conflict Management in India; Sustainable Development Policy Institute (Islamabad) SDPI and Islamabad Policy Research Institute (IPRI) in Pakistan; Center for Policy Alternatives in Sri Lanka; and Center for Policy Dialogue and Bangladesh Enterprise Institute in Bangladesh. Local philanthropy as well as the indigenous capital of the corporate sector has still not been tapped for funding international studies, though this is beginning to change.[5] The quantum of foreign funding in IR also remains small and is confined to research institutions based in capital cities along with a few other metropolitan centers. International NGOs have also become much more active in the region.

The growing strength of the new genre of think-tanks and international NGOs influences the production of IR knowledge in three significant ways. First, they often take a lead in introducing and popularizing the non-traditional agenda of IR studies including issues such as governance, environmental and energy security, human security, ethnic conflicts, gender, refugees, and terrorism. Significantly, however, such shifts in their discursive focus were often triggered or shaped by their respective funders'/foundations' research agendas in their countries of origin (Behera 2004). Second, a near-universal trademark of these institutes is their privileging of "policy-relevant" research, which further shrinks the space for basic academic research in IR. Most look down upon the latter as a "waste of time" partly because there is no "clientele" for the consumption of basic research. In other words, the "saleability" of research ideas tends to determine their research agendas. Third, the growing number of funded research projects and the increasing opportunities for undertaking consultancy work for international NGOs institutionalizes the phenomenon of "commissioned research" in the subcontinent. Many scholars give priority to "paid" research over their other research commitments that might yield few monetary benefits.

Finally, the relationship of universities and research institutes with the foreign policy bureaucracy needs to be understood. Although the state is instrumental in setting the agenda for IR studies, there is an iron curtain that divides the two sides. The foreign policy bureaucracy and academia in every South Asian country live in separate, almost self-contained worlds that operate from fundamentally different information bases. There is no sharing of information, no reliance on institutional memory, and no light thrown on decision-making processes. No government in South Asia respects a freedom of information act; classified documents are *never* made public. So, when the state does make any information available, at its own discretion of course, there is an implicit *quid pro quo* by privileging and rewarding those scholars who support government policies.

Explaining the impoverishment of IR

Two factors have made IR an impoverished, limited, and handicapped field from the onset. These pertain to the epistemological character of the discipline and the wider context of social sciences and processes of knowledge production in the region that are designed to cater to the state's needs and demands.

Epistemological character of the IR discipline

IR in South Asia has steadfastly refused to critically interrogate the character and efficacy of the state system by historicizing it. It takes the state as a given and unproblematic entity, which is the *starting point* of all its scholarly endeavors. This discipline shares an umbilical relationship with the state not in an institutional sense, since IR was taught in Dhaka University even before India became independent, but in terms of the location of its epistemological bases. The state in the contemporary international system is modeled after the Westphalian state born out of the European context. Since the Indian state – as indeed any other South Asian state – is supposed to be an emulation of the Westphalian model, its own historical repository of statecraft has proved to be of little relevance. Thus students of IR in South Asia do not learn about the ontological origins of their respective states in terms of the social and political formations in the pre-modern period that would show that a state is not a reified "given" but a "historical product." This, too, is of a particular kind because it follows a different trajectory of undergoing colonial rule, which is why it is intrinsically different from that of the historical Westphalian state that ubiquitously forms the bases of *all* realist analysis in IR.

India, for example, had no formal political philosophy but the science of statecraft was much cultivated. An individual's loyalty in ancient India was primarily to the tribe, clan, or caste group, and his/her relationship with political authority was limited to paying taxes. Political allegiance to territorial states was a tenuous affair under traditional conditions and political authority, and control tended to be dispersed and distributed between various levels of authority: vassal states, regional kingdoms and empires, as distinct from a centralized political unity of the modern sovereign state. In the Vedic texts, terms like *adiraja* and *samrat*, often loosely translated as "emperor," seem actually to imply lordship over a number of feudatories. The Indian system also differed from that of Europe in that the relations of overlord and vassal were not regularly based on contract (Basham 2004: 95). If a king was decisively defeated in battle, he could render homage to his conqueror and retain his throne.

Thus vassals usually became so by conquest rather than by contract and "lawful conquest" (*dharamvijya*), according to the epics and *Smrti* literature, did not involve the absorption of the conquered kingdom, but merely its reduction to a vassal status and the suzerain's hand mostly weighed lightly especially on the more powerful and remote vassal states. This created a fluid and malleable political system in which "society, the age-old divinely ordained way of Indian life, transcended the state and was independent of it. The king's function was the protection of society, and the state was merely an extension of the king for the furtherance of that end" (Basham 2004: 90).

From the personalized rule of kings, colonial rule transformed the nature and form of political authority in a fundamental and irreversible manner. The modern state's concept of sovereignty and the impersonal nature of public power eliminated the intermediary layers of political authority, encroached upon the autonomy of social processes, and appropriated the role of indigenous social regulatory mechanisms and organizations such as the caste system and the *Sangha* – societal definition in the Hindu and the monastic order Buddhist traditions, respectively. The British centralized the administration of the subcontinent and imposed political unity, thus creating a unitary, sovereign state which ruptured the old, indigenous, and creative mechanisms of compromise and collaboration between various identities and political authority (Jalal 1995: 9–10). Although this became a source of several security dilemmas for almost every South Asian state (Behera 2001: 21–28), few IR scholars have sought to explore the relevance of these historical experiences for understanding or ameliorating modern problematiques of IR.

At a deeper level, IR stands divorced from the Indian cosmology and its conceptions of subject–object, knowledge, individualism, and secularism bear no weight in this discipline. Scholars theorizing IR rarely, if at all, draw upon the myriad ways of knowing, ideas, and practices of India's "pasts" because the two operate in completely separate epistemological domains (Behera 2007). In other words, modern Indian IR has little to do with its own history and philosophy because there is a huge implicit, albeit untested, assumption that the latter has nothing to offer in terms of enhancing knowledge about its key subject matter – the state.

These intellectual traditions have, therefore, been discredited or rendered irrelevant as a source of knowledge creation. For instance, though political realism provides the principal foundation of Indian IR, it does not recognize its *own* Indian political philosopher Kautilya as "the father of *realpolitik*." Kautilya is not taught in any principal IR theory courses and though *Arthashastra* has much to offer for theorizing IR, applicability of his ideas is not acknowledged – almost universally. Kautilya's theory of *Mandala* (sphere or circle of influence, interest, and ambitions) assumes and is prepared for a world of eternally warring states by stressing "perpetual preparedness" or the doctrine of *Danda* (punishment, sanction) (Sarkar 1921: 83–89). International relations conceived in this political tradition derives from a purely secular theory of state with power as its sole basis permitting no ethical or moral considerations. Kautilya is, thus, the forerunner of the modern fathers of the realist traditions in IR as *Arthashastra* presupposes Hobbes' "state of nature," Machiavelli's "prince" as well as Kenneth Waltz's anarchic international system and the "security dilemma" of modern states. However, the disciplinary subject matter of Indian IR is completely silent on Kautilya.

The story of nationalism is not much different. Modern IR privileges the idea of territorial nationalism *à la* European style and therefore precludes the debate on how such key concepts of nationalism, nation-state, and territoriality could acquire different meanings. This may be briefly explained with reference to the Indian and Pakistani notions of nationalism.

Several conceptualizations and critiques of nationalism by Mahatma Gandhi, Jawaharlal Nehru, Rabindranath Tagore, M.S. Golwalkar, V.D. Savarkar, Bankim Chandra Chatterjee, and Sri Aurobindo Ghosh were at play in the political arena in pre-independence India. Most of these were not territorial in their vision, nor conceptualized in rationalist terms as understood in the modern instrumental sense. Ghosh wrote:

> For what is a nation? What is our mother country? It is not a piece of earth, nor a figure of speech, nor a fiction of the mind. It is a mighty *Shakti* (power), composed of all the *Shaktis* of all the millions of units that make up the nation.
>
> (Quoted in Singh 1967: 70–71)

He looked upon India as a living and pulsating spiritual entity, and nationalism was envisioned as a "deep and fervent religious *sadhana*," a spiritual imperative essential for the emancipation of the motherland from colonial rule (cited in Singh 1967: 74). Savarkar argued that the Hindus "are not only a nation but race-*jati*. The word *jati*, derived from the root *jan*, to produce, means a brotherhood, a race determined by a common origin, possessing a common blood" (1969: 84–85). He rejected the idea of a nation state based on an abstract social contract with individualized citizens dwelling within its administrative frontiers. From a very different vantage point the Gujrati text of Gandhi's *Hind Swaraj* makes a significant distinction between a genuine nation formed as *praja* (community) and a nation of individuals merely held together by state power characterized as *rashtra* (Gier 1996: 267). A most powerful critique of nationalism came from Tagore (1998 [1917]: 131–132):

> What is a Nation? It is the aspect of a whole people as an organised power. This organisation incessantly keeps up the insistence of the population on becoming strong and efficient. But this strenuous effort after strength and efficiency drains man's energy from his higher nature where he is self-sacrificing and creative. For thereby man's power of sacrifice is diverted from his ultimate object, which is moral, to the maintenance of this organisation, which is mechanical.

Thus nation "controls the life of the individual insofar as the needs of the State or Nation make it necessary" (quoted in Fenn Jr. 1929: 321).

The story of Pakistani nationalism, which, for the most part, evolved in juxtaposition to Indian nationalism, followed a similar trajectory. Those demanding Pakistan also rejected the notion of territorial nationalism, claiming that Islam transcended narrow ethnic and lingual differences. Allama Mohammad Iqbal, the poet-philosopher who had first proposed the idea of Pakistan in 1930, believed that "it is not the unity of language or country or the identity of economic interests that constitutes the basic principle of our nationality. . . . We are members of the society founded by the Prophet (PBUH)" (Vahid 1964: 396). Paradoxically, it was opposed by many *ulema* who thought that Muslim nationalism was un-Islamic. Followers of the Deoband movement who had sought to sustain their religion and culture apart from the colonial state could not reconcile territorial nationalism with concern for the solidarity of the worldwide Muslim community, the *umma*. Maulana Abdul Ali Maududi – the most influential exponent of Islamic nationalism in post-1947 Pakistan – unequivocally opposed the campaign for Pakistan as it was based on a secular notion of nationalism. He then insisted that "in the sight of God, Muslim nationalism is just as cursed as Indian nationalism" (quoted in Syed 1982: 35).

Alongside pan-Muslim nationalism, alternative conceptualizations of nationalisms on ethnic (the Pakhtun) and linguistic (Bengali) bases were also at play in the areas that later formed Pakistan. The people of the North-West Frontier Province (NWFP) demanded

Pakhtunistan, which envisaged Pathans and Punjabis as "two major nations by any definition or test of a nation," and argued that "the very thought of grouping the NWFP with the Punjabis [was] revolting to the Pathan mind." In East Bengal, Abdul Mansur Ahmad, President of the Bengal Muslim League, had declared in 1944 that

> religion and culture are not the same thing. Religion transgresses the geographical boundary but *tamaddum* (culture) cannot go beyond the geographical boundary. . . . For this reason the people of *Purba* (Eastern) Pakistan are a different nation . . . from the "religious brothers" of Pakistan.
>
> (Talbot 2003: 83)

After the creation of Pakistan in 1947, however, the stories of all such competing nationalisms were consigned to the dustbin of history. Successive rulers of Pakistan including Jinnah sought to build a "strong state" based on the principle of "one nation, one culture and one language." Hence, provincial mobilization of any ethnic identities was not only denounced as a threat to the Pakistani state, but in academia, students of political science and IR were not equipped with the tools for understanding the political pluralities of their social system which they experience on a day-to-day basis. This in turn creates a disjuncture between their theoretical frameworks and realities on the ground.

Overall, the impoverishment of Indian or Pakistani IR's disciplinary character cannot be understood without a thorough examination of their umbilical relationship with their respective states, born as they both were in August 1947. Following the footsteps – metaphorically and substantively – of its "Master Creator" (read Western IR) wherein "the realist power ritual administers silence regarding the historicity of the boundaries it produces, the space it historically clears and the subjects it historically constitutes" (Ashley cited in Tickner 2003: 300), Indian/Pakistani IR has also shied away from critically interrogating the story of its birth. Unless they do so, they cannot come to terms with *exclusions* that have long been taken for granted, accepted, and internalized even as they have stripped away its intellectual terrain.

Social sciences and the "project" of the state

Most social science inquiry in South Asia is accomplice to the project of the state (Uyangoda 1994). Hence there is an overwhelming insistence that social science must be policy relevant – though this is not unique to the discipline of IR or to South Asia. This emanates from the long-standing presumption that

> given the scarcity of economic resources in the Global South, resources devoted to higher education represent at best a luxury given their opportunity cost, and at worst a payoff or subsidy to keeping potentially dangerous members of the intelligentsia quiet. Under these circumstances, woe betide any academic who wants to engage in theory building "for its own sake" or conduct research for reasons of "pure curiosity."
>
> (Abraham 2004: 8)

Because the social sciences are primarily "valued for their utility; applied knowledge to further state goals. If theory came via this path, so be it" (Abraham 2004: 8). There is little realization that consistent and continuous production of high-quality theoretical research is the motor that drives any discipline's growth. In IR especially, a weak theoretical base that is often divorced from its ground of social realities poorly equips its scholars to produce useful policy-relevant research. Denigration of theoretical research in South Asia has had a devastating impact on the development of the IR discipline because unlike other social sciences, which offered some robust critiques of the nation state phenomenon, IR, as argued above, has shied away from critiquing the state, which in turn has completely stifled the scope of its intellectual inquiries.

Within the social sciences, economics has acquired a special significance particularly in the Nehruvian vision of a modern and industrialized India. "We want experts in the job," Nehru wrote in his autobiography, "who study and prepare detailed plans" (2004: 608), and the Indian state did indeed help create a critical mass of very able economists and world-class institutions. IR had no such luck, ironically because Nehru himself provided the much-needed and much-valued "expertise."

Prospects of IR in South Asia

The future of the IR discipline in South Asia will be determined by those critical choices which its scholarly community makes with respect to rebuilding its institutional infra-structure, rethinking its epistemic foundations, and augmenting its intellectual resource base by reworking its disciplinary boundaries.

Rebuilding the institutional infrastructure calls for undertaking a series of initiatives for revamping this discipline in the university system. This entails introducing it on a mass scale at the undergraduate level, substantially increasing the number of universities offering a Masters program, and institutionalizing mechanisms to fund these programs. A concerted effort is required to develop good-quality textbooks that explain IR to students in view of their historical, political, sociological, and geo-cultural contexts and experiences. Such books also need to be translated into various local/regional languages. Syllabi must impart a firm disciplinary grounding as well as enable students to use this knowledge in the marketplace. This will attract good talent to the IR discipline. Every country in South Asia must establish (if none exists) a professional body of IR scholars who will provide an intellectual platform for the seniors as well as to new entrants in the field.

The real challenge lies in rethinking the discipline's epistemic foundations by stepping out of the box of Western political realism and indigenizing the academic discourses of IR. This is necessary because standard realist tools have proved to be ineffective in understanding the diverse local realities and internal political character of the South Asian states. Hence few IR scholars have been able to explain the turmoil in states like Pakistan, Nepal, and Sri Lanka. Their state-centric worldview also does not suffice for making sense of a globalizing world that is characterized by a rapid diffusion of state authority. Most important, the "given" value system, foundational knowledge claims, and fixed parameters of the realist paradigm have allowed little room to create regional IR knowledge. This is because they have fought this intellectual battle on a turf chosen by the West, with tools designed and provided by the West and rules-of-game set by the West enforced, as they were, not just by its political and military might but, more importantly, by its all-pervasive discursive power. South Asian scholarship of IR has thus remained on the margins of the larger discipline.

South Asians must draw upon their own knowledge traditions and explore alterna-tive, non-traditional sites of IR scholarship for understanding their contemporary problema-tiques. Modern IR, for instance, privileges the claims of state sovereignty over all other kinds of political communities and assumes that "difference," especially cultural difference, is "debilitating to the purpose of establishing order" (Inayatullah and Blaney 2004: 94).

Hence, its overwhelming emphasis on "universalization" of state-making processes – the Westphalian state becoming the role model for *all* states. However, many plural societies of the third world are torn by conflicts precisely because their socio-cultural diversities are viewed as a political threat by the homogenizing impulses of the modern nation state. What lies at the root of most such conflicts – between various ethnic, linguistic, or religious communities and/or between such communities vis-à-vis the state – is a fundamental inability on the part of their political leadership to view differences and diversity as a source of strength rather than fear and danger. Internationally, there are divisive ramifications of externalizing the "other" in constructing a nationalist identity. A nationalist worldview inevitably generates hatred for an alien community or foreign country and makes these biases and prejudices a part of its national psyche. Against this backdrop, an alternative worldview of IR may be generated by drawing upon Indian ideas and practices, especially its non-dualistic mode of thinking (Behera 2007). These cultivate a political imagination that recognizes, understands, and nurtures differences and precludes the need to impose a particular set of norms as "universal values."

This intellectual endeavor does *not* aim at producing a "native" Indian, Pakistani, or Sri Lankan IR. Nativism is the exact reverse of universalism; both lack certain forms of self-reflexivity. The idea is to create spaces for alternative thinking on IR, which cannot be accomplished without a critical self-awareness *and* questioning of the a priori assumptions, procedures, and values embedded in the positivist enterprise. It means that "the question of what we keep and what we discard from the heritage of modernity needs explicit and ongoing discussion" (Inayatullah and Blaney 2004: 201). In addition, as argued earlier, there is a small albeit significant body of scholars in South Asia that is engaged in this critical endeavor. It is important to strengthen such voices and, most importantly, to bring them into the fold of IR by reworking its disciplinary boundaries. Throwing open the disciplinary gates of IR entails risks but taking such risks is not only worthwhile; they are also integral to the churning process which South Asian IR must go through to redefine itself and open up to the possibilities of alternative futures.

Notes

1   Research notes and review articles in all journals were not included in the survey. For *Alternatives*, the survey was done from 1980 to 2004. The 2005 and 2006 issues and that of 1977 (vol. 22), no. 2; 2002 (vol. 25), nos 1 and 4; and 2003 (vol. 26), no. 4 were not available. For *International Studies*, the survey was done from 1959 to 2006. This journal appears to have undergone a transition between 1968 and 1973 when only two volumes (nos 10 and 11) were published. Hence, no separate data were available for the years 1969 to 1972. In addition, the 2005 issue was missing as was the case for the *BIISS Journal* for which 2005 and 2006 issues were not available. *Strategic Studies* from 1977 to 2000 and *International Studies* from 1959 to 1972 did not have a straight co-relation in terms of volumes and years of publication as some volumes were published over a two-year period. In all such cases the data for all issues of a particular volume have been amalgamated in a single (first) year. The missing issues included 1979 (vol. 2), no. 2; 1980 (vol. 3), no. 2; 1990 (vol. 14), no. 4; 1992 (vol. 15), no. 1. *Strategic Studies* combined the publication of years 1995 and 1996 in a single vol. 18 and that of 1999, 2000, and 2001 in vol. 20. These have been listed under the years 1995 and 1998 respectively.

2   For the purposes of content analysis of these journals, an article that researches theoretical approaches (existing or new)/debates among different theoretical approaches or methodological issues of IR has been classified as a "theoretical" piece of research. If a research article deploys an existing/new theoretical framework to undertake an empirical analysis of any particular problematique in IR, it has been classified as "theoretically informed" research. In addition, if an article offers a historical or narrative account of any issue whether it is about foreign relations of a

particular state or addresses a disciplinary issue, for example, the working of the United Nations, it has been classified as an "empirical" research category.

3   JNU professors narrate interesting anecdotes of the easy availability of Morgenthau's low-priced book in the university campuses.

4   CSDS's work has been equated to the early Frankfurt School critiques of Enlightenment (Dallmayr 1996).

5   The Observer Research Foundation, a think-tank based in Delhi with another office in Chennai, is supported by the Reliance industries. Another center, the Delhi Policy Group, receives support from the Sriram Group of industries.

References

Abraham, Itty (1998) *The Making of the Indian Atom Bomb: Science, Secrecy and the Post-colonial State*, London: Zed Books.

Abraham, Itty (2004) "The Changing Institutional–intellectual Ecology of Knowledge-production in South Asia," paper presented at the UNESCO Forum on Higher Education, Knowledge and Research, Paris, December 1–3.

Acharya, Amitav and Barry Buzan (2007) "Why Is There No Non-Western IR Theory: Reflections on and from Asia," *International Relations of the Asia-Pacific*, 7 (3): 285–286.

Alavi, Hamza and Fred Halliday (eds) (1988) *State and Ideology in the Middle East and Pakistan*, London: Macmillan.

Ali, Mahmud S. (1993) *The Fearful State: Power, People and Internal War in South Asia*, London: Zed Books.

Appadurai, Arjun (1996) *Modernity at Large: Cultural Dimensions of Globalization*, Minneapolis: University of Minnesota Press.

Armstrong, H.F. (1956–1957) "Neutrality: Varying Tunes," *Foreign Affairs*, 35: 57–83.

Ayoob, Mohammed (1995) *The Third World Security Predicament: State Making, Regional Conflict and International System*, Boulder, CO: Lynne Rienner.

Bajpai, Kanti (2003) "Indian Conceptions of Order and Justice: Nehruvian, Gandhian, Hindutva and Neo-liberal," in Rosemary Foot *et al.* (eds), *Order and Justice in International Relations*, New York: Oxford University Press, pp. 236–261.

Basham, A.L. (2004) *The Wonder That Was India*, London: Picador.

Basrur, Rajesh (2005) *Minimum Deterrence and India's Security*, Stanford, CA: Stanford University Press.

Bastian, Sunil (ed.) (1994) *State and Devolution in Sri Lanka*, New Delhi: Konark.

Behera, Navnita Chadha (ed.) (2001) *State, People and Security: The South Asian Context*, New Delhi: Har-Anand.

Behera, Navnita Chadha (2004) "Meta Narratives and Subaltern Voices: Role of the Ford Foundation in South Asia," paper presented at the annual meeting of the International Studies Association (ISA), Montreal, Canada, March 17–20.

Behera, Navnita Chadha (ed.) (2006) *Gender, Conflict and Migration*, New Delhi: Sage.

Behera, Navnita Chadha (2007) "Re-imagining IR in India," *International Relations of the Asia-Pacific*, 7 (3): 341–368.

Bhabha, Homi (1994) *The Location of Culture*, London: Routledge.

Chenoy, Anuradha M. (2002) *Militarism and Women in South Asia*, New Delhi: Kali for Women.

Chimni, B.S. (1993) *International Law and World Order: A Critique of Contemporary Approaches*, New Delhi: Sage.

Dallmayr, Fred R. (1996) *Beyond Orientalism: Essays on Cross-cultural Encounter*, Albany, NY: SUNY Press.

Darby, Phillip (2003) "Reconfiguring 'the International': Knowledge Machines, Boundaries, and Exclusions," *Alternatives*, 28 (1): 141–166.

Debrah, E.M. (1961) "Will Uncommitted Countries Remain Uncommitted?," *Annals of the American Academy of Political and Social Science*, 336 (July): 83–97.

Dinh, Tran Van (1975) "Non-aligned but Committed to the Hilt," *Pacific Community*, 7 (1): 118–131.

Dutt, Sri Kant (1984) *India and the Third World: Altruism or Hegemony?*, London: Zed Books.

Fenn Jr., Percy Thomas (1929) "An Indian Poet Looks at the West," *International Journal of Ethics*, 39 (3): 313–323.

Gardezi, Hasan H. (1991) *Understanding Pakistan: The Colonial Factor in Societal Development*, Lahore: Maktaba.

Gier, Nicholas F. (1996) "Gandhi: Pre-modern, Modern or Post-modern?," *Gandhi Marg*, 17 (3): 261–281.

Hagerty, Devin (1991) "India's Regional Security Doctrine," *Asian Survey*, 31 (4): 351–363.

Harshe, Rajen (1997) *Twentieth Century Imperialism: Shifting Contours and Changing Perceptions*, New Delhi: Sage.

Harshe, Rajen (ed.) (2004) *Interpreting Globalisation: Perspectives in International Relations*, New Delhi: Rawat.

Hussain, Neelam, Samiya Mumtaz, and Rubina Saigol (eds) (1997) *Engendering the Nation-state*, Volumes I and II, Lahore: Simorgh.

Inayatullah, Naeem and David L. Blaney (2004) *International Relations and the Problem of Difference*, New York: Routledge.

Jaipal, Rikhi (1983) *Non-alignment: Origins, Growth and Potential for World Peace*, New Delhi: South Asia Books.

Jalal, Ayesha (1995) *Democracy and Authoritarianism in South Asia: A Comparative and Historical Perspective*, New Delhi: Foundation Books.

Kalam, Abul and Akmal Hussain (2003) "Teaching of International Relations at University Level in Bangladesh," in USEFI Report, *Teaching of International Relations in South Asian Universities*, New Delhi: USEFI.

Karnad, Bharat (2002) *Nuclear Weapons and Indian Security: The Realist Foundations of Strategy*, New Delhi: Macmillan.

Khan, Rasheeduddin (ed.) (1981) *Perspectives on Non-alignment*, New Delhi: Kalamkar.

Khatri, Sridhar H. (2003) "Teaching of International Relations in Nepal," in USEFI Report, *Teaching of International Relations in South Asian Universities*, New Delhi: USEFI.

Kothari, Rajni (1979–1980) "Towards a Just World," *Alternatives*, 5 (1): 1–42.

Kothari, Smitu and Zia Mian (eds) (2001) *Out of the Nuclear Shadow*, Karachi: Oxford University Press.

Lal, Vinay (ed.) (2000) *Dissenting Knowledges, Open Futures: The Multiple Selves and Strange Destinations of Ashis Nandy*, New Delhi: Oxford University Press.

Manchanda, Rita (ed.) (2001) *Women, War and Peace in South Asia: Beyond Victimhood to Agency*, New Delhi: Sage.

Muni, S.D. (1980) "South Asia," in Mohammed Ayoob (ed.), *Conflict and Intervention in the Third World*, New York: St. Martin Press.

Nandy, Ashish (1987) *Traditions, Tyranny and Utopia*, New Delhi: Oxford University Press.

Nehru, Jawaharlal (2004) *An Autobiography*, New Delhi: Penguin.

Rais, Rasul Bakhsh (2005) "Teaching of International Relations in Pakistani Universities," in N. Inayatullah *et al.*, *Social Sciences in Pakistan: A Profile*, Islamabad: Council of Social Sciences.

Rajagopalan, Swarna and Farah Faizal (eds) (2005) *Women, Security, South Asia: A Clearing in the Thicket*, New Delhi: Sage.

Rana, A.P. (1988a) *Reconstructing International Relations as a Field of Study in India, Studying International Relations: The Baroda Perspective*, Occasional Review I, Baroda: The M.S. University.

Rana, A.P. (1988b) *The International Relations Study of the Political Universe*, Occasional Review II, Baroda: The M.S. University.

Rana, A.P. and K.P. Misra (2004) "Communicative Discourse and Community in International Relations Studies in India: A Critique," in Kanti Bajpai and Siddharth Mallavarapu (eds), *International Relations in India: Bringing Theory Back Home*, New Delhi: Orient Longman, pp. 71–122.

Riaz, Ali (1994) *State, Class and Military Rule*, Dhaka: Nadi New Press.

Samaddar, R. and Helmut Reifeld (eds) (2001) *Peace as Process: Reconciliation and Conflict Resolution in South Asia*, New Delhi: Manohar.

Sarkar, Benoy Kumar (1921) "The Hindu Theory of the State," *Political Science Quarterly*, 36 (1): 79–90.

Savarkar, V.D. (1969) *Hindutva: Who Is a Hindu?*, Bombay: S.S. Savarkar.

Sheth, D.L. (1983) "Grass Roots Stirrings and the Future of Politics," *Alternatives*, 9 (1): 1–24.

Singh, Karan (1967) *Prophet of Indian Nationalism: A Study of the Political Thought of Sri Aurobindo Ghosh, 1893–1910*, New Delhi: Bhartiya Vidya Bhavan.

Srestha Anand, P. and Hari Uprety (eds) (2003) *Conflict Resolution and Governance in Nepal*, Kathmandu: NEFAS.

Syed, A.H. (1982) *Pakistan, Islam, Politics and National Solidarity*, New York: Praeger.

Tagore, Rabindranath (1998 [1917]) *Nationalism*, USA: Kessinger Publishing.

Talbot, Ian (2003) "Back to the Future? Pakistan, History and the Nation Building," in Charles H. Kennedy *et al.* (eds), *Pakistan at the Millennium*, Karachi: Oxford University Press.

Tickner, Arlene B. (2003) "Seeing IR Differently: Notes from the Third World," *Millennium*, 32 (2): 295–324.

Uyangoda, Jayadeva (1994) "The State and the Process of Devolution in Sri Lanka," in Sunil Bastian (ed.), *State and Devolution in Sri Lanka*, New Delhi: Konark.

Vahid, S.A. (1964) *Thoughts and Reflections of Iqbal*, Lahore: S.L. Ashraf & Sons.

Vanaik, Achin (1995) *India in a Changing World*, New Delhi: Orient Longman.

Wignaraja, Ponna and Akmal Hussain (eds) (1989) *The Challenge in South Asia: Development, Democracy and Regional Cooperation*, New Delhi: Sage.

9 Iran
Accomplishments and limitations in IR

Mahmood Sariolghalam

This chapter addresses how the field of International Relations evolved in Iran before and after the Islamic Revolution. A close connection is drawn between the aura and priorities of the state and the evolution of political science and IR. Historical, economic, and, most important, sociological variables are presented to explain this evolution. The study of politics in its modern sense is a new phenomenon in Iran. However, alongside economics, it has become a prestigious and socially influential area of study in the post-revolutionary period. This chapter surveys the challenges and paradoxes of the IR discipline in Iran's university system and society at large. It examines the hypothesis that although IR theories and methodologies have had virtually no impact upon the way in which the Islamic Republic defines the global system and conducts its foreign relations, its influence today among students, the intellectual community, and the interested public is unprecedented. IR has emerged as a conduit between Iran and the global community under conditions where state institutions systematically defy the international system, its patterns, and its logic. The chapter concludes that as Iran undergoes changes in its political and social orientation, political science and IR will play an even larger role not only in providing raw data about the world but also by introducing knowledge on how other countries are being transformed and what Iran could learn from them.

IR before the Iranian Revolution

As an ancient state dating back more than 3,000 years, political writings in Iran have generally been produced in the form of memoirs, travel journals (*Safar Nameh*), or books of advice to political leaders (*Siasat Nameh*). In international relations categories, these writings symbolize the traditional school represented by the classic works of Niccolò Machiavelli, and in the twentieth century by E.H. Carr and Hans Morgenthau. Almost all of these books take a philosophical approach to discussions of man, society, politics, and ways of governing societies. They end with prescriptions on effective governance and statecraft. Often, the authors of these writings served in the royal courts or were political and social philosophers of their times. For example, Abu Nasr Farabi (870–952), in his *Utopia*, focuses on how to achieve prosperity and serve the public good. Farabi is interested in reform and encourages leaders to expand their learning horizons by drawing from the Egyptian and Greek civilizations. Specifically, Farabi pays attention to how the Greeks interpret the universe and define man and society. Moreover, he believes that the fate of societies is intertwined with their construction of reason, and that reason reflects their understanding of the environment (Tabatabaee 1989: 19–20). In his monumental work *Seirol-Mollook* (A Journey through Nations), Neza-mol Molk (987–1064) concentrates strictly on prescriptions. At the order of

King Malekshah Saljoughi, Neza-mol Molk wrote a critical work emphasizing the deficiencies of governance under the king. His writings are still a source for Iranian political theory. Their relevance, even today, suggests that political traditions and behavior in Iran have changed surprisingly little, and that ironically the rules of the political game have endured for centuries (Sariolghalam 1992: 3). Abu Hamed Ghazzali (1029–1084) is another prominent Iranian political philosopher whose work on the problems of the day and his prescriptions to correct them drew on the experiences of other nations and empires. His *Naseehatol-Molook* (Advice for the Kings) is a critical analysis of everyday conditions and provides extensive problem-solving prescriptions (Sariolghalam 1992: 38).

As was the case with most other ancient societies, writings in philosophy, ethics, and religion received vast public attention. Politics and particularly international politics were matters for the ruling elites and their courts. The elites relied primarily on oral communications and exchanges both within the courts and with their counterparts visiting from other countries or empires. These writings mirror the nature of social construction in ancient Iran. Persia, as it used to be called, was a huge empire extending from the Mediterranean to the borders of China. Although status quo doctrines were widely used to rule the empire, the geography of the empire and the experience that people gained through their travels along the Silk Road brought new knowledge and wisdom to the courts. A philosophical mind-set also breathed new air into Iranians' historical interest in other cultures and civilizations. The aforementioned writings echo a deep concern to learn, improve, and advance; concerns that are still being pursued in modern Iran.

It was only in 1934 that the University of Tehran, the first university in its modern sense, was established in Iran. The School of Law and Political Science was one of three schools. Following the French tradition, law and politics were placed together (Azghandi 2003: 41). Similar to the Chinese, Russian, and Arab intellectual traditions, students and faculty of politics and international relations in Iran prided themselves in studying political theory and political philosophy. Not only were Iranian philosophers such as Farabi carefully studied, but more attention was paid to Kant, Rousseau, Montesquieu, and Weber. This tradition, which began under Reza Shah (1920–1941) and continued through the reign of his son (1941–1979), led to several important consequences. First, the analysis of contemporary issues was considered unsophisticated and journalistic, while attention to abstractions was highly valued because such analytical exercises were considered to be closer to philosophy. While philosophy was considered the mother of all knowledge, focus on contemporary problems required some proximity to power to be able to have access to data and inside information. Second, positivist methodology was never widely accepted and advanced by the majority of those involved in knowledge building, given that scholarly value was judged according to the abstractness of academic analyses rather than their concreteness and precision. This tendency is still apparent in Iran's institutions of higher education.

Moreover, for academics on the Left, conventional wisdom demanded that true intellectuals keep their distance from centers of power. Such an atmosphere led academic and intellectual work to revolve primarily around abstractions and theoretical approaches. Ambiguity and subtlety were considered virtues; it was widely understood that one had to read between the lines to understand exactly what an author meant. Because of state control and the dictatorial nature of the Shah's regime, it was also safer to avoid critical thinking and direct commentary on everyday matters. At the time, political correctness dictated that the Western-oriented policies of the Iranian government be promoted, particularly Iranian–American strategic relations. Criticism of the state, its policies and practices normally led to serious repercussions. Therefore, critiques, when they were formulated, were conceived theoretically.

Iranian academics were divided along nationalist, liberal, and Marxist lines. To a large extent, divisions in daily politics extended into the study of international politics. There were those who based Iran's foreign policy outlook exclusively on Iranian nationalism. They believed that the country had to maintain its monarchical traditions and integrate itself into the Western world. The liberal tradition distanced itself from monarchy and promoted civil society and competitive politics. It believed that monarchism was outdated and that Iran should move towards liberal democracy. The Iranian Left focused on socialist ideas and methods. Between the 1950s and the onset of the Iranian Revolution of 1979, among the three groups it was the Marxists who were the most organized, sophisticated, and influential in the field of politics and in international politics.

Another prominent university with a Department of Politics was established in 1965. The School of Economics and Political Science at the National University of Iran, modeled somewhat after the American tradition of integrating IR and political economy studies, expanded the teaching of international relations and politics in the country (Azghandi 2003: 59). In both politics and economics, liberal views commanded theoretical approaches in this new school. Islamic approaches to politics, which became prevalent in the post-revolutionary period, were almost non-existent in departments of politics during this period. On both campuses, International Relations were taught in the form of a number of courses, notably international relations theories, politics of the great powers, American foreign policy, state and politics in Europe, China, the Soviet Union and the Middle East. Historical accounts, descriptive foreign policy, and patterns of state behavior were emphasized in these courses. The field of IR was initially introduced in Iran during the late 1960s through a number of scholars, who were typically educated in the United States and Britain. Most taught at the Tehran and National Universities and relied upon their own personal accounts and interpretations of the field, using translated texts from Hans Morgenthau, E.H. Carr, and Charles McClelland (Azghandi 2003: 44–50; 61–68).

Traditionally, Iran's schools of political science have exerted almost no influence in the actual political decision-making processes of the country; a tradition that has continued in the post-revolutionary period. Politics in Iran has usually served the interests of individuals and rarely the interests of the country. This may explain why ideas, whatever their ideological bent – liberal, Marxist, or even Islamic – have not found their way into the decision-making process. In consequence, the majority of scholars and theoreticians have found themselves alien, irrelevant, and even an annoyance in the political arena. Within IR studies, the focus was on foreign policy theories. Some instructors dubbed as "court academics" made use of modernization theories to justify the Shah's policies and international conduct. Many of the subdivisions of IR, including IPE, strategic studies, conflict resolution, regional studies, third world studies, cognitive studies, and political psychology, received scant attention by instructors. Finally, most academics based their teaching upon personal notes drawn substantially from Western literature. Research was not a strict requirement for tenure or promotion. Rather, networking with individuals in high places or prestigious institutions in the West was considered far more important in providing academic security and status in higher education and in the larger society.

In the field of International Relations, there was only one textbook in Farsi during this period (Behzadi 1975). It focused on power politics and gave a classic account of foreign policy analysis as substantiated by Hans Morgenthau. In 1965, the Center for Advanced International Studies was established at the University of Tehran. This Center produced policy series and organized roundtables on the issues of the day. The Center also offered graduate programs in international politics (Azghandi 2003: 55–57). In sum, from classroom teaching to student dissertations, the study of IR in pre-revolutionary Iran concentrated on historical, journalistic, and descriptive accounts of international issues and country studies. Rigorous methodological and theoretical approaches to studying politics were not prevalent. While scholars, particularly in the United States, constructed new positivist paradigms in IR and engaged in sophisticated methodological debates in realism, idealism, behavioralism, and globalism, the Iranian university system remained traditional and uninterested in the new approaches. Iran's academic community focused fundamentally on realist theories of international relations. New approaches and schools of thought in IR did not reach Iran until after the Revolution.

IR in the first decade of the Revolution

The Iranian Revolution was the historical outcome of defying foreign rule in Iran. Foreign and especially Western ideas and commodities were perceived as a threat to national sovereignty, indigenous culture, and the political integrity of the country. The mindset of the Iranian post-revolutionary leadership was anti-colonial, anti-imperialist, and anti-Western. During the first decade of the revolution, the Islamic Republic of Iran promoted economic self-sufficiency, political sovereignty, cultural indigeneity, and Islamic identity. While most successful members of the developing world, including Malaysia, Turkey, Brazil, China, and South Korea, sustained development by further integrating themselves to the world, Iran took the opposite path, defying the international system, its theories, constructs, and applications (Sariolghalam 2003: 69–82).

Given this political context, those academics who remained in Iran after the revolution immersed themselves further in abstractions and deductive thinking, mainly because none of them had been exposed to Islamic thought. The revolution forced everyone to adopt Islamic outlooks and ways of thinking. During the first two years, a stand-off emerged between Islamic, Marxist, and liberal thinking, while in the years preceding the revolution, the majority of intellectuals in Iran's universities were either Marxist or liberal. With Islamic thinking streaming into the country's political life as a result of the revolution, the well-organized and well-reasoned Marxists and liberals found themselves debating political, social, and economic issues with the Islamists. Politically, however, and for the duration of the Iran–Iraq war (1980–1988), Marxism and liberalism were marginalized. As in the case of the "Leninizing" process of the Soviet system during the 1930s and the "Maoizing" of the People's Republic of China in the 1950s, the Iranian university system focused on "Islamizing" the social sciences in the 1980s. Almost every notion and idea was customized into some kind of Islamic interpretation recalling examples from the early days of Islam in the sixth century. As a result of state directives and rules guiding political correctness, curricula, lectures, and conceptual frameworks were universally developed and assessed according to Islamic axioms. Ideologically oriented instructors in various social sciences departments began to deconstruct engraved Western notions of the individual, society, the state, economic development, the logic of social cohesion, and finally, "materialistic international relations."

An ideological breakthrough occurred during the cultural revolution of 1981 to 1984, when the universities were forced to shut down. Since the university campuses were the main forum for discussion among the advocates of various ideological leanings in the early days of the revolution, the cultural revolution marginalized liberal and Marxist ideologies and advocates on distinct campuses. The Islamic paradigm then emerged as the dominant mode of thinking. The Iran–Iraq war also provided the security grounds for such practices to intensify, permeate, and become institutionalized. Because the country was facing a foreign enemy and had to fight a war and defend its borders, the mainstream Islamic paradigm overruled other paradigms in the name of national security. The bulk of the intellectual community of liberals and leftists left Iran during the war. Once settled in Europe and North America, they reorganized and began undermining the Islamic paradigm and methods of governance.

Consequently, the kinds of political science and International Relations developed in North America and Britain were curbed during the first decade of the revolution. Leaders of Iran argued that the Iranian Revolution set an example not only for the Muslim world but also for the developing world. They argued that it defied the global system institutionalized by the West and that it was creating a new international order based on egalitarianism and ethics. This fantasy never moved beyond rhetorical pronouncements. Aside from pockets of Shii communities in the Muslim world, Iran's model of state and its idealist foreign policy were not even accepted by Muslim countries, let alone by the developing world which increasingly concentrated its efforts on integrating with the West for economic gain. It was claimed that it was only a matter of time and people's unity before such objectives were achieved. The divisive international system and its capitalist foundations had to be abandoned by Muslims and those striving for justice and liberty.

The nature of the Iranian revolutionary polity thus provided new thinking about the country's international relations (Sariolghalam 1998: 426–427). Iran rejected the idea that countries should be categorized according to their economic power. According to Iranian interpretations, power stemmed from spiritual and moral sources rather than gross national product or technological innovation. Based upon Islamic traditions, Iran divided the world between the believers and non-believers. However, despite a vigorous drive to build new institutions and orient daily politics towards Islamic principles, scholarly literature was produced neither by the clerics nor by the academics. Unlike the Chinese and Soviet cases, where a body of literature and somewhat theoretical works on international relations were published by both the universities and the Communist parties, literature on world politics in post-revolutionary Iran remained polemical, descriptive, ideological, resentful, and prescriptive. In other words, there was no model for how Iran could launch its Islamic paradigm at the foreign policy level. As a result, the country's external conduct was beset by contradictions and paradoxes. At one level, Iran desired normal relations with its neighbors. At another, it promoted the Islamists in the neighboring states. These contradictory behaviors resulted in distrust, oscillatory relations, and even complete breakups.

Iranian–Saudi relations are a classic example. In a period of five years (1992–1997), Iran shifted from a characterization of Saudi Arabia as an enemy of Islam to one in which that country became its most significant pillar. At one level, Iran conducted commercial relations with the Europeans. At another, it rejected liberal democracy, secularism, and their support of Israel. At one level, Iran worked hard to join the World Trade Organization. At another, it rejected capitalism, globalization, and the Western role in managing the global economy. Layers of contradictory behavior characterized Iran's foreign policy behavior and this behavior drastically reduced its chances of emerging as a model for Muslim and developing countries.

Within the Shii seminaries, theorizing on politics was a minor preoccupation. Even those clerics who were politicized became activists, preachers, and organizers of popular protests against the Shah's regime. Few clerics who chose to enter the Iranian university system in the early 1970s to challenge the dominant Marxist thinking among students began to present Islam in a theoretical construct. The works and the activities of Morteza Mottahari stand out as an example. He produced a considerable number of books and pamphlets on Islam written in an orderly and analytical manner. However, international politics were not part of his research concerns. In a culture that values oral interaction far more than written expression, most Iranians heard about ideological interpretations of politics and international issues on state-run television, or at public sermons and Friday prayers. However, theorizing on global patterns, structures, and interactions from Islamic premises was almost non-existent. The temperament was one of defiant practice rather than scholarship. Anger at foreign intervention and expansionist policies of the Europeans and Americans was so deep that all things foreign came to be seen through the lens of a past in which Iran and Iranians had been mistreated.

The Iranian Foreign Ministry experienced an almost complete overhaul after the revolution. Most of the new diplomats entering the foreign service had training in engineering and medicine. There was a simple reason for this development. In the 1960s and the 1970s almost all Islamists chose to study engineering while some entered medical school. However, some 15 years after the revolution many engineers began their graduate work in political science and International Relations. Part of the explanation for interest in these fields was most likely a need to better understand how the rest of the world conducted politics and directed its foreign policy. In addition, Iran's political science and International Relations community became increasingly resentful of engineers' and physicians' involvement in politics and foreign policy decision-making, leading the latter to seek out formal training.[1] In 1988, following the Iran–Iraq war, as the Islamic Republic began an era of economic reconstruction and political engagement with the rest of the world, liberal modes of thinking returned to media, campuses, and classrooms. President Akbar Rafsanjani (1989–1997) sought out national economic development, which in turn required an accommodative foreign policy. Increasingly, while at the rhetorical level Iran spoke in terms of Islamism, at the political and practical levels the country's economy was run according to international norms, and its foreign policy focused increasingly on national interests.

IR during the second decade of the revolution

During the second decade of the revolution, at least initially, the confrontational mood in Iran's approach to international relations was tempered down. Rafsanjani's presidency introduced considerable degrees of caution in coming to grips with global realities. It paid lip-service to revolutionary idealism at the same time that it pursued national economic interests by promoting trade, privatization, and industrialization. Economics, at least for some five years, dominated national politics. Although revolutionary ideas about the global order, the Western world, and Middle Eastern issues continued to occupy a central role in official discourse, Iran gradually returned to its traditional trade partners. This situation also set the tone for academia. Academics produced and for the most part translated Western writings on globalization, modernization, democratization, interdependence, and postmodernism. In turn, defiant foreign policy approaches were downplayed (Ehteshami 1995: 115–121).

In response to this shift, political science and International Relations departments were established even in remote parts of the country. Islamic Azad University, a private institution, created 73 departments of political science between 1995 and 2006 in 21 provinces. In contrast to previous educational traditions in Iran, whereby engineering and medicine were considered the ultimate sciences, throughout the 1990s obtaining a degree in political science or economics became highly fashionable, partly because graduates in these fields could write articles in journals and newspapers and appear on television shows to explain both domestic and international phenomena. In other words, education in these fields provided opportunities for greater visibility and demonstration of intellectualism. Thus it is not surprising that political science and IR schools mushroomed throughout Iran (Azghandi 2003: 126–131). Even in the religious city of Qum, five schools of political science were opened in the early 1990s. For many clerics, holding a university degree brought considerable social and academic prestige.

Nonetheless, the literature that was used in classrooms remained liberal, Western, and particularly American. The availability of Western literature far exceeded that of domestic literature, which was basically abstract and idealistic. In addition, Western literature provided an opportunity to translate books and to respond to market demands. At the same time, however, the national state-run television station promoted anti-Westernism and aired lectures and roundtables that ridiculed Western philosophy and Western lifestyles. In tandem, national religious leaders encouraged academics and students to engage in the process of "indigenization" of the social sciences. Throughout the duration of the Revolution, senior Iranian leadership has relied on indigenization to move away from Western literature and towards Islamic interpretations. In fact, several research institutes have received state funding precisely in order to produce "Islamic social sciences." Although many attempts have been made to do just this, especially in economics, and in reference to the principles of the Islamic state, such efforts remain primitive and highly abstract; they have been unsuccessful in influencing mainstream scholarship, let alone becoming the mainstream.

With the presidency of Mohammad Khatami in 1997, which promoted civil society and democracy in the country, anti-Western campaigns were revitalized. New formulations forging Islam with democracy surfaced. During the Rafsanjani government, divisions had begun to take shape within the Iranian polity and society at large concerning the accommodative–confrontational spectrum of both domestic politics and Iran's international relations. However, under Khatami's rule these divisions deepened and were consolidated. Although there has been a consistent national political stand-off between accommodative and confrontational paradigms since 1989, the IR literature produced and translated by academics and taught at universities has remained liberal. This partly explains the conceptual divide between the state and the university system in Iran. Prominent scholars of political science and IR in Iran have found it very difficult to provide consultation to the state because the overwhelming majority of individuals running Iran's politics and foreign policy have either engineering or medical backgrounds. There are huge gaps in understanding political phenomena. Interestingly, in terms of education, Islamic fundamentalists are either engineers or physicians. Throughout the Muslim world, there is hardly a single social scientist with fundamentalist leanings. It can be safely claimed that in post-revolutionary Iran not a single respected political science or IR scholar has been able to reach the higher echelons of the Iranian government. There is a simple explanation. Dominant paradigms in political science and IR scholarship counter those that prevail in the halls of the government. The two sides lack a vocabulary for conceptual communication. Writings that tend to adopt an Islamic outlook on international relations reflect a defiance of the current order without providing an alternative. However, over the past decade, literature on the philosophical and epistemological foundations of the Islamic political system has been produced by some clerics, as well as ideologically oriented academics. This kind of literature on international relations with an Islamic outlook in the form of newspaper editorials or essays tends to be rhetorical. Part of the explanation for this has to do with the fact that Islamic scholarship in Iran has remained abstract for centuries and has never had the opportunity to be applied to real-life situations. Former President Rafsanjani is almost the only Iranian cleric who developed an interest in statistics, mathematics, and raw data. He is the only post-revolutionary Iranian leader who has spoken in concrete terms. Even former President Khatami spoke in abstract terms when outlining his thinking on justice, liberty, and the dialogue of civilizations.

The confrontational–accommodative dichotomy in the evolution of Iranian IR is indicative of larger dynamics in Iranian political life. Undoubtedly, sociological explanations are needed to analyze this political divide within the country and the ways in which it manifests itself at the level of academic practice. The majority of the scholarly community is conscious of changes at the international level and is interested in integrating and interacting with the rest of the world. It is interested in learning from outside experiences and knowledge but also in contributing to their enrichment. However, another part of academia, along with the policy establishment, resents the world and especially the West. This resentment ranges from traffic rules to interpretations of the universe in the West. Nonetheless, when studied carefully, the resentment has less to do with reason and more with temperament. Ideologically oriented individuals are not willing to forgive and forget the Western historical record in Iranian politics and culture. It seems that this constant reference to the past behavior of the West is more an indication of weakness and frustration rather than a political ideology based upon calculation and strategy. It is ironic that the resentful group has consistently had the upper hand in politics because of its populist appeal.

As suggested above, there appears to be a connection between the nature of the polity and the revolutionary focus of the international outlook in Iran's political establishment. Whereas within the state, normative and revolutionary idealism dominates foreign policy approaches, academic institutions are more or less free to concentrate on realist and liberal schools of thought that account for mainstream thinking around the world. As stated previously, revolutionary thinking in Iran does not recognize power differentiations among states, given that all states are equal. In addition, GNP, per capita income, and technological leverage are totally dismissed. What differentiates states is how they regard justice, spirituality, and egalitarianism in their conduct – ambiguous terms that are hard to measure. Moreover, the confrontational–accommodative dichotomy mirrors the revolutionary-internationalist political spectrum in post-revolutionary Iran. The revolutionary paradigm reflects a pan-Islamist view of politics, downplays the notion of the nation state, and considers the international system as its analytical unit. Clearly, these beliefs are rooted in Islamic principles. Therefore, it is rejectionist and strives to replace the current system with an Islamic one. In contrast, the internationalist outlook views the nation state as the prevailing unit of analysis. Moreover, the internationalist aims at developing the state and its economic and social capacity. For the advocates of internationalism, the international system is an opportunity. While the internationalists can simply draw on the liberal literature to develop a strategy of action and follow the examples of Malaysia, South Korea, and China, Islamists apply a politics of opposition to the logic and "materialistic" principles of the current global system (Sariolghalam 2005: 174–178).

For the most part, Iran's schools of International Relations have upheld internationalist principles by relying on translated liberal writings. Ironically, much of the university system and almost all social science research institutes in Iran are state-owned. Privatization of higher education in Iran began in the early 1990s. In the private sector too, IR education draws on the Western and liberal literature. Because liberal views in the university system are so dominant, accounting for some 50,000 academics, there is not much the state can do to redirect the educational system. Nonetheless, it should be mentioned that Iranians, clerics included, have three layers in their intellectual construct: Islamic, socialist, and liberal. Of course, the relative weight of each layer varies from one individual to another. As citizens and politicians, Iranians pick and choose from these baskets of knowledge depending on the particular situation. In consequence, the last thing one can expect is for Iranians to be harmonious in the way they define phenomena and practice politics.

As to the foreign policy decision-making apparatus in the country, the revolutionary paradigm has continued to dominate debates, discussion, and decision-making processes. Despite attempts to improve Iran's global standing, both Presidents Rafsanjani and Khatami, who believed in the accommodative school of thought, failed to sustain and institutionalize their initiatives. One fundamental reason is that the major institutions of the country were led by the revolutionary groups and thus had the authority and resources to maintain their confrontational momentum.

Iran's foreign policy conduct is based neither on research originating from the university system nor relevant research institutes. Foreign policy officials usually distrust political science or International Relations scholars; the latter's non-revolutionary frame of reference cannot serve the officials' cognitive constructs and policy priorities and preferences. Mainstream IR knowledge within the academic community is drawn from the Western world and especially literature produced in the United States. Ideological approaches to IR in the university system are a very small and minority view, and the proponents of these ideological perspectives are somehow linked to the institutions of the state. Part of the distance between the academic community and the state arises from the nature of the foreign policy of the Islamic Republic; a foreign policy that does not account for the nation state, the power configuration of the contemporary international system and dissociates economic interactions from political undertakings. This analysis suggests that there is some space and recognizable distance between Iran's academic community in general, and the field of IR in particular, and state preferences and obligations. In this sense, the Islamic Republic is markedly different from the state–university modalities of the former Soviet Union.

In the post-revolutionary period, not a single person in the higher echelons of Iran's foreign policy establishment has had training in political science or International Relations. The IR-educated academic elite have presented their views in conferences or at best have served as occasional advisors to foreign policy officials. Much of the academic discussion in official circles has also been reframed in ideological terms in order to gain acceptance on the part of the foreign policy establishment. If an IR scholar wishes to be influential in foreign policy circles, he or she is obliged to provide ideological window dressing in analyzing IR phenomena and Iranian foreign policy. One particular stance that is indispensable in gaining recognition is opposition to United States policies and condemnation of the state of Israel. In a country where ambiguity is a virtue, this practice has not been an arduous task. As a result, mainstream IR theories and methodologies have remained outside the decision-making processes and debates in the country.

One underlying reason for the survival and even expansion of classical and realist paradigms in Iran's academic community is the lack of an alternative. Compared to economics, sociology, and anthropology, IR and political science tend to be fields that are critical of society and the state. Therefore, rigid local frameworks and methodologies to study the country are consciously shunned. Furthermore, given that IR and political science are the only fields in which students and faculty learn about developments around the world, they are better equipped to understand their own country in a comparative perspective. Having remained a fundamentally endogenous state following the revolution, students of IR compare Iran's standing with the rest of the world and immediately become critical of state policies and approaches.

Viewed from another perspective, the field of IR in Iran is captive to the political confrontation between tradition and modernity. This confrontation dates back nearly two
centuries in the country. Before the revolution, political systems in Iran tended towards the
West, but they failed to deliver modernity and full-scale development. Disillusionment with
the shortcomings of this model gave rise to the traditional and Islamist schools of thought in
the post-revolutionary period. In order to find solutions for national problems, the political
mood in Iran has shifted from one school of thought to another. Sociologically, Iranian
society is stratified and divided into many layers of belief systems. Even the Shii clerics are
accustomed to diverse opinions. Given its financial independence from society, the state in
Iran is the ultimate arbiter, balancer, and decision-maker. In post-revolutionary Iran it has
emerged as all-encompassing, forcing individuals to at least practice caution in expressing
their potentially distinct ideas from those of the state. The country's geographical diversity
is considerable. Interestingly, people living along the borderline provinces tend to subscribe
to the internationalist school and are more tolerant of other cultures and societies. Perhaps,
at the national level, one can opt for a rainbow portrait of belief structure where individuals
pick and choose from various schools of thought as they wish and as it fits their interests.
Therefore, owing to socio-economic differences, it is an almost impossible task to try to
produce an internally consistent belief system towards the global milieu throughout the whole
country. Because of weaknesses in consensus building processes among Iranians, the bureaucracy ultimately intervenes, sets the national agenda, and defines issues. Conceptually, Iran
may be described as a country with a strong state and a weak, fragmented, and disorganized
society.

However, at the end of the second decade of the Iranian Revolution, vivid patterns in the
substantive and political direction of IR studies and research in Iran can be put forth. The
concept of the national interest dominates IR writings and research. Even in newspaper
editorials, attention is drawn to what constitutes national interests. Inadvertently, the
ideological approaches of the state have given rise to the relevance and predominance of the
ideas of Hans Morgenthau. Revolutionary and rhetorical approaches to international politics
by government are the antithesis of the teaching of realist and neorealist theories of
international relations at the universities. Even in most dissertations at the Masters and Ph.D.
levels, conceptual frameworks tend to draw largely from realist and neorealist approaches.
There is also a minority that has increasingly become interested in postmodern literature.
Although translation of Western literature is the dominant way of producing IR materials in
university and research center settings, overall there is greater methodological awareness in
producing IR materials than before. Whereas, in the past, description was the only recognized
method for producing literature, greater attention is paid today to field research, content
analysis and methodological rigor. Whereas before the revolution there was almost no
emphasis or awareness of methodology, there are now several authored and translated books
on political science and IR methodological approaches. Almost everywhere in the country,
students are asked to submit research proposals that include a clear explanation of their
research problems, hypotheses, and research methods. This is a relatively new development,
following a long historical and descriptive French tradition in the Iranian social sciences.
Unlike the pre-revolutionary period where translations and personal notes were the usual
sources of scholarship of IR academics, creative thinking and inductive approaches are now
fashionable among mid-career and younger academics. It may be confidently concluded that
in the area of Iranian foreign policy, competing conceptual frameworks among Iranian
academics and fresh Ph.Ds abound. Comparative, cross-cultural, and issue-based analyses
of Iranian foreign policy are now available. Due to the liberal and realist outlooks of the

majority of faculty, the university system has been rather successful in promoting positivist methodology, empirical approaches, and integrative formulations. Of course, this does not mean that ideological advocacy on all campuses has disappeared. Rather, the two approaches coexist and there is little interaction and debate among them. This is largely an Iranian cultural trait, whereby instead of attempting to learn from different perspectives they tend to be ignored. However, conventional wisdom does not acknowledge the ideological approach to be "academic" or "scientific." In contrast, internationalist and liberal propositions and conceptual frameworks are regarded with respect and applicability among academics and institutions of higher education. Among others, two particular reasons may be postulated. First, there is a subtle tendency in Iran's university system to believe that what is produced in the West is more rational. Second, because bureaucratic inertia has sidelined those who do not subscribe to state views, sophisticated and confident academics rely on differences of thinking to draw attention and demonstrate their distinctiveness.

Due to great interest and market demand, significant steps have been taken in the past decade to expand IR programs and curricula. Political science and IR curricula are basically structured after the American system. IR texts mostly translated and some authored now exist in Farsi. IR Masters and Ph.D. programs are offered in more than 25 departments throughout the country. Graduate students increasingly use the internet for original research and make extensive application of internet materials in their theses. Subdivisions of IR particularly into regional studies, foreign policy analysis, and international organizations are prevalent in IR departments. Most research centers now require field surveys and rigorous methodologies to process proposals and analyze data. Some 2,000 students study political science and international relations at various levels of higher education throughout the country in both state and private institutions. There is an annual exam to enter the Masters program in political science and International Relations in about nine universities in various state universities where over 2,500 applicants take the exam and only about 100 are accepted into the programs due to limited capacity. Some six departments offer Ph.D. programs in IR. At the present time, some 50 students are at different phases of the Ph.D. program. The prestigious universities that offer IR programs are Tehran, Shahid Beheshti, Allameh Tabatabaee, and Tarbiat Moddares. Private universities have about the same number of Masters and Ph.D. students (Azghandi 2003: 143–153; 163–167). A fundamental shortcoming among an overwhelming number of students is a weak command of the English language, forcing them to rely on limited Farsi sources as well as providing a huge market for Farsi literature. Furthermore, due to financial restrictions as well as political problems between Iran and the rest of the world, travel opportunities for social science students are also constrained.

A sizeable contribution to IR and political science (as well as sociology and economics) reaches Iran through the literature produced by expatriate Iranian social scientists in Europe and North America. Although parts of these books and articles critical of the Iranian state may be deleted by the translators in order to acquire permission for publication, overall, citations indicate how influential this literature has become. However, it should be pointed out that judgments by the state on what should be allowed to be published and what should not are rather arbitrary. Much of the literature produced by the expatriate community particularly in the United States deals with Iran's foreign policy. Among the authors who have gained recognition within the IR and political science community in Iran are Farhad Kazemi, Roy Mottahedeh, Mohsen Milani, Bahman Baktiari, Abbas Milani, Houchang Chehabi, Anoush Ehteshami, Farhad Khosrokhavar, Mehrzad Boroujerdi, and Nayereh Tohidi. These scholars barely travel to Iran but have greatly contributed to a better understanding of Iran's domestic and foreign behavior. The application of theories and rigorous methodologies to a better comprehension of Iranian politics by these scholars who have the freedom to analyze and formulate recommendations have helped introduce IR students in Iran to a diverse and sophisticated literature. Unlike the rigidities of the Soviet system, fundamental shifts occur from one government to another and even during the tenure of a particular government.[2]

Prospects of IR in Iran

The fate of IR in Iran no longer depends on the nature of the Iranian state. This is due in large part to processes of globalization and ease of inter-societal communications. Access to the internet, a great interest in what others think about Iranian affairs, and the conceptual fault lines between the state and IR educators and students direct these studies to international standards. Given the negative image of Iran at the global level, there is a strong proclivity among the professional, intellectual, and academic communities in the country to reach out to the world, to be accepted, recognized, and respected, and ultimately to contribute to the global processes in trade, energy, science, and culture. Such an inclination is a constant source of integration with the rest of the world. IR literature serves as a penetrating and effective source of linkage between the internal–external environments. More than other social science fields, IR literature provides understanding about other societies, how they define issues, the strategies they adopt, and their accomplishments. Traditionally, philosophy used to dominate the social sciences in Iran. Today, however, the new generation is far more empirical, realistic, and concrete. Induction is gradually replacing pure deduction as a method of analysis. The idealistic nature of the Iranian Revolution has also contributed to the weakening of philosophically based arguments especially among the youth and the professionals. The quality of work of many expatriate Iranians in Europe and North America who continue to focus their research on Iranian studies has also influenced the scope and the substance of teaching and research at home.

A review of the 2005 presidential campaign strategies indicates that candidates' references to statistics and tangible issues (in contrast to idealistic and philosophical abstractions) were far more important in the mindset of the average voter. A significant challenge facing the next generation of politicians in the country is how Iran is going to define itself in the global system. Will a confrontational approach serve Iran's national interests? With a population reaching 100 million people in the year 2018, can Iran continue to depend on its petroleum income to feed itself? In this context, IR literature underlines the conduit between Iran and the international community since it is almost the only field of study that provides comparative analysis between what is happening at home and the breakthroughs beyond Iran. Although travel is limited, other avenues of exploring the world such as the internet, libraries, and satellite television are readily available. Some 100,000 Iranian students study abroad in places such as Malaysia, India, Armenia, Hungary, and Western Europe. This suggests that Iran is by no means another North Korea. The curious mentality of the average Iranian does not allow the state to fully limit its citizens. More than 100 Iranian websites and thousands of weblogs, overwhelmingly outside the country, provide data, analysis, and intellectual communication. This literature explains global trends and developments not only to the student body but also to the population at large. There is great interest in Turkey, Malaysia, the UAE, China, and India, all of which have some degree of resemblance to Iran. In this context, the political and the economic aspects of globalization will certainly continue to dominate the mainstream media and intellectual debates in the country.

In the course of a decade, the fields of political science and International Relations in Iran have advanced considerably. Many members of faculty and increasing numbers of students have admirable command over the mainstream IR literature. However, levels of theoretical innovation remain weak. A number of reasons may be outlined. First, competitiveness in Iran's academic system is only recognized when students want to take the university entry exam. Once students are accepted into the program, competition fades and there are no incentives to remain competitive. Second, innovation is not encouraged. There are no institutional and societal mechanisms to reward innovation. Third, Iran's academic system is not organizationally linked with the rest of the world. Yet it has great capacity to be aware of what takes place elsewhere and to translate current Western literature into Farsi. With the exception of a small minority of faculty and students, the overwhelming majority of those involved in academic and research activities are confined to print and internet materials. Inability to communicate in foreign languages, the difficulty in securing travel funds, and a feeling of uneasiness in dealing with the world beyond Iran all contribute to limiting knowledge and mobility among academics. Fourth, Iran's higher education system is basically structured for teaching and not for research. Original research in the social sciences capable of competing internationally remains extremely scant. A key indicator for the future of IR in Iran will be how quickly the country will be able to join global processes.

There appears to be a relationship between the development, expansion, and creativity in the field of International Relations on the one hand and the level of penetration in the international system by the country on the other. Populism in Iranian politics hinders greater involvement in global economic, political, and cognitive processes. The nuclear crisis and the stand-off between Iran and the United States have intensified Iran's foreign relations not only in commercial banking and technological fields but also in limiting how Iranian academics interact with universities and think-tanks. But Iran is headed for significant changes when a generational shift occurs in its leadership cadre. Iran's geo-politics, geo-economics, size, natural cultural and political influence and, perhaps more salient of all, the cosmopolitan nature of its population, are all contributing factors for its entry into the international system. In this context, the constructs, theories, and approaches of IR will be far more influential than any other social science field in Iran because they introduce knowledge and even raw data about other countries and global trends. As a country of paradoxes and contradictions, however, Iran faces galactic challenges in the path towards stability and institutionalization of politics. In meeting these challenges and against the traditions of the past where engineering and medicine ruled the university system, it appears that the social sciences and particularly economics and International Relations will play a determining role in the future of Iran.

Notes

1 The reform movement under Mohammad Khatami (1997–2005) was founded on such a group of advocates.

2 Regarding the state of IR literature in the Iranian university system, some of the International Relations classics that have been translated into Farsi are: *Politics among Nations* by Hans Morgenthau, *Man, the State and War* by Stephen Waltz, *Turbulence in World Politics* by James Rosenau, *Contending Theories of International Politics* by James Dougherty and Robert Pfaltzgraff, and *Political Order in Changing Societies* by Samuel Huntington. Two translated books by the Iranian expatriates stand out: *The Making of Iran's Islamic Revolution: From Monarchy to Islamic Republic* (1994) by Mohsen Milani, and *After Khomeini: The Iranian Second Republic* (1995) by Anoush Ehteshami. Some of the works authored by Iranian scholars in the Iranian universities are: *Principles of Foreign Policy and International Relations* (1991) by Seyed Abdulali Ghavam, *Theories of International Relations* (1996) by Seyed Hossein Seifzadeh, and *The Evolution of Method and Research in International Relations* (1992) by Mahmood Sariolghalam. It should be

pointed out that hundreds of articles written in Iranian newspapers and quarterlies draw from European and especially American academic journals as well. Furthermore, it needs to be emphasized that the overwhelming volume of political translations in Iran has dealt with issues such as civil society, democracy, and identity.

References

Azghandi, Alireza (2003) *The Science of Politics in Iran*, Tehran: Baz Press (in Farsi).

Baktiari, Bahman (1996) *Parliamentary Politics in Revolutionary Iran*, Tampa: University Press of Florida.

Behzadi, Hamid (1975) *Principles of International Relations and Foreign Policy*, Tehran: Chapakhsh.

Boroujeridi, Mahrzad (1996) *Iranian Intellectuals and the West: The Tormented Triumph of Nativism*, Syracuse: Syracuse University Press.

Chehabi, Houchang and Juan Linz (1998) *Sultanistic Regimes*, Washington, D.C.: Johns Hopkins University Press.

Ehteshami, Anoush (1995) *After Khomeini: The Iranian Second Republic*, London: Routledge.

Ghavam, Seyed Abdulali (1991) *Principles of Foreign Policy and International Relations*, Tehran: Samt Publications.

Kazemi, Farhad (1980) *Poverty and Revolution in Iran: The Migrant Poor, Urban Marginality and Politics*, New York: New York University Press.

Khosrokhavar, Farhad (2000) *Anthropologie de la révolution iranienne: Le rêve impossible*, Paris: L'Harmatten.

Milani, Abbas (2006) *The Persian Sphinx*, Washington, DC: Mage Publishers.

Milani, Mohsen (1994) *The Making of Iran's Islamic Revolution: From Monarchy to Islamic Republic*, Boulder, CO: Westview Press.

Mottahedeh, Roy (1985) *The Mantle of the Prophet*, New York: Pantheon.

Sariolghalam, Mahmood (1992) *The Evolution of Method and Research in International Relations*, Tehran: Shahid Beheshti University Press (in Farsi).

Sariolghalam, Mahmood (1998) "Arab–Iranian Rapprochement: The Regional and International Impediments," in Kair el Din Haseeb (ed.), *Arab–Iranian Relations*, New York: St. Martin's Press, pp. 425–435.

Sariolghalam, Mahmood (2003) "Understanding Iran: Getting Past Stereotypes and Mythology," *Washington Quarterly*, 26 (4): 69–82.

Sariolghalam, Mahmood (2005) "Iran's Emerging Regional Security Doctrine: Domestic Sources and the Role of International Constraints," in The Emirates Center for Strategic Studies and Research (ed.), *The Gulf Challenges of the Future*, Abu Dhabi: The Emirates Center for Strategic Studies and Research, pp. 163–184.

Seifzadeh, Seyed Hossein (1996) *Theories of International Relations*, Tehran: Samt Publications (in Farsi).

Tabatabaee, Seyed Javad (1989) *A Philosophical Outlook on Iran's Political Thought*, Tehran: Institute for Political and International Studies (in Farsi).

10 Arab countries
The object worlds back

Editors' introduction

The Arab case is in many ways a particularly interesting one. The region was the original object of "orientalist" knowledge practices (Said 1979), and again today it is for large parts of Western debate the primary global exception: exceptions to the global security order, to modernity, to secularism, to the form of knowledge and reason that constitute the "we" talking about these very exceptions (Pasha 2007). In this situation, it becomes exceptionally important to interrogate the kinds of thinking that form the basis of agency in this region, which is so often constructed in mental frames that ultimately deny it any autonomous agency. Arab actors are construed as so weak and vulnerable as to not really matter as agents, even in stories about the region. And when local actors make meaningful and "good" choices, this is recounted as part of a narrative of Western expansion, so the subject is ultimately still in the West (Rumelili 2007). The only quasi-subjects in the region taken seriously in most news coverage and even policy research are radical and especially terrorist groups, and there is strong political pressure in the direction of defining them as irrational (Wæver 2006) – whereby again the relevance is lost for trying to understand any cognitive productivity in the region. How do scholars of IR in the Arab world work, and what kinds of knowledge are produced for whom, how and why?

However – and maybe partly for these reasons – this has been a chapter particularly diffi- cult to attain. During the – long – process of recruiting expert authors for all of the chapters and getting their chapters in, the Arab case stood out as the most challenging. Relatively little has been published on IR in the Arab countries compared to some of the other regions and countries in this book, and more potential authors were contacted for this chapter than for any other. We are not saying that no scholar in the region was up to the task – with a bit more luck this chapter could have been written in a format closer to the rest of the book by either of our two authors below. However, it is also true that the chapter *did* prove particularly compli- cated, not only due to unfortunate coincidences but also to a systematicity in both scarcity of potential authors and low propensity to do this kind of chapter. Among the reasons are probably that the international relations of the region are so dramatic and problematic that it seems to many local scholars luxurious to engage in the present kind of second-order reflec- tions. In addition, the status of the IR discipline in the region is unclear, partly because "area studies" which have generally – as discussed in several chapters of the book – formed a kind of alternative to IR in and especially about much of the third world, has done so particularly strongly in the case of the Middle East (Valbjørn 2008). With the increasing predominance of the region on the policy agenda in the US, funding for Middle Eastern area studies has been increasing. The main institutional home for scholarship globally on the international relations of the Middle East has probably been area studies, not the IR discipline. Therefore, in the region, a particularly complicated definition of disciplines and specialties emerged at the intersection of strong policy demands, different local academic traditions and the international, disciplinary dualism of area studies and classical disciplines. Finally, local political and institutional conditions make the task harder for a number of reasons, including the fragmented international structure of the region and the domestic brittleness of the political situation in many countries.

Especially in the current political situation, where the Arab case is all too often made the exception, and where agency and voice from the region are habitually discounted, it would have been particularly unbearable to publish this book without an Arab chapter, even if it was by pure coincidence that the predictable impossibility of lining up 15 chapters from around the world happened to hit exactly this case. Luckily, we found a very fortunate way of providing a Chapter 10, even if technically it does not completely fit the standard format followed by the other chapters. We first reprint a classical article by Bahgat Korany, "IR Theory: Contributions from Research in the Middle East"[1], following which Karim Makdisi has produced, with surprisingly short notice, an essay that addresses many of the issues discussed by the other case studies in this volume.

Korany's text brings out the tense but also possibly productive relationship between IR and area studies. Within both fields and in relation to the region in general, the article shows powerfully how scholarship from the West makes problematic assumptions and deals with Middle Eastern international relations in ways that are beginning to be challenged by scholars from the region. The interaction between the two dichotomies of IR/area studies and external/internal perspectives is particularly complicated and important in the case of the Middle East. Korany then suggests that for IR research on the Middle East to have credibility, it has to be context-sensitive and field-based. IR discipline-oriented area specialists can be of great help in this respect and constitute the needed bridge that mutually reinforce these two fields of knowledge.[2]

Makdisi's snapshot of IR studies throughout the Arab world downplays the centrality of area studies and presents us instead with a field that has evolved in various disciplinary and institutional settings. The author suggests that the main tension or divergence in teaching and research trends in the region is between Western-funded institutions catering to the academic interests of the West (including area studies, which are concentrated on here) and Pan Arab institutions and networks, and increasingly, Islamic ones, whose scholarly practices tend to challenge this orthodoxy.

IR THEORY: CONTRIBUTIONS FROM RESEARCH IN THE MIDDLE EAST

Bahgat Korany

Introduction

At a time when advances in technology and communication have brought countries together in what some have termed the "global village," the concept of area studies often evokes an impression of narrowness and parochialism. Moreover, the field of area studies is under pressure from the declining availability of research funds and, in particular, from the changing priorities of many funding agencies. It is against this background that Rashid

Khalidi, President of the Middle East Studies Association (MESA) in 1994, used the occasion of his Presidential Address at the annual MESA Conference to issue an unambiguous wake-up call concerning the future of area studies.

This challenge to area studies also provides the context for this chapter, which in some ways is more nuanced and less defensive than the remarks offered by Khalidi in 1994. In particular, I wish to emphasize the dynamic and dialectical relationship that has for more than three decades characterized interaction between area studies and traditional academic disciplines. Even more specifically, I wish to advance three propositions about this relationship.

1   A longitudinal perspective is necessary to understand the dialectical relationship between area studies and disciplinary social science, including that in my own field, International Relations. Area studies today is very different than it was in the 1950s or the 1960s. It is much less impressionistic and descriptive than in the past. Thus, much of the criticism directed at area studies is outdated.

2   We should avoid creating inappropriate and unnecessary dichotomies in the pursuit of scholarly knowledge, one of which is the unproductive separation of area expertise and analytical social science. Rather, the two perspectives must be integrated, with both kinds of knowledge and expertise brought to bear on the study of issues of international significance. In most instances, opposition to this kind of integration comes not from area specialists but from social science generalists.

3   Middle East specialists, like other area specialists, should continue to work within the traditions of established disciplines, but they should also bring a critical perspective. They must not blindly borrow social science concepts and methodologies. They must also refine them, in part by investigating their operationalization and applicability in particular social and cultural settings. This is necessary for the kind of comparative inquiry that is required for social science to make progress toward its declared goal of generalizable insights. The contribution of area specialists is not only valuable, it is indispensable.

I contend that the area specialists of today, and even more those of the future, are also discipline-oriented specialists (i.e., economists, political scientists, sociologists, anthropologists). Indeed, many have gone so far in establishing a bridge between area and disciplinary specialization that it is often their counterparts, those who regard themselves as social science generalists, who are in danger of parochialism. To illustrate and support these contentions, I shall draw upon two examples from my own research in international relations.[3] In concluding, I shall also offer some ideas about the future of area studies, since my attempt to correct misconceptions about area specialization is not intended to obscure the need for continued evolution in the field.

Middle East studies under fire – from within

The relationship between area and disciplinary studies was confronted by Khalidi during his Presidential Address at the 1994 annual MESA Conference. Khalidi was responding to a recent article by Stanley Heginbotham, Vice-President of the Social Science Research Council, in which the possibility was raised that area studies have become obsolete in the post-Cold War period and that what is needed today is research which is global and thematic in nature. Taking up this theme, Khalidi voiced his concerns by posing a serious question to his colleagues: "Is there a future for Middle East studies?"

Some may ask why I have chosen this ominous-sounding title. For most of us, the MESA Conference is a time for socializing, browsing among the latest books and hearing papers on recent research, generally in that order. It is certainly not a time for serious, intro-spective, potentially boring questions like this one. In the beautiful environment of this resort, it is even harder to focus on such unpleasant matters. In one of my last acts as President of MESA, however, I have decided to spoil the party, if only for a few minutes.

Khalidi then continued by identifying what he believed to be the most important way to save Middle East studies from "stagnation, provincialism, and ultimately extinction."

[T]o be part of the internal discourse within the disciplines, whereby new ideas are resisted or accepted, instead of standing outside, in splendid isolation, turning up our noses at such ideas. In other words, it is time for people studying the Middle East to partake of some of the excitement which characterizes many of their respective disciplines, and to realize that the future of the field is ultimately there.

A more nuanced view

My counter-argument is that Middle East studies, except for some Orientalist and purely descriptive historical works, is already doing what Khalidi asks. Many younger and middle-aged scholars have been studying what he qualified as the rising "trendy themes": the shift to market economies, the process of democratization, the growth of civil society, the resurgence of nationalism, national identities, and ethnic and religious rivalries. This is confirmed by a look at the contributions to the volume where this chapter originally appeared, as well as by the book review sections of such area-oriented journals as the *Middle East Journal* and the *International Journal of Middle East Studies*. These scholars have managed to address the issues of concern to social science generalists, who themselves often develop their "universally applicable" theories and "law-like generalizations" without feeling a need to visit, or even consult basic books about any of the world regions to which they believe their insights apply.

Briefly, then, we can agree that the advancement of knowledge requires familiarity with both disciplinary and area studies. What must be added is that most Middle East specialists, contrary to past practices and to Khalidi's extreme defensiveness, are today following this prescription. Their initial frame of reference is their own social science discipline; they read general disciplinary books and journals, and they conceptualize their research problems in disciplinary terms. Many generalists, by contrast, have not managed to avoid the trap of "contextual bankruptcy."

To support these assertions, I shall briefly discuss two general works on international relations and one book with a Middle East area focus. The first of these is a stimulating book entitled *Traditions of International Ethics* (1992), which draws attention to the normative dimension of the International Relations field. The editors, Terry Nardin and David Mapel, deal with an extended array of topics, including international law, classical and twentieth-century realism, natural law, Kant, utilitarianism, Marxism, liberalism, the contractarian tradition, individual human rights, and biblical arguments pertaining to international ethics. Although they select representatives of the most important voices in relevant ethical debates, they also admit to "obvious omissions," most notably "the traditions of Islamic, Chinese, and other non-Western civilizations." To explain these omissions, they state that "we did not attempt to examine these partly because the debate about international ethics for many years has been so decisively shaped by Western ideas, and partly because we were afraid to take on a task so obviously beyond our abilities."

To their credit, Nardin and Mapel are at least aware of the limits of their work. Moreover, Nardin deserves praise for his subsequent efforts to rectify this situation. He thus brings a more contextual perspective to the study of ethics and international affairs in his 1996 work *The Ethics of War and Peace*. This volume contrasts the attitudes toward war and peace found in various religious and normative traditions, including those associated with Islam and Judaism.

A second and more blatant example is a recent collection entitled *International Relations Theory Today* (1995). This volume has much to recommend it. It extends beyond any single national perspective and includes prominent authorities from Europe and North America. Its co-editor, Steve Smith, was then editor of the Cambridge University Press/British International Studies Association series on international relations, which is the most prestigious and influential in the field.

In the very first chapter, Smith himself analyzes in an encyclopedic and stimulating manner as many as ten self-images of the subdiscipline. Yet not one of the 108 references he cites refers to the Middle East, to any other region in the third world, or even to the third world as a whole. Thus, if the third world exists at all, it does not appear to influence theory-building endeavors in the presumably universally oriented field of International Relations.

The volume's 15 chapters cover such varied topics as international political economy, the environment, security, identity, and gender. There are a total of 611 references to these chapters, yet of these only four pertain to the Middle East, only three to Africa, and only six to the third world as a whole. Moreover, none of these references or their authors is deemed important enough to appear in the appendix, and this despite the fact that one of the contributing theoreticians, Fred Halliday, has frequently published on the Middle East.

The work of many Middle East specialists is different. This is illustrated by an important American–Egyptian research project, initiated almost two decades ago by the late Malcolm Kerr, a confirmed area specialist as well as a political scientist. The book that resulted from this project (Kerr and Yassin 1982) reflects the increasing enrichment of Middle East area studies that was already becoming evident. First, the project has a strong interdisciplinary perspective, bringing together three sociologists, six economists, and three political scientists, all of whom worked as a unified team. Second, the 615 notes and references, 69 tables, and five figures contained in the published volume not only confirm this interdisciplinary orientation, they also reflect the conceptual and methodological preoccupations of the research. Third, with respect to substantive considerations, the work at this relatively early time period addressed the themes of low politics and interdependence that are becoming increasingly central in present-day international relations research.

The actor level

Additional studies may be reviewed to reinforce my assessment, and toward this end I shall comment briefly on both earlier and more recent scholarship, including several of my own published works. I shall also make use of a consensual division among international relations theorists, the distinction between actor and system, agent and structure, or, as it is also sometimes described, between micro- and macro-level analysis, and between foreign policy and international system analysis.

In two surveys of more than 200 periodicals for the periods 1975 to 1981 and 1982 to 1988, it was found that the field of Middle East International Relations was still unclear about the "what" of foreign policy (Korany and Dessouki 1991: ch. 1). Does this mean the consequence of a specific action or behavior, or, alternatively, a strategy and general orientation, or perhaps both? The field also frequently devoted itself to current affairs. With very few exceptions, then, the analysis of foreign policy during the 1970s was more chronological and descriptive than analytical and theoretical. Decision-making analysis in particular was noticeably absent. This state of affairs corresponded to the characterization of Middle East area studies offered by Khalidi.

One notable exception was Michael Brecher's three-volume study of the structure and outcomes of Israel's foreign policy system (1972, 1974; Brecher and Geist 1980). The importance of this work lies in the amount and quality of the data it presents, in the elaboration of an explicit and detailed framework for the analysis of foreign policy, in the systematic and consistent application of this framework to the Israeli case, and in the incorporation of foreign policy theory.

While Brecher's work on Israel illustrates the behavioral or "scientific" study of foreign policy, his study has not been replicated in other countries of the Middle East. One possible reason may be the huge commitment of time (and funding) required for such research. Brecher himself had hoped to add a comparative dimension and extend the application of his framework to the analysis of India's foreign policy, but he subsequently shied away from this effort. On the other hand, his work has influenced and inspired quite a few younger scholars who study the Middle East. A notable example is Adeed Dawisha, who has studied Egyptian foreign policy (1976), that country's intervention in the Yemeni civil war (1975), and Syria's 1976 decision to invade Lebanon (1980). Moreover, because Dawisha had difficulty acquiring all the data required for the application of Brecher's framework, he devised adaptations that made use of the framework more "do-able," and in this way contributed to the further evolution of foreign policy analysis. This is illustrated by the works of Abu Diyya (1991), Khalidi (1986), and Gamal Zahran (1987, 1993) pertaining to political systems in the Arab East, and those of Mary-Jane Deeb (1991), Nicole Grimaud (1984), and Said Ihrai (1986) focusing on countries of the Maghrib.[4]

Despite their conceptual and methodological sophistication, these analyses were still single-case studies. Although their findings were potentially generalizable, the basis for this generalizability needed to be complemented by comparative multi-case studies. Other researchers have subsequently tried their hand at comparative analysis in order to fill this void, and two studies, published at seven-year intervals, provide an illustration. Both explicitly undertake to bring a conceptual perspective to the study of foreign policy in the Middle East.

The first work, by R. D. McLaurin, M. Mughisuddin, and P. A. Wagner (1977), is a seven-chapter book that examines four cases: Egypt, Iraq, Israel, and Syria. The emphasis was on domestic sources of foreign policy, and to allow "maximum comparability" the authors focused on three elements: people, processes, and policies. One of this book's strengths is its attempt to link the political structures and processes of the four countries to their foreign policy outputs. It is only partially successful in this endeavor, but it is nonetheless an important early attempt to apply a theoretical framework to the analysis of foreign policy in the Middle East.

Rather than limiting itself to domestic inputs, the second attempt, undertaken by myself and a colleague, was influenced by a political economy perspective and integrated global dynamics into the analysis of foreign policies in third world countries (Korany and Dessouki 1984). In addition to elaborating the book's analytical framework, my co-author and I, individually or together, wrote seven of its 13 chapters. The six remaining chapters were written by Middle East specialists from Canada, the United States, and the Middle East. Since the comparative study of foreign policy is essentially a collaborative enterprise, the objective of the volume was for researchers to adapt and apply a conceptual framework that they had not themselves developed. The framework itself was based on the three building blocks of foreign policy theory: the *why*, or foreign policy sources; the *what*, or foreign policy outputs; and the *how*, or decision-making processes (Korany 1983). In addition to dealing with some nagging problems of theory and method, such as the definition of foreign policy outputs and comparability, the book attempted to widen the range of Middle Eastern cases considered by bringing in the Maghrib (i.e., Algeria) and nonstate actors (i.e., the PLO).

In undertaking this study, we not only sought to contribute to the analytical understanding of foreign policy in the Arab states, we also wished to encourage the continuing evolution of research on the Middle East that employs conceptual and methodological tools from the disciplines of political science and International Relations. The project was thus a collective endeavor in which borrowing from a discipline was as important as, or even more important than, a contribution to that discipline. Indeed, while there was a concern for advancing theory construction by offering insights based on area-oriented research, my co-author and I also offered a critical assessment of much of the work on foreign policy that had previously been carried out by area specialists. We noted, for example, that "much of it belongs to the tradition of diplomatic history or commentary on current affairs" (Korany and Dessouki 1984: 1). Our goal in this connection, as with the volume as a whole, was to encourage students of Arab foreign policy to draw upon disciplinary tools and to integrate their work into a disciplinary matrix.

The system level

Integration into a disciplinary matrix remained the objective when I shifted the focus of my research to the systemic or structural level. In this instance, however, a primary objective of my project on national security was to address some deficiencies in the existing conceptual literature on strategic studies, particularly the dual separation of domestic and international politics and of high politics and low politics. Further, the state was often "black-boxed" in this literature, meaning that there was inadequate attention to its historical evolution and social dynamics (Korany 1986, 1989).

It was, therefore, necessary to revise some of the literature's basic assumptions and to provide an alternative framework that took into consideration the characteristics of states in the Middle East and other regions of the third world. More specifically, it was important to move beyond a perspective that reified domestic and external military factors in the assessment of national security, and to emphasize as well such issues as debt, ethnic fragmentation, and low regime legitimacy, all of which are in the domain of low politics and assigned only secondary importance in much of the disciplinary literature on strategic studies. In fact, however, these latter attributes are of central importance in the Middle East and need to be treated as key independent variables in the analysis of national security.

The task of testing hypotheses derived from this new framework exceeded the capacity of a single researcher, and I accordingly undertook a collaborative project with two colleagues from McGill University, Paul Noble and Rex Brynen. We established the Inter-University Consortium for Arab Studies, and in 1993 we published our first volume, *The Many Faces of National Security in the Arab World*.

In contrast to the project on Arab foreign policies, the national security project from the beginning sought not merely to borrow, but rather to refine, the dominant paradigm in the relevant disciplinary literature. In this instance, in other words, a critical eye was directed not so much at the previous work of area specialists but rather at generalists and at the state of discipline-oriented scholarship. Commenting on the basic literature on strategic studies and national security, the introduction to our book accordingly noted that

> the discussion is still terribly U.S.-centric. Moreover, the problems of the majority of the global system, the third world, were not dealt with directly. Thus, in Stephen Walt's systematic review of the field, third world problems do not impinge on the analysis nor appear in the references. Moreover, there seems to be little awareness among many specialists of security studies, even the most open-minded, of the specific historical–sociological context of issues of state-building in these countries and how they could affect the pattern of their conflicts.
>   This is why this book takes as its starting point state properties in the Arab world. Rather than continuing the tradition by limiting itself to the inter-state wars, the book aims to investigate the link between the specificities of these states and various types of security problems existing in the region. The aim is not only to draw attention to other types of threat to national security, and thus widen the definition of this basic concept, but also potentially to add to the explanation of the various inter-state wars that plague the region.
>
> (Korany *et al.* 1993: xvii–xix)

Eleven scholars subsequently joined our research team, providing expertise in different areas and hence a solid empirical base for testing our conceptualization. As noted, this conceptualization emphasized the impact on national security issues of the internal fragility and other characteristics of third world states. In order to prevent our project from resulting in a "conventional" reader, the research team worked together to ensure that the volume we were preparing would possess analytical coherence. The first chapter thus introduced and explicated our conceptual framework. Subsequent chapters were divided into three parts, each introduced by a discussion that explicitly linked the specific contribution of each chapter to the volume's overall theme. A concluding chapter provided additional integration and also picked up where the authors left off by discussing Arab security issues in the post-Gulf War era. Tables containing social, military, and economic data were annexed in support of the book's critical arguments.

While it is for others to evaluate the contributions of this research, a recent follow-up project suggests that our effort to bring area expertise to bear on disciplinary issues has been productive. This is a Harvard project on New Frontiers of National Security in the Middle East, which builds on the *Many Faces* study by developing a "comprehensive framework" that moves beyond the military focus of traditional national security research (Martin 1996). Similarly, an earlier project, focusing on Asia, was inspired by the political economy approach of the Arab foreign policies study described earlier (Wurfel and Burton 1990). All of this suggests that area specialists can contribute, and indeed have been contributing, to the analytical cumulativeness required for scientific progress.

Conclusion

None of this means that area specialists should be satisfied with their achievements and resist calls for the further evolution of their research agenda and perspectives. Not at all. This chapter's main concern has been to correct misconceptions about area studies, but certainly not to advocate an end to the field's evolution.

At the turn of the century, two directions suggest themselves for the future evolution of area studies research. Both are of value and hold promise. First, there are dynamic subfields of international relations research where students of the Middle East and other world regions could both profit from and contribute to ongoing efforts at theory construction. One such subfield is concerned with international regime analysis (Krasner 1983; Rittberger 1993; Levy *et al.* 1995). Despite its salience, very little work in this area has been explicitly devoted to the third world. In fact, however, Middle East regional specialists could make an important contribution by investigating the utility of analyzing Arab groupings and coalitions from the perspective of international regimes, and, if necessary, suggesting conceptual refinements to make insights from this subfield applicable more broadly.

Another example is the growing body of international relations research which focuses on the hypothesis that democracies do not go to war against one another. With both democratization and regional conflict prominent items on the political agenda of the Middle East, regional specialists are particularly well positioned to examine this hypothesis with a degree of depth that goes beyond the aggregate studies that characterize much of the disciplinary research in the field. Indeed, there have already been a number of important contributions by Middle East specialists along these lines (Hudson 1995; Tessler and Grobschmidt 1995).

Second, the other direction for the evolution of area studies research involves reaching out to specialists in other world regions, such as Latin America, Africa, or Asia, and designing collaborative projects. This would contribute to scholarly cumulativeness in the study of many important issues, including processes of state formation, political liberalization and democratization, and privatization and structural adjustment. By comparing patterns and processes across regions, it will be possible both to identify generalizable insights and to determine whether and when the political dynamics characterizing a particular region are unique. This is not to say that generalizability and breadth should be sought at the expense of accuracy and depth, a concern that has been properly raised by another MESA President (Kazemi 1996). But cross-regional comparison is important, particularly in an age of increasing globalization, and in this respect, as in others, area studies has no choice but to adapt to new conditions and continue its evolution.

The opportunities and benefits of this cross-regional approach to scholarly inquiry are evident in numerous areas, including, among others, ethnic conflict, international diasporas, the relationship between domestic politics and foreign policy, international migration, gender and international relations, the impact of the global communications revolution, and the nature and consequences of economic liberalization programs. This in no way reduces the importance of area studies knowledge, however. On the contrary, the investigation of these and other global issues, or themes, should be pursued by examining the relevant experiences of different world regions, in each case drawing both on the appropriate conceptual and methodological disciplinary tools and on the area studies expertise needed for their valid and reliable application to real-world situations. In this way, not only will currently fashionable terms like "globalization" and "thematic perspective" help to shape the agenda for future research, it will also be clear that such research will fulfill its potential only if informed by the kind of knowledge associated with area studies, as well as that associated with social science disciplines.

REFLECTIONS ON THE STATE OF IR IN THE ARAB REGION

Karim Makdisi

This article offers preliminary reflections on the discipline of International Relations (IR) in the Arab region.[5] As explained by the volume editors, it is not intended as a comprehensive contribution in line with other chapters in this volume. Rather, it makes a few key points related to the context within which IR (and other social science) scholars work, the types of institutions that teach or conduct research within the field of IR, and the problematic self-understanding of "IR" in a region whose scholars have had little impact on the discipline and its principal journals and forums.[6] An overview of influential IR journals shows not only that voices and research from the Arab region are notable only by their general absence, but also that those IR "conversations" dealing with the Arab region routinely eschew Arabic sources, let alone oppositional Arab voices. Indeed, the discipline's general lack of interest in, even deliberate neglect of, the work of Arab scholars is not new and reflects a long pattern of academic and intellectual hegemony and orientalism exposed in the path-breaking work of Edward Said.[7]

The fact that the volume editors had such difficulty in tracking down a contributor from the Arab region offers a good starting point for this discussion, as it reflects the near-complete disengagement between Arab international relations scholars working in the region and their colleagues operating within the U.S. academic and policy spheres. The original and profound idea behind the envisioned three-volume project is to understand how global affairs are read by scholars around the world given the editors' correct assumption that the field of IR has "very little knowledge about how it is itself shaped by global and international relationships of power, knowledge and resources" (Tickner and Wæver 2006). Yet, the venue within which the original workshop and subsequent meetings to elaborate on and solicit contributions from scholars were held at successive annual meetings of the International Studies Association (ISA) in Montreal (2004), Hawaii (2005), and San Diego (2006). Given Arab scholars' perennial lack of resources, obvious language barriers, poor publication record in mainstream IR journals, and the perceived irrelevance (and lack of accessibility) of such academic forums as the ISA to the congenital state of crisis in the region, it is clear that many Arab scholars working in Arabic and within national institutions would not appear on the ISA's radar screen.

Contextualizing knowledge production and social science research in the Arab region

There has been very little written let alone published on the state of International Relations in the region. Instead, what exists of such literature covers periodic attempts over the past three decades to assess (and improve) the state of social science research as a whole, and indeed the knowledge-production process itself. It is thus worth exploring this literature briefly in order to contextualize the conditions and political realities under which most IR scholars work.[8]

While universities and other knowledge-production systems, of course, have a very long tradition in the Arab and Islamic worlds, their evolution in the modern period may be broken down into a number of phases (some overlapping) that were naturally shaped by the broader historical, socio-economic, and political contexts. During the colonial period, the first Western-style universities were established (e.g., the American University of Beirut in 1866 and American University in Cairo in 1919) in order to "modernize" the region and "enlighten" it by spreading liberal values.

The subsequent post-colonial and state-building phase, for its part, was marked by a surge of national universities (most importantly Cairo University, founded in 1908) and research centers in conjunction with the rise of the contemporary Arabic public systems of education that ushered in an era of universal and free education. The strong Arab nationalist sentiment fueled by anti-colonialism and support for the Palestinian struggle, coupled with the oil boom of the early 1970s, also led to the creation of a number of significant social science institutions with a pan-Arab outlook (e.g., the Arab Planning Institute in 1972; the Center for Arab Unity Studies in 1975). Significantly, indigenous financial organizations or benefactors funded many of these pan-Arab research institutions in order for them to pursue their agenda without perceived neocolonial interference. Finally, in the post-Cold War period the Western foreign donors (e.g., the World Bank) have reasserted their influence by funding the foundation of key regional social science research centers and development networks such as the Economic Research Forum (ERF) and Global Development Network (GDN).

Today, Western-funded research projects are generally hegemonic in terms of influence in the public policy of Arab regimes (which have increasingly accepted neo-liberal reforms) but not necessarily among scholars in the region. Pan-Arab institutions and networks such as the Center for Arab Unity Studies (CAUS) and, increasingly, Islamic bodies continue to challenge this orthodoxy and remain popular among Arab academics in national universities and research centers. The divergence between these two research trends may be illustrated by the struggle over what "region" Arab social scientists were supposed to cater to. The nationalist and pan-Arab trends strongly advocated an "Arab" region that was distinct from its neighbors. Conversely, since the 1970s foreign donors have often sought to break up an imagined Arab community into the more nebulous "Middle East" that could accommodate Israel – thus forcing a political project of Arab–Israeli "normalization" on the Arab research community before Palestinian self-determination was reached and occupied Arab territory liberated – and even Turkey and Iran. Thus, the Organization for the Promotion of Social Science in the Middle East (OPSSME), for instance, established in the 1970s, was countered by CAUS's creation of national Arab political science, economics, and sociology associations in the 1980s (Fergany 2000). Of course, Islamist research creates a third main trend as it envisions a wider Muslim region not limited necessarily by the geographical and material constraints of the Arab world.

Notwithstanding the politicization of social science research agendas in the Arab region, there is a consensus in the literature that the quality of research itself has been generally "questionable" and that the notable increase in the number of social science institutions has not been converted into an improvement in the quality of research in the region (Jamal 2006: 7). Indeed, the Egyptian sociologist Saad Eddin Ibrahim has even argued that there has been a decline in such research quality over the years (Ibrahim 1997: 549). Core issues are the inhibiting political context, generally dire level of resources, and difficult working conditions (including high teaching loads and low wages) that force academics and independent researchers to become consultants and conform to governmental or foreign donor agendas. Other problems encountered by Arab researchers include

> [the lack of resource incentive structure which does not encourage social science research, restrictive political environments, cultural norms which place little value on social science research, the absence of a tradition of peer review, the "elitism" of social science research and its lack of accessibility to the general public, and language

constraints especially since a declining number of students are trained in non-Arabic languages.

(Jamal 2006: 7–8)

The brain-drain phenomenon is another important factor that affects social science research in the region, just as it does most research-oriented fields. Arab researchers migrate at alarming rates in search of educational opportunities and professional satisfaction (generally obtaining high positions in many of the OECD countries in which they work). A recent study commissioned by the United Nations Education and Social Commission (UNESCO) estimates that as many as 85 percent of the approximately 12,000 Ph.Ds obtained abroad by Arab students annually do not return to their home countries, resulting in a total of 150,000 Arab Ph.Ds working abroad compared to only about 50,000 to 60,000 in the region itself (Zahlan 2007: 4).

Still, the social science picture today in the Arab region is not all bad. The demise of the Cold War has accelerated the opening up of many Arab countries whose leaders and political elites are adapting themselves to the realities of U.S. hegemony and the increasing local demand for education and participation. By 2004, there were over 230 universities in the region compared to 140 in 1993 and 45 in 1973 (Bashshur 2004: 92). An IDRC study estimates that there are currently around 50,000 social scientists working in the region – including 20,000 senior scholars (Ibrahim 2000) – while social science disciplines in the region represent some of the highest enrollments in Arab universities (e.g., Morocco social science enrollment figures represent 46 percent of the total enrollment, while in Lebanon the figure is 40 percent, and in Palestine and Jordan it is 32 percent) (UNESCO 2006: 139). It is not clear, however, if this rise in demand for education and social sciences in particular will be translated into serious research agendas that are both independent and adequately funded. As the *Arab Human Development Report* reminded us, scholarly output from the region remains poor (in terms of internationally refereed journals), with an average output per million inhabitants of only 2 percent of that of an industrialized country (UNDP 2002: 68).

Observations on the state of International Relations in the Arab region

To my knowledge, no indigenous studies or evaluations of the state of IR in the region exist, nor any reflections on it specifically as a discipline or subdiscipline within political science. This reflects the reality that IR in the region is, for the most part, not so much a distinct empirical field of study as an amalgam of pressing current affairs and short-term public policy concerns. In the absence of comprehensive statistics, empirical studies, or comparative data, this section will highlight notable institutions in the Arab region that teach or engage in IR research before exploring the content of the 30-year-old journal *al-Mustaqbal al-Arabi* ("The Arab Future"), which is considered to be fairly representative of the social science, policy, and international affairs research concerns emanating from the Arab region. While by no means comprehensive, it is possible to draw some observations from this content analysis exercise that can be generalized for the research community as a whole.

Historically, IR has not been an important field of study in Arab universities with relatively few of the 230-plus universities actually offering IR degrees. The resulting lack of resources and investment in IR has meant that scholars interested in serious academic IR research generally migrate outside the Arab region (mostly to OECD countries) in order to both complete their degrees and pursue employment opportunities.

A rudimentary survey of key universities in the region reveals that the dominant tradition among those that do offer some form of IR track usually do so within political science departments in Faculties of humanities, social sciences or law. Notable examples of such universities include:

- American University of Beirut (Lebanon), Faculty of Arts and Sciences, Department of Political Studies and Public Administration;
- American University of Cairo (Egypt), Faculty of Humanities and Social Sciences, Department of Political Science;
- Birzeit University (Palestine), Faculty of Law and Public Administration, Department of Political Science;
- Cairo University (Egypt), Faculty of Economics and Political Science;
- Jordan University (Jordan), Faculty of Humanities and Social Sciences, Department of Political Science;
- Kuwait University (Kuwait), College of Social Sciences, Department of Political Science;
- Mohammad V University-Agdal (Morocco), Faculty of Law, Economics and Social Sciences, International Relations major;
- United Arab Emirates University (UAE), College of Humanities and Social Sciences, Department of Political Science;
- University of Algiers (Algeria), Faculty of Information and Political Science;
- University of Khartoum (Sudan), Faculty of Economic and Social Studies, Department of Political Science;
- Yarmouk University (Jordan), Faculty of Arts, Department of Political Science.

The political science and IR courses offered in these programs are generally the standard courses offered in U.S. academic institutions, albeit with significantly less overall depth (in terms of variety of courses and topics). Relatively few IR tracks in the region offer non-traditional courses such as international environmental politics or go beyond a superficial survey of traditional IR theoretical approaches. Textbooks used in survey courses are usually drawn from U.S. or European publishing houses. In short, the traditional political science departments that offer IR tracks essentially follow the lead of Western (U.S.) academic departments. Generally speaking, moreover, it is mainly the American universities in the region (such as the American University of Beirut's Center for Arab and Middle East Studies) that have created distinct Middle East studies programs as an object of academic study, and these generally cater to foreign students who want to live in the region for a period and learn its language, history, and politics.

The growing interest in the study of international affairs in some parts of the Arab region has created a new trend that allows IR some autonomy from the more rigid political science department model by recasting it as "international affairs." Birzeit University (Palestine) established the Ibrahim Abu Lughod Institute for International Studies to cater to graduate students interested in pursuing Palestine's international dimension. Similarly, the Lebanese American University now offers an international affairs major – distinct from its political science track – within its Division of Social Sciences and Education (in the College of Arts and Sciences). This trend, however, is perhaps most apparent in the smaller Gulf Cooperation Council (CGG) countries such as Qatar and the UAE which have been trying to use their wealth, and relative stability, to carve out a niche in regional public policy and international affairs. Qatar University, for instance, has recently established an autonomous international affairs program within its College of Arts and Sciences. Qatar also invited Georgetown University to open a branch of its School of Foreign Service (SFS), which is a well-known brand among Arab elite circles, in 2005. In turn, SFS in Doha has opened a Center for International and Regional Studies. A number of other, similar initiatives are being pursued in the Gulf region, but it is too early to tell if these will actually provide a solid base for independent and innovative research, or if they are simply in the business of manufacturing bureaucrats and policy-makers that can spread U.S. and Western hegemony more efficiently.

There are also a number of independent research and policy centers/think-tanks that conduct varying degrees of international relations research in the region and publish journals of interest to national or regional scholars and policy-makers. These include the following:

- *Al-Ahram Center for Political and Strategic Studies* (Cairo, Egypt): Established in 1968 as an independent research unit functioning within the framework of the Al-Ahram Foundation. It publishes the only journal that purports to deal exclusively with international relations issues, namely the regionally prominent *al-Siyasiyya al-Dawliyya* ("International Politics"). It also publishes the monthly *Al-Ahram Strategic File*.
- *Center for Arab Unity Studies*: The independent pan-Arab center that pursues "independent, scientific research into all aspects of Arab society and Arab unity, free of ties to any Government and in an atmosphere far removed from partisan politics."[9] It publishes a large range of books, conference proceedings, and journals including its flagship journal, the monthly *Al-Mustaqbal Al-Arabi* ("Arab Future"). The Center has also recently started publishing the journal of the Arab Political Science Association, *Al-Majalla Al-Arabiyya Lil-'Ulum Al-Siyassiyya* ("the Arab Journal of Political Science").
- *Emirate Centers for Strategic Studies and Research* (Abu Dhabi, UAE): An independent center that "serves as a focal point for scholarship on political, economic, and social issues pertinent to the UAE, the Gulf, and the greater Middle East through the sponsorship of empirical research and scientific studies conducted by scholars from around the globe."[10]
- *Center for Strategic Studies* (Amman, Jordan): Established in 1984 as an academic unit of the University of Jordan concerned mainly with research in the fields of regional conflicts, international relations, and security.
- *Institute for Palestine Studies* (Beirut, Lebanon): The independent and internationally renowned research and documentation center that deals with Palestinian issues and the general Arab–Israeli conflict. Its flagship journal is the refereed *Journal of Palestine Studies* (published by the University of California Press), but it also disseminates Arabic and French journals.
- *Issam Fares Institute for Public Policy and International Affairs* (Beirut, Lebanon): Established in the American University of Beirut, the Institute's mission is "to raise the quality of public policy-related debate and decision-making in the Arab World and abroad, to enhance the Arab World's input into international affairs, and to enrich the quality of interaction among scholars, officials and civil society actors in the Middle East and abroad."[11]

In order to explore the kinds of issues being discussed and researched in the region by scholars interested in IR issues, I turn now to a brief content analysis of the CAUS flagship journal, *al-Mustaqbal al-Arabi* ("Arab Future"), which broadly represents the community of Arab social science scholars. This Beirut-based monthly journal is currently celebrating its 30th anniversary, its first issue having been published in May 1978 in the midst of the

Lebanese civil war, and indeed just after Israel's first invasion of southern Lebanon. As Kheir Eddin Haseeb, CAUS's influential director, notes, the journal did not once halt its publication schedule despite the violence and pressure resulting from the long civil war in Lebanon (that continued until 1991) and large-scale Israeli invasion of Lebanon and siege of Beirut in 1982 (not to mention 2006). When the journal could not be published or distributed from Beirut due to frequent airport closures, the journal was shipped off to Cyprus or carried overland via Damascus or Amman (Haseeb 2008: 6). In this sense, the 30-year life of *al-Mustaqbal* mirrors the constraints under which research and knowledge are both produced and disseminated in the Arab region.

Looking at the recently compiled index of *al-Mustaqbal* covering the period 1978 to 2008, several observations may be made that are broadly consistent with an impressionistic overview of IR scholarship in the region (CAUS 2008):

1   The vast majority of the articles that deal with political (including international relations) issues are not "scientific" in terms of methodological rigor or self-reflection. Indeed, only four references to "political science" were found in the *al-Mustaqbal* 1978 to 2008 index. This continues the trend found by Nader Fergany (2000), who found only two references dealing with "political science" in *al-Mustaqbal* during the years 1978 to 1998.

In one of the rare articles dealing with the discipline and theories of political science, published in 1991, Abd al-Khaliq Abdullah makes the point that the subdiscipline of IR was becoming more autonomous within the academy and its main branches – such as international law, international organizations, and international economics – had each spawned its own set of specialized theories and associations (Abdullah 1991: 23). If this was a call for new research agendas in the region, a quick review of the *al-Mustaqbal* indices shows:

   •   No references dealing with the role of international organizations since 1991, and those dealing with the United Nations (27 references) are generally descriptive and specific to the UN role in the various regional wars, particularly the U.S.–Iraq war and the sanctions regime of the 1990s.
   •   Only two references dealing with international law, neither theoretical in nature.
   •   Only one reference to international economics.

2   There is very little engagement with, or analysis of the classical (let alone new) IR theories that form the backbone of the IR discipline in the West. The *al-Mustaqbal* index does not even have one entry for "theory." Of course this does not mean there are no implicit theoretical or conceptual frameworks, including realist, liberal, Marxist and anti-colonial and Arab nationalist ones. In general, it is possible to infer that the realist tradition of power politics remains hegemonic within the Arab IR community, while three other trends may also be clearly seen: a liberal trend that focuses on various reform initiatives; a leftist (centered in Cairo) and nationalist (secular) trend that focuses on anti-imperialism and Arab unity; and of course a growing Islamist framework that challenges the core understanding of state-centric international relations.

3   Most of the topics covered respond to classical issues deemed international in the region such as democracy (104 references), development (89), Arab unity (79), security (49), weapons of mass destruction (32), and of course analysis of the various regional crises (e.g., 74 references on the general Arab–Israeli conflict, 62 references on the 2003 U.S.–UK war on Iraq in 2003, and already 16 references to Israel's July 2006 war on Lebanon). It should be noted that the various subcomponents of these seminal conflicts

receive much more attention. Fundamentalism and terrorism are referred to 11 and 12 times respectively over the 30-year period considered. Interestingly, since many scholars assume that internal matters in the Arab region are influenced by external factors, most internal issues are considered within the purview of IR. For instance, the recent events in Lebanon, presumably an internal matter dealing with elections and distribution of power, was not only finally mediated by and in Qatar in May 2008, it was effectively settled by a Saudi–Iranian agreement that included U.S. and Syrian support. Similarly, democratization is a matter of IR concern as is the notion of development itself, given the reliance of all non-oil Arab states on donor funds.

Concluding remarks

This reflection piece has tried to briefly contextualize the objective conditions under which scholars working on IR issues in the Arab region operate, and highlight the way in which IR is taught and researched. Its prognosis that most IR scholarship in the region lacks methodological rigor and explicit theoretical or conceptual frameworks explains, at least in part, why such scholars have had little impact on the IR discipline itself. Although outside the scope of this piece, the introduction also touched on the orientalist and hegemonic tendencies of U.S. knowledge production, including academia, as another main reason for Arab scholars' exclusion from mainstream debates. What is left to posit is why Arab scholarship lacks such theoretical insights and why so few scholars have engaged in an Arab perspective that would challenge the clearly unsatisfactory categories standard in IR discourse. Such a question, of course, is worthy of a major research agenda that would start with questioning the very core unit of International Relations: the state. Some of the most interesting research being carried out today in the region is that which explores the inadequacy of the state in organizing an otherwise strong Arab society (or societies) from both the nationalist and Islamic perspectives, and the emergence of non-territorial concepts of governance which would require a radical re-thinking of what international relations means in the Arab context (see, e.g., Al-Barghouti 2008). After all, a dominant strand of secular Arab scholarship for four decades has been the concept of Arab integration or unity in the context of abject failure of Arab states to provide security or development; and today this is being challenged by Islamic notions of the wider *ummah* or Islamic community (see, e.g., Ahmad 2006).

Notes

1 Originally published in Mark Tessler, Jodi Nachtwey and Ann Banda (eds), *Area Studies and Social Science: Strategies for Understanding Middle East Politics*, Bloomington: Indiana University Press, 1999, pp. 148–158. It should be noted that the contributors to that book were instructed that the objective was not only to survey the field, but also importantly to bring in the author's own contribution to the field. In the present context, it should therefore be explained that Bahgat Korany uses his own work as illustration for this reason. The chapter has not been updated content-wise for the current publication, but a few technical changes have been made.

2 In directing a research team that is both inter-cultural and inter-generational, Korany and Dessouki (2008) give a concrete form to this bridge area.

3 See note 1.

4 These last three paragraphs are taken from Korany (1988).

5 I would like to thank a number of scholars who have helped me think through this assignment, including As'ad Abu Khalil, Ziad Hafez, and Kheir Eddine Haseeb, though of course any mistakes are my own. I would also like to thank the staff of the library and documentation center in the Center for Arab Unity Studies for their kind assistance.

6 While the subject of the IR discipline's relationship with and representation of the Arab region is not the main issue of this contribution, this author is currently pursuing it in an ongoing research project.

7 See, for instance, Edward Said's seminal book *Orientalism* (Said 1979) and its follow-up work, *Culture and Imperialism* (Said 2000). Said's main contribution rested on exposing the relationship between the Western colonial project to "know" the Arab and Islamic worlds and its power over it by denying Arab and Islamic self-representation.

8 This section draws on the recent (unpublished) literature reviews conducted by Necla Tschirigi (Tschirigi 2006) and Manal Jamal (Jamal 2006) in the context of an ongoing multi-year project by key regional institutions and scholars to strengthen social science research in the Arab region and to set up a proposed Arab council for the social sciences. This author was elected on to the steering committee charged with pursuing this. The workshop discussions and literature collected by the participants and secretariat (provisionally based in the Dubai School of Government) have provided an invaluable base to explore the social science literature in the region.

9 See http://www.caus.org.lb/Home/contents1.php?id=25.

10 See http://www.ecssr.ac.ae/ECSSR_Index_en.

11 See http://wwwlb.aub.edu.lb/~webifi/aboutIFI/About_the_IFI.html.

References

Abdullah, Abd el Khaliq (1991) "Al-Itjihat al-Jadida wa al-Mustaqbaliyya fi 'ilm al-Siyassa," *Al-Mustaqbal al-Arabi*, 149 (July): 21–37.

Abu Diyya, Saad (1991) *Decision-making Process in Jordan's Foreign Policy* (in Arabic), Beirut: Center for Contemporary Arab Studies.

Ahmad, Ahmad Youssef (2006) "Kharitat al-Waq'I al-Siyassi al-Arabi (1975–2006)," in *Al-'Awam al-Thalathoun al-Oula fi Hayat Markaz Dirasat al-Wihda al-Arabiyya*, Beirut: Center for Unity Studies, pp. 32–55.

Al-Barghouti, Tamim (2008) *The Umma and Dawla: The Nation State and the Arab Middle East*, New York: Pluto Press.

Bashshur, Munir (2004) *Higher Education in the Arab States*, Beirut: UNESCO.

Booth, Ken and Steve Smith (eds) (1995) *International Relations Theory Today*, Philadelphia: University of Pennsylvania Press.

Brecher, Michael (1972) *The Foreign Policy System of Israel*, Oxford: Oxford University Press.

——— (1974) *Decisions in Israel's Foreign Policy*, Oxford: Oxford University Press.

Brecher, Michael and Benjamin Geist (1980) *Decisions in Crisis: Israel 1967 and 1973*, Berkeley: University of California Press.

Center for Arab Unity Studies (CAUS) (2008) *Fahras Majallat al-Mustaqbal al-'Arabi min al-Sana al-Oula hatta al-Sana al-Thalatheen*, Beirut: CAUS.

Dawisha, Adeed (1975) "Intervention in Yemen: An Analysis of Egyptian Perception and Policies," *Middle East Journal*, 29 (winter): 47–63.

——— (1976) *Egypt in the Arab World: Elements of Foreign Policy*, London: Macmillan.

——— (1980) *Syria and the Lebanese Crisis*, New York: St. Martin's Press.

——— (1983) *Islam in Foreign Policy*, Cambridge: Cambridge University Press.

Deeb, Mary-Jane (1991) *Libya's Foreign Policy in North Africa*, Boulder, CO: Westview Press.

Fergany, Nader (2000) "Science and Research for Development in the Arab Region," *Research and Development in the Middle East and North Africa*, Cairo: International Development and Research Center, viewed 15 May 2008, http://www.idrc.ca/en/ev-41620-201-1-DO_TOPIC.html.

Grimaud, Nicole (1984) *La politique extérieure de l'Algérie*, Paris: Karthala.

Haseeb, Kheir Eddin (2008) "*Al-Mustaqbal al-Arabi* 'ala a'tab dukhuliha al-'am al-hadi was al-thalatheen," *Al-Mustaqbal al-Arabi*, 350 (April). Beirut.

Heginbotham, Stanley J. (1994) "Rethinking International Scholarship," *Items*, 48 (2–3): 33–40.

Hudson, Michael (1995) "Democracy and Foreign Policy in the Arab World," in David Garnham and Mark Tessler (eds) *Democracy, War and Peace in the Middle East*, Bloomington: Indiana University Press.

Ibrahim, Saad Eddin (2000) "Arab Social Science Research in the 1990s and Beyond: Issues, Trends, and Priorities," Cairo: International Development and Research Center, viewed May 15, 2008, http://www.idrc.ca/en/ev-41625-201-1-DO_TOPIC.html.

Ihrai, Said (1986) *Pouvoir et influence: Etat, partis et politique étrangère au Maroc*, Rabat: Edino.

Jamal, Manal (2006) "Background Paper: Regional Social Science Research in the Arab World." Papers prepared for the workshop "Strengthening Social Science Research in the Middle East/Arab Region: Exploring the Feasibility of an Arab Social Science Research Council," Dubai, November 26–27.

Kazemi, Farhad (1996) "Changes for Area Studies: Impact Could Be Great," *MESA Newsletter*, 18 (2).

Kerr, Malcolm and S. Yassin (eds) (1982) *Poor and Rich States in the Middle East*, Boulder, CO: Westview Press.

Khalidi, Rashid (1986) *Under Siege: PLO Decision-making during the 1982 War*, New York: Columbia University Press.

—— (1995) "Is There a Future for Middle East Studies?," *MESA Bulletin*, 29 (1): 1–6.

Korany, Bahgat (1974) "Foreign Policy Models and Thin Empirical Relevance to Third World Acts: A Critique and an Alternative," *International Social Science Journal*, 26 (1): 70–94.

—— (1983) "The Take-off of Third World Studies? The Case of Foreign Policy," *World Politics*, 33 (April): 465–487.

—— (1986) "Strategic Studies and the Third World: A Critical Evaluation," *International Social Science Journal*, 38 (1).

—— (1989) "Vers une définition des études stratégiques," in Charles David *et al.*, *Les études stratégiques: approche et concept*, Montreal: Méridien.

—— (1998) "Middle East International Relations," in B. Reich and M. Deeb (eds) *Handbook of Political Research on the Middle East and North Africa*, Westport: Greenwood Press.

Korany, Bahgat and A. E. H. Dessouki (eds) (1984) *The Foreign Policies of Arab States*, Boulder, CO: Westview Press.

Korany, Bahgat and A. E. H. Dessouki (eds) (1991) *The Foreign Policies of Arab States* (2nd edn), Boulder, CO: Westview Press.

Korany, Bahgat and A. E. H. Dessouki (eds) (2008) *Foreign Policies of Arab States: The Challenge of Globalization*, New York and Cairo: American University in Cairo Press.

Korany, Bahgat, Paul Noble, and Rex Brynen (eds) (1993) *The Many Faces of National Security in the Arab World*, New York: St. Martin's Press.

Krasner, Stephen D. (ed.) (1983) *International Regimes*, Ithaca, NY: Cornell University Press.

Levy, Mark, Oran Young, and Michael Zurn (1995) "The Study of International Regimes," *European Journal of International Relations*, 1 (3): 267–330.

Martin, Lenore (1996) "Towards a Comprehensive Approach to National Security in the Middle East," paper presented at the second meeting of the project New Frontiers of National Security in the Middle East, Bellagio, Italy, June 24–28.

McLaurin, R. D., M. Mughisuddin, and P. A. Wagner (1977) *Foreign Policy-making in the Middle East*, New York: Praeger.

Nardin, Terry (ed.) (1996) *The Ethics of War and Peace: Religious and Secular Perspectives*, Princeton, NJ: Princeton University Press.

Nardin, Terry and David Mapel (eds) (1992) *Traditions of International Ethics*, Cambridge: Cambridge University Press.

Pasha, Kamal Pasha (2007) "Human Security and Exceptionalism(s): Securitization, Neo-liberalism and Islam," in Giorgio Shani, Makoto Sato, and Mustapha Kamal Pasha (eds) *Protecting Human Security in a Post 9/11 World: Critical and Global Insights*, Basingstoke: Palgrave.

Rittberger, Volker (1993) *Regime Theory and International Relations*, Oxford: Clarendon Press.

Rumelili, Bahar (2007) "Roundtable: International Relations, Pluralism or Hegemony," written basis for a presentation made at the Pan-European Conference of ECPR's SGIR, Torino, Italy, September.

Said, Edward W. (1979) *Orientalism*, New York: Vintage Books.
—— (2000) *Culture and Imperialism*, New York: Vintage Books.
Sprout, Harold and Margaret Sprout (1965) *The Ecological Perspective in Human Affairs*, Princeton, NJ: Princeton University Press.
Tessler, Mark and Marilyn Grobschmidt (1995) "Democracy in the Arab World and the Arab–Israeli Conflict," in David Garnham and Mark Tessler (eds) *Democracy, War, and Peace in the Middle East*, Bloomington: Indiana University Press.
Tickner, Arlene B. and Ole Wæver (2006) "Global Scholarship in International Relations: A Book Proposal," Mimeo.
Tschirigi, Necla (2006) "The Middle East Under Pressure: What Role for Regional Social Sciences?" Paper prepared for the workshop "Strengthening Social Science Research in the Middle East/Arab Region: Exploring the Feasibility of an Arab Social Science Research Council," Dubai, November 26–27.
UNDP (2002) *Arab Human Development Report 2002: Creating Opportunities for Future Generations*, New York: UNDP.
UNESCO (2006) *Global Education Digest 2006: Comparing Educational Statistics Across the World*, Montreal: UNESCO Institute for Statistics, accessed May 20, 2008, http://www.uis.unesco.org/TEMPLATE/pdf/ged/2006/GED2006.pdf.
Valbjørn, Morten (2008) *A "Baedeker" to IR's Cultural Journey Before, During and After the Cultural Turn. Explorations into the (Ir)Relevance of Cultural Diversity, the IR/Area Studies Nexus and Politics in an (Un)Exceptional Middle East*, Ph.D. thesis, University of Aarhus.
Wæver, Ole (2006) "What's Religion Got to Do With It? Terrorism, War on Terror and Global Security," keynote lecture at the Nordic Conference on the Sociology of Religion, Aarhus; print version is in preparation.
Wurfel, David and Bruce Burton (eds) (1990) *The Political Economy of Foreign Policy in South East Asia*, London: Macmillan.
Zahlan, A.B. (2007) "Higher Education, R&D, Economic Development, Regional and Global Interface." Paper presented at UNESCO regional seminar "The Impact of Globalization on Higher Education and Research in the Arab States," Rabat, Morocco, May 24–25.
Zahran, Gamal (1987) *Egypt's Foreign Policy* (in Arabic), Cairo: Madboli.
—— (1993) *Who Governs Egypt? A Study in Political Decision-making in Egypt and the Third World* (in Arabic), Cairo: Madboli.

11 Israel

The development of a discipline in a unique setting[1]

Arie M. Kacowicz

Introduction

In this chapter I examine the development of the discipline of International Relations (IR) in Israel over the past four decades. Because of its geopolitical uniqueness as an "island" surrounded by hostile Arab neighbors, its strong links to Europe and the U.S., and its Jewish political culture, Israel represents a singular case. IR has contributed to understanding the intricacies of the Arab–Israeli conflict by setting it in a more general context and by offering a comparative framework (Harkabi 1989). Moreover, although realism has obviously thrived in the quintessential "security dilemma" neighborhood of the Middle East, peace study research has surged since the 1990s, along with other theoretical approaches to International Relations and social sciences in general, including constructivism and cultural studies.

One may argue, following Klieman's seminal research on the state of IR in Israel, that "the Israeli study of international relations does not differ in basic outlines and contours from the leading centers of teaching and research elsewhere" (Klieman 1989: 303). The fact that Israeli research today is in the mainstream of the discipline – a large number of Israelis present their research annually at meetings of the International Studies Association (ISA) and many Israeli scholars are recognized worldwide – should not be taken for granted, due to the relative youth of the discipline in the country (and even of the State of Israel itself). The study of IR in Israel has come a long way. Booming in the 1980s and the 1990s and moving into the new millennium, IR has transformed itself: it is now a recognized and established field of study, reflected in the numbers of its students and published books and articles. In 2001, an Israeli Association for International Studies (IAIS, formally linked to the ISA) was established that today includes about 30 faculty members and 40 graduate students. Two prominent members of the Israeli community of IR have received the Karl Deutsch Award of the ISA (Zeev Maoz in 1989 and Alexander Mintz in 1993). Israeli scholars teach at top universities overseas, and are editors and members of advisory boards of journals and research centers around the world (like Emanuel Adler in *International Organization*).

But what is it that is unique about the study of international relations in Israel? Traditionally, it has been a pluralistic and interdisciplinary field. The development of the discipline in Israel is distinct from the trajectory in the U.S., where International Relations is definitively "an American social science" (Hoffmann 1977). Israel has had more outside influences: in addition to the obvious and paramount impact of the U.S., it has been affected by European traditions and paradigms, including the English school of international relations, international law, diplomatic history, as well as the humanities. This theoretical synthesis between American and European influences has made the discipline in Israel one that bridges the Atlantic divide.

Thus, our university departments sustain a mixture of U.S. and European-raised scholars, a scenario not found in Europe (where American political science is mostly criticized), or in the U.S. (where many scholars are very skeptical of, if not condescending towards, their European colleagues). In this context, the Department of International Relations at the Hebrew University of Jerusalem represents a quite unique synthesis and amalgamation, a kind of "confederation" among diplomatic historians, international lawyers, and international relations theorists. Moreover, this department has played a pivotal role in the development of IR in Israel, as the "core" from which numerous undergraduate and graduate students became faculty members elsewhere in Israel and beyond its borders.

Israel is a relatively small country, with a distorted resonance of domestic and foreign politics. The percentage of the population reading daily newspapers is among the highest in the world, everybody is aware of the hourly news on the radio, and politics is a usual subject even in "small talk." In the academic world, we research and publish in English and teach in Hebrew, and many of us hold Ph.Ds from European and American universities. General public interest in foreign and defense affairs is also widespread – perhaps more so than in other Western countries – for obvious reasons related to the lingering state of war with some of Israel's neighbors. Paradoxically, the wide interest of broader segments of the public in foreign affairs means that the study of IR in Israel is perhaps stigmatized as "less academic" than other disciplines, since everyone knows (or pretends to know) something about international politics without studying it systematically. Moreover, research activity is disproportional to the size and resources of the country (Heller 1982: 757). The proportion of R&D as part of the national budget is relatively high compared to other developed countries, but at the same time there are only a small number of research universities. This has serious and obvious professional implications for Israeli scholars, who have to fight hard to get or keep their academic jobs. As a result, Israel "exports" IR scholars (graduate students and faculty) who prefer to research and teach in North America and Europe to the academic community beyond its borders.

In the following pages, I examine the state of IR in Israel. First, I summarize, by academic departments and research institutes, the institutional development of the discipline at the major Israeli universities. Second, I address the question of how we theorize about the field locally. I map the state of the art and the subfields we tend to emphasize and neglect. Third, I consider the relationship between the academic field of IR and the real world of politics in Israel. Finally, I attempt to explain and understand the state of IR in Israel by referring to the uniqueness of Israeli foreign policy and the Jewish component of its political culture.

The state of International Relations in Israel

The community of IR scholars in Israel (and of Israeli scholars overseas) currently includes about 150 members, most of whom teach and research in seven universities and several research centers (as specified below). They may be grouped into five waves or generations on the basis of age and professional training:

1   The first generation came from Central and Eastern Europe and taught in the early years of the State of Israel with a strong European inclination and emphasis on law, history, and normative theory.
2   The second generation includes scholars who received their Ph.Ds in Europe and North America in the late 1960s and taught at Israeli universities through the rapid development of IR programs here since the 1970s.

3   The third generation refers to Israeli-born scholars and/or immigrants who received their education in Israel and overseas, and became faculty in the late 1970s and the 1980s.

4   The fourth generation completed their Ph.Ds in the late 1980s and early 1990s and represents the mid-career phase of the profession in Israel.

5   Finally, the new generation of IR scholars includes those who have completed their Ph.Ds in the past six years, both in Israel and overseas.

Academic departments

The Department of International Relations, Hebrew University of Jerusalem

The story of the study of IR in Israel dates back to the pre-state period of the British mandate for Palestine, before 1948. Following the establishment of the Hebrew University in 1925, the instruction of International Relations began in 1932. Starting in 1946, students could receive an MA degree in International Relations, and in 1953, a BA, both of these within the framework of political science (Klieman 1989: 305; Gazit 2002).

In the aftermath of the Six Day War of 1967, and in view of the increasing importance of the field of IR, an independent Department of International Relations was re-created in 1969 under the leadership of Saul Friedlander and Michel Brecher as a teaching and research entity separate from the Department of Political Science. The department was initially built around diplomatic historians, IR theorists, and international lawyers. The Hebrew University of Jerusalem remains to this day the only institution offering all three academic degrees in International Relations in the country. In 1972, the Leonard Davis Institute for International Relations was created as an independent research institute that closely collaborates with members of the department.

Since its re-establishment in 1969, the department has kept its pluralistic structure, bringing together IR theoreticians, diplomatic historians, and international lawyers at the intersection of the humanities and the social sciences, providing a unique background for the development of the discipline. The foundational interdisciplinary nature of the field is reflected in the number of its joint appointments with other university departments, such as the Faculty of Law, Islamic and Middle Eastern Studies, East Asian Studies, Russian and Slavic Studies, and Political Science. Faculty members research issues of international political economy, international cooperation and conflict, theories of IR, diplomacy and negotiations, peace research, international history, and public international law. Currently, the department has 19 faculty members and about 900 students, including about 100 MA students and 30 Ph.D. candidates. Their research covers a gamut of subjects in the discipline, including issues of war, peace, and strategy; Israeli foreign policy and the Arab–Israeli conflict; international law; diplomatic history; and international political economy.

The current members of the department agree that the traditional separation of theory, history, and international law is rather artificial. Since the mid-1990s, graduate studies have been reorganized around issue areas: international security and diplomatic studies; international political economy and global studies; and international law, organizations, institutions, and the normative dimension of IR. Some international lawyers currently adopt theoretical constructs and methodologies of social sciences (Hirsch 1999, 2003; Broude and Kacowicz 2006; Broude 2006); conversely, IR theoreticians address major subjects of international law (Kacowicz 1994, 2005; Press-Barnathan 2004). Diplomatic historians and IR theoreticians similarly produce work that is mutually informed by their counterparts (Kacowicz 1998, 2005; Kochavi 2002; Bialer 2005). This coming-of-age beyond the traditional (and sterile) debates among historians, theoreticians, and international lawyers of the 1970s and the 1980s indicates the maturation of the IR field.

Beyond the Department of IR, several members of the Department of Political Science at the Hebrew University have engaged in research at the intersection of comparative politics, political theory, and International Relations. At the Faculty of Law, several faculty members address paramount issues of international relations, including human rights, international organizations, and Jerusalem.

The Department of Political Science, Tel-Aviv University

International relations and strategic studies is one of the fields of study – alongside political thought; Israeli politics; comparative politics; politics, society and law; methodology and political communication; and public administration – within the Department of Political Science at Tel-Aviv University, founded in 1956. The department, a portion of whose scholars focus on International Relations, includes about 900 undergraduates, 400 MA students, and 30 Ph.D. students. Among a faculty of 20 members of the department, at least six may be clearly identified as IR scholars. Their research approaches the discipline from various angles.

Several research institutes are associated with the Department of Political Science in areas related to IR, including the Institute for National Security Studies (international security and national security); the Tami Steinmetz Center for Peace Research (peace and conflict studies); the Dayan Center for Middle Eastern Studies; and the Curiel Center for International Studies (history and regional studies).

The Department of Political Studies, Bar-Ilan University

The Department of Political Studies (founded in 1967) is one of the largest academic departments in this university. Approximately 1,700 students are enrolled, among them some 600 Master's degree candidates and 40 doctoral students. International Relations comprises one of the nine subfields in this department, alongside political philosophy (Western and Jewish); comparative politics; Israeli politics; strategy and national security; politics in the Middle East; public communications; public administration and public policy-making; and the politics of the Jewish people.

Among the 36 faculty members of the department, about one-third conduct research on international relations and strategic studies, with a special emphasis on strategic studies, national security, Israel, and the Middle East. Most are also research associates with the Begin-Sadat Center for Strategic Studies (BESA). Only a small number of scholars address general issues of international relations theory *unrelated* to strategic studies and the Middle East.

In addition to the Department of Political Studies, a number of scholars at the Faculty of Law address paramount issues of international law, including the WTO, the European Union, international economic law, international environmental law, and international humanitarian law.

The Division of International Relations, School of Political Sciences, Haifa University

The Division of International Relations was established in 2000 within the framework of the current School of Political Sciences at the University of Haifa. Upon completion of the accreditation process, the division will become a graduate department of International Relations, offering specialization in the following subfields: theories of international relations; foreign policy, national security, and strategy; diplomacy and conflict resolution; international relations of the Middle East; and nationalism and multiculturalism in international relations. The division currently includes nine faculty members.

The Department of Politics and Government, Ben-Gurion University (Beer Sheva)

The study of international relations at the University of Ben-Gurion (founded in 1969) is an integral part of the Department of Politics and Government, which was established in 1999. This department believes in a multidisciplinary approach to the study of politics, focusing on three core areas – comparative politics, political theory, and IR – and employing the insights of several other disciplines in the social sciences and humanities, such as sociology, geography, and history. The department has a strong European focus, as it houses the Center for the Study of European Politics and Society. Furthermore, David Newman, a prominent member of the department, is co-editor of the journal *Geopolitics* (along with John Agnew from UCLA), which is a resurgent field at the interface of geography and International Relations.

   Among the 11 faculty members of the department, three are directly concerned with core issues of international relations, and four others stand at the intersection of IR with other fields of political science: political theory and comparative politics.

The Department of Sociology, Political Science and Communication, Open University of Israel

A special mention should be made of the Open University given the numbers of students taking courses related to international relations since its creation in 1976 (Klieman 1989: 305). Of the 25 faculty members of the political science and International Relations division, three work at the core of the discipline. Among the courses dictated at the Open University dealing with IR we should mention Diplomatic History of the Twentieth Century, The Emergence of New States in Africa, Foreign Policy of the Soviet Union/Russia, Introduction to International Relations, Selected Topics in Israeli Foreign Policy, The United States in the International Arena since 1945, and War and Strategy.

The Lauder School of Government, Diplomacy, and Strategy, Interdisciplinary Center, Herzlyia

This private college, created in 1994, includes a School of Government that "aspires to prepare the next generation of leaders for Israel's public sector and to conduct research in order to find practical solutions to this sector's problems." It takes an interdisciplinary approach with respect to International Relations, linking political science and international relations theory to economics, law, technology, and communications (http://pow.idc.ac.il/portal). Among the 16 full-time faculty of the Lauder School, eight teach IR subjects.

   Two institutes, chaired by Faculty members, epitomize the policy orientation of the Lauder School: the Institute for Policy and Strategy (in charge of the Annual Herzlyia Conference Series on Israel's Balance of National Security), and the International Policy Institute for Counter-Terrorism (ICT).

Academic research institutes

A partial list of the major institutes dealing with international relations research in Israel includes (1) The Leonard Davis Institute for International Relations; (2) The Harry S. Truman Research Institute for the Advancement of Peace; (3) The Begin/Sadat (BESA) Center for Strategic Studies; (4) The Jaffee Center for Strategic Studies; and (5) The Tami Steinmetz Center for Peace Research. All those institutes are affiliated within the major research universities in the country.

The Leonard Davis Institute for International Relations (The Hebrew University of Jerusalem)

The Institute was established in 1972, and it is considered the leading institution for the research of international relations in Israel. Its programs aim at deepening the understanding of Israel's foreign relations and diplomacy, Middle Eastern affairs, and the subject of world order. This embraces, in particular, the critical choices Israel faces as part of the international community – in such domains as international political economy, the environment, human rights, global security and conflict resolution, and international organizations.

The formal aims of the Institute include promoting scientific research in the theory of international relations; adopting a broad interdisciplinary perspective; presenting universal themes of international politics to the Israeli public (thereby enhancing the national discourse on these matters); and rendering its expertise and consulting capability to the service of national institutions that conduct the security and foreign affairs of the country.

Research sponsored and supported by the Davis Institute covers a wide range in the discipline. A partial list of research projects from the past five years includes the following subjects: the Palestinian refugee problem in a comparative perspective; the influence of international norms in a regional perspective; religious and ethnic minorities in the Middle East; the United States and regional cooperation in Asia and Europe since World War II; wars as a social and historical construct of constitutive rights; identities and transitions from war to peace; the Palestinian–Israeli interaction as a game theory analysis of territorial conflict; the global sources of regional transitions from war to peace in the Middle East; Israel and the *intifada* as a case of adaptation and learning; Israeli diplomacy in the back channel; uncertainty and risk-taking in Israeli peacemaking; ethos as an expression of Israeli identity and its changes in the transition from conflict to peace; stable peace among nations; the transition from conflict resolution to reconciliation; and population resettlement in international conflicts.

The Harry S. Truman Research Institute for the Advancement of Peace (The Hebrew University of Jerusalem)

Founded in 1965, the Institute is dedicated to fostering peace and advancing cooperation in the Middle East and among the peoples of the world through research, sponsorship of conferences and colloquia, and provision of fellowships for local and visiting scholars. The Truman Institute focuses on peace studies, the Middle East, and particularly the third world through an interdisciplinary approach to regional studies.

The Institute specializes in studies on Middle Eastern issues, with an emphasis upon Israeli–Palestinian relations and the promotion of cooperation and welfare in the region as a whole. In addition, the institute specializes in studies concerning the third world in general, in search of a better understanding of the roots of domestic and international conflicts in the global South. It is divided into six geographical units – Africa, Asia, the Balkans, Central Asia and the Caucasus, Latin America, and the Middle East.

The Begin–Sadat Center for Strategic Studies (BESA) (Bar-Ilan University)

The BESA Center has been affiliated with the Department of Political Studies at Bar-Ilan University since 1991. The Center provides policy-oriented research on matters of strategy, security, and peace in the Middle East. Its publications and policy recommendations are directed at a number of audiences, including senior Israeli decision-makers (in military and civilian life), the Defense and Foreign Affairs establishments in Israel, the diplomatic corps, the press, the academic community, the broader public, and leaders of the Jewish communities around the world.

The research fields associated with this institute include Israeli strategic thinking; deterrence and regional security; strategic options in the peace process; domestic and foreign policy of the Palestinian Authority; Israeli public opinion on national security; U.S.–Israel relations; terrorism and low-intensity violence; Israeli–Turkish strategic ties; security in the Eastern Mediterranean basin; Middle East water resources; proliferation of weapons of mass destruction; Middle East arms control; and regional security regimes.

The Institute for National Security Studies (formerly the Jaffee Center for Strategic Studies (JCSS)) (Tel-Aviv University)

The JCSS was founded in 1973. It initiates and conducts research on a multiplicity of factors – political, military, economic, psychological, and socio-cultural – that involve strategic issues, with an emphasis on those related to Israeli national security. The Center thus relates to the concept of "strategy" in its broadest sense, namely the complex of processes involved in the identification, mobilization, and application of resources in peace and war aimed at solidifying and strengthening national and international security.

According to Mark Heller, a leading researcher in the Center, the creation of the JCSS has been symptomatic of a growing interest in policy analysis, reflecting Israel's national policy priorities. Considerable attention has been paid to containment, management, and resolution of international conflicts; military issues such as arms races, escalation, deterrence, and boundaries and other geographic dimensions; and studies on intelligence (surprise, early warning, and misperceptions) that have been particularly salient since the debacle of the Yom Kippur War of October 1973 (Heller 1982: 760).

In 2006, the Center experienced a process of "privatization" and structural change, becoming currently the Institute for National Security Studies, a think-tank independent from Tel-Aviv University.

The Tami Steinmetz Center for Peace Research (Tel-Aviv University)

The Tami Steinmetz Center for Peace Research is an academic research institution that since 1994 has surveyed public opinion of the peace process, the Israeli–Palestinian conflict, and the Arab–Israeli conflict in general. The Center publishes monthly surveys about the current state of public opinion, including the "Peace Index." In addition, it supports research related to peace theory and international relations, including issues such as the causes and origins of war; the conversion of armaments and sites; intra-social and ethnic conflicts (national identities); psychological peace research; feminist aspects of peace research; peace education; and nonviolent conflict management.

The "Peace Index" assesses the way the Israeli public perceives the peace process with the Arab countries and the Palestinians, and the probable and desirable ramifications of the process – political, social, and economic – in the short and long term. Other permanent projects of the Center include a database on Israeli–Arab cooperation, which systematically collects studies on cooperation by government agencies, voluntary organizations, and academic and nonacademic institutes in Israel and abroad.

An assessment of the state of the art

In the following pages, I examine first how theorizing about international relations takes place locally. Second, I assess the kind of discipline we have developed in Israel, emphasizing both the well-developed and the "underdeveloped" areas. Finally, I refer to the important policy question of the relationship between the study of international relations and the "real world" (of politics) in the country.

How theory (of IR) takes place locally? An Israeli story

Members of the academic community of IR scholars in Israel seem to agree that although we develop international relations theory and contribute significantly to the progress of the field in general, no distinct Israeli approach to or theory of the study of international politics exists. The contribution of the Israeli community to the global one is based in the large participation of Israeli scholars in ISA meetings and publications, their research and teaching abroad, and the publication of their articles in U.S. and European journals of international relations. Based on meetings, interviews, and e-mail exchanges with about 25 colleagues, I have traced a number of explanations for this absence of a unique Israeli IR theory. First, Israeli international studies are not informed by a dominant school of thought or a predominant thinker; therefore, they have evolved in an eclectic and pluralistic fashion, based on individual preferences and national developments (Klieman 1989: 312). Personal and academic backgrounds have shaped individual preferences, such as whether or not an Israeli academic was educated in Israel or overseas. The national developments that have prevailed, obviously, have been the lingering state of war since 1948 and the recent (and truncated) peace process of the 1990s. As for the discipline as a whole, we do not have an accepted text or a governing theory. Some academic departments emphasize security studies and realism (for instance, Bar-Ilan), while others take a "softer," more idealistic approach (like Jerusalem). What characterizes the structure of the IR department in Jerusalem, as a paradigmatic case, is the singular and fruitful dialogue among theoreticians, historians, political economists, and international lawyers dealing with international studies from their particular theoretical, historical, economic, and legal angles.

Second, as Israeli culture bearers *and* academicians, we tend to be very individualist, independent, eclectic, and critical. This makes the nature of the field atomized rather than a collective enterprise. Israeli society is very heterogeneous and its members argumentative, and this is clearly reflected in academia. Because of a weak sense of community, little work is undertaken by teams or through inter-university cooperation. Hence, major gatherings of Israeli scholars of IR from all over the country usually take place at the annual meetings of the International Studies Association in far-away places such as San Diego or Honolulu (this anomaly has been partially amended since 2002 by the recent creation of the IAIS and its annual gatherings at local universities). The lack of local cooperation is directly related to the hegemonic role of "American" (i.e., U.S.) political science, which makes most of us focus outside Israel and invest our energy in building ties with American (and other non-Israeli) academics.

Third, although the realist mainstream has thrived in the country for obvious (and "objective") reasons, there is no "official" approach to international relations. The field has developed in the country under the encompassing shadow of the Arab–Israeli conflict, which epitomized a reality of *realpolitik* (Harkabi 1989: xxv). In this sense, one can discern particular epistemological and methodological styles in the field that reflect the existential conflict with Israel's neighbors. As Klieman (1989: 309) succinctly suggested almost 20 years ago:

> Israel offers an extraordinary opportunity for testing conventional political wisdom and for explaining new directions. In turning political adversity into scholarly advantage the Israeli community of IR researchers tends as a whole more toward the state-centric approach than to the transnational one, to concentrate somewhat less on the thematic, or theory and methodology, and more on substantive aspects usually of direct concern to Israel.

For instance, scholars naturally focus on inter-state relations, international security, and security studies – including subjects like military intelligence, strategic surprise, low-intensity war, and nuclear weapons – and neglect areas such as international political economy and globalization. Moreover, a predilection for empiricism and implementation of case studies and issues of real-life *problematique* is also apparent, as opposed to abstract theorizing or formal modeling, deriving from the direct concern with the Arab–Israeli conflict.

Yet, during the 1990s and into the new millennium, research projects dealing with conflict resolution and peace research (Kacowicz 1994, 1998; Adler and Barnett 1998; Kacowicz *et al.* 2000); regional cooperation (Press-Barnathan 2003, 2009); and constructivism and the cultural and sociological dimensions of IR (Adler 1997, 2005; Cohen 1997; Sofer 1998, 2001) are all becoming more common. Moreover, the particular role attributed to international law and to diplomatic history at the core of the discipline, at least in the case of the Hebrew University of Jerusalem, reflects a Grotian, or English school, approach to IR study (Press-Barnathan 2004). These new themes and directions do not contradict the predominance of themes such as security and strategic studies, but rather offer a welcome addition to the "mainstream" of the discipline. Although the movement in the direction of peace studies was clearly affected by the initial optimism of the Israeli–Palestinian peace process in the early 1990s, the academic trend has survived the apparent demise of that process.

Fourth, Israeli scholars base their research on American and European sources, so it is hard to imagine a theory or approach developed in the country as entirely original. This is due to the Western orientation of the country, and the academic background and education of its faculty members. To stay relevant worldwide, an established Israeli theory would have to truly regard the whole world. Hence, Israeli scholars prefer to be hooked into the general academic discourse of IR, which is eminently American, rather than offering a particular(istic) Israeli perspective. At least geographically we are in the periphery, so the only way to remain "relevant" and to "be heard" is to build strong ties with the hub of contemporary political science – North America and Western Europe. Likewise, the critical mass of academic journals ranked in Israel for promotion purposes are based in those two key regions as well.

Fifth, since we are a small and very globally interconnected academic community, and several of us are former immigrants who studied overseas, we tend to adopt the tendencies and overall "fashions" of the discipline. Although U.S. textbooks and approaches pre-dominate, we have disciplinary affinities with the English school of international relations (the Grotian approach), as well as more cosmopolitan views. At the same time, our theoretical concerns are informed by and partly derived from the overwhelming context of the Arab–Israeli conflict, and the almost perennial search for an elusive peace.

Sixth, the issue of language complicates the relationship between teaching and research (Cohen 2001: 156). We teach in Hebrew and assign reading material in English to our students. For professional advancement, we are obliged to publish in English at the top overseas journals in North America and Europe. The fact that publishing articles in Hebrew garners almost no recognition provides little incentive to do so, which is unfortunate for the national language and the Israeli academic community as a whole. As the academic editor of *Politika* (in 2000–2002 and again since 2007), published twice a year by the Davis Institute of the Hebrew University, I encounter difficulties in getting submitted articles to review, since non-tenured faculty prefer to publish in leading, ranked journals in English. The result is a wide gap and even a marked disjuncture between the requirements of teaching and those of research, as well as the fact that many times we identify ourselves more with the broader community of IR scholars worldwide (through the International Studies Association) than with our "local" colleagues in Israel. Hence, it is not uncommon for Israeli scholars to be more recognized and praised overseas than in their own country.

There are a few Israeli journals dealing with political science in general, and International Relations in particular, most of them in Hebrew. Between 1975 and 1992 the Davis Institute published the only IR journal in English, *The Jerusalem Journal of International Relations*. Since 1975 it has published in Hebrew a journal called *State, Government, and International Relations*, re-named in 1998 *Politika: An Israeli Journal for Political Science and International Relations*. There are two journals in Hebrew that address issues of national and international security: *Ma'arachot* (published by the Israeli Ministry of Defense); and *Adkan*, published by the Institute of National Security Studies. It is worth mentioning *Israeli Studies* as well, a multidisciplinary journal on Israeli scholarship dealing with history, politics, society, and culture. Most recently, the Israeli Council of Foreign Relations, a think-tank associated with the Jewish Congress, has started publishing the *Israel Journal of Foreign Affairs* (in English).

What kind of discipline did we develop in Israel: what do we study?

Traditionally, the study of international relations in Israel has focused in particular on the subfield of security and strategic studies, with a bias towards issues related to Israel's own security agenda. Mentionable subjects researched are superpower regional contests; crisis management and conflict resolution; patron–client relationships; decision-making and domestic–external linkages; perceptual models of rationality and irrationality; national security policy; intelligence and strategic surprise; conventional and nuclear deterrence strategies; and arms race dynamics. The emphasis on security studies might be related as well to the sociological fact that most faculty members are Israeli males, many of them having a past record in the Israeli army or the intelligence community.

In addition, the local discipline of IR has emphasized Israel and Middle East political and diplomatic history; Middle East regional politics; Arab–Israeli conflict patterns; Israeli foreign policy; and international law. Since the 1990s, interest in peace and conflict studies, European studies, and the more general nexus between international law and international institutions has been growing.

Conversely, important areas of study in the discipline of International Relations have been neglected, first and foremost the study of international political economy with just a few exceptions (Tovias 1990, 1997; Press-Barnathan 2009; Sadeh 2006). This bias against political economy is again based in the former (and wrong) distinction between "high" and "low" politics, and between international and domestic politics. This is despite (or perhaps because of) political attempts made during the Oslo process of 1993 to 2001 to foster mechanisms of (asymmetrical) economic interdependence (with Israel being the dominant party in economic terms). The failure of the process could be analyzed then as either an indication that a liberal economic approach was not the right approach to take, or that considerations of narrow security concerns and sheer power should eventually trump the logic of economic interdependence. Even in the context of the Arab–Israeli conflict, issues such as the economics of defense have been relatively neglected, due to the almost monolithic concern with the potential use of force and military power, rather than its economic logics.

Furthermore, although Israel is one of the most globalized countries in the world, we barely focus on globalization and global studies as central phenomena and processes of international relations. The few exceptions are related to international governance and environmental law, and are usually addressed by international lawyers, not by political scientists. Transnationalism is considered only in the context of terrorism and terrorist groups. Few Israeli scholars tackle global issues such as environmental concerns or the promotion of human rights. The reason for the scarcity of studies on globalization derives, again, from the traditional bias against international political economy and the relative novelty of the subject, at least in scholastic terms.

Similarly, ethical and normative concerns have been absent from the academic research of IR in Israel until recently. This poses an interesting question regarding the absence of ethical/normative concern in a country whose Jewish national identity and interests have such a strong religious base, and in which the very conflict with its neighbors encompasses, at least partially, religious and normative foundations as well. But it is precisely the constant state of war since 1948 that has precluded the concern with "soft" issues of international relations, including normative ones. Hence, the paramountcy of security concerns and the traditional adoption of a "hard-nosed" Hobbesian version of realism partially explain the neglect of normative studies, which started to thrive only with the launching of the peace process in the 1990s. The overall sociological explanation for the fact that security concerns crowd out religious/normative ones is again related to the existential threats posed to the state since 1948. Moreover, until recently the conflict between Israel and its Arab neighbors (first and foremost with the Palestinians) was regarded as secular and national, rather than as an extreme religious dispute confronting Jews and Muslims.

Other neglected areas include feminist or gender studies, IR and third world, and political communications. Even the study of U.S. foreign policy is very limited in scope. Moreover, in methodological terms, most IR scholars are still reluctant to utilize quantitative and formal methods, with a few prominent exceptions. This reluctance is perhaps related to the initial evolution of the discipline in Israel, with a strong European orientation, as a stepchild of history and the humanities, far away from the exact sciences and behaviorism.

What is the relationship between IR and the real world (of politics) in Israel?

Paradoxically, despite the huge impact of the real world of politics that frames the context of the academic study of international relations in Israel, academia has not had a similar impact upon the practitioners of international politics in the country. In this context, it is

difficult to pinpoint any policy implementation or impact of the academic or research institutions described here, with the exception perhaps of the Jaffee Center's policy options project
in the 1980s on alternative futures for the Arab–Israeli conflict in general and the Israeli–
Palestinian conflict in particular. Hence, the "real" world has no institutionalized cooperation
with the academic world. The Israeli political establishment evinces little interest in listening
to academics, and it does not rely upon our work. Unlike the U.S. model, there is little (open)
movement back and forth between academia and the government, which reinforces the
conceptual and practical gap between scholars and decision-makers. This disconnection
exists for several reasons.

First is a series of "attitudinal" or perceptual reasons (Heller 1982: 762). Receptivity to
academic input is limited owing to the general preference of experience over theory.
Practitioners – in both the security and Foreign Ministry establishments – have been focused
essentially on the "here and now." They have short-term views and little if any patience for
theory, long-term perspectives, or what they consider philosophical speculation. Academics
on the other hand have been engaged in largely theoretical or historical work of relatively
little relevance to the practitioners. There are only few formal think-tank institutions that
attempt to bridge the gap between theory and policy, without any significant impact upon
either the academic world or the practical one. Any mutual movement between academics
and practitioners is further affected by the obsession with secrecy in security affairs, which
limits exchanges to informal, hidden, or underground contacts. Although the academic
community and the world of policy-making has no open and clear link, there exists a "shadow
community," a security network that works as a closed epistemic community involving
security officers with an academic background, or alternatively, faculty members with a
security background from their military service and professional life (before academia).
Hence, mutual impact takes place at the informal, individual level. For instance, former
military officers (in the military intelligence and/or IDF Strategic Planning) commonly
pursue academic careers at one of the major research centers on strategy and national
security, or through a university department. Conversely, many professional diplomats from
the Israeli Foreign Ministry hold academic degrees in International Relations and political
science.

Second, any fruitful dialogue between the small community of IR scholars and the political
security establishment faces structural limitations. Unlike the U.S. political system, the
executive and legislative branches of government experience no constitutional tension. As a
result, the legislature does not have an independent research capacity like that of many
Western countries, which provide access for Western academics concerned with foreign and
security affairs (Heller 1982: 762). Moreover, the Israeli Foreign Ministry is rather small,
both in terms of its allocation in the national budget (about 0.5 percent) and the amount of
political leverage vis-à-vis the omnipotent security establishment (Sofer 1998: 6).

Unfortunately, there is a void about the knowledge the Israeli political establishment
requires on issues of national security from academia and think-tanks. That knowledge is
ultimately provided from within the security establishment itself, so there are not sufficient
civilian and professional filters to assess or monitor the input of the knowledge provided by
the security establishment (essentially the Israeli army) upon the decision-making apparatus.
This has become particularly evident in the decision-making process during the Second
Lebanon War (July–August 2006). For all these reasons, relations between government and
academics have been sporadic. The "inner and outer" phenomenon is less pronounced in
Israel; the few exceptions include scholars such as Yehoshafat Harkabi, Shlomo Avineri,
Nimrod Novick, Uzi Arad, and Dore Gold (in the discipline of IR), Yehuda Zvi Blum and

Ruth Lapidot (in international law), and Itamar Rabinovitch, Shlomo Ben-Ami, Shimon Shamir, and Eli Bar-Navi (in the related fields of the Middle East and history). These academics did serve as political and security advisors, senior diplomats and officers, and even ministers, but they have been the exception to the rule. This is very unfortunate, since studying international relations can provide the practitioners in the security and diplomatic realms with a systematic road map of how to cope with the world (Harkabi 1989: 206).

Explaining and understanding the state of IR in Israel

To make sense of the state of the discipline of IR in Israel, we have to refer as well to the actual state of its international relations in broader terms. In other words, the political, geopolitical, and cultural contexts of the country inform, shape, and affect (though they do not cause in a positivistic fashion) the way we study, explain, and understand international relations. In this section, I refer to two major components: (1) the geopolitical context (of the Arab–Israeli conflict); and (2) the cultural context (of Israel as a Jewish state). Those two components complement and complete the picture of the state of IR in Israel as outlined above, including unique characteristics such as the participation of the academic community in global academic circles *more* than in the national discourse, and the relative lack of interaction between the state and the scholarly community.

The geopolitical context of the Arab–Israeli conflict: the primacy of security I

As a small nation, a democracy (at least within the pre-1967 borders), and the only Jewish state in the world, Israel is a unique international actor, one with a certain exclusiveness or exceptionalism regarding its place in the world. Because of the lingering state of war with its Arab neighbors since its creation in 1948, Israel's lack of strategic depth, its numerical inferiority, and its exposed frontiers have created a feeling of insecurity. The constant preoccupation with the Arab–Israeli conflict as an existential conflict has led to a clear discrepancy between the aspirations of Israel to meet universal norms and the necessity of adopting *realpolitik* rules of behavior vis-à-vis its neighbors (Sofer 1998: 5). This discrepancy also explains the relative neglect of the normative dimension of IR, both in theory and in practice. The tragic and paradoxical condition of the Jewish people in its renewed exercise of national sovereignty within the State of Israel resides in the fact that it cannot fulfill the lofty ideals and the cosmopolitan vocation of their biblical prophets until peace is reached with its neighbors so that Israel becomes more of a "normal" country.

Living in what might be considered a quintessential realist region of the world, Israel has emphasized, for geopolitical and "objective" reasons, the primacy of security. Even when the realities of world politics and Israel's own technological and economic edge over its neighbors do not warrant a sense of insecurity, security considerations have remained the central constraint of Israeli domestic and foreign politics at the cognitive level, profoundly shaping and affecting the Israeli discipline of IR as well, as it cannot dissociate itself from the context of real life and politics. This partly explains the bias towards the study of pressing issues dealing with Israeli security over theory about global political issues, and the predilection for a realist worldview.

In comparative terms, the Israeli case is quite singular. Israel is one of three nation-states in the world, along with Ireland and Armenia, whose national majority (i.e., the Jewish people) remains outside of the state's geographical borders (Epstein 2004: 89). This furthers the sense of Israel as a geopolitical island (in relation to its direct, Middle Eastern environment) and its global outreach to the Jewish diaspora around the globe. Israel is also one of the few states in the world without clear and recognized borders (except for its borders with Jordan and Egypt). Moreover, the legitimacy of the state and its very existence are still questioned by some of its neighbors and by some intellectual circles around the world. Hence, the uniqueness of Israel's hostile environment must be taken into account when placing the Israeli study of international relations in a comparative perspective.

Israel as a Jewish state: the primacy of security II

We should add to the "objective" unfriendly geopolitical conditions of Israel the primordial fact of Israel as a (or the) Jewish state. Jewish political culture permeates Israel's approach to international relations, and, indirectly, the way Israeli scholars study and research it. Two thousand years of persecution of the Jewish people in the diaspora, which culminated in the Holocaust of six million Jews, have created what Alan Dowty cogently refers to as the *gevalt syndrome* ("expecting the catastrophe"): Jewish politics, even after almost 60 years of Israeli independence, are still dominated by a deep sense of insecurity with long historical roots (Dowty 1997: 10).

The primacy of security concerns in Israel meshes very well with proclivities rooted in Jewish political culture: the sense of an unfriendly world of gentiles (*goim*) resolved to doom the Jews and the need ultimately for self-reliance. Ironically, the state founded to resolve the perennial problem of Jewish security has itself been plagued, since the beginning and well into the present, by a constant sense of insecurity (Dowty 2001: 321–322).

International relations in the modern sense depend on a conception of plurality of nations, which is quite foreign to this Jewish tradition of politics. Jewish thought traditionally divided the world into two: the Jewish people versus the "gentiles" full of malice (Harkabi 1989: 201). Jews can traditionally rely upon their own people, but are reluctant to reach out to their non-Jewish neighbors. In terms of international relations (and of international relations theory) this predisposition creates an attitude cogent to a hard realist perspective based on self-reliance, anarchy, and self-help. Moreover, in comparative terms the Jewish people have had little practical experience in handling power as a sovereign nation until 1948. Hence, the modern study of international relations in contemporary Israel should have a particular significance: as a corrective heuristic tool to make sense of the world and to reduce the paramount and overwhelming Arab–Israeli conflict to more modest and comparative terms, by reaching out to other cultures, traditions, concepts, and ideologies, and by studying other conflicts and alternatively, zones of peace. In this sense, the study of international relations in Israel should incorporate the cosmopolitan (universal) element in Jewish religious tradition, according to which Jewish/Israeli culture should enlighten the world as a whole (the element of *or lagoim*, literally providing a spiritual light to the gentiles).

To sum up, Israeli general skepticism in foreign policy, rooted in traditional Jewish insecurity, helps us to explain why the Israeli public in general and our students in particular consider realism as the predominant (and even natural) paradigm of international relations. As in many other countries of the world, the public discourse about international relations often reflects a self-centered, ethnocentric view of the world (Cohen 2001: 159). Against this parochial tendency that constrains our academic agenda, it is our moral and intellectual duty to reach out to the broader community of IR and to break the stereotypes of the rest of the world. This explains also why our theoretical contributions to the field are not coined in specific or uniquely Israeli terms, but rather are placed in a more general, universal vein.

Conclusions and future perspectives

In this chapter, I have presented a succinct review of the development of the study of IR in Israel against the background of its unique setting. In geopolitical terms, Israel is an island. In disciplinary terms, IR in Israel is directly related to the West (we publish in Western Europe, especially in England and North America, and we partly teach and research in American and European universities). Hence, the level of cooperation between Israeli scholars and Arab scholars is minimal, if not virtual. Exceptions perhaps are the Truman Institute at the Hebrew University of Jerusalem and the Steinmetz Center from Tel-Aviv University, especially before 2001. The level of academic interaction between Israelis and Palestinians has been a function of the transition from war to peace (and back) in the past two decades.

The discipline of IR as an independent field of research and teaching has grown in Israel since the early 1970s, reflecting a parallel movement of the thriving of international studies in the world in general. Israeli students and scholars of IR have contributed substantially to the development of the field, relative to the size of the academic community (currently about 150 scholars with Ph.Ds in IR and political sciences) and the small population of the country. However, their contribution has been as individuals rather than from a distinctive school or way of theorizing about international relations in Israel. Moreover, a significant number of Israeli scholars currently teach (either full- or part-time) overseas, and a majority of them have a previous affiliation, either as students or lecturers, with the Department of International Relations at the Hebrew University of Jerusalem, which has remained the core institution for the development of IR as an academic discipline in the country.

Although the realist paradigm of international relations seems to have a natural affinity with the Middle Eastern setting where Israel is located, the study of IR in Israel does not deal only with *realpolitik* concerns, since it is informed as well by the Grotian approach, as it becomes apparent in research and studies dealing with diplomatic history and international law. In both theoretical endeavor and practical implementation, a delicate balance between Realism and idealism, between national goals and attentiveness to the external world, must be found (Sofer 1998: 17). In the long cultural and religious Jewish tradition we have evidence of both the national and particularistic messages of the Jewish nation and state from a realist standpoint, along with the universal, cosmopolitan credo as predicated by Isaiah long before Jesus, Kant, and Marx. Thus, understanding international relations in general, and in Israel in particular, can help refute the notion that it is so stereotypically embedded in the Israeli collective public that such relations are motivated solely by calculations of national interest in the domain of necessity. As Yehoshafat Harkabi pointed out: "Actions in the international sphere are not ruled by morality, but neither do they ignore it" (Harkabi 1989: 202–203). Hence, qualifying the power politics approach can act as a heuristic corrective for the practice of international relations in the country and for the overwhelming impact of security concerns.

The geopolitical and cultural constraints of Israel have partly determined the contours of the discipline of IR in the country, emphasizing subfields such as security studies and neglecting areas such as international political economy and global studies. The remaining challenge for us is to broaden our horizons and extend our links both to the region and to the world. To that end, we should aim at having some impact upon the shaping of the *realities* of international relations and not just its academic discipline.

Looking at the evolution of the discipline of IR in Israel in the past 40 years, it seems that it has reflected, even in some distorted ways, the general trends we know elsewhere. There has been a move towards eclecticism and pluralism, realism has become challenged but not superseded, and new themes and perspectives have emerged following the end of the Cold War, including global issues and concerns. At the same time, only the resolution of the long and simmering Arab–Israeli conflict might set the context for the development of more normal international politics for Israel and its neighbors, thus creating the conditions for an agenda for the study of international relations more in tune with the current developments in Europe and North America.

Note

1   I would like to thank colleagues and friends from the Israeli community of IR scholars for their comments and suggestions, including Orit Gazit, Aharon Klieman, Galia Press-Barnathan, Yael Krispin, Sasson Sofer, Zeev Maoz, Emanuel Adler, Ziv Rubinovitz, David Freilich, Chanan Naveh, Edy Kaufman, Jonathan Rynhold, Yasmin Schindler, Noam Kochavi, Shachar Nativ, Piki Ish-Shalom, Alan Dowty, Uri Bialer, Stephen Cohen, Yaacov Vertzberger, Michla Pomerance, Neve Gordon, David Newman, Amir Lupovici, Galit Ben-Israel, Alex Mintz, Alfred Tovias, Roni Bart, Eitan Barak, and Abraham Ben-Tzvi. I also greatly appreciate the editorial suggestions of Orly Kacowicz, Michla Pomerance, the editing of Colette Stoeber in Canada, the comments of Arlene Tickner and Ole Wæver, as well as the support by the Leonard Davis Institute of International Relations. This is a revised version of a paper published by the Leonard Davis Institute of International Relations in November 2006 (*Davis Papers on Israel's Foreign Policy*).

References

Adler, Emanuel (1997) "Seizing the Middle Ground: Constructivism in World Politics," *European Journal of International Relations*, 3 (3): 319–363.

Adler, Emanuel (2005) *Communitarian International Relations*, London: Routledge.

Adler, Emanuel and Michael Barnett (eds) (1998) *Security Communities*, Cambridge: Cambridge University Press.

Bialer, Uri (2005) *Cross on the Star of David: The Christian World in Israel's Foreign Policy, 1948–1967*, Bloomington, IN: Indiana University Press.

Broude, Tomer (2006) "Between *Pax Mercatoria* and *Pax Europea*: How Trade Dispute Procedures Serve the EC's Regional Hegemony," in Padideh Ala'I, Tommer Broude, and Colin Picker (eds), *Trade as the Guarantor of Peace, Liberty and Security? Critical, Historical and Empirical Perspectives*, Washington, DC: American Society of International Law, pp. 47–62.

Broude, Tomer and Arie M. Kacowicz (eds) (2006) *The Role of International Trade in the Promotion of Regional Peace*, Jerusalem: Leonard Davis Institute for International Relations (in Hebrew).

Cohen, Raymond (1997) *Negotiating Across Cultures*, Washington, DC: U.S. Institute of Peace.

Cohen, Raymond (2001) "Living and Teaching Across Cultures," *International Studies Perspectives*, 2 (2): 151–160.

Dowty, Alan (1997) "Is There a Jewish Politics?," in Sasson Sofer (ed.), *The Role of Domestic Politics in Israeli Peacemaking*, Jerusalem: Leonard Davis Institute for International Relations, pp. 1–12.

Dowty, Alan (2001) "Jewish Political Culture and Zionist Foreign Policy," in Abraham Ben-Zvi and Aharon Klieman (eds), *Global Politics: Essays in Honour of David Vital*, London: Frank Cass, pp. 309–326.

Epstein, Alex D. (2004) "The Current Sociological Agenda of Israel Studies in Israel/U.S.A. and Russia: A Reexamination," *Israel Studies Forum*, 19 (3): 83–98.

Gazit, Orit (2002) "The Department of International Relations at the Hebrew University of Jerusalem: Characteristics, Approaches, and Research Areas," Jerusalem: Department of International Relations, Hebrew University of Jerusalem (unpublished manuscript in Hebrew).

Harkabi, Yehoshafat (1989) *Israel's Fateful Hour*, New York: Harper & Row.

Heller, Mark (1982) "International Relations Research in Israel," *Orbis*, 26 (1): 757–764.

Hirsch, Moshe (1999) "Game Theory, International Law, and Environmental Cooperation in the Middle East," *Denver Journal of International Law and Policy*, 27 (1): 75–119.

Hirsch, Moshe (2003) "Compliance with International Law in the Age of Globalization: Two Theoretical Perspectives," in Eyal Benvenisti and Moshe Hirsch (eds), *The Impact of International Law on International Cooperation*, Cambridge: Cambridge University Press, pp. 166–193.

Hoffmann, Stanley (1977) "An American Social Science: International Relations," *Daedalus*, 106 (3): 41–60.

Kacowicz, Arie M. (1994) *Peaceful Territorial Change*, Columbia, SC: University of South Carolina Press.

Kacowicz, Arie M. (1998) *Zones of Peace in the Third World: South America and West Africa in Comparative Perspective*, Albany, NY: SUNY Press.

Kacowicz, Arie M. (2005) *The Impact of Norms in International Society: The Latin American Experience, 1881–2001*, Notre Dame, IN: University of Notre Dame Press.

Kacowicz, Arie M., Yaacov Bar-Siman-Tov, Ole Elgstrom, and Magnus Jerneck (eds) (2000) *Stable Peace among Nations*, Lanham, MD: Rowman & Littlefield.

Klieman, Aharon (1989) "The Study of International Relations in Israel," in Hugh C. Dyer and Leon Mangasarian (eds), *The Study of International Relations: The State of the Art*, London: Macmillan, pp. 303–318.

Kochavi, Noam (2002) *A Conflict Perpetuated: China Policy during the Kennedy Years*, New York: Praeger.

Press-Barnathan, Galia (2003) *Organizing the World: The U.S. and Regional Cooperation in Asia and Europe*, New York: Routledge.

Press-Barnathan, Galia (2004) "The War Against Iraq and International Order: From Bull to Bush," *International Studies Review*, 6 (2): 195–212.

Press-Barnathan, Galia (2009) *The Political Economy of Transitions to Peace*, Pittsburgh, PA: Pittsburgh University Press.

Sadeh, Tal (2006) *Sustaining European Monetary Union: Confronting the Cost of Diversity*, Boulder, CO: Lynne Rienner.

Sofer, Sasson (1998) "Israel in the World Order: Social and International Perspectives," *Davis Occasional Papers*, 61, Jerusalem: Leonard Davis Institute for International Relations.

Sofer, Sasson (ed.) (2001) *Peacemaking in a Divided Society: Israel After Rabin*, Portland, OR: Frank Cass.

Tovias, Alfred (1990) *Foreign Economic Relations of the European Community: The Impact of Spain and Portugal*, Boulder, CO: Lynne Rienner.

Tovias, Alfred (1997) *Options for Mashrek–Israeli Regionalism in the Context of the Euro-Mediterranean Partnership*, Brussels: Center for European Policy Studies.

12 Turkey
Towards homegrown theorizing and building a disciplinary community[1]

Ersel Aydinli and Julie Mathews

The International Relations (IR) discipline has existed in Turkey for well over half a century, yet in many ways it is still struggling to come together as a coordinated disciplinary community. Perhaps the most distinctive characteristic that emerges when trying to understand the discipline's development and current state is the complex and uncomfortable relationship it holds with the world of IR theory and theorizing. Over the past 15 to 20 years in particular, "theorizing" and the professional identities associated with how – and whether – one does it have resulted in a divide in the local disciplinary community between "theorists" (a title claimed by most) and "others" (a title generally bestowed by "theorists" on the rest). This divide splits along academic generations, educational backgrounds, professional interests, and socio-economic classes, and is inextricably intertwined with a desperate competition for disciplinary power. Ironically, given the pivotal role that theory has come to play within the local discipline, it is in the realm of theory in particular that Turkish IR has achieved the least. In this chapter we look at this inconsistency in Turkish IR by focusing on the issue of IR theory – when and how it was introduced to the local disciplinary community, the factors surrounding its emergence as a privileged and therefore often claimed disciplinary activity, and the forms of scholarly activity that fall under the title of "theorizing." We end by considering the prospects for change in these established patterns and the implications these might have on broader core–periphery relations within the discipline.

Mapping the state of IR in Turkey

Monopoly of the Mulkiye

The foundations for Turkish IR came out of the Mulkiye Mektebi, a carry-over from higher education during the Ottoman times, that has been described less as a school of international relations and more as a "vocational school" (Karaosmanoglu 2005: 137) for those preparing to enter state agencies, including a distinct track for those joining the diplomatic service. Instruction in the Mulkiye Mektebi focused on topics such as the teaching of diplomacy, diplomatic techniques, and protocol, with an added element of political indoctrination for those who would be representatives of the state abroad. This general approach and content continued – at least up until the late 1970s – even as the Mulkiye Mektebi was moved in the Republican era from Istanbul to the new capital of Ankara, and as it later came to be known as *Siyasal Bilgiler Fakultesi* (SBF, or Political Science Faculty). The curriculum became formally divided into administrative, financial, and political studies sections. A distinct IR track within the school was established by the 1950s, and produced its first Ph.D. student in 1956.

In those early years of the 1960s and 1970s, the Mulkiye held an incontrovertible monopoly over training and scholarship in the field of IR. Although a few other faculties offered somewhat related programs, such as economics and trade or administrative sciences, the prestigious Mulkiye was the only one that truly mattered, as its graduates alone were eligible for service in the Foreign Ministry. Small and exclusive, the Mulkiye became the world of the elite. A grooming ground for future diplomats, policy-makers, or policy advisors, the curriculum focused on diplomatic history and international law, and served a student body which, more often than not, was made up of the children of the country's wealthier families, often past diplomats and policy-makers. These students were not only familiar with the world they were training to enter, but had the foreign living experience and often the language skills to ease their transition into the field. Professors in the field were often diplomatic historians or retired diplomats. In fact, this description of the Mulkiye is not unlike those of early IR in the U.S. in the first half of the twentieth century, which has been described as a discipline dominated by "enlightened men of learning and leisure," and noted for the unclear boundaries between academia and politics (Wallace 1994: 140).

With the entire local IR disciplinary community essentially reduced to one department, whatever happened in that department had a huge impact on the local discipline. The retirement of certain faculty members, the firing of others, or the particular politicization of the Mulkiye students and faculty, had the potential to disrupt the overall progress of the local discipline. Major national events, such as political disruption within the country in the 1970s, or the coup of 1980 were all reflected in the department. When a significant percentage of the Mulkiye faculty were fired or sent to jail after the 1980 coup, it took nearly a decade for the department – and thus the discipline – to recuperate and regroup. (Though, of course, one could equally argue that this huge upheaval actually helped the local IR community in that it finally allowed other departments to emerge from under the Mulkiye's shadow, as will be seen below.)

The Mulkiye excelled at producing well-informed policy-makers and diplomats, but neither the school's Ottoman-age style of teaching and learning nor its primary curricular focus on policy was conducive to the development of theory and theorizing, a criticism raised early on by a leading faculty member (Bilge 1962). Teaching and learning was based on discipline and memorization, with minimal requirements for reading but rather a focus on taking vigilant notes from the professors' lectures and writing exams based on those lectures. This style did not accommodate critical engagement with the ideas being presented, nor did it promote reading diverse material and comparing and evaluating arguments, all of which are essential aspects to conceptual development. Rather than being questioned, the style remained largely unchanged over the years as those students who performed best in this system were taken on as graduate students and eventually faculty members. One could hardly expect theoretical breakthroughs to come out of such a context.

Moreover, the fact that the graduates of this leading department for IR in Turkey almost all went on to serve in the Foreign Ministry meant that policy-relevant research was dominant in the Mulkiye, and thus in Turkish IR – at the expense of theory. As is the case in most of the world, the policy community was not then, nor is it now, necessarily sympathetic to theoretical works. A retired Turkish diplomat recently expressed his belief that "theory and practice do not fit," and that theory does not "provide solutions" to urgent problems (personal communication 2007). Unsurprisingly, when the Turkish Foreign Ministry sponsored Mulkiye faculty members to produce the first volume on Turkish foreign policy, a book that would constitute the primary textbook for generations of future IR students, they particularly demanded a descriptive, policy-relevant work, not theoretical abstractions. In its training and scholarship, therefore, the Turkish IR community was in its first decades entirely focused on Turkey and on meeting the demands of daily foreign policy issues and foreign policy-makers.

An expanding discipline

In the 1980s, the growth worldwide in the number of IR departments and students began to strike Turkey as well. Following the 1980 coup, the newly formed Higher Education Council, designed to bring under governmental control the universities that had served as the front lines for much of the political turmoil of the 1970s, also sought to streamline various university programs. Departments of Economics and Trade or Administrative Sciences that existed at a handful of universities in the 1970s were renamed in 1982 as Departments of Political Science and Public Administration. Either as part of these or as newly developed separate departments, instruction in International Relations was included. While numerically the 1980s witnessed this increase in IR departments, the instruction in these departments for the most part followed the Mulkiye tradition of treating IR as a combination of international politics, international law, and diplomatic history. The one possible exception to this rule was the Department of IR at Middle East Technical University, where an effort was made to instead introduce two main tracks of theoretical studies and area studies (Middle East and Europe).

Along with an overall opening up and political liberalization of the country in the 1980s and the 1990s, the discipline saw not only a numerical growth but an increasing number of students from non-elite socio-economic backgrounds joining International Relations pro-grams. This was not due to a particular effort to include a broader demographic base of students, but can probably be simply linked to the growing numbers of students being admitted into newly created IR departments. With the influx of students there was a dividing of the student body between the small numbers of elite who had traditionally made up the full population and a still small but growing minority of non-elite students – as noted in the words of some self-described "non-elite" students of the era:

> In the classroom you could always tell who was who because the aristocrat kids all sat together. There were only a few of us kids from poor backgrounds and we always sat together too. . . .

> I came from a family that was not rich . . . I started out in IR to be a diplomat. To be a diplomat, a Turkish representative abroad, it is a very interesting and challenging task. But in the later stages, say, in the middle of my undergraduate education, I understood it was very difficult for us to enter the foreign ministry because of some, well, obstacles.

> I soon realized it was practically impossible to become a diplomat because I only had weak German skills, and I didn't know French or English.

The divide between the elite and non-elite operated like a domestic core and periphery – with all of its accompanying restrictions. With the domestic "core" dominating the discipline in foreign policy, the domestic "periphery" faced a struggle, complicated by their lack of family connections and foreign language skills. As a weak but growing minority group that was gradually advancing up the ladder of the local disciplinary community, it is unsurprising that the domestic periphery students would seek new ways of proving themselves, new ways to compete, and new means to compete with – ways and means that were not within the exclusive control of the domestic core.

At about the same time – the mid-1980s and the early 1990s – there was a push by the Turkish Ministry of Education and later by the Higher Education Council to send large numbers of students abroad for graduate studies. This coincided with the opening of several new universities across Turkey and, among them specifically, the launching of 13 new departments of IR. The peak of the foreign studies effort was the 1993 to 1995 dispatching of more than 4,000 students, who were intended to return and make up the faculty for these newly opening universities. To give a sense of the concurrent scope of growth of the IR discipline from those years up until the present, in recent years the number of undergraduate students enrolled in IR departments has reached nearly 13,000, up from 1,800 in 1986 and from only a couple of hundred at any one time in the 1970s. By 2005 there were over 200 Ph.D. students alone registered in IR departments across Turkey. Turning to faculty members, from only a handful throughout much of the early decades of the discipline (even by 1986 there were only 13 actual professors – assistant, associate or full – of IR), in recent years the number has topped 400 and is growing.

Turning back to the early 1990s, for the discipline of IR in Turkey, graduate study abroad for more than just the occasional individual student was a dramatic – one might even say revolutionary – turning point. For these scores of students of international relations, studying in North America or Europe meant being exposed for the first time to the world of IR theory, and in many cases to the understanding that producing theory was the highest role to achieve in the discipline. Significantly, many of those studying abroad were not from the traditional elite. The nature of the 1993 to 1995 scholarship program was such that for the first time, masses of students from all geographical and socio-economic backgrounds were able to go abroad for graduate studies – including in the field of IR. In this case, the "de-eliticization" of the student body, and ultimately, faculty of IR was a more deliberate one, brought on by a Higher Education Council president who pointedly strove to make the scholarships accessible to students outside of the main cities and without the advanced foreign language skills that mark a private school education in Turkey (Mathews 2007). For these non-elite IR students/junior faculty returning to Turkey, "theory" meant a new area in which they could compete and excel without family connections. Armed with Western knowledge, the domestic "periphery" began using theory as a shield to balance against the domestic core and even to penetrate the core itself.

Throughout the 1990s, we can see a growth in works of a generally theoretical nature being produced by Turkish IR scholars, as one scholar after another tried to show himself (or frequently, herself, as the numbers of females in the field were also on the rise) as more "theory-driven" than the rest, or simply, as one IR scholar who was an assistant professor at the time, says, "to try and prove to people that they knew theory." To draw an analogy with IR terminology, what we see in the 1990s is a grand-scale literary attempt at balance of power. To balance against the older elite generation of IR scholars (and their traditional discourse of diplomacy, history, and international law), the younger, often non-elite products of the foreign study-abroad programs began making use of the means of the Western IR community – the discourse, genres, and topics of IR theory.

There is no doubt whatsoever that they were successful in their goal of balancing against the local IR elite by introducing a new and powerful discourse to the Turkish disciplinary community. It is difficult to find an IR scholar in Turkey today who will not in some way attempt to explain how his or her works incorporate a theoretical perspective into their analyses. The prioritizing of "theory" has become so widely accepted that scholars of all backgrounds try to claim their position as "theorists," but it is most noticeable among the generations of the late 1980s and afterwards. The phenomenon manifests itself vividly when you hear Turkish IR scholars say something along the lines of, "Yes, I write primarily about Turkey . . . *but* I do it in a theoretical way." The two following excerpts from interviews with scholars who completed their Ph.Ds in England and returned to Turkey in the early and the mid-1990s not only reveal the attempt to identify themselves as part of the new, "theoretical" community, but also to draw a generational line between themselves and the past:

> The scholars in Turkey before the 1990s focused on Turkish foreign policy issues, or some other empirical, national issues . . . case studies. Nowadays in Turkey I see that, like me, some other scholars have started to teach theories of IR. This should be taken as a positive contribution made by the new generation of IR scholars. Of course, still the majority of IR scholars in Turkey focus on issues which are concerned with Turkey or Turkish foreign policy . . . this is normal, most of the time we are occupied by national problems and issues. Because of this I am very sad to say that I am one of those whose writings are concentrated on issues of Turkish foreign policy. *But*, what I try to do even as I am studying and writing on these issues, I try to look at the problem in a theoretical perspective.

Or another scholar:

> IR teaching began in the 1950s in Ankara University. The people who were teaching there were imported from diplomatic history or international law. Even in the 1990s when I came back from England I found the tradition was still the same. When you talk to people they wouldn't admit this, but you have to look at how they teach in their classes or how they write their books, and when you look at those, you'll see that most of the IR writing and teaching in Turkey in the early 1990s was still using the tools of diplomatic history, not social science research tools. And still this is very much a problem. Turkish IR is not grounded in theory, it's mostly about Turkish–Russian relations, or Turkish–Iraqi relations between certain years. My own writings tend to be about Turkish foreign policy too, *but* I try to distinguish myself. The difference between a couple of guys and myself and the rest is that since we have this IR theory understanding, I start by developing a big picture and drawing a framework, then start analyzing the issue.

When speaking to those older generation members who were themselves educated abroad, the divide becomes less clear, and the overall theory issue takes on greater complexity. While most senior scholars generally recognize the importance of theorizing both in the core and in the local IR community, they are sometimes more willing than the younger scholars to admit that they generally don't "do theory." One senior scholar dismisses one of her own works somewhat bitterly:

> This is purely empirical and descriptive, a product of my own research. It has no link to a body of theoretical literature on the topic because I never had a chance to look at that literature. And I seriously doubt I will have a chance.

One of the very first Turkish scholars to go abroad and receive training in IR theory at a prestigious U.S. institution in the late 1970s blames his admitted lack of theoretical works on time constraints and easier alternatives, and draws attention to a dilemma of the older generation's finest academic potential being drawn prematurely into leadership roles that prevented them from doing challenging, theoretical research:

> When I returned to Turkey the discipline was so small here that I immediately became promoted and took on important administrative duties. This kept me extremely busy. I had to build up our department. It still keeps me busy. So when people come to me and ask, I write chapters for their books, usually concrete things on Turkey's relations with Europe, European politics, and so on. Since I don't have much time to publish, I like the work because easily then I can publish. . . . If I were able to work in my own tempo, I could probably have formed my own agenda more, looked for different publishing spaces, journals . . . but I don't have the time and there is always the demand. I work according to that demand.

Still another senior scholar, one well respected and published internationally, carefully keeps the door open to the idea of his own works having at least a "theoretical perspective," but dismisses overall the assertion of any actual "theorizing" being done in Turkey at all:

> As you know, I'm not doing theoretical work. Nobody's doing theoretical work in Turkey. I'm rather doing policy-oriented work, but I use IR theories.

His statement raises the obvious question of what we mean when we speak of "doing theory." Do we mean "using" IR theories? Do we mean – as implied in the previous quote – drawing a framework before analyzing? Or do we mean something else?

Categories of theory

Attempting to define the "types" of theory being somehow used or applied in the research and writing practices of scholars in the Turkish IR community is a complex task, and one which could undoubtedly result in very different answers. Our effort here draws on and compiles the ideas of various Turkish IR scholars on this issue, taking into consideration the purposes these various types of theorizing serve for these scholars in terms of their professional development and advancement in Turkey. Despite some slight overlap, it is possible to define four general categories of what has been considered and labeled by Turkish IR scholars as "theorizing": pure theorizing, homegrown theorizing, application, and translating.

Pure theorizing

The same professor who claimed that "nobody" is doing theoretical work in Turkey explained in this way what he meant by theoretical work:

> Pure theoretical work, which is to be published in theory journals like *International Organization*, *International Security*, or *International Studies Quarterly*. Original theoretical work . . . no work like that is being done here. Sure, there are some people doing some kind of theoretical work in Turkey, but they don't publish it in good journals. Most of it is published in Turkish and they are borrowed works. They repeat what the theory people are saying in the U.S. You see, they are translations.

His description of pure theorizing resembles others' efforts to distinguish types of theorizing, in particular Lepgold's "pure" theorizing category (Lepgold 1998), which specifies that the goal of such "pure" or "referent-free" theorizing is to find coherent explanations for broad phenomena while remaining unattached to specific areas. Such a definition would be questioned by some as unattainable. As one young Turkish IR scholar pointed out to us, "You won't see an Alexander Wendt in Turkey because Wendt was writing from Wisconsin!" In other words, even if actual theory construction does take place in Turkey, it will not likely be the same as that carried out by core IR scholars. His point recalls Cox's well-known position that so-called "pure" theorizing is in any case affected by the contexts in which the theorist operates. The questions theorists choose to speculate on, the ways they choose to do so, and the interpretations they give to the answers they find, are all affected in multiple ways by the theorists' own backgrounds and the social worlds they interact with. This debate temporarily aside, any existing theoretical literature that does not explicitly address a particular country may be considered for the moment as "pure" theorizing.

Homegrown theorizing versus application and translation

A second category of theorizing may be found in the words of a junior scholar who spoke of her aspirations to produce original theory based on local contexts and questions:

> I would like to be someone who can combine theory and policy. I would like to first take the theories that the core produces and use them in my efforts to explain things in Turkey. But better yet, I would like to be someone who could not only explain things on a conceptual level, but also somehow build up some original perspective out of looking at Turkey's international relations or Turkey's experiences. That's my goal. I would call myself really successful if I could come up with a work identified as an original theoretical perspective originating out of these lands, out of Turkey or Turkey-like countries. That would certify that knowledge has accumulated in this country and finally produced something.

We can conceive from this statement of a second level of theorizing, a "homegrown" theorizing in which entirely new patterns, understandings, and frameworks of analysis are sought through the construction of theories stemming from "local" experiences. These "local" experiences do not mean simply the last century's history of the Turkish republic, nor does it mean that the resulting theoretical activity is relevant only to Turkey or her neighbors. Examples of "local" Turkish contexts out of which theorizing might come include the context of mid-size powers in global affairs, Islamic democracies, former Empires, democratizing countries located in anarchic regions, or multicultural nations. These and many other categories describing aspects of Turkey's past and present could provide valuable starting points for original, homegrown theorizing. Homegrown theorizing may also involve existing theoretical questions or debates, but using local experiences, history, and contexts to locate gaps within and build on to those existing theories.

Following this level is a third, the one that most Turkish IR scholars seem to mean when they say they "apply a theoretical framework." This "application-level theorizing" has various subcategories of its own, but at its most basic seems to refer to leading off a written work with some kind of literature review, rather than jumping straight into a description of the particular event or issue. At a slightly more sophisticated level, application may also refer however to those scholars who take an existing theoretical model, and draw on the Turkish or regional experience to provide evidence of the model's usefulness as a way of looking at things. Thus, for example, a study using a constructivist approach to explain Turkey's relations with the

EU is a form of application theorizing. Application theorizing may also be nonconfirming if the local context is used as a ground for "testing" and finding fault with an existing theoretical approach or body of literature. A subtle distinction may be made between such non-confirmative application theorizing and actual homegrown theorizing in that the latter should either introduce an entirely new approach or perspective (based on the local context but applicable beyond it) or should at a minimum draw on the local context to add original perspectives or concepts addressing shortcomings or gaps in an existing theoretical approach.

An interesting example (though a missed opportunity) of how homegrown theorizing might take place comes from balance of power theory. At a time when the prevailing Waltzian view was that countries balance against rising powers, Stephen Walt looked to the Middle East and alliance patterns there and wrote that in fact they balanced against the threat potential (Walt 1987). The work received great attention and admiration, and quickly became part of the core theoretical literature. While legitimate questions can be raised as to whether such a reformation of an existing theory, coming from a local Middle Eastern scholar, would have been received with equal praise by the core, it would (at least hypothetically) have been a powerful example of homegrown theorizing. The irony from this example is that at a time when most Middle Eastern "theoreticians" were teaching and translating Waltzian balance of power theory, Waltz's own student was busily using the local neighborhood to further the original theory.

Finally, there is a fourth level of theorizing, implied by the earlier cited senior professor's reference to "borrowed works." In this case, someone writes a piece in Turkish that basically translates ideas or concepts that have already been expressed abroad. This "translation-level" theorizing would include works that provide overviews of particular core theoretical paradigms or perspectives, translating them into Turkish to make them accessible to the average Turkish IR student. It also happens to include the major textbooks of IR (e.g., Gonlubol 1993; Sonmezoglu 2000; Ari 2002), which present in Turkish major ideas from the Western disciplinary community.

By numbering these levels of theorizing, the intention is not to prioritize them in terms of value, though there is a logical progression in a disciplinary community of one building on the other. Not only homegrown theorizing, but all levels should be seen as necessary and interdependent elements in the process of community-wide theory-building. Translations are necessary to expose the broader disciplinary community, beyond those few who have access through language and study abroad experiences, to existing theoretical ideas. For example, as-yet-undeveloped theoretical ideas and concepts may be hidden in areas of Turkey where the very idea of "IR theory" and its use is available only in translation. Such unexplored ideas and concepts could include ideas on multiculturalism (experienced in the southeast of Turkey), or conceptualizations of religious coexistence (as may be found in Central Anatolia in the writings on human-centric peace by Rumi). In order for such potential theoretical ideas or concepts to be explored, the scholars familiar with them must be aware of the purposes, goals, and value of theorizing – yet these scholars are very often unable to access these ideas and gain this familiarity due to limited foreign-language skills. A first step therefore is to ensure that widely known theoretical concepts in the international IR community are made available through translations to the full Turkish IR disciplinary community. Applications of existing theory are also necessary, both to add confirmations to those existing theories (of use to the larger disciplinary community) and to provide examples of and practice in the use of theory (of use to the local community).

Having said that all levels are important, the experience in Turkish IR over the past 15 to 20 years has shown instead that a hierarchical perspective is generally taken. There is the tendency for Turkish IR scholars to either deny the existence of or to put down others' theory efforts as less important than their own. Thus, scholars involved in the translation of theory criticize those who do "only" policy studies, scholars doing some form of application theorizing tend to criticize the translators, and scholars who participate in homegrown theorizing put down the application studies.

Confusing matters further, differing interpretations or misrepresentations of what may or may not constitute examples of certain levels become manipulated for purposes of building up professional identities or supporting professional rivalries. Scholars sometimes claim to conduct different levels of theorizing than they actually do. In most cases there is just a general claim to "theorizing," but in others there is the implication that scholars are conducting, for example, "pure" theorizing, when, according to our definition, their works would more likely fit under the heading of application studies. For example, a scholar claiming to be a "theoretician" because s/he works on questions of strong state traditions in anarchic environments, but who explores this issue by using existing neo-liberal concepts and frameworks to analyze the Turkish case, is doing application-level theorizing.

There may be a very few examples of Turkish scholars now who participate entirely in existing core theoretical discussions at an abstract level, without any reference to Turkey. If these scholars are truly doing this without any connection to Turkey or to regional experiences, if they are, in that sense, indistinguishable from their core colleagues in terms of the contribution they are making to that theoretical discussion, then in light of Cox's arguments that there can be no truly "context-free" theorizing, it would appear that such scholars were in fact fully assimilated into the core disciplinary community, and can no longer really be categorized as "periphery" scholars.

Still underachieving

With the monopoly of the Mulkiye broken, and with the numbers of IR departments, students, and foreign-trained scholars skyrocketing in the past 15 years, why is it that we see only a booming of application-level theorizing (and a domination in recent years of applications of critical theories and approaches)? Why is there still an underachievement of homegrown theorizing?

Periphery-based causes

Perhaps the first reason for this underachievement is the fact that although talk of theorizing has become commonplace, its use has not been for purely academic purposes. With theory being used as a "balance of power" tool, its practice often remains elusive, unsubstantiated, and shallow. IR departments have seen cases of professors who have never undergone graduate level exams in IR theory or perhaps have never even taken a comprehensive, graduate-level IR theory class, becoming known as "theorists" and being assigned the task of training future Turkish IR scholars in IR theory simply because they have come from abroad. In many cases this results in teaching a very limited picture of IR theory – focusing on whatever theory(ies) the professor is familiar with, from selected epistemological and methodological approaches to formal IR theories. Over the years this has led to the importation into Turkish IR of waves of theories and approaches – whatever represents the cutting edge at the time of the professor's own foreign study experience. Students become exposed to a particular wave and remain unaware of the fuller spectrum of theories, concepts, and approaches. Such a pattern prevents any accumulation of debate over IR theory in Turkey as each successive generation dismisses or fails to recognize any value in the previous generation's efforts.

Many other factors have contributed to the lack of homegrown theorizing. As scholars here point out, even without the Mulkiye monopoly, training in analytical thinking remains under-emphasized throughout the entire Turkish educational system, and memorization-based learning still prevails. This style rewards replication and eliminates any real need for learning alternative ways of looking at subjects. There is little investment in methodology training in Turkey, and thus training in the art of scholarship remains extremely weak. Even the leading IR departments often fail to recognize the value of teaching methodology, with some having done away with or at least questioning the value of having separate methodology courses for their graduate students. A former chair of a leading IR department connects the lack of methodology with the underachievement in theorizing when he says that Turkish IR "never promoted the value of comparative studies, and therefore learning about other cases, comparing, producing generalizations, remained weak. We only studied our case. Without generalization, theorizing becomes impossible." The natural outcome of this single-minded emphasis on the Turkish case has been a limiting of chances for theorizing. Either the lack of or poor quality of methodology training results in students/scholars skipping the crucial stage of "pre-analysis" that must occur in theoretically based scholarship. Clearly defining the research question, locating a gap in the theoretical and empirical literature, discussing alternative methods for analyzing the question, identifying appropriate theoretical framework and methodological tools – all of these stages critical to both theorizing and well-argued research receive only passing attention.

Ironically, given the importance apparently given to theorizing on the level of self-identification within the Turkish disciplinary community, many IR scholars nevertheless note that in Turkey theoretical work simply doesn't pay back – it doesn't get you media coverage or project funding and it doesn't even guarantee you a better job (a process still sometimes based on personal connections and a touch of luck). Theorizing is considered by many therefore as a luxury. Two professors from leading Turkish state universities both referred to the envy they felt for their European and North American colleagues, whom they believe are able to gain special professional recognition for theorizing and publishing theoretical works in particular venues, whereas in Turkey they are kept overly busy with teaching (often having to supplement low pay standards by teaching extra courses at private universities) and are not recognized for serious publishing efforts. In the words of one, "They don't slap your face if you publish, but they don't pat you on the back either." Instead, recognition, status, and money for the Turkish IR scholar is still more likely to come from writing policy pieces – these get you television spots, invitations to write newspaper columns, and opportunities for government contracts.

A deeper structural problem that works against the possibility of conceptual works being produced here is the lack of established criteria for publication standards. In the West, the most prestigious journals often have a theoretical emphasis. Since publishing in them carries the promise of widespread recognition, promotion, and better employment, the effort seems worthwhile. In Turkey there remains little incentive to opt for the seemingly more difficult venue of theoretical research. True, for promotion in Turkish universities a greater number of points are now credited to articles published in Social Science Citation Index journals, but the overall total requirement of points remains very low, so points can easily be achieved through other routes. Among these other routes are Turkish-medium, non-theoretical journals, among which there is little in the way of agreed-upon standards. When an article quickly published in a newly launched "refereed" journal out of a newly established IR department in a new university in rural Turkey can be counted for academic promotions across the country, why struggle against huge odds to get published in *International Security*?

In order to set such standards, and therefore even more critical for the long-term development of theorizing from the local IR community, there is the need for a cohesive, conscious, organized, and institutionalized Turkish IR disciplinary community. This community should have a yearly convention, a flagship journal, and a national index of acceptance criteria to evaluate Turkish publications as well as standards for quality research and training. Unfortunately, even after 50 years, such a community does not yet seem to exist.

Evidence of the Turkish IR community's lack of such cohesiveness and organization may be seen in the fact that there have been only a handful of occasions in its history when scholars have come together to discuss the state of the discipline. Two early meetings, in 1959 and 1961, were followed 35 years later by a third, a fourth in 2001, and the most recent in 2005.[2] Except at the last of these meetings, the participants were exclusively from Ankara and Istanbul – reflecting the ongoing division of the domestic core and periphery. More disturbing from the view of disciplinary development is the observation made in 2005 by a senior scholar who was personally familiar with the earlier meetings, that in all of them the challenges and questions debated remained the same: what is IR, what should we teach, and how can we build an IR discipline (Onulduran 2005)? Clearly little or no progress has been made on these most basic of questions, a sobering note suggesting that Turkish IR remains at best a loosely knit, fragmented community, unable to build a coherent accumulation of research agendas and findings or offer suggestions for future research.

Core-based causes

Turkish scholars are of course not the only source of blame for the lack of Turkish theorizing. A large share must fall on the core, where training patterns, advisor–student relationships, core prejudices, and scholarly competition all tend to push the periphery student and scholar away from engaging fully in theoretical discussions. Examples from the experiences of two Turkish scholars may strike familiar bells with other periphery students who have studied in the core. In one case, a female IR scholar reported asking for advice on how to pursue IR-track studies in her political science department from a Turkish scholar who had lived and worked in the U.S. for many decades. His response was, "You might as well go right into comparative politics. We all start off in IR, and we all end up in comparative politics." Yet another scholar who studied in Europe in the early 1990s reported experiencing the same attitude:

> Core scholars are looking for people to work on their theories and prove them in new lands so that they can tell their colleagues that their ideas are being read about and applied in China or the Middle East. They aren't looking for new theoreticians. They're looking for native colonials to sell core products in new lands, whether these are new epistemological fixations or hardline methodological preferences or concrete theories. The best they do for their developing world pupils is perhaps to force them into applying their own theories. Of course, when they tell them to do this, they don't expect them to question or revise those theories with some Oriental input. The problem with this though is once the pupil adapts the advisor's theoretical identity and assumes this confirming role, it's very hard to make the jump to a critical, revisionist mode for generating new theories. Once you become the agent and franchiser of someone, it's not easy to try and produce your own product. We see McDonald's pushing aside the old age kofte stands in Turkey in the same way.

Prospects

On the Turkish front, there are several hopeful signs that we will see greater achievements in IR theorizing in the years to come. The fact that three of the handful of Turkish IR disciplinary gatherings have taken place within the past decade suggests that there are increasing efforts for community-building and for coming to terms with the challenges that face the local discipline. The 2005 gathering in particular was exceptional in the sense that it gathered together the domestic "core" and "periphery." Though the minutes of the meetings show that core voices still remain dominant, the effort gives hope that a relatively integrated Turkish IR community can grow before this distinctive domestic core–periphery structure becomes further consolidated. Useful ideas to this effect came during the meeting from a senior scholar and graduate of the Mulkiye, who proposed that scholars from rural Turkish universities be encouraged to teach as visiting scholars at the leading universities in the major cities, thereby allowing them to play more active roles in the community. She also suggested developing a program to support these scholars' attendance at international conferences (Sezer 2005: 113). The good news is that these ideas are already being partially supported by government policies. The Scientific and Technological Research Council of Turkey (TUBITAK) is organizing a program to promote scholarly exchanges within Turkey, and the Higher Education Council is working to place graduate students from rural areas for training in the domestic core universities, so that they will later go back to teach in periphery institutions.

In terms of Turkish publishing venues, the 1990s witnessed an explosion in the number of think-tanks in Turkey and consequently in journals reflecting the policy priorities of these think-tanks. At the same time, major universities shied away from publishing journals. There seems however to be some signs of a shift. Though not coming directly out of a university, the new journal *Uluslararasi Iliskiler Dergisi* (International Relations Journal) was launched by two SBF professors, and appears to be an exception, promoting the publication of theoretical research. Another hopeful sign of community-building and progress is the now annual international IR conference held at Middle East Technical University – a conference that tries each year to combine theory, policy, and area studies.

Homegrown theorizing and becoming a community

If these trends continue, and if able and interested scholars begin producing increasing examples of successful homegrown theorizing efforts, these activities may become the driving energy behind a new image and substance for the Turkish IR community. Turkish IR still seems mired in questions about what the discipline should be doing. IR communities in the West have not necessarily resolved their existential debates about "what is IR?," but have rather gone beyond these basic questions by building up long-term research agendas and research paradigms often based on "great debates" – e.g., realism vs. idealism. These Western communities have become communities through hands-on practice of IR, not through meta-cognitive debates of the question. The growth of homegrown theory in Turkish IR can play a similar leading role in defining such debates, from epistemological and methodological questions through the formation of formal IR theories. It is surprising, for example, that given Turkey's critical relations with the European Union, Turkish IR over the years has not taken a leading role in debating and contributing to integration theories.

Turkish theorists can also take a leading role in helping fight the IR community's fears of infiltration of poor-quality scholarship, of an epidemic of "conspiracy theorizing" (attractive to the masses in its simplicity and parsimony but empty of methodology), and an overlap between journalism and IR. It has been pointed out that these challenges to the discipline are best met by standing firmly behind vigorous theoretical and methodological work with global standards (Dedeoglu 2005: 49; Kut 2005: 51). Turkey's theoretically inclined IR scholars should draw on their own training, produce quality examples of scholarship, and make clear the differences between scholarly research and speculation.

Of course, such noble efforts cannot be achieved unless the quality of the research supports it. "Theorizing" will have to come to mean more than just a balancing tool, and simply claiming to do theory can no longer be enough to provide ammunition for self-identification and superiority. The burden of going beyond the current image, misrepresentations, and misuse of theory lies with those who claim to be theorists. Turkish scholars have to recognize that theory does not mean better, but in fact demands the close support and cooperation with case studies, area studies, and policy studies. This attitude must be transferred in the class-room. Teaching IR theory both in the U.S. and in Turkey has shown us that if you fail to communicate to students the use of theory for their needs and contexts, you immediately lose the goodwill of a large portion, and may even encounter resistance from those heading towards government work or area studies. The Turkish IR theory classroom must be the front line in calling a halt to the local disciplinary community's domestic core–periphery structure before it becomes consolidated under labels of "theorists" and "others."

Homegrown theorizing and core–periphery IR disciplinary relations

The question remains as to what such positive developments in local IR theorizing might mean for future relations between the Turkish and core IR communities. Turkish IR scholars currently complain that their attempts to have their voices heard in core IR theoretical discussions go unheard. Their scholarly efforts, when recognized by the core, seem to hold importance only as far as they represent a national view (e.g., a Turkish perspective on the Iraqi situation, or a Turkish perspective on energy politics in Eurasia). As one senior IR scholar noted several years ago:

> What happens is that you become good for area studies. So I do get to teach at good universities in the U.S. and Europe, but it's all on Middle Eastern politics. And when you get invited to conferences, it's not for the contributions that you might make to theory or conceptual thinking, but more to sort of case studies, or area studies, or sort of empirical descriptive analyses, and that, to be honest, hurts. That hurts.

His dismay extended beyond the personal affront, however, to concern over the resulting construction of disciplinary knowledge in such a compartmentalized environment:

> What I have noticed over the last few years is that I find colleagues in the West slipping into generalizations, and theorizing that is really remote from what one might consider as the reality out there. And that really is at times almost scary. What happens is that maybe the lack of very in-depth knowledge of cases or areas by and large leaves this group ignorant of all this, and then they get involved in an exercise that reinforces each other. And when, say, someone like me comes in and I throw a question at them, it really generates a moment of silence, and we can sense that the whole thing is thrown off balance. There is a moment of insecurity there, but it's only a moment and then they push on.

In such an environment, what might an increase in homegrown Turkish theorizing mean for local-core disciplinary relations? The potential is a positive one. Rather than Turkish scholars attempting to participate as outsiders in core theoretical discussions by trying to explore the same questions – and possibly being viewed therefore as either superfluous to the discussion or worse yet as trying to "trip up" core theorists with examples from the Turkish experience – Turkish IR scholars may be better off participating as newcomer theorists, with their own set of questions, stemming from different contextual conditions.

In the natural tendency to create hierarchies, homegrown theorizing out of the periphery would probably in the short run take second seat to theorizing out of the core. On the other hand, such theorizing would recognize (*à la* Charles Taylor) the politics of difference of periphery theorists, and allow for the possibility of discovering what, for example, a Turkish version of IR theorizing might be like. The alternative seems to be a seemingly futile quest for Turkish (and other periphery) scholars, the ultimate goal of which is the dubious one of assimilation into one core theory community or another.[3] Periphery scholars engaging in homegrown theorizing would trade the loss of some equality (which never really existed anyway) for a boost to distinctiveness, which may be the only route to another kind of equality. It seems a worthwhile exchange. An increase in homegrown theorizing out of the periphery will naturally spawn greater core–periphery dialogue on theory in IR – including projects such as this one on geocultural epistemologies – help to reduce the negative experiences of pigeon-holed periphery scholars, and ultimately improve IR theorizing overall by enriching its sources and perspectives.

Notes

1   A different version of this chapter has been published as "Periphery Theorizing for a Truly International Discipline: Spinning IR Theory Out of Anatolia," in the *Review of International Studies*, 34 (4), 2008.
2   "Workshop on IR Teaching in Turkey", held in 1996 at Middle East Technical University, Ankara; "Deconstructing and Redefining IR", held in May 2001 at Marmara University in Istanbul; "Workshop on the Study and Education of IR in Turkey", the minutes of which published in a special volume of the journal *Uluslararasi Iliskiler*, 2 (6), summer 2005.
3   One wonders whether theorizing in the periphery might not turn out to be the next battlefield for transatlantic paradigm battles, as countering schools of thought from North America and Europe seek to gain prominence in newly emerging arenas. It could be argued, for example, that a work like Callahan's 2001 discussion of how IR theory is being built up in the Chinese context is critical of peripheral embracing of "rationalist" views on theorizing not due to concerns over incompatibility or inappropriateness of the perspective for that context, but rather due to concerns that American views on social science seem to be gaining prominence there.

References

Ari, Tayyar (2002) *Uluslararasi iliskiler teorileri*, Istanbul: Alfa Yayinlari.

Bilge, Suat (1962) *Politika ogretimi sympozyumu*, Ankara: Sevinc Matbaasi.

Callahan, William A. (2001). "China and the Globalisation of IR Theory: Discussion of 'Building International Relations Theory with Chinese Characteristics'," *Journal of Contemporary China*, 10 (26): 75–88.

Dedeoglu, Beril (2005) "Workshop on the Study and Education of IR in Turkey," *Uluslararasi Iliskiler*, 2 (6).

Gonlubol, Mehmet (1993) *Uluslararasi politika: ilkerler, kavramlar, kurumlar* (4th edn), Ankara: Attila Kitabevi.

Karaosmanoglu, Ali (2005) "Workshop on the Study and Education of IR in Turkey," *Uluslararasi Iliskiler*, 2 (6).

Kut, Gun (2005) "Workshop on the Study and Education of IR in Turkey," *Uluslararasi Iliskiler*, 2 (6).

Lepgold, Joseph (1998) "Is Anyone Listening? International Relations Theory and the Problem of Policy Relevance," *Political Science Quarterly*, 113 (1): 43–63.

Mathews, Julie (2007) "Predicting Students' Academic Success . . . Is Not Always Enough: Assessing the Turkish Foreign Scholarship Program," *Higher Education*, 53 (5): 645–673.

Onulduran, Ersin (2005) "Workshop on the Study and Education of IR in Turkey," *Uluslararasi Iliskiler*, 2 (6).

Sezer, Duygu (2005) "Workshop on the Study and Education of IR in Turkey," *Uluslararasi Iliskiler*, 2 (6).

Sonmezoglu, Faruk (2000) *Uluslararasi politika ve dis politika analizi* (3rd edn), Istanbul: Filiz Kitabevi.

Taylor, Charles (1992) *Multiculturalism and the "Politics of Recognition": An Essay*, Princeton, NJ: Princeton University Press.

Wallace, William (1994) "Between Two Worlds: Think Tanks and Foreign Policy," in C. Hill and P. Beschoff (eds) *Two Worlds of International Relations*, London: Routledge.

Walt, Stephen M. (1987) *The Origins of Alliances*, Ithaca, NY: Cornell University Press.

13 Russia
IR at a crossroads

Alexander Sergounin

Introduction

The end of the Cold War, the breakdown of the Soviet Union, and the intensification of globalization processes have compelled Russia to redefine its national interests and the conceptual basis of its international strategy. The changing domestic and global environment and the challenges they pose have led to fierce debate on matters of foreign policy among scholars and practitioners. Although this discussion is ongoing, neither a coherent international strategy nor a solid theoretical footing for it has yet been found.

This chapter examines the evolution of Russian international relations studies during the post-Soviet period. In addition to identifying the main theoretical approaches observable in Russian IR, it describes the *problematique* posed by Russian international relations discourse. The text also discusses the ways in which the nature of Russian IR has been shaped by the interaction between the political situation of the country and the institutional organization of the discipline itself. In particular, I examine how the Soviet Marxist heritage has affected present-day scholarship, how the latter has adapted to the post-Soviet environment, how institutional settings have changed, what themes are researched, and which major IR schools can be identified.

The Soviet legacy

Russian IR theory of the early 1990s was heavily influenced by the Soviet legacy in terms of theory and methodology. Classical Soviet approaches to international affairs drew primarily upon Marxist teachings, which argued that the world was undergoing radical social upheaval and transformation, manifest in revolutions, and worker and national liberation movements. The main historical mission of the U.S.S.R. was to facilitate this revolutionary process through various means, including financial assistance to anti-capitalist forces, propaganda campaigns, and even military intervention.

Class struggle was considered the key motor of revolutionary change. The working class was viewed as a progressive force because it represented a more advanced socio-economic system and thus it was a natural leader of a society headed towards socialism. Conversely, the capitalist class constituted a reactionary group that should be deprived of power. In the post-World War II period, class struggle was manifested primarily through the Cold War confrontation between socialism and capitalism which, it was argued, would eventually result in the victory of Communism.

In line with this globalist paradigm, Soviet IR also emphasized the overall structure of the international system. In its analysis of world affairs, Soviet theory judged the global context within which states and other entities interacted extremely important. Another of its premises was that the foreign policy behavior of states could not be adequately understood by studying only the internal factors shaping their external policies. Rather, it was argued that the ways in which the economic and political structure of the international system conditioned actors to behave in certain ways was fundamental. This approach also emphasized the centrality of a historical perspective for understanding international relations. The rise of capitalism, its development, changes, and expansion were deemed to be the defining characteristic of the international system. Contrary to Western theories such as realism and liberalism that saw states as given and independent variables, Soviet theory considered them dependent variables.

The particular focus of Marxist analysis was on how some states, classes, or elite groups created and used mechanisms of domination by which they benefited from the capitalist system at the expense of others. Therefore, Soviet IR specialists were typically concerned with the development of dependency relations among industrialized states and the poorer countries. They viewed this North–South disparity as a major source of global instability and revolutionary movements. In addition, more so than other schools of thought, Soviet IR theory emphasized the critical importance of economic factors in the workings of the international system.

Soviet IR theory differed from Western schools in its selection of key units of analysis too. Contrary to state-centric paradigms, it assumed that states were not unitary actors. Social classes that spanned national boundaries, such as the capitalist class, cooperated inter-nationally to preserve a political and economic environment that was conducive to multi-national corporation investment. Workers from different countries also demonstrated their solidarity through collective forms of action. In consequence, where realists saw anarchy, Soviet IR observed a hierarchy of classes and states in which the weak were subordinated to the strong. For these reasons, the key units of analysis were social class, race, and gender rather than nation-state, which was viewed as a secondary actor (Arbatov 1970).

By the mid-1970s to the early 1980s, Soviet IR theory had undergone a rather unusual change. Despite its differences with realism, which was deemed a major rival among the Western paradigms, Soviet IR had tacitly incorporated a number of neorealist postulates into its analysis. In contrast with traditional Soviet Marxism's emphasis on social classes as key international actors, this new strain of Soviet IR paid greater attention to realist-type cate-gories such as the state, national interest, power balance, and spheres of influence. Among the political conditions explaining this shift, the long-term impact of the Cold War, declining political dynamism and leadership within the U.S.S.R., and a perceived global change from offensive to defensive Soviet position are worth mentioning. Contrary to neorealists, Soviet scholars denied the anarchical nature of the international system, although they did develop a systems approach to world politics (Gantman 1984; Pozdnyakov 1976). In addition to system analysis, rational choice approaches, modeling, simulation, and game theory became popular research methods among IR specialists. As a result of these conceptual changes, theorists lent support to a Soviet foreign policy that became less messianic and more pragmatic – compared to the more ideological and self-righteous Marxist theory.

The Gorbachev era brought about radical transformations in Soviet thinking about world affairs. There was a shift from the quasi-realist approach to a combination of liberalism and globalism (with a prevalence of the latter). This mixture of Marxism with Western-derived concepts was coined "New Political Thinking" (NPT). Its key principles included the prevalence of "all-humankind" interests over national ones; the end of confrontation between socialism and capitalism, concentration of international efforts on solving global problems;

creation of an efficient worldwide mechanism to prevent potential conflicts; a multi-dimensional understanding of international security; overcoming political divisions in various parts of the world; and promotion of arms control and disarmament, and conversion of the defense industry (Gorbachev 1987).

Despite the innovative and far-reaching character of some Soviet IR thinking in the 1970s and 1980s (including NPT), the field continued to face numerous problems both in theoretical and practical terms. Ideologically colored, Soviet IR viewed the world through the simplistic lens of either the class struggle principle or "planetary values" and rejected all other views that clashed with official doctrines. This inevitably led to scholastics and self-isolation from global IR discussions. Although mutually opposed, both of these Soviet approaches were performative truth installments rather than explanatory theories, and they were not structured in a format that allowed for debate among theories or close interaction with Western-style theories. Both the traditionalist Marxist IR theory and NPT ignored the very existence of national interests; instead, they developed the concepts of state or class interest, or that of "all-humankind." Both were either too narrowly focused or too abstract, and failed to fit into the post-Cold War political context. Soviet IR basically existed at the macro-level ("grand theories") while mezo- and micro-level theories were lacking. This made it difficult to translate IR thinking into concrete recommendations for foreign policy practice. Furthermore, Soviet theories were unable both to explain the end of the Cold War and to provide Moscow with a new vision of an emerging world order.

Post-Soviet IR: adapting to change

A considerable amount of time elapsed before Russian post-Soviet IR was able to shift from paradigmatic uniformity, Marxist–Leninist concepts and self-isolation to ideological pluralism and participation in the global IR discourse. Following the collapse of Marxism, which had served as an official theoretical basis for the social sciences, a conceptual vacuum emerged. For some time, Russian scholars were either unable or unwilling to fill it with new theories of their own making or borrowed from abroad. The fact that the very professors trained during the Soviet period were charged with establishing International Relations departments in diverse Russian universities in the early 1990s also led to significant degrees of institutional inertia.

An added institutional aspect of this problem was that before the collapse of the U.S.S.R., international relations was taught in only two elitist Soviet universities that trained future diplomats – Moscow State Institute of International Relations (MGIMO) and the Institute of International Relations (Kiev State University). IR itself was viewed as an empirical and historical rather than theoretical discipline. In the 1990s, when several Russian universities decided to introduce International Relations into their curricula, they were confronted by both a scarcity of qualified academics and of appropriate programs of study. The fact that most scholars lacked strong foreign-language skills and regular contact with academic communities in other parts of the world slowed this process even further. Therefore, courses and curricula had to be developed almost from scratch, a process that lasted until the late 1990s and is still in progress at some Russian universities.

Defining the status of IR within the system of the social sciences also proved difficult. Traditionalists denied that International Relations could enjoy the same status as, say, history, political science, or international law. At best, they recognized it as a rather amorphous multidisciplinary field or underdeveloped, second- (if not third-) rate discipline.

The domestic political environment exerted myriad kinds of influence upon Russian IR as well. Scholars were constantly pressed by government institutions and political parties to respond to the real challenges posed by the post-Cold War global environment by producing policy-oriented knowledge. With the rise of numerous think-tanks and a more or less independent mass media, the demand for foreign policy experts increased dramatically. Many IR scholars abandoned academia altogether or tried to combine scholarly practice with these other activities. One result was that international relations studies became more popular but their quality and standards of expertise worsened. Chronic economic crises and changes in public attitudes towards scientific enterprises exerted another negative effect upon the field. The state and society as a whole lost interest in science and higher education (at least for a time), and their prestige declined accordingly. In addition to migrating from academia to other professional sectors, scholars also migrated abroad. The situation began to change in the early 2000s, when university enrollment began to rise and the Russian state decided to raise public investment in the higher education system.

The aforementioned factors inhibited rather than facilitated the development of IR in Russia. Moreover, they were conducive to an ideologization of the field and its inclination towards policy-relevant, applied research rather than theoretical reflection. As a result, academic debate on the status of IR as a field of study, and its subject matter, *problematique* and theories and research methods is still underway.

Mapping post-Soviet IR: institutions and research topics

Theoretical pluralism in post-Communist Russia has been accompanied by a quantitative growth of research and training institutions dealing with IR. Four main categories of institution can be identified: university departments and centers; the Russian Academy of Sciences; ministerial institutes and research centers; and independent think-tanks.

Universities

Despite the lack of funding and governmental support for Russia's leading universities during the 1990s, institutions such as MGIMO, Moscow State University (MSU), and St. Petersburg University not only survived but actually broadened the scope of their research and improved their curricula. Although, as suggested previously, scholarly practice became largely captive to Russia's new foreign policy needs, on the other hand the dissolution of the U.S.S.R. provided greater freedom to those scholars who remained in academia to choose their desired theoretical approaches and teaching methods. University administrators succeeded in securing Russian and foreign grants, and attracting promising candidates willing to pay for undergraduate and graduate training. In the case of IR, Western foundations and donors also began sponsorship programs to help build up the field. Finally, in the 1990s Moscow allowed peripheral universities to establish IR training programs of their own. This move resulted in the mushrooming of institutions harboring International Relations programs around the country. In addition to bringing an end to Moscow's monopoly over international studies, it enriched Russian IR scholarship with regional perspectives and added theoretical polyphony. Moreover, the growth and diversification of IR studies in the country has facilitated the training of personnel for local diplomatic and international business structures that are developing rather dynamically in many regions. By providing regional political, security, and economic elites with expertise on world politics, it has allowed them to become more independent (from the federal government) in the foreign policy sphere. Therefore, peripheral

IR has implicitly facilitated the process of democratization and decentralization of Russia's foreign and security policy in the post-Communist era.

Notwithstanding the diversification of IR's geography over the past 15 years – over 30 universities offer IR and area studies degrees at present – many of the most influential institutions continue to be based in Moscow. Among them, MGIMO and MSU are still the strongest both in terms of the academic training they offer and their contributions to the development of theoretical approaches to the field. In the post-Soviet period MGIMO's research has focused on a number of topics, including IR theory (Bogaturov *et al.* 2002; Ilyin 1995; Khrustalev 1991; Kokoshin and Bogaturov 2005; Lebedeva 2000, 2003/2006; Lebedeva and Tsygankov 2001; Torkunov 1997, 1999, 2001, 2005; Tyulin 1991, 1994); national, regional and global security (Bogaturov 1997; Davydov 1993; Kulagin 2006; Torkunov 1995, 1997, 1999, 2001, 2005); the foreign services of different countries (Lapin 2002; Popov 2004; Selyaninov 1998; Torkunov 1997, 1999, 2001; Zonova 2003, 2004); and diplomatic history (Bogaturov 2000; Narinsky 1995; Nezhinsky *et al.* 1995). Moscow State University (MGU) focuses on international relations history (Manykin *et al.* 1996, 1997) and IR theory (Fel'dman 1998; Gadzhiev 1997; Kokoshin and Bogaturov 2005; Lebedeva and Tsygankov 2001; Panarin 1997, 2003; Tsygankov 1995, 1996, 1998, 2002, 2007; Tsygankov and Tsygankov 2005, 2006), among others. Among the non-Moscow-based universities, the St. Petersburg State University also stands out.

During the past 15 years, the entire Russian higher education system, including international studies, has been completely transformed. Since 2003, when Russia pledged to join the Bologna process, a new round of reforms was initiated, whose aim is to harmonize the Russian university system with that of Europe by introducing a two-level system (Bachelor and Masters degrees), ECTS (European Credit Transfer System) and more flexible curricula.

The Russian Academy of Sciences (RAS)

The RAS – dating from 1724; before, during and after the Soviet Union a structure of research institutes parallel to and relatively separate from the main universities – was less successful than the universities in adapting its research, financial, and administrative structures to post-Soviet realities. The Academy is more dependent on the government in terms of financing and has less opportunity to develop commercial projects. Foreign foundations and private sponsors also prefer to deal with institutes of higher education, independent think-tanks, and NGOs because they are viewed as being less conservative, more dynamic, and more influential in terms of affecting society and foreign policy-making. Similar to academia in general, the RAS also faced competition from other segments of the expert community, including universities, consulting firms, NGOs, mass media, and, especially, public service. Low salaries and lack of resources and opportunities for professional career development thus provoked an exodus of foreign policy experts from the RAS in the 1990s.

Nonetheless, the RAS managed to keep some skilled personnel to develop international studies. The Academy's institutes are particularly good in area studies because many of them are organized according to geographic principles. Unfortunately, however, it pays little attention to IR theory. Few RAS units – the Institute for U.S. and Canadian Studies (Bogaturov *et al.* 2002; Shakleina 2002), the Institute of Europe (Razuvaev 1993; Sorokin 1995), the Institute of World Economy and International Relations (Kosolapov 1999) and the Institute of Philosophy (Gadzhiev 1997) – publish theoretical works. Universities still retain their advantage in this particular area.

Ministerial centers and institutes

Since the Soviet period, many foreign policy, economic, security, and defense agencies have think-tanks and training institutions of their own. For example, MGIMO has a dual affiliation, given that it is subordinate to both the Ministry of Higher Education and the Foreign Ministry. In addition, there is a Diplomatic Academy which trains or retrains mid-career diplomats. Similar to the Foreign Ministry, the Defense Ministry, Federal Security Service (FSS), and Foreign Intelligence Service (FIS) have educational and research institutes, including the General Staff Academy, Military University, FSS Academy and FIS Academy. All focus mainly on studying national and international security policies. They are also active in examining the role of the military and intelligence agencies in shaping and implementing world politics. In addition, they take part in debates on Russian national security doctrine and organization.

The Presidential Administration and the Cabinet of Ministers run a number of specialized higher education institutions which basically train personnel for federal and regional public service. Some of them, such as the Russian Academy of Public Service (and its regional branches), the Public Economy Academy, and the Academy of Finance conduct research on international relations, world economy, and international law.

The Russian Institute for Strategic Studies (RISS) is the most authoritative organization among state-run research institutes that deal with international affairs. In accordance with the presidential decree of 1992, the RISS is a state research organization assigned to provide governmental bodies with analytical information and recommendations related to national security. The RISS has a staff of over 70 research fellows and is funded mainly from the state budget, although it also receives grants from NATO and other foreign donors. The Institute maintains close relationships with the Presidential Administration, Foreign and Defense Ministries, security services, and the Parliament.

The RISS's main areas of research include national security and Russia's strategic interests in different regions of the world; developments in the CIS countries; the European security system; Russia–NATO and Russia–EU relations; disarmament and global stability; non-proliferation of weapons of mass destruction; and peacekeeping operations (Antonenko 1996: 42).

Due to their official status and proximity to governmental agencies, these institutes have a unique opportunity to influence Russian foreign policy decision-making. Some of them, including the Diplomatic Academy, General Staff Academy, and the RISS, are highly influential. However, their closeness to the political establishment also makes them more policy-oriented and less academic. In order to contribute to the Russian IR debate more productively these institutions would need to seek out greater coordination and interaction with the university and RAS centers.

Independent research centers

The rise of public policy centers is an important characteristic of Russian political and intellectual life in the post-Communist era. Most of them have been created for purely political purposes such as monitoring, providing expertise and prognoses, servicing election campaigns, and human rights protection. For this reason, few have been oriented towards basic research. In contrast with some other countries such as the United States, think-tanks and public policy centers in Russia are relatively few in terms of their numbers, centrally located (mostly in Moscow and St. Petersburg), and with less influence upon the public policy process.

Some of these centers aim at influencing foreign policy-making. The Council on Foreign and Defense Policy (CFDP) is the largest and most influential of these and is governed by an assembly of some 50 prominent figures in government, business, academia, and the mass media. The second group of think-tanks seeks to combine basic and applied research. Over the past 10 to 15 years it has included various organizations that range from representative offices of foreign think-tanks (the Moscow Carnegie Center and East–West Institute), expert institutions (the Center for Strategic Assessments, Center for Russian Political Research, Center for International Research and Programs, the Baltic Research Center), to public policy centers (the Gorbachev Foundation, "Strategy" Foundation).

Professional associations

Prior to the collapse of the U.S.S.R., the Soviet Political Science Association coordinated academic activities related to International Relations. Although the Russian Political Science Association (www.rapn.ru) replaced the SPSA in 1991, it quickly became a fighting arena between the former "scientific Communists" and the new generation of political scientists. As a result, it was unable to function for nearly a decade. In the late 1990s the RPSA was able to resume its activities, beginning with the first all-Russian Congress of Political Scientists held in Moscow in 1998. Currently, the Association has three sections related to IR – world politics, foreign policy studies, and war and peace studies.

In December 1999 the first convention of a newly established Russian International Studies Association was held in Moscow. This development has facilitated both the maturation of national IR schools and their integration into global scholarship. RISA organizes a convention every two to three years, and publishes a newsletter and a quarterly academic journal (*Cosmopolis*) (www.rami.ru).

Professional journals

In contrast with the West, professional journals in Russia are rather few and they do not play an organizing or socializing role in the local IR community. Prior to the establishment of *Cosmopolis* (1999) and RISA, the Russian IR community lacked a specialized organ within which to develop its professional debates. Other social science journals, such as *Social Sciences and Modernity*, *Polis (Political Studies)*, *Political Science*, *World Economy and International Relations*, and *Socio-Political Journal*, published (and still publish) articles on IR theory and foreign policy on a regular basis. In turn, *International Affairs,* the Foreign Ministry's semi-official periodical, touches upon theoretical aspects of contemporary world politics from time to time. Several foreign institutions have also provided funding to create Russian-language IR journals, including *Pro et Contra* (Moscow Carnegie Center) and *International Trends* (Ford Foundation).

Notwithstanding these developments, there is nothing comparable to Western journals that serve as a forum for developing theoretical discussions, following the state of the art in the field, distributing power and careers, and socializing young scholars. Moreover, the circulation of the above journals is very limited. They are read mostly by Moscow- and St. Petersburg-based scholars and reach a very limited target audience in the periphery. The Russian IR community is still underrepresented in professional journals and quite weak in developing its own socializing mechanisms.

Russian IR schools

Several schools of thought have developed in post-Communist Russia, differing both in their conceptual foundations and their approaches to specific international issues. Along with purely Russian schools, almost all of the classic IR paradigms – realism, idealism/liberalism, and globalism (or state-centric, multi-centric, and global-centric approaches to international politics) – can be identified. It goes without saying that these schools have been relatively fluid coalitions, and condensing the complex debate into just a few categories obviously risks oversimplification. However, they do provide a helpful framework for analyzing Russia's post-Communist IR discourse.

Russian Realpolitik

The realist paradigm is dominant in present-day Russia. Politically, the realists have belonged to different groups, although with a predominant orientation towards the democratic camp. The realist conception of global affairs simply provides them with a common theoretical framework and ideas, which easily cross party lines.

According to the realists, Russia's national security concept should be grounded in the real potential of the state, provide for the rational use of resources, and combine and interact with internal, foreign policy, socio-economic, scientific, technological, informational, and all other aspects of life and work. The realists were one of the first schools of thought in Russia to propose extending the concept of national security to include not only "hard security" issues, but "soft security" topics as well. In doing so, they argued that a working security concept should contain a comprehensive analysis and classification of the existing and potential threats to Russia's security, as well as considering internal and external mechanisms for both the prevention and operational elimination of these threats. In other words, the concept should combine both security goals and ways of ensuring them in accord with Russia's historical position and future role. It should ensure a coordinated effort on the part of both the state and the people as a whole to provide security at the national, regional, and global levels, as well as the organization of internal and international interaction in solving urgent and long-term security problems (Shaposhnikov 1993).

As far as the post-9/11 world order is concerned, the realists believe that the Afghanistan and Iraq wars demonstrate the return of the world to a nineteenth-century-type anarchical model which is based on power politics, selfish national interests, and hard competition between major players. They emphasize the inability of international organizations and international law to prevent new wars and the rise of hegemonic powers. Instead, they suggest several possible models for the "neo-anarchical" world. Some Russian realists believe that an era of U.S. unilateralism looms ahead and advise the Russian leadership to choose sides, either joining the U.S.-led pole as a junior partner (Dmitrieva 2003a) or trying to counter-balance the American superpower with the help of other power poles, including the EU, China, and CIS (Lukin 2003).

Another group of realists visualizes the future world as a chaotic combination of *ad hoc* and shifting coalitions where different states pursue their national interests. The realists warn Russian leaders that since these coalitions will be of a temporary rather than permanent nature, Russia should not invest too much in them and should change allies and alliances when they stop serving Russia's national interests (Satanovsky 2003). They point to U.S.– Russian cooperation on Afghanistan (2001) and the Russian–French–German strategic triangle in the case of Iraq (2003) as examples of such *ad hoc* coalitions.

Finally, there are realists who believe that a multipolar model of the world is still possible and that Russia could become one of the power poles (especially in the post-Soviet geostrategic space) (Nikolaev 2003). More specifically, this model of the "manageable anarchy" could create a "concert of powers" international security system where Russia could play a significant role. The G-8 is seen as an embryo of such a less informal but more flexible and reliable security regime. President Putin's speech at the Munich Conference on International Security in February 2007 reflected this line of thinking (Putin 2007). Some realists suggest that China and India be included in the G-8 in order to make this institution more authoritative and representative (Dmitrieva 2003b). The UN Security Council should not be neglected either. It could be useful when there is a consensus between the five permanent members or it could be used by Russia (and its allies) to block (or delegitimize) undesirable initiatives and strategies.

The realist legacy has had a fairly mixed record in Russian IR. On the one hand, realism has directly influenced the Russian foreign policy debate. The realists succeeded in articulating Russia's security interests and priorities with both domestic and foreign audiences. Moreover, the spread of their ideas made Russian security thinking more predictable and understandable for the West. The Russian national security concept of 1997 (and revised in January 2000) drew heavily upon realist ideas. On the other hand, realism's emphasis on national interests, national security, and national sovereignty implied a return to the older paradigms of classical modernity, leading to underdevelopment of concepts addressing the challenges of postmodernity.

Geopolitics–Eurasianism

Along with realism, its close "relative" – geopolitics – is currently in fashion in Russia. In part, it could be viewed as a counter-reaction to Marxist theories and Gorbachev's NPT, which both denied the role of geopolitical factors in international relations. The geopolitical paradigm was seen by many thinkers as having a solid theoretical basis compared to other IR concepts.

Initially, geopolitics in Russia took shape by way of so-called Eurasianism (*evraziistvo*). The concept drew heavily on a philosophical school of the 1920s émigrés who had tried to seek a compromise with the Stalinist regime. This discourse stresses the uniqueness of Russia. One of its key postulates is that in civilizational terms Russia has never been part of Europe. Hence, it should choose a "third way" between the West and the East. Globally, Russia should be a bridge between these civilizations. As apparent from the term Eurasianism itself, its geographic frame of reference implied first of all the Eurasian continent. Other regions were of peripheral interest for Eurasianism. Hence, as methodology, Eurasianism was close to classical geopolitics (comparable to Mackinder's "Heartland" theory).

Eurasianism is grounded in the thesis of Russia's special mission in history. According to Stankevich (1992: 94):

> Russia's role in the world is . . . to initiate and maintain a multilateral dialogue between cultures, civilisations and states. It is Russia which reconciles, unites, and co-ordinates. It is the good, Great Power that is patient and open within borders, which have been settled by right and with good intentions, but which is threatened beyond these borders. This land, in which East and West, North and South are united, is unique, and is perhaps the only one capable of harmoniously uniting many different voices in a historical symphony.

The Eurasianists believed that the government had paid too much attention to the Western direction of its foreign policy, while Russia's most compelling needs were in the South and East. The Eurasianists argued that, first of all, Moscow should deal with "the arc of crisis" developing on Russia's southern borders, and with the problems that had arisen in relations with its own sizeable Muslim population. They persuaded the Yeltsin government to make CIS the highest priority for Moscow's international policy, and to initiate the Commonwealth's integration. They argued that Russia needed to develop an active diplomacy to meet the challenges posed by Turkey, Iran, Saudi Arabia, and other Islamic countries. Coping with these threats and challenges, the Eurasianists contended, was more important than dialogue with the West.

However, Eurasianists have never denied the importance of maintaining good relations with the West. They did not object to Russia entering either the international economy or the "defence structure of the advanced part of the world community" (Bogaturov *et al.* 1992: 31). In their view, Russia's main "Western" interest is improving relations with the EU, and gradual integration into the European economic and political system. Russia should oppose the transformation of Europe into a closed economic system and military–political union, just as it should oppose the appearance of a dominant regional power (Germany). For the Eurasianists, it is best to preserve both the multipolar nature of European politics and the role of the U.S. in the region. Simultaneously, the role of NATO should be reconsidered. Like the realists, Eurasianists have been successful in influencing IR debates in Russia. The theoretical framework of Russia's 1993 foreign policy doctrine (especially the setting of regional priorities) was clearly affected by Eurasianist ideas.

By the mid-1990s, the Eurasianist school had been transformed into a more typical geopolitical vision. Contemporary Russian geopolitics is grounded in the assumption that every state consists of three indispensable components: territory, population, and political organization. Wherever people may live, and under whatever political system, their activities are invariably conditioned by the physical environment. Every state has unique geographical features. Its territory has a location, landscape, form, size, and natural resources. These specifics account for the equally unique historical background of any country. Of the numerous factors influencing people's activities, geography changes least of all. It underlies the continuity of national policy provided that the geographical area remains unchanged (Pozdnyakov 1992: 4).

Many Russian adherents of geopolitics accept the classical concept of two geostrategic regions: the maritime world dependent on trade (with the U.S. as its core) and the Eurasian continental world (where Russia is the core). According to Pozdnyakov (1992: 7), the U.S. is now the only remaining superpower. In addition, it is trying to take advantage of this situation to achieve some of its goals which, until recently, had been largely unattainable. In the geopoliticians' mind, two things are of paramount importance for the maintenance of world order and stability: (1) establishing a clear boundary between Western sea power and Eurasian land power in Europe, and (2) preserving the unity of the Heartland. According to some analysts, both of these principles are seriously challenged by the reunification of Germany and the collapse of the Soviet Union. The boundary between the West and Eurasia has shifted eastward. To date, this boundary has not been properly defined. Russia, which controlled most of the Heartland, has shrunk in terms of territory and is currently unable to play the role of balancer in a geopolitically unstable world. A geopolitically unbalanced Eurasia might provoke a universal redivision of the world with its resources and strategic boundaries. In turn, it could imply a protracted period of turbulence, rift, and bloody conflict. The Kosovo war, Chechnya, the civil wars in Tajikistan and Afghanistan have already demonstrated some implications of the lack of such a geopolitical balance. To avoid an even worse scenario, both Russia and the West should make joint efforts to stabilize the post-Soviet geopolitical space. It could restore Russia's historical mission to be the mediator and to serve as a safeguard against forces aiming at worldwide domination. Echoing Mackinder's three geopolitical theses, Pozdnyakov (1992: 12) coined his own geopolitical formula: "He who controls the Heartland can exercise effective control over world politics, above all by maintaining a global geopolitical and power balance, without which lasting peace is unthinkable."

Despite the seemingly old-fashioned argumentation, the geopolitical paradigm is likely to retain its influence in the Russian IR debate in the foreseeable future. Not only the existence of a theoretical vacuum, but the current geopolitical challenges and the need to define Russia's national identity, national interests, and security politics make this paradigm both significant and attractive to Russian policy-makers and analysts.

The idealist/liberal paradigm

Despite the dominance of realist and geopolitical thinking, the idealist/liberal perspective on international relations has also taken hold in Russian IR. Idealism emphasizes globalizing trends in the world economy which point towards global management of economic and political developments and increases the relevance of international legal frameworks, thus reducing global anarchy. Idealists believe that multilateral institutions and regimes could guarantee the stability of the international system. Although the trend towards a multipolar world is not neglected within the liberal perspective, it argues that the future development of the international system is no longer predominantly determined by the shape and outcome of rivalries among the major centers of economic and military power, but increasingly by the dynamics of their common development and interdependence (Zagorski *et al.* 1992). The liberals argue that the geopolitical drive for control over territories does not matter any more, and suggest that it should be replaced by geo-economic thinking.

The debate between realists and idealists in Russia on more practical aspects of diplomacy has mainly concentrated on two issues: CIS integration and European security. For instance, Zagorski (1995) argues that the real dilemma of Russian politics in the CIS is not further disintegration versus integration, but rather reintegration versus eventual "natural" new integration on the basis of democratic and market reforms yet to be completed. Zagorski also argues that to pursue the latter option one needs to recognize that the major building blocks of the EU experience do not apply to the CIS and another type of soft integration should be the goal.

As for European security, the major controversial issue was NATO enlargement. While mainstream thinking made a geopolitical argument against enlargement, the liberals have argued for a cooperative solution to the issue, which would strengthen and institutionalize interaction between Russia and the West. Their basic argument has been that the predominant interest of Russia in Europe should be the strengthening of multilateralism as a guarantee against a return to balance of power politics in Europe.

Pro-Western liberals viewed no serious threat stemming from NATO enlargement. They believed that NATO extension was a natural reaction of the former Soviet satellites to Russia's unpredictable behavior. The liberals considered NATO as the main guarantor of stability in Europe (in particular in relations between Western and Eastern Europe) (Maksimychev 1994). They believed that Russia was interested in NATO's responsibility for the stability of borders in Central and Eastern Europe, a region with a number of potential hotbeds of instability that could endanger Russia and the CIS member-states. The liberals thought that once NATO accepted the Central and Eastern European countries, which are currently anti-Russian, they will no longer have an incentive to be hostile to Moscow and that they would become more benevolent neighbors to Russia. In this view, partnership between NATO and Russia could become an instrument of conflict resolution in Russia's relations with its neighbors.

The liberals want Russia to focus on its domestic problems such as economic decline, organized crime, environmental decay, nationalism, and separatism which they consider much more dangerous than NATO enlargement. They proposed that Russian diplomacy should be focused not on resistance to NATO expansion, but on dialogue with NATO about disarmament and confidence-building (Churkin 1995).

Realists and idealists disagree on the nature of the post-Cold War European security model. Realists believe that in an age of multipolarity only a flexible pan-European security system can guarantee a balance of power on the continent and the national sovereignty of particular countries. They hope that the OSCE, the only organization where Russia acts on an equal footing with other major Western powers, can be the core of such a security system. Liberals, however, are quite pessimistic as regards the possibility of creating an effective pan-European structure where Russia could have a major say. Transformation of the EU into the pillar of a "Big Europe" cannot but result in the marginalization of current pan-European structures, in particular of the OSCE. This reduces the available options for Russia's integration into European developments. The main objective of Russia's foreign policy should not be joining Western European organizations, but using cooperation with them to facilitate its own integration into the world economy and the community of democratic states. This aim may be attained not only through membership, but also by creating mechanisms of "extra-institutional" cooperation between Russia and the EU, NATO, and other organizations. For example, they are satisfied with projects and initiatives such as the EU's Northern Dimension that aims at integrating Russia's northwestern regions into a single European economic, social, and cultural space or Russia–NATO Permanent Council cooperative format.

As far as the global security regime is concerned the Russian liberals are anxious about the decreasing role of international organizations and international law, and the rise of unilateralism in the aftermath of 9/11 (Volkov 2003: 7). There was a split among the liberals on the nature of the emerging world order. One group insisted that Russia should aim to restore the crucial role of international organizations and law in world affairs. In particular, they advised the Russian government to bring the Iraqi question back to the UN and handle it within the world community rather than within the "coalition of winners" (Ivanov 2003: 1, 6). Another group came close to the realist camp by suggesting a switch from traditional international organizations to more flexible and informal institutions (such as G-8) and the "concert of powers" model. They hope that this could help to prevent the complete collapse of the world order and keep the chaos of international politics at a manageable level.

Although liberals are unable to dominate or even influence Russian IR discourse significantly, they play a useful role by challenging realism/geopolitics and providing these schools with an intellectual alternative.

Globalism/neo-Marxism

There are two main versions of Marxist-inspired political thought in Russia. The first is exemplified by the Communist Party of the Russian Federation (CPRF). The second is close to social democracy. The traditionalists or Communists have been unable to reconcile themselves with the demise of the Soviet Union and the country's loss of great power status. They believe that Gorbachev and Yeltsin led the U.S.S.R. to defeat in the Cold War and finally to its collapse. These two leaders are in fact regarded as national traitors (Elections 1995). Some pro-Communist experts have suggested that Russia's security choice is between the domination of national state interests over cosmopolitan ones with an independent, Russian position in the international relations system, or an orientation towards "Western values and the joining to a community of civilized countries" (Podberezkin 1996). The CPRF opts for the first alternative. The Communists, in contrast to traditional Marxism, emphasize the invariable nature of the country's national interests, which do not depend on a concrete regime or dominant ideology. They believe that the main Russian national interest inherited from its history consists of preserving the country's territorial and spiritual integrity. The idea of a powerful state based on multi-ethnicity is equivalent to the Russian national idea. Thus, the breakdown of the Soviet Union and the weakening of the Russian state have undermined Russian security and worsened its geostrategic position.

The Communists believe that Russia is part neither of the West nor of the East. It should define its own, independent way. At the same time, the Communists are not really fascinated with Eurasianism, seeing both Russian and world history as the result of objective processes rather than messianic ideas. However, they acknowledge the need for a national ideal or doctrine that could consolidate Russian society (Podberezkin 1995). Contrary to the domestic sphere, the CPRF has failed to produce any coherent and clearly pronounced foreign policy doctrine. Instead, it has operated with an amalgam of the party leadership's statements and remarks, making it difficult to reconstruct the CPRF's foreign policy platform. Despite its significant domestic influence, the CPRF has, in fact, been unable to influence Russian discourse on IR theory.

Social Democratic foreign policy thinking has focused on the concept of stability. Internal stability has been defined as cohesion within the political system, adherence to normal democratic procedures concerning the rotation of ruling elites, the absence of pressing ethnic and social conflicts, and a healthy functioning economy. International stability has been seen as the balance of interests among major international players (contrary to the balance of power in the past) (Kolikov 1994: 12).

Along with other schools of thought, the Social Democrats have contributed to the Russian discussion of national interests. Contrary to Gorbachev's NPT which was grounded in the unconditional priority of "all-human" interests over national interests, the Social Democrats have admitted that national interests are of fundamental concern for any country. They define national interests as a manifestation of the nation's basic needs (survival, security, pro-gressive development) (Krasin 1996). National interests may be subjective in terms of their form or way of expression, but they are definitely objective in terms of their nature. In a nation-state, national interests are usually synonymous with state interests. In multinational countries (like Russia) the articulation and representation of national interests are a much more complicated process involving numerous political actors and requiring more time and effort to achieve a public consensus.

The Social Democrats, however, do not limit themselves to the acknowledgment of the significance of national interests. They believe that in an interdependent world, international actors cannot afford to solely pursue their own interests. Since the international environment has become multidimensional, state actors should take into account both the national interests of other players and universal (all-human) interests. According to the Social Democrats, narrow-minded nationalism is outdated and detrimental not only to the world community but, in the end, also to a nation conducting a nationalist policy (Utkin 1995). They realize that democracy in the international relations system is still in its infancy, and few "all-human" values have taken root in humankind's mentality. The Social Democrats regard the creation of a global civil society as the only way of replacing national interests with "all-human" values. In their view, a world civil society could be based on a system of horizontal links between both inter-governmental and non-governmental organizations dealing with economic, political, environmental, and cultural issues (Krasin 1996: 12). Some experts have proposed the creation of a world government to resolve global problems and to save humankind from imminent catastrophe (Shakhnazarov 1995: 79). Thus, the Kantian project of "perpetual peace" – the methodological basis of the NPT and its current proponents – could be put into practice.

The Social Democrats perceive the world as moving from a unipolar towards a multipolar structure. None of the countries or ideologies will be able to impose its model on the others. Various civilizational models will compete in the foreseeable future. A future world will be born out of the process of the interaction of two contradictory processes – integration and regionalization. The future poles of power will emerge on the basis of economic, religious, and cultural differentiation. In any case, these developments will make the world less predictable and more multidimensional than has been the case so far.

As far as Russia's strategic orientation, the Social Democrats have proposed a model of "multidimensional partnership" directed at cooperation with the major players of the world regardless of their geographical location. According to this model, Russia's policy should not be based on playing geopolitical "cards" (Chinese, American, European). Instead, it should be oriented towards establishing long-term and stable bilateral relations as well as to promoting multilateralism (Voskresensky 1996: 99). However, it remains unclear which methods should be used to create such relations and how to convince other powers to accept this model.

Post-positivism in Russia?

Until now, Russian scholarship has been quite indifferent to post-positivism. Few social scientists have tried to implement post-positivist approaches in their research, although post-modernism has been studied as one of the schools of Western political thought (Sergounin and Makarychev 1999). In the case of IR, post-positivism is largely considered irrelevant, mainly because it fails to provide analysts with a theoretical framework for producing practical advice on concrete issues. Nevertheless, since the late 1990s social constructivism has become popular in some Russian academic settings, in particular to analyze issues such as identity and security (Makarychev 2007; Medvedev 1998).

Two cases that are marginal in the bigger picture might be worth mentioning as illustrations of the way international theoretical trends are inflicted through particular mental and political conditions in Russia. Some have suggested that a certain postmodern insight could be evolving in Russia due to some peculiarities in the national mentality. Russians have never been happy with the project of modernity grounded on rationalism, a belief in linear progress, and the decisive role of science and knowledge. Even Marxism, a typical product of modernity, has been adapted to Russian conditions (Arbatov 1970; Antyukhina-Moskovchenko *et al.* 1988). Another peculiarly Russian adoption of post-structuralist inspiration emphasized the "grammatological" focus on *writing* and used this to improve on Huntington to interpret the lines of global conflict as falling between the different alphabets (Kuznetsov 1995: 98–99). This form of postmodernism also used their skepticism and instability focus to spell out how international institutions were unable to cope with the destabilizing potential of alphabetic frictions around "small" civilizations on the fault-lines.

It is hard to imagine that post-positivism will become an influential school in Russian IR in the foreseeable future. Given that Russia is still in the process of trying to define its own national identity, realist concepts such as national interest, national security, and balance of power continue to hold significant sway among academics and policy-makers alike.

Conclusions

Several conclusions emerge from the above analysis. Russian international studies has experienced a very quick and dramatic transformation from a discipline dominated by Marxist ideology to multiparadigmatic discourse. Although the realist/geopolitical school is currently dominating the discipline, other perspectives such as idealism/liberalism, globalism, and post-positivism do exist and form alternatives to the prevailing paradigm. In the foreseeable future, Russian foreign policy discourse will be a polyphony rather than a monophony or cacophony. The mainstream of Russian IR has managed to avoid xenophobic/extremist views on international affairs and to develop more or less moderate and well-balanced concepts.

Russian authors have taken great strides in exploring international problems such as diplomatic history and present-day Russian foreign policy. However, Russian IR remains too dependent on policy-relevant/government-oriented research. Russian scholarship still lacks profound theoretical work.

Russian IR has managed to establish itself as an independent academic discipline with a status equal to other social sciences. The "democratization," "demonopolization," and "normalization" of international relations studies have had many implications at the institutional level: the number of research centers dealing with international studies has dramatically increased, and new regional centers have emerged. This has made Russian scholarship even more diverse and interesting. However, the Russian IR community remains fragmented; its professional associations, journals, and other constitutive/socializing mechanisms are still weak. There is a long way to go for Russian IR to take a form similar to North America and Europe, which are generally viewed as the "international standard."

References

Antonenko, Oksana (1996) *New Russian Analytical Centers and Their Role in Political Decisionmaking*, Cambridge, MA: John F. Kennedy School of Government, Harvard University.

Antyukhina-Moskovchenko, V.I., A.A. Zlobin and M.A. Khrustalev (1988) *Osnovy Teorii Mezhdunarodnykh Otnosheniy* (Basics of International Relations Theory), Moscow: Mezhdunarodnye Otnosheniya (in Russian).

Arbatov, Georgy (1970) *Ideologicheskaya Bor'ba v Sovremennykh Mezhdunarodnykh Otnosheniyakh* (Ideological Struggle in Contemporary International Relations), Moscow: Politizdat.

Baluev, Dmitry (2002) *Sovremennaya Mirovaya Politika i Problemy Lichnostnoi Bezopasnosti* (Contemporary World Policy and Problems of Human Security), Nizhny Novgorod: Nizhny Novgorod State University Press.

Bogaturov, Alexei (1997) *Velikiye Derzhavy na Tikhom Okeane* (Great Powers in the Pacific), Moscow: Konvert-MONF (in Russian).

Bogaturov, Alexei (ed.) (2000) *Sistemnaya Istoriya Mezhdunarodnykh Otnosheniy* (Systemic History of International Relations), Moscow: Moskovskiy Rabochiy.

Bogaturov, Alexei, Nikolai Kosolapov, and Mark Khrustalev (2002) *Ocherki Teorii i Politicheskogo Analiza Mezhdunarodnykh Otnoshenoy* (Essays on Theory and Policy Analysis of International Relations), Moscow: NOFMO.

Bogaturov, Alexei, Mikhail Kozhokin, and Konstantin V. Pleshakov (1992) "Vneshnyaya Politika Rossii" (Russia's Foreign Policy), *USA: Economics, Politics, Ideology*, 15 (10): 28–37.

Churkin, Vitaly (1995) "U Rossii s NATO Nikogda ne Bylo Konfliktov" (Russia and NATO Never Had Conflicts), *Segodnya* (13 April): 3.

Davydov, Yuri (1993) *Russia and Eastern Europe*, Providence: Brown University Press.

Dmitrieva, Olga (2003a) "Plyusy Odnogo Polyusa" (Pluses of a Single Pole), *Rossiyskaya gazeta*, 20 (May): 6.

Dmitrieva, Olga (2003b) "Vosmyerka Budet Pravit Mirom?" (Will the G-8 Rule the World?), *Rossiyskaya gazeta*, 31 (May): 1, 4.

Elections (1995) "Parties' Foreign Policy Views," *International Affairs* (Moscow), 41(11–12): 3–13.

Fel'dman, Dmitry (1998) *Politologiya Konflikta* (Political Analysis of Conflict), Moscow: Strategy.

Gadzhiev, Kamaludin S. (1997) *Geopolitika* (Geopolitics), Moscow: Mezhdunarodnye Otnosheniya.

Gantman, V.I. (1984) *Sistema, Struktura I Protsess Razvitiya Sovremennykh Mezdunarodnykh Otnosheniy* (System, Structure and Process of Development of Contemporary International Relations), Moscow: Nauka.

Gorbachev, Mikhail (1987) *Perestroyka dlya Strany I Vsego Mira* (Perestroika for the Country and the Whole World), Moscow: Politizdat.

Ilyin, Mikhail (1995) *Ocherki Khronopoliticheskoi Tipologii* (Essays on Chronopolitical Typology), Moscow: MGIMO.

Ivanov, Igor (2003) "Irakskiy Vopros Snova v OON" (The Iraqi Question is Again in UN), *Nezavisimaya gazeta*, 30–31 (May): 1, 6.

Kamenskaya, Galina *et al.* (eds) (2007) *Istoriya Mezhdunarodnykh Otnosheniy* (International Relations History), Moscow: Logos.

Kapustin, Boris (1996) "Natsionalnyi Interes kak Konservativnaya Utopiya" (National Interest as Conservative Utopia), *Svobodnaya Mysl*, 6: 13–28.

Khokhlysheva, Olga (2002) *Miroponimanie, Mirotvorchestvo, Mirosokhranenie: Opyt XX Stoletiya* (Peace-understanding, Peace-making and Peace-keeping: XXth Century's Experience), Nizhny Novgorod: Nizhny Novgorod State University Press.

Khrustalev, Mark A. (1991) *Teoriya Politiki i Politicheskiy Analis* (Political Theory and Political Analysis), Moscow: MGIMO Press (in Russian).

Kokoshin, Andrei and Alexei Bogaturov (eds) (2005) *Mirovaya Politika. Teoriya, Metodologiya, Prikladnoi Analiz* (World Politics. Theory, Methodology, Applied Analysis), Moscow: KomKniga.

Kolikov, Nikolai (1994) "Rossiya v Kontekste Globalnykh Peremen" (Russia in the Context of Global Transition), *Svobodnaya Mysl*, 2–3: 3–18.

Kolobov, Oleg A. (ed.) (2001) *Istoriya Mezhdunarodnykh Otnosheniy* (International Relations History), Vols 1–2, Nizhny Novgorod: Nizhny Novgorod State University Press.

Kolobov, Oleg A. (ed.) (2004) *Teoriya Mezhdunarodnykh Otnosheniy* (International Relations Theory), Vols 1–2, Nizhny Novgorod: Nizhny Novgorod State University Press.

Kolosov, Yuri and Emilia S. Krivtchikova (1994) *Mezhdunarodnoye Pravo* (International Law), Moscow: Mezhdunarodnye Otnosheniya.

Konyshev, Valery (2004) *Amerikansky Neorealizm o Prirode Voiny: Evolutsiya Politicheskoi Teorii* (American Neorealism on the Nature of War: Evolution of Political Theory), St. Petersburg: Nauka.

Kosolapov, Nikolai (1999) "Analiz Vneshnei Politiki: Osnovnye Napravleniya Issledovaniy" (Foreign Policy Analysis: Main Directions), *Mirovaya Economika i Mezhdunarodnye Otnosheniya*, 2: 75–81.

Krasin, Yuri (1996) "Natsionalnye Interesy: Mif ili Realnost?" (National Interests: Myth or Reality?), *Svobodnaya Mysl*, 3: 3–29.

Kulagin, V.M. (2006) *Mezhdunarodnaya Bezopasnost* (International Security), Moscow: Aspect Press.

Kuznetsov, Artur (1995) "A New Model for Traditional Civilisations," *International Affairs* (Moscow), 41 (4–5): 95–100.

Lantsov, S.A. and V.A. Achkasov (2007) *Mirovaya Politika i Mezhdunarodnye Otnosheniya* (World Politics and International Relations), St. Petersburg: St. Petersburg State University Press.

Lapin, G.E. (2002) *Konsul'skaya Sluzhba* (Consular Service), Moscow: Mezhdunarodnye Otnosheniya.

Lebedeva, Marina M. (1997) *Politicheskoye Uregulirovanie Konfliktov: Podkhody, Reshenya, Tekhnologii* (Conflict Resolution: Approaches, Solutions, Techniques), Moscow: Aspect Press.

Lebedeva, Marina M. (2003/2006) *Mirovaya Politika* (World Politics), Moscow: Aspect Press.

Lebedeva, Marina and Pavel Tsygankov (eds) (2001) *Mirovaya Politika i Mezhdunarodnye Otnosheniya v 1990-e Gody: Vzglyady Amerikanskikh i Frantsuzskikh Issledovatelei* (World Politics and International Relations in the 1990s: Views of American and French Scholars), Moscow: MONF (in Russian).

Lomagin, Nikita (ed.) (2001) *Vvedenie v Teoriyu Mezhdunarodnykh Otnosheniy i Analiz Vneshnei Politiki* (Introduction to International Relations Theory and Foreign Policy Analysis), St. Petersburg: St. Petersburg State University Press.

Lukin, Vladimir P. (2003) "Prishla Pora Igrat v Komandnuyu Igru" (It's Time Now to Play Staff Game), *Nezavisimaya gazeta*, 24 (March): 15.

Makarychev, Andrei (2000) *Mezdunarodnye Otnosheniya v 21-m Veke: Regional'noe v Global'nom, Global'nke v Regional'nom* (International Relations in the 21st Century: Regional in Global, Global in Regional), Nizhny Novgorod: Nizhny Novgorod Linguistic University Press.

Makarychev, Andrei (2005) "Russia as Seen from its Edges. Discursive Strategies of Russia's Western Borderlands," in Andrei Makarychev (ed.), *Russia's North West and the European Union: A Playground for Innovations*, Nizhny Novgorod: Nizhny Novgorod Linguistic University Press, pp. 7–54.

Makarychev, Andrei (2006) "Russia's Discursive Construction of Europe and Herself: Towards New Spatial Imagery," in *EU–Russia: The Four Common Spaces*, Working Paper Series, No. 1, Nizhny Novgorod: Nizhny Novgorod Linguistic University Press, pp. 5–29.

Makarychev, Andrei (2007) "Terrorism: Encyclopedia, Arkheologiya, Grammatika" (Terrorism: Encyclopedia, Archeology and Grammar), *Index Bezopasnosti*, 13 (2): 133–142.

Makarycheva, Marina (2006) *Rossiskiy Diskurs v SShA: Formirovanie, Structura, Politicheskaya Transformatsiya* (The Russian Discourse in the U.S.: Formation, Structure, Political Transformation), Nizhny Novgorod: Nizhny Novgorod Linguistic University Press.

Maksimychev, Igor (1994) "Nuzhna li Evrope NATO?" (Does Europe Need NATO?), *Nezavisimaya gazeta*, 8 (April): 3.

Malhotra, Vinay Kumar and Alexander A. Sergounin (1998) *Theories and Approaches to International Relations*, New Delhi: Anmol Publications Pvt. Ltd.

Manykin, Alexander S., Yuri N. Rogulev and Evgeny F. Yazkov (eds) (1996) *Novyi Kurs Franklina D. Ruzvelta: Posledstviya dlya SShA i Rossii* (The New Deal of Franklin D. Roosevelt: Implications for the USA and Russia), Moscow: Moscow State University Press (in Russian).

Medvedev, Sergei (1998) "Riding into the Sunset: Russia's Long Journey into Europe," in Jouko Huru, Olli-Pekka Jalonen, and Michael Sheehan (eds), *New Dimensions of Security in Central and North Eastern Europe*, Tampere: Tampere Peace Research Institute, Research Report No. 83, pp. 221–251.

Medvedev, Sergei (2006) *EU–Russian Relations. Alternative Future*, Finnish Institute of International Affairs.

Mezhevich, Nikolai (2002) *Globalism i Regionalism – Tendentsii Mirovogo Razvitiya i Factor Sotsial'no-Ekonomicheskogo Razvitiya Rossii* (Globalism and Regionalism – Tendencies of the World Development and Factor of Russia's Socio-Economic Development), St. Petersburg: St. Petersburg State University Press.

Morozov, Vyacheslav (2005) "New Borderlands in a United Europe: Democracy, Imperialism, and the Copenhagen Criteria," in *EU–Russia: The Four Common Spaces*, Working Paper Series, No. 1, Nizhny Novgorod: Nizhny Novgorod Linguistic University, pp. 74–84.

Narinsky, Mikhail M. (1995) *Kholodnaya Voina: Novye Documenty* (The Cold War: New Documents), Moscow: Pamyatnimi Istoricheskoi Mysli (in Russian).

Nezhinsky, Leonid N. *et al.* (1995) *Sovetskaya Vneshnaya Politika v Gody "Kholodnoi Voiny"* (Soviet Foreign Policy in the "Cold War" Period), Moscow: Mezhdunarodnye Otnosheniya (in Russian).

Nikolaev, Andrei (2003) "Staraya Strategiya na Noviy Lad" (A New Strategy in an Old Shape), *Nezavisimaya gazeta,* 12 (May): 9, 14.

Panarin, Alexander S. (1997) *Politologiya* (Political Science), Moscow: Prospect (in Russian).

Panarin, Alexander S. (2003) *Strategicheskaya Nestabil'nost v XXI-m Veke* (Strategic Instability in the 21st Century), Moscow: Algoritm-kniga (in Russian).

Podberezkin, Alexei (1995) "Cherez Dukhovnost – k Vozrozhdeniyu Otechestva" (Restoring Motherland Through Spirituality), *Svobodnaya Mysl*, 5: 87–99.

Podberezkin, Alexei (1996) "Geostrategicheskoe Polozhenie i Bezopasnost Rossii" (Russia's Geostrategic Position and Security), *Svobodnaya Mysl*, 7: 86–99.

Popov, V.I. (2004) *Sovremennaya Diplomatiya: Teoriya i Praktika* (Modern Diplomacy: Theory and Praxis), Moscow: Mezhdunarodnye Otnosheniya.

Pozdnyakov, Elgiz (1976) *Sistemniy Podkhod I Mezhdunarodnye Otnosheniya* (System Approach and International Relations), Moscow: Nauka.

Pozdnyakov, Elgiz (1992) "The Geopolitical Collapse and Russia," *International Affairs* (Moscow), 38 (9): 3–12.

Putin, Vladimir (2007) Speech and Discussion at the Munich Conference on Security Policy, February 10, available at http://www.kremlin.ru/appears/2007/02/10/1737_type 63374type63376type63377 type63381type82634_118109.shtml.

Razuvaev, V. (1993) *Geopolitika Postsovetskago Prostranstva*, Moscow: Institute Europe, Russian Academy of Sciences.

Reut, Oleg (2000) *Republic of Karelia: A Double Asymmetry or North-Eastern Dimensionalism*, COPRI Working Paper No. 13, Copenhagen: Copenhagen Peace Research Institute.

Satanovsky, Yevgeny (2003) "Nastupaet Ocherednoi Peredel Mira" (The New Redivision of the World Is Coming), *Nezavisimaya gazeta*, 24 (March): 1.

Selyaninov, O.P. (1998) *Tetradi po Diplomaticheskoi Sluzhbe Gosudarstv* (Notes on Foreign Services of States), Moscow: MGIMO Press (in Russian).

Sergounin, Alexander (2003) *Rossiyskaya Vneshnepoliticheskaya Mysl: Problemy Natsional'noi i Mezhdunarodnoi Bezopasnosti* (Russian Foreign Policy Thought: Problems of National and International Security), Nizhny Novgorod: Nizhny Novgorod Linguistic University Press.

Sergounin, Alexander (2004) "International Relations Discussions in Post-Communist Russia," *Communism and Post-Communism Studies*, 37: 19–35.

Sergounin, Alexander and Andrei Makarychev (1999) *Sovremennaya Zapadnaya Politicheskaya Mysl: Postpositivistskaya Revolutsiya* (Contemporary Western Political Thought: Postpositivist Revolution), Nizhny Novgorod: Nizhny Novgorod Linguistic University Press.

Shakhnazarov, Georgi (1995) "Vostok i Zapad: Samoidentifikatsiya na Perelome Vekov" (East and West: In Search for Identity on the Turn of the Century), *Svobodnaya Mysl*, 8: 73–9.

Shakleina, Tatyana (2002) *Vneshnyaya Politika i Bezopasnost Sovremennoi Rossii* (Russia's Foreign Policy and Security), Moscow: ROSSPEN, Vols 1–4.

Shaposhnikov, Yevgeny (1993) "A Security Concept for Russia," *International Affairs* (Moscow), 39 (10): 10–19.

Sorokin, Konstantin (1995) "Geopolitika Sovremennogo Mira i Rossiya" (Contemporary Geopolitics and Russia), *Politicheskie Issledovaniya*, 3 (1): 3–12.

Stankevich, Sergei (1992) "A Transformed Russia in a New World," *International Affairs* (Moscow), 38 (4–5): 81–104.

Torkunov, Anatoly V. (1995) *Koreyskaya Problema: Noviy Vzglyad* (The Korean Problem: A New Outlook), Moscow: ANKIL (in Russian).

Torkunov, Anatoly V. (ed.) (1997, 1999, 2001) *Sovremennye Mezhdunarodnye Otnosheniya* (Contemporary International Relations), Moscow: ROSSPEN.

Torkunov, Anatoly V. (ed.) (2005) *Sovremennye Mezhdunarodnye Otnosheniya i Mirovaya Politika* (Contemporary International Relations and World Politics), Moscow: Prosveshenie.

Tsygankov, Andrei and Pavel Tsygankov (eds) (2005) *Rossiskaya Nauka Mezhdunarodnykh Otnosheniy: Novye Napravleniya* (Russian International Relations: New Perspectives), Moscow: PER SE.

Tsygankov, Andrei and Pavel Tsygankov (2006) *Sotsiologiya Mezhdunarodnykh Otnosheniy: Analiz Rossiyskikh i Zapadnykh Teoriy* (Sociology of International Relations: Analysis of Russian and Western Theories), Moscow: Aspekt Press.

Tsygankov, Pavel A. (1995) *Mirovaya Politika: Problemy Teorii i Prakitki* (World Politics: Problems of Theory and Practice), Moscow: MGU (in Russian).

Tsygankov, Pavel A. (1996) *Mezhdunarodnye Otnosheniya* (International Relations), Moscow: Novaya Shkola.

Tsygankov, Pavel A. (ed.) (1998) *Mezhdunarodnye Otnosheniya: Sotsiologicheskie Podkhody* (International Relations: Sociological Approaches), Moscow: Gardariki (in Russian).

Tsygankov, Pavel A. (2002) *Teoriya Mezhdunarodnykh Otnosheniy* (International Relations Theory), Moscow: Gardariki.

Tsygankov, Pavel A. (ed.) (2007) *Mezhdunarodnye Otnosheniya: Teorii, Konflikty, Dvizheniya, Organizatsii* (International Relations: Theories, Conflicts, Movements, Organizations), Moscow: Alfa-M/INFRA-M.

Tyulin, Ivan G. (1991) *Politicheskaya Nauka: Vozmozhnosti i Perspectivy Mezhdistsiplinarnogo Podhoda* (Political Science: Opportunities and Prospects on Inter-Disciplinary Approaches), Moscow: MGIMO Press (in Russian).

Tyulin, Ivan G. (1994) *Theory and Practice in Foreign Policy Making: National Perspectives on Academics and Professionals in International Relations*, London: Pinter Publishers Ltd.

Utkin, Anatoly (1995) "Natsionalizm i Buduschee Mirovogo Soobschestva" (Nationalism and the Future of the World Community), *Svobodnaya Mysl*, 3: 78–86.

Volkov, Alexander (2003) "Bez Suda I Sledstviya" (Without Justice and Investigation), *Rossiyskaya gazeta*, 18 (March): 7.

Voskresensky, Alexei (1996) "Veter s Zapada ili Veter s Vostoka? Rossiya, SShA, Kitai i Mirovoe Liderstvo" (Is There Wind from the West or East? Russia, the USA, China, and World Leadership), *Svobodnaya Mysl*, 10: 89–100 (in Russian).

Voskresensky, Alexei (ed.) (2002) *Vostok/Zapad: Regional'nye Podsistemy i Regional'nye Problemy Mezhdunarodnykh Otnosheniy* (East–West: Regional Sub-systems and Regional Problems of International Relations), Moscow: ROSSPEN.

Zagorski, Andrei (1995) "Was fur eine GUS. erfullt thren Zweck," *Aussenpolitik*, 46 (3): 263–270.

Zagorski, Andrei, Anatoly Zlobin, Sergei Solodovnik, and Mark Khrustalev (1992) "Russia in a New World," *International Affairs* (Moscow), 38 (7): 3–11.

Zamyatin, D.N. (2004) *Vlast' Prostranstva i Prostranstvo Vlasti: Geograficheskie Obrazy v Politike i Mezhdunarodnykh Otnosheniyakh* (Power of Space and Space of Power: Geographic Images in Politics and International Relations), Moscow: ROSSPEN.

Zonova, Tatyana (2003) *Sovremennaya Model Diplomatii: Istoki Stanovleniya i Perspectivy Razvitiya* (The Modern Model of Diplomacy: Origins and Prospects for Development), Moscow: ROSSPEN.

Zonova, Tatyana (ed.) (2004) *Diplomatiya Inostrannykh Gosudarstv* (Diplomacy of Foreign Countries), Moscow: ROSSPEN (in Russian).

14 Central and Eastern Europe
Between continuity and change[1]

Petr Drulák, Jan Karlas, and Lucie Königová

Introduction

To the best of our knowledge, there is no study that maps out and analyzes the state of the discipline of International Relations (IR) in the Central and Eastern European region (CEE) as a whole.[2] Yet there are at least two reasons for which IR in the CEE represents a topic that is worth exploring. First, IR has become more self-reflective in recent years. Whereas Stanley Hoffmann's path-breaking contribution defining IR as "an American Social Science" remained isolated in the 1970s (Hoffmann 1977), the 1990s was witness to a host of articles fueled by a new wave of sociological reflexivity, reviewing the discipline as such, or national IR traditions (see e.g. Wæver 1998). Second, like the CEE societies, IR in the region has also presumably undergone some transformation.

In this chapter, we will describe and assess how the discipline of IR in the CEE looked a decade and a half after the fall of the communist regimes.[3] Before we present our analytical approach, it is necessary to mention that there are several acute limitations to such a project, especially given the constraints in collecting relevant data. Most books, journals, and syllabi are available only in their local languages and are difficult to access unless visiting the local institution itself. Thus, relying on an incomplete command of local languages and somewhat "filtered-out" evidence available in English, one receives an incomplete picture, despite good intentions and reasonable effort. Research outputs, moreover, tend to be rather scattered. The CEE is not a common culture-based region with intensive cross-border contacts as is, for example, the Nordic region.

Hence, it is extremely difficult to make any generalizations about the region. To limit the scope of our study we chose to focus on six countries: the Czech Republic, Lithuania, Poland, Romania, Slovakia, and Slovenia. This choice was determined by our linguistic skills and the availability of respective national journals in the Czech libraries. Nevertheless, the selected countries also happen to represent a fair distribution in terms of their size, geography and cultural, religious, and political/imperial backgrounds.

The chapter combines two perspectives: national and regional. First, we examine individual national IR disciplines. Thus, six national IR scholarly journals[4] have been selected and analysed. Furthermore, we looked at 11 major research institutes/think-tanks active in the field of IR in the six countries under review. In addition, in spite of the data collection constraints, we have managed to undertake an analysis of the local university syllabi.

Second, we examine the IR studies within a wider, regional frame of reference, zooming in on those IR institutions that appear to represent the CEE region as a whole. This perspective allows us to address (once again) one journal, one professional organization (instead of a "regional" research institute), and one university. Despite the concentration of the IR discipline on the national level and continuing scarcity of truly regional projects, regional institutions have been going through a tremendous development recently.

The following questions were of particular interest to us:

* What topics are researched most heavily within the country/region?
* What are the external and internal influences?
* What are the internal structures of the IR community?
* What is the position of the regional discipline in the global IR structure?

This chapter gives some preliminary answers to these questions. First, the most researched topics relate to regional issues, international security, and European integration. Second, Anglo-American influence has been significant since the early 1990s, in terms of the literature that scholarly articles refer to, in terms of assistance in the development of the Central and Eastern European International Studies Association (CEEISA), in terms of its impact on the Central European University (CEU) curricula, and in terms of its impact on the CEEISA's journal (*Journal of International Relations and Development*; JIRD). The Western European influence was equally important and manifested itself mainly in literature references and the funding of some research institutions. Third, IR in the CEE seems to be marked by a diffusion of power. Generally speaking, there is no hierarchy of publications as the main source of academic reputation. In addition, the control over publications is shared by the local academic representatives, editors of domestic journals as well as editors of foreign collective volumes. Fourth, the data also demonstrate that the regional discipline belongs to the peripheral part of IR. The bulk of IR professional activities concentrates on empirically oriented research, and the nature of professional communications also indicates a peripheral status.

National perspectives

Journals

We set out to analyze five national scholarly IR journals available in Czech libraries from the years 1998 through 2006.[5] The five journals selected were: *Mezinárodní vztahy* (Czech Republic), *The Lithuanian Foreign Policy Review* (Lithuania), *Medzinárodné otázky* (Slovakia), *The Polish Quarterly of International Affairs* (Poland), and *the Romanian Journal of International Affairs* (Romania).[6]

In each journal, four features were examined. First, referring only to the topics of the articles, we sought to identify the most popular themes. Second, looking at the books reviewed, our aim was to find out what the IR community was reading (looking again at topics and the province of the reviewed publications). The latter criterion may give us some hints about the position of foreign IR communities in each particular state and provide, at the same time, a good parameter to measure the strength of local IR book production. Third, for a more accurate yardstick to determine what intellectual sources influence local IR research, we made an analysis of references[7] along geographical lines. Moreover, the frequency of source citations may give us a rough idea of the quality of a particular academic journal. Fourth, we examined the background of authors. In the first step we asked what percentage of authors was from civil service sectors as compared to those based at universities and research institutes. In the second step, we looked at the proportion of authors coming from abroad as compared to local authors, using their institutional affiliation as the ultimate criterion. The answer to the last question invites quite ambiguous interpretations: if the authorship is purely local in province, then the domestic status of the discipline may be very strong but at the same time parochial and isolated (and the other way round, of course).

Our analysis of the data compiled from the journals reveals, among other things, that IR in CEE countries is rather government-centric. The journals are usually published either directly by the countries' foreign ministries or by foreign ministry-funded institutions. This influence is sometimes carried over into the editorial boards, where former and active diplomats sit alongside academics and scholars. The editor-in-chief often is or used to be a political appointee. Compared to university-affiliated IR journals in the West, these five journals have a less academic framework. As shown in Table 14.1, only the Czech publication is dominated by contributors from universities and research institutes. A significant proportion of contributions to the other four are made by civil service personnel.

In general, the discipline also continues to lack strong academic standards and local foundations. Journal articles are usually written without reference to any explicit theoretical framework. They are mainly descriptive and based on intuitive insights. Only one journal consistently required the use of references to other academic texts. Just two journals have well-established review sections. Moreover, according to the editorial information of the journals, only one of them is based on a peer-review system. The small share of local books in book review sections (except for Poland) indicates insufficient domestic scholarly output.

The prevalence of research themes differs from country to country but the CEE, EU, and international security are highly researched everywhere. As Table 14.3 indicates, there are

Table 14.1 Distribution of characteristics of authors contributing to IR journals in the Czech Republic, Lithuania, Poland, Romania, and Slovakia (%)

Authors (1998–2006)	Czech	Lithuanian	Polish	Romanian	Slovak
By country					
• Local	86	61	90	49	59
• From abroad	14	39	10	51	41
By profession					
• Academic/research	82	55	62	56	58
• Civil Service	10	4	36	34	33
• Others	8	5	2	10	9
Authors in total	251	75	179	180	192

Table 14.2 Regional origin of references made by authors contributing to IR journals in the Czech Republic, Lithuania, Poland, Romania, and Slovakia (%)

References by origin (1998–2003)[a]	Czech	Lithuanian	Polish	Romanian	Slovak
Local	29	25	45	9	19
Anglo-American	48	32	28	51	36
Western Europe	16	19	15	24	17
CEE	10	11	1	6	15
Others	2	10	0	9	8
Articles in total	159	35	40	67	101

Note
[a] As mentioned, we exclude possible references to documents or speeches.

certain themes that make up between 13 and 30 percent of the articles published. Each journal except for the Lithuanian one seems to focus on two such dominant themes. In all the five journals, CEE and international security emerge as either dominant or secondary themes. Yet, the high proportion of contributions dealing with CEE themes does not mean that the analysed journals would offer genuine and valuable research on local concerns and questions. Unfortunately, this research often lacks any theoretical or methodological underpinnings. third world issues and the global agenda are principal or secondary themes in three journals. Only the Czech and Romanian journals have an increasingly flourishing portfolio of IR/social theory articles. Finally, a dominant theme in one journal is usually either dominant or secondary in each of the others.

To evaluate outside influences, we examined the origin of reviewed books (Table14. 4) and the geographical distribution of references (Table 14.2). According to those indicators, Anglo-American intellectual influence strongly prevails, followed by local production and Western Europe (especially Germany). In the Czech and Slovak journals, Anglo-American publications were most frequently reviewed. On the contrary, the Polish and, to some extent, also Lithuanian and Romanian journals were dominated by a domestic review trend. Anglo-American literature is also the greatest source for external references (and, besides Poland, it is the most frequent reference source of all), followed by Western European literature.

Table 14.3 Articles in IR journals in the Czech Republic, Lithuania, Poland, Romania, and Slovakia, by topic (%)

Articles (1998–2006)	Czech	Lithuanian	Polish	Romanian	Slovak
CEE	12	2	8	10	34
EU	12	6	20	11	18
International law	4	0	7	3	2
International security	13	6	18	21	8
IPE	7	0	3	2	4
IR history	1	9	4	0	0
IR theory/social theory	13	2	6	20	4
Middle East	4	0	2	0	4
Third world	6	0	0	0	0
UN, global issues	6	0	5	10	10
Western Europe, U.S.A.	7	0	14	2	5
Others	15	75	13	17	11
No. of articles in total	237	76	160	236	229

Table 14.4 Book reviews in IR journals in the Czech Republic, Lithuania, Poland, Romania, and Slovakia, by language of the publication reviewed (%)

Book reviews by language of the publication (1998–2006)	Czech	Lithuanian	Polish	Romanian	Slovak
English	38	50	11	0	33
Western Europe	21	0	3	25	2
Russian	1	0	0	0	28
Mother tongue	32	50	81	50	22
Translations	8	0	5	25	15
Reviews in total	192	8	449	4	54

Unlike in Slovakia, Russian literature receives a smaller share of attention in the Czech journal and is almost disregarded in its Polish, Lithuanian, and Romanian counterparts. A review series on Russian geopolitics generated a high share of Russian books in the Slovak journal.

Institutions of research

This part of our research focused on selected research institutes that deal with IR and foreign policy analysis (FPA) and are based in the six above-mentioned countries.[8] Our findings suggest that think-tank activity in the field of IR is still in its nascent stages in CEE, and the core of current research remains in universities, academies of science[9] and state-founded (and funded) institutions. More specifically, we have identified two types of IR research institutes in these countries. Traditional research institutes are the former analytical centres of Foreign Ministries that have revamped their research agendas and undergone major organizational reform. For instance, the Institute of International Relations in the Czech Republic and the Polish Institute of International Affairs represent this category. The structures of these institutes are by and large comparable to the structures of Western European "foreign policy institutes" such as Deutsche Gesellschaft für Auswärtige Politik, L'Institut Français des Relations Internationales or the Royal Institute of International Affairs.

CEE think-tanks, on the other hand, are typically post-1989 entities, often consisting of highly effective and up-to-date networks organized around specific issues. Only Poland can boast a genuinely significant and vibrant think-tank community that addresses all areas of research.[10] The research interests of the majority of think-tanks in the six analysed countries are quite broad, and in most of the cases IR represents a rather marginal part of their activities.

The IR research institutes in these countries demonstrate three particular funding profiles. First of all, traditional research institutes receive varying levels of support from their own country's foreign ministry. Think-tanks whose major source of income is grants from NGOs and private foundations make up the second profile. Finally, some post-1989 think-tanks can be characterized by their diversified funding portfolios.

Generally speaking, the primary research interests of the examined research institutions are highly area and currency driven. The EU and NATO enlargements have been at the top of all IR research institutes' agendas. Various schemes of neighborhood cooperation and of regional organization rank next. What is quite notable about the region is the strong strategic and security focus of some of these institutions (this is rivaled only by an international economy perspective) – unsurprisingly given the understanding of IR as peace and war research, which traditionally prevailed within the discipline.

Furthermore, we also explored the academic robustness of IR research. Drawing upon the Freedom House's think-tank directory listing percentage information on the institutes' activities, we have taken three IR and FPA research institutes from the Czech Republic (CERGE-EI, Centre for Democracy and Free Enterprise, and the Institute of International Relations), three from Slovakia (Slovak Institute for International Studies, Slovak Foreign Policy Association, and the Institute for Public Affairs), four from Poland (Adam Smith Research Centre, MCRD Foundation – International Centre for the Development of Democracy Foundation, Centre for Political Thought, and Institute for Public Affairs) and four from Romania (Centre for Euro-Atlantic Studies, Institute for Political and Economic Research, EURISC Foundation, and the Romanian Institute for International Law and International Relations Studies). Subsequently, we divided their activities portfolio shares into two major groups: "soft output," i.e., conferences and seminars; education and training; consulting; public outreach; and advocacy, and "hard output," i.e., publications. Percentage share of the institutes' activities identified as "research" by the Freedom House's directory on the basis of information provided by the organizations themselves was not accounted for, as the final output may be both "soft" and "hard" in this case.[11]

When applying these criteria, we found that most of the research institutes focus on the "soft" rather than the "hard" output of their work. The institutions we examined promote a great deal of academic activity, but most of it consists of "social" academic activity, such as conferences, round tables, and seminars. Most publications are the products of these endeavors, taking the form of conference volumes and working papers. At the same time, however, there is a real dearth of monographs and articles based on genuine research. On average, "soft output" represented nearly 51 percent of the research institutes' initiatives, set against roughly 16 percent of "hard output" activities. Research institutes in the Czech and Slovak Republics demonstrated the highest publishing activity (18.3 percent of all activity), with Poland following at 15.8 percent and Romania last at 10.0 percent. Each of the six countries analyzed, however, has at least three research institutes with active publishing departments, with the exception of Slovenia.

In terms of external influence, all the institutes have been engaged in establishing links with numerous Western institutions, ranging from NGOs and private foundations to universities and partner IR institutes. The strongest extra-regional influence comes from Western Europe. Intensive partnering and networking are shaping both the funding and the research profiles of regional institutions. Although the presence of U.S. funding is strong in the region (for example, the German Marshall Fund and the Ford Foundation, in Slovakia and Poland), extensive funding also comes from Germany in the form of research partnerships (the Konrad Adenauer, Friedrich Ebert, Bertelsmann, and Friedrich Naumann Foundations contribute to the financial and research portfolios of at least one research institute in each country, excluding Slovenia). George Soros' Open Society Fund and the EU's PHARE (Poland and Hungary: Aid for the Restructuring of Economies) programmes also had considerable influence on the institutes we looked at.

The region's IR research institutes more closely resemble European think-tanks and research organizations than American ones. They tend to be organized according to research topics or along political, even party lines. They are often co-funded by their respective governments, and their target audience includes chiefly elites in the civil service sector. This pattern probably at least partially results from the above-mentioned intellectual inspiration and financial support coming from Western European countries into the region.

Universities

Due to the incomplete data obtained – and sometimes even the difficulties in obtaining any data at universities running IR programs[12] – it was not easy to examine IR teaching in the six CEE countries under review.[13] In our analysis, we focused on the three following categories: (1) the institutional background of IR teaching, (2) individual IR teaching institutions, and (3) individual curricula and courses. To analyze the individual teaching institutions, we proceeded from the following five criteria: (1) the number of teaching staff, (2) the nationality of teaching staff, (3) the Ph.D. background of teaching staff, (4) the number of students, and (5) the nationality of students. Lastly, we examined the courses taught in the respective programs by reviewing their syllabi. More specifically, we assessed, in the first place, what areas are covered by the courses.[14]

One of our most important conclusions is that there are three different models of the institutional background of IR teaching at the respective faculties of CEE universities. First, in some cases (Lithuania and Poland) the institution devoted primarily to IR constitutes a self-existing department within a faculty (there is even an IR faculty in Lithuania). Second, in other cases (the Czech Republic and Slovenia) there are IR departments existing as subunits of political science departments. Third, some faculties (Romania and Slovakia) do not have an IR department at all and IR is taught within political science departments.

At most of the faculties a separate IR program exists only at the MA level.[15] In fact, only a minority of faculties has a separate IR program already at the BA level. Whereas this is the case in Poland and Slovenia, in the Czech Republic, Lithuania, Romania, and Slovakia IR is combined with political science at the BA level.[16] Moreover, the number of political science courses in those BA programs prevails considerably over IR courses offered. At the Slovak faculty a separate IR program does not even exist at the MA level.

The typical CEE IR teaching body has between 10 and 20 faculty members,[17] and there are between 50 and 150 students in the related IR MA program(s). On the one hand, there are quite large institutions, such as the Polish IR institute with more than 30 teaching faculty members and the Romanian teaching body of 25 members specializing in IR. In contrast, the Slovak department has only a few IR scholars. The average type is represented by the institutes of the Czech Republic, Lithuania, and Slovenia that have between 10 and 20 IR specialists. Typical IR-related programs at the MA level, such as those of the Czech Republic, Lithuania, Romania, and Slovakia, have altogether between 50 and 150 students in total.

Even though we have only partially succeeded in our "hard" research, regarding the teaching staff's country of origin, drawing on more "soft" indicators such as surnames we can reach the conclusion that institutions under review almost never have foreign members. At the same time, in cases where data regarding Ph.D. backgrounds were available to us (the Czech Republic, Lithuania, Slovakia, and partially Slovenia) we found that the majority of teaching staffs received their Ph.Ds from the same country in which they teach. In addition, domestic students totally prevailed over foreign ones in all institutions that we assessed (again the Czech Republic, Lithuania, Slovakia, and Slovenia). Hence, the characteristic of all university institutions is largely national and not international.

On the contrary, the course topics reflect the IR teaching as it developed in the Anglo-American and Western European domain. In the first place, a great number of courses deal with general IR topics. Only afterwards do courses on area studies and the history of international relations follow. At the same time, all the study programs contain at least one course on IR theories. On the one hand, the lack of data prevents us from judging whether theory courses include an appropriate balance of classical IR theories and later introduced critical approaches. On the other hand, the presence of theory courses in the regional curricula could be as such considered a progressive element. In this way, students get acquainted with at least some conceptual and theoretical issues.

In sum, even though the vast majority of IR teaching staff did their Ph.D. studies at national institutions, those institutions switched during the 1990s to the mainly Anglo-American way of teaching IR. This implies that despite the lack of personal experience with studying IR abroad, IR teaching staff has sought to follow the internationally recognized patterns of teaching. Yet the content and structure of the courses does not, of course, guarantee an overall quality of education. On the contrary, it seems that even though IR teachers were rather flexible as course conveyors, as researchers they have mostly remained to be socialized in the rather low standards of IR research in the region.

Table 14.5 Education at the national level – the main data

	Level of IR institution within university hierarchy	Degree level of IR program (number of programs)	Number of internal teaching staff (specializing in IR)	Number of students (students in programs involving some IR courses)[a]
Czech Republic	A subdepartment within a social science faculty department	MA (1)	10	340 BA – 240 MA – 100
Lithuania	Faculty	MA (3)	17	553 BA – 423 MA – 130
Poland	A faculty department	MA (1, but a 5-year program)	31	1000
Romania	Not existing	MA (1)	25	1060 BA – 1000 MA – 60
Slovakia	Not existing	Not existing (only courses in a 5-year MA political science program)	2	120
Slovenia	A subdepartment within a political science faculty department	BA (1), MA (2)	10	400[b]

Notes
[a] In the case of the Czech Republic, Lithuania, and Romania the BA students study IR courses within their political science programs.
[b] Distribution among BA and MA could not be ascertained.

Regional perspectives

In this section, we examine three IR institutions that may represent the CEE region as a whole: the Central and Eastern European International Studies Association, its journal, the *Journal of International Relations and Development*, and the Central European University. As our analysis will reveal, the discipline seems to be much more qualitatively developed at the regional than at the national level. Unlike the national IR communities, the regional institutions (especially the JIRD and CEU) place a strong emphasis on theories and methods. Nowadays, it seems that regional institutions provide more powerful tools for cultivating local IR research practices and succeeding in its presentation outside of the region than did existing national institutions.

Central and Eastern European International Studies Association (CEEISA)

The CEEISA constitutes a professional organization of CEE IR scholars and has been developing on the regional level since 1996. It was launched by the European Director of the International Affairs Network (IAN) as an organization modeled on the American International Studies Association (ISA). IAN sponsored the first CEEISA annual convention in Prague in 1999 with the participation of leading ISA figures. Anglo-American participants were for a long time the most numerous "outsiders" at the CEEISA conventions (Table 14.6). In particular, the 2003 convention, co-organized with the ISA, saw a massive presence of Anglo-American scholars, the convention's overarching theme being "Global Tensions and Their Challenges to Governance of the International Community," with the September 11 and international security issues becoming quite a "conference within a conference."

Most CEEISA activities have been organized by IR communities in Russia, the Czech Republic, and Slovenia. Due to their size, IAN initially viewed Russia and Poland as regional hubs for the CEEISA. The first president of the CEEISA was Russian. Russian scholars always constituted a large number of participants at annual conferences and the 2002 convention held jointly with RISA and NISA[18] was convened in Moscow. The Polish IR community also played a key role in CEEISA's development as organizers of the second annual convention in 2000 – the first convention held without IAN funding. Later on, however, the Polish presence declined. The Czech connection to the CEEISA resides mainly in the fact that the European IAN Director used to be based in Prague. Prague (University of Economics) also provided infrastructure and support for the CEEISA president between 1999 and 2005 and its secretariat. In addition, for a long time Slovenia (University of Ljubljana) produced the CEEISA's official journal (see below) and convention staff. The described activity of the aforementioned local IR communities indicates that the CEEISA is self-sustaining, which was further reinforced by introducing fee-based membership,[19] again modeled on the Western IR community.

The analysis of papers presented at the past CEEISA annual conferences shows that the most favored topics include international security, European integration, regional issues, and Russia (Table 14.7). Besides "Russia," these topics coincide with the most popular issues addressed by articles published in the regional journals. The convention papers dealing with Russia are usually presented by Russian participants to explain their quantitative prominence, especially at the 2002 Moscow convention. In addition, the huge number of papers on international security and global issues must be attributed to the presence of ISA scholars at the 2002 and 2003 conventions.

Table 14.6 Participants at the CEEISA conventions (chairs, panelists, and paper-givers)[a]

	Prague 1999	Warsaw 2000	Moscow 2002	Budapest 2003	Tartu 2006
U.S.A.	8	7	16	384[b]	16
UK	0	11[c]	32	88	21
Western Europe	1	9	36	142	61
Central and Eastern Europe	33	38	97	116	86
Other	1	2	13	150	21

Notes
[a] By institutional affiliation.
[b] A very large but not a dominant proportion of U.S.-based scholars at the 2003 joint convention were CEE students/academics currently at U.S. universities and/or research institutes.
[c] Most of the participants from the UK were Central and Eastern Europeans currently at British universities. The same applied in 2002 and, to a much lesser extent, in 2003.

Table 14.7 Topics of the papers presented at the conventions

	Prague 1999	Warsaw 2000	Moscow 2002	Budapest 2003	Tartu 2006
EU enlargement	7	10	27	48	19
CEE as a region	7	11	16	24	25
Russia and CIS	4	14	40	33	21
European security	5	7	88	40	22
Global issues, IR theory	6	6	26	201	19
Culture and ethnicity	4	0	14	42	4
IR studies	3	2	3	18	12
Other	2	4	15	223	67

Journal of International Relations and Development (JIRD)

JIRD was launched by the University of Ljubljana in 1998. Since 1999, JIRD has been the official journal of the CEEISA. There is a significant "regional division of labor" in the production of the journal. Although the main editorial office was opened in Ljubljana, JIRD's book review section is edited in Prague at the Institute of International Relations. As of 2004 the journal is now published by Palgrave Macmillan, joining the family of quality IR journals. JIRD clearly differs from the journals discussed above. First of all, the members of the editorial board are mostly from outside the region. Only approximately a quarter of almost 70 board members work at institutions in the CEE region. Furthermore, the editorial board is composed of the most prominent IR scholars. The journal is currently being co-edited by a scholar residing outside the region (Stefano Guzzini, Danish Institute of International Studies and Uppsala University) and a scholar working at a regional institution (Milan Brglez, University of Ljubljana).

Moreover, JIRD has introduced the strict standards of Western scholarly journals, using a double-blind peer review system, and has included prominent IR scholars as reviewers. The consequence of this policy is that articles published in JIRD are competitive by Western academic standards. JIRD articles typically exhibit a solid theoretical framework and their authors – almost all of them academics – are familiar with the "state-of-the-art" literature on their topics. Table 14.8 reveals that the distribution of topics is comparable with those of the national journals. A rather stark exception to this has been the very high share (40 percent) of theoretical articles, which perhaps would not be surprising in a Western journal. Similarly, much more attention is paid to global issues. Otherwise, regional issues rank among the top themes and the share of European integration coverage is similar to the shares in national journals. The data assembled in the 1998 to 2003 period revealed that sources from the Anglo-American province were quoted in 96 percent of the articles, Western European sources coming second (80 percent).

Although JIRD represents an official journal of CEEISA, only a small share of articles published in the journal is produced by scholars from the region. In fact, only about 15 percent of JIRD writers worked in institutions in CEE countries. The proportions of authors from German-speaking countries and Nordic contributors reached a similar level (approximately 15 percent for each). The share of Anglo-American contributors was almost 40 percent. Unlike other national IR journals, the high proportion of foreign authors in JIRD may be seen as a contribution to the professionalization of IR in CEE. Since the articles published by foreign authors in JIRD reveal a high level of theoretical and methodological quality, their presence can help increase academic standards in the regional IR.[20]

Table 14.8 Articles in the *Journal of International Relations and Development* (JIRD), by topic (%)

Articles	1998	1999	2000	2001	2002	2003	2004	2005	2006	Total	Ratio
CEE	60	4	50	6	36	6	13	8	0	26	18
EU	10	32	0	18	12	0	6	15	18	20	14
IR theory/social theory	30	44	7	41	18	56	56	46	47	59	40
UN, global issues	0	20	36	12	0	17	13	23	35	28	19
Other	0	0	7	23	34	21	12	8	0	14	10
Total	10	25	14	17	17	18	16	13	17	147	
Ratio	7	17	10	12	12	12	11	9	12		

Central European University (CEU)

The CEU is an internationally recognized postgraduate social science and humanities institution. Established in April 1989 as the Inter-University Centre, it has been funded by George Soros. As of 2001 to 2002, 858 students from more than 40 countries were enrolled. The Department of International Relations and European Studies (IRES) launched its first MA program in IR and European Studies in June 1994, originally accredited by the Open University (UK). In 2004, the program was registered with the Department of Education in the State of New York. IRES offers two degree programs: an MA in IR and European Studies (a ten-month course) and a Ph.D. specialization in IR, available under the Ph.D. program within the Department of Political Science (a three-year course).

When exploring IR teaching at CEU, we drew upon our analysis of the IRES 2000/2001, 2001/2002, 2002/2003 and 2003/2004 curricula, 2001/2002 newly enrolled student profile, and 2000/2001 and 2003/2004 Ph.D.-awarding universities of teaching staff. These data reveal that the CEU (thus IRES as well) has become the regional academic hub. In the academic year of 2001/2002, there was a total of 485 applications to IRES from 28 CEE and former Soviet states.

While functioning as an important academic center of the region, the CEU has also built upon, has been shaped by, and currently displays distinct features of the Anglo-American academic tradition. As the authors of IRES curricula claim and the syllabi clearly reveal, the programs seek to build on the strong tradition of the discipline in the United States. Thus, the most prominent feature is their focus on training students in analytical thinking, critical research methods, and comprehensive study, accompanied by clear and mature academic writing and presentation skills. Clearly, this is an imported feature in the region (in terms of its recent history). During the communist era, not only IR but virtually all of the social sciences did not exist as academic subjects and the fall of communism brought about their rapid development. Strangely enough, although the development of social sciences led to a greater awareness of the importance of theory, methodological standards have not been considered equally significant. Thus, academic writing has hardened a string of never-ending, complex, and almost unreadable phrases lacking clearness of argument, dynamics, taste and invention and, last but not least, comprehensive and evidence-backed conclusions.

One explanation for this could be the absence of methodological courses in the university curricula. Although the younger generation of students or scholars was introduced to theories, they have hardly had an occasion to make themselves familiar with methods. This can be accounted for by the fact that most of the regional scholars (and teachers) do themselves a purely descriptive form of research lacking any theoretical and methodological framework. It seems that even though the regional IR community has come to be (in theory) aware of the significance of theories, it has not yet understood the importance of methodologies without which a relevant application of theories is not possible.

Apart from training in research methods, all IRES students receive an education in the major theories of IR, IPE, and European integration. The strength of Anglo-American tradition may also be seen in the curricula vitae of the IRES teaching staff. In 2000 to 2001 and 2003 to 2004, most of the IRES faculty members had Ph.Ds from Western universities (with a majority from the Anglo-American area).

The internal structures of IR in the CEE

To make a deeper assessment of IR in the CEE, we analyze both its internal structures and position in the global IR structure. With regard to internal structures, we concentrate on identifying the actors who determine the process in which the discipline's members seek to be recognized as competent specialists. In other words, we ask who holds power in the regional discipline. In order to tackle this question, we proceed from Ole Wæver's application of Richard Whitley's model to the sociology of IR (Wæver 1998, 2007). We thus explore mutual dependence and task uncertainty as two crucial features of any scientific field.

Mutual dependence

The Whitley model highlights two distinct types of dependence: functional and strategic (Whitley 1984 in Wæver 2007: 23–27). Functional dependence basically refers to the extent to which researchers depend on the results of other researchers of the very same discipline. It thus reflects the degree to which "researchers have to use the specific results, ideas and procedures of fellow specialists" (Whitley 1984: 88 in Wæver 2007: 23). If functional dependence is high, the coordination of task outcomes and adherence to common competence standards become crucial. Strategic dependence is the extent to which researchers need to persuade their colleagues of the importance of their research problem and approach to achieve a high reputation. When strategic dependence is high, researchers have to primarily coordinate their research strategies.

Like in IR in general, functional dependence is low in IR in the CEE (see Wæver 2007: 23–24). On the contrary, the regional discipline appears to differ from the global IR model[21] due to a rather low level of strategic dependence. This is so because IR research in the CEE is heavily oriented on purely empirical analysis and more theoretical discussions about specific research strategies as the most important precondition of a high strategic dependence are virtually absent.

Nevertheless, IR scholars in the CEE do of course need to obtain some recognition from their colleagues if they want to pursue an academic career. In this respect, the regional IR coincides with the global IR due to the importance of publications as a means of recognition-seeking. Regarding the value of the various types of publications, there is little indication that one particular type of publication (monographs, book chapters, journal articles) would be privileged over others. For instance, there is no hierarchy of journals which exists in the global IR and which puts a premium on publishing in top journals. Furthermore, not many local IR researchers are able to publish in international journals or at prestigious foreign publishers. Domestic publications are thus perceived as relevant proof of an academic qualification.

This state of affairs crucially influences the power of individual actors in national IR fields. Unlike in the global IR, power is not concentrated in the CEE around journals and their editors and reviewers. This is not to say that editors and editorial boards do not affect reputation prospects at all. Journal publications certainly constitute one of the relevant publication outputs, and the general absence of a peer-review system actually provides journal editors with a unique control over what is published. Still, the editors of collective volumes play a similarly or even more significant role in the process of recognition-seeking. Considerable power is therefore held by heads of local research institutions since they function most frequently as initiators and editors of collective volumes, and in this way give individual researchers an opportunity to publish.

Recognition-seeking in IR in the CEE is to some extent also determined by academic entrepreneurs from abroad, namely from Western Europe (particularly from Germany). It is a matter of fact that the majority of IR researchers in the region publish mostly at the domestic level. Still, national IR communities do also recognize the significance of publishing outside the region. Since most of the regional researchers have little chance of presenting their work in prestigious international journals due to the absence of any theoretical and methodological basis, they concentrate their quest for foreign publications on contributing to edited volumes. For this reason, Western European scholars acting as volume editors also play an important role in the IR publication system in the CEE. In fact, they give the majority of local scholars the only opportunity to publish outside the region. Local researchers typically contribute to such volumes with articles presenting some data on a particular CEE country or countries.

Task uncertainty

The Whitley model also distinguishes two types of task uncertainty: technical and strategic task uncertainty (Whitley 1984 in Wæver 2007: 27–29). Whereas technical task uncertainty is equal to the extent to which work techniques are well understood and research results reliable, strategic uncertainty is mainly related to uncertainty about intellectual priorities and the relevance of research topics, strategies, and outcomes.

Unlike in the global IR model, technical task uncertainty is quite low in IR in the CEE. As we have repeatedly mentioned above, the IR research in the region usually lacks any theoretical and methodological elements. Published books and articles typically offer chronological (historical) or thematically structured descriptions of the analyzed processes and events. Consequently, local researchers do not face a high technical uncertainty because the empirical collection of facts as the underlying procedure of descriptive research is simple and quite comprehensible.

Strategic task uncertainty also appears to be low since research priorities and topics are structured by the heritage of the communist era and current political developments. First, let us recall that IR research was rather limited and ideologically biased during communist times. Individual IR subdisciplines (e.g. foreign policy analysis, conflict studies) did not exist at all. After the fall of the communist regimes, there has therefore been a large intellectual vacuum in the IR field. Under those circumstances, one dominant and apparent research priority emerged – to carry out some basic research on the most significant IR topics previously studied in the global IR discipline before the fall of communism. A high number of monographs, textbooks, and articles basically surveying the state of the art have subsequently been published. Second, as our analysis of topics dominating in journals confirms, research has also been substantially guided by the perceived importance of the EU, and also NATO and the effort of CEE countries to join those organizations. Hence, the low task uncertainty limits the ability of any actor to manipulate what qualifies as a relevant research output.

Up until now, we have discussed the recognition-seeking pursued by individual researchers and the power of actors that influence this process. To make the outline of the internal structures of IR in CEE complete, we also need to take into account the material dependence of collective IR research institutions on various actors providing the necessary financial resources. In our above-presented research, we have already highlighted the considerable involvement of state funding in IR research in the CEE. As described, a high number of research institutions in the region are funded by state ministries. In addition, a large part of research institutions (especially think-tanks) rest on the financial resources coming from especially foreign NGOs and private foundations. Hence, while the careers of individual scholars rely mainly on their publications and the related mutual recognition, the very existence of collective research institutions is based on state, public, or private funding.

In sum, our preliminary conclusion would be that the internal structures of IR in the CEE are marked by a rather diffused distribution of power. The academic reputation of individual researchers depends on their publication results, but there is no clear hierarchy of publications. The control over academic reputation is thus shared by the heads of local academic institutions, editors of domestic journals as well as foreign academic entrepreneurs. What somehow diminishes the power of those actors is that IR research in CEE is based on relatively apparent and comprehensible research procedures and priorities. The diffusion of power may also be observed at the level of collective research institutions, where in general no monopoly of funding exists.

The CEE discipline in the global IR structure

As the existing literature shows, regional IR disciplines are often evaluated in terms of whether they are part of the core or the periphery within the entire IR discipline (Aydinli and Mathews 2000: 291; Friedrichs 2004: 1–23; Jørgensen 2000; Tickner 2003: 326; Wæver 1998). More specifically, we rely on two established methods of distinguishing the core from the periphery. First, we judge the level of abstractness of the professional activities of IR in the CEE. Second, we focus on the nature and intensity of communication between the IR community in CEE and IR communities in other parts of the world (both methods are described in more detail below).

The level of abstractness

In line with several existing studies we assume that core parts of the discipline concentrate not only on empirically but also on theoretically focused research. In this way, Sonia Lucarelli and Roberto Menotti, drawing on Joseph Lepgold, make a distinction between two basic types of literature and professional activities in IR: theory-building and policy applications (Lucarelli and Menotti 2006: 49–51). While theory-building involves both general theoretical and issue-oriented research, policy applications include case-oriented explanations and policy-making. Similarly, Ersel Aydinli and Julie Mathews (2000: 292–293) divide theoretical/conceptual contributions from policy/case studies. In our analysis we use the two mentioned categories of theoretically and empirically focused research, not just for the classification of journal articles, but also for the assessment of the relevant features of research institutes and the educational process. We presume that while the center deals both with theory-building and policy applications, policy applications dominate in the periphery.

Our inquiry about the state of IR in the CEE clearly demonstrates that in most professional activities significantly more attention is paid to empirically oriented research rather than theoretical. With regard to journals, theoretical and conceptual research does not exceed 20 percent in any of the analyzed titles. In the majority of the journals the theoretically driven work actually drops below 6 percent. Similarly, the output of research institutions is also marked by the prevalence of empirical contributions.

Nevertheless, it is IR education which lessens the limited presence of theory within the regional discipline, since all examined study programs offered at least one course on IR theories. In addition, the curricula place a stronger emphasis on general IR issues rather than international history or area studies. The theoretical wheel is furthermore fueled by the regional level of the discipline. The regional journal, academic conferences, and teaching style display a domination of theoretical and conceptual issues over purely empirical ones.

External and internal communication

Proceeding from the often quoted model of IR's center and periphery, developed by Kalevi J. Holsti, we also categorize IR in the CEE on the basis of its communication with the other parts of the discipline. According to Holsti's model, the periphery is defined by these three features: (1) marginality, (2) penetration, and (3) fragmentation (Holsti 1985: 145 in Friedrichs 2004: 51). First, a regional IR discipline may be considered marginal if the periphery relies more on its communication with the core than the core does on its communication with the periphery (marginality). Second, another significant feature of the periphery is that communications with other peripheries are underdeveloped compared to the density and intensity of communication with the center (penetration). Third, communication of the periphery with the center is more dense and intense than communication within the periphery (fragmentation).

Our data as well as our "anthropological" experience lead us to claim that IR in the CEE may be described according to Holsti's terminology as marginal, weakly penetrated, and fragmented. First, it appears to be indisputable that IR in the CEE relies on its communication with the Western core more than vice versa. To emphasize this, in all the examined journals (including the regional journal JIRD) except for the Polish one, the references to Anglo-American and Western European literature amount to more than 50 percent. In addition, the share of Anglo-American contributors in JIRD was higher than the share of scholars from the region. With regard to research institutes, many of them, including the regional association CEEISA, depended or still depend on funding from the U.S. or Western Europe. The general profiles and curricula of IR study programs in the CEE have also been inspired by U.S. and Western European models.

By contrast, the Western core does not depend on the CEE in any of the ways outlined above. Contributions by CEE scholars to journals of the core, as well as references to CEE literature, are marginal from the overall perspective. In addition, the region does not provide the core with any substantial material aid or intellectual models.

Second, communication of the CEE discipline with the Western core is far more developed than communication with other peripheries. Briefly, in all examined indicators the authors, literature sources, financial resources, or intellectual models related to the core massively dominate the same factors flowing into the CEE discipline from other peripheries.

Third, external communication with the Western core is also more dense and intense than internal communication within the regional discipline. Again, references to CEE sources occupy a much lower share in the CEE IR journals than references to the Anglo-American and Western European literature. Even though there is some cooperation among CEE research institutes and universities, more developed exchanges certainly occur between CEE institutions and institutions from the core. More specifically, CEE institutions concentrate their outside relations primarily on research networking (research institutions) or student exchange (universities) with Western European countries and to some extent also with the U.S.

The fragmentation of the CEE discipline is partially weakened by the existence of regional institutions. The most important of these, the CEEISA, is a stable institution and its conference platforms ensure that there is some lasting communication among CEE scholars. However, the described activities of regional institutions do not alter the fragmented character of the regional discipline. First of all, the substance of the discipline's life certainly resides in the national communities, which remain in some respects closed and in others one-sidedly open to the Western core.

In addition, one cannot overlook the fact that regional institutions represent channels of regional communication only to a limited extent. As mentioned above, CEEISA's functioning is largely based on the activities of a few national communities. In the same vein, JIRD can hardly be interpreted as a forum of exchange among regional scholars since they make up only a small part of the journal's authors. Lastly, the existence of the CEU IR study program and limited exchanges of students among CEE universities do not substantially diminish the fact that the large majority of CEE IR students either graduate solely at the national level or conduct some of their studies at Western European universities.

Resemblance to other models of IR

Finally, the analysis of internal structures and global position of IR in the CEE give us an opportunity to assess (or rather summarize) its resemblance to IR communities in other parts of the world. The character of the internal structures of the regional IR community in CEE does not reveal a stronger resemblance to any other regional IR.[22] After assessing all the similarities and differences, one could tentatively conclude that the CEE region is probably closest to the German model in which local heads of IR institutions (professors) have the greatest leverage over the publication achievements of scholars. Yet we have also emphasized that in CEE countries this leverage is balanced by a significant role of foreign academic entrepreneurs and, to some extent, also domestic journal editors. On the contrary, IR in CEE does not have an affinity with the U.S. system, where the discipline is dominated by key journals controlled by leading theorists. CEE countries also appear to be far from the French model (a hierarchy within specializations).

In terms of its global position, IR in the CEE also does not really follow any of the European IR models that were previously described in the literature (Friedrichs 2004; Schmidt 2006: 264–265). Due to low abstraction and the one-sided significance of communication, CEE countries are not similar to those parts of Europe that have managed to develop their own distinct research and simultaneously participate in the American agenda. The countries belonging to this group such as Britain, Germany, and the Nordic countries do in fact constitute part of, or at least a "periphery" of, the core. Unlike France, CEE countries have not produced original, even though rather isolated, theoretical findings. Furthermore, the CEE even seems to be distanced from the Italian way of marginalized research, the reason being that although the Italian IR relies solely on theoretical imports from the core, a large part of Italian research is still theoretically informed (Friedrichs 2004; Lucarelli and Menotti 2006).

Conclusion

Our analysis of the national level of IR in the CEE reveals that national IR communities are marked by a continued lack of sophistication in theories and methods. In terms of the research focus, there is a distinct drive towards topicality and a CEE-centered approach. While the CEE is topically centered, regional research still fails to draw on the general, Western mainstream set of concepts. Moreover, CEE research simultaneously has not developed any appropriate general concepts and perspectives that would refer to the local context.

Furthermore, we also observe a strong state influence in the funding sources of IR research as well as state presence on editorial boards. The more independent regional research institute community is still in its earliest stages. In terms of extra-regional intellectual influence, it is the Anglo-American and Western European literature that seem to have taken hold in the six countries we examined. This is largely due to the fact that the domestic institutional and educational background is still rather unproductive. Clearly, the histories of totalitarian rule, the shortage of academic human resources, and the relative youth of the discipline contribute to this state of affairs.

In contrast, at the regional level, the discipline seems much more robust. Driving these strengths is the Anglo-American "know-how" that was identified as the model. This reliance on Anglo-American models allows the regional discipline strict academic standards for research but poses questions of autonomy.

In terms of the internal power distribution within national IR communities, the control over academic reputation is shared by several types of actor. The position of CEE countries in the global IR structure indicates their peripheral status. Overall, the regional discipline displays peculiar features rather than a proximity to any particular IR communities existing in other parts of the world.

Despite the obvious weaknesses of IR in the CEE which we have pointed out, our data also show the possibility of alleviating weaknesses over a period of time, in which the regional discipline could reach a less peripheral status. There are several prospects of such a change in the near future. First, theory has achieved its place in the analyzed national IR curricula. This implies that recent or future IR graduates who will begin their work in academia are more likely to be able to produce theoretically informed research. At the regional level, the teaching of theory is also supplemented with a regional journal that involves a high proportion of theoretically inclined articles. Second, the fragmentation of the CEE discipline may be weakened by the continual development of regional institutions. Third, the small size of IR national communities allows those entrepreneurial individuals interested in importing a professional academic culture the opportunity to do so.

Notes

1   This chapter draws upon findings from a more extensive research the initial phase of which was captured in Petr Drulák and Lucie Königová: "The Discipline of IR in Central and Eastern Europe," discussion paper prepared for the ECPR Conference on Political Science Research in Eastern Europe, November 9–10, 2001. A summary of these findings was published in a special issue of the EPS journal (Drulák and Königová 2002). The authors would like to thank Vít Beneš, Denis Gibadulin, Georgis Krahulík, Jana Krajčíková, Petr Reimer, and Zuzana Vilčeková for their assistance with data collection.
2   Even though several attempts have already been made at reflecting on the state of the discipline in some parts of the CEE (Drulák and Druláková 2000, 2006; Sergounin 2000).
3   Our analysis is particularly strongly anchored in the state of the discipline in the first half of 2004 when most of the data were collected or completed, but the analytical reflections are current as of late 2007.

4 Scholarly journals may be considered the flagships of the discipline, serving to inform about various topics, methodologies, and contributors. They reflect the life of the discipline as well as the quality of the research (Wæver 1998).

5 Unfortunately, our analysis of the *Lithuanian Foreign Policy Review* and *Romanian Journal of International Relations* covers only the years 1998 to 2003 as the 2004 to 2006 volumes of those journals were not available to us. Besides this main limitation, one of the 2002 *Lithuanian Foreign Policy Review* issues was not available. Neither were the 2003 and 2005 issues of the *Polish Quarterly of International Affairs* available completely. Finally, the 4/2003 issue of *Medzinárodné otázky* was not available for research.

6 There is no English-language IR journal in Slovenia (the one dealing with political science and published in Slovenian is unavailable in the Czech Republic). On the other hand, this is quite understandable and easily explicable since the University of Ljubljana has long provided the ground and both infrastructural and academic support for the JIRD, the regional IR journal analyzed later in this chapter.

7 We take into account only references to books and articles and we exclude references to documents, speeches, and so on.

8 We had previously compiled a basic list of CEE think-tanks using the second edition of *Freedom House's Think Tanks in Central and Eastern Europe* (http://www.ngonet.org/ttd2idx.htm), the updated version of the *National Institute for Research Advancement's (NIRA) World Directory of Think Tanks* (http://www.nira.go.jp/ice/tt-info/nwdtt/index.html) and the ISN Partner Network (http://www.isn.ethz.ch/index.cfm). Our analysis was largely based on information about research institutes that we found through the internet.

9 Academies of science usually represent scientific non-university institutions. They involve a high number of research institutions ranging from natural to social sciences and humanities. The primary aim of academies of science is to conduct theoretical as well as applied research.

10 As many as eight IR/FPA research institutes have been identified in Poland. In Lithuania, on the other hand, there is neither an IR think-tank nor an IR research institution similar to the other CEE countries researched since the main research institution in Lithuania is the Institute of International Relations and Political Science (IIRPS) at the Vilnius University, functioning primarily as a place of education, and only then as a research center – though a highly influential one. The other think-tank identified is linked personally and otherwise to the IIRPS but we have not been able to obtain any specific information on this one, collecting and analyzing only scattered data in effect.

11 No information in that respect has been found on the two Lithuanian IR think-tanks (see above), and no Slovenian IR think-tank or research institute that meets our criteria has been identified.

12 We have not managed to obtain, by any means, any data on the curriculum and syllabi of the Department of International Relations, Faculty of Political Science, University of Bucharest (Romania).

13 IR is taught at a few universities in each of the six countries examined. For our analysis of IR curricula, however, we have chosen only the institutions that have built (perhaps) the most developed and extensive undergraduate and postgraduate IR study programmes in the respective countries, to reflect on the six countries' "national academic IR hubs." The institutions under review were: Department of International Relations, Institute of Political Studies, Faculty of Social Science, Charles University, Prague (Czech Republic); Institute of International Relations and Political Science, Vilnius University, Vilnius (Lithuania); Institute of International Relations, Faculty of Journalism and Social Science, University of Warsaw, Warsaw (Poland); Department of International Relations, Faculty of Political Science, University of Bucharest, Bucharest (Romania); Department of Political Science, Faculty of Arts, Comenius University, Bratislava (Slovakia); and Department of Political Science, Faculty of Social Science, Ljubljana (Slovenia).

14 As far as the nationality of teaching staff is concerned, we were ultimately forced to draw on rather "soft" though clear-cut indicators (see below). Regarding the syllabi, we managed to get at least the course lists of all the faculties. Nevertheless, in some cases the lists or syllabi available to us indicated only the mandatory courses (Poland, Romania).

15 Here we do not pay particular attention to Ph.D. programs as more concrete data from the public sources on those programs are relatively limited.

16 However, it is necessary to point out that at the Slovak and Polish faculty, the BA and MA levels are, at least regarding IR, not separated from each other. In effect, they are five-year MA programs covering both the otherwise distinguished BA and MA level.

17 In the numbers of teaching staff we include only the internal members of the institution.
18 RISA is the Russian International Studies Association and NISA is the Nordic International Studies Association.
19 As of March 10, 2004 there were 333 records in the CEEISA Membership Database.
20 We thank Ole Wæver for suggesting this interpretation. According to the World of Science database, JIRD became indexed in the Social Science Citation Index as late as 2008.
21 Here we refer to "the American-partly-turned-global discipline." See Wæver (1998: 717).
22 On different models of internal IR structures, see Wæver (1998: 719–720).

References

Aydinli, Ersel and Julie Mathews (2000) "Are the Core and Periphery Irreconcilable? The Curious World of Publishing in Contemporary International Relations," *International Studies Perspectives*, 1 (3): 289–303.

Drulák, Petr and Radka Druláková (2000) "International Relations in the Czech Republic: A Review of the Discipline," *Journal of International Relations and Development*, 3 (3): 256–282.

Drulák, Petr and Radka Druláková (2006) "The Czech Republic," in Knud Erik Jørgensen and Tonny B. Knudsen (eds), *International Relations in Europe: Traditions, Perspectives and Destinations*, London: Routledge, pp. 172–196.

Drulák, Petr and Lucie Königová (2002) "The Discipline of IR in Central and Eastern Europe. European Political Science," *European Political Science*, 1 (3): 47–53.

Friedrichs, Jörg (2001) "International Relations Theory in France," *Journal of International Relations and Development*, 4 (2): 118–137.

Friedrichs, Jörg (2004) *European Approaches to International Relations Theory: A House with Many Mansions*, London: Routledge.

Guzzini, Stefano (2001) "The Significance and Roles of Teaching Theory in International Relations," *Journal of International Relations and Development*, 4 (2): 98–117.

Hoffmann, Stanley (1977) "An American Social Science: International Relations," *Dædalus*, 106 (3): 41–60.

Holsti, Kalevi J. (1985) *The Dividing Discipline: Hegemony and Diversity in International Theory*, Boston, MA: Allen & Unwin.

Jørgensen, Knud E. (2000) "Continental IR Theory: The Best Kept Secret," *European Journal of International Relations*, 6 (1): 9–42.

Krupavičius, Algis (1997) "The Development of Political Science in Lithuania: Years of Breakthrough," *European Journal of Political Research*, 31 (4): 499–517.

Lopata, Raimundas (1999) "Political Science in Lithuania: The Formation and Development of a New Academic Discipline and Scientific Investigations," *Lithuanian Foreign Policy Review*, 2 (4), available at http://www.lfpr.lt/uploads/File/1999-4/Political.pdf.

Lucarelli, Sonia and Roberto Menotti (2006) "Italy," in Knud Erik Jørgensen and Tonny B. Knudsen (eds), *International Relations in Europe: Traditions, Perspectives and Destinations*, London: Routledge, pp. 47–71.

Schmidt, Brian C. (2006) "Epilogue," in Knud Erik Jørgensen and Tonny B. Knudsen (eds), *International Relations in Europe: Traditions, Perspectives and Destinations*, London: Routledge, pp. 253–269.

Sergounin, Alexander (2000) "Russian Post-Communist Foreign Policy Thinking at the Cross-roads: Changing Paradigms," *Journal of International Relations and Development*, 3 (3): 216–255.

Tickner, Arlene (2003) "Hearing Latin American Voices in IR," *International Studies Perspectives*, 4 (4): 325–350.

Wæver, Ole (1998) "The Sociology of a Not So International Discipline: American and European Development in International Relations," *International Organization*, 52 (4): 687–727.

Wæver, Ole (2007) "The Social and Intellectual Structure of the IR Discipline," paper presented at the annual meeting of the International Studies Association (ISA), Chicago (Illinois), U.S.A., February 28 to March 3.

Whitley, Richard (1984) *The Intellectual and Social Organization of the Sciences*, Oxford: Clarendon Press.

15 Western Europe

Structure and strategy at the national and regional levels

Jörg Friedrichs and Ole Wæver[1]

Is IR in Western Europe moving from a situation of American hegemony towards a more balanced pattern based on national or regional professionalization (Wæver 1998)? Is there a chance that Western European IR may become "a house with many mansions" where national communities of scholars are integrated into a wider community (Friedrichs 2004)?[2]

To provide an answer to these questions – and a few more along the way – this chapter starts with a typology of the "mansions" that may constitute a common European "house." Since American hegemony is a fact of life for any IR community worldwide, our typology follows the distinctive ways in which peripheral communities cope with American hegemony. A distinction is made between three typical "coping strategies": academic self-reliance as in France, resigned marginality as in Italy, and multi-level research cooperation as in the Nordic countries. Each strategy represents a distinct way of coping with American intellectual hegemony. Statistics from leading journals published in the English lingua franca are provided to show how each strategy impacts on the international presence of scholarly production.

In the second section we reflect on the reasons for the systematic differences between these "typical" IR communities in Western Europe. We consider different modes of intellectual and social organization, the different political and theoretical agendas to which they correspond, the relations to the political and societal structures of authority in which they are embedded, and the historically evolved relationship of IR with other academic disciplines.

The third section looks at the standing of European IR within the global discipline. How does Europe contribute to the global discipline in qualitative and quantitative terms? We will not look from the bottom up as in the first half of the chapter, surveying local settings. Instead, we will look from the top down, asking how much European IR is present in the discipline at large in terms of publications, personalities, and production of theory.

The fourth section takes a more sociological view. If not necessarily an explanation, it will provide at least a contextualization. Under what conditions is IR scholarship produced in Europe? To which forces are scholars exposed, both in terms of opportunities and constraints? We will draw on concepts from the sociology of science introduced in the third section (and in Chapter 1 of this book): Robert Merton's "CUDOS-norms" and "mode one" versus "mode two" research.

Finally, we reflect on the prospects for European IR. Is European IR bound to fall back into a situation where different national communities of scholars share little apart from their continued subordination to the American core of the discipline? Are national IR communities heading towards gradual emancipation and autonomy, at the level of either individual states or language areas? Or can Europe become, as far as IR scholarship is concerned, "a house of many mansions where there will be room for all" (Churchill 1940)?

Coping with marginality

From a bird's-eye view, Western European communities of International Relations scholars are all peripheries to the American core, or at least to its mainstream.[3] This is not to deny that other regions of the world are even more on the periphery – so much so that Western European IR is a semi-periphery rather than a true periphery to American IR (Aydinli and Mathews 2000; Giesen 2006: 20; Guzzini 2007). But regardless of whether we define them as peripheries or semi-peripheries, all Western European IR communities stand in a center–periphery relationship to the American mainstream. For reasons that will become clear during this chapter, intellectual deference to American intellectual hegemony is particularly intense in Europe because American IR is vividly present to European scholars – keenly followed, journals read, debates interpreted – in contrast to much of the rest of the world, where current American IR is given much less attention (cf. concluding chapter in the book).

It is in the very nature of such a constellation that the peripheries cannot help but try to cope with their own marginal position. Given the relative isolation of the peripheries from one another, which is a typical corollary of the center–periphery constellation, it is not surprising that different peripheries try different solutions to this fundamental problem. This provides a common ground of comparison between Western European IR communities.

In the face of American intellectual hegemony, three different coping strategies have been adopted by European IR communities: academic self-reliance, resigned marginality, and multi-level research cooperation. The first strategy, academic self-reliance, consists in the dissociation of a community of scholars from the American core. French IR provides the epitome of this strategy in Western Europe.[4] The opposite way, resigned marginality, is taken by those scholarly communities which have learnt to accept their position at the fringes of the discipline. Italian IR is a typical case, while the situation in Spain does not seem to be very different. A third strategy consists in multi-level research cooperation, where academic resources are pooled at different levels in order to create a more vibrant arena for research competition and a larger body of resonance for scholarly production. IR scholars from the Nordic countries have been very successful with the third strategy, but one may speculate whether scholars from the German- and Dutch-speaking areas are embarking, or have already embarked, on a similar path. With a gradual strengthening of the European level, one may further speculate if multi-level research cooperation will be the dominant strategy.[5]

French, Italian, and Nordic IR are interesting because they represent three characteristic strategies for coping with intellectual hegemony. Other European IR communities may be associated, and we can therefore limit ourselves to a brief summary of French, Italian, and Nordic IR (see Table 15.1 for an overview; further details in Friedrichs 2004: 25–83).[6]

Western European IR is too "big" to list all major theorists or textbook authors. Within the scope of this chapter, it is only possible to identify the most relevant trends and patterns. For at least two reasons, we risk making ourselves unpopular among colleagues: first, due to our failure to mention some valuable contributions; and second, because we treat what

Table 15.1 Typology of IR communities in Western Europe

	Academic self-reliance	*Resigned marginality*	*Multi-level research cooperation*
Paradigmatic example	France	Italy	Nordic countries
Other examples	–	Spain	Dutch- and German-speaking areas

most country/region travelogues are reluctant to talk about: power structures and disciplinary mechanisms.

Academic self-reliance

During most of the past half-century, the French community of IR scholars has been pursuing a strategy of academic self-reliance. Already in the 1950s, American IR was construed as an "Other" from which French IR should keep as distant as possible (Duroselle 1952; Grosser 1956). Since then, three post-war generations of leading IR scholars have deliberately opted for academic self-reliance in the face of American intellectual hegemony.[7]

The deliberately inward-looking character of the French IR community has had two important consequences. First, French IR is at a greater distance from the Anglo-American mainstream than any other Western European community of scholars (Lyons 1982; Hopmann 1994; Groom 2005). Second, this distance is reciprocated both by the Anglo-American mainstream and by most Western European communities of International Relations scholars.

With few exceptions, IR scholarship from France is ignored abroad. Probably the French scholar most prominent in the wider international public is the late Raymond Aron (1962), one of the godfathers of realism in the 1960s, who was popularized in the United States by his Franco-American disciple Stanley Hofmann. Other historical figures of French IR theory, such as Pierre Renouvin and Marcel Merle, are hardly known abroad (Frank 2003).

Only in the 1990s was Bertrand Badie identified as a French representative of the "reflective" approach to IR theory (Leander 1997). In fact, the "political sociology" of this author offers an interesting synthesis of historical sociology, comparative politics, international relations, and diplomatic studies (Badie 1999, 2008). He provides powerful tools to account for the ongoing transformation of the international system, which are ready to be applied by scholars from other countries or regions of the world – for example, from Africa (Sindjoun 2002).

Another interesting case is Didier Bigo who became, in one decade, the second most visible French scholar abroad. After a promising start in the study of police cooperation and collective violence (Bigo 1996; *Cultures et conflits*), Bigo became a leading European player in the emerging field of critical security studies and securitization theory (Wæver 2004; Huysmans 2006; C.A.S.E. 2006). Partly as an outgrowth of active participation at ISA, he also became co-editor of the new ISA journal *International Political Sociology*. This may serve as a conduit for a new generation of young French IR scholars, who are often trained in English and sometimes go to ISA, to join the international scene and insert themselves into the field.

Since academic IR mostly did not produce for the needs of society at large, paradoxically it was for French public intellectuals such as Pierre Hassner (1995),[8] and for other disciplines such as geopolitics (Lacoste 1997), to fill the void. In general, public intellectuals tend to be more visible in the French media than IR scholars. Quite often, they perform as polemic simplifiers. Take as an example a debate from the time of the 2003 Iraq War, when a public intellectual condemned "heinous Islam" and celebrated the United States as the harbinger of freedom (Glucksmann 2003, 2004). To correct this kind of simplification, Bertrand Badie (2004) provided a more sophisticated – and less clamorous – picture of the dialectics of American power and powerlessness in a world where friend and enemy are hard to distinguish.[9]

Overall, academic self-reliance is not the most successful strategy to cope with U.S. hegemony. Over the 1990s, French IR scholars started taking an increased interest in theoretical developments in other parts of the world, and particularly in the Anglo-American core (Giesen 1992; Vennesson 1998). Leading French IR scholars have come to consider the results of academic self-reliance to be largely unsatisfactory (Smouts 1998; Martres 2003).

Regardless of whether or not one considers academic self-reliance to be a successful strategy, one should recognize that French theorizing about international relations can be highly original. In fact, there is a specifically French approach to IR theory: the sociology of international relations. Subsequent generations of leading scholars have undertaken progressive attempts to develop this sociology of international relations (Aron 1962; Merle 1974; Badie and Smouts 1992; Badie 1999, 2008).

Resigned marginality

In Italy, International Relations scholars mostly oscillate between two different but related strategies. Sometimes they try to establish direct links with the American core, imitating the deans of Italian political science who were learning and teaching in the United States, such as Giovanni Sartori and Gianfranco Pasquino. But, alas, the interest of Italian scholars in American scholarship is usually not reciprocated. When frustrated in their endeavor, many Italian scholars turn towards the protected domain of domestic academia.

On the one hand, Italian scholars try to be wide open towards American and, to a lesser degree, British IR. On the other hand, they are relatively closed with regard to theoretical developments in the rest of Europe. Sometimes they are not even aware of theoretical developments at other Italian universities. At least this is the impression one gets from the self-reflection of Italian scholars: "We are very weak in university and research. Who knows how much we will still have to go to school in America or Great Britain to keep up" (Cerutti 2000: 15). While Italian IR is characterized by an astounding propensity towards self-critical reflection (Silj 1976; Pasquino 1977; Bonanate 1984; Papisca 1984; Attinà 1987; Lucarelli and Menotti 2006), most surveys paint a fairly bleak picture. Most Italian scholars tend to believe that there is reason to be frustrated with the marginality and fragmentation of Italian IR.

Statistics on publications in leading journals confirm this picture. Italians are much less represented than Scandinavians and Germans, as well as less than the Turks and the Dutch, but more than the French (at least in our particular, rather limited, dataset: see Table 15.2).

In fact, the relationship between Italian and American IR is mostly one-way. For example, there is an excellent textbook in Italian, co-authored by five Italian and five American scholars (Ikenberry and Parsi 2001a, 2001b). Just imagine how unlikely it would be the other way around: to have a textbook for American university students co-authored with Italian scholars.[10] Moreover, American theorizing is mostly digested in Italy with a considerable time-lag. The extreme case is a 1959 book by Kenneth Waltz translated in 1998. Well into the 2000s, Italian IR is still haunted by polemical debates between undeconstructed "realists" and "idealists."

Due to their numerical weakness and internal fragmentation, the visibility of Italian scholars is mostly limited to their own academic environment. The work of most Italian scholars hardly resonates in Italian politics and society. Very few are visible at the international level (exceptions include Fulvio Attinà, Luigi Bonanate, and Fabio Petito).

This is not to deny that Italian scholars have made some highly original contributions, spanning from "Democratic Peace" (Panebianco 1997) to "Post-Westfalian IR" (Parsi 1998). As in the case of France, however, the most spectacular theorizing on international relations takes place far off the beaten track of academic IR. Take, for example, the pacifism of the late

Table 15.2 National residence of authors of articles in leading English language journals; intra-European distribution. Based on all articles from every fifth year, 1970 to 2005, IS from 1980, RIS from 1975 and EJIR from 1995.

	International Organization (IO)	*International Studies Quarterly* (ISQ)	*International Security* (IS)	*Review of International Studies* (RIS)	*European Journal of International Relations* (EJIR)	*Sum*
UK[a]	15,33	17,66	7,83	246,66	45,22	(332,7)
Germany	6,82	1,5	0,2	9	16,5	34,02
Norway	3,75	4,33	–	5	3,33	16,41
Sweden	1	2	–	3	8,5	14,5
Denmark	1	0,66	–	6	6	13,66
The Netherlands	–	1	0,2	2,5	4	7,7
Switzerland	2,5	0,5	–	–	3,5	6,5
Ireland[a]	–	1	–	4	1	(6)
Turkey[a]	–	1	1,33	2	1,33	(5,66)
Italy	–	1	–	2	2	5
Hungary[a]	–	1	–	1	2	(4)
Finland	–	–	–	1	2	3
France	1	–	–	–	1	2
Austria	–	–	–	1	–	1
Greece	–	–	–	1	–	1
Belgium	–	–	–	0,5	0,5	1
Czech Republic[a]	–	–	–	–	1	(1)
Cyprus	–	–	–	–	0,5	0,5
Spain	–	–	–	–	–	–
Portugal	–	–	–	–	–	–
Sum Western Europe	16,07	13,99	1,73	38	53,16	106,29
Total sum	303	320	251	511	184	1569

Notes
[a] UK, Turkey, Hungary, Ireland and the Czech Republic are covered by other chapters in this book, but are included here for the sake of comparison (not included in "Sum Western Europe").

political philosopher Norberto Bobbio (1989, 1997), the iconoclastic realism of lawyer– philosopher Danilo Zolo (1995, 2000), the constructivist ethics of diplomat Roberto Toscano (2000), or the geopolitics of army general Carlo Jean (2003).[11]

The existing surveys show that Italians themselves are quite unhappy about this state of affairs. Apart from Italy, Spain is another exemplar of resigned marginality. Spanish IR is even more marginal to the American core and perhaps a little more open towards the rest of Western Europe, but these are differences in degree rather than in kind (Segura 2006).

Multi-level research cooperation

Both at the regional level and beyond, IR in the Nordic countries has slowly become more integrated since the mid- and late 1960s.[12] The national IR communities in Denmark, Sweden, Norway, and, to a lesser extent, Finland[13] are now integrated into a network of multi-level research cooperation that extends far beyond Scandinavia and the Nordic region.

As a result, Nordic scholars dispose of a variety of attractive outlets for their academic production. First, most of them have gained access to the academic "world market" by getting their books and articles published by British and American editors (Goldmann 1995). Second, many Nordic scholars are networking with scholars from other European countries, producing excellent edited volumes (e.g. Eriksen *et al.* 2004). Third, some extend their tentacles to other world regions, from Russia to the developing countries. Fourth, Nordic scholars meet at conferences of the Nordic International Studies Association and publish their articles in Nordic (or Nordic-based) journals, namely *Cooperation and Conflict*, *Journal of Peace Research*, *Security Dialogue* and *Scandinavian Political Studies*. Fifth, they do not neglect their national audiences either, producing textbooks for national markets, using journals in the vernacular languages as an outlet for some of their academic production, working in national policy think-tanks, and addressing civil society via the mass media and popular publications.

In short, Nordic IR scholars operate and cooperate at many levels simultaneously. By this, they are players in a sort of "multi-level game" of intra- and inter-academic relations. Their position at the intersection of the various different layers yields them clear advantages. They gain international visibility, benefit in terms of intellectual diversity, and can shift from one editorial outlet to the other, which increases their professional detachment.

In terms of scholarly output, Nordic scholars excel in two distinct regards. On the one hand, their particular strength lies in the sympathetic correction of mainstream approaches. On the other hand, they are strong in the concoction of new approaches to challenge the mainstream.[14] Typical representatives of the former current – "scientific revisionism" – are the Danish scholars Mouritzen (1998) and Wivel (Mouritzen and Wivel 2005), with their revisionist critique of structural neorealism, as well as a group of scholars centering around the University of Lund who apply a multi-disciplinary approach to diplomacy, bargaining, and EU studies (Elgström and Jönsson 2005; Jönsson and Hall 2005). Representatives of the latter current – "scientific revolutionism" – are typically concerned with genealogical critique and deconstruction (e.g. Bartelson 2001), critical realism (e.g. Patomäki 2002), deliberation in the European Union (e.g. Eriksen 2005) or re-inventing the study of diplomacy on the basis of anthropology and fieldwork (Neumann 2007). The most influential Scandinavian contribution to international security studies, the quasi-constructivist "Copenhagen School" (Buzan *et al.* 1998), is probably an odd mix of the two approaches (and often criticized accordingly).

In a previous peak period of Scandinavian disciplinary successes, the mid-1970s, the institutional structure was thinner than today, and the core–periphery pattern clearer. The journal *Cooperation and Conflict* published the majority of work and had quite a high rank internationally, but academic status mainly accrued from a group of scholars participating actively in a particular (very) American subdiscipline, "comparative foreign policy" or "foreign policy analysis." This was in line with "Scandinavian behavioralism" (Anckar 1987) in political science at large. In the beginning, status came partly from contributing particular "small state" insights, and thus in some way working as "local informants" for this American programme, but increasingly also from developing original theory with a distinct profile (culminating in works like Carlsnaes 1987 and Goldmann 1988; for reviews emphasizing the Scandinavian nature of these, see Wæver 1990a, 1990b).

The pooling of academic resources has provided the Nordic IR communities with the critical mass that was necessary to become visible at the international level, channel their theoretical contributions to the English-speaking audience, and thereby gain access to the discipline via the centre. In recent years, Scandinavians have diversified their networking activities to include research cooperation with scholars from Western Europe and from other parts of the world. As a result, there is now a "Nordic network" of multi-level research cooperation that makes the Nordic countries a uniquely successful integrated IR periphery.

The figures in Table 15.2 support the interpretation of Nordic IR as a success story. Although individually Nordic countries are behind German IR, in combination Norway, Sweden, and Denmark publish 50 percent more than Germany. This becomes even more impressive when one considers that Germany has a population more than three times larger than Scandinavia.

Nordic IR is by now the most long-standing and the most typical, but not necessarily the only example of multi-level research cooperation. Since the 1990s, a majority of German scholars have also given up their isolation from each other and from the discipline at large, and started seeing scientific production more as a cooperative endeavor (Hellmann *et al.* 2003; Humrich 2006).[15] This trend at least in part encompasses the German-speaking IR communities in Austria and Switzerland. The Dutch-speaking communities of the Netherlands and Belgium are perhaps another case in point. However, it is left for future researchers to explore to what extent multi-level research cooperation is taking place beyond the Nordic countries.[16]

Socio-disciplinary explanation

How are we to explain these three characteristic and contrasting strategies to cope with American intellectual hegemony? With a modified version of the explanatory scheme suggested in Wæver (1998), and integrating suggestions from, among others, Breitenbauch and Wivel (2004) and Breitenbauch (2008), we will operate with the following three categories:

1   Status and delimitation of disciplines – how is political science positioned vis-à-vis other disciplines? How does IR relate to political science and area studies?
2   Power structures and hierarchies – where does disciplinary power rest? With chairs or professor(s) in local departments, with influential figures at the national level, with editors of journals, or with political decision-makers?
3   Policy link – how important is policy orientation for IR scholars?

France

The French political system is notorious for its age-old tradition of centralization and *dirigisme*.[17] This has created the social and institutional conditions for a mainstream in political science that devoutly ignores theory. Most courses taught at the Ecole Nationale d'Administration (ENA) and the Grandes Ecoles deal with theory only at the margins. The main objective of these courses is to prepare students for a political or administrative career. Unsurprisingly, area studies is widely recognized as one of the strengths of French IR.

However, this is only part of the story. Ever since the demise of Napoleon, French political society is struggling to reintroduce the revolutionary element into the mainstream. As a result, society as such is recognized as a rewarding object of study. This explains the high profile of sociology from Comte and Durkheim to Touraine and Bourdieu. French political science has been strongly influenced by this tradition. As we have seen, the same holds true for IR.[18]

Since theory is held in high esteem by intellectuals (French or otherwise), there is a burgeoning industry of theoretical scholarship. However, theoreticians tend to relate to their fellow theoreticians rather than to policy-oriented scholars or "real-world" phenomena. Conversely, policy-oriented scholars do empirical or policy work without feeling an obligation to explicitly engage theory or justify themselves by pointing to theoretical implications. French IR theory is probably even more divorced from policy than in most other countries.

In the most extensive study of French IR (in contrast to American) Henrik Ø. Breitenbauch (2008) has pointed to the importance of *form*. The French conception of legitimate scientific expression is different from the American research article format, where the French educational system all the way privileges a form of "literary Cartesianism," which values clear conceptual thinking but in a different mode of expression from what "counts" in international IR journals. This form is deeply entwined with French state formation and social structures, and has increasingly also become an aesthetic–political representation of national identity. Thus, it is not a minor "form" thing or "formality" to adjust in order to "score higher" in international publications. "Academic self-reliance" is therefore not well understood if seen as a strategic choice of how to compete with others about doing the same – it is about doing things so differently that it leads to a separate academic system. In contrast to many other cases studied in other chapters of this book, an incongruity with the form of knowledge demanded from leading U.S. journals is not experienced as a contrast between theory in the U.S. and empirical/practical scholarship locally – in the French case, theory is highly valued, but it takes its own forms, and especially the mode of theoretical reasoning is distinct.

Disciplinary power is concentrated in Paris. Scholarly prestige rests with a handful of universities and research institutes in Paris, while the recruitment of prominent IR scholars from other countries and awareness of their scholarship is kept to the minimum. As we have already seen, the French IR community has deliberately isolated itself from the American core and has developed its own intellectual center in the French capital. While excellent scholarship in the subfields of the discipline and in area studies is also conducted in the French province, the road to recognition leads almost exclusively via Paris. Within Paris, disciplinary power is shared between a theoretical and a policy-relevant apex. An upcoming scholar can gain recognition either via theoretical sophistication, connecting his work to the theoretical center in Paris, or via policy relevance, raising the interest of the political establishment and attracting the attention of the leading policy think-tanks.[19] Either way, the framework of reference will be the top ranks of institutional hierarchies in Paris. This is where most funding comes from, and only rarely will one find any theoretically important or politically influential French contribution originating from elsewhere. The same applies to the French editorial market: almost all important books about IR are published in Paris.

French IR this way becomes a "closed shop" with internal mechanisms of regulation, not in need of a coupling to a transnational discipline. Furthermore, the pattern of orientation to other disciplines – split between administration and sociology – does shape the discipline very differently from the U.S. version, as do micro-mechanisms related to the form of training and writing (Breitenbauch 2008). The primacy of Paris makes the system less run on an accreditation system separate from the main institutes as in the U.S. (journals), and more through position won in the Parisian departments.

Italy

The institutional vicissitudes of Italian IR are complex, and the sources of its present weakness are manifold (Friedrichs 2004: 48–51; Lucarelli and Menotti 2006: 59–65). The most important fact is that Italian IR is the result of a double emancipation struggle. In the 1970s, IR emerged as a subdiscipline of political science and positioned itself alongside diplomatic history and a few other subdisciplines. At the same time, political science itself was challenged to break free from law's embrace. Particularly the latter point is of crucial importance.

Substantively, political science in Italy may be traced as far back as the renaissance philosopher Niccolò Machiavelli[20] and Gaetano Mosca (1896), the dean of Italian elite theory. Institutionally, however, it started after the unification of Italy in the late nineteenth century. The problem was that law faculties were exceedingly important for the production and reproduction of the political and administrative elite of the recently unified country. As a remedy, bourgeois entrepreneur Carlo Alfieri tried to position political science as an alternative breeding ground for the elite of the young state.[21] Apart from the foundation of one School in Florence, however, this first attempt was by and large unsuccessful (Curcio 1963).

The next time something similar was attempted was in the "constitutional phase" of fascist rule, in the mid-1920s. Minister of Education Giovanni Gentile for the first time managed to put political science on a firm institutional basis, with *La Sapienza* in Rome at the center. Again, the objective was to create an alternative to law faculties for the production and reproduction of the elite. Despite increasing political pressure from Mussolini's regime, not all professors were stout fascists (D'Addio 1993; Gentile 2003).[22]

After the war, the experiment was rehearsed once again. This time, the objective was the rebirth of political science in the "true," i.e. liberal and empirical, sense of the word (Bobbio 2001 [1986]). This happened under strong U.S. influence and with considerable American start-up funding. The "re-founding fathers" were Giovanni Sartori, Norberto Bobbio, and a few others.[23] They tried to import from the United States an empirical and social-scientific understanding of politics (Morlino 1991). There was a great deal of funding by American foundations. Several political scientists went to the United States for training (Graziano 1991: 133–137). The 1950s and 1960s saw the gradual development of a scholarly community, intellectual production, editorial outlets, and mass universities (Cotta *et al.* 2001: 11–12). Formal recognition of political science as an indispensable element of Italian academia came around 1970. Since then, Italian political science has seen further growth, professionalization, and institutionalization; but also fragmentation and institutional differentiation (Sola 1996).

Disciplinary power in Italy is very much exercised through a centralized selection procedure called the *concorso*. In theory, the procedure guarantees the equality of chances via the centralization of recruitment at the national level. However, it is notoriously open to manipulation. In practice, the *concorso* has led to the concentration of control over academic appointments in the hands of a few mandarins. Wagging tongues have it that the system is very much based on clientele and the anticipation of favors on the part of appointees.

As we have already seen, academic IR in Italy is not particularly focused on policy relevance. However, there are a number of more policy-oriented institutes.[24] These institutes provide an interesting, albeit limited, career outlet for graduates from Italian universities. In many cases, however, incipient scholars enrol at these at least as much due to the limited availability of career opportunities at Italian universities as to personal predilections.

Scandinavia

In Sweden, a "science of the state" was influential already in the nineteenth century (allowing, for example, a Swedish political science professor, Rudolf Kjellén, to coin the term "geopolitics" around 1900). In other parts of Scandinavia, political science became an independent discipline much later, often under inspiration from – and modeled after –

the U.S. One illustration could be the contrasting routes of the two main departments in Denmark: Aarhus and Copenhagen. Aarhus was set up in 1959 largely by disciplinary pioneers who took the lead from U.S. political science (even though the International Relationist among the pioneers was a Francophile: Erling Bjøl), and to compete with law and economics in training civil servants. The Copenhagen department, in contrast, was only set up in 1965 as an effect of a reform in high school curricula creating a need for teachers of "social science" (political science, sociology, economics and IR). Therefore, this department was more inter-disciplinary, spun out of a department of contemporary history, and originally located in the humanities faculty. Although leaving long-lasting differences in profiles for the two departments, the trend here as in all of Scandinavia is a convergence on the "Aarhus model" with a strict political science discipline as an independent social science, sending most of its candidates into service in the state administration, and subdividing the discipline largely as in the U.S. Independent departments of IR were never attempted in Scandinavia, but peace research institutes played an important role (see below).

The net effect was a relatively strong and autonomous discipline of political science, compared to other parts of Europe, and one unequivocally defined as a social science – not very close to law or humanities. More often it was the (little) sister of economics – one more thing to making the set-up compatible with the U.S.

The second level of explanation is the organizational structure of the university system and especially hiring practices, formal and informal. The Scandinavian discipline is semi-mobile. Especially at the professorial level, there has always been a certain mobility within and across countries in the subregion. Hiring is done according to public procedures and conceived in "rule of law" terms (often confusing to outsiders who apply for a job in the area). Much power rests with a hiring committee, usually of three, where typically one is from the department, one from another university in the country, and one from another Nordic country. The evaluation was until recently done purely on the basis of publications, without any interviews. Lengthy assessments of each applicant were circulated, and dissenting opinions were common. While causing much animosity and frustration, this also created awareness of the criteria that led to success in academic careers. The decisions were of course never fully "automated," and local concerns influenced outcomes through the selection of committees and assessment criteria, but still the process underlined the importance of academic standing in the discipline as such. Publications matter – until recently, mostly books and articles published in the Nordic IR journal *Cooperation and Conflict*. Increasingly, the demand is for publications in leading international peer-reviewed journals and even sometimes citation counts. These criteria trickle down from the criteria according to which departments are evaluated. Deans and department chairs have been strengthened, but the judgement by the discipline still counts, because the new power-holders seek the high scorers on these criteria.

Quantitatively, mobility is still very low compared to the U.S., and local criteria and research cultures vary more.

Power was concentrated until the student revolt of the 1960s in the IR professor in each department (with power shared among all professors of political science on other decisions). Since the "revolt against professorial reign," power was shared between faculty as a collegiate body and departmental chair, dean and chancellor in a changing relationship (as university reforms come and go). Pre-1970, power and criteria were local, from the 1970s to the 1990s there was increasing power of an all-Scandinavian discipline (and indirectly, the global discipline), and in recent years power has gone increasingly to university leadership. It in turn tries to impose international standards, but is also tempted to follow local concerns, so we get a weakening of the self-regulating Scandinavian discipline (with its intra-disciplinary professorial elite) and an uneasy mix of localism and internationalization (market mechanism imposed via plan economics).

The third level of the explanatory model is that in all Scandinavian countries, think-tank-like foreign policy institutes have helped to create a relatively productive set-up. IR as a discipline has been neither directly exposed to many policy demands, nor risked charges of irrelevance or lack of policy access when sought. The foreign policy institutes (in recent years supplemented by a plethora of other smaller units) to some extent operate as a go-between. University researchers do not go in and out of office as often as they do in the U.S. (although Norway comes close), but they often go in and out of policy research. Policy relevance pushed development research higher in the discipline since the 1970s and EU studies since the 1980s.

Peace research had periodically high visibility and since the 1970s independent institutes (except most of the time in Denmark). Especially for the security part of IR, peace research was in the 1970s a source for confrontation and competition often energizing the field. Since the end of the Cold War there has been more synergy between peace research and IR, where developments originating in peace research institutes both draw on IR theory and feed back into the discipline also in university departments (e.g. region-building theory, securitization theory, critical geopolitics). The sometimes surprising productivity of these environments can probably be explained by the balance of closeness/insulation in relation both to practical issues (searching reality, but not advising to the prince) and simultaneously vis-à-vis the discipline (IR identity of some peace researchers, but autonomous spaces) (Jørgensen 2000: 17–18; Wæver 2000, 2004; Guzzini 2004; Wæver and Buzan 2007); cf. section below on dynamic fields within IR in Europe.

In general, the position of IR in relation to policy has been fortunate: policy-makers do not twist or constrain the discipline as such, and actually show little interest in university IR (except as training), while the field at large establishes its overall relevance and thus legitimacy due to the policy institutes, and there is access to policy for those in the discipline who so prefer.

Multi-level cooperation emerged as the orientation of Nordic IR owing to a basic compatibility of the local form of political science with American IR in combination with a sufficiently large publications market to allow for dynamic intellectual processes in the region as well as publications at all levels towards the global. A key factor has been hiring criteria that favored publications and have been gradually adjusted from the local to the global.

Europe's Standing in Global IR

First, let us look at quantity (or what in national research assessment exercises tends to be called "quality"): the number of articles in leading "international" – i.e. mostly American and to some extent British – journals. Revisiting Wæver (1998: 698), we examine three American, one British, and one European/British journal. Within these five journals, we find a highly unequal distribution of authors as regards their geographical location. This becomes clear from Table 15.3, which shows the current institution of authors (not their "ethnic" or training origin).

Authors from North America[25] are hugely dominant in the three American journals *International Organization* (widely seen as *the* leading IR journal), *International Studies Quarterly* (in addition to being generally a top journal, also the main journal of ISA) and *International Security* (the top journal for security studies, with a very high impact factor),

Table 15.3 Residence of scholars publishing in leading journals; global distribution

	North America (%)	British based (%)	Rest of Europe (%)	Rest of the world (%)
International Organization				
1970	92.3	0	3.8	3.8
1975	100	0	0	0
1980	66.7	14.3	4.8	14.3
1985	80	10	5	5
1990	78.1	0	18.8	3.1
1995	85.7	4.8	9.5	0
2000	92.6	0	7.4	0
2005	81.5	9.3	1.9	7.4
International Studies Quarterly				
1970	95.4	4.5	0	0
1975	92.9	0	0	7.1
1980	88.5	0	7.7	3.8
1985	88.5	0	7.7	3.8
1990	90.9	0	9.1	0
1995	83.3	8.3	8.3	0
2000	87.5	5.4	0	7.1
2005	82.2	11.1	3.3	3.3
International Security				
1980	68.8	18.8	0	12.5
1985	100	0	0	0
1990	86.4	9.1	0	4.5
1995	96	0	4	0
Note: Vol. 25 2000	95.5	0	0	4.5
Note: Vol. 30 2005	96	4.0	0	0
Review of International Studies				
1975	0	100	0	0
1980	40	40	6.7	13.3
1985	26.1	65.2	0	8.7
1990	14.7	73.5	5.9	5.9
1995	45.6	42.1	5.3	7.1
2000	34.9	58.5	1.9	4.7
2005	25.4	56.8	6.8	11.0
European Journal of International Relations				
1995	30.8	30	39.2	0
2000	35.3	23.5	41.2	0
2005	44.7	26.3	21.1	7.9

with most years ranging between 80 and 100 percent. Except for *International Security*, non-British Europeans are publishing slightly more than UK-based scholars but obviously on a much larger population basis, and thus proportionally less. In the UK-based journal *Review of International Studies* (RIS), a lot of the articles come from the UK, but far more American-based authors publish there than from Europe. In the *European Journal of International Relations* (EJIR), Europeans (East and West, but excluding UK) made up around 40 percent in 1995 and 2000, but only 21 percent in 2005.

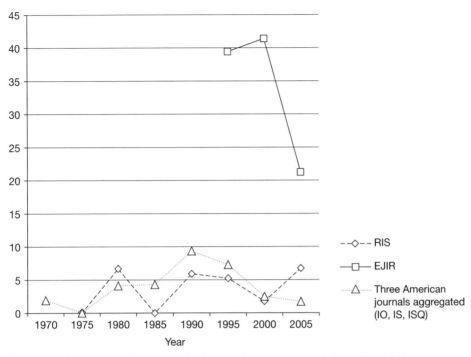

Figure 15.1 Percentage of authors in five leading journals who work in continental Europe

The trend is not encouraging. The European presence in American journals peaked in the early to mid-1990s and has been declining ever since (Figure 15.1). This is to some extent offset by – and possibly partly caused by – more European articles in the *European Journal of International Relations*.[26] For the trend during the1990s, this would work as a possible interpretation. However, the European proportion of articles in the main European journals has been declining recently. Figure 15.2 zooms in on the most comparable cases: UK versus rest-of-Europe in two of the most important non-American journals, RIS and EJIR. It shows an unmistakable trend in the relative decline of Europe-based compared to UK-based authors.[27]

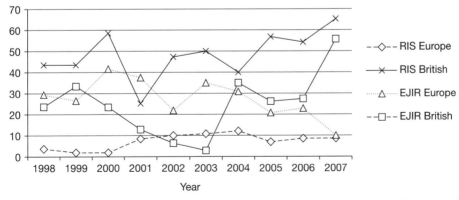

Figure 15.2 Percentage of authors in two European journals who work in continental Europe and Britain

Going back to the general picture, including all authors and including the U.S. journals, Figure 15.1 and Table 15.3 and Figure 1.1 in Chapter 1 (p. 5) give a picture of continued or even solidified American dominance. Contrary to widely held expectations, there is not a trend towards a more balanced pattern of publications with Europeans – or for that matter, "rest-of-world" authors – gradually taking a proportionally larger part compared to authors based in North America.

"Quantity," however, is one thing (although it is sometimes seen as quality, because publishing in the leading journals is measured as a sign of quality). Another issue is "quality" in the sense of making distinct contributions that actually shape the discipline.[28] The question here is whether European authors produce their own influential contributions to theory, or if they only apply American theories while possibly criticizing them a little. Seen from other parts of the world, one might expect to find Europeans on a slightly more privileged semi-periphery, but the "parochialism of hegemony" in American IR remains pervasive, and European IR has certainly not penetrated it to any significant degree. Despite the presence that European IR after all has – small but still larger than most other parts of the world – it is striking how rarely theories or debates come from Europe.

If we accept for now that scholarly awareness in the U.S. is a valid criterion of impact, it is revealing to look at the TRIP survey where 1,112 scholars from the U.S. and Canada answered an extensive questionnaire. Among other things, scholars were asked to list up to four scholars having had the largest impact on IR over the past 20 years. Strikingly, the U.S. top 26 based on the answers to this question has not a single scholar resident in Europe – the most European is probably Peter Katzenstein (No. 10) and Morgenthau (No. 15). The Canadian list has some British-based scholars, but nobody from continental Europe. The next question searches for upcoming shooting stars, asking neatly, "Aside from you, who has been doing the most interesting work in international relations in recent years?" The U.S. top 25 again has only North Americans, and the Canadian list includes scholars from Britain and *one* "real" European, Iver B. Neumann from Norway (Maliniak *et al.* 2007).[29]

Leaving aside the impossible criterion of "making it in New York," a related question is if European theories and debates are still structured by "positioning games" vis-à-vis the U.S., or if they are becoming more autonomous. We have no quantitative measurement, but this seems to be the case at least in two areas: European studies and security studies.

Within European studies, it would seem natural to find Europeans defining the main theories. Therefore, it was probably a rather discouraging experience for many Europeans to find, after the end of the Cold War and the regained momentum for European integration, that the theoretical debates were largely structured around the theory of the American scholar Andrew Moravcsik and his liberal intergovernmentalism (re-enacting institutionally the performance of Ernest Haas and neo-functionalism in a previous generation of integration theory). However, the main theoretical counter-position was more European: multi-level governance. Increasingly, this rather polarized debate gave way to a more creative scene, where at first most of the European contributions were to some extent mutations of the general anti-statist, post-sovereign and more comparative politics-inspired multi-level governance (Diez and Wiener 2004; Rosamond 2007a, 2007b). But increasingly, European scholars have also begun to make inroads into the more rationalistic, institutionalist side of the literature.

One way of seeing this would be that Europeans increasingly exploit their comparative advantages. American scholars are trapped in theory-driven presumptions about what the EU is and can be, while the lived experience of Europeans generates a more complex understanding, even for those who then set out to explore Europe with rational choice theories. The European scholars in this context benefit from some of the general patterns in European scholarship: a less clear-cut divide between IR and comparative politics, and more sensitivity towards history, law, and social theory. With some justification we can count in the influential work of Thomas Risse, who is possibly the most cited European-based scholar.[30]

Diez and Wiener (2004) indirectly offer a possible explanation for the increased role of theory "made in Europe" based on phases of European integration itself. They see the most recent phase of European integration theory as shaped by questions of legitimacy and policy-making. In contrast to the first phase of explaining integration as such (classical integration theory) and a second one of "understanding the nature of the beast," the third phase generally politicizes – or accepts the politicization of – European issues. This would point towards more constructivist and critical work. Ben Rosamond has argued that while this suggests a pluralistic, multifaceted research agenda, EU studies also witnesses continued attempts at creating a period of "normal science" and cumulation according to methodological "best practices." Interestingly, European scholars are at the forefront of both kinds of theory. They also see themselves increasingly as EU scholars rather than IR scholars.

The other field where European scholars seem to be able to generate "theory" that is picked up, at least, by other scholars in Europe, and to some extent even in the U.S., is *security studies* (formerly known as "strategic studies"). In recent years, the otherwise conservative field of security studies has seen a distinct European hotbed, where a lively research environment has emerged drawing from, discussing, criticizing and sometimes cross-fertilizing (C.A.S.E. 2006) approaches such as critical security studies (Krause and Williams 1997), securitization theory (Buzan *et al.* 1998), feminism, governmentality studies, and the "Paris school" (Bigo 1996). The subfield of security studies took unusually different paths in Europe and the U.S. during the 1990s (Wæver 2004; Wæver and Buzan 2007). While taking a very different stance on the relationship between theory, expertise, and policy-making, European security scholars are, like American ones, placed in a dual-reference system in relation to academic IR and security as a political field. This duality is often – as we discuss in the final section – materialized in institutional relations to both universities and think-tanks, especially for Ph.D. students.

Both fields have strong policy links and a certain subdisciplinary identity. The theorists operate at the intersection of IR as a discipline and strong, semi-autonomous subfields that are partly interdisciplinary. Such locations might turn out to be particularly conducive to theoretical and epistemic innovation. Some of the reasons for this are explored in the next section.

Institutional conditions in Europe: before and after CUDOS

In recent times, European scholars have often expressed frustration. They feel under heavy pressure from constant waves of institutional reform entailing enhanced doses of administrative control, measurement, and documentation of productivity. Although this frustration is typically expressed over lunch and not given scholarly form, it can be explained in terms of a simple but brutal scheme from the sociology of science.

As a starting point, let us take Robert Merton's CUDOS scheme of academic self-regulation (see Chapter 1, this volume). The assumption was that the intellectual quest for recognition by other intellectuals would automatically produce the most dynamic growth of science. In a way, American IR has been as close to this ideal as it can get. Academic careers in the U.S. rest less on patronage by the local professor than on publishing and peer recognition. The intellectual trend-setters, including the editors of leading journals, are therefore the gatekeepers of the discipline at large.

A recent body of literature on "the new production of knowledge" calls this form of science "mode one": aims are set internally to a discipline, products are assessed by the discipline, and the societal relevance or irrelevance is judged only *ex post facto*. Against this classical ideal stands the increasingly influential "mode two," where knowledge production is negotiated from the onset between economic, political, and academic stakeholders, and funds are increasingly channeled into interdisciplinary issue-driven projects (Gibbons *et al.* 1994; Nowotny *et al.* 2001). In the knowledge society science becomes too important (Weingart 2001) and too risky (Beck 1992) to be left to the scientists alone.

Where does Europe fit into this scheme? Arguably, Europe is moving from a sort of pre-CUDOS "mode zero" towards a challenging mixture of modes one and two. Traditionally, power in most European IR communities rested with feudal lords at university departments or research councils. Differently from the U.S., power had not been made anonymous through mobility on a large academic job market. Without such a market it was not rational for European scholars to struggle for an entire year to produce one article to be *almost* accepted by IO and one more year revising it for final acceptance. Increasingly, however, the value of such publications is touted in Europe as well.

At the same time, much energy goes into the post-disciplinary format of mode two. This is not least because most of the new funding is there. In almost all European countries public research funding is shifted from research council and university budgets towards more "relevant" programs aimed at making research more valuable to society. This format certainly characterizes EU grants, especially the large framework programs that enjoy increasing popularity and prestige among European scholars.

As a result, European scholars feel under pressure. They are expected to show political and economic utility when negotiating their research agendas and priorities with stakeholders from outside academia. Paradoxically, however, part of the attempt of these external actors to increase the quality of research is to impose a more intense measurement culture which is based on refereed journals, citation scores, and so forth. Thus, whereas mode one and mode two are according to the theory opposite to each other, European IR scholars find themselves simultaneously under pressure to accommodate more to *both* of them – a possibility not envisioned by the original Gibbons *et al.* exposé. The explanation for this is both that European IR is coming from what could be called a pre-CUDOS, "mode zero" (to coin a term) situation, and that current research policy is less neat in moving from mode one to mode two (as envisioned by Gibbons *et al.*), but trying to strengthen both.

From a sociology-of-science perspective, there seems to be a trend in two opposite directions simultaneously. On the one hand, there is an increased emphasis on publishing in leading peer-reviewed journals and similar classical expressions of academic self-regulation (this is nevertheless often resented because the focus on peer review comes precisely not as self-regulation but as a tool of state regulation); on the other hand, academic self-regulation is directly challenged by increasing emphasis on "targeted" funding, i.e. specific money for "relevant" themes instead of blanket money for departments. This does not necessarily mean more "applied" research or direct political control, but the themes are chosen not through academic self-regulation but from the outside.

Consequently, a new breed of organizer–gatekeepers and politician–academics are gaining pride of place. We basically see a shift from feudal lords (German *ordinarius* or French *mandarin* as ideal cases) to disciplinary elites excelling in citation scores and controlling journals. Simultaneously, we also see a shift to the politician-academic who combines presumable policy relevance with reputable academic "excellence."

As a result the academic discipline is weakened but far from irrelevant. Even the politician– academic needs peer recognition in the form of refereed publications and citation figures. But funding goes less to the academic discipline than to policy-relevant research regardless of its disciplinary or interdisciplinary context. As we have seen, examples include the dynamic fields of European studies and security studies. These fields receive comparatively generous funding on the basis of criteria that are beyond the control of any particular academic discipline.

This situation can (but does not have to) lead to a productive interplay between think-tanks and universities. Ph.D. students often undertake a tightrope walk between a think-tank where they conduct their project and where policy relevance is specific and central, and their supervisor at a university where they have to justify their project to a self-defining disciplinary community. This can lead to tough cross-pressure on young scholars, but when it works well they are pushed towards creativity by having to make sense both in the policy and the theory world with basically the same research. Disciplinary blinders are removed while at the same time the disciplinary frame of reference is maintained.

When looking at the key criteria regarding publications, we probably have to conclude that Europeans are lagging behind. When taking a more Broad Church approach to criteria of academic merit, however, we may argue that Europeans do not feel pressured to give the same priority to premium publications as their American colleagues. Even if their research is actually at the same intellectual level, it is communicated in a different way. Europeans simply do not go to the same lengths as Americans to squeeze their work into a few key articles placed in leading journals. While American scholars tend to put long hours into such premium publications and often make heavy concessions to the demands of top journals, this is simply not the game whole-heartedly played by European scholars.[31]

In line with the general project of this book, we should avoid seeing European IR in terms of what it is not (American IR), and understand what it is and how it is this. European IR is an intellectual field of activity producing analyses that make sense out of international relations with a combination of theory and empirical work that often finds an outlet in research reports and edited volumes that are not of high prestige in the formal systems of the global discipline, but circulate in the wider network in Europe among not only researchers and policy-makers but also research administrators. Much research is organized within specific projects, networks and collaborations, and output is delivered because it is promised – not because it fulfils career aims about getting into particular journals (Guzzini 2007). The very securing of funding – especially for big EU grants – gives the scholar credit in itself. The grant entails research obligations, and this research is judged among peers in the network but by different standards from the "research journal" ones. When most successful, the resulting knowledge production becomes more collective and cumulative – a process of gradually pushing forward in a certain area without each piece being able to stand alone and out of time as a perfect unit with theory section and case study and synthesis of the two. This format is probably more conducive than the classical method for bringing in researchers from traditionally less IRish countries, especially in Southern and Eastern Europe. EU projects demand the participation of many countries, and the partners who come in can contribute to this flow more easily than by meeting the either/or threshold of international publications. In this sense, larger intersecting issue-defined European networks take shape and build a kind of parallel world of European IR, not clearly observable through the normal measures (see tables and figures above), nor a strict alternative to it, because disciplinary standing counts as well and is measured through that other universe. But in this dual world of European IR, much knowledge, theory and analysis is produced, while the number of participating nations grows, and both researchers and policy-makers play many simultaneous games separately and jointly.

Increasingly it is European in the form of a certain density of networking at this level too. Generally it does not make sense to interpret IR in terms of separate national units, nor as a homogeneous global discipline. Discussion on whether European IR exists should not be conducted in these terms either, and in the emerging multi-layered process the European level is gradually gaining importance. This may be seen by surveying the main institutions of IR in Europe.

The most important institution for the IR discipline is still the university. These are 99 percent anchored nationally. Europe is home to the original universities, so there are some very old and self-conscious ones in the region, but also a spectrum of younger universities. Many countries have witnessed a growth of small universities sometimes due to regionalist policies, sometimes due to polytechnics successfully being redefined and politicians welcoming the increased competition. At the European level, the most important university is the European University Institute in Florence, Italy (and a Masters programme at the College in Europe in Bruge, Belgium), although the Geneva-based Graduate Institute *de facto* is close to also being an international graduate school. Quantitatively their share is small, but given the lack of separate graduate schools in much of Europe they have become attractive institutions helping to focus a European discipline.

Think-tanks too are mostly national with "foreign policy institutes" the central ones in most countries, but many others are being added. However, with the growing importance of EU policy-making, Brussels has become the home of around 50 think-tanks, some of which include IR issues (Villumsen 2007). These are, however, more policy focused and less academic than the average think-tank in Europe, less integrated with universities, and therefore so far not very important for IR theory and disciplinary developments.

Regarding funding, it has already been mentioned that the EU share is gradually growing. By being the source of some of the largest grants, it exerts more influence than the total figure would suggest. National research policies increasingly take clues from EU policy and try to shape national research support to help capture EU grants.

The picture regarding associations is messy. Some countries have IR associations, others only IR sections in political science associations. For most Europeans, the main annual meeting is the ISA in the U.S., followed for some by BISA in the UK. However, increasingly the oddly named "Standing Group on International Relations" (under the European Consortium for Political Research, ECPR) has had some success in organizing a pan-European conference every third year. This drew around 400 at the first two meetings (Heidelberg 1992 and Paris 1995), and 800 at the last four (Vienna 1998, Canterbury 2001, The Hague 2004 and Torino 2007). For some subfields, the general political science organization, ECPR, has been an important network with a very productive format for its all-European conferences.

Last but not least, the landscape of journals is important. To Scandinavians, their "own" journal *Cooperation and Conflict* was important in the "middle period," and to Germans, *Zeitschrift für Internationale Beziehungen* has been important for the past 15 years. As outlined above, the rest of Europe mostly has policy journals (or intellectual generalist ones), not theoretically inclined IR journals. The main journals have therefore increasingly been the international ones (see Tables 15.2 and 15.3). However, a factor of immense importance to European IR is the launch, success and potential of the *European Journal of International Relations* (EJIR). Since its 1995 launch – under the auspices of the "Standing Group" – it has strived to assist European IR being a journal that both competed with the top U.S. ones on their own terms and differing in a European way, i.e. it aimed to publish articles that would easily have found their way into IO or ISQ too, but also to be more open and pluralistic than these journals. To some Europeans it is just another good journal, to others it has become the preferred one due to dissatisfaction with American narrowness. Other European-level journals are – in addition to the subregional ones mentioned: CoCo and ZIB – some subdisciplinary ones: the *Journal of Common Market Studies* and *Journal of European Public Policy* to Europeanists, and *Security Dialogue*, *Cultures et Conflits*, and maybe *International Political Sociology* to participants in the new security theories. Although "international" journals, not formally "European," they have been the arenas of the articulation of independent European scholarship. Finally, JIRD, although technically the journal of the East Central European IR organization (see Chapter 14, this volume), is also an important part of the pan-European IR community because it has published much of the self-reflective literature on European IR.

Conclusion

This chapter has shown a heavy variation within Europe in the ways IR has emerged and the way this found expression in different "coping strategies" towards the hegemonic U.S. discipline. French, Italian, and Nordic IR were used to illustrate three ideal types: academic self-reliance, resigned marginality, and multi-level research cooperation. Different forms of IR scholarship were produced with different degrees of visibility on the global register – from the French style of work that is both theoretical and sophisticated but with minor presence outside France to the Scandinavian (and German) production of scholarship that is sufficiently compatible with U.S.-style IR to achieve a certain presence while also showing characteristic traits that made it distinguishable.

The social organization of research in Europe has specific features that among other things have generated some major cases of independent theorizing in areas like European integration and security theory, where a mix of distance and connection to both policy and academe was achieved by semi-autonomous subfields. Partly linked to this, the recent trends in research policy were discussed and the dual pressure on European scholars for both publishing more in international journals and labouring in "relevance"-guided networks tend to hamper growth in the European scores in international publications but also generates novel forms of international cooperation that deliver its own forms of academic expression, a distinct genre of collective, cumulative, and networked issue knowledge. Especially in these spheres, we also see the pan-European elements strengthened.

These developments do not necessarily lead to regional convergence as to the disciplinary communities. Thus in terms of the vision of "a house with many mansions," there are signs that while the mansions keep to their distinct styles, the house is solidifying both in the disciplinary system around the SGIR and the post-disciplinary system around EU-sponsored research projects.

Notes

1 The authors would like to thank Kim B. Olsen for energetic and effecient work on the tables and figures.
2 Our account is limited to the continental part of Western Europe. Britain and Ireland, as well as Central and Eastern Europe, are covered by other contributions to this volume (Cox and Nossal; Drulák *et al.*).

3 For a collection of articles on different European IR communities see Jørgensen and Knudsen 2006.
4 Perhaps Soviet IR may be seen as a further example (Lebedeva 2004; Sergounin, Chapter 13, this volume); and Japan until recently had some of these features (Inoguchi, Chapter 5, this volume).
5 Due to a lack of critical mass, there is nothing approaching an IR community in Portugal and Greece (although for the beginnings hereof, see Mikelis 2003; Rigueira 2007).
6 The justification for interpreting French, Italian and Nordic IR as embodying the three strategies has been developed at length elsewhere (Friedrichs 2004: 1–23).
7 The three generations may be labeled "a-theoretical research" in the 1950s, "social and socialist theory" from the 1960s to the 1980s, and a trend towards "post-theory" in the 1990s and 2000s (Friedrichs 2004: 25–46). For alternative categorizations see Giesen 2006; Breitenbauch 2008.
8 See Le Gloannec and Smolar 2003; Wæver and Buzan 2007. Hassner has a strong international presence in strategic studies. He has also retained a more broadly defined profile as a public intellectual in France. It is revealing that neither of these roles has made him very powerful within French IR, not least because his main institutional basis was "think-tanks" such as CERI combined with teaching in the U.S., Italy, and at Sciences Po.
9 A similar case is the exchange between the "simplifier" Revel 2002 and the "rectifiers" Hassner and Vaïsse 2003.
10 It is revealing that no other European scholars, not even from Great Britain, were called on to participate in the endeavor. This does not necessarily impair the quality of the textbook, but it is clearly indicative of the type of centre–periphery relationship within which the Italian IR discipline is located. For a textbook with a slightly stronger European component see Cesa 2004.
11 On the post-Cold War "hype" in Italian geopolitics see Brighi and Petito 2008.
12 See Friedrichs 2006. For a previous survey of Scandinavian IR see Jönsson 1993; for Denmark see Breitenbauch and Wivel 2004; for Norway see Underdal 1997; for political science in Sweden see Angstrom *et al.* 2003; Ekman 2007.
13 In other scientific fields there are often a few internationally (very) influential Finnish scholars who link up directly to American circles without Nordic "mediation." This is the case in IR only to some extent.
14 Even here it seems to be a Scandinavian particularity to be less "confrontational" than in the U.S. and UK (see, for example, the willingness of Scandinavian post-structuralist discourse analysts to talk "methodology" (Hansen 2006), or the exchange between Iver Neumann 1999 and David Campbell 1998.
15 Humrich 2006 is critical of this development for principled reasons; cf. already the controversy between Hellmann 1994 and Zürn 1994; on the older generation of German IR see Gantzel-Kress and Gantzel 1980; Czempiel 1986. In any case German IR has exhibited new dynamism and ambition in recent years, as evidenced by the new – and peer-reviewed – journal *Zeitschrift für Internationale Beziehungen* and more recently large research centers in Bremen and Berlin (more on Germany in the final section of this chapter).
16 To our knowledge, there are no recent surveys of IR in Austria, Switzerland, the Netherlands, and Belgium (except Goetschel 1999 for Switzerland; older surveys include Everts 1976; Yakentchouk 1978; Gärtner *et al.* 1980; Baehr 1982; Skuhra 1994).
17 Tocqueville 1988; Elias 2000: 277–362.
18 Where IR has been influenced by history, it was the sociological tradition of the Annales School.
19 It is hard to do both, and most scholars do not even try.
20 One may add Pareto, Michels, and even Gramsci for Italy (Pasquino 1990), and compare this to more radical attempts in Spain, during the dictatorship of General Franco, to construct a national history of political science with origins in medieval theology and jurisprudence (Beneyto 1949).
21 The model was France, with its École Libre de Sciences Politiques.
22 There was some continuity with the ideas of Gaetano Mosca.
23 On Sartori see Pasquino 2005.
24 For example, the Istituto Affari Internazionali (IAI), close to the Ministry of Foreign Affairs in Rome; the independent Centro Studi di Politica Internazionale (CeSPI), also in Rome; and the Centro Einaudi in Turin.
25 For good arguments why Canada and the U.S. should not be lumped together see Cox and Nossal, Chapter 16, this volume.
26 Other possible explanations are intensified competition in American IR and the drift of IR towards intra-paradigmatic "normal science" following the peak of the "fourth debate" in the mid-1990s (Wæver 2007).

27 Especially in a short-term analysis like the one in Figure 15.2, it is possibly unfortunate to have only the data referring to country of residence, not origin. Britain has attracted quite a few young continental Europeans, not least Germans in recent decades (possibly linked to both the economic situation in Germany and intellectual working conditions), and the graphs might reflect neither the productivity of different soils, nor the long-term strength of the different research communities, but mostly the specific distribution at a given time, where these people do work in the UK.

28 Where we so far relied on statistics regarding publication patterns, in this context it would be more relevant to look at citation figures, but these are hard to generate on a geographical format.

29 Similarly, Biersteker's contribution to this volume (Chapter 17) shows how texts written by European scholars continue to be almost totally absent from the syllabi of key courses in the U.S.

30 According to the Social Science Citation Index and Google Scholar, the four most cited scholars within the region defined by this chapter are Thomas Risse, Ole Wæver, Friedrich Kratochwil, and Iver B. Neumann. It is interesting to note that all four are either German (with significant careers in the U.S.) or Scandinavian (without U.S. careers), which illustrates the prevalence of output from the "multi-level research cooperation" strategy.

31 Another way to explain the limited presence of European scholars in leading journals and the lack of independent theory could be to focus on the kind of theory preferred in Europe compared to the U.S. It may be argued (Ross 1992; Wæver 1998) that there are deep forces pushing Americans towards a nomothetic, anti-historical form of science while Europeans are more inclined towards a historically sensitive, less scientist view of social science. The problem with this explanation is that it does not explain the low publication profile of European scholars. It is simply not true that the leading journals want grand theorizing all over, but they actually publish a lot of applications and mid-range theory.

References

Anckar, Dag (1987) "Political science in the Nordic countries," *International Political Science Review*, 8 (1): 73–84.

Angstrom, Jan, Erik Hedenstrom and Lars-Inge Strom (2003) "Survival of the most cited? Small political science communities and international influence: the case of Sweden," *European Political Science*, 2 (3): 5–16.

Aron, Raymond (1962) *Paix et guerre entre les nations*, Paris: Calman Lévy; trans. (1966) *Peace and War: A Theory of International Relations*, Garden City, NY: Doubleday.

Attinà, Fulvio (1987) "The study of International Relations in Italy," *Millennium*, 16 (2): 325–332; reprinted in Hugh C. Dyer and Leon Mangasarian (eds) (1989) *The Study of International Relations: The State of the Art*, Basingstoke: Macmillan, pp. 344–357.

Aydinli, Ersel and Julie Mathews (2000) "Are the core and periphery irreconcilable? The curious world of publishing in contemporary international relations," *International Studies Perspectives*, 16 (1): 289–303.

Badie, Bertrand (1999) *Un monde sans souveraineté: Les Etats entre ruse et responsabilité*, Paris: Fayard.

Badie, Bertrand (2004) *L'impuissance de la puissance: Essai sur les nouvelles relations internationales*, Paris: Fayard.

Badie, Bertrand (2008) *Le diplomate et l'intrus: L'entrée des sociétés dans l'arène internationale*, Paris: Fayard.

Badie, Bertrand and Marie-Claude Smouts (eds) (1992) *Le retournement du monde: Sociologie de la scène internationale*, Paris: Presses de la Fondation Nationale de Sciences Politiques.

Baehr, Peter R. (1982) "International relations research in the Netherlands," *Orbis*, 26: 517–525.

Bartelson, Jens (1995) *A Genealogy of Sovereignty*, Cambridge: Cambridge University Press.

Bartelson, Jens (2001) *The Critique of the State*, Cambridge: Cambridge University Press.

Beck, Ulrich (1992) *Risk Society: Towards a New Modernity*, London: Sage.

Beneyto, Juan (1949) *Los Orígenes de la Ciencia Política en España*, Madrid: Instituto de Estudios Políticos.

Bigo, Didier (1996) *Polices en réseaux: L'expérience européenne*, Paris: Presses de Sciences Po.

Bobbio, Norberto (1989) *Il Terzo Assente: Saggi e Discorsi sulla Pace e la Guerra*, Turin and Milan: Sonda.

Bobbio, Norberto (1997 [1979]) *Il Problema della Guerra e le Vie della Pace*, Bologna: il Mulino.

Bobbio, Norberto (2001 [1986]) "La scienza politica e la tradizione di studi politici in Italia," in id., *Saggi sulla Scienza Politica in Italia*, Roma-Bari: Laterza, pp. 245–263.

Bonanate, Luigi (1984) "Gli studi delle relazioni internazionali in Italia: la sindrome del 'brutto anatroccolo'," in Antonella Arculeo *et al.*, *La Scienza Politica in Italia: Materiali per un Bilancio*, Milan: FrancoAngeli (= Fondazione Feltrinelli, Quaderni 28–29), pp. 49–76.

Breitenbauch, Henrik Ø. (2008) "Cartesian Limbo: A Formal Approach to the Study of Social Sciences: International Relations in France," Ph.D. dissertation, University of Copenhagen.

Breitenbauch, Henrik Ø. and Anders Wivel (2004) "Understanding national IR disciplines outside the United States: political culture and the construction of international relations in Denmark," *Journal of International Relations and Development*, 7 (4): 413–443.

Brighi, Elisabetta and Fabio Petito (2008) "IR? No thanks, in Italy we prefer geopolitics: or on Italy's foreign policy discourse and practice," *International Politics*, forthcoming.

Buzan, Barry, Ole Wæver and Jaap de Wilde (1998) *Security: A New Framework for Analysis*, Boulder, CO: Lynne Rienner.

Campbell, David (1998) "Epilogue: the disciplinary politics of theorizing identity," in *Writing Security: United States Foreign Policy and the Politics of Identity* (2nd revised edn), Manchester/ Minneapolis: Manchester University Press/University of Minnesota Press, pp. 207–228.

Carlsnaes, Walter (1987) *Ideology and Foreign Policy: Problems of Comparative Conceptualization*, Oxford: Blackwell.

C.A.S.E. Collective (2006) "Critical approaches to security in Europe: a networked manifesto," *Security Dialogue*, 37 (4): 443–487.

Cerutti, Furio (ed.) (2000) *Gli Occhi sul Mondo: Le Relazioni Internazionali in Prospettiva Interdisciplinare*, Roma: Carocci.

Cesa, Marco (ed.) (2004) *Le Relazioni Internazionali*, Bologna: il Mulino.

Churchill, Sir Winston (1940) Radio broadcast on January 20.

Cotta, Mauricio, Donatella della Porta and Leonardo Morlino (2001) *Fondamenti di Scienza Politica*, Bologna: il Mulino.

Curcio, Carlo (1963) *Carlo Alfieri e le Origini della Scuola Fiorentina di Scienze Politiche*, Milano: Giuffrè.

Czempiel, Ernst-Otto (1986) "Der Stand der Wissenschaft von den internationalen Beziehungen und der Friedensforschung in der Bundesrepublik Deutschland," in Klaus von Beyme (ed.), *Politikwissenschaft in der Bundesrepublik Deutschland*, Opladen: Westdeutscher Verlag (= *Politische Vierteljahresschrift*, Sonderheft 17), pp. 250–263.

D'Addio, Mario (1993) "Gaetano Mosca e l'istituzione della facoltà romana di scienze politiche (1924–1926)," *Il Politico*, 166 (3): 329–373.

Diez, Thomas and Antje Wiener (2004) "Introducing the Mosaic of Integration Theory", in Antje Wiener and Thomas Diez (eds), *European Integration Theory*, Oxford: Oxford University Press, pp. 1–21.

Duroselle, Jean-Baptiste (1952) "L'étude des relations internationales: objet, méthode, perspectives," *Revue Française de Science Politique*, 3 (2): 676–701.

Eberwein, Wolf-Dieter and Knud Erik Jørgensen (2005) "The Standing Group on International Relations: looking back – moving ahead. An internal evaluation report," August.

Ekman, Joakim (2007) "The times they are a-changing: the internationalisation of Swedish political science," *European Political Science*, 6 (3): 268–275.

Elgström, Ole and Christer Jönsson (2005) *European Union Negotiations: Processes, Networks and Institutions*, London: Routledge.

Elias, Norbert (2000 [1939]) *The Civilizing Process: Sociogenetic and Psychogenetic Investigations*, Malden, MA: Blackwell.

Eriksen, Erik Oddvar (ed.) (2005) *Making the European Polity: Reflexive Integration in the EU*, London: Routledge.

Eriksen, Erik Oddvar, John Erik Fossum and Augustín José Menéndez (eds) (2004) *Developing a Constitution for Europe*, London: Routledge.

Everts, Philip P. (1976) "International studies in the Netherlands," in Ford Foundation (ed.), *International Studies in Six European Countries: United Kingdom, France, Federal Republic of Germany, Sweden, Netherlands, Italy*, New York: Ford Foundation, pp. 191–260.

Frank, Robert (2003) "Penser historiquement les relations internationales," *Annuaire Français des relations internationales*, 4: 42–65.

Friedrichs, Jörg (2004) *European Approaches to International Relations Theory: A House with Many Mansions*, London: Routledge.

Friedrichs, Jörg (2006) "The Nordic countries," in Knud Erik Jørgensen and Tonny Brems Knudsen (eds), *International Relations in Europe: Traditions, Perspectives and Destinations*, London: Routledge, pp. 125–148.

Gantzel-Kress, Gisela and Klaus Juergen Gantzel (1980) "The development of international relations studies in West Germany," in Ekkehart Krippendorff and Volker Rittberger (eds), *The Foreign Policy of West Germany: Formation and Contents*, London: Sage, pp. 197–269.

Gärtner, Heinz, Otmar Höll, Helmut Kramer and Hanspeter Neuhold (1980) *Internationale Beziehungen in Österreich: Eine Bestandsaufnahme*, Laxenburg: Österreichisches Institut für Politikwissenschaft.

Gentile, Emilio (2003) "La Facoltà di scienze politiche nel periodo fascista," in F. Lanchester (ed.), *Passato e Presente delle Facoltà di Scienze Politiche*, Milan: Giuffrè, pp. 45–85.

Gibbons, Michael, Camille Limoges, Helga Nowotny, Simon Schwartzman, Peter Scott and Martin Trow (1994) *The New Production of Knowledge: The Dynamics of Science and Research in Contemporary Societies*, London: Sage.

Giesen, Klaus-Gerd (1992) *L'éthique des relations internationales: Les théories anglo-américaines contemporaines*, Brussels: Bruylant.

Giesen, Klaus-Gerd (2006) "France and other French-speaking countries (1945–1994)," in Knud Erik Jørgensen and Tonny Brems Knudsen (eds), *International Relations in Europe: Traditions, Perspectives and Destinations*, London: Routledge, pp. 19–46.

Glucksmann, André (2003) *Ouest contre ouest*, Paris: Plon.

Glucksmann, André (2004) *Le discours de la haine*, Paris: Plon.

Goetschel, Laurent (1999) "Außenpolitikanalyse in der Schweiz: Paradigma oder Sonderfall? Zum Einfluss von Entscheidungsprozessen auf nationale Rollenkonzepte," *Zeitschrift für Internationale Beziehungen*, 6 (2): 349–370.

Goldmann, Kjell (1988) *Change and Stability in Foreign Policy: The Problems and Possibilities of Détente*, Princeton, NJ: Princeton University Press.

Goldmann, Kjell (1995) "Im Westen nichts Neues: seven international relations journals in 1972 and 1992," *European Journal of International Relations*, 1 (2): 245–258.

Graziano, Luigi (1991) "The development and institutionalization of political science in Italy," in David Easton, John G. Gunnell and Luigi Graziano (eds), *The Development of Political Science: A Comparative Survey*, London: Routledge, pp. 127–146.

Groom, A. J. R. (2005) "International Relations in France: a view from across the channel," *European Political Science*, 4 (2): 164–174.

Grosser, Alfred (1956) "L'étude des relations internationales, spécialité Américaine?," *Revue Française de Science Politique*, 6 (3): 634–651.

Guzzini, Stefano (2004) "'The Cold War is what we make of it': when peace research meets constructivism in international relations," in Stefano Guzzini and Dietrich Jung (eds), *Contemporary Security Analysis and Copenhagen Peace Research*, London: Routledge, pp. 40–52.

Guzzini, Stefano (2007) "Theorising International Relations: lessons from Europe's periphery," Copenhagen: *DIIS Working Paper*, no. 2007/30.

Hansen, Lene (2006) *Security as Practice: Discourse Analysis and the Bosnian War*, London: Routledge.

Hassner, Pierre (1995) *La violence et la paix: De la bombe atomique au nettoyage ethnique*, Paris: Editions Esprit; trans. (1997) *Violence and Peace: From the Atomic Bomb to Ethnic Cleansing*, Budapest: Central European University Press.

Hassner, Pierre and Justin Vaïsse (2003) *Washington et le monde: Dilemmes d'une superpuissance*, Paris: Autrement.

Hellmann, Gunther (1994) "Für eine problemorientierte Grundlagenforschung: Kritik und Perspektiven der Disziplin 'Internationale Beziehungen' in Deutschland," *Zeitschrift für Internationale Beziehungen*, 1 (1): 65–90.

Hellmann, Gunther, Klaus Dieter Wolf and Michael Zürn (eds) (2003) *Die neuen Internationalen Beziehungen: Forschungsstand und Perspektiven in Deutschland*, Baden-Baden: Nomos.

Holden, Gerald (2006) "Approaches to IR: the relationship between Anglo-Saxon historiography and cross-community comparison," in Knud Erik Jørgensen and Tonny Brems Knudsen (eds), *International Relations in Europe: Traditions, Perspectives and Destinations*, London: Routledge, pp. 225–252.

Hopmann, P. Terrence (1994) "French perspectives on international relations after the Cold War," *Mershon International Studies Review*, 38: 69–93.

Humrich, Cristoph (2006) "Germany," in Knud Erik Jørgensen and Tonny Brems Knudsen (eds), *International Relations in Europe: Traditions, Perspectives and Destinations*, London: Routledge, pp. 73–99.

Huysmans, Jef (2006) *The Politics of Insecurity: Fear, Migration and Asylum in the EU*, London: Routledge.

Ikenberry, G. John and Vittorio E. Parsi (eds) (2001a) *Teorie e Metodi delle Relazioni Internazionali: La Disciplina e la Sua Evoluzione*, Rome and Bari: Laterza.

Ikenberry, G. John and Vittorio E. Parsi (eds) (2001b) *Manuale di Relazioni Internazionali: Dal Sistema Bipolare all'età Globale*, Rome and Bari: Laterza.

Jamison, Andrew (1977) "The sociology of science in Scandinavia," in Robert K. Merton and Jerry Gaston (eds), *The Sociology of Science in Europe*, Southern Illinois University Press, pp. 335–358.

Jean, Carlo (2003) *Manuale di Geopolitica*, Rome and Bari: Laterza.

Jönsson, Christer (1993) "International politics: Scandinavian identity amidst American hegemony?," *Scandinavian Political Studies*, 16 (2): 149–165.

Jönsson, Christer and Martin Hall (2005) *Essence of Diplomacy*, Basingstoke and New York: Palgrave Macmillan.

Jørgensen, Knud Erik (2000) "Continental IR Theory: The Best Kept Secret," *European Journal of International Relations*, 6 (1): 9–42.

Jørgensen, Knud Erik and Tonny Brems Knudsen (eds) (2006) *International Relations in Europe: Traditions, Perspectives and Destinations*, London: Routledge.

Krause, Keith and Michael C. Williams (1997) *Critical Security Studies: Concepts and Cases*, London and New York: Routledge.

Lacoste, Yves (1997) *Vive la nation: Destin d'une idée géopolitique*, Paris: Fayard.

Le Gloannec, Anne-Marie and Aleksander Smolar (eds) (2003) *Entre Kant et Kosovo: Etudes offertes à Pierre Hassner*, Paris: Sciences Po.

Leander, Anna (1997) "Bertrand Badie: cultural diversity changing international relations," in Iver B. Neumann and Ole Wæver (eds), *The Future of International Relations: Masters in the Making?*, London: Routledge, pp. 145–169.

Lebedeva, Marina M. (2004) "International Relations studies in the USSR/Russia: is there a Russian national school of IR studies?," *Global Society*, 18 (3): 263–278.

Lucarelli, Sonia and Roberto Menotti (2006) "Italy," in Knud Erik Jørgensen and Tonny Brems Knudsen (eds), *International Relations in Europe: Traditions, Perspectives and Destinations*, London: Routledge, pp. 47–71.

Lyons, Gene M. (1982) "Expanding the study of international relations: the French connection," *World Politics*, 35 (1): 135–149.

Maliniak, David, Amy Oakes, Susan Peterson and Michael J. Tierney (2007) "The view from the ivory tower: TRIP survey of IR faculty in the United States and Canada," *Reves Center/Art and Sciences*, College of William and Mary, Williamsburg, VA, February.

Martres, Jean-Louis (2003) "De la nécessité d'une théorie des relations internationales: l'illusion paradigmatique,"*Annuaire Français de relations internationales*, 4: 19–41.

Merle, Marcel (1974; 4th edn 1988) *Sociologie des relations internationales*, Paris: Dalloz.

Mikelis, Kyriakos (2003) "The self-reflection of the Greek I.R. community: the decade of the 1990s," 1st LSE Ph.D. Symposium on Social Science Research in Greece, June 21.

Morlino, Leonardo (1991) "La scienza politica Italiana: tradizione e realtà," *Rivista Italiana di Scienza Politica*, 21 (1): 91–124; trans. (1991) "Political science in Italy: tradition and empiricism," *European Journal of Political Research*, 20 (4): 341–358.

Mosca, Gaetano (1896) *Elementi di Scienza Politica*, Turin: Bocca.

Mouritzen, Hans (1998) *Theory and Reality of International Relations*, Aldershot: Ashgate.

Mouritzen, Hans and Anders Wivel (eds) (2005) *The Geopolitics of Euro-Atlantic Integration*, London: Routledge.

Neumann, Iver B. (1999) *Uses of the Other: "The East" in European Identity Formation*, Minneapolis: University of Minnesota Press.

Neumann, Iver B. (2006) "Sublime diplomacy: Byzantine, early modern, contemporary," *Millennium*, 34 (3): 865–888.

Neumann, Iver B. (2007) "'A speech that the entire ministry may stand for,' or: why diplomats never produce anything new," *International Political Sociology*, 1 (2): 183–200.

Nowotny, Helga, Peter Scott and Michael Gibbons (2001) *Rethinking Science: Knowledge in an Age of Uncertainty*, Cambridge: Polity.

Panebianco, Angelo (1997) *Guerrieri Democratici: Le Democrazie e la Politica di Potenza*, Bologna: Il Mulino.

Papisca, Antonio (1984) "Gli studi di relazioni internazionali in Italia: La politologia dell'integrazione Europea," in Antonella Arculeo *et al.*, *La Scienza Politica in Italia: Materiali per un Bilancio*, Milan: FrancoAngeli (= Fondazione Feltrinelli, Quaderni 28–29), pp. 77–115.

Parsi, Vittorio E. (1998) *Interesse Nazionale e Globalizzazione: I Regimi Democratici nelle Trasformazioni del Sistema Power-Westfaliano*, Milan: Jaca Books.

Pasquino, Gianfranco (1977) "Le relazioni internazionali in un paese senza politica estera," in Istituto di Studi Nordamericani di Bologna (ed.), *L'Insegnamento e la Teoria delle Relazioni Internazionali Negli Stati Uniti e in Italia*, Bologna: Cooperativa Libraria Universitaria Editrice, pp. 27–40.

Pasquino, Gianfranco (1990) *Political Science in Italy: Recurrent Problems and Perspectives*, Barcelona: Institut de Ciencies Politiques i Socials, Working Paper no. 26.

Pasquino, Gianfranco (ed.) (2005) *La Scienza Politica di Giovanni Sartori*, Bologna: Il Mulino.

Patomäki, Heikki (2002) *After International Relations: Critical Realism and the (Re)construction of World Politics*, London: Routledge.

Revel, Jean-Francois (2002) *L'obsession anti-américaine: Son fonctionnement, ses causes, ses inconséquences*, Paris: Plon.

Rigueira, Paulo (2007) "International relations in Portugal: The dominant tradition, the critics and the future. I bet that we will look good on the (inter)national dancefloor," unpublished.

Rosamond, Ben (2006) "Disciplinarity and the political economy of transformation: the epistemological politics of globalization studies," *Review of International Political Economy*, 13 (3): 516–532.

Rosamond, Ben (2007a) "The political sciences of European integration: disciplinary history and EU studies," in Knud Erik Jørgensen, Mark. A. Pollack and Ben J. Rosamond (eds), *Handbook of European Union Politics*, London: Sage, pp. 7–30.

Rosamond, Ben (2007b) "European integration and the social science of EU studies: the disciplinary politics of a subfield," *International Affairs*, 83 (1): 231–252.

Ross, Dorothy (1992) *The Origins of American Social Science*, Cambridge: Cambridge University Press.

Segura, Garcia (2006) "Spain," in Knud Erik Jørgensen and Tonny Brems Knudsen (eds), *International Relations in Europe: Traditions, Perspectives and Destinations*, London: Routledge, pp. 100–124.

Silj, Alesandro (1976) "Italy," in Ford Foundation (ed.), *International Studies in Six European Countries: United Kingdom, France, Federal Republic of Germany, Sweden, Netherlands, Italy*, New York: Ford Foundation, pp. 261–312.

Sindjoun, Luc (2002) *Sociologie des relations internationales africaines*, Paris: Karthala.

Skuhra, Anseln (1994) *International Studies in Austria 1945–1991*, Salzburg: Institut für Politikwissenschaft (= Schriftenreihe 1994/2).

Smouts, Marie-Claude (ed.) (1998) *Les nouvelles relations internationales: Pratiques et théories*, Paris: Presses de Sciences Po; trans. (2001) *The New International Relations: Theory and Practice*, London: Hurst & Company.

Sola, Giorgio (1996) *Storia della Scienza Politica: Teorie, Ricerche e Paradigmi Contemporanei*, Roma: Carocci.

Sørensen, Georg (2004) *The Transformation of the State. Beyond the Myth of Retreat*, Basingstoke: Palgrave Macmillan.

Tocqueville, Alexis de (1988 [1856]) *The Ancien Régime*, trans. John Bonner, London: Dent.

Toscano, Roberto (2000) *Il Volto del Nemico: La Sfida dell'etica nelle Relazioni Internazionali*, Milan: Guerrini e Associati.

Underdal, Arild (1997) "Studiet av internasjonal politikk," *Norsk Statsvitenskapelig Tidsskrift*, 13 (3): 299–324.

Vennesson, Pascal (1998) "Les relations internationales dans la science politique aux Etats-Unis," *Politix*, 41: 176–194.

Villumsen, Trine (2007) "Think tanks in Europe: shaping ideas of security," *Militært Tidsskrift*, 136 (2): 143–160.

Wæver, Ole (1990a) "The language of foreign policy" (Review Essay on Carlsnaes, *Ideology and Foreign Policy*), *Journal of Peace Research*, 27 (3): 335–343.

Wæver, Ole (1990b) "Thinking and rethinking in foreign policy" (Review Essay on Goldmann, *Change and Stability in Foreign Policy*), *Cooperation and Conflict*, 25 (3): 153–170.

Wæver, Ole (1998) "The sociology of a not so international discipline: American and European developments in international relations," *International Organization*, 52 (4): 687–727.

Wæver, Ole (2000) "The strange successes of Scandinavian peace research: why the inter-twined disciplines of peace research and international relations develop differently in the U.S., Scandinavia and other parts of Europe," presentation at the conference "In Search of Peace in the Twenty-First Century" in Seoul, January 25, organized by the Korean Peace Research Association and the Korean National Commission for UNESCO.

Wæver, Ole (2004) "Aberystwyth, Paris, Copenhagen: new 'schools' in security theory and their origins between core and periphery," paper prepared for the 45th Annual Convention of the International Studies Association, Montreal, March 17–20; revised version to appear in A.B. Tickner and O. Wæver (eds), *Thinking the International Differently: Worlding Beyond the West*, Vol. 2, London: Routledge.

Wæver, Ole (2007) "The social and intellectual structure of the IR discipline," paper prepared for the 48th Annual Convention of the International Studies Association, Chicago, February 28 to March 3.

Wæver, Ole and Barry Buzan (2007) "After the return to theory: the past, present and future of security studies," in A. Collins (ed.), *Contemporary Security Studies*, Oxford: Oxford University Press, pp. 383–402.

Waltz, Kenneth N. (1959) *Man, the State, and War: A Theoretical Analysis*, New York: Columbia University Press; trans. (1998) *L'Uomo, lo Stato e la Guerra: Un'Analisi Teorica*, Milan: Giuffrè.

Weingart, Peter (2001) *Die Stunde der Wahrheit? Zum Verhältnis der Wissenschaft zu Politik, Wirtschaft und Medien in der Wissensgesellschaft*, Weilerswist: Velbrück Wissenschaft.

Yakentchouk, Romain (1978) "La science politique et l'étude des relations internationales en Belgique," in *Belgisch Buitenlands Beleid en Internationale Betrekkingen: Liber Amicorum Prof. Omer de Raeymaeker*, Leuven, pp. 107–125.

Zolo, Danilo (1995) *Cosmopolis: La Prospettiva del Governo Mondiale*, Milan: Feltrinelli; trans. *Cosmopolis: Prospects for World Government*, Cambridge: Polity Press.

Zolo, Danilo (2000) *Chi dice Umanità: Guerra, Diritto e Ordine Globale*, Turin: Einaudi; trans. (2002) *Invoking Humanity: War, Law and Global Order*, London and New York: Continuum International.

Zürn, Michael (1994) "We can do much better! Aber muss es auf amerikanisch sein? Zum Vergleich der Disziplin 'internationale beziehungen' in den USA und in Deutschland," *Zeitschrift für Internationale Beziehungen*, 1 (1): 91–114.

16 The "crimson world"

The Anglo core, the post-Imperial non-core, and the hegemony of American IR

Wayne S. Cox and Kim Richard Nossal

In any mapping exercise of the global contours of International Relations, a focus on the English-speaking countries of the world makes considerable sense: so much of the discipline of IR has evolved in the academy in English-speaking countries; so much of the research in IR is published in English; and so much of the debate about the discipline occurs in English. What Holsti (1985: ix) called an "Anglo-American core of 'producers'" has dominated the discipline, creating an "intellectual condominium" (Holsti 1985: 103) or a hegemonic educational duopoly (Jarvis 2001: 274–275; see also Wæver 1998; Crawford and Jarvis 2001). And attached to the "core" have been "small appendages in other anglophone countries," notably Australia and Canada (Holsti 1985: ix).

The purpose of this chapter is to examine IR on the "Anglo" side of the putative Anglo-American condominium. However, what constitutes the "Anglo" world of IR is more problematic than it might at first appear. We would start with Britain as a "core" producer – despite the obvious inappropriateness of using "Anglo" to mean all of the United Kingdom.[1] But what beyond that "Anglo core" should be included? Holsti might have recognized the contributions of "small anglophone appendages," but these "anglo"[2] appendages have often been difficult to see. For example, in Wæver's examination of global IR, Canada simply disappears into "North America" (1998: 696). Likewise, in their historiography of IR, Groom and Mandaville (2001: 152–159) discuss "North American" IR, even though there is not a single Canadian, anglophone or francophone, among those they cite. The contributions of the Australian academy have not suffered the same fate, perhaps because there is no wider geographic unit into which Australians can as readily be tossed. But Australian IR does share with Canadian IR that same invisibility accorded to IR in other English-speaking parts of the world that are not deemed "core."

What might comprise the "non-core"[3] of "anglo appendages"? One might include all those sites of IR scholarship where English is the usual language of instruction: Ireland, Canada, the anglophone Caribbean, the English-speaking South Pacific, New Zealand, Australia, Hong Kong, Singapore, the countries of South Asia, and the countries of East, Southern, and West Africa. However, the problem with terming all these places "anglo" or "English-speaking" is that a number of other languages, official and unofficial, are also spoken. Thus, for example, it makes no sense to refer to the Canadian academy as "English-speaking" (or anglo), since francophone scholars (even if they are perfectly fluent in English) would most definitely not consider themselves "anglo"! One could make the same observation about scholars in Ireland, Hong Kong, or South Africa.

We argue that instead of focusing on language, we should consider the one other obvious commonality of these places: they were all at one time part of the British Empire. Indeed, since we are engaged in a mapping exercise, we borrow a cartographic trope to describe both the UK "core" and the "non-core" locales that were at one time a part of the British Empire. In that era, maps of the world invariably showed the various parts of the Empire in crimson: the UK at the imperial center, together with the various dominions, colonies, territories, and dependencies across the globe, the Mercator projection invariably overmagnifying the extent of the Empire on which the sun never set.

Therefore, in this chapter we seek to map the professing of IR in those parts of this post-Imperial (with a capital I) "crimson world" not surveyed by other authors. We look at the United Kingdom, Ireland, Canada, Australia, and New Zealand, and survey the professoriate, their research interests, and the institutions of IR research. We show that there are clear similarities in how IR is being professed in these locales and how the IR community is being socially reproduced in these countries.

While we demonstrate the *similarities* of approaches to IR in these countries, we also demonstrate the *differences* between how IR is professed in the United States and how it is professed in these other locales. Historically, there was little agreement on the nature of the Anglo-American "condominium." For example, Fitzpatrick saw little difference between the "Anglo" and the "American" approaches to IR (1987: 51). By contrast, Lyons claimed that there was a "distance" between British and American scholars (1986: 629); likewise, Smith argued that he could see an "Atlantic divide" in the Anglo-American condominium (Smith 1985: ix–xiv). We suggest that, more recently, the divide has become much wider: the divide is now between these post-Imperial "crimson" locales (the "Anglo core" and the "anglo non-core") on the one hand, and the U.S. on the other. In particular, we will show that the theoretical approaches to IR that enjoy dominance in the American academy, such as rational choice, formal modeling, and quantitative approaches, are generally not employed at all in the "crimson world."

What explains this "crimson" divide – not only the similarities across the five "crimson" countries, but also the differences between the professing of IR in those places and IR in the U.S.? While there are long-term, historical, and underlying causes at work that could explain the evolving shape of the academy on each side of the divide, this chapter focuses on the more immediate and *proximate* causes: the pattern of academic social reproduction over the past decade. In particular, there is an increasing lack of transboundary scholarly cross-fertilization between the academy in these five "post-Imperial" locales on the one hand, and the U.S. on the other. We show that in Britain and Australia, and to a lesser extent in Canada, Ireland, and New Zealand, there has been a tendency to hire indigenously trained Ph.Ds to fill IR positions, or Ph.Ds from other "post-Imperial" countries. The result is that fewer American-trained Ph.Ds now occupy IR posts in these countries. At the same time, however, IR in the U.S. continues to be professed almost entirely by American-trained Ph.Ds. This, we argue, constitutes the emergence of (at least) two separate English-speaking IR "research communities" – in the Kuhnian sense of the term paradigm (Kuhn 1962). Unlike the plethora of paradigmatic typologies that emerged to explain the development of contending theories in IR in the 1970s and 1980s – based variously on such elements as basic assumptions, units of analysis, values, assumptions about the state of nature, or the role of structure and theory – the emergence of an American and Anglo set of IR research communities is built on (at least) two social and academic contexts that have evolved into distinct, but not entirely disconnected, research traditions. Within the Anglo research community, our data show that through hiring practices, preferences of theories and methods, and research interests, the Anglo core and the post-Imperial non-core (the "crimson world") are partially integrated with one another, and they are growing increasingly distinct from the "American" IR core. The "American" core has (rightly or wrongly) been increasingly accused of parochialism, self-referentiality, and working in the interests of the U.S. state in a post 9/11 world – a connection that concerns many non-American IR scholars uncomfortable with the practices and the consequences of uncontested American hegemony.

These developments, we conclude, have considerable implications for the longer term durability of the hegemony of American IR. A decade ago, Wæver argued that we were increasingly seeing the "de-Americanization of IR" in other parts of the world (1998: 726). Our survey of the academy in Britain, Ireland, Canada, New Zealand, and Australia confirms Wæver's contention: the professing of IR in these parts of the world is distinctly more different from the professing of IR in the U.S. than it was even a quarter of a century ago.

We acknowledge that focusing on this divide might be useful for examining differences in how IR is professed in the U.S. and how it is professed in these locales, but it is not without its limitations. First, a focus on division disguises the many differences *within* each of these geographically defined sides of the divide. However, in many ways, American and British realist scholars have much more in common with each other than they do with their national compatriots working within more liberal or radical traditions. Likewise, those more critical traditions that seek to challenge the basic assumptions of the dominant discourses in IR (both liberal and realist) have become increasingly important in the non-core and more firmly grounded outside the American academy (Murphy and Tooze 1991; Onuf 1997). Furthermore, the American academy is so vast and diverse that there are considerable differences in American IR, including significant contributions to the critical school.[4]

We recognize that, to some extent, how IR is professed in many places in the world goes well beyond territoriality. In particular, many of those who receive doctorates in IR from English-speaking universities, whether in the United States or in the post-Imperial locales surveyed in this chapter, go on to profess IR in the non-English-speaking world – in continental Europe, post-colonial Africa, and elsewhere. They might teach in their own language, but their training, their research agendas, and their tendency to publish in English-language journals all place them firmly within a *Western* core of IR. In this sense, the colonialism of Western IR as a discipline has been even more expansive and total than the legacies of British imperialism and later American (neo)colonialism. Indeed, some would argue that this is more properly a form of academic dependency. The form of "colonial present" (Gregory 2004) that IR's "Anglo-American" core has established is one whose territorial expansiveness is arguably greater than that of colonialism itself. However, if indeed there are profound epistemological differences between the "Anglo" and "American" traditions in IR, one should consider which (if any) of the dominant traditions is more closely associated (or perhaps more aptly put, of more use to) IR's dependent colonies of English-speaking scholarship.[5]

The mapping operation: methodology

As with other contributions to this volume, the "mapping exercise" in this chapter seeks to outline the nature of IR as it is professed (or, as Jarvis (2001: 374) likes to put it, "done") in Britain, and, working westward, Ireland, Canada, New Zealand, and Australia. Since the professing of IR in these places is primarily conducted in the confines of universities, we look at IR under three main headings:

- *The university setting* for the professing of IR; in other words, the institutional sites in which IR is taught and researched.
- *The professoriate*, particularly the research interests of IR faculty and their scholarly training. Given the importance of the permanent professoriate for research, (post)-

graduate supervision, and undergraduate teaching, for each country we sought to identify all those who contribute to IR in one way or another. Since the vast majority of the universities offering International Relations programs of some sort have fully developed websites, much of the information about IR programs and the professoriate who offer them was taken from university websites, with follow-up information elicited from colleagues by email. We noted each scholar's research interests as outlined on their unit's website, or inferred it from their publications – though we acknowledge that it is not possible to identify these interests in precise tabular form.[6] Because a scholar's epistemological and ontological approaches to the discipline are so heavily influenced by their (post)graduate education, we also noted the doctoral "pedigree" of each scholar. Our database includes 688 scholars: 319 in the UK, 15 in Ireland, 228 in Canada, 20 in New Zealand, and 106 in Australia.

- *The institutions of IR research*, including the primary scholarly associations, and the main journals for IR scholarship, on the grounds that journals are "the crucial institution of modern sciences" (Wæver 1998: 697).

Three caveats should be entered. First, this chapter focuses on the professoriate and their research interests rather than on their actual research outputs or their teaching activities. A complete mapping of the terrain would require a detailed examination of the actual scholarship of the approximately 700 IR scholars in these four countries, including a characterization of methodologies and epistemologies and a listing of the scholarly outlets selected. It would also require a survey of how IR is actually taught at both the undergraduate and (post)graduate levels at universities in these locales by looking at course outlines/syllabi and the readings, particularly the textbooks (Nossal 2001), assigned to IR students.

Second, the portrait of IR in each of these places is a snapshot taken in 2006; the data are therefore approximate. Universities in most of the locales surveyed in this chapter are in the midst of a major rejuvenation in the ranks of the professoriate, with large-scale retirements and new hirings. Moreover, there will be grey areas. For example, we did not count emeritus or retired faculty. And with increasing "workforce dualization" (Barrow 1995; Nossal 2006) considerable teaching is being done by non-permanent and part-time academics who often do not show up on departmental web-pages.

Finally, our mapping exercise seeks to capture how IR is professed. We attempt to identify those who "do" IR – through their research interests, supervisory interests, or course teaching. The problem, of course, is that the boundaries between IR and other subdisciplines within political science, and between IR and other disciplines such as history, sociology, and international development studies, have grown increasingly blurred. The result is that a mapping exercise runs the risk of pigeon-holing scholars inappropriately – usually by excluding those whose statements of research, supervisory, or teaching interests understate the IR component.

The "Anglo" core: the United Kingdom

A great deal has been written about IR in the United Kingdom (see e.g. Suganami 1983; Holsti 1985; Smith 1985; Lyons 1986; Wæver 1998; Crawford 2001; Little 2002; Kennedy-Pipe and Rengger 2006; Linklater and Suganami 2006, among many others), in particular its contribution to IR theory. These contributions are a key aspect of the evolution of the field itself. From what was eventually termed the English School through to the contemporary debates on post-positivist IR, one can trace a lineage of British scholarship that was, at least in part, distinct from its American counterpart. IR's first "great debate" between idealists and realists was clearly articulated in Carr's *The Twenty Years' Crisis*. Although commonly labeled a realist, Carr and his contemporaries like Wight spent a great deal of time considering the earlier works of Hobbes, Kant, and most importantly Grotius. Carr and Wight (as well as their followers like Hedley Bull and R.J. Vincent) may have shared certain assumptions with popular realists in the United States like Morgenthau, but the British scholars tended to pay more serious attention to the idea of an international society. Moreover, Carr in particular was well trained in the dialectical approach to social philosophy, and he, like many other English School scholars, was far less interested in an applied and "scientific" approach to understanding world politics than his (mostly later) American counterparts (Carr 1939, 1961).

During the Cold War era, the problem-solving emphasis of American realism could be closely linked to the foreign policy interests of the American state. In Britain, the societal aspects of the English School continued to be a more important component of IR approaches. By the time of IR's second discipline-defining debate in the late 1960s that pitted behavioral approaches against those whose method of establishing "fact" was embedded in normative historical explanations, a fairly clear demarcation between (at least part of) the Anglo and American traditions was obvious (Smith and Hollis 1991; Buzan 1993). Many members of the English School (especially early members like Carr) were trained as historians, and most were skeptical of the utility of applied behavioralism when discussing such macro questions as those in world politics (Carr 1961).

Thus, the perceived limitations of realism as the dominant lens in IR fostered alternative approaches to realism, notably liberal and radical schools. These alternatives were not just about a different set of primary assumptions from the realist core of IR as described by Holsti and Banks in the 1980s; they were also further developments of the English School's notion of international society (e.g. Bull 1977), or, in the case of Marxists, a structural system, and, most of the alternatives to realism also shared concerns about positivist/behavioral claims to truth (Banks 1985; Holsti 1985). Almost ironically, the rejection of realism became increasingly associated with a rejection of positivism/behavioralism in the wake of the "second debate." The melding of realism and positivism/behavioralism was mostly (but not exclusively) an American enterprise (Wæver 1997).

By the advent of neorealism in the 1980s (especially Waltz's version of structural realism), the scientific method of positivism had become an integral aspect of neorealist assertions (Waltz 1979). Although there were varying degrees to which neorealists built on or used behavioral methods, Waltz's claim that a good theory is only good to the extent to which it can accurately explain the "world as it is" was particularly difficult for many outside of the U.S. to accept. The idea that theory could be objective, or that IR theorists should aspire to be objective, flew in the face of an understanding of all theories as inherently political – whether intended or not. For an increasing number of scholars outside of the U.S., theoretical claims about the "world as it is" are a reflection of social context from which those claims are made, who is making the claims, and for what purpose. Such an understanding of theory came from a set of epistemological assumptions that were incommensurable with those of positivism. These two epistemological paradigms became the basis of IR's "third debate" between positivism and dialectics (Heilbroner 1980). By the early 1990s, the relevance of the various versions of neorealism seemed to be seriously challenged by the end of the Cold War system. However, while neorealism itself did not disappear, the alternatives to realism and neorealism within the American academy (mainly liberal and later social constructivist approaches) had also become heavily enmeshed in a wider trend throughout American political science towards problem-solving and positivist traditions. For Ricci, the "tragedy" of American political science was its preference for the scientific and applied aspects of IR; by contrast, the British tradition (along with many within English-speaking IR in Europe, Canada, Australasia, and elsewhere) was marked by a wider mistrust of the implied politics of the so-called attempts at theoretical and empirical objectivity (Ricci 1984). While this, of course, was not exclusively true in either case – there are many post-positivist IR scholars at work within the American academy, and many positivists at work within the British and other academies – one cannot deny that the roots of post-positivist IR are linked to the differences between the American and Anglo traditions. Our "mapping exercise" of the UK demonstrates these differences.

The university setting

Hoffmann claimed that IR was "born and raised in America" (1977: 60), but such a claim of paternity would not stand up well in a DNA test. Professorial chairs in International Relations and departments of international politics emerged in Britain long before IR emerged as a discipline in the United States. In 1919, a professorial chair at the University College of Wales at Aberystwyth was endowed as a memorial to those who had died in the Great War. This Woodrow Wilson Chair was intended to explore the causes of war and the conditions of peace in international politics, and around this Chair was organized the first Department of International Politics, with Alfred Zimmern as the Wilson Chair and Sydney Herbert as the first lecturer in the field. In 1920 the Stephenson Chair in International History was created at the University of London; in 1924 the Sir Ernest Cassel Chair in International Relations was created, with Philip Noel-Baker as its first incumbent. These chairs, together with a readership in international law, formed the basis of a new Department of International Studies that gave courses on international relations, diplomatic and international institutions, and inter-imperial relations of the British Empire. In 1924, Sir Montague Burton, owner of a tailoring firm which, inter alia, provided uniforms for the British army during World War II, endowed a professorship at Oxford University to give, in the words of the university's statutes, "instruction on the theory and practice of International Relations," and in 1930 gave the London School of Economics and Political Science a bequest to support Noel-Baker's professorship (Suganami 1983; Lyons 1986; Wæver 1998: 709–712; Bauer and Brighi 2003).

These early developments had at least two lasting impacts on the evolution of IR in Britain. First, the establishment of specific chairs and institutes in the UK meant that IR as an academic discipline was in many instances institutionally insulated from larger departments of politics or political science. The early scholars of IR were often trained in the related disciplines of history, diplomacy, international law, or political philosophy (among others) and, as a result, they brought to the study of IR intellectual tools and traditions from their related fields of study. In most instances, behavioral and rational-choice methods were not the preferred means for making claims about the world as it was (or is).

The institutional isolationism that came with specific schools of IR also meant that the behavioral revolution which swept through the American academy in the 1950s and 1960s was far less prevalent in British IR. For those trained as social historians or those whose intellectual links were to debates in contemporary philosophy, applied behavioral methodologies seemed to be irrelevant to the key issues of IR. For some at least, IR's second great debate was less about a choice and more about an American flirtation with a method of particular use to policy-makers and think-tanks.

Second, IR in Britain was transformed by the rapid expansion of the university system over the course of the twentieth century – most recently by the "promotion" of a large number of polytechnics to universities. In particular, this has had the effect of dramatically increasing the size of the IR professoriate, and, as we will argue below, diversifying it.

Today, IR is taught at 65 of the UK's 89 universities. Whereas in the U.S. most IR teaching and research is lodged almost exclusively in departments of political science (or government), in Britain IR is professed in a variety of institutional settings. First, the historical legacy of the British origins of IR may be seen in the maintenance of separate departments, schools or centers of international politics (University College of Wales at Aberystwyth and City University) or International Relations (London School of Economics, St. Andrews, and Nottingham Trent). At 14 universities, IR is taught in departments or schools of politics, political studies, or government (only one university – Birmingham – has a "political science" department). The most common disciplinary unit is politics and the international: at 22 universities IR is taught in units of International Relations or international studies and government or politics. A number of universities have abandoned the departmentalized model that remains standard in North America, so that at many institutions IR is taught as a subject or a discipline within larger divisions, schools, or faculties that combine politics with cognate (and sometimes not-so-cognate) academic disciplines. At some universities, IR is conducted outside the rubric of politics or political studies altogether: at the University of Bradford, for example, the home of IR is in the Department of Peace Studies.

The professoriate

The "location" of IR within the British academy is crucial for the way in which the discipline is professed. As Wæver (1998: 710) put it, in Britain "IR is much less one-dimensionally defined as political science than is the case in the United States." This is certainly reflected in the research/teaching interests that may be identified for the 319 individuals in this study. While there are some scholars who list their primary interests in the IR subfields of security studies or British and/or American foreign policy, much larger numbers list interests in such areas as international political economy; IR theory of different kinds; critical studies; globalization; gender; and regional international relations. Moreover, the research interests of these scholars tend to be less applied and not so concerned with problem-solving. Most importantly, there are virtually no professors of IR in the British academy who embrace methodologies popular in American IR, such as rational choice or formal modeling.

Contrasting the working groups of the British International Studies Association with the various sections of the International Studies Association (see Table 16.1) shows not only the pattern of research interests in Britain, but also the degree to which research interests differ between the U.S. and the UK. While the ISA is markedly international for a scholarly organization based in the U.S. – in 2006, its 4,000 members came from approximately 70 countries – it is nonetheless dominated by scholars at U.S. universities, and is thus a useful reflection of research interests in American IR.

While there are many similarities between the sections of the two associations, there are also some notable differences. First, a large percentage of ISA sections (10 out of 23) deal with issues, or are dominated by research problems that tend to work within an applied, behavioral, rational-choice, or problem-solving way. By contrast, only about one-third of BISA's working groups deal with applied or problem-solving issues.

Second, ISA's sections are more closely tied to established university disciplines such as education, law, communication, and environmental studies, whereas BISA's sections are

Table 16.1 Research interests and associational subdivisions: BISA and ISA

BISA working groups	ISA sections
Working Group on Art and Politics	Active Learning in International Affairs
Working Group on the Balkans	Comparative International Studies
Working Group on British Foreign Policy	Diplomatic Studies
Working Group on Diplomacy	English School
Working Group on the English School	Environmental Studies
Working Group on Gendering IR	Ethnicity, Nationalism and Migration
Working Group on Global Ethics	Feminist Theory and Gender Studies
Working Group on Historical Sociology and IR	Foreign Policy Analysis
Working Group on International Mediterranean Studies	Global Development Studies
Working Group on Security and Intelligence Studies	Human Rights
Working Group on Small States	Intelligence Studies
Working Group on Sovereignty and its Discontents	International Communication
Working Group on U.S. Foreign Policy	International Education
International Political Economy Group	International Ethics
BISA Network of Activist Scholars of Politics and IR	International Law
	International Organization
	International Political Economy
	International Political Sociology
	International Security Studies
	Peace Studies
	Post-Communist States in IR
	Scientific Study of International Processes
	Women's Caucus

Sources: http://www.bisa.ac.uk/groups/Groups.htm;
http://www.isanet.org/sections.html

organized more around the subfields of IR such as foreign policy and political economy. This may be a reflection of the fact that IR in the UK has had a more distant relationship from the wider field of political science.

However, perhaps the most striking difference between ISA and BISA is the inclusion in the ISA of highly specific applied research working groups such as those on the Scientific Study of International Processes and Active Learning in International Affairs. Although there is usually a higher percentage of American participants at the ISA's annual conventions, a quick review of the program of ISA's 2007 Chicago meeting (http://isanet.ccit.Arizona.edu/chicago2007) reveals that about 80 to 85 percent of those papers with titles indicating a "scientific" approach were given by scholars from American universities.

Finally, also notable is the absence of the kind of "neo/neo" positivist–rationalist research agenda (Wæver 1997) that is so common among IR scholars in the U.S. Certainly the listing confirms the frequent observation that there is a marked absence of any indication of followers of rational choice or quantitative approaches at UK universities (Wæver 1998; Jarvis 2001). Only at the University of Essex did we find an indication that scholars are pursuing the kind of IR research agenda which dominates American IR.

As Table 16.2 shows, the doctoral backgrounds of the UK scholars in this study are overwhelmingly domestic: 233, or 80 percent, received (or actively finished) their doctorate from a UK university; the percentage would be higher still if we added those 16 individuals who profess IR without a doctorate, since the vast majority of them have first or second degrees from UK universities. Only 8 percent have doctorates from American universities. (The remaining 12 percent have Ph.Ds from European, Australian, Canadian, and other universities.)

Table 16.2 IR scholars in the United Kingdom: country where doctorate granted

Country	No.	%
UK	233	79.5
U.S.	24	8.2
Other Europe	16	5.5
Australia	8	2.7
Canada	8	2.7
Other	4	1.4
Totals	293	100.0

The institutions of IR research

As noted above, the main scholarly association for IR in the United Kingdom is BISA. Formed in 1975 to promote interaction and interchange between scholars professing International Relations, BISA holds an annual conference in December at universities around Britain (Kennedy-Pipe and Rengger 2006). It has an active membership of over 1,000: approximately 40 percent of BISA members are postgraduate students; approximately 10 to 12 percent of the membership are from outside the UK, mostly from Europe.

Mention should also be made of Chatham House, the premier international affairs think-tank in the UK. This organization emerged out of an initiative by members of the British and American delegations to the Paris Peace Conference in 1919 to create an Anglo-American Institute of International Affairs with branches in London and New York to discuss international issues and promote international peace. In the event, two national organizations emerged. While the British side of the institute was created quickly in 1920, by contrast, in the United States isolationism slowed the creation of the American branch of the organization. This meant that a joint organization, even with "close" foreigners like the British, was out of the question. As a result, an all-American Council on Foreign Relations was created in 1921. For its part, the Institute of International Affairs moved into the home of former British prime ministers, Chatham House, and received a royal charter in 1926 as the Royal Institute of International Affairs. Today, the organization is known simply as Chatham House. It has over 2,300 members and a considerable research operation overseen by International Relations scholars in their own right.

Journals widely regarded as the "leading" IR journals in Britain are *Review of International Studies*, the journal of BISA; *Millennium*, a student-run journal founded by LSE professor F.S. Northedge in 1971; *International Affairs*, the quarterly journal of Chatham House; and *The Round Table: Commonwealth Journal of International Affairs*, founded in 1910 and now published by Taylor & Francis and edited at the University of Kent. However, there are a large number of journals published by British publishing houses, and edited by scholars at UK universities, that could be added to this list. Most of these journals are more "diverse" in terms of their scholarship than comparable American IR journals. For example, *Millennium* and *Review of International Studies* routinely publish critical IR scholarship; by contrast, *International Studies Quarterly*, *International Organization*, and other leading American journals tend to be dominated by rational-choice, problem-solving scholarship.

The post-Imperial "non-core"

This section looks at the professing of IR in Ireland, Canada, New Zealand, and Australia. We follow the same format used in the case of the "Anglo core" by looking at general contributions to the field, followed by a survey of each country. Less has been written about contributions to IR from the "non-core" countries than has been written about the United Kingdom. This is not to say, however, that there have not been significant contributions made by Irish, Canadian, Australian, and New Zealand scholars – especially in regard to IR theory. Like the case of "Anglo" IR, the evolution of IR in these non-core countries has been a part of the evolution of the discipline itself. Any serious reading list on IR theory would likely include the works of Canadian and Australian scholars such as Kal Holsti or Hedley Bull. Although it has been common to bemoan Canadian IR as a miniature replica of American realist thought (Rioux *et al.* 1988: 57–58; Melakopides 1998: 14; Keeble and Smith 1999: 9–10), recently Canadian IR has come to be known theoretically for contributions to critical theory.

In his seminal and discipline-defining piece on IR's "third debate," Lapid acknowledged that his call for more reflexive theorizing came out of his experiences as a visiting scholar to Canada in the late 1980s (Lapid 1989). At that time, Canadian-based neo-Gramscian and post-structural scholars like Robert W. Cox, Stephen Gill, and R.B.J. Walker were beginning to question the implications of a dominant form of theorization that was firmly rooted in an understanding that theory itself could be an objective reflection of the "world as it is" (Cox 1987; Gill 1993; Walker 1993; Cox and Sinclair 1996). In the wake of Lapid's call for methodological and theoretical pluralism (a pluralism that included space for critical and reflexive approaches that claimed all theory to be inherently political), a number of scholars in Canada sought to redefine the critical school (e.g. Cox 1987; Gill 1993; Walker 1993; Sjolander and Cox 1994; Whitworth 1994; Neufeld 1995). Indeed, by the mid-1990s, so many critical scholars in Canada had embraced a neo-Gramscian perspective that in 1995 Steve Smith referred to the "Canadian–Italian" school of International Relations (Smith 1995).

As in Canada, there was a marked transformation in the IR community in Australia and New Zealand in the 1990s. While the Australian contribution to the English School in the 1960s and the 1970s was very much in the realist tradition, by the 1990s this had changed dramatically. In 1987 Kubalkova and Cruickshank might have been criticizing Australian IR for its tendency "to peddle Europocentrism of whatever variety," and calling for an "authentic Australian voice" in the global conversation on IR (Kubalkova and Cruickshank 1987: 118). But in the 1990s, a number of Australian and New Zealand students of IR established themselves as contributors in their own right to global IR theory (e.g. Campbell 1992; Linklater 1992; George 1994; Pettman 1996; and, in New Zealand, True 1996, 2006). Importantly, all of these Australasian voices were writing IR from a critical perspective. For our purposes here, it is interesting to note that while the American IR research paradigm has evolved into a research tradition that values problem-solving approaches, those approaches that are "Anglo" non-core have clear ties to (and in some cases are at the leading edge of) those non-positivist, non-rationalist, and often critical perspectives that one sees in the UK.

Ireland

Ireland has eight universities: Dublin City University; the University of Limerick; National University of Ireland, Galway; National University of Ireland, Maynooth; Trinity College Dublin; University College Dublin; University of Dublin; and University College Cork.

While an undergraduate program in politics is offered at all universities, at two universities (NUI Galway and NUI Maynooth) politics is taught in conjunction with sociology, but at neither university is there a full-time permanent faculty member in IR.

In the other six universities there are 15 scholars of IR teaching in departments or schools of political science (Trinity College Dublin), government (University College Cork), government and law (Dublin City), and politics and public administration (Limerick). Only at University College Dublin is IR taught in a School of Politics and International Relations. The research interests of the 15 scholars of IR include: Irish foreign policy, European Union security, IR theory, IPE, and globalization. Fully 80 percent of these scholars received their doctorates from Irish or UK universities; only 6.7 percent had degrees from U.S. universities.

The Political Studies Association of Ireland (PSAI) provides the main organizational network for political scientists in Ireland, holding an annual conference in October and a postgraduate conference each spring. It maintains seven specialist groups, including an International Relations and Area Studies Specialist Group and the Democratization, Conflict and Peace Studies Specialist Group. PSAI's peer-reviewed journal, *Irish Political Studies*, tends to publish research on domestic Irish politics. Research on IR may be found in *Irish Studies in International Affairs*, published by the Royal Irish Academy and its National Committee for the Study of International Affairs, a scholarly and general interest forum for the discussion of international affairs in Ireland. This journal, published annually, contains scholarship concerned not only with Irish foreign policy, but also with broader issues of international relations.

Canada

IR is taught at virtually all of Canada's 50 universities. Canadian universities remain heavily departmentalized, not having (yet) been affected by the academic managerialism that has almost entirely "de-departmentalized" the Australian academy (see below). As in the United States, IR in Canada is overwhelmingly professed in departments of political science (or political studies, or politics): the only Department of International Studies is at University of Northern British Columbia, where it exists alongside the Department of Political Science; and the only exclusively international affairs department is to be found at the graduate level, the Norman Paterson School of International Affairs (NPSIA) at Carleton University. Doctoral programs in IR are offered at 18 universities: Alberta, British Columbia, Calgary, Carleton, Concordia, Dalhousie, Laval, McGill, McMaster, Montréal, Ottawa, UQAM (Université du Québec à Montréal), Queen's, Royal Military College, Simon Fraser, Toronto, Western Ontario, and York.

A total of 228 full-time/permanent scholars were identified as doing IR in Canada, a marked increase since the late 1990s when Porter (2001: 139) identified 188 full-time IR scholars for his survey. Among the most mentioned research interests are: international relations theory, international political economy, Canadian foreign policy, globalization, and global governance. There is a notable absence of interest (and expertise) in the Canadian academy in many of the methods of IR found in the American academy: rational choice, game theory, formal modeling, or quantitative methods.

This is perhaps particularly surprising given the number of Canadian IR scholars who received their doctoral training in the United States. As Table 16.3 shows, of the 225 scholars with doctorates, nearly 30 percent have doctorates from American universities. However, it should be noted that there has been a particular pattern in the recruitment of individuals with Ph.Ds from U.S. universities: of the 66 scholars with U.S. doctorates, 10 are at francophone

Table 16.3 IR scholars in Canada: country where doctorate granted

Country	No.	%
Canada	120	53.3
U.S.	66	29.3
UK	25	11.1
France/other francophonie	8	3.6
Australia	2	0.9
Other	4	1.8
Totals	225	100.0

universities, and 20 are concentrated at only three English-speaking universities: the University of British Columbia, the University of Toronto, and McGill University. While the departments at UBC, Toronto, and McGill do not exclusively recruit IR scholars with American doctorates – 10 of the 30 IR scholars in the three departments have non-American doctorates – an examination of recruiting patterns over the past three decades suggests that these departments generally hire candidates with an American doctorate in a way not seen at other Canadian universities (Nossal 2000).

The primary associational outlets for IR research are the ISA meetings, the annual meetings of the Canadian Political Science Association, and the Société québécoise de science politique. Graduate students in IR tend to gravitate to the CPSA meetings; to the Colloque de la recherche étudiante en science politique (CRESP), an annual bilingual meeting run by the Société Québécoise de Science Politique involving graduate students from Québec, Ontario and New England. In 2004, Canadian IR scholars formed themselves into a separate region of ISA; there are approximately 250 members of ISA-Canada, which holds its annual regional meeting in conjunction with the CPSA meetings.

There are five main Canadian journals for IR scholarship. The *Canadian Journal of Political Science* (CJPS), the journal of the Canadian Political Science Association, publishes articles in both English and French. While CJPS is primarily an outlet for students of Canadian politics, the journal also publishes IR scholarship. The quarterly journal of the Canadian Institute of International Affairs, formed in 1928 on the model of Chatham House, is the *International Journal*. It is peer-reviewed and edited by university-based scholars. *Canadian Foreign Policy* is a peer-reviewed journal published by the Norman Paterson School of International Affairs at Carleton University, and, as its title suggests, focuses on scholarship in Canadian foreign policy. *Studies in Political Economy* is a peer-reviewed interdisciplinary journal, also published at Carleton University, which since 1979 has provided scholars who work in the traditions of socialist political economy with an outlet for their research. IR scholarship in French appears in *Études Internationales*, published by the Institut québécois des hautes études internationales at Université Laval in Québec City. The *Revue Politique et Sociétés*, the peer-reviewed journal of the Société Québécoise de Science Politique, is not dissimilar to the *Canadian Journal of Political Science* in that it tends to focus on Québec/Canadian politics, comparative politics, and political theory rather than IR (though there have been issues on North American integration and post-Cold War foreign policy).

Australia

Of the 38 universities in Australia 30 teach politics or international relations. Nearly all Australian universities have "de-departmentalized" their teaching, locating political science as "disciplines" or "areas" within larger units, usually schools or faculties. As in Britain, a number of universities have combined government/politics with International Relations/studies (Deakin, Flinders, Macquarie, New England, New South Wales, Queensland, Sunshine Coast, Sydney, and Western Australia).

There is one major dedicated department of International Relations in Australia. The Department of International Relations at Australian National University (ANU) has been a long-standing site of "production" of IR theory, dating back to the 1960s, when Bull was a professor in the department. In 1977, he moved to Oxford as the Montague Burton Professor of International Relations; likewise, Vincent, another leading "English School" scholar, completed his Ph.D. in the ANU department before moving to the UK, as the Montague Burton Professor of International Relations at the London School of Economics. In addition to the DIR, IR is also offered at both the undergraduate and postgraduate levels in the School of Social Sciences in the Faculty of Arts.

The Ph.D. in IR is offered at a number of universities, including Adelaide, ANU, Deakin, Flinders, LaTrobe, Melbourne, Monash, Murdoch, New South Wales, Queensland, Sydney, Tasmania, and Wollongong. However, ANU enjoys a major position in the Australian academy: nearly 40 percent (26 out of 67) of Australians currently teaching IR have doctorates from the ANU.

A total of 106 IR scholars in Australia was identified; five do not have doctorates. Of the remaining 101, 67 (66.3 percent) have doctorates from Australian universities. A further 20 scholars have doctoral degrees from the UK; fewer than 10 percent have doctorates from American universities (see Table 16.4).

While Australian IR scholars identify an array of research interests, the most frequently mentioned is IR theory, with many indicating a non-realist/anti-realist orientation, confirming the conclusion of observers like Higgott and George in the early 1990s that the English School realism of the 1960s and the 1970s was increasingly being challenged by alternative approaches, particularly critical theory and international political economy (Higgott and George 1990; Higgott 1991). Australian foreign policy is the next most frequently mentioned, followed by international political economy and security issues of different sorts. As in other locales surveyed in this chapter, there is little evidence of interest in rationalist approaches to IR.

While many IR scholars routinely attend the annual meetings of the ISA, there are two major indigenous locations for the presentation of IR research. One is the IR stream of the annual meetings of the Australasian Political Studies Association. The other is the biennial Oceanic Conference on International Studies, designed to be a forum for the presentation of research from Australia, New Zealand, and the South Pacific. Inaugurated in 2004 by the

Table 16.4 IR scholars in Australia: country where doctorate granted

Country	No.	%
Australia	67	66.3
UK	20	19.8
U.S.	9	8.9
Canada	3	3.0
Other	2	2.0
Totals	101	100.0

Department of International Relations at ANU, OCIS meetings were held at the University of Melbourne in 2006 and at the University of Queensland in 2008.

There are three major scholarly journals for IR research published in Australia. The *Australian Journal of Political Science* is a peer-reviewed journal published by the Australasian Political Studies Association; while most of its articles focus on aspects of Australian politics, IR research is also published. The *Australian Journal of International Affairs* is published by the Australian Institute of International Affairs, created in 1933 on the model of Chatham House and the Canadian Institute of International Affairs. Published since 1946, and edited by university professors at the ANU, it provides an outlet for both scholarly and policy-relevant studies on IR. The *Australian Journal of Politics and History* also publishes scholarship on international politics, Australian foreign policy, and Australian relations with the Asia-Pacific region.

New Zealand

IR is taught at six of the eight universities in New Zealand: Auckland, Canterbury, Otago, Massey, Victoria University of Wellington, and Waikato. We identified 20 IR scholars whose research interests are dominated by IR theory (with eight scholars mentioning this as their primary research interest), and foreign policy and security coming in at second place.

Unlike other locales surveyed in this chapter, there is no dominant doctoral pedigree of IR scholars in New Zealand: rather, Ph.D. backgrounds are almost evenly divided between New Zealand (15 percent), Australia (25 percent), the UK (25 percent), the U.S. (20 percent), and Canada and South Africa (15 percent).

The Australasian Political Studies Association and the Oceanic Conference on International Studies are the main venues for the presentation of IR research – other than local conferences and the International Studies Association annual meetings. New Zealand also has an Institute of International Affairs. Founded in 1934, the NZIIA is affiliated with the Victoria University of Wellington. It publishes the *New Zealand International Review*, which is a bimonthly magazine rather than a scholarly journal. The School of Political Science and International Relations at Victoria University of Wellington publishes *AntePodium*, the world's first online academic journal (http://www.vuw.ac.nz/atp/). *AntePodium* is self-consciously anti-mainstream: its website calls for contributions that will develop "critical, subversive, and innovative theoretical approaches to the study of world affairs."

Analysis

How can we explain the patterns of IR outlined above? Our focus is on the proximate rather than the underlying causes at work in the academy in each of these countries. We argue that the *proximate* cause lies in the sociology of the contemporary academy, and particularly in the distinctive patterns of academic social reproduction in the academy in each of these locales. Of considerable importance are the hundreds of hiring decisions that, in the aggregate, give shape to the academy and to how IR is professed. But each hiring decision is a microcosmic exercise in the privileging of some epistemological and methodological approaches, and the rejection of other approaches.

Staffing and the social reproduction of IR

Where scholars receive their doctoral training will have a marked impact on both teaching and research. Our data suggest that in all the locales surveyed in this chapter, there has been

Table 16.5 IR scholars in the Anglo core and the post-imperial non-core

Country	Population (millions)	Universities	# IR scholars identified	% IR scholars with indigenous Ph.Ds	% IR scholars with U.S. Ph.Ds	% IR scholars with other Ph.Ds
United Kingdom	60.6	89	319	79.5	8.2	12.3
Ireland	4.1	8	15	33.3	6.7	60.0
Canada	33.1	47	228	53.3	29.3	17.4
New Zealand	4.2	8	20	15.0	20.0	65.0
Australia	20.3	38	106	66.3	8.9	24.8

a tendency to staff IR positions with those who have received their doctoral training "in country," though this varies considerably, as Table 16.5 shows.

British universities are most inclined to hire those with indigenous Ph.Ds and least inclined to hire those with U.S. doctorates. In the case of Australia, Canada, Ireland, and New Zealand, there has been a progressive abandonment of the practices of their Imperial pasts, born of necessity when universities were being replicated in Imperial possessions, of hiring those with degrees from universities in the Imperial center. In the past, these were either locals who had traveled to the Imperial center for higher education and returned "home" to teach, or those from the Imperial center who moved to the "colonies" (or who were induced to take up positions there by favorable tax regimes[7]).

In both Ireland and New Zealand there is still a reliance on foreign Ph.Ds, a function in part of the small size of the academy in both of those countries. By contrast, in both Australia and Canada we have seen a growing abandonment of reliance on the imperial centre/center and a growing "Canadianization" and "Australianization" of IR.

In Canada, Nossal (2000) has shown that Canadian IR has been increasingly "Canadianized" over the past 30 years. However, Canada does still have the largest concentration of U.S. Ph.Ds within its professoriate (at nearly one-third), and as discussed, these are highly concentrated within three of its larger departments. On pedigree alone, McGill, Toronto, and UBC are the most "Americanized" Canadian departments of political science. It is not coincidental that the largest centers of critical and "alternative" IR are found in more diversified departments, such as York, Carleton, Laval, Simon Fraser, and UQAM, among others. At the same time however, with a large number of Ph.D.-granting institutions in IR and a large cohort of graduate students and recently completed Ph.Ds entering the system, the tradition of a distinct and often less "applied" approach to IR in Canada remains healthy, with a large number of scholars committed to contributing to broader IR debates globally.

The survey here suggests that the same trend is occurring even more robustly in Australia.[8] Two-thirds of those who profess IR in Australia have indigenous Ph.Ds, and their research interests and publications tend to focus, as noted above, on international political economy and critical approaches, as a survey of the 2004 and 2006 Oceanic Conferences on International Studies suggests.[9] While Australian IR theorizing, like Canadian or British theorizing, does not appear to have made an impact in the U.S., there appears to be considerable cross-fertilization between and among academics in the five countries surveyed in this chapter.

In the "Anglo" core, by contrast, we have not seen a similar trend towards a "Britishization" of IR, since the vast majority of those professing IR in the UK have always been UK-educated. So while the "Anglo" core has sustained (and reproduced) itself as primarily Anglo, one would suspect that those differing approaches to the study of IR that have been so strong within the British research and literature will remain distinct from those in the "American" core. It is likely that the close research and paradigmatic relationship between British, Irish, Canadian, and Australian critical post-positivist perspectives will continue. Certainly an examination of a BISA conference program (for example, http://www.bisa.ac.uk/2006/index.htm), or a glance at the topics in publications like *Millennium* or *Review of International Studies* demonstrates the extent to which there is a clear demarcation at the level of epistemological assumptions between the "Anglo"/British and "American" cores in IR.

In this sense, the British "core" reproduces itself in exactly the same way as the American "core": American political science departments are almost completely staffed by scholars who have Ph.Ds from American universities. As American IR has evolved an increasingly unique worldview, with its own preferences for methodologies that are deemed relevant to the core (rational choice, behavioral, positivist, policy relevant, some would argue a-theoretical, or at very least a-historical, and decidedly empirical), the rift between the "Anglo" and "American" cores of IR is often perpetuated by parochial hiring practices. In keeping with Kuhn's notion of a research paradigm, each of these increasingly independent "research communities" has been perpetuating itself, while the common epistemological and methodological preferences within the "crimson world" have resulted in more national cross-fertilization than happens in the case of the "American" core and the outside world.

But as universities in the "non-core" progressively abandon what in Australia is called "colonial cringe" – the almost fawning reverence for the "product" of the core and a concomitant self-deprecation of indigenous "product" – and more like the British and American "cores" – i.e., to increasingly hire those with indigenous Ph.Ds – we are likely to see an acceleration of the second major development we identify in this chapter: the divide between the United States and others.

The crimson divide

The survey in this chapter confirms what many others have argued: that there is a considerable divide between IR as it is professed in the American academy and IR as it is professed in these countries. First, some of the dominant approaches in the United States academy – rational choice, quantitative methods, formal modeling – are simply not found in the "crimson world," a cultural/anthropological oddity given the number of "products" of the American academy who teach in the locales surveyed in this chapter. This, however, merely entrenches the trend noted above: without individuals on staff to reproduce those approaches, Ph.D. programs in the "non-core" will tend to graduate those who are not familiar with, or sympathetic towards, those "American" approaches.

Second, it is true that the American academy remains an important referent for the academy in the non-core. For example, publishing in a leading American journal is still widely perceived to be a mark of scholarly excellence, particularly by those higher up the academic food chain who like any measure that allows them to claim that their institution is "world-class" in the various bean-counting exercises that are deeply entrenched in the contemporary academy. Likewise, some "theoretical products" of the American academy tend to be "consumed" by those outside the United States more eagerly than others: consider the degree to which constructivism has been embraced in the academy in Britain, Canada, Australia, and New Zealand and the degree to which rational choice is actively shunned.

Moreover, it is also important to note that the research interests listed by those who are teaching and researching IR in the locales surveyed in this chapter strongly suggest that the theoretical product of the American academy in IR is frequently used in a largely negative way: referred to in order to be criticized and rejected in favor of different, and distinctly non-American, perspectives. As Jarvis notes, "the would-be challengers to positivist–rationalist-based epistemologies derive almost universally from non-American pedigrees. British, European, Canadian and Australian theorists have been the originators and driving force of most of these alternative perspectives" (Jarvis 2001: 373). The survey in this chapter confirms this, to the extent that we can infer theoretical perspectives from research interests and publications.

Conclusion: implications for the hegemony of American IR

It is often argued that American IR is hegemonic, and that theoretical and methodological fashions in the U.S. academy dominate academic discourse and fashion in other parts of the world. Likewise, it is often argued that American journals of IR remain the "gold standard" no matter where in the world one professes IR. Yet, as Wæver noted almost a decade ago, global IR was fragmenting into a "not so international discipline." He predicted that the

> result is likely to be a slow drift from a pattern with only one professional and coherent national market – the United States, and the rest of the world more or less peripheral or disconnected – toward a relative American abdication and larger academic communities forming around their own independent cores . . . in short, the "de-Americanization of IR".
>
> (Wæver 1998: 726)

The "divide" identified in this chapter confirms not only Wæver's prediction of greater pluralism in IR, but also his argument that we would see the progressive de-Americanization of IR. The hiring practices in both the American academy itself and those locales surveyed in this chapter suggest that, as IR becomes increasingly nationalized, and nationally self-reproducing, the gulf between American IR and the way in which IR is professed outside the United States will deepen and widen.

Moreover, academic-reproductive feedback mechanisms are likely to entrench these trends. First, as hirings of those with indigenous Ph.Ds increase, the attraction of going to the U.S. for the doctorate will diminish. This, in turn, is likely to cause a diminution in the "colonial cringe" that has historically privileged American Ph.Ds over indigenous doctorates. Second, as the paranoia that washed across the U.S. after 9/11 has made it increasingly difficult for all foreigners to attend American universities, the number of International Relations Ph.Ds trained in the U.S. will diminish, and reduce further the transmission of American methodologies and epistemologies abroad. By the same token, it is likely that more and more students seeking to go abroad for a doctorate in IR will end up in one of the countries surveyed in this chapter. These students are likely to be exposed to an IR that is highly critical of problem-solving approaches; that does not have a central security focus; that is more skeptical of the dominant, or hegemonic, role played by actors such as the U.S.; and that tends towards a worldview of systemic or structural subordination.

Third, this will entrench the absence of certain methodological and epistemological practices that are already noticeable. The almost complete absence of IR scholars in the locales surveyed in this chapter who do rational choice, formal modeling, or quantitative methods is a stark reminder that the jeremiads about American hegemony in IR simply have it wrong. And since virtually no IR doctoral program in Australia, Britain, or Canada teaches methodologies like rational choice or formal modeling in a positive way, it is likely that these are methodologies and epistemologies that will become increasingly more Americo-centric.

Likewise, although the theoretical "production" of the American IR "core" will likely continue to be consumed by those in the non-core, that production is less and less likely to be persuasive to non-American scholars of IR, particularly as other sites of scholarly "production" become more accepted as a "gold standard" in their own right. Certainly, as *International Studies Quarterly* and *International Organization* have become less accessible to scholars who do not employ certain methodologies, and thus less relevant, it is likely that their "value" in non-American eyes will diminish, and other publication outlets will acquire increased value as a place in which to publish.

In short, the hegemonic position of American IR has been seriously challenged by the way in which IR has been "done" in the Anglo core and the post-Imperial non-core in the past decade. IR as it is professed in these countries will never supplant American IR – the American academy is too vast, too self-referential, and too Americo-centric. But our survey of the professoriate in Britain, Ireland, Canada, New Zealand, and Australia strongly suggests that the days of American hegemony in IR are already gone.

Notes

1 As Little (1995), Dunne (1998), and Linklater and Suganami (2006: 12–42) note, the "English School" of IR is similarly misnamed, given the non-English roots of so many of its primary exponents.
2 In Canadian usage, "anglo" – uncapitalized – is both a noun and an adjective for "English-speaking."
3 Although we follow Wallerstein (1976) in seeking to identify a "core," we categorize other places as "non-core" rather than trying to identify the semiperiphery or periphery. See Crawford 2001: 240, n1; Jarvis 2001: 369.
4 R.B.J. Walker (interview, February 25 2004) noted that when Richard Ashley was co-editing *International Studies Quarterly* in the 1980s, an active group of critical theorists was working in American political science departments; by the early 2000s, however, many had moved to departments of history, philosophy, and sociology; indeed, some had left the U.S. altogether. Many were no longer publishing in IR journals but in journals of comparative politics, development studies and post-colonialism, critical social geography and history, contemporary philosophy, and sociology.
5 The approach used in this volume is, of course, just one way of understanding the process of intellectual hegemony. For one of many possible alternatives, see Agnew 2007.
6 While the approaches used by some scholars may be inferred from titles of books and articles, not all faculty members identify their preferred approach. In addition, some professors list more than one research interest.
7 For example, Canada staffed a massive expansion of its university system in the 1960s by negotiating a "tax holiday" with the U.S. Internal Revenue Service for U.S. academics who took positions at Canadian universities.
8 See Jarvis (2001: 374), who claimed that 70 percent of recent IR hires in Australia's seven research-intensive universities had non-Australian degrees.
9 See http://rspas.anu.edu.au/ir/Oceanic/OCISPapers/index.html (2004); and http://www.politics. unimelb.edu.au/ocis/draft.pdf (2006).

References

Agnew, John (2007) "Know-where: Geographies of Knowledge of World Politics," *International Political Sociology*, 1(2): 138–148.
Banks, Michael H. (1985) "The Inter-paradigm Debate in International Relations," in Margot Light and A.J.R. Groom (eds), *International Relations: A Handbook of Current Theory*, London: Pinter, pp. 7–26.

Barrow, Clyde W. (1995) "Beyond the Multiversity: Fiscal Crisis and the Changing Structure of Academic Labour," in John Smyth (ed.), *Academic Work*, Buckingham: Society for Research into Higher Education and Open University Press, pp. 159–178.

Bauer, Harry and Elisabetta Brighi (eds) (2003) *International Relations at LSE: A History of 75 Years*, London: Millennium Publishing Group.

Bull, Hedley (1977) *The Anarchical Society: A Study of Order in World Politics*, New York: Columbia University Press.

Buzan, Barry (1993) "From International System to International Society: Structural Realism and Regime Theory Meet the English School," *International Organization*, 47(3): 327–352.

Campbell, David (1992) *Writing Security: United States Foreign Policy and the Politics of Identity*, Minneapolis: University of Minnesota Press.

Carr, E.H. (1939/2001) *The Twenty Years' Crisis*, London: Palgrave.

Carr, E.H. (1961/2002) *What Is History?*, New York: Penguin Classics.

Cox, Robert W. (1987) *Power, Production and World Order: Social Forces in the Making of World History*, New York: Columbia University Press.

Cox, Robert W. with Timothy Sinclair (1996) *Approaches to World Order*, Cambridge: Cambridge University Press.

Crawford, Robert M.A. (2001) "Where Have All the Theorists Gone – Gone to Britain, Every One? A Story of Two Parochialisms in International Relations," in Robert M.A. Crawford and Darryl S.L. Jarvis (eds), *International Relations – Still an American Social Science? Toward Diversity in International Thought*, Albany: State University of New York Press, pp. 221–242.

Crawford, Robert M.A. and Darryl S.L. Jarvis (eds) (2001) *International Relations – Still an American Social Science? Toward Diversity in International Thought*, Albany: State University of New York Press.

Dunne, Tim (1998) *Inventing International Society: A History of the English School*, Basingstoke: Macmillan.

Fitzpatrick, John (1987) "The Anglo-American School of International Relations: The Tyranny of A-historical Culturalism," *Australian Outlook: The Australian Journal of International Affairs*, 41(1): 45–52.

George, Jim (1994) *Discourses of Global Politics: A Critical (Re)Introduction to International Relations*, Boulder, CO: Lynne Rienner.

Gill, Stephen (1993) *Gramsci, Historical Materialism and International Relations*, Cambridge: Cambridge University Press.

Gregory, Derek (2004) *The Colonial Present: Afghanistan, Palestine, Iraq*, Malden, MA: Blackwell.

Groom, A.J.R. and Peter Mandaville (2001) "Hegemony and Autonomy in International Relations: The Continental Experience," in Robert M.A. Crawford and Darryl S.L. Jarvis (eds), *International Relations – Still an American Social Science? Toward Diversity in International Thought*, Albany: State University of New York Press, pp. 151–166.

Heilbroner, Robert L. (1980) *Marxism, For and Against*, New York: W.W. Norton.

Higgott, Richard (1991) "International Relations in Australia: An Agenda for the 1990s," in Richard Higgott and J.L. Richardson (eds), *International Relations: Global and Australian Perspectives on an Evolving Discipline*, Canberra: Department of International Relations, Australian National University, pp. 394–426.

Higgott, Richard and Jim George (1990) "Tradition and Change in the Study of International Relations in Australia," *International Political Science Review*, 11(4): 423–438.

Hoffmann, Stanley (1977) "An American Social Science: International Relations," *Daedalus*, 106 (3): 41–60.

Holsti, K.J. (1985) *The Dividing Discipline: Hegemony and Diversity in International Theory*, Boston, MA: Allen & Unwin.

Jarvis, D.S.L. (2001) "Conclusion: International Relations: An International Discipline?," in Robert M.A. Crawford and Darryl S.L. Jarvis (eds), *International Relations – Still an American Social Science? Toward Diversity in International Thought*, Albany: State University of New York Press, pp. 369–380.

Keeble, Edna and Heather A. Smith (1999) *(Re)defining Traditions: Gender and Canadian Foreign Policy*, Halifax: Fernwood Publishing.

Kennedy-Pipe, Caroline and Nicholas Rengger (2006) "BISA at Thirty: Reflections on Three Decades of British International Relations Scholarship," *Review of International Studies*, 32(4): 665–676.

Kubalkova, V. and A.A. Cruickshank (1987) "The Study of International Relations in the South Pacific," *Australian Outlook: The Australian Journal of International Affairs*, 41(2): 110–129.

Kuhn, Thomas (1962) *The Structure of Scientific Revolutions*, Chicago, IL: University of Chicago Press.

Lapid, Yosef (1989) "The Third Debate: On the Prospects of International Theory in a 'Post-Positivist' Era," *International Studies Quarterly*, 33(3): 235–254.

Linklater, Andrew (1992) "The Question of the Next Stage in International Relations Theory: A Critical–Theoretical Point of View," *Millennium: Journal of International Studies*, 21(1): 77–100.

Linklater, Andrew and Hidemi Suganami (2006) *The English School of International Relations: A Contemporary Reassessment*, Cambridge: Cambridge University Press.

Little, Richard (1995) "Neorealism and the English School: A Methodological, Ontological and Theoretical Reassessment," *European Journal of International Relations*, 1(1): 9–34.

Little, Richard (2002) "The English School's Contribution to the Study of International Relations," *European Journal of International Relations*, 6 (3): 395–422.

Lyons, Gene M. (1986) "The Study of International Relations in Great Britain: Further Connections," *World Politics*, 38(4): 626–635.

Melakopides, Costas (1998) *Pragmatic Idealism: Canadian Foreign Policy, 1945–1995*, Montreal and Kingston: McGill–Queen's University Press.

Murphy, Craig N. and Richard Tooze (eds) (1991) *International Political Economy Yearbook: The New International Political Economy*, Boulder, CO: Lynne Rienner.

Neufeld, Mark A. (1995) *The Restructuring of International Relations Theory*, Cambridge: Cambridge University Press.

Nossal, Kim Richard (2000) "Home-grown IR: The Canadianization of International Relations," *Journal of Canadian Studies*, 35(1): 95–114.

Nossal, Kim Richard (2001) "Tales That Textbooks Tell: Ethnocentricity and Diversity in American Introductions to International Relations," in Robert M.A. Crawford and Darryl S.L. Jarvis (eds), *International Relations – Still an American Social Science? Toward Diversity in International Thought*, Albany: State University of New York Press, pp. 167–186.

Nossal, Kim Richard (2006) "A Question of Balance: The Cult of Research Intensivity and the Professing of Political Science in Canada", Presidential Address to the Canadian Political Science Association, Toronto, Ontario, June 2, 2006, *Canadian Journal of Political Science*, 39(4): 735–754.

Onuf, Nicholas (1997) "A Constructivist Manifesto," in Kurt Burch and Robert A. Denemark (eds), *International Political Economy Yearbook,* Vol. 10: *Constituting International Political Economy*, Boulder, CO: Lynne Rienner, pp. 1–17.

Pettman, Jan Jindy (1996) *Worlding Women: A Feminist International Politics*, London: Routledge.

Porter, Tony (2001) "Can There Be National Perspectives on Inter(national) Relations?," in Robert M.A. Crawford and Darryl S.L. Jarvis (eds), *International Relations – Still an American Social Science? Toward Diversity in International Thought*, Albany: State University of New York Press, pp. 131–147.

Ricci, David M. (1984) *The Tragedy of Political Science: Politics, Scholarship and Democracy*, New Haven, CT: Yale University Press.

Rioux, Jean-François, Ernie Keenes and Gregg Legare (1988) "Le néo-réalisme ou la reformulation du paradigme hégémonique," *Études internationales*, 19(1): 57–80.

Sjolander, Claire Turenne and Wayne S. Cox (eds) (1994) *Beyond Positivism: Critical Reflections on International Relations*, Boulder, CO: Lynne Rienner.

Smith, Steve (1985) "Introduction," in Steve Smith (ed.), *International Relations: British and American Perspectives*, Oxford: Blackwell, pp. ix–xiv.

Smith, Steve (1995) "The Canadian–Italian School of International Theory," *Mershon International Studies Review*, 39(1): 164–166.

Smith, Steve and Martin Hollis (1991) *Explaining and Understanding International Relations*, Oxford: Clarendon Press.

Suganami, Hidemi (1983) "The Structure of Institutionalism: An Anatomy of British Mainstream International Relations," *International Relations*, 7(5): 2363–2381.

True, Jacqui (1996) "Feminism," in Scott Burchill *et al.*, *Theories of International Relations* (2nd edn), New York: St. Martin's Press, pp. 231–276.

True, Jacqui (2006) *Feminist Methodologies in International Relations*, Cambridge: Cambridge University Press.

Wæver, Ole (1997) "Figures of International Thought: Introducing Persons Instead of Paradigms," in Iver B. Neumann and Ole Wæver (eds), *The Future of International Relations: Masters in the Making?*, London: Routledge, pp. 1–37.

Wæver, Ole (1998) "The Sociology of a Not So International Discipline: American and European Developments in International Relations," *International Organization*, 52(4): 687–727.

Walker, R.B.J. (1993) *Inside/Outside: International Relations as Political Theory*, Cambridge: Cambridge University Press.

Wallerstein, Immanuel (1976) *The Modern World-system: Capitalist Agriculture and the Origins of the European World-economy in the Sixteenth Century*, New York: Academic Press.

Waltz, Kenneth N. (1979) *Theory of International Politics*, New York: McGraw–Hill.

Whitworth, Sandra (1994) *Feminism and International Relations: Towards Political Economy of Gender in Interstate and Non-Governmental Institutions*, Basingstoke: Macmillan Press Ltd.

17 The parochialism of hegemony
Challenges for "American" International Relations

Thomas J. Biersteker[1]

Stanley Hoffmann famously described International Relations as "an American social science" in his classic article about the subject first published in *Daedalus* in 1977. Hoffmann's students, and a great many others, have picked up on the phrase and the ideas embedded within it in subsequent citations and publications about the development of the field (Kahler 1997). There is good reason for this, because the phrase contains a great deal of truth. The integration of the study of the international with the analytical methods of social science has been most assiduously pursued in the United States. There are more IR degree-granting institutions, more IR faculty, and more IR dissertations, degrees, associations, and conferences in the U.S. than in any other country on the globe. Most of this development has taken place in the U.S. since 1945, coinciding with the dawn of what many have described as "the American century," and there is a broad consensus in the U.S. about the importance of using the most sophisticated methods of social science to pursue the analysis of international relations.

At the same time, the phrase "an American social science" can be misleading in two important respects. First, much of the activity in international relations, as well as scholarship about the subject, takes place outside of the United States, as evidenced by this volume. Second, the field of International Relations begins long before the advent of "the American century" that began with the U.S. rise to power and hegemony following the end of World War II. Important works of twentieth-century International Relations scholarship – from Norman Angell's *The Great Illusion* to V.I. Lenin's *Imperialism* and E.H. Carr's classic *The Twenty Years' Crisis* – were published and widely discussed long before the application of American social science methods to international relations. The first endowed chair in International Relations, the Woodrow Wilson Chair, was established at the University of Wales, Aberystwyth, in 1919, and one of the first schools of international studies was founded in Geneva in 1927.

Although Hoffmann's classic has been read literally by many as equating the study of international relations with American social science, much of the work is not a commentary on the potential consequences of this equation. Hoffmann devotes much of the article to an assessment of the "peculiar problems" of policy engagement, the dangers of capture by one's subjects, and the extent to which his former Harvard colleague Henry Kissinger personally embodied both. His prescient concerns remain relevant to this day, a point I will return to at the end of this chapter.

There have been many other important surveys of American (by which I mean largely U.S.) International Relations scholars.[2] I co-authored an article with the late Hayward R. Alker Jr. on the parochialism of International Relations scholarship in the U.S., first published in the *International Studies Quarterly* more than 20 years ago in 1984. Kal Holsti wrote an insightful comparative analysis of IR scholarship around the world, including the U.S., published the following year, in 1985. More recently, Colin and Miriam Elman (2003), Miles Kahler (1997), and Ole Wæver (1998) have each more recently written insightful analyses of the subject.

In this chapter, I intend to update the analysis of American International Relations first presented in Alker and Biersteker (1984). I will begin in the next section with a discussion of how American intellectual hegemony operates in general terms. Next, I will describe the nature of contemporary parochialism in American international relations scholarship, with an analysis of the international relations syllabi currently being taught in the leading departments of political science, where most scholarly IR is taught, in the United States. Following this statistical survey and analysis, I will illustrate how many major theoretical debates in the U.S. are essentially driven by immediate American foreign policy concerns, rather than global aspects of the operation of the international system. I will conclude the chapter with a discussion of the implications of American parochialism for the U.S. understanding of the world (and for the rest of the world which consumes American IR scholarship), with some self-reflection on how American my analysis of American IR is, despite my current bi-national base.

The operation of American intellectual hegemony

American International Relations scholarship is globally hegemonic. American International Relations scholars are disproportionately read, assigned, and debated across the globe. Wherever one travels, IR scholars of almost every nationality are familiar with the canons of American realist and liberal thought – from Morgenthau, Kissinger, and Waltz to Gilpin, Nye, and Keohane. They also tend to be at least familiar with the latest theoretical debates currently fashionable in the U.S., even if that tendency is not well reciprocated by American scholars, a point I will illustrate in greater detail in the next section. How has this intellectual hegemony been created?

At least in part, American intellectual hegemony is a simple product of the sheer volume of American IR scholarship. Whether indicated by the number of universities, think-tanks, or academic and research positions, there are more active IR research scholars working in the U.S. than in any other country in the world. The number of scholarly and research positions is out of proportion to its relative demographic size, considered alone. More IR scholarship is also written and published in the U.S. than in any other country in the world, producing the structural benefits of sheer market size. There are more publication outlets and more research libraries to house the works of IR scholars in the U.S. than anywhere else on the globe. Some European-based journals with a scholarly and research content which is distinctly different from the mainstream of American International Relations literature rely heavily on the U.S. market for a significant share of their subscription sales.[3]

Beyond the structural benefits of market size (though probably at least in part because of it), many prominent non-American scholars of international relations were educated in leading U.S. institutions of higher education. This is very much the product of American hegemony and the number of scholarship programs provided historically for scholars from other parts of the world to study in the United States. Because of their U.S. training, it is not surprising that many of the works that American-educated scholars subsequently assign to their own students are works they originally mastered while studying the subject in the United States. This is not a universal tendency, and certainly did not apply to the vast majority of the International Relations scholars educated in the former Soviet Union or in China during the height of the Cold War (or in France both during and after the Cold War). Even in these cases, however, there are prominent scholars who regularly engage American scholarly works, and who are engaged by their American counterparts at professional conferences on a regular basis.

Another source of American hegemony is the fact that many leading non-American IR scholars publish some of their most important works in English and in U.S.-based journals or presses. In some instances, the extent to which a given work is considered of "international standard" is determined by its publication venue. A major publication, or as I have recently learned in the instance of one of my Asian graduate students, a first academic appointment in the U.S., can be critical for subsequent advancement in one's home country. In many instances a publication in a leading U.S. journal is important for a scholar's status and legitimacy as an "international"-level scholar in their home domain.

Not only is the U.S. academic market globally hegemonic in international relations, but within the U.S. there is hegemony of a relatively small number of leading research departments and universities. These are the institutions that both house and subsequently produce the overwhelming majority of scholars who are assigned and cited by others. These departments perform a critical selection and disciplinary (or subfield) gatekeeping function. Who they select for admission, who they hire to teach their students, who they promote (and who they deny promotion), and where they publish, are critically important for the development of the academic discipline of International Relations. Moreover, as will be discussed in more detail in the next section, the readings they assign and require their Ph.D. students to master prior to their advancement to candidacy and for writing the doctoral dissertation matter a great deal. The questions they ask on their qualifying examinations, as well as whom they pass, and whom they fail, are critically important. These are all practices of intellectual reproduction and of disciplining and defining the field of study.

Not only are a relatively small number of institutions of higher education engaged in the training of scholars who go on to be widely cited and assigned by others in the United States, but departments of political science, politics, or government, rather than schools of international studies, produce most of the leading scholars in the field. Political science tends to be more important than International Relations as a disciplinary identity, as indicated by the fact that political science departments tend disproportionately to hire the graduates of other political science departments, and are often rather skeptical of individuals with multi-disciplinary IR degrees, whose disciplinary depth in political science is likely to be less extensive because of the requirement that their graduates take courses in more than one discipline. Even leading schools of international studies in the United States tend to select their faculty from disciplinary political science departments, rather than from multi-disciplinary IR programs relatively more similar to themselves. This further reinforces the hegemony of a small number of institutions of higher education (which will be identified in the following section). The fact that IR is grounded in political science affects the contours of the field in other important ways.

Beyond the institution and discipline from which an individual receives her or his Ph.D., the social structure of the field is governed by a broadly based consensus on the hierarchy of leading journals (*International Organization*, *International Security*, *World Politics*, *International Studies Quarterly*, and more recently the *American Political Science Review*), of leading scholarly presses (Cambridge, Princeton, Harvard, California, Cornell), of prestigious dissertation funding sources (Social Science Research Council, National Science Foundation, U.S. Institute of Peace), of major private foundations (especially Ford,

MacArthur, and Carnegie), and of key postdoctoral fellowships (from the Council on Foreign Relations to a variety of postdoctoral fellowships offered by leading university-based institutes of international studies). In each of these venues, groups of peer-reviewing scholars serve without financial compensation to make the difficult and critical choices about who will receive recognition and financial support.

The selection of the editors of key journals, of the reviewers of manuscripts and proposals, and of the members of the leading fellowship selection committees are invariably politicized enterprises.[4] These individuals play critical gatekeeping and discipline-defining roles, at times with a relatively narrow conception of the field, though rarely self-consciously so. They are constantly engaged in making critical appointments of other reviewers (of manuscripts, programs, and fellowship applications). They tend to be united in the common enterprise of improving the quality of the social science. In this sense, Stanley Hoffmann was correct to describe the fusion of International Relations and social science in the American academy. While everyone may be pursuing "science," however, there are competing conceptions of how to define "science."

There tends to be a strong tendency toward intellectual reproduction, particularly with regard to epistemological orientation. This is true not only with regard to the publication of articles in leading journals and the award of prestigious fellowships. Leading scholars in top-ranked disciplinary departments typically assign what they consider to be "good" social science (although a few also assign works that they consider to be "bad" in an effort to illustrate how *not* to conduct research), and this work tends to be broadly similar in approach to the way in which those same individuals were trained to conduct social science research themselves. Therefore, what is understood or recognized as "good" research, something that is reproduced in hiring, promotion, and examination results, is usually broadly similar to one's own research approach and orientation. The consequences of this phenomenon are explored more fully in the following section, but it is important to note that this general tendency is not unique to the United States.

The nature of contemporary American parochialism

All nationally constituted communities of International Relations scholars are parochial in one way or another. They may be linguistically parochial, assigning works exclusively or largely in their national language. It is a practical necessity that the vast majority of Russian students of international relations be taught in Russian or Chinese students in Chinese. Communities of IR scholars may be geographically parochial, giving primacy to consideration of issues as defined within a single region (such as Asia or Europe) or from the shared experience of being a small or regional power. This may, in turn, lead to a form of topical parochialism, where the focus in developing countries of Africa or Latin America is on bargaining and negotiating strategies of the relatively weak, the focus in Europe is on the challenge of forging a common foreign policy or the changing meaning of sovereignty, and the focus in China and India is on the global challenges facing emergent great powers. Finally, nationally based scholarly communities may be epistemologically parochial, giving primacy to a single approach to scholarly analysis, or a synthesis of different traditions, as in the case of the English School's integration of history, philosophy, and law. As I illustrate below, while the American International Relations community is most certainly parochial, it is hardly alone in the world for being so. I suspect, however, that if the same analysis were systematically applied to other national communities, the degree of U.S. parochialism would probably be exceptional, for some of the reasons already identified above.

In order to assess the nature of contemporary American parochialism, I have conducted a survey of the assigned or required readings for Ph.D. candidates concentrating in International Relations in the leading departments of political science, politics, or govern-ment in the United States. This is in many respects a revisiting of the survey of American IR which Hayward Alker and I conducted 25 years ago. Our hypothetical future global arche-ologist of international savoir faire discovered at the time that "behavioral–scientific approaches concerned with explaining and managing a complex world order have predom-inated in the United States" (Alker and Biersteker 1984: 123). We focused on an analysis of the syllabi of prominent IR theory instructors whose course reading lists had been assembled into a single volume.[5] We concluded that "not only were the bulk of readings on their syllabuses written by other American scholars, but those readings were almost exclusively from . . . behavioral science" (p. 128). We went on to argue that therefore "the questions asked, the values assumed, the issues addressed, and the debates considered . . . have all been addressed from within the narrow confines of a single epistemological tradition" (ibid.). Our concern was that this focus on one approach did "not do justice to the world-wide variety of substantively and politically significant approaches to international relations," which we argued included dialectical, as well as traditional (historical, philosophical, or legal) approaches (ibid.).

Has this American parochialism lessened or changed significantly over the past 25 years? Does behavioral science still dominate the teaching and analysis of international relations in leading departments of political science in the United States? Times change, and as Hayward Alker and I pointed out in 1984, historical context matters significantly. We argued that "intimate, often reciprocal and sometimes constitutive connections exist between the historical context of . . . research and the research activities themselves" (p. 122). Thus, with the end of the Cold War and the consequent diminution of the global ideological struggle between capitalism and socialism at the end of the twentieth century, there are far fewer representatives today of dialectical–materialist analyses of international phenomena than existed globally in the mid-1980s (though a few may still be found today in some critical assessments of globalization). Hence, this is not a direct replication of our study, which dif-ferentiated between the three categories of traditional, behavioral–scientific, and dialectical approaches.

Rather, I have adapted the categories applied by Ole Wæver in his 1998 comparative analysis of the "metatheoretical orientations" of articles published on different sides of the Atlantic. Wæver differentiated between "(1) formalized rational choice, game theory, and modeling; (2) quantitative studies; (3) nonformalized rationalism, that is 'soft rational choice,' which includes most neorealism, all neoliberal institutionalism, and a few 'independents'; (4) non-postmodern constructivism; (5) the 'radicals,' be they poststructuralists, Marxists, or feminists" (1998: 701), and a sixth category reserved for what he termed "other."

Categories 1 through 3 constitute the descendants of behavioral science, as we defined the general approach in 1984. Dialectical approaches are largely subsumed under Wæver's category 5 for radicals, though it also includes some approaches that were just beginning to emerge in IR in the 1980s, such as post-structuralism and feminism. Our category of traditional is subsumed under his "other," and constructivism had not yet emerged as a separate approach. On reflection, our emphasis on constitutive relationships and interest in social context may be read retroactively as an early illustration of one aspect of the approach.

Adapting Wæver's more recently developed categories has some advantages. First, it enables a comparative assessment of his survey of the published journal literature and my analysis of contemporary lists of required readings. Second, it unpacks the category "behavioral–scientific" and expands it beyond quantitative analysis. Third, it takes account of contemporary developments, for example, the emergence of constructivism, which was only evident in the work of a few people like John Ruggie at the time when Alker and I wrote our original article. In the analysis that follows, I have also switched the focus from an evaluation of the syllabi of individual instructors to an analysis of the required reading lists of leading departments, something facilitated by the emergence of the internet and the relative ease of access to electronic postings of required reading lists.[6]

Determining the top-ranked or leading departments of political science and/or government in the United States, like deciding on any "top-ten" list, is a highly problematic enterprise. The selection of a single or small number of quantitative indicators can mislead or skew the results, the reputation of institutions tends to lag behind current developments, and the actual learning experience for graduate students may diverge from the scholarly reputation of an institution's faculty. There are a multitude of indicators one can derive to determine departmental impact or influence – from citation scores and publication volume to surveys of reputation and placement records – along with the biases inherent in relying upon existing citation indices (which tend to discount or ignore publications outside of the U.S.). There are also a large number of different rankings, based on multivariate assessments of different criteria or indicators of quality, prominence, and/or influence, different time periods, and on different sample bases (from the U.S. and Canada to the entire world).

Different ranking systems, not surprisingly, produce different rank orderings. Despite the variation in rank ordering and identity of which institution tops the list, however, there is something to this ranking exercise that has a "we all know who they are . . ." quality to it. That is, while there is considerable debate about the top institution, about the particular rank ordering below number one, or around the margins and toward the bottom of the list of the top ten institutions, there is little debate about the top half-dozen or so. One may think the reputations are undeserved or based on reputations established a generation ago, but like great powers in the international system, hegemonic institutions of political science graduate training in the United States have changed relatively little in the past 50 years. Harvard, Yale, Princeton, Stanford, Chicago, Berkeley, and Michigan consistently top all of the lists. Determining which institutions deservedly fill the remaining three to five slots to make up the top ten departments, which will form the basis of my survey of what is currently being taught in leading departments in the U.S., is more challenging.

Rather than trying to perfect a ranking instrument or argue for the "best" set of criteria, I simply looked at the frequency with which departments were listed in the top 10, 12, 15, and 20 institutions in the lists from seven different surveys.[7] This is analogous to constructing an index based on indicators, a practice common in the behavioral tradition of quantitative analysis. I weighted each of the lists equally, such that if an institution received a top 10, 12, 15, or 20 ranking in one of the lists, it would be given a score of one. For each list in which a department received a top ranking it would be given an additional score of one. I then simply added up the results of the seven different rank orderings, as displayed in Table 17.1. Yale leads the list, with a top-ten ranking on all seven lists, closely followed by Harvard, Princeton, Stanford, Berkeley, Chicago, and Michigan. Table 17.1 summarizes the frequency with which different institutions appeared on the top 10, top 12, top 15, and top 20 lists in these seven different surveys.

Identifying the top ten departments was one challenge. The next was to obtain copies of the required reading lists for Ph.D. candidates concentrating on International Relations within each of them. Some departments (Chicago and Yale) post their lists of required readings on

Table 17.1 Frequency with which departments are listed in the top 10 to top 20 lists

University	Top 10	Top 12	Top 15	Top 20	Total
1 Yale	7	7	7	7	28
2 Harvard	6	7	7	7	27
3 Princeton	6	6	7	7	26
4 Stanford (tie)	6	6	6	6	24
5 Berkeley (tie)	6	6	6	6	24
6 Chicago	5	6	6	6	23
7 Michigan	5	5	5	6	21
8 Columbia	4	4	4	5	17
9 UCSD	4	4	4	4	16
10 MIT	0	4	5	5	14

their department websites. Other departments post their lists of courses, and sometimes they or their faculty also post the syllabi for their graduate-level IR theory course. In contrast to the mid-1980s when Alker and I did our survey of IR syllabi, there appears to be a growing tendency for departments to require or expect their International Relations Ph.D. candidates to take more than one IR theory course, typically one in international political economy and one in security studies or in general IR theory. This is the case at Stanford, Princeton, and Berkeley. In some departments the required IR theory course is usually taught by the same individual, as in the case of Columbia and Michigan. In others, the core graduate IR theory course is rotated among several faculty members, often with a common reading list that is supplemented by or tailored to the particular interests of the different instructors from year to year. In most instances, IR students are either required to take these courses, or are strongly recommended to take them if they are planning to take their qualifying examinations and/or writing a thesis in international relations.

For the top ten departments in which the required reading list was available online, I downloaded the latest version and did the same for the syllabi for general IR theory courses at the Ph.D. level which were available from an individual instructor's web page. In those instances where the latest version was not available online, I contacted the most recent instructors of the courses, explained the purpose of the request, and asked for copies of their latest syllabi. I am deeply grateful to colleagues at Harvard, Princeton, Stanford, UCSD, Michigan, and UC Berkeley who responded to my request for copies of their syllabi. I also solicited syllabi from a few other highly ranked departments, especially those identified in the TRIP survey (focused specifically on IR Ph.D. training), syllabi that I draw on to supplement and compare with the top ten, and I am grateful to colleagues at UCLA, Duke, and Cornell for their cooperation. In all cases, I used the most recently taught syllabus, and the syllabi range in date from 2005 to 2007.

As indicated above, rather than trying to replicate the Alker and Biersteker coding categories, which for reasons already discussed would be inappropriate for an analysis or characterization of the readings currently being assigned, I adapted the categories that Wæver (1998) employed in his analysis of journal publications in the U.S. and Europe. I have slightly adapted his classifications into the following seven categories:

1   *Formal theory (FT)*, which includes formalized rational choice, game theory, and modeling.

2   *Quantitative (Q)*, which most closely replicates the behavioral science category from Alker and Biersteker.
3   *Behavioral (B)*, a category not employed by Wæver which includes conceptual works on human behavior, decision-making, and political psychology.
4   *Applied rational choice (ARC)*, which contains non-formalized rationalism, or what Wæver termed "soft rational choice," and includes most neorealism, and most neoliberal institutionalism.
5   *Constructivism (CON)*, which includes non-postmodern constructivism.
6   *Radicals (RAD)*, which includes poststructuralists, Marxists, post-Marxists, critical theorists, interpretivists, and most writing by feminist scholars.
7   *Other (O)*, which includes works of methodology, political theory, contributions from other disciplines (including history, economics, law, sociology, or philosophy), classic texts (e.g. Thucydides), surveys of the field, and most of the English School.

To give heuristic examples of each of these different categories, Table 17.2 contains a list of exemplary works that serve well to define them. There are, of course, works which straddle more than one category or which combine several of these theoretical approaches or orientations. In those instances where a single work could be characterized as illustrative of more than one category, an effort was made to identify the central tendency, or principal focus of the work. These classifications are subject to interpretation and legitimate differences of opinion no doubt exist, but the list of exemplars is intended to summarize the basis for the literally hundreds of codings involved in the analysis.[8]

Generalizing about theoretical orientation is probably the most important aspect of characterizing the nature of International Relations education in the leading departments of political science in the United States. In addition to coding each assigned reading item for its general theoretical orientation, however, each item was also coded for the national base of its author or authors, the original language in which it was written, the date of publication, the gender of the author or authors, and the geographical location of the publication of the assigned work. The national base and publication outlet are important for assessments of geographical or regional orientation. The original language in which the piece was written is important for an analysis of linguistic parochialism, although the lingua franca of IR globally is increasingly English. The original date of publication is important for gauging the degree to which recently published works are favored over the assignment of classics. Gender of the author is important for assessing the extent to which international relations remains disproportionately, as Lloyd Etheredge (1978) once described the State Department, "a world of men."

Just as in the case of coding for theoretical orientation, there are challenges and difficult decision rules in coding for these other aspects of the assigned readings. National base was defined operationally not as the current or original nationality of the author, but rather by where the author of the work had spent the bulk of his or her professional career from the time they entered graduate school.[9] In cases of joint authorship, both nationalities were listed. The primary goal here was to determine the extent to which scholars writing in other parts of the world are assigned, read, and debated in the United States.

All of the assigned readings are in the English language, but there are instances in which works have been translated from another language into English. Thucydides would be one obvious example, Machiavelli, or Cardoso and Faletto would be others. The date of publication was taken either from the edition assigned or the date of publication of the original edition of the work. Gender was coded into the gender of the author or authors, accordingly

Table 17.2 Exemplars of different categories of works assigned

Formal theory

Bueno de Mesquita, Bruce, James D. Morrow, Randolph M. Siverson, and Alastair Smith, "An Institutional Explanation of the Democratic Peace," *American Political Science Review* 93 (1999).

Fearon, James and David Laitin, "Explaining Interethnic Cooperation," *American Political Science Review* 90(4) (1996).

Morrow, James, "Modeling the Forms of International Cooperation," *International Organization* 48 (1994).

Quantitative

Doyle, Michael and Nicholas Sambanis, "International Peacebuilding: A Theoretical and Quantitative Analysis," *American Political Science Review* 94(4) (2000).

Hiscox, Michael, "Class Versus Industry Cleavages," *International Organization* 55 (2001).

Huth, Paul and Bruce Russett, "General Deterrence between Enduring Rivals: Testing Competing Models," *American Political Science Review* 87(1) (1993).

Behavioral

Jervis, Robert, *Perception and Misperception in International Politics* (1976).

Larson, Deborah Welch, "Trust and Missed Opportunities in International Relations," *Political Psychology* 18 (1997).

Levy, Jack, "Learning and Foreign Policy: Sweeping a Conceptual Minefield," *International Organization* 48 (1994).

Applied rational choice

Keohane, Robert O., *After Hegemony: Cooperation and Discord in the World Political Economy* (1984).

Milner, Helen, "International Theories of Cooperation among Nations: Strengths and Weaknesses," *World Politics* 44 (1992).

Waltz, Kenneth, *Theory of International Politics* (1979).

Constructivist

Barnett, Michael and Martha Finnemore, "The Politics, Power, and Pathologies of International Organizations," *International Organization* 53(4) (1999).

Finnemore, Martha, *National Interests in International Society* (1996).

Wendt, Alexander, *Social Theory of International Politics* (1999).

Radical

Ashley, Richard and R.B.J. Walker, "Conclusion: Reading/Writing the Discipline: Crisis and the Question of Sovereignty in International Studies," *International Studies Quarterly* 34(2).

Campbell, David, *Writing Security*, Revised Edition (1998).

Cardoso, F.H. and E. Faletto, *Dependency and Development in Latin America* (1979).

Other

King, Gary, Robert Keohane, and Sidney Verba, *Designing Social Inquiry* (1994).

Koh, Harold, "Why Do Nations Obey International Law?," *Yale Law Journal* 106 (1997).

Wight, Colin, "Philosophy of Social Science and International Relations," in Carlsnaes *et al.*, *Handbook of International Relations* (2002).

into male, female, or jointly authored by male and female. Publication outlet was determined by the location of the publisher of the book or journal article assigned, using the same general criteria described above for determining national base.

Of the readings assigned in a given course or included on a departmental list, only those that were *required* readings were coded for each of the institutions surveyed. That is, recommended or background readings were not included, assuming that the list of required readings provided the best indication of instructor or department faculty assessment of the most important work in the field. In cases where both departmental and individual course lists were available, preference was given to the departmental list, assuming that it was the product of a collective determination of the International Relations faculty, most probably based on discussion and consensus formation (also probably involving some negotiation, bargaining, and logrolling) among the faculty. Finally, unpublished material, usually by the instructor of the course, was not included for coding, since it was not necessarily available online and since each work had to be examined before it could be coded for theoretical orientation.

The results

There is wide variety and a considerable range of different authors and topics assigned as required reading in international relations theory in the top ten departments. A total of 454 different authors and 809 different publications were assigned in the ten departments surveyed. From the sheer magnitude of the numbers of scholars and different works alone, one might be inclined to infer that there is a great diversity and pluralism among the assigned readings in the leading institutions. There is certainly not a single approach to teaching international relations theory in the U.S., nor is there a common sequence to the introduction of different topics. Nonetheless, realism and liberalism are always represented, and constructivism appears on nine of the ten lists.[10] Kenneth Waltz and Robert Keohane appear on every IR assigned reading list, while Alexander Wendt appears on seven of the ten lists. Despite the so-called "constructivist turn in international relations theory" (Checkel 1998), however, a simple frequency distribution of the number of constructivist works assigned suggests that they rarely (in only three out of ten cases) account for more than 10 percent of the assigned readings. Radicals are even more scarce, appearing on only two of the ten lists.

Just as Wæver concluded about the theoretical orientation of journal publications in the U.S. in the late 1990s, the leading departments today overwhelmingly assign readings with a rationalist and positivist orientation. On average across all ten institutions, 69 percent of the required readings are both rationalist and positivist, with applied rational choice theory being the most common, followed by formal theory and analyses based on quantitative analytical methods. Table 17.3 summarizes the results. There is some predictable inter-institutional variation. Michigan, for example, tends to give more attention to formal theory, Yale and Princeton to quantitative approaches, and Harvard, Stanford, Chicago, Berkeley, and UCSD to applied rational choice theory. Constructivists appear on nearly all of the lists, but only occasionally (two out of ten times) do they manage to exceed the category of "other" in total frequency with which they are assigned. When they are assigned, they range from a high of 13.9 percent at UCSD to only 6.5 percent at Harvard. Radicals are virtually nowhere to be found on any of the lists. Wæver used Ann Tickner's *Gender in International Relations* as an exemplar for the "radical" category in his survey, but her treatment is not the most radical among applications of feminist theory to international relations, and even Tickner is rarely assigned, appearing on only two of the ten lists. More radical feminists are even less commonly assigned, and readings from critical theorists, postmodernists, post-structuralists,

Table 17.3 Theoretical orientation (% of assigned works in different traditions)

Department	FT	Q	B	ARC	CON	RAD	Other
Yale	13	19	5	42	10	0	12
Harvard	12	16	4	48	7	0	13
Princeton	29	32	0	32	0	0	6
Stanford	18	16	1	45	11	0	10
Berkeley	0	5	0	70	10	0	15
Chicago	7	5	0	59	10	0	19
Michigan	31	14	0	36	7	0	11
Columbia	7	6	9	33	12	5	28
UCSD	17	10	6	46	14	0	8
MIT	2	6	0	29	10	5	48

Notes
FT = Formal theory
Q = Quantitative
B = Behavioral
ARC = Applied rational choice
CON = Constructivist
RAD = Radical
Other = Other

and post-Marxists never make it to the required reading lists.[11] This is not to say that scholars with publications with a radical orientation are not to be found in the U.S. A great deal is taught and written in the United States, as evidenced by the wide variety of approaches represented at any annual meeting of the International Studies Association. There is an extraordinary diversity and a broad range of scholars and approaches across the different institutions in the country. Works with a radical orientation, however, are simply not taught in the leading research departments in the U.S. They are presumably considered not to be of sufficient scientific quality, and therefore not worthy of serious scholarly attention.

There are some exceptions to this general characterization of the theoretical orientation of the leading departments in the U.S. Although it did not make the top ten, based on its cumulative ranking in the seven different surveys that determined the list, the Department of Government at Cornell was ranked tenth on the TRIP survey, the one survey that specifically asked scholars to rank the top departments for Ph.D. training in International Relations. The Cornell required reading list provides some interesting contrasts to the general tendencies described above. The number of required readings with a rationalist orientation (as defined by the number of readings that are principally applied rational choice, formal theory, or quantitative and behavioral) was only 44 percent, as compared to an average of nearly 70 percent for the institutions included in Table 17.3. Constructivists make up 24 percent of the assigned readings at Cornell, while radicals constitute 9.3 percent of the list. Constructivists and radicals jointly make up a full one-third of the list. Formal theory and quantitative works are significantly less represented, with only one formal theory reading assigned and two quantitative readings. Despite the strong convergence around the teaching of rationalist works among top-ten institutions, other leading departments in the U.S. offer the possibility of more pluralism in the teaching of international relations. Even within these islands of intellectual pluralism, however, the hegemony of rationalist positivism is reproduced. A market socialization process ensures that Ph.D. candidates are educated in the canon of the discipline in order to enable them to engage in the core debates, as well as to be marketable in the broader discipline of political science. This is one reason why

American constructivists tend to be more positivistic in orientation than their European counter-parts. If a department decided to teach only constructivist or radical works to its Ph.D. candidates to the exclusion of formal theory, quantitative, behavioral, or applied rational choice, they would never be able to get jobs in the top ten institutions and would probably have great difficulty being employed anywhere. There is a "trickle-down" process which ensures that rationalist positivism is reproduced throughout U.S. international relations.

With regard to national base of the assigned authors and publication venue, the institutions on the top-ten list are overwhelmingly American. An average of 94 percent of the assigned readings in leading U.S. departments were written by scholars who have spent most or all of their careers in the United States. Michigan appears to be the most U.S.-centric, with 99 percent of its readings from U.S.-based scholars. Harvard is somewhat less American-focused than the others, but even there, 89 percent of the required readings were written by scholars residing in the U.S. The same pattern is observed with regard to publication venue. Although there has been an expansion in the activity of UK-based publishers in international relations in recent years, 95 percent of the assigned works in the leading departments were published in U.S. journals and presses. Despite the increasing ease with which scholarly material can be circulated on the worldwide web and the growing tendency of many Europeans to publish their scholarly work in the global lingua franca, English,[12] Americans tend only to read other Americans.[13]

It is not at all surprising, therefore, that all of the assigned works are in English. Linguistic parochialism is the norm globally, and with a few exceptions,[14] the language of instruction in nearly all universities is the indigenous language of the country in which the university is located. What is most striking about the assigned readings at the top ten institutions in the U.S., however, is not that there are no works assigned in languages other than English, but the fact that there are so few translated works on the reading lists. In nearly all of the top ten departments, 100 percent of the required readings were originally written in English. Yale and MIT are the exceptions in that they both assign Thucydides' *Melian Dialogue*, in a translation from the original Greek. With regard to this indicator, Cornell does not provide much of a contrast, since only 2 percent of its readings were originally written in a language other than English.

There is also a pronounced tendency to assign relatively recently published materials in the top ten leading departments. There is a natural tendency to want to expose one's students to the latest publications, intellectual innovations, and debates. It is striking, however, to realize that the average date of publication across all ten institutions is 1987. The modal date of publication is more recent, coming in at 1996. MIT, Chicago, and Yale have the earliest average date of publication, thanks once again to Thucydides who published his original edition in 431 BC. If we suppress that outlier, however, the Yale average is much closer to the median and mode at 1997. Chicago comes in as one of the most historically oriented, possibly reflecting the institutional culture of the College of the University of Chicago with its legacy as a place where classics and the great books are still taught. Princeton, Stanford, Michigan, and UCSD are the most contemporary, with an average date of publication of between 1996 and 2001.

With regard to gender, there is not much variation across the top ten departments. International Relations as a field is still predominantly populated by men, but the number of required readings written by women or jointly authored by women and men has reached between 8 percent and 35 percent of the total in different departments.[15] Unfortunately, this is not a longitudinal survey, so it is not possible to assess the extent to which there are more women being assigned today than there were 20 or 30 years ago, but given the growth in the number of women in the field, it is likely that this is the case. If you want to read relatively more works written by women, you should plan to attend Princeton, Harvard, or Stanford, where "only" 65 percent to 77 percent of the assigned readings are written by men. Chicago has the fewest female authors at 8 percent, followed by Berkeley and MIT with 12 percent. This time Cornell does not provide much of a contrast. While it offers the most pluralism in theoretical orientation, 84 percent of its authors are men.

To summarize, the leading departments producing Ph.Ds in International Relations in the U.S. today are overwhelmingly rationalist and positivist in their theoretical orientation. They tend only to assign other U.S.-based authors, individuals who publish their works predominantly in U.S. publication venues. Virtually all of the works assigned to Ph.D. candidates were originally written in English, and most of them were written by men in the past ten to 15 years. The nature of American IR parochialism is that it is rationalist, positivist, U.S.-centric, monolingual, recently published, and written by men.[16]

Hayward Alker and I argued in 1984 for a theoretical cosmopolitanism in the teaching of International Relations, one which would give serious consideration to major theoretical traditions taught and practiced in other parts of the world (Alker and Biersteker 1984: 132). Over the course of the past 25 years, only the English School, and for a brief time the Dependencia tradition from Latin America, have been actively engaged by U.S. scholars in leading research departments. Like the other works in the radical tradition, the dependency approach is no longer assigned in any of the top ten departments.[17] Even the English School tradition, however, is not required reading in all of the leading departments and only makes it on to the assigned reading lists in half of them. Hedley Bull is assigned at Harvard, Yale, Columbia, MIT, and Chicago, and Barry Buzan makes it on to the lists at Harvard, Columbia, and Chicago. By contrast, no examples of the English School are assigned and actively engaged (even if it means to point out the flaws in their analysis) at Princeton, Stanford, Berkeley, Michigan, and UCSD. Thus, in contrast to the situation in the mid-1980s, there appears to be a decreased tendency to engage theoretical traditions developed outside of North America (a tendency confirmed by the summary data presented in Table 17.4).

Table 17.4 National base, language, date, and gender (% of assigned works)

Department	U.S.-based	U.S. published	English	Date	Gender
Yale	93	95	99	1979	85
Harvard	89	93	100	1993	77
Princeton	88	100	100	2001	65
Stanford	97	99	100	1996	77
Berkeley	94	85	100	1988	88
Chicago	97	97	100	1972	92
Michigan	99	99	100	1996	84
Columbia	92	87	100	1981	85
UCSD	96	98	100	1996	80
MIT	94	96	97	1967	88

Notes
U.S.-based = % based at U.S. institutions
U.S. published = % published by U.S. institutions
English = % published originally in English
Date = average year of publication
Gender = male authors

Consequences of American parochialism

Sure the U.S. is parochial. So is everyone else. So what? Why does it matter that much anyway? One reason to be concerned about the insularity of American International Relations is that it prevents U.S. scholars from recognizing the extent to which so many of our theoretical constructs, frameworks, and debates are essentially driven by American foreign policy concerns. The issues that motivate our research, the concepts we employ, the global scope of the problems we address, and even the terminology we use (often without any self-reflection on its consequences),[18] mirror many of the concerns of U.S. policy-makers and the problems they confront on a global scale. This is not to say that they are entirely driven by them, as there is also simultaneously an intertextual engagement with previous scholarly works that motivates scholarly research. There are times, of course, when attention to U.S. foreign policy concerns can be incredibly productive. It is important, however, to be able to step outside of the American context and reflect upon just how much of what are assumed by many U.S. scholars to be global, timeless patterns, experiences, or universalizing tendencies are in fact the product of a particular American concern and perspective at a given point in time. Let me illustrate with three examples.

Take first the development of hegemonic stability theory in the 1970s, an important precursor to the emergence of theories of international regimes in the 1980s. Hegemonic stability theory developed in the 1970s in a context of intense concern within the United States about the decline of American power and influence in the world. The 1970s was a difficult decade for the U.S. The decade began auspiciously, with the suspension of the convertibility of the U.S. dollar into gold and the collapse of the U.S.-led Bretton Woods monetary order in August 1971. It was succeeded two years later by the first global oil shock and a major increase in the price of petroleum in 1973 to 1974. The following year saw the U.S. loss in Vietnam, symbolized by the ignoble departure from the rooftop of the U.S. Embassy in Saigon in April of 1975. Later in the decade, Soviet parity with the U.S. in nuclear weapons was acknowledged in arms control negotiations, and the decade concluded with the Iranian Revolution, the humiliating seizure of U.S. diplomatic hostages in Tehran, and the Soviet invasion of Afghanistan. It is not surprising, therefore, that one of the principal theoretical innovations of the decade focused on the importance of hegemonic stability and explored the consequences of hegemonic decline – from Charles Kindleberger's classic analysis of the lessons of the Great Depression (1973) to Robert Gilpin's expansion of Kindleberger's analysis into a more general theory,[19] and culminating in Paul Kennedy's (1987) broad historical contextualization of American decline.

These are important works, but like all social science scholarship they are also very much the product of their time. They were motivated by contemporary events, potential foreign policy challenges facing the U.S., and situated in an intertextual context that motivated, shaped, and influenced their development. They could be extended historically (as Kennedy most certainly did) and projected into the future (as Gilpin did), but they were not developed from pure theoretical abstraction or experimentation, but were addressing American foreign policy and popular concerns of the time. They became broadly discussed and globally debated theories, and there were efforts to apply them across time and space to the rise and decline of the great powers; former, present, and future. They stimulated rich subsequent theoretical developments like the emergence of regimes analysis in the 1980s and the argument about why an existing order might be sustained even after hegemony (Keohane 1984), but their very universality was constrained by the context of their origins in ways not always perceived by their creators. It is hard to see this if you do not consciously try to take yourself out of the context and/or unless you engage with theoretical traditions developed simultaneously in other parts of the world. They are, therefore, inevitably only *partial* explanations of global order, not comprehensive ones. They did not adequately comprehend the evolution of international society, the emergence and persistence of norms, or the critical readings of hegemony from subaltern critiques and dependency approaches.

A second illustration of the extent to which major theoretical debates can be projections of American foreign policy concerns unmediated by perspectives or insights from other parts of the world is the debate about the post-Cold War order that emerged in the U.S. in the early 1990s. Francis Fukuyama (1992) proclaimed the end of history, while Samuel Huntington (1993) warned about the coming clash of civilizations. John Mearsheimer (1990) argued that we would soon miss the stability of the Cold War order, Joseph Nye (1990) proclaimed that the U.S. was bound (in both senses of the word) to lead, and Robert Kaplan (1994) warned ominously of the coming anarchy. There was a broad consensus that the international system was undergoing a major transformation, and each of these U.S.-based authors offered a different theoretical formulation about the basis of, and prospects for, the emerging world order. Like theories of hegemonic stability and international regimes before them, however, these theoretical contributions were once again principally addressing American foreign policy concerns. The debate was motivated by the question of who or what would be the next major security threat to the United States.[20]

A third illustration of the centrality of American foreign policy concerns in the development of international relations theory in the U.S. stems from the reaction of many American scholars to the attacks of September 11, 2001. The analysis of terrorism went from a relatively marginal concern on the fringes of security studies to one of its central preoccupations. While American scholars (myself included)[21] have become increasingly interested in the emergence of new types of threat from non-state actors and the many normative issues and other challenges this creates for existing analyses, many of our colleagues in the rest of the world see the principal threats to security as stemming from other sources. Some are concerned with environmental change, from global warming and global climate change to increased local competition over scarce water resources. Many colleagues from Latin America are more concerned with the threat from the proliferation of small arms and the incapacity of the state to effectively police urban areas, while some colleagues from the Middle East are concerned that the principal threat to security may come from the United States itself. Many Europeans share this view, at least as it applies to the U.S. doctrine of preventive intervention.

In each of these three instances – hegemonic stability and regimes theory, conceptualizing the post-Cold War world order, and the discussion of the threat from global terrorism – the theoretical arguments initiated in the U.S. became globalized. They were not just exported as global IR theory by American scholars, but they were actively engaged by scholars and publics across the globe. It is difficult to travel virtually anywhere in the world where a reference to the "clash of civilizations" does not provoke a (usually negative) reaction. The fact that scholars globally appear to be engaged with U.S.-produced theories of international relations tends to reinforce the impression among American scholars that their works are of universal, and at times even of timeless, application. Everyone, at least superficially, appears to be engaged in the U.S.-dominated debates. This engagement is not reciprocated, however. If U.S. scholars do not actively engage with the insights from theoretical traditions in other parts of the world, they will be less able to see the reaction, rejection, or reinterpretation of their arguments. This is why Alker and I argued that the "oppositions and penetrations (of different theoretical traditions from different parts of the world) make up both the substance and the promise of a truly global 'interdiscipline' of International Relations" (1984: 132).

Beyond acknowledging the extent to which major U.S. theoretical debates are not simply the product of abstract reasoning but are significantly motivated by U.S. foreign policy concerns, another reason to be concerned about the lack of U.S. engagement with the scholarly communities and contributions from other parts of the world is that not every important new theoretical conception or idea emanates from the U.S. The idea of international society is one obvious example, just as the concept of structural constraints on the possibility of development in a world economy conducted according to liberal free market principles is another. A more recent example from Europe is the articulation of the Copenhagen School's idea of "securitization" and the analysis of the normative and political implications of declaring an issue a matter of security (Buzan *et al.* 1997). As Ole Wæver argues, in contrast to Europe, in the U.S. "the concept of security is not present *in the analysis* as such" (2004: 17). Contributions from the analysis of post-colonialism and attention to the subaltern would be another illustration, with their focus on socially marginalized populations globally and the consequences of their absence of agency (Spivak 1988). Consideration of this work could enrich both analyses of globalization and the idea of global civil society.

A final reason to be concerned about the non-reciprocal engagement of the American IR community with scholarly counterparts in the rest of the world is the consequence this has for reproducing both existing methods of analysis employed predominantly in American scholarship and the practices of American policy itself. As Wæver, following Dorothy Ross, has argued, there is a tendency in U.S. scholarship to deny historicist arguments and embrace positivist methods, a point emphatically illustrated in the preceding analysis of syllabi from leading departments (Wæver 2004: 14). The primary interest in causal explanation (over interpretive understanding or critical theory) conforms to the complex needs of U.S. global hegemony and the challenges of "managing" the international system. From the vantage point of the state currently residing at the pinnacle of the global hierarchy in structural terms, there is a strong interest in managing economic interdependence and maintaining international peace and security. To manage is to control, and the responsible "manager" that tries to lead the world needs to understand its dynamics in causal terms. Scholars become engaged in this larger project, not because they all necessarily want to "advise the Prince" (something that is increasingly difficult to do, given the sharp distinctions between the academy and policy intellectuals in the United States), but because they tend to share the assumptions of the political leadership that the world needs to be managed, that we should conceptualize and address issues on a global scale, and that it is important to try to make the world a better place.[22] Causal models and arguments serve this function, and the academy is actively engaged in their production. This is not an argument against causal explanation, which has many important contributions to make, but an argument for the legitimacy of something other than causal explanation: for pluralism and for recognition of the legitimacy of both interpretive understanding and of critical theory in graduate International Relations education.

The virtual absence of critical theory in the canon of American IR theory in the leading departments ultimately contributes to the reproduction of American hegemony and explains why otherwise generally liberal and internationalist IR scholars in the U.S. sometimes find themselves engaged in a discipline that reproduces not only American hegemony, but even some rather unpleasant forms of hegemony like providing justifications for preventive intervention and the use of exceptional measures during war. While many of the substantive concerns of American IR are strongly influenced by events and policy concerns, the kind of understanding and analysis produced in the academy reciprocally feeds back into the formation of policy itself. The channels of influence are not always immediate or direct, but are manifested in participation in policy task forces, in Congressional testimony, in writing op-ed articles, in engaging in issue advocacy, and ultimately in publishing articles, books, and reports. There is certainly nothing wrong with this kind of engagement,[23] but if we think we are simply doing objective social "science" with our causal models and explanations, and if we are not engaged in a critical self-reflection on our various engagements and consciously aware of the crucial legitimating function served by our scholarship, we are doing our students, and our government, a disservice.

Conclusion

It is easy to be content as a U.S. scholar of international relations. You do not have to "bother" with other languages. Everyone speaks your language (English), and appears to be using your principal frameworks and theoretical understandings. You can travel throughout the world making references to IR theory entirely produced by other American scholars, and most of your audience will be familiar with the basic texts, if not all of the latest arguments. The problem is, however, that "they" can speak in languages and discourses that "we" Americans cannot understand. They may also have important insights and adaptations of our arguments that we cannot comprehend or benefit from, either due to linguistic or epistemological barriers. English has become the global lingua franca, not only for global business, but for global academia. While everyone may be speaking the same language, however, the core concepts and ideas may not always have the same meaning in translation. Identical concepts may be interpreted or understood differently, and these differences can at times be profound.[24] Thus, there is a danger that by reading only other American scholars, by assigning virtually no translations of works published in other parts of the world, and by operating largely within a single rationalist and positivist theoretical framework, American International Relations will be less able to perceive counter-hegemonic developments, trends, resistances, and tendencies in the world.

In the final analysis, a lack of reflexivity and self-understanding of the nature of parochialism in American International Relations tends to mimic the policies of the American state. Most of the scholarly International Relations community in the United States has been strongly opposed to the foreign policy of the Bush administration, and in particular to the U.S.-led intervention in Iraq.[25] Parochialism in policy leads to ignorance, arrogance, and an inability to anticipate the tragic consequences of disastrous foreign policy choices. Just consider the American experiences in Vietnam and Iraq. Why should parochialism in academe, however, be any different? Why should it also not lead to ignorance, arrogance, and an inability to anticipate the tragic consequences of unreflective analysis?

I know that I am not immune from the tendency to see the world in American terms. My reliance on quantitative indicators of department quality and diligent effort to code systematically each of the assigned readings in the leading departments is indicative of an American behavioral science approach to establishing an empirical basis for an argument, even if it does rely on a presentation of fairly elementary descriptive rather than inferential statistics. My interpretation of the central theoretical debates of the past three decades in the preceding section also undoubtedly reflects an American narrative and chronology of the major arguments. Self-reflective acknowledgement of this is a first step toward theoretical cosmopolitanism, but as Alker and I argued, "real scientific universalism must be a skilled human achievement" (Alker and Biersteker 1984: 136). It also requires a deliberate effort to conceptualize the field of International Relations as composed of interpenetrating, but opposed approaches to knowledge cumulation, to engage different theoretical traditions and epistemologies of understanding seriously, to investigate their normative underpinnings, to examine the contextual bases of all theoretical work (including one's own), and to proceed with sensitivity, humility, and openness in the process of global theory development (ibid.: 136–139).

Notes

1 I would like to acknowledge and thank Jesse Finkelstein and Jonas Hagmann for their excellent research assistance. At different stages of this project, they assisted with the identification of rankings of political science departments, the location of web-based syllabi, the creation of spreadsheets for empirical analysis, the suggestion of criteria for comparative assessment, and a portion of the coding of required international relations readings assigned in leading departments of political science in the United States. I would also like to thank David Sylvan, Arlene Tickner, and Ole Wæver for their extensive and helpful comments on a previous draft of this chapter.

2 With all due respect to my many friends and colleagues in Canada (not to mention Mexico and the rest of the Americas), I am going to use "American" and "U.S." interchangeably in this chapter, as is consistent with the usage in the U.S. While there are important differences in U.S. and Canadian scholarship – as pointed out elsewhere in this volume and as reflected in the latest TRIP survey of IR – the similarities override major differences (particularly with reference to IR scholarship in English-speaking Canada). The fact that the leading journal of U.S. International Relations scholarship, *International Organization*, is now housed at the University of Toronto and that there is no separate Canadian International Studies Association (although there is a Mexican ISA) are good operational indicators of the extent to which American and U.S. can often be interchangeable in practice.

3 The *Journal of Peace Research*, edited in Oslo, Norway, on whose international advisory board I have sat for many years, represents a tradition (peace research) with a far stronger base in Europe than in the U.S., but whose circulation is historically dependent on sales in the U.S. market.

4 Consider, for example, the widespread interest (both substantive and personal) in the recent change in the editorship of *International Organization*. I would assume that my appointment as Chair of the SSRC's MacArthur-funded Global Security and Cooperation Committee a few years ago probably raised more than a few eyebrows in the traditional security studies community.

5 This is something that prompted one senior IR scholar to comment to me at the time that the article "had something to offend everyone in the discipline."

6 This also addresses the personal concern expressed about our original analysis. I also benefited from the willingness of many faculty members teaching assigned IR theory courses in leading departments to send me the latest copies of their syllabi.

7 The seven surveys were: (1) the National Research Council (http://209.85.135.104/custom?q= cache:5QYTkX0YxrAJ:www.nap.edu/dataset/pub/research_doctorate_programs_in_the_united_st ates/appendix_p/sthpol.xls+Political+Science+rankingsandhl=enandct=clnkandcd=1andclient= google-coop-np), (2) the Chronicle of Higher Education (http://chronicle.com/subscribe/ login?url=/weekly/v53/i19/19a00801.htm), (3) the TRIP survey (Maliniak *et al.* 2007), (4) the U.S. News and World Report ranking of graduate departments (http://gradschools.usnews.rankingsand reviews.com/usnews/edu/grad/rankings/phdhum/brief/polrank_brief.php), (5) Hix's 2004 global ranking of departments, (6) Masuoka *et al.*'s 2007 evaluation of the number of Ph.Ds produced, and (7) McCormick and Rice's 2001 ranking of research productivity.

8 The master list of different readings assigned in the ten leading departments contains 809 discrete items from a total list of 1027 works.

9 Someone like Peter Katzenstein, for example, would be coded as U.S.-based, since he has spent most of his career in U.S. institutions, while Lars-Erik Cederman (who has spent some time at Harvard and UCLA) would by this time in his career be coded as European-based.

10 Princeton does not assign any works by constructivists, but this result may be a reflection of the fact that the syllabus for only one of the two required IR theory courses was available for coding.

11 One of the rare exceptions to this was on a syllabus I did not include in the survey because its author had recently moved from one top ten institution to another and was no longer teaching the required IR theory course at the new institution. The readings assigned were in a section devoted to "anti-scientific" works of international relations, however.

12 Both the *European Journal of International Relations* and the *Journal of Peace Research* publish in English.

13 Once again, Cornell appears to be the exception, with 83 percent of its assigned readings originally written in English.
14 The Graduate Institute of International Studies, Geneva (Institut Universitaire de Hautes Études Internationales, Genève) was one of the earliest exceptions globally in being bilingual, but has been joined more recently by bilingual programs at the European University Institute in Florence, the School of International Studies at the University of Trento, and several new programs in Germany and Switzerland.
15 Once again, the figure for Princeton may be skewed, because it is based on only one of two lists, and one of relatively small size (of only 34 required readings).
16 While I did not examine this systematically, it appears that if a woman is teaching a required IR theory course, a higher percentage of works written by women are assigned.
17 This is true, with the notable exception, once again, of Cornell.
18 For an insightful illustration of this phenomenon in the scholarly analysis of U.S. bombing policy in Indochina, see Milliken and Sylvan (1996).
19 Robert Gilpin first introduced the idea in *US Power and the Multinational Corporation* (1975) and later developed it into a broader IR theory application in his *War and Change* (1981).
20 Indeed, Huntington's original formulation of the clash of civilizations idea was in a paper he presented at the Harvard seminar on future threats to U.S. national security.
21 I applied my knowledge of the design of targeted financial sanctions to the construction of the counter-terrorist financing regime and in my most recent book, co-edited with Eckert (Biersteker and Eckert 2007).
22 As the Princeton Project described it, "America must stand for, seek, and secure a world of liberty under law." See Ikenberry and Slaughter (2007: 6). Or as the CSIS Commission on Smart Power put it, "The goal of US foreign policy should be to prolong and preserve American preeminence as an agent for good" (2007: 5).
23 Indeed, I have done most of these things myself.
24 Consider, for example, the offense taken by Americans to French statements of concern about the U.S. as a hyper-power or *hyper-puissance*.
25 Consider, for example, the range of scholarly traditions reflected in the list of 700+ U.S. scholars of IR who signed a statement circulated by Stuart Kaufman that opposed the policies of the Bush Administration in Iraq during the summer of 2004.

References

Alker Jr., Hayward R. and Thomas J. Biersteker (1984) "The Dialectics of World Order: Notes for an Archeologist of International Savoir Faire," *International Studies Quarterly* 28(2): 121–142.

Armitage, Richard L. and Joseph S. Nye, Jr. (2007) CSIS Commission on Smart Power (Washington, DC: CSIS) available as a PDF file at
http://www.csis.org/media/csis/pubs/071106_csissmartpowerreport.pdf.

Biersteker, Thomas J. and Sue E. Eckert (eds) (2007) *Countering the Financing of Global Terrorism*, London and New York: Routledge.

Buzan, Barry, Ole Wæver, and Jaap de Wilde (1997) *Security: A New Framework for Analysis*, Boulder, CO: Lynne Rienner.

Checkel, Jeffrey T. (1998) "The Constructivist Turn in International Relations Theory," *World Politics* 50(2): 324–348.

Elman, Colin and Miriam Fendius Elman (2003) *Progress in International Relations Theory: Appraising the Field*, Cambridge, MA: MIT Press.

Etheredge, Lloyd S. (1978) *A World of Men: The Private Sources of American Foreign Policy*, Cambridge, MA: MIT Press.

Fukuyama, Francis (1992) *The End of History and the Last Man*, New York: Free Press.

Gilpin, Robert (1975) *US Power and the Multinational Corporation*, New York: Basic Books.

Gilpin, Robert (1981) *War and Change*, New York and London: Cambridge University Press.

Hix, Simon (2004) "A Global Ranking of Political Science Departments," *Political Science Review* 2: 293–313.

Hoffmann, Stanley (1977) "An American Social Science: International Relations," *Daedalus* 106(3): 41–60.

Holsti, Kal J. (1985) *The Dividing Discipline*, Boston: Allen & Unwin.

Huntington, Samuel P. (1993) "The Clash of Civilizations?," *Foreign Affairs* 72(2): 22–49.

Ikenberry, G. John and Anne-Marie Slaughter (eds) (2007) *Forging a World of Liberty under Law: U.S. National Security in the 21st Century,* Princeton Project report (Princeton University), available as a PDF file at http://www.wws.princeton.edu/ppns/report/FinalReport.pdf.

Kahler, Miles (1997) "Inventing International Relations: International Relations Theory after 1945," in Michael W. Doyle and G. John Ikenberry (eds), *New Thinking in International Relations Theory*, Boulder, CO: Westview Press, pp. 20–53.

Kaplan, Robert D. (1994) "The Coming Anarchy," *Atlantic Monthly* 273(2): 44–76.

Kennedy, Paul (1987) *The Rise and Fall of Great Powers*, New York: Random House.

Keohane, Robert (1984) *After Hegemony*, Princeton, NJ: Princeton University Press.

Kindleberger, Charles (1973) *The World in Depression: 1929–1939*, Berkeley: University of California Press.

McCormick, James M. and Tom W. Rice (2001) "Graduate Training and Research Productivity in the 1990s: A Look at Who Publishes," *Political Science* 34(3): 675–680.

Maliniak, Daniel, Amy Oakes, Susan Peterson, and Michael J. Tierney (2007) "The View from the Ivory Tower: TRIP Survey of International Relations Faculty in the United States and Canada," A publication of the Program on the Theory and Practice of International Relations, College of William and Mary, Williamsburg, Virginia.

Masuoka, Natalie, Bernard Grofman, and Scott L. Feld (2007) "The Production and Placement of Political Science PhDs, 1902–2000," *Political Science* 40(2): 361–366.

Mearsheimer, John J. (1990) "Why We Will Soon Miss the Cold War," *Atlantic Monthly* 266(2): 35–50.

Milliken, Jennifer and David Sylvan (1996) "Soft Bodies, Hard Targets, and Chic Theories: US Bombing Policy in Indochina," *Millennium: Journal of International Studies*, 25(2): 321–359.

Nye, Joseph (1990) *Bound to Lead: The Changing Nature of American Power*, New York: Basic Books.

Spivak, Gayatri Chakravorty (1988) "Can the Subaltern Speak?," in Cary Nelson and Lawrence Grossberg (eds), *Marxism and the Interpretation of Culture*, Chicago, IL: University of Illinois Press, pp. 271–313.

Wæver, Ole (1998) "The Sociology of a Not So International Discipline: American and European Developments in International Relations," *International Organization* 52(4): 687–727.

Wæver, Ole (2004) "Aberystwyth, Paris, Copenhagen: New 'Schools' in Security Theory and Their Origins between Core and Periphery," Paper presented at the annual meeting of the International Studies Association, Montreal, March 17–20.

18 Conclusion
Worlding where the West once was

Arlene B. Tickner and Ole Wæver

What have we learned after taking this global tour of International Relations scholarship? Each of the chapters offers a number of fascinating and unique insights into the ways in which IR has evolved and is practiced in distinct sites around the world. These different snapshots, in and of themselves, are invaluable, especially given the paltry state of knowledge about the discipline in nearly all corners of the globe. Furthermore, although a fair degree of literature actually does exist about the political, social, and economic environments that characterize these diverse countries and regions, exploring the ways in which their varying geocultural traits inform and condition scholarly activity in International Relations serves our dual purpose of stretching the field's boundaries (thus doing justice to its "international" label) and contributing to greater self-reflexivity within it.

In addition to the individual appeal of the 16 case studies presented in this book, are there observable patterns worth mentioning? Can anything meaningful be gleaned about "IR" from examining them as a whole or, for that matter, about "geocultural epistemologies" and "worlding" in general?

As in the case of the introductory chapter, in the conclusion we will refer to the two bodies of theory that have been at play, often implicitly, throughout the book: sociology of social science and postcolonial theory. The former will be reintroduced, following which we present a first group of observations related to the more social side of the project (the *how*, the working conditions, and organization of IR). Gradually, this expands into a second set of remarks concerning the intellectual aspects at play in different settings, namely the "content" of the IR scholarship produced (or not), the *what*. Several puzzles and surprises we come across lead to a brief revisiting of postcolonial theory, and finally we return to the center–periphery question as such: how does IR look in terms of global structure, as its own case of "International Relations"?; and from this we launch some final reflections on the next stages in the project of "worlding beyond the West."

Professionalization of IR?

One way to start cutting across the chapters is to look at a particular issue that is central, both in the general sociology of (social) science literature and in many of the more everyday reflections that take place within the discipline: what is often known as "professionalization." This problematic term refers to the extent to which the academic community of IR scholars has achieved sufficient autonomy from political and economic powers in society to establish purely academic-based internal principles of regulation, so that debate over the truth and/or quality of research becomes the primary format for regulating practices. The regulation of its own affairs is what constitutes a discipline as a profession, and is what professionalizes it in the sense of allowing it to become what it claims to be: a science, or in this case social science, that abides by the characteristic practices and institutions of this sphere, rather than those of other types of system.

In contrast to the earliest versions of this sociology of science argument, one does not have to make the heroic (and naïve) assumption that truth actually becomes the arbiter of scientific developments. Only that debate conducted *in terms of*, or *as if about*, truth becomes the main venue through which various battles are fought, where we can still allow for a number of social and intellectual processes to be active, from both outside and inside academe. Nor is the term meant to idealize this situation, mainly because intra-academic regulations constitute relations of power and control too. Instead, we employ it here in order to crystallize the question of internal and external forces operating on the discipline, which we think is crucial for understanding variation in IR in distinct national and regional sites.

When looking at IR in any given national or regional setting, a specific complication adds to the complexity of investigations traditionally done within sociology of (social) science: the global structure and the pervasive but inconsistent presence of the U.S.-centered discipline. Traditionally, sociology or history of science looked at a given discipline at large or at its avant garde. When examining local cases (for example, French physics in "x" decade), relations to other countries were normally studied as competing research programs or simply looked at comparatively. Our case is more difficult, given that the nature of International Relations in a given place does not grow out of local soil alone, but rather, the U.S. brand of IR is always present as a reference point. In consequence, the nature of the IR – both as knowledge and as social system – that greets scholars anywhere in the world is a complex mixture of U.S./global IR and its local variant. Attempts to discuss power structures or intellectual patterns in individual cases must necessarily take both levels into account.

The U.S. form of IR is simultaneously a single local instance of the field and an integral component of everyone else's universe. It is, so to speak, the top of the mountain that we all stand at the base of (although admittedly, some of us prefer simply to look at it instead of actually trying to climb it). It provides the defining criteria of success, which are expected to rub off or trickle down into the kinds of publications or theories that count locally. As the case studies suggest, however, this process occurs to highly varying degrees and in different ways. This claim is crucial, given that it provides clues as to how the global structure of the discipline intersects with local patterns and practices. In this vein, a series of observations about the "professionalization" of IR – the formation or not of inner-directed academic communities of scholars – may be derived from the chapters.

1   One facet of the consolidation of an autonomous and academic IR discipline is related to the extent to which the political – or the economic – system interferes directly and limits, orders, manages, and prioritizes scholars, research projects and institutions. This defines the classical Mertonian criterion of autonomy. Universities and research are generally more tightly state-controlled in authoritarian than in democratic systems, although several Western democracies have decreased university autonomy through administrative reforms adopted during the past decade (Karran 2007). Based on Cirino Hiteng Ofuho's assessment of the African continent, state intervention in the university system there is fairly widespread. In the case of India, too, Navnita Behera points out that universities depend almost exclusively on the public sector for funding, and that state support is largely driven by political imperatives and the priorities of individual governments. The South African chapter highlights another type of external regulation – the bureaucratization of academic practice – that took place as a result of

neoliberal reform in the early 1990s, and that has influenced scholarship throughout the non-core and to some extent in Europe, too. According to Maxi Schoeman, neoliberalism's main effect was to introduce performance criteria into the university system that valued form and practical outcomes over intellectual content, thus limiting academia's potential. See Seng Tan's critical portrayal of Southeast Asian IR scholars in the 1980s and 1990s as scholar–bureaucrats promoting elite interests and eventually legitimating authoritarian rule through their closeness to the state constitutes a distinct type of political interference. Surprisingly, similar levels of direct interference do not occur in the Iranian context (according to Mahmood Sariolghalam's chapter), even though universities in that country are state-owned. Even with all of these forms of political influence, it should be noted that contrary to what some in the core might expect, the IR discipline in the non-core is not characterized by extensive direct interference and political ordering. Sites such as the university as well as academic practices such as research do enjoy some degree of autonomy in all places. The basic norm that this is an important part of the idea of the university has been globalized (Drori *et al.* 2003), not in the sense that the norm is uniformly followed, but – as with most other norms – that it exerts a significant influence even in the breach. The world of research receives impulses from society in all parts of the world, but they are mostly in an indirect format and their degree placed on a scale not in a dichotomous format where internal factors are overruled by external factors in some places (more on the economic factor below in point 6).

In many countries around the world IR provides the important service of training future diplomats, through both officially sponsored or acknowledged diplomatic schools and, more broadly, by producing personnel for the foreign service. Generally, the more central this role is the more direct intervention becomes by politicians. This is clearly the case with African IR, which revolves around such a training role, and with a number of Latin American sites, where university autonomy, especially at private institutions, is relatively high, but IR students are trained with an eye towards gaining entrance into the foreign service.

2   The kinds of foundations and research councils, if any, that support investigation in different places is important. Disciplinary autonomy generally grows as more money is apportioned to basic university budgets, universities gain internal autonomy, and additional grant opportunities are provided by them for basic research. In contrast, the autonomy of both disciplines and universities is low in systems providing only limited funding and/or that target specific programs and applied research. Normally, top universities in the United States have massive endowments, making them less vulnerable to influence by external economic or political actors, that try to shape research by changing the criteria for research support. Although a substantial literature laments the marketization of U.S. research universities, this process operates more through intense competition over students, placements, and profile, rather than through the loss of autonomy, strictly speaking. In many other parts of the world, most notably in the non-core, universities are much less independent financially, especially if they are public. While the majority of the case studies do not address this issue, it seems that direct control filters down to the disciplinary or departmental level only to a very limited degree, and that universities generally operate at some distance from the powers that be. Direct routes of command from politics to "content" are relatively rare (see factor 1), but research policy regulates research through attempts to control its format. Generally, such policies shape organizational frameworks, overarching regulation of internal university forms of rule, and principles for dispensation of public funds. This practice has evolved

over the decades, gradually becoming more ambitious – in most places – in terms of indirect steering. The conditions and histories of such regulation differ: the U.S. situation displays most financial autonomy for universities but also the longest history of conscious research policy; Western Europe has the strongest state sway over universities that are almost universally public and one-source dependent, but also the longest history of universities as institutions with their own claim to legitimacy and tradition; and in parts of the non-core research policy is a more recent phenomenon and has in many places not yet developed the instruments for indirect rule (governmentality) where meta-strategies of the state attempt to rule academics through their self-rule (i.e. to mold academics who act according to *their* logic by channeling this according to state aims). In these non-core settings, research policy is often more oriented towards quantity – budget size, what areas of research to have – and is less concerned about sophisticated calculations as to how to actually mold the behavior of researchers through indirect means (Drori *et al.* 2003). In our chapters, this variation is visible mostly indirectly. While it is not addressed by all the authors – quite understandably – it is taken up in those cases where ambitious research policy is a major shaping force for the working conditions and criteria of success of researchers, relative to other constraining factors: Western Europe, the "Anglo-core", South Africa, Israel, and Japan–Korea–Taiwan.

3   The role of the think-tank industry constitutes an interesting and complicated variant on the first two themes – the influence of the political and/or economic system upon academic practice – that comes out most clearly in the chapters on South Africa, Russia, and to some extent Central and Eastern Europe. The rise and fall of local and global, public and private interest in funding applied research in international studies conducted by think-tanks has important direct and indirect implications for the field's development in settings such as universities. By placing certain research forms and themes on the general academic agenda, direct pressure is exerted upon the framing questions that determine scholarly practice (to the extent that the think-tanks and universities are seen in some respects as part of the same academic universe). Conversely, by captivating monies and researchers, the think-tank industry also saps universities' capacity to engage in their own preferred practices. However, in contrast to the first factor, the university world – where the discipline of IR is normally anchored – retains a formal autonomy with changes in this third one, but it is influenced nevertheless by state action on a neighboring object, research units for applied research.

4   A fourth, somewhat related, factor is the role of the foreign policy agenda of the country, or, as Mahmood Sariolghalam puts it in his chapter on Iran, "the aura and the priorities of the state." The link here is that the political agenda translates into a research agenda, even if there is no direct line of command. Clear cases of this include Africa, Latin America, Southeast Asia, Israel, South Asia, South Africa, and maybe particularly strongly Russia, China, and, at least until recently, Japan. The criterion of success is to develop scholarship that makes sense out of the challenges faced by "x" country and, in some instances, that offers concrete policy recommendations for overcoming them. In cases such as Africa, Latin America, and South Africa, this essentially means becoming "think-tank-like" by engaging in problem-solving and providing specific answers to distinct policy challenges. However, in other settings the relation between foreign policy needs and IR scholarship operates more at the level of identity. The different schools in Russian IR, security thinking in Southeast Asia, Israeli approaches to the field, and its historical phases in Japan and China, have been guided by the overarching questions faced by each country or region as to their place in the world and their identity in relation

to it. In such instances politicians set the academic agenda, not necessarily through a direct policy link to the researchers, but through the general agenda that is set for all of society in the public sphere. Scholars in all of these sites typically have little influence over these issues. In the first group of cases where they try to play an advisory role, their limited influence stems from the weak institutional authority and institutional misfit of universities in relation to such tasks; in the second type of situation, academics do not even enjoy an advisory relationship, and influence mainly emerges if scholars play a role in public debate, personal networks, and more long-term through the training of candidates who go into jobs in foreign ministries, parties, and the legislation.

5   The importance of global criteria, in other words recognition in the United States and U.S.-based journals, is a fifth factor, whose weight is highly variable in the countries and regions studied. In Western Europe it has become the ultimate path to local scholarly power. In Israel and Southeast Asia too, a prime value is placed on publishing in Western journals, while doing so in local venues garners significantly less recognition and stature. To a lesser degree, in East Central Europe and some parts of Latin America (Brazil and Mexico, in particular), this is also true. For much of the rest of the world of IR scholars, however, trying to get an article published in a leading journal – unless you actually aspire to a career in the United States or Europe – is not the most relevant or strategic career move. This is partly due to the lack of attention given to this factor by the relevant power holders, but it also reflects just how unrealistic it is to try and publish in a leading IR journal, given the extreme non-publication of non-Western scholars (see Figure 1.1, p. 5).

6   Another kind of dependence upon the center is produced by foreign money, mostly U.S. and European. The cases of India, East Central Europe, Latin America, and South Africa in particular illustrate that private foundations (such as Ford) have been major shapers of the discipline. The resources invested in IR programs have been so significant compared to local sources and relatively clearly targeted that they have been key factors in orienting research at several stages. Ironically, despite philanthropic foundations' ambition to build up local research environments, in practice they have delivered relatively few independent, self-reliant, and full-blown social science disciplines worldwide, mainly because they did not fund high theory, operating instead under specific assumptions of (policy) relevance. This kind of funding has often risked strengthening local IR quantitatively at the cost of marginalizing it qualitatively, by re-enforcing the classical intellectual division of labor whereby theory is produced in the center and consumed and applied in and by the periphery.

7   Finally, what kind of power structure exists internally? Professionalization is not produced exclusively through the fencing off of external control; it depends on internal institutions and structure. Here, the cases exhibit considerable variation. In the United States, power is largely vested in the rulers of the discipline at large. To a significant degree, local decisions on hiring and promotion weight publication records heavily, and thus judgments made by editors and other all-discipline leaders are of significant import. In the Anglo almost-core, especially England, Canada, and Australia, Wayne S. Cox and Kim Richard Nossal show that this is also the case to almost the same degree. In Europe, however, although publications increasingly influence decisions, up until now, Jörg Friedrichs and Ole Wæver argue, articles in "international publications" are increasingly extolled as the key, but local biases have played a significant role in this process, and as a result European IR has much lower mobility than its North American colleague. For the rest of the world this is even more the case: international publications are

not the key route to influence. Moreover, what then "counts" instead within the field in different settings differs greatly. National associations and individual leaders of the national discipline in a more organizational or personal capacity are important in countries such as Japan and Korea, as discussed by Takashi Inoguchi, in which the discipline is relatively well organized at a national level, but does not operate primarily through the publication-merit model. In most other places, the local university seems to be the site of power, and, correlating with this, standards and criteria vary from one department to the next. Many chapters do not spell this out in explicit detail, probably because social forms of this nature are so taken for granted that they are not easily observed. In addition, it is highly controversial to reflect explicitly on the nature and place of power in the local academic community in which one works. Nevertheless, it does transpire from the chapters, in which cases power and judgment ultimately reside at the departmental or university level, at the national disciplinary level, or beyond in the U.S./global discipline.

In several cases, Western publications matter in a slightly different way than the standard format; and not least education in the West does count, for instance, in Israel and Southeast Asia. At least the top of the local pyramid will usually be occupied by professors with international publications and some presence on the international scene, but this is not the regulatory criterion all the way down in hiring for lower positions. Therefore, this status becomes less a ladder to climb and more a kind of threshold criterion, where appointments ultimately depend on a mix of research, closeness to policy-makers, and various other forms of power and capital.

The total picture that emerges regarding professionalization is that in major parts of the world there is actually a relatively high degree of autonomy, but this does not necessarily trigger the expected dynamics and mechanisms of academic regulation. One plausible explanation for this is that the original sociology of science theory assumed that disciplines were formed as a novelty. In the periphery of the current world system, however, any formation of an academic research community necessarily takes place in the shadow of already-existing, larger, and predefining IR communities. This basically means that it is difficult to create the dynamics of academic standards as the primary regulator of scholarly activity due to the fact that the pinnacle is already occupied. Therefore, a pure publication-merit system cannot be brought to function as a local form of organization. Instead, local IR disciplines constitute themselves as niches within a global structure, neither directly "instructed" from the center nor able to make much headway at this level. However, through their status as part of an international discipline they are partially insulated from local political control, and thereby manage to create an academic sphere distinct from other forms of discourse in society. The point is that the discipline exists as a source of authority locally. Therefore, even scholars who do not read journals from the U.S. or Europe very intensively, do not attend ISA meetings or participate in edited, international volumes, or have not studied abroad are able to take a specific position locally by force of the nested institution of university/faculty/department/specialty. It is a global norm to have these things, and there is therefore a position to be held – even if it is then filled in a different way from the place where that norm originated. The Stanford School has shown that many practices including universities and ministries of research spread globally less because of an instrumental ends–means solution to local problems, but because of norms of modernity which tell us that to be a modern state and achieve a certain standing one has to have these things (Drori *et al.* 2003). When institutions are created in this symbol-driven manner, control by local powers is constrained by the fact that the institution partly derives its legitimacy from the global norm, not from the local context. The local scholar can thereby establish a platform based on institutional position that is stronger than if the setting had to be invented and justified purely *de novo* in relation to local relations of power and finance. This explains some of the characteristic features of non-Western IR, most notably the low standing of theory, which is discussed in the next section.

The way this interplay between global and local dynamics shapes particular social structures for the practice of IR is important for understanding why IR is not on one linear trajectory where some are further ahead. Socially, doing IR means something different in different parts of the world. While the entire exercise of this volume – and the book series – might seem self-evidently interesting to some, this point cannot be taken for granted. It should be recalled that the mainstream view on this and nearly all of the other issues brought up in the book is basically that it does not matter! Challenges launched in the 1990s by Steve Smith (1995, 2000), Ole Wæver (1998) and others were most often responded to with claims that it was irrelevant to show that IR differed in distinct parts of the world or that publication patterns were unbalanced. According to the mainstream, this only confirmed that the United States had started operating according to the pure format first – with no socially induced deviations – that the U.S. thus produced "true" IR scholarship, and that when other communities started to do so they too would produce the same kind of knowledge (Katzenstein *et al.* 1998; Crawford and Jarvis 2001). The discussion above shows why this is not the case. The global structure of IR is much more complex and differentiated, and varying scientific norms and forms of organization produce distinct kinds of IR disciplines around the world. In which ways the form of IR knowledge then varies is addressed next.

The kinds of IR made around the world

The second set of insights derived from the chapters in this volume is related to the content of International Relations and the kinds of disciplines being practiced around the world. This brief discussion could never do justice to the richness of detail and analysis presented in all of the case studies; nor is it our intention to summarize each author's arguments. Instead, we single out a number of recurring themes we find particularly noteworthy and/or that puzzle us and thus demand further attention.

Scholarly communities in IR throughout the world share a state-centric ontology that in most cases is manifest in the internalization of realist-based ideas concerning concepts such as power, security, and the national interest. Different authors offer distinct reasons for the primacy of state-centrism and realism. For example, in the Israeli context Arie Kacowicz argues that the salience of security concerns in realist thinking meshes particularly well with the political culture of insecurity that characterizes that country. A similar argument could be made in the case of Iran, given the post-revolutionary state's confrontational relationship with the international system. Although Soviet Marxist thinking did not privilege the state as a key unit of analysis, Alexander Sergounin traces a shift in post-Soviet Russian IR thinking by which scholars began to borrow from realist categories and to revive a long-standing tradition of geopolitical thought. In Southeast Asia, See Seng Tan associates state-centrism with the post-Cold War emergence of the Asia-Pacific as a global power, the rise of ASEAN, and the academic community's closeness to the state. Arlene B. Tickner suggests that Latin American IR's love affair with the state and realism is deeply rooted in the state's historical role as the principal expression of national identities and interests. In addition, as in most other peripheral contexts, this tendency was reinforced by the fact that the social sciences were created in order to produce knowledge susceptible to being converted into policy recommendations of use to state actors. This view is echoed in the South Asia chapter.

More than a problem of ontology, however, the centrality of the state to IR thinking around the globe reminds us of the importance of epistemology. Over two decades ago, critical theorists such as Richard Ashley (1987) and R.B.J. Walker (1993) began to contend that as an offspring of the modern sovereign state system, the International Relations discipline is essentially a social and political practice involved in the interpretation and normalization of specific forms of order rooted in that very system. Moreover, "state-speak" imposes categories through which all readings of the "international" are interpreted. Therefore, as Navnita Behera discusses in her analysis of South Asia, the epistemological base of IR is anchored in the idea of the Westphalian state. Not only is this actor the point of departure for most inquiries into international politics, but it is also viewed in ahistorical and unprob-lematic terms. In postcolonial contexts in particular, this view is highly problematic given that it inhibits the IR community from historicizing the state and from dialoguing with other ways of knowing about the past.

In addition to its robust state-centrism, the lack of theoretical production in IR and scholarly interest in this enterprise is striking in most of the cases studied, especially in the non-core. An interesting exception is Turkey, where Ersel Aydinli and Julie Mathews explain that the primary way in which the younger generation of International Relations scholars has vied for influence in the field is by playing the "theory" card against older generations who prefer policy-relevant knowledge and have enjoyed closer relations with the political establishment. Although IR scholarship in this country has not become highly theoretical, the fact that theory is viewed by the academic community as a "good" thing has become increasingly relevant to understanding the discipline.

In trying to make sense of the invisibility of theory in much of the world, both global and local explanations need to be explored. Within a perspective of geocultural epistemologies it would be tempting to see the near absence of non-Western theory as the sole effect of Western dominance, or of the core setting rules of the game whereby theory cannot originate in the periphery. Without a doubt, IR *does* exhibit an intellectual division of labor in which the center has come to be viewed as the primary producer of scientific theory while peripheral sites are deemed incapable of theoretically based thinking and therefore constitute sources of "data" or, in the best cases, local expertise. By claiming authority over decisions con-cerning what qualifies as "theory" the core reproduces this hegemonic arrangement. Sadly, academic communities in the South (not to mention political and economic elites) also internalize and reproduce it by favoring core knowledge as more authoritative and scientific in comparison to local variants. In Latin America, for example, dependency and liberation theology have been largely overlooked by scholars in the social sciences and especially in IR as legitimate theoretical contributions. In South Asia too, Jawaharlal Nehru's principle of non-alignment was never recognized as theory (as Navnita Behera points out in the chapter on South Asia). Still, it is too "easy" – albeit politically correct and "critical" – and paradoxically also too core-centric to rely wholly on an interpretation based upon how hegemony blocks local theory. More effort has to be put into understanding the *local* dynamics behind low-theory IR.

One of the key local explanations for theory's low standing is that it is not deemed especially helpful or relevant and is thus dreaded by many IR scholars. In addition, given the "real world" problems that many countries of the non-core are forced to address, theory is commonly viewed as a luxury they can ill afford. In war-torn and poverty-stricken areas throughout Africa, the Arab world, and Latin America, for example, what academic honestly has time for theoretically based scholarship? This argument is certainly not trivial. In general terms, the function that IR has in most settings makes abstract, generalizable knowledge less interesting and concrete, specific, situational analysis with a policy angle more valuable. This tendency is reinforced by the discipline's proximity to the state and to the foreign policy agenda in a considerable number of the countries and regions studied, which exercises between significant and tremendous impact in framing the context of academic practice. In addition, in countries in which foreign monies are a crucial source of research funding, the disincentives to think theoretically are quite substantial, given most foundations' clear preference for knowledge that can be translated into policy influence.

Therefore, there is little reward in producing theory locally and the road to influence in the discipline moves through other channels. When theories are then required for teaching purposes or to make publications fit some expected academic format, a common tendency is that IR scholars outside the core pick and choose from the ones at hand, rather than investing too much time (which is ultimately considered a waste) in developing new ones. In this perspective, the lack of theorizing is less a question of "prevention" or unthinkability deriving from the center and more one of *irrelevance* locally. The greater engagement with theory observable in cases such as Turkey and Southeast Asia may be related to the growing numbers of IR scholars being trained in the United States and Europe, on the one hand, and the growing international relevance of these countries. And yet, in the case of the latter, See Seng Tan is somewhat skeptical towards the field's theoretical turn, given its "mimetic reliance" on U.S. IR – its terms of reference, categories and language – an attitude that the author describes as self-orientalism.

Notwithstanding the preeminence of the state to IR scholarship, nationalist wishes for one's own theory are visible in relatively few cases, including China, Russia, and Japan. Special accent on this is found in China, where Yiwei Wang discusses a clear consciousness among scholars of the absence of a national perspective – a Chinese IR school – and a sense that this is problematic, both for symbolic reasons (a great power needs considerable paraphernalia, not least of which an independent IR school) and for political–practical reasons (if Marxist sociology of knowledge taught that the dominant ideas were the ideas of the dominant, then for China to use U.S. theories when trying to limit American world dominance would seem counterproductive). In Russia too, the conceptual underpinning of this country's place in the world has been a source of fierce academic debate, although the field's rebirth after the end of the Cold War has not yet translated into the same kind of theoretical quest that characterizes the Chinese IR community. The Eurasian "School" in particular benefited from a symbolism of the theory being uniquely Russian and thus having form correspond to content in its message.

The literature on United States dominance in International Relations has normally assumed that this state of affairs is problematic mainly because it imposes an "American" set of questions on other scholarly communities as well as a form of social science that is not relevant in other contexts. Nonetheless, if we examine the case studies for three types of domination – framing questions, theories, and meta-theory – a crude generalization would be that it is mainly theories that come from the United States. The *questions* are not imported. Each academic community is guided by distinct research interests based largely upon its respective country's foreign relations. Nor are the *meta-theories*. IR outside the core is mainly of a rather traditional form, somewhere between classical realism, neorealism and security studies, sometimes with a bit of interdependence theory, but never rational choice or quantitative analysis, nor post-positivist frameworks for that matter. What is clearly provided by the center and not produced locally is *IR theory*. Textbooks and studies, if they use theory at all, employ "American" theories. But usually, theories are not used in very disciplined or tight ways, but are subject to a fair amount of "picking and choosing" based upon local needs and readings. Therefore, these theories do not necessarily "control" very much.

In the Anglo-core and post-Imperial non-core, Wayne S. Cox and Kim Richard Nossal observe that the hegemony of U.S. IR is challenged by the ways in which the discipline is practiced there. This is basically due to the fact that none of the meta-theoretical approaches currently fashionable in the United States are employed by scholars in Britain, Canada, Australia, Ireland, or New Zealand. According to the authors, the fact that indigenously trained scholars are hired almost exclusively to fill IR posts in these countries and that a separate "crimson world" research community seems to be forming points to a growing divide in the "Anglo-American condominium." In contrast, in Western Europe Jörg Friedrichs and Ole Wæver argue that U.S. hegemony cannot be ignored (as in the former case) but rather that individual countries have developed different strategies for coping with it. In distinct ways, both of these chapters point to the parochialism of "American" IR and, in Tom Biersteker's analysis, the strong isolation of International Relations scholarship in the United States from the rest of the world is confirmed.

A strange absence in ancient, self-conscious, and large cultures like China, India, Iran, Japan, or the Arab world, and in countries like Israel and Iran with deeply ingrained religious traditions, is that IR seems to receive hardly any influence from strong cosmologies. In such cases one would expect to find, at least as a part of International Relations scholarship, approaches that differ in fundamental ways from Western ones. If the basic understandings of categories such as subject–object, individual–collective, earthly and transcendent, time and knowledge, among others, are different from standard Western thinking, it seems reasonable that they would be incorporated into IR too. India seems a particularly good place to look, given that it has a very different philosophical and religious tradition, and a relatively old IR community. Why then do we not find what we are looking for? Part of the explanation is that it happens in other disciplines. Although non-traditional critical thinking such as subaltern studies and postcolonial theory have been incorporated into cultural and literary studies, history and sociology within India, and has even influenced critical scholarship in the West, it is not recognized as IR in South Asia.[1]

Iran poses another curious case, in that specific attempts by the post-revolutionary state to introduce Islamic principles into political, social, economic and cultural institutions, daily life, and scholarly practice have been only partially effective. In the case of IR, Islamization has been even more unsuccessful according to Mahmood Sariolghalam, primarily because no model exists for converting the Islamic paradigm into a concrete foreign policy strategy. This delinking from local traditions may be seen partly as a purposeful, defensive shielding for liberal scholars in particular, whose goals include reaching out to the world, gaining academic acceptance and respect, and introducing knowledge about other countries into the Iranian context.[2]

Difference – in a different way

This brief comparison between the 16 case studies suggests that although a number of social and intellectual factors differentiate IR in many parts of the world, the discipline also exhibits rather strong similarities. Along with the factors already discussed, the salience of security issues, the absence of normative concerns, and the proximity to state cues, particularly with regard to foreign policy (not to be equated with scholarly influence upon foreign policy itself), also deserve to be mentioned. What this means is that the prevalent notion that non-core, non-Western readings of International Relations are essentially "different" needs to be thought through.

The problem of critical Western scholarship idealizing subordinate versions of IR is discussed by Pinar Bilgin (2008), who argues that it is characteristic of the Western mindset and its scholarship to look beyond the West in search of difference and novelty. Instead of seeking out radical difference in otherness, Bilgin urges the discipline to examine more carefully practices in the periphery that at first glance look "the same" but – in the words of Homi Bhabha – are usually "almost the same but not quite." She argues that

> the seeming "similarity" may be rooted in policies of survival shaped in an international political context chararcterised by an unequal division of labour and distribution of power. What is more, this may be true not only for "non-Western" policy making, but also for "non-Western" scholarly studies of IR. That is to say, if "non-Western" scholars come across as "social science socialized" products of "Western" IR, the domestic and international politics of such socialisation is worth inquiring into. Arguably, such inquiry into the agency of the "non-West" in the production of ways of thinking and doing that are "almost the same but not quite" will allow the project of thinking past "Western" IR to further flourish.
>
> (Bilgin 2008: 19–20)

Surely this is an important and astute observation about what is going on in International Relations, especially in a book such as this. However, as mentioned in the Introduction, relying excessively upon the Bhabha-inspired valoration of hybridity as a productive and promising position risks underplaying the power and asymmetries involved in its very construction. In this vein, it is necessary to confront and historicize some of the central Western categories and presuppositions that inform scholarly activity in the non-core more actively and directly, most importantly state-centrism and national security. If the local role of IR in the periphery is to change, which is most likely the key to a distinct dynamic in its development, redefining what IR is and thereby what types of knowledge constitute legitimate contributions to it is indispensable.

Where to now?

Returning to the questions we posed at the beginning of this book – how is the world understood around the world? Are there distinct ways of thinking about international relations? How do scholars of IR interact as a global community? What kinds of worlding are produced by global IR scholars and especially IR theorists? – the dominant set-up for these types of question is: *either* we have a situation of center–periphery, United States dominance and uniformity *or* one of diversity and increasing pluralism (see e.g. Crawford and Jarvis 2001). This is probably not the most useful way to present the problem. As may be inferred from the case studies presented in this volume, different IR communities are not completely separate universes, so that a better balance between them does not necessarily entail variation, nor does dominance automatically lead to uniformity. International Relations the world over is clearly shaped by Western IR. And yet, the situation is certainly not one of "uniformity" and the "same," precisely because Western IR translates into something different when it travels to the periphery.

In this respect, the dynamic at play comes closer to classical *dependencia* theory: because center and periphery occupy distinct positions in a global structure they produce different types of IR. In contrast to some versions of dependency, however, this is not because peripheral conditions are shaped exclusively by relations to the core, nor does it imply that the center "imposes" its version of IR. On the contrary, it is striking how the currently dominant forms of U.S. IR do *not* travel. Rather, since the core dominates the discipline as such, an indirect effect is produced whereby the classical sociology of science dynamics do not work in the non-core. Simultaneously, due to practical conditions and needs, the function of IR in most peripheral locales is defined primarily in direct relation to foreign policy, and less as distinct theory. The end result is that we see relatively independent local communities in relation to the core, but they practice a kind of IR that fails to mirror that which is valued there. Without producing that much of its own IR theory and perspectives, IR "works" in many places, but this means something markedly different than in the core. Instead of comparing it to IR in the core – and defining peripheral IR in terms of what it is *not* – it is necessary to see what it *is*. To take seriously what IR *does* by doing what it does. Real existing IR in non-privileged parts of the world is a purposeful, meaningful, and socially relevant activity, only under conditions different from those in the core.

This interpretation should not be taken to imply that IR in the center is somehow better because theory is done there. As Gabriel Abend (2006) has argued in a comparative study of "styles of sociological thought" in Mexico and the U.S., both communities "allege they are in the business of making true scientific knowledge claims about the social world" (2006: 2), but their work is "consistently underlain by significantly different epistemological assumptions" (ibid.). Most noteworthy are the varied understandings of "what is a theory?," whereby the two communities use theories of a different kind, in a different manner, and to a different degree. Both approaches have their heroic assumptions and their built-in criteria of quality, so they respectively find faults in the other approach. In their given context, the other kind of work would be less efficient in fulfilling social tasks both internal to the university and vis-à-vis society.

The aim of bringing such legitimate variation to light is not to move towards a world of national perspectives – "the Chinese School", "Indian theories" – and thus lowered international communication and a kind of internal monopoly of criticism and assessment (Callahan 2001; Xinning 2001). Standpoint arguments should not lead to the conclusion that criteria of validity are somehow relative to the geographical origins of a work. But communication can only begin if voices actually emerge from around the globe, and not only echoes of one voice (Holsti 1985).

So, where do we turn now? As mentioned in the Introduction, this book is both freestanding and part of a larger project: a trilogy that mutates into a book series. In the first volume, our intention has been to provide a comprehensive overview of the development of IR throughout the world. Despite some of the general trends that were discovered in the diverse case studies, our conclusion is that International Relations is not the same everywhere, although probably for reasons different from those usually assumed. However, by asking that the "international" be talked about primarily within the boundaries of the discipline, our analysis cannot end here. The second volume of our trilogy explores how key concepts are conceived differently in distinct geocultural settings. The concepts included are authority/state, security, secularism, globalization, and "the international." In contrast to the current volume, we do not aim for full geographical coverage in this second exercise, but rather for "important" or "representative" thinking on the concepts highlighted. In addition, our analysis begins to move outside the "box" created by the IR discipline, in that the volume's distinct authors are asked to discuss how "x" concept is experienced and problematized in their respective locale, both within and outside of International Relations. In this way, volumes 1 and 2 are complementary.

In the third volume, our aim is to seek out more explosive mechanisms for exposing IR's claims of universality and singularity of its categories and for interrogating alternative global imaginaries. This will necessarily include discussion of the implications of geoculturally based reflections for the field of IR. What kind of discipline are "we" and what do (and do not) "we" study? How is the discipline shaped today by its privileging of Western/core experiences in terms of boundary, issues, and forms of knowledge? What are the boundaries of IR according to the "center" and "periphery" and the role of non-core thinking in creating a "post-Western discipline" (Inayatullah and Blaney 2004)? Is it important to redefine "IR" as such, or should innovation at the periphery be celebrated locally, while the core is left to its own parochialism? Does post-Western and post-hegemonic necessarily also mean interdisciplinary and post-IR?

By playing out difference in these distinct ways and exploring what it means to be different in a field such as International Relations, these initial volumes, and the monographs and edited books to follow in the "Worlding beyond the West" series, seek to disrupt current conceptions of IR and tune in to emerging alternatives for thinking otherwise. In doing so, our aim is to engage the issue of where and how intellectual exchange can take place other than in the spaces created by hegemonic, positivist, and Western IR.

Notes

1   So the explanation is disciplinary delineation. This, however, just moves the question; it does not answer it. Because, why are the lines drawn like that? A major part of the explanation is that political science and IR came late and remained small. Thus the larger and deeper issues were located elsewhere, while political science was viewed as partly a rather technocratic art of the state, partly a very Western science housed mainly as a duty.
2   IR quite often seems to have been a politically moderating force in times of confrontation: Iran, U.S., Israel. The TRIP survey (Maliniak *et al.* 2007) shows, for the U.S. discipline, a much more liberal/leftist profile than society at large.

References

Abend, Gabriel (2006) "Styles of Sociological Thought: Sociologies, Epistemologies, and the Mexican and U.S. Quests for Truth," *Sociological Theory*, 24(1): 1–41.

Ashley, Richard K. (1987) "The Geopolitics of Geopolitical Space: Toward a Critical Social Theory of International Politics," *Alternatives*, 12(4): 403–434.

Bilgin, Pinar (2008) "Thinking Past 'Western' IR," *Third World Quarterly*, 29(1): 5–23.

Callahan, William A. (2001) "China and the Globalisation of IR Theory: Discussion of 'Building International Relations Theory with Chinese Characteristics'," *Journal of Contemporary China*, 10(26): 75–88.

Crawford, Robert M.A. and Darryl S. Jarvis (eds) (2001) *International Relations – Still an American Social Science? Toward Diversity in International Thought*, Albany: State University of New York Press.

Drori, Gili S., John W. Meyer, Francisco O. Ramirez, and Evan Schofer (2003) *Science in the Modern World Polity: Institutionalization and Globalization*, Stanford, CA: Stanford University Press.

Holsti, K.J. (1985) *The Dividing Discipline: Hegemony and Diversity in International Theory*, Boston, MA: Allen & Unwin.

Inayatullah, Naeem and David Blaney (2004) *International Relations and the Problem of Difference*, London: Routledge.

Karran, Terence (2007) "Academic Freedom in Europe: A Preliminary Comparative Analysis," *Higher Education Policy*, 20: 289–313.

Katzenstein, Peter J., Robert O. Keohane, and Stephen D. Krasner (1998) "International Organization and the Study of World Politics," *International Organization*, 52(4): 645–685.

Maliniak, Daniel, Amy Oakes, Susan Peterson, and Michael J. Tierney (2007) "The View from the Ivory Tower: TRIP Survey of IR Faculty in the U.S. and Canada," Reves Center/A&S, College of William and Mary, Williamsburg VA, February.

Smith, Steve (1995) "The Self-Images of a Discipline: A Genealogy of International Relations Theory," in Ken Booth and Steve Smith (eds), *International Relations Theory Today*, University Park: Pennsylvania State University Press, pp. 1–37.

Smith, Steve (2000) "The Discipline of International Relations: Still an American Social Science?," *British Journal of Politics and International Relations*, 3(3): 216–255.

Tickner, Arlene B. (2003) "Seeing IR Differently: Notes from the Third World," *Millennium: Journal of International Studies*, 32(2): 295–324.

Wæver, Ole (1998) "The Sociology of a Not So International Discipline: American and European Developments in International Relations," *International Organization*, 52(4): 687–727.

Walker, R.B.J. (1993) *Inside/Outside: International Relations as Political Theory*, Cambridge: Cambridge University Press.

Xinning, Song (2001) "Building International Relations Theory with Chinese Characteristics," *Journal of Contemporary China*, 10(26): 61–74.

Index

Abend, Gabriel 339
Abraham, Itty 146, 152
Acharya, Amitav 16, 23, 25, 98, 125–6, 129, 142
Afghanistan 135, 230, 232, 321; *see also* Arab countries
Africa 71–83; African Union (AU) 58, 66–7, 81; Africanization 54–6; career opportunities 57, 65, 72, 82; cold war 74–5, 80–1; critical issues facing 76–7; dependency theory 74, 76, 79; disciplinary autonomy 76–8; educational system 73; foreign policy establishment and IR 79–81; funding 72–3; language 73; liberation movements 75, 77, 80; modernization 73–4, 83; nationalism 75; Organization of African Unity (OAU) 72, 75, 81; political regime 77, 80; power theory 75–6; realism 73, 75–6, 81; social sciences 74–5; syllabi 73; teaching 71–3, 75–9, 82; theorizing 71, 76, 81; universities 72–3; war 77–8; *see also* South Africa
Akinyemi, Professor A.B. 72
Alavi, Hamsa 146
Algeria 178, 184
Alker Jr., Hayward R. 50, 308–9, 312–15, 320, 322, 324
America *see* United States; Latin America
Amin, Samir 74–5
Anarchy 114, 150, 204, 216, 224, 230–1, 233
Angell, Norman 308
Angola 53, 73, 77, 80; *see also* Africa
Anti-colonialism 73, 182
Apartheid 53–7, 64–8
Appadurai, Arjun 137, 142, 146
Arab countries 172–87; area studies 172–80; associations 174–5, 178, 181; career opportunities 183; disciplinary autonomy 184; foreign policy analysis 177; foreign policy establishment and IR 176–8; funding 172–3, 182; journals 175, 181, 183, 185; language 181, 183; liberalism 175, 186; Marxism 175; methodology 174, 176–8, 180, 186–7; nationalism 182, 186; orientalism 172, 175, 181, 188; political regime 173, 178,

182; publishing 181; realism 175, 186; research institutes 181–2, 184–5; salaries 182; teaching 173, 184; textbooks 176, 184; think-tanks 185; theorizing 177, 180, 186; training abroad 183; universities 181–4; working conditions 182
Arad, Uzi 202
Area studies: Arab 172–80; Japan 86, 88, 92, 95; Central and Eastern Europe 248, 256; East Asia 86, 88, *92*, 95–6; Russia 227; South East Asia 126; South Asia 136–41; Turkey 210, 219–20; Western Europe 267–8
Argentina 34, 36–9, 45, 49; *see also* Latin America
Aron, Raymond 263
Ashley, Richard 152, 304, 316, 335,
Asia-Pacific Economic Cooperation (APEC) 95, 125 *see also* Southeast Asia
Associations (professional): Arab 174–5, 178–82; Australia 299–300; Canada 297–8; Central and Eastern Europe 242–3, 249–50, 257; China 116–17; Israel 191, 198; New Zealand 300; Russia 229, 237; Scandinavia 250, 260, 266; Turkey 218; United Kingdom 292–7, 302; Latin America 39, 46, 49; United States 181, 191, 198, 200, 249, 293–4, 298, 318; Western Europe 263, 266, 278
Association of Southeast Asian Nations (ASEAN) 95, 117, 121–5, 127, 334; *see also* Southeast Asia
Atsushi, Kusano 93
Australia 4, 23, 90, 106, 287–90, 294–304, 332, 337; *see also* Crimson world
Austria *265*, 267, 280 *see also* Western Europe
autonomy 12, 22, 33–6, 47–9, 74, 87, 143, 146, 150, 184, 258, 261, 328–31, 333; *see also* disciplinary autonomy
auto-orientalism 120, 128
Avineri, Shlomo 202

Badie, Bertrand 263
Balance of power 123, 135, 216, 224, 230–7; theory 215–16